Social, Political, and Health Implications of Early Marriage

Emaj Uddin
University of Rajshahi, Bangladesh

IGI Global
Scientific Publishing
Publishing Tomorrow's Research Today

Vice President of Editorial	Melissa Wagner
Managing Editor of Acquisitions	Mikaela Felty
Managing Editor of Book Development	Jocelynn Hessler
Production Manager	Mike Brehm
Cover Design	Phillip Shickler

Published in the United States of America by
IGI Global Scientific Publishing
701 East Chocolate Avenue
Hershey, PA, 17033, USA
Tel: 717-533-8845
Fax: 717-533-8661
E-mail: cust@igi-global.com
Website: https://www.igi-global.com

Copyright © 2025 by IGI Global Scientific Publishing. All rights reserved. No part of this publication may be reproduced, stored or distributed in any form or by any means, electronic or mechanical, including photocopying, without written permission from the publisher.
Product or company names used in this set are for identification purposes only. Inclusion of the names of the products or companies does not indicate a claim of ownership by IGI Global Scientific Publishing of the trademark or registered trademark.

Library of Congress Cataloging-in-Publication Data

CIP Pending
ISBN: 979-8-3693-3394-5
EISBN: 979-8-3693-3395-2

British Cataloguing in Publication Data
A Cataloguing in Publication record for this book is available from the British Library.

All work contributed to this book is new, previously-unpublished material.
The views expressed in this book are those of the authors, but not necessarily of the publisher.
This book contains information sourced from authentic and highly regarded references, with reasonable efforts made to ensure the reliability of the data and information presented. The authors, editors, and publisher believe the information in this book to be accurate and true as of the date of publication. Every effort has been made to trace and credit the copyright holders of all materials included. However, the authors, editors, and publisher cannot assume responsibility for the validity of all materials or the consequences of their use. Should any copyright material be found unacknowledged, please inform the publisher so that corrections may be made in future reprints.

Table of Contents

Preface xiv

Chapter 1
Family Social Origins of Age-Heterogamous Marriage Across Societies: The Case of Bangladesh 1
    Emaj Uddin, University of Rajshahi, Bangladesh

Chapter 2
Family Socio-Cultural Values and Early Marriage Across Ethnic Groups: The Case of Bangladesh 27
    Emaj Uddin, University of Rajshahi, Bangladesh

Chapter 3
Breaking the Chains: Understanding and Combating Early Marriage-Induced Violence Against Girls 61
    Tripti Bhushan, O.P. Jindal Global University, India

Chapter 4
Child Marriage in Indonesia: Exploring Social Culture and Gender Inequality . 93
    Hari Harjanto Setiawan, Research Center for Social Welfare, Villages and Connectivity, National Research and Innovation Agency (BRIN), Jakarta, Indonesia
    Yanuar Farida Wismayanti, Research Center for Public Policy, National Research and Innovation Agency (BRIN), Jakarta, Indonesia
    Nyi R. Irmayani, Research Center for Social Welfare, Villages and Connectivity, Research Center for Social Welfare, Villages and Connectivity, National Research and Innovation Agency (BRIN), Jakarta, Indonesia
    Adhani Wardianti, Bandung Correctional Center, Ministry of Immigration and Corrections, Bandung, Indonesia

Chapter 5
Early Marriage and High School Dropout Among Poor Girls Across the Globe: Family Life Course Perspective 115
    Emaj Uddin, University of Rajshahi, Bangladesh
    Shara Antara, University of Rajshahi, Bangladesh

Chapter 6
Early Marriage and Mental Health in India: A Socio-Ecological Approach..... 141
    Lalhriatpuii Fanai, Christ University, India
    Vaishnavi Jeyachandran, Christ University, India
    Deepthi Jose Maliakkal, Christ University, India

Chapter 7
Mental Health Impact of Early Marriage: Exploring the Psychological Consequences of Early Marriage 163
    Mohit Yadav, O.P. Jindal Global University, India
    Ajay Chandel, Lovely Professional University, India
    Ta Huy Hung, Vietnam National University, Hanoi, Vietnam

Chapter 8
Health Consequences of Early Marriage: Examining Morbidity and Long-Term Wellbeing.. 189
    R. Vettriselvan, Academy of Maritime Education and Training, India
    A. Deepan, Sambhram University, Uzbekistan
    Geetanjali Jaiswani, Saraswathi Institute of Medical Sciences, Hapur, India
    A. Balakrishnan, Gandhigram Rural Institute, India
    R. Sakthivel, DMI-St. Eugene University, Zambia

Chapter 9
Early Marriage From a Health Perspective: Risks and Intervention Strategies. 213
    Sevinç Sütlü, Burdur Mehmet Akif Ersoy University, Turkey
    Özge Kutlu, Burdur Mehmet Akif Ersoy University, Turkey

Chapter 10
Enormities of Early Marriages of Girls Lensing Physical-Mental Health Impairments: Projecting Socio-Legal Implications in Global Context.............. 237
    Bhupinder Singh, Sharda University, India

Chapter 11
Social and Economic Consequences of Early Marriage on Women's Education and Workforce Participation 261
    Ajay Chandel, Lovely Professional University, India
    Mohit Yadav, O.P. Jindal Global University, India
    Ta Huy Hung, Vietnam National University, Hanoi, Vietnam

Chapter 12
Early Marriage as a Model of Child Trafficking: Exploring the Legal
Safeguards to Victims 291
    Ramy El-Kady, Police Academy, Egypt

Chapter 13
Teenage Pregnancy and Health Implications 327
    Shafia Jan, University of Kashmir, Srinagar, India
    Bilal Ahmad Bhat, Sher-e-Kashmir University of Agricultural Sciences
      and Technology, India

Chapter 14
Causes, Effects, and Remedies of Early Marriage: Social Work Implication.... 341
    Iranna Ronad, Shree Sangameshwar Arts and Commerce College,
      Chadchan, Karnataka, India

Chapter 15
The Role of International Mechanisms in Preventing Early Marriage:
Empowering Asylum Seekers Through International Protection in Türkiye..... 369
    Bekir Güzel, Recep Tayyip Erdoğan University, Turkey
    Sema Nur Beserek, Independent Researcher, Turkey

Compilation of References 393

About the Contributors 455

Index 463

Detailed Table of Contents

Preface xiv

Chapter 1
Family Social Origins of Age-Heterogamous Marriage Across Societies: The Case of Bangladesh 1
    Emaj Uddin, University of Rajshahi, Bangladesh

Family social background factors influence age-heterogamous marriages across societies. This chapter examines how social background factors such as ethnicity, gender socioeconomic status, traditional marriage norms, and patriarchal family structure exert negative effects on age-heterogamy than age-homogamy in first time marriage in collectivistic societies. Using empirical data from Bangladesh as a collectivistic society, the results indicated that most of the couples were age-heterogamous than age-homogamous in first time marriages. The results of bivariate correlation and binary logistic regression analysis suggested that age-heterogamous marriages were significantly associated with social bacground factors. Of the predicting factors, ethnicity, gender SES, middle family income, arranged marriage, middle family size, patrilocal residence, and autocratic family authority were the greatest (1-3% times) risks factors for age-heterogamous marriages in Bangladesh. The findings have implications in future causal research and policy practice in Bangladesh.

Chapter 2
Family Socio-Cultural Values and Early Marriage Across Ethnic Groups: The Case of Bangladesh 27
    Emaj Uddin, University of Rajshahi, Bangladesh

This chapter examines and compares how family socio-cultural values exert effect on early marriage across ethnic groups, focusing on Bangladesh. In doing so, 585 pairs of couples (295 for Muslim and 290 for Santal) were randomly selected from Bangladesh. Data were collected, applying questionnaire method in family setting. Then the collected data were analyzed, using X2 test and binary logistic regression (BLR) technique. The frequency distribution showed that most of the Santal couples compared to the Muslim were married before the minimum legal age in Bangladesh. Results of BLR analysis suggested that early age at first marriage was significantly ($p<0.01$ & $p<0.05$) associated with family socio-cultural values studied. It is argued that ethnicity, family pattern, residence pattern, illiteracy and ascriptive occupational status were the risk factors to persist early marriage among the Santal couples than the Muslim ones in rural Bangladesh.

Chapter 3
Breaking the Chains: Understanding and Combating Early Marriage-Induced Violence Against Girls 61
Tripti Bhushan, O.P. Jindal Global University, India

Early marriage remains a pervasive issue worldwide, particularly in developing countries, where cultural norms, poverty, and lack of education perpetuate its prevalence. This proposed book chapter aims to delve into the complex dynamics surrounding early marriage-induced violence against girls, examining its root causes, manifestations, and impact on the physical, emotional, and psychological well-being of young brides. Further this book chapter will talk about the mental issues of bride. The chapter will begin by providing an overview of the prevalence of early marriage globally, highlighting the socio-economic and cultural factors that contribute to its persistence. Finally, the chapter will conclude with recommendations for policymakers, practitioners, and activists on effective strategies to combat early marriage-induced violence against girls, emphasizing the importance of multi-sectoral collaboration, empowerment approaches, and holistic support services.

Chapter 4
Child Marriage in Indonesia: Exploring Social Culture and Gender Inequality . 93
Hari Harjanto Setiawan, Research Center for Social Welfare, Villages and Connectivity, National Research and Innovation Agency (BRIN), Jakarta, Indonesia
Yanuar Farida Wismayanti, Research Center for Public Policy, National Research and Innovation Agency (BRIN), Jakarta, Indonesia
Nyi R. Irmayani, Research Center for Social Welfare, Villages and Connectivity, Research Center for Social Welfare, Villages and Connectivity, National Research and Innovation Agency (BRIN), Jakarta, Indonesia
Adhani Wardianti, Bandung Correctional Center, Ministry of Immigration and Corrections, Bandung, Indonesia

Child marriage has become an important issue in recent years, both nationally and globally. This is detrimental to children's growth and development. Many children throughout the world experience problems with child marriage, including in Indonesia. The difficulties they experience include reproductive health, emotional aspects, exploitation, violence and harassment. This paper uses critical discourse analysis methods to explore conceptual and practical gaps. This chapter was written qualitatively, using literature observations and previous research findings on early marriage. The results show that cultural factors and gender equality play a role in the high rate of child marriage in Indonesia. This chapter explains the socio-cultural aspects of early marriage and gender equality based on research in Indonesia. This chapter contributes to the academic and practitioner literature on preventing early marriage in Indonesia. The implication is that child marriage has become a reality in child protection efforts in Indonesia.

Chapter 5
Early Marriage and High School Dropout Among Poor Girls Across the
Globe: Family Life Course Perspective 115
    Emaj Uddin, University of Rajshahi, Bangladesh
    Shara Antara, University of Rajshahi, Bangladesh

Despite school process-based measures taken, high school dropout (HSD) associated with early marriage (EM) among teenage girls is increasing across countries, including Bangladesh. Based on family life course approach and comprehensive literature review, this chapter explains potential pathways of EM such as early transition to family responsibility, pregnancy, child bearing and rearing and household chores, leading girls to dropout from high school. Based on the FLCA, literature over the past several decades suggests that EM and its subsequent events (e.g., pregnancy, childbearing and rearing, early family role transition) partially explain high school risk behaviors that, in turn, affect girls to drop out from high school. Evidence in this chapter is important for developing effective programs or measures to prevent teenage girls' EM and HSD across developing countries.

Chapter 6
Early Marriage and Mental Health in India: A Socio-Ecological Approach..... 141
    Lalhriatpuii Fanai, Christ University, India
    Vaishnavi Jeyachandran, Christ University, India
    Deepthi Jose Maliakkal, Christ University, India

Child marriage constitutes an extreme breach of the United Nations Convention on the Rights of the Child. It is estimated that the total number of women who get married before reaching the age of 18 will surpass 60 million. Out of these women, more than one-third live in South Asia. India has experienced the most rapid decrease in early marriage (EM) at a rate of 3.8%. However, the eradication of EM will not happen at the current pace until there are advancements in girls' education, an increase in marital household wealth, and a deeper understanding of the negative repercussions of child marriage. Consequently, it is crucial to implement comprehensive and cross-sectoral initiatives to decrease the occurrence of EM. This study utilized the socio-ecological approach to comprehensively explore the intricate phenomenon of EM in the Indian context.

Chapter 7
Mental Health Impact of Early Marriage: Exploring the Psychological
Consequences of Early Marriage 163
    Mohit Yadav, O.P. Jindal Global University, India
    Ajay Chandel, Lovely Professional University, India
    Ta Huy Hung, Vietnam National University, Hanoi, Vietnam

Early marriage poses significant psychological and societal challenges, impacting both individuals and communities worldwide. This abstract examines the mental health consequences of early marriage, including depression, anxiety, and PTSD. It explores the cultural and societal contexts that perpetuate early marriage, emphasizing the roles of traditional norms, gender inequality, and societal pressures. The intergenerational impact of early marriage is also highlighted, revealing how it affects children of young mothers and strains community resources. Effective interventions and support mechanisms, including preventive measures, psychological support, and successful case studies, are discussed. The need for comprehensive approaches that integrate education, empowerment, and policy reforms is emphasized. This analysis underscores the importance of addressing early marriage's root causes and implementing tailored strategies to mitigate its psychological impact.

Chapter 8
Health Consequences of Early Marriage: Examining Morbidity and Long-
Term Wellbeing.. 189
    R. Vettriselvan, Academy of Maritime Education and Training, India
    A. Deepan, Sambhram University, Uzbekistan
    Geetanjali Jaiswani, Saraswathi Institute of Medical Sciences, Hapur, India
    A. Balakrishnan, Gandhigram Rural Institute, India
    R. Sakthivel, DMI-St. Eugene University, Zambia

Early marriage, defined as marriage occurring before the age of 18, has significant health implications that affect individuals throughout their lives. Based on life course approach, this chapter investigates the health risks associated with early marriage, emphasizing both immediate and long-term consequences. It highlights increased vulnerability to various health issues, such as higher rates of maternal and infant complications, chronic illnesses, and mental health disorders. Additionally, the chapter explores the interplay between socio-economic factors and health outcomes, revealing how these factors exacerbate existing disparities and restrict access to healthcare services. Through an examination of current research and case studies, this chapter provides a comprehensive overview of the health challenges associated with early marriage and offers recommendations for strategies to mitigate these risks. By addressing these issues, the chapter seeks to contribute to a deeper understanding of the broader implications of early marriage on individual and public health.

Chapter 9

Early Marriage From a Health Perspective: Risks and Intervention Strategies. 213
Sevinç Sütlü, Burdur Mehmet Akif Ersoy University, Turkey
Özge Kutlu, Burdur Mehmet Akif Ersoy University, Turkey

Early marriage is one of the most significant global issues created by traditional and patriarchal cultures, particularly impacting girls and women and hindering societal development. Mostly prevalent in impoverished and rural areas of underdeveloped and developing countries, early marriages are now recognized as a violation of women's and girls' human rights. Early marriage has various adverse effects on individuals' health. It increases the likelihood of fertility-related health risks such as pregnancy and childbirth complications, particularly for young people who haven't completed their physical and emotional development. The health implications of early marriage are extensive and diverse, emphasizing the importance for youth to comprehend its risks and consequences for a healthy and secure future. Hence, it's imperative to develop comprehensive strategies and supportive policies to prevent early marriages and safeguard young people's health rights.

Chapter 10

Enormities of Early Marriages of Girls Lensing Physical-Mental Health Impairments: Projecting Socio-Legal Implications in Global Context.............. 237
Bhupinder Singh, Sharda University, India

Early marriages have long been a source of worry because of the possible negative impacts on one's physical and mental health, especially when they involve females. Child marriage continues to be a common practice in many places, affecting millions of girls globally, despite global attempts to abolish it. Gender inequality, socioeconomic circumstances and cultural expectations are some of the main causes of early marriages. The physiological immaturity of young brides poses risks during pregnancy and childbirth, leading to higher rates of maternal and infant mortality. Legislation and enforcement play a pivotal role in preventing and combating child marriages. This chapter explores existing legal frameworks globally and highlights the importance of stringent laws, effective implementation and awareness campaigns to curb this harmful practice via- Policy Recommendations; Education and Awareness: Support Systems; Community Engagement because early marriages can have profound effects on the physical health of girls.

Chapter 11
Social and Economic Consequences of Early Marriage on Women's
Education and Workforce Participation 261
    Ajay Chandel, Lovely Professional University, India
    Mohit Yadav, O.P. Jindal Global University, India
    Ta Huy Hung, Vietnam National University, Hanoi, Vietnam

This chapter explores and explains the effects of the significant social and economic consequences of early marriage on women's education and workforce participation. Early marriage, often driven by cultural, religious, and economic factors, disrupts educational opportunities for young girls, leading to lower education attainment and limited access to formal employment. These poor socioeconomic attainments perpetuate the cycles of poverty and reinforce gender inequality, trapping women in economic dependency and social marginalization. The chapter employs theoretical frameworks such as social reproduction theory, human capital theory, and intersectionality to analyze how early marriage sustains these inequalities. It also examines the historical, cultural, and legal contexts that underpin the practice, highlighting the need for targeted, culturally sensitive interventions. The findings underscore the importance of comprehensive strategies to empower women, challenge patriarchal norms, and promote education and economic participation.

Chapter 12
Early Marriage as a Model of Child Trafficking: Exploring the Legal
Safeguards to Victims 291
    Ramy El-Kady, Police Academy, Egypt

The chapter deals with the issue of early marriage as one of the most prominent issues plaguing societies. The family is the entity of society, and women are the cornerstones of the family. There is no doubt that forming a family requires the availability of several conditions, the most important of which is the woman's ability to manage family affairs, as practical reality has resulted in the spread of the phenomenon of underage marriage. As one of the reflections resulting from poverty, the spread of ignorance, and adherence to some customs and traditions. This chapter aims to shed light on the psychological, health, and social aspects of early marriage and explain why it has become more and more common in society. It also aims to explain the legal framework that governs its confrontation as one of the most prominent forms of child trafficking. The study concluded that the need for an integrated community confrontation plan or strategy depends on enforcing laws and adopting large-scale mass media campaigns to spread public awareness of this issue and establish emergency lines.

Chapter 13
Teenage Pregnancy and Health Implications 327
    Shafia Jan, University of Kashmir, Srinagar, India
    Bilal Ahmad Bhat, Sher-e-Kashmir University of Agricultural Sciences
        and Technology, India

Adolescent pregnancy and parenthood have emerged as major social issues in recent years, which is an issue of life and death to the teenagers. Poverty and ignorance magnifies this problem to a greater extent. According to National Family Health Survey-3, the incidence of teenage pregnancy in India was 16%, with majority of them occurring in uneducated rural population (Saloi, 2017). Teenage mothers face numerous health complications, both physical and mental. Pregnancy-induced hypertension and preeclampsia are more common in teenage pregnancies, posing significant health risks. Additionally, obstructed labour is a frequent issue due to immature pelvic structures, often necessitating caesarean sections. Maternal mortality rates are also higher among teenage mothers compared to older women, underscoring the severe risks involved.. Efforts can be made to empower teenagers to make informed decisions about their sexual health and reduce the incidence of teenage pregnancy.

Chapter 14
Causes, Effects, and Remedies of Early Marriage: Social Work Implication.... 341
    Iranna Ronad , Shree Sangameshwar Arts and Commerce College,
        Chadchan, Karnataka, India

Abstract Despite the fact that marriage has a unique character, variety, and significance in all communities on the planet, sociologists contend that early marriage has had a number of detrimental effects. There is a wide range of views and attitudes in society about early marriage. While some believe that it is highly advantageous for the family, others think that getting married young is not a good idea and that it will only cause troubles and negative outcomes. Even though it is against the law, early weddings are never less common in many civilizations throughout the world. These types of marriages involve girls under the age of eighteen for various reasons. Many low-income parents wed their daughters before the age of eighteen. Due to their lack of resources, high expectations of their children, and intense feelings, many poor people complete their responsibility by marrying off their daughters at the young age of eighteen or younger.

Chapter 15
The Role of International Mechanisms in Preventing Early Marriage:
Empowering Asylum Seekers Through International Protection in Türkiye..... 369
  Bekir Güzel, Recep Tayyip Erdoğan University, Turkey
  Sema Nur Beserek, Independent Researcher, Turkey

Early marriage is an increasing global problem all over the world. International mechanisms play a critical role in combating this problem, which is even more prevalent in underdeveloped or developing countries. These mechanisms make important contributions in many areas from raising awareness to creating a legal framework, from developing programmes/interventions to providing funds. Türkiye has the largest population of asylum seekers in the 21st century. [..] The Ministry of Family and Social Services is the primary ministry authorised for child protection in Türkiye. These institutions (NGOs and MFSS) in Türkiye implement different empowerment-based practice models in the field. These include information and advocacy on judicial processes and legal procedures, medical intervention, psychosocial support, education and counselling as well as protective-preventive and empowering activities. This chapter indicates that international mechanisms play an important global role in ending early marriage.

Compilation of References 393

About the Contributors 455

Index 463

Preface

Early marriage, a practice deeply rooted in sociocultural traditions, continues to be a significant and harmful phenomenon that transcends geographic and cultural boundaries. Despite legislative efforts such as the Early Marriage Prohibition Act, as well as strides in sociocultural development and a global commitment to achieving the United Nations Sustainable Development Goals, the practice remains prevalent. Globally, 20-60% of girls between the ages of 13 and 19 are still married in contexts of poverty, low socio-economic status, and traditional societal structures. The consequences of early marriage are manifold and devastating, spanning across social, political, and health domains. These consequences have far-reaching implications for the individual lives of young girls and for society at large.

The purpose of this edited volume is to offer a comprehensive examination of the multifaceted impacts of early marriage on teenage girls, utilizing a life course perspective and a critical review of longitudinal literature. The evidence gathered in this book reveals the deep and pervasive effects early marriage has on girls' lives, ranging from diminished educational and occupational opportunities to poor health outcomes, early family formation, social exclusion, and increased vulnerability to violence, trafficking, and other forms of exploitation. Such consequences not only diminish the potential of these young girls but also perpetuate cycles of poverty and inequality that span generations.

Through contributions from scholars, researchers, and practitioners across diverse fields—including sociology, psychology, health, demography, law, political science, social policy, and social work—this book provides both theoretical and practical insights into understanding and addressing the challenge of early marriage. By exploring theories such as life course perspectives, human development, family life cycles, and empowerment, as well as drawing on longitudinal evidence, we offer a well-rounded view of the issue and its profound impact on adolescent girls.

CHAPTER OVERVIEW

Chapter 1: Family Social Origins of Age-Heterogamous Marriage across Societies: The Case of Bangladesh

Drawing on empirical data from Bangladesh, this chapter explores how family social backgrounds—such as ethnicity, socioeconomic status, and patriarchal norms—contribute to age-heterogamous marriages, where there is a significant age gap between spouses. The findings suggest that age-heterogamy is more common in collectivist societies like Bangladesh and is influenced by factors like ethnicity, arranged marriages, and autocratic family structures. These insights have important implications for understanding marriage dynamics and informing future policy and research on age disparities in marriage.

Chapter 2: Family Socio-Cultural Values and Early Marriage across Ethnic Groups: The Case of Bangladesh

This chapter examines the influence of family socio-cultural values on early marriage practices among different ethnic groups in Bangladesh, with a focus on Muslim and Santal communities. It highlights significant differences in early marriage rates and explores the risk factors such as illiteracy, traditional family patterns, and ascriptive occupational statuses that contribute to early marriages, especially in rural settings. The findings shed light on the complex socio-cultural underpinnings of early marriage and suggest targeted interventions to address these practices.

Chapter 3: Breaking the Chains, Understanding and Combating Early Marriage-Induced Violence against Girls

This chapter investigates the prevalence of violence linked to early marriage, with a focus on its physical, emotional, and psychological impacts on young girls. It identifies socio-economic, cultural, and educational factors that perpetuate early marriage and provides an in-depth analysis of the violence experienced by young brides. Through evidence and case studies, the chapter proposes strategies to combat early marriage-induced violence, emphasizing multi-sectoral collaboration and the importance of empowering girls through holistic support services.

Chapter 4: Child Marriage in Indonesia: Exploring Social Culture and Gender Inequality

This chapter examines the socio-cultural and gender dynamics of child marriage in Indonesia, where cultural norms and gender inequality significantly contribute to its persistence. It uses critical discourse analysis to highlight the emotional, reproductive, and societal consequences of early marriage on children. The chapter draws from research findings to offer insights into the socio-cultural contexts of early marriage in Indonesia and stresses the importance of addressing these issues through policy reforms and community-based interventions.

Chapter 5: Early Marriage and High School Dropout among Poor Girls across the Globe: Family Life Course Perspective

This chapter explores the relationship between early marriage (EM) and high school dropout (HSD) rates among teenage girls globally, with a particular focus on Bangladesh. It argues that early marriage accelerates the transition to family responsibilities, including pregnancy and child-rearing, leading many girls to drop out of school. Using a family life course perspective, the chapter analyzes how EM contributes to high school dropout and suggests effective programs and policies to prevent these outcomes, particularly in developing countries.

Chapter 6: Early Marriage and Mental Health in India: A Socio-Ecological Approach

Focusing on India, this chapter uses a socio-ecological framework to explore the mental health consequences of early marriage, including depression, anxiety, and PTSD. Despite a decrease in early marriages, the chapter argues that ongoing educational, economic, and cultural factors continue to contribute to the prevalence of child marriage and its mental health implications. It emphasizes the need for comprehensive, cross-sectoral interventions to reduce the occurrence of early marriage and address its mental health consequences.

Chapter 7: Mental Health Impact of Early Marriage: Exploring the Psychological Consequences of Early Marriage

This chapter provides a comprehensive analysis of the psychological effects of early marriage, including depression, anxiety, and PTSD. It explores the cultural and societal contexts that sustain early marriage and examines its intergenerational impact on children born to young mothers. The chapter advocates for multi-faceted approaches, including prevention, psychological support, and policy reforms, to mitigate the mental health challenges faced by young brides.

Chapter 8: Health Consequences of Early Marriage: Examining Morbidity and Long-Term Wellbeing

This chapter investigates the immediate and long-term health risks associated with early marriage, emphasizing maternal and infant health complications, chronic diseases, and mental health disorders. By integrating socio-economic factors and health outcomes, the chapter highlights how early marriage exacerbates existing health disparities and restricts access to healthcare. It provides a thorough overview of the health challenges faced by early brides and proposes strategies to mitigate these risks.

Chapter 9: Early Marriage from a Health Perspective - Risks and Intervention Strategies

This chapter highlights the severe health risks posed by early marriage, particularly for young girls in underdeveloped and developing countries. It examines the fertility-related health complications, such as pregnancy and childbirth risks, faced by adolescent brides. The chapter stresses the need for comprehensive strategies, including education, policy reforms, and awareness campaigns, to prevent early marriages and safeguard the health rights of young people.

Chapter 10: Enormities of Early Marriages of Girls Lensing Physical-Mental Health Impairments: Projecting Socio-Legal Implications in Global Context

This chapter explores the physical and mental health impairments caused by early marriage, focusing on its impacts on young girls. It discusses the physiological risks during pregnancy and childbirth, leading to higher maternal and infant mortality rates. The chapter also examines the global legal frameworks aimed at preventing child marriage, proposing stronger enforcement, awareness campaigns, and community engagement strategies to address the issue.

Chapter 11: Social and Economic Consequences of Early Marriage on Women's Education and Workforce Participation

This chapter explores how early marriage disrupts women's education and workforce participation, perpetuating cycles of poverty and gender inequality. By analyzing early marriage through the lens of social reproduction theory and human capital theory, the chapter highlights how early marriage limits educational attainment and access to formal employment. It stresses the need for targeted interventions that challenge patriarchal norms and promote women's economic participation.

Chapter 12: Early Marriage as a Model of Child Trafficking: Exploring the Legal Safeguards to Victims

This chapter addresses early marriage as a form of child trafficking, emphasizing the health, psychological, and social consequences for young brides. It outlines the legal frameworks governing early marriage and advocates for the enforcement of laws and large-scale awareness campaigns to prevent this harmful practice. The chapter stresses the importance of integrating community-based strategies and legal reforms to protect young girls from child trafficking through early marriage.

Chapter 13: Teenage Pregnancy and Health Implications

This chapter discusses the health risks associated with teenage pregnancy, including physical complications like pregnancy-induced hypertension, preeclampsia, and obstructed labor. It highlights the higher maternal mortality rates among teenage mothers and emphasizes the need for empowering teenagers to make informed decisions about their sexual health to reduce the incidence of teenage pregnancy and its associated health risks.

Chapter 14: Causes, Effects, and Remedies of Early Marriage: Social Work Implications

This chapter examines the causes and effects of early marriage, focusing on its detrimental impacts on young girls. It highlights the role of social work in addressing early marriage, discussing legal, cultural, and economic factors that perpetuate the practice. The chapter proposes remedies, including comprehensive social work interventions and policy reforms, to prevent early marriage and support affected individuals in overcoming its consequences.

Chapter 15: The Role of International Mechanisms in Preventing Early Marriage: Empowering Asylum Seekers through International Protection in Türkiye

This chapter explores the role of international mechanisms in combating early marriage, particularly in the context of asylum seekers in Türkiye. It discusses the contributions of global institutions in raising awareness, developing legal frameworks, and implementing protective programs for victims of early marriage. The chapter highlights the importance of empowerment-based practice models and multi-sectoral collaboration in preventing early marriage and protecting vulnerable populations.

This volume aims to shed light on how the negative consequences of early marriage can be mitigated, if not entirely prevented, and how affected young girls can be supported to lead healthier, more empowered lives as they progress through different stages of their life course. We believe that the insights provided in this book will be of value not only to scholars and researchers but also to practitioners and policymakers across a variety of fields. Social workers, health professionals, law enforcement agencies, and governmental and non-governmental organizations engaged in the fight against early marriage and its consequences will find this book an essential resource in their efforts to prevent and address this pervasive issue.

The chapters included in this volume cover a broad spectrum of topics critical to understanding the scope of early marriage's impacts. These include:

- The background and historical context of early marriage
- Theoretical frameworks for understanding the complex social, political, and health ramifications of early marriage
- The relationship between early marriage and family formation, educational attainment, occupational opportunities, and social participation
- The psychological and physical health consequences, including the increased risk of violence, trafficking, morbidity, and mortality
- Social policy implications and recommendations for intervention and prevention

By offering this collection, we aim to contribute to global efforts to end early marriage and its devastating effects. This work also seeks to encourage collaboration among researchers, practitioners, and policymakers to create a future where teenage girls are empowered to pursue their potential, free from the harmful practice of early marriage.

We invite readers from diverse disciplines and practices to engage with this book, as it represents a collective effort to combat early marriage and improve the lives of teenage girls worldwide.

Chapter 1
Family Social Origins of Age-Heterogamous Marriage Across Societies:
The Case of Bangladesh

Emaj Uddin
https://orcid.org/0000-0002-6721-6856
University of Rajshahi, Bangladesh

ABSTRACT

Family social background factors influence age-heterogamous marriages across societies. This chapter examines how social background factors such as ethnicity, gender socioeconomic status, traditional marriage norms, and patriarchal family structure exert negative effects on age-heterogamy than age-homogamy in first time marriage in collectivistic societies. Using empirical data from Bangladesh as a collectivistic society, the results indicated that most of the couples were age-heterogamous than age-homogamous in first time marriages. The results of bivariate correlation and binary logistic regression analysis suggested that age-heterogamous marriages were significantly associated with social bacground factors. Of the predicting factors, ethnicity, gender SES, middle family income, arranged marriage, middle family size, patrilocal residence, and autocratic family authority were the greatest (1-3% times) risks factors for age-heterogamous marriages in Bangladesh. The findings have implications in future causal research and policy practice in Bangladesh.

DOI: 10.4018/979-8-3693-3394-5.ch001

INTRODUCTION

Family origins such as ethnicity, gender, family socioeconomic status, and family patterns influence age-gap in marriages across societies and cultures (McKenzie, 2021). Family researchers over the past several decades have much interested in analyzing age-homogamous vs. age-heterogamous marriages (e.g., Atkinson & Glass, 1985; Bytheway, 1981; Derenski & Landsberg, 1981; Styron, 1979; South, 1991). Evidence in the family literature has shown that age-homogamous marriage in developed societies (e.g., U.S.A., E.U., Australia) is remarkable (Atkinson & Glass, 1985; Glenn, 1982; Labov & Jacobs, 1986; Morgan, 1981), but age-heterogamous marriage in developing and less-developed societies is widely prevalent (van den Berghe, 1973; Casterline et al., 1986; South, 1991; Vera et al., 1985). Internationally and in Bangladesh current research (Dommaraju, 2023; Silva & Percheski, 2024) has found that age differences in marriages are higher in Africa (5-8 years) and South Asia (3-5 years) than western/European countries (1-3 years). Bangladesh Bureau of Statistics, BBS, (2012) has shown that although mean age difference between men and women in marriage is shrinking from 7.1 years in 1991 to 5.2 years in 2010 at national level, the findings from periodical studies have shown that men are markedly older (5 to 20 years) than women in marriage relationship in rural and urban Bangladesh (Chowdhury, 2004; Islam & Ahmed, 1998; ICDDR B, 2007; Mitra, Ali, Islam, Cross, & Saha, 1994; Roy, 2008; Uddin, 2015).

Structural family sociologists assume that family cultural and structural patterns lead to age-heterogamous marriages in traditional societies. Age-heterogamous marriages than age-homogamous ones are the most likely to affect women's economic, social, and physical well-being than men's after death of husbands (Klinger-Vartabedian & Wispe, 1989; Kemkes-Grottenthaler, 2004) in the under-developed societies, including Bangladesh. McKenzie (2021) systematically reviewed over century literature on age differences in couples and found age-dissimilar marriages associated with social and cultural factors across the societies. Despite these effects of age-heterogamous marriages on women by family sociologists (Atkinson & Glass, 1985; Casterline et al., 1986; Mensch, 1986), previous research in sociology, particularly in 0family science has given less attention on how social origins of family (ethnicity), hyper marital SES, value of children, traditional marriage and family pattern influence age-heterogamous marriage than age-homogamous marriages in the less-developed societies, including Bangladesh (Berardo et al., 1993; Barbieri & Hertrich, 2005; Lloyd, 2006; Malhotra & Tsui, 1996; Malhotra, 1997; Uddin, 2010, 2012).

In this chapter, this section works as a background for knowledge gap and research purpose. In second section we review relevant family sociological theories and its empirical evidence to explain age-heterogamous marriages presented and then representative sample will be drawn and that examined whether these family cultural and structural factors influence age-heterogamous marriages in rural Bangladesh (See, methodology third section). The results of the study presented in section four would help family sociological researchers to develop causal framework to study age-heterogamous marriages in under-developed societies, depending on the researchers' interests. The fifth section presents discussion and interpretation. The findings of the study would also help social policy makers and family practitioners to understand and design social programs to change in family cultural and structural factors that perpetuate age-heterogamous marriages in rural Bangladesh (See, conclusion and implication section).

THEORETICAL BACKGROUND

Family Social Origins of Age-Heterogamy in Marriages

Family social scientists search complex and diverse reasons for people enter into age-heterogamous marriages across societies (McKenzie, 2021; Schwartz, 2013). There are several models to identify reasons for people's age-heterogamous marriages. The rational choice model suggests that people look for partners who can provide life course social and economic support for them. As men earn more as they get older, their partners (women) prefer older men in marriages. Although this reason is changing as more women enter the labor force (McKenzie, 2021; Schwartz, 2013), many of the women still prefer older partners in their marriages in developing and the least developed counties. The demographic model is concerned with sex ratio between men and women in the society, the marriage squeeze, and migration patterns to reason age-dissimilar marriages (McKenzie, 2021). The cultural model explains that the higher the value placed in having children, the higher the age-gap will be. Sociologists prefer structural and social factors of families such as family status and family patterns to explain age differences in marriages (Luke, 2005; Uddin, 2012, 2015).

A great deal of scientific research has shown that age differences in marriages are varied by ethnicity (Labov & Jacobs, 1986), gender SES (Morgan, 1981), marriage pattern (Mensch, 1986; Wilson, 1982), and family structural background factors (Atkinson & Glass, 1985; Casterline et al., 1986). First of all, race/ethnicity background has independent effects on age differences in spouses in first time marriage pattern (Bytheway, 1981; Dressel, 1980; Labov & Jacobs, 1986; Tucker & Mitchell-Kernan, 1990). General trends in first time marriage pattern suggest that although median age differences between men and women in the United States have shrunk, black, African, and Mexican women than white or Hispanic women are the most likely to marry more older men with low socio-economic attainment and previous marriage history due to imbalanced sex ratio and unfavorable marriage market (Mensch, 1986; Spanier & Glick, 1980; Schoen et al., 1989; Wilson, 1982). Atkinson & Glass (1985), analyzing secondary data in 1900-1980, found that age-heterogamous marriages were more likely to occur in black women than in white women in the US. Glick et al. (2006) and other research (see also Michael & Tuma, 1985; Teachman et al., 2000) found that age differences in Black, African, and Mexican couples with collectivistic community identity in first time marriage were markedly higher than its counter-parts in the US and European countries.

In Bangladesh, BBS (2020) reveals that although both men and women currently select mates in similar socio-economic background and their median age differences in marriage are shrinking in urban area, husbands are markedly older than wives in the conservative, collectivistic community groups in rural Bangladesh. Although both Muslim and Santal communities are collectivistic in nature, the findings of Uddin's (2009a, 2015) studies have shown that average age-heterogamy in the Muslim couples (mean=7.71, SD= 4.63) is slightly higher than in the Santal couples (mean=7.51, SD= 4.15) in rural Bangladesh. In this chapter, we expect that collectivistic ethnic communities prefer more age-heterogamous marriages than individualistic ethnic ones across societies.

Hyper Marital Socio-Economic Status

Marital age differences in married couples are reflected in relative gender socio-economic status attainments (e.g., education, occupation, & income) in the family (Malhotra, 1997; Shafer & James, 2013; Uddin, 2009c, Uddin, 2009e, 2015). Richman (1977) suggests that the more egalitarian gender norms in socio-economic status (SES) attainments the society becomes, the men and women hold the less traditional attitudes towards their age differences in marriages. Cross-cultural research (Blumberg, 1978; Lee, 1977) has shown that similarities in SES attainments between men and women lead more likely to age-homogamy in the democratic/egalitarian societies (e.g., U.S., E.U.), while differentials in SES attainments between men and women lead more likely to age-heterogamy in first time marriage in the traditional, polygamous, and authoritarian societies. Further studies reveal that age-heterogamy is higher among those couples who are illiterate or educated at primary level and occupationally traditional (e.g., husbands work outside the home for earning, but wives are home-makers) in nature than those couples who are literate and both work outside the home for earning (Malhotra & Tsui, 1996; Parrado & Zenteno, 2002; United Nations, 1988, 1990, 2000; United Nations Children's Fund, 2001).

In developing countries, some research has shown those couples whose annual family income is below the poverty level than those couples who have higher living standards are more age-heterogeneous in marriages (Malhotra, 1997; Shafer & James, 2013; United Nations, 1990). The lower SES characteristics are the most likely to prevail in under-developed, rural societies, including Bangladesh. Several studies in Bangladesh have found that men with middle class, rural background are the most likely to select younger women than men with lower or higher SES, urban residence background (Uddin, 2009b). The studies argue that middle class people maintain more stable socioeconomic life and observe traditional social norms than the lower and upper class people who are more likely to fluctuate from social norms, because of socioeconomic uncertainty or poverty situation (Malhotra, 1997; Parrado & Zenteno, 2002; Shafer & James, 2013; Uddin, 2009d). Recently, Uddin (2023, 2024) found that there were large differences in family socioeconomic status attainment between majority Muslim and minority ethnic groups in Bangladesh. These socioeconomic differences may influence age-dissimilar marriages between the ethnic groups in the country.

Marriage Pattern

Marriage pattern (e.g., type of marriage, marital arrangement) is an important indicator to explain categorical variances in age-homogamy and age-heterogamy in the married couples (Uddin, 2009d, 2010). In studying marriage pattern, sociologists and anthropologists broadly classify it into two types: (1) monogamy and (2) polygyny. Although *monogamy* (the marriage of one man with one woman at a time or *serial monogamy* remarriage of one man with one woman after divorce) is widely practice, some families permit *polygyny* (the marriage of one man to more than one wife at a time, sororate and levirate, widow or widower' remarriage). In a study of 1681 married men, only 19 cases had two wives and only one had three wives (Uddin, 2010).

Marital arrangement refers to the marriage practice by which a marital bond is developed. There are two types of marital arrangement: (1) contracted marriage and (2) romantic marriage. Although people, in general, prefer *contracted marriage* or arranged marriage (marital arrangement in which parents or elder members of the family choose or select mates for their sons or daughters with or without their concern), *romantic marriage* (marital arrangement in which marital partners fall in love and select themselves as mates for marriage) is increasing day-by-day. These marriage patterns may affect age differences in married couples. Some research has shown that serial monogamous couples are more age-heterogeneous, while the monogamous couples are more age-homogamous (Uddin, 2010, 2012). Further evidence shows that the couples with arranged marriage are more age-heterogamous than the couples with romantic marriage are age-homogenous in marriage relationship in the least-developed societies, including Bangladesh (Crissey, 2005; Malhotra & Tsui, 1996;United Nations, 1988, 1990). In Bangladesh, Uddin (2009b, 2010) found that as Muslims are relatively conservative, they prefer more arranged marriages than other ethnic groups. Differences in marriage patterns may influence age-gap in marriages in Bangladesh.

Family Pattern

Family pattern is an influential factor that explains variances in age-heterogamy and age-homogamy in first time married couples (Lloyd, 2006; United Nations, 1988, 1990; Uddin, 2009a, 2009b). Although people in the collectivistic peasant economy usually prefer more *complex/joint family* (where two or more generations live and maintain *familism* a culture, feeling or subordination of individual goals to the family and belonging to the family for co-ordination of family activities to achieve family goals, assist family members, and maintain intergenerational family ties for adaptation), most of the couples live in simple family (e.g., conjugal family or nuclear family) where one or two generations live.

In Bangladesh, Rahaman (1995) found that out of 203 families simple family was 75.37 percent and complex family was 24.63 percent. In a village study, Sarker (1997) explored that out of 132 families, Muslim nuclear family was 56.8 percent, supplementary nuclear family was 12.1 percent, joint family was 24.9 percent and extended family was 6.2 percent. In a study, Uddin (2012) argues that although nuclear families are increasing due to changes in socioeconomic pattern and urbanization, these families are concerned with their origin of families (family of procreation). In several studies, Uddin (2010, 2012) found that 20-40% of the families are joint or extended. These trends of family patterns may determine age-heterogamous marriage in Bangladesh.

Although evidence on family pattern in this country is abundant, less research has analyzed a link between family pattern and age gap in couples. Some empirical research has found that extended or joint family pattern than nuclear family pattern is closely associated with age-heterogamy than age-homogamy in the married couples (United Nations, 1988, 1990). In this chapter, we expect that extended or joint family pattern with familism than nuclear family pattern with individualistic value is closely linked with age-heterogamy than age-homogamy in the first time married couples (Pyke & Adams, 2010; Uddin, 2009c, 2012).

Family Size

Age differences are associated with family size preference in the first time married couples. Previous research has found that the higher the family size preference is significantly associated with the younger the wife in marriages. BBS (2022) over the decades shows that average family size has changed from 5.36 in 1974 to 2.8 in 2020. Although average family size has gradually shifted into smaller one, overall family size of the census years is too much higher than the expected family size (two or one-child family size).

There are also variations in average family size among the major religious groups with rural, urban, and municipal background. In this respect average family size of Muslim was higher than that in the Hindu, Budhist, Christian and Tribals. Although evidence on family size in Bangladesh is huge, minor previous research has found that higher the family size than the lower family size has independent effects on the couples' age-heterogamy (e.g., husband older, wife younger) than age-homogamy (the same age) in first time marriages (Uddin, 2008). Currently, family size is becoming smaller, 30-50% of the families prefer higher family size. Despite this, higher family size norms still influence age-heterogamous marriage than age-homogamous one (Uddin, 2010, 2012).

Family Residence

Residence refers to the norms by which couples after marriage reside with the bride or groom's parents' family (Malhotra & Tsui, 1996). When people marry they must decide where to live. Decisions about the place of residence are typically determined by cultural rules and occupational status that conform to one or more residences: *Neolocal* is a norm of residence in which newly married couple establishes residence separate from those of both the sides of parents, *biolocal* is a norm of residence in which a newly married couple establishes residence with or near the parents of either spouse, *patrilocal* is a norm of residence by which a married couple lives with the husband's parents' family or husband family, *and matrilocal* is another norm by which a couple lives with the wife's parents' family.

Although couples in a patriarchal society usually prefer patrilocal residence, many of them reside in neolocal residence (when newly married couples live outside the village or town), or biolocal residence (when married couples live in the parents' territory, or matrilocal residence (when husband is died), depending on social, economic, and demographic situations. Relevant popular research has shown that patrilocal residence than other residential patterns (e.g., neolocal, biolocal, matrilocal) are more likely to have a significant association with age-heterogeneous than age-homogamy in the first time married couples in the under-developed cultures, including rural, agricultural economy of Bangladesh (Lloyd, 2006; Malhotra & Tsui, 1996; United Nations, 1988, 1990; Uddin, 2012). In Bangladesh, despite increasing neolocal residence pattern, most of the families are patrilocal. This residence pattern still influences higher age-gap in couples (Uddin, 2012).

Family Authority

Family authority (also formal power) is an influential factor to explain variances in spouses' age differences in marriages (Komter, 1989; Vogler & Pahl, 1994; Uddin & Arefin, 2007). *Family authority* refers to the norms by which legitimate power is assigned on the older family member who controls behavior in the family and makes important decisions about family matters. According to Wolfe (1959), *family authority pattern* is classified into three categories: (1) *Autocratic authority* is an authority type in which a husband is more dominant than his wife and has larger the range of relative and shared authority than wife in the family, (2) *Syncratic authority* is an authority type in which both husband and wife have bal8ance of relative authority, but the range of shared authority is equal to or greater than the combined ranges of the husband and wife, and (3) *Autonomic type* in which both husband and wife have nearly a balance of relative authority, but one has greater range in the shared authority than other within the family.

Although the patriarchal communities, where females are subjugated, are male-dominated, there are wide cultural differences in family authority patterns between men and women in the family. Uddin (2009d) found that most of the Muslim couples would follow autocratic authority (62.07%), while most of the Santal couples would practice Syncratic authority (71.33%) compared to other authority patterns to manage and lead their families. Although evidence on family authority patterns are widely studies, few studies analyze relationships between family authority pattern and age-gap in couples across societies. Some extant studies have shown that the couples with patriarchal authority pattern than matriarchal authority than egalitarian authority pattern in the families are more likely to be age-heterogamous than age-homogamous in marriage pattern (Blumberg & Coleman, 1989; Komter, 1989; Pyke & Adams, 2010; United Nations, 1988, 1990; Vogler & Pahl, 1994; Uddin, 2010). In this chapter, we expect that autocratic family authority than other authority patterns (e.g., syncratic, autonomic) are the most likely to affect age-heterogamy than age-homogamy in the first time married couples in rural Bangladesh. Uddin and Arefin (2007) found that Muslim community was more like to practice patriarchal family authority than other communities. Differences in family authority patterns influence age-gap in couples.

Hypothesis

In light of literature review and its findings on the given areas described above, in this chapter we formulate the following seven research hypotheses:

1. *The ethnic hypothesis*: The Santal couples than the Muslim couples are more likely age-heterogeneous than age-homogenous in first time marriage in rural Bangladesh.
2. *Gender socioeconomic status hypothesis*: The couples who attain lower socioeconomic status than the couples who attain higher socioeconomic status will be more likely age-heterogeneous than age-homogenous.
3. *Marriage pattern hypothesis*: The couples who are married more times (serial monogamous marriage) than the couples who are married one time (monogamous marriage) will be more likely age-heterogeneous than age-homogenous; the arranged married couples than the romantic married couples will be more likely age-heterogeneous than age-homogenous.
4. *Family pattern hypothesis*: The couples who live in extended or joint family pattern than the couples who live in nuclear family will be more likely age-heterogeneous than age-homogenous.
5. *Family size preference hypothesis*: The couples with higher family size pattern than the couples with lower family size pattern are more likely age-heterogeneous than age-homogenous.
6. *Family residence hypothesis*: The couples who live in patrilocal residence pattern than the couples who live in matrilocal residence or other (e.g., neolocal, biolocal) pattern will be more likely age-heterogeneous than age-homogenous.
7. *Family authority hypothesis*: The couples who live in autocratic family authority than the couples who live in syncratic or autonomic family authority will be more likely age-heterogeneous than age-homogenous in the first time marriage.

METHOD

Data and Sample

The data to test the above-mentioned hypotheses were collected from the first time married couples in *Tanore Upazila* of *Rajshahi* district, Bangladesh from January to May in 2013. The couples studied were ethnically Muslim and Santal and that were widely practiced early marriage for their respective family living. First of all through snow-ball process and checking of marriage documents we carefully identified 3500 couples who were married the first time between 1995 and 2004 years and whose age range was 12 to 48 years for husbands and 10 to 45 years for wives. From the preliminary list, 1755 pairs of couples were randomly selected through cluster sampling. The selected couples (e. g., both husband and wife) who sincerely informed their consent to participate in the study were individually interviewed with semi-structural questionnaire, including open-ended and close-ended questions.

In order to collect data we followed several strategies: (1) rapport-building with the selected respondents to create consciousness about the research purposes and objectives, (2) recruiting one female interviewer (who was trained up) to collect data from women who observe *purdah*, and male interviewer with the male respondents. The questions designed were presented to them and answers of the questions asked were written down by the interviewers. Sometimes probing was made when somebody could not understand any question asked. Duration of interview was one and half hours. By the given procedure the data were collected at afternoon when the respondents were leisured, because most of the respondents as farmers and day laborers who would work in the agricultural field from morning to midday and even round the day. After the completion of each interview, some token money with special thanks was given to each pair of couples if it was necessary again for any errors.

Dependent Variable

The dependent variable (DV) for this study is a binary measure of whether or not the couples are age-heterogamous vs. age-homogamous in first time marriage. To distinguish age-heterogamous couples from age-homogamous ones previous research has operationalized for age-heterogamous marriages in which husbands are four or more years older or younger than wives and for age-homogamous marriages in which husbands are no more than three years older or younger than wives in either directions (Atkinson & Glass, 1985; Vera, Berardo, & Berardo, 1985; Spanier & Glick, 1980). As men younger-women older marriages in rural Bangladesh are socio-culturally odd, so we slightly modified earlier definitions and we operationalize age-heterogamous marriages in which husbands are three or more years older than wives, while age-homogamous marriages in which husbands are one or two years older than wives. First of all we accounted for chronological age of the couples in year and then husbands' age was separated from wives' age. Later the actual age differences in the spouses were categorized into two groups, following our operational definition and coded as 0= age-homogamy (23.42%) and 1= age-heterogamy (76.58%) in first time marriage.

Independent Variable

Independent variables (IV) or predictor variables for this study are regressed to explain variances in age-heterogamy from age-homogamy in first time marriages in rural Bangladesh. The predictor variables derived from Atkinson & Glass (1985) and Vera, Berardo, & Berardo (1985) lists are couples' socioeconomic status (SES) in the family (e.g., husband's education, wife's education, husband's occupation, annual family income), ethnicity, marriage pattern (e.g., type of marriage, marital arrangement), and family structural patterns (e.g., family size, family type, residence, family authority). Of the predictor variables ethnicity or ethnic identity derived from single, close-ended question (South, 1991) was nominally measured and coded as 0= Muslim, and 1= Santal. Couples were categorized into two groups and coded as 0= husband and 1= wife. Of the sample, self-reported ethnic identity of Muslim couples (42.74%) than the ethnic identity of Santal couples (33.75%) was more likely to have an association with age-heterogamous than age-homogenous (X^2= 66.36, df= 1, p= 0.000) in first time marriages (see, Table 1).

A measure of couples' SES in the family was used open-ended questions, following Nam & Terrie's (1981) and South's (1991) framework: Education, occupation, and income. Especially, husband's and wife's education was numerically measured and accounted for in years. Later the numerical values were categorized into three groups and coded as 0= Illiterate (there is no formal education), 1= primary (1-5 years of education), and 2= secondary and above (6+ years of education). Husband's and wife's occupational status was nominally measured and coded as 1= farming, 2= small business, 3= day laboring for husband and 0= housewife only and 1= housewife and day-laboring for wife. Annual family income was numerically measured in Taka (1 US$ = 77 Bangladesh Taka in currency exchange) and then it was categorized into 1= low income family (10,000-14,000), 2= middle income family (15000-19,000), and 3= high income family (20,000+). Frequency distribution on the SES indicators shows that the couples with illiteracy (55.56% for husbands & 53.50% for wives), farming (31.62%) and day-laboring (40.34%), and middle income (44.10%) are more likely to be age-heterogamous than age-homogamous (see, Table 1).

The type of marriage was coded as 0= monogamy (one time married) and 1= serial monogamy (two or more times married). Marital arrangement was coded as 0= romantic marriage, and 1= arranged marriage. Family size was accounted for as the number of live births for per couple and coded as 1= low family size (1-2 children), medium family size (3-4 children), and 3= high family size (5+ live children) in the family. Family structure was nominally measured and coded as 1= nuclear family (the married couples and unmarried children), 2= joint, and 3= extended family (more than two generations in the family). Residence pattern was measured and coded as 1= patrilocal residence, 2= matrilocal residence, 3= others. Family authority was nominally measured and coded as 1=autocratic authority, 2=syncratic authority, and 3=autonomic authority in the family (Author, 2009). Of the marriage and family structural characteristics the couples with arranged marriage (56.92%), medium family size (42.91%), patrilocal residence (52.14%), and autocratic authority (42.22%) except other categories of marriage and family structural patterns are significantly associated with age-heterogamous marriages than age-homogamous marriages (see, Table 1).

Analytic Approach

We began simple analysis using percentage differences in age-homogenous vs. age-heterogeneous (DV) by a set of categorical predictor variables: Couples' SES in the family, ethnicity, marriage pattern, and family structural patterns (IV) for the first time married couples. As our tendency to find out co-variations and predictions age-heterogeneous marriages than age-homogenous marriages by the categorical predictor variables, including couples' SES in the family, ethnicity, marriage pattern, and family structural patterns, so we first of all apply Spearman's rank order bivariate correlation, including X^2 test (data shown in table 1 & 2) for sample distribution. Overall frequency distributions of the sample reveal that age-heterogamous marriages than age-homogeneous ones are more likely associated (significantly different at p<0.01 & p<0.05 level) with (affected by) ethnicity, couples' SES, marital arrangement, family size, family residence, and family authority in which the couples live. To reassure co-variations in age-homogenous vs. age-heterogeneous marriages by the categorical predictor variables, then we apply bivariate correlation test to find out one-to-one relations and strength of relationships. The results shown in table 2 confirm our earlier X^2 test's findings (Ishii-Kuntz, 1991).

To specify and substantiate categorical co-variations or predictions of IVs on DV we apply binary logistic regression (BLR) analysis, using backward stepwise likelihood ratio (Wald) method (Ishii-Kuntz, 1991; Morgan & Teachman, 1988). In so doing, current age, sex, and age at first marriage of the couples that are categorized into dummy variables are selected one-by-one in the analysis. Overall result in step 0 shows that there are correct percentages 76.6%, predicting age-heterogeneous marriages than age-homogenous ones (reference category) by the categorical predictor variables included (Uecker & Stokes, 2008). In addition, to fit the model chi-squire values and its degree of freedom are gradually decreased from step 1 (X^2= 195.94, df= 21, p= 0.000) to step 4 (X^2= 191.91, df= 16, p= 0.000) and values of degree of freedom are lesser than the chi-squire values (Morgan & Teachman, 1988). In addition, the correct percentages increase from 79.1 in model 1 to 79.5 in model 4.

We use coefficients of β, SE, Exp. β, and its 95% confidence intervals (CI) to predict variances in DV by IVs. The results of the analysis, in detail, are presented in Table 3.

RESULTS

Table 1 reveals respondents' self-reported percentages of age-heterogamy vs. age-homogamy by categorical predictor variables. Of the predictor variables ethnicity, couples' SES status in the family, annual family income, marital arrangement, family size, family residence, and family authority except type of marriage and family are significantly associated with age-heterogamy (p<.01, p<.05) than age-homogamy in first time marriage. In order to specify positive and negative relations and strengths between the variables we analyze bivariate correlation.

Results presented in table 2 show that age-heterogamy than age-homogamy is positively associated with husband's education ($r_s = .08$, p<.01), husband's occupation ($r_s = .11$, p<.01), marital arrangement ($r_s = .05$, p<.05), family residence ($r_s = .10$, p<.01), and family authority ($r_s = .15$, p<.01), but negatively associated with ethnicity ($r_s = .-11$, p<.01), wife's education ($r_s = .-19$, p<.01) and occupation ($r_s = .-08$, p<.01) and family size ($r_s = -05$, p<.05). Bivariate correlation analysis also shows that there is no linking age-heterogamy with family income, type of marriage, and family structure. Of the categorical predictor variables husband's occupation, family residence, and authority, however, may have the greatest positive effects, but wife's education has the greatest negative effects on age-heterogamous marriages than age-homogamous marriages.

Table 1. Frequency and Percentages of Age-Homogamy vs. Age Heterogamy by Family Socio-Economic Background Characteristics (N=1755)

Background Variables Descriptions	Age-Homogamy	Age-Heterogamy	df	X^2
Ethnicity Muslim	135 (7.69)	750 (42.74)	1	66.36*
Santal	276 (15.73)	594 (33.85)		(0.000)
Husband's Education Illiterate (0 year)	300 (17.09)	975 (55.56)	2	7.09**
Primary (1-5 years)	51 (2.91)	222 (12.65)		(0.030)
Secondary+ (6+ years)	60 (3.42)	147 (8.38)		
Wife's education Illiterate (0 year)	321 (18.29)	939 (53.50)	2	10.55*
Primary (1-5 years)	69 (3.93)	312 (17.78)		(0.005)
Secondary+ (6+ years)	21 (1.20)	93 (5.30)		
Husband's occupation Farming	96 (5.47)	555 (31.62)	2	65.99*
Small business	69 (3.93)	282 (16.07)		(0.000)
Day-laboring	246 (14.02)	507 (28.89)		
Wife's education Housewife only	249 (14.19)	636 (36.24)	1	22.15*
Housewife-day-laboring	162 (9.23)	708 (40.34)		(0.000)
Annual family income Low (10,000-14,000)	84 (4.79)	312 (17.78)	2	16.84*
Medium(15,000-19,000)	279 (15.73)	774 (44.10)		(0.000)
High (20,000+)	48 (2.74)	258 (14.70)		
Types of marriage Monogamy	345 (19.66)	1092 (62.22)	1	1.54
Serial monogamy	66 (3.76)	252 (14.36)		(0.242)
Marital arrangement Romantic marriage	126 (7.18)	345 (19.66)	1	3.99**
Arranged marriage	285 (16.24)	999 (56.92)		(0.046)
Family size pattern Low (1-2)	111 (6.32)	465 (26.50)	2	12.10*
Medium (3-4)	270 (15.38)	753 (42.91)		(0.002)
High (5+)	30 (1.71)	126 (7.18)		
Family structure Nuclear family	336 (19.15)	1089 (62.05)	2	0.49
Joint family	42 (2.39)	153 (8.72)		(0.785)
Extended family	411 (23.42)	102 (5.81)		
Family residence pattern Patrilocal	324 (18.46)	915 (52.14)	3	22.40*
Matrilocal	30 (1.71)	150 (8.55)		(0.000)
Others	51 (2.91)	207 (11.79)	2	43.34*
Family authority pattern Autocratic	210 (11.97)	741 (42.22)		(0.000)
Syncratic	171 (9.74)	447 (25.47)		
Autonomic	30 (1.71)	156 (8.89)		

Note: Percentages in parentheses.
*p>0.01, **p>0.05,

Table 3 presents coefficients and odds ratios from a binary logistic regression model (backward stepwise method) predicting age-heterogamy in the first time married couples. Overall results revealed that approximately 76.6% of the variance of age-heterogamous marriages was accounted for by the categorical predictor variables (β= 1.185, SE= .06), exp. (β) = 3.270, $p<.01$): Ethnicity, couples' SES, marriage pattern, and family structural characteristics. Of the categorical predictor variables, Muslim ethnicity (β= .70, SE= .15, exp. β = 2.01, $p<.00$; CI for exp. β = 1.49-2.71), husband's primary education completed (β= .56, SE= .31, exp. β = 1.76, $p<.05$; CI for exp. β = 1.12-2.78) and farming for husband's occupation (β= .60, SE= .17, Exp. β = 1.82, $p<.00$; CI for exp. β = 1.29-2.53), housewife only for wife's occupation (β= .70, SE= .15, exp. β = 2.01, $p<.00$; CI for exp. β = 1.49-2.71), medium family income (β= -.61, SE= .18, Exp. β = .54, $p<.00$; CI for exp.

β = 1.49-2.71), arranged marriage for mate selection (β= .77, SE= .17, exp. β = 1.75, *p*<.00; CI for exp. β = .60-1.03), medium family size(β= -.68, SE= .23, exp. β = .51, *p*<.00; CI for exp. β = .47-1.23), patrilocal residence (β= -1.65, SE= .44, exp. β = .52, *p*<.00; CI for exp. β = 1.7 9-2.79) and autocratic family authority (β= -.73, SE= .24, exp. β = .52, *p*<.00; CI for exp. β = .53-1.29) shown in model (step) 1 were positively or negatively linked to age-heterogamy than age-homogamy.

The next models (2-4) also suggest that the categorical predictor variables were significantly associated with age-heterogamy with slight decreasing of coefficients or values, but the ranges of CI for exp. β were increased. It is interesting to note that ethnicity of Muslim, couples' occupation, medium family income, and family size, arranged marriage for mate selection process, patrilocal family residence, and autocratic family authority were the greatest (1% - 3%) risks factors to persist age-heterogamous marriages than age-homogamous ones.

Table 2. Inter-correlation coefficients (r_s) between Family Socio-Economic Status and Age-Heterogamy in First Time Marriage (N=1755)

Variables	2	3	4	5	6	7	8	9	10	11	12	13
1. Age heterogamy	.106* (.000)	.077* (.001)	.191* (.000)	.112* (.000)	.080* (.001)	.030 (.216)	.030 (.215)	.048** (.046)	.046** (.053)	.006 (.791)	.102* (.000)	.152* (.000)
2. Ethnicity	1.00	-.164* (.000)	.577* (.000)	.036 (.134)	-.041 (.088)	-.001 (.971)	.013 (.589)	-.001 (.956)	.014 (.545)	.042 (.079)	.019 (.421)	.032 (.178)
3. Husband's education		1.00	-.033 (.165)	-.141* (.000)	.246* (.000)	.035 (.139)	-.013 (.597)	-.015 (.534)	.188* (.000)	-.075* (.002)	-.021 (382)	-.110* (.000)
4. Wife's education			1.00	-.126* (.000)	.134* (.000)	.084* (.000)	.067* (.005)	.069* (.004)	-.012 (.617)	.006 (.817)	.080* (.001)	-.007 (.756)
5. Husband's occupation				1.00	-.019 (.434)	.011 (.633)	.005 (.844)	.013 (.599)	.093* (.000)	.003 (.898)	-004 (.874)	.053** (.026)
6. Wife's occupation					1.00	.013 (.593)	-.040 (.091)	.045 (.060)	-.102* (.000)	.067* (.005)	.059** (.014)	.447* (.000)
7. Family income						1.00	-.004 (.871)	.048** (.045)	.071* (.003)	.083* (.000)	-.010 (.685)	.061** (.011)
8. Type of marriage							1.00	.085* (.000)	-.058* (.015)	.080* (.001)	.142* (.000)	-.001 (.954)
9. Marital arrangement								1.00	.007 (.779)	.068* (.000)	-.066* (.006)	.087* (.000)
10. Family size									1.00	-.001 (983)	.037 (.119)	.047** (.050)
11. Family structure										1.00	-.030 (.214)	.100** (.000)

continued on following page

Table 2. Continued

Variables	2	3	4	5	6	7	8	9	10	11	12	13
12. Family residence											1.00	.055** (.020)
13. Family authority												1.00

Note: **p<0.01, *p<0.05 (2-tailed test)

DISCUSSION

Despite age-homogamous marriages are increasing associated with changes in sociodemographic status, social structure, and personal characteristics in the urban couples, a significant number of rural couples widely practice age-heterogamous marriages in Bangladesh. Interviewing representative sample of the rural couples from *Tanore Upazila* of *Rajshahi* district, Bangladesh we find that most of the couples (76.58%) are age-heterogamous than age-homogamous (23.42%) in first time marriage. The age-heterogamous marriage in the rural couples is significantly associated with the Muslim collective ethnicity, couples' lower SES, traditional marriage pattern, high family size norms, patriarchal residence, and authoritarian family structure in traditional, agricultural economy of Bangladesh.

The major findings suggest that of the categorical predictors Muslim ethnicity than Santal ethnicity, hierarchical gender SES status in the family (e.g., husband's educational and occupational attainment is higher than wife, husband income-earner, wife home-maker), middle family income, traditional mate selection (arranged marriage), middle family size, patrilocal family residence, and autocratic (authoritarian) family authority are significantly associated with age-heterogamy ($p<.01$, $p<.05$) than age-homogamy in first time marriage. These findings partially support our gender status, family size, family income, marital arrangement, family residence, and family authority hypotheses. It is interesting to note that the findings of ethnic community identity status are different from some previous literature (Atkinson & Glass, 1985; Glick, Ruf, White, & Goldscheider, 2006; Parrado & Zenteno, 2002). For example, Atkinson & Glass (1985) find that age-heterogamous marriages are more likely to occur in the blacks than in the whites. Glick, Ruf, White, & Goldscheider (2006) found that although both men and women of Hispanics and Whites are the most likely to marry earlier than Black, African, and Mexican, age differences in Black, African, and Mexican couples are markedly higher than its counter-parts.

Age-heterogamous marriages also are varied by hierarchical gender SES in the family in which husbands' SES attainment is higher than its counter-parts, wives. The findings of the study suggest that lower education (husband's primary school completed) than illiteracy and occupation (husbands' breadwinner and wives' home-maker) than both the couples' breadwinning and medium family income attainment than lower or higher ones are significant predictors of age-heterogamy than age homogamy in first time marriages. These findings are consistent with previous research's findings dating back to the 1970s (Blumberg, 1978; Lee, 1977). They found that differentials in gender or couples' SES attainments in the families are more likely to lead age-heterogamy in first time marriage in the traditional, hierarchical, and authoritarian societies. Recent past studies reveal that age heterogamy is higher among those couples who are illiterate and occupationally traditional (e.g., husbands work outside the home for earning, but wives are home-makers) in nature (Parrado & Zenteno, 2002; Pyke & Adams, 2010; United Nations, 1990, 2000; United Nations Children's Fund, 2001).

Table 3. Coefficients, Standard Error (SE), and Odds Ratios From Binary Logistic Regression Analysis Predicting Age-Heterogamy

Variables in the Equation	Model 1	Model 2	Model 3	Model 4
	B SE Exp(β)	B SE Exp(β)	B SE Exp(β)	B SE Exp(β)
Ethnicity	.70* .15 2.01	.70* .15 2.01	.70* .15 2.01	.72* .15 2.06
Muslim	.35 .10 0.98	.35 .10 0.94	.35 .10 0.92	.35 .10 0.96
Santal				
Husband's education	.22 .19 1.25	.22 .19 1.21	.22 .18 1.24	.19 .19 1.21
Illiterate (0 year)	.56** .31 1.76	.56** .23 1.70	.57** .23 1.76	.57** .23 1.77
Primary (1-5 years)	.10 .09 0.75	.11 .09 0.74	.12 .10 0.76	.12 .10 0.75
Secondary+ (6+ years)				
Wife's education	-.22 .27 0.80	-.23 .27 0.79	-.23 .27 0.79	- - -
Illiterate (0 year)	.02 .30 1.02	-.01 .30 0.98	-.01 .30 0.97	- - -
Primary (1-5 years)	-.01 .23 0.73	-.02 .20 0.72	-.02 .24 0.70	- - -
Secondary+ (6+ years)				
Husband's occupation	.60* .17 1.82	.59* .17 1.81	.59* .17 1.81	.60* .17 1.81
Farming	.27 .18 1.30	.27 .17 1.31	.26 .18 1.30	.29 .17 1.31
Small business	.05 .15 0.45	.04 .08 0.44	.01 .08 0.42	.01 .18 0.42
Day-laboring				
Wife's occupation	-.34** .15 0.71	-.32** .15 0.73	-.29** .14 0.75	-.28** .14 0.75
Housewife only	.03 .03 0.08	.03 .04 0.23	.02 .22 0.80	.02 .22 0.80
Day-laboring				
Family income	-.32 .21 0.73	-.32 .21 0.73	-.32 .21 0.74	-.35 .21 0.70
Low (10,000-14,000)	-.61* .18 0.54	-.61* .18 0.55	-.60* .18 0.56	-.64* .18 0.53
Medium (15,000-19,000)	.09 .07 0.09	.08 .05 0.36	.08 .10 0.36	.08 .10 0.36
High (20,000+)				
Types of marriage	-.13 .16 0.88	-.13 .16 0.88	-.12 .16 0.83	- - -
Monogamy	-.52 .21 1.89	-.53 .21 1.91	-.52 .21 1.90	- - -
Serial monogamy				
Marital arrangement	-.24 .13 0.79	-.25 .14 0.81	-.25 .13 0.80	-.27 .13 0.81
Romantic marriage	.77* .17 1.57	.76* .15 1.56	.75* .15 1.57	.73* .15 1.58
Arranged marriage				
Family size pattern	-.28 .24 0.76	-.26 .25 0.77	-.26 .24 0.76	-.23 .25 0.80
Low (1-2)	-.68* .23 0.51	-.69* .23 0.50	-.69* .23 0.50	-.66* .23 0.51
Medium (3-4)	.03 .01 0.28	-.02 .02 0.22	-.22 .18 0.19	-.22 .18 0.19
High (5+)				
Family structure	-.05 .22 0.95	- - -	- - -	- - -
Nuclear family	-.22 .30 0.81	- - -	- - -	- - -
Joint family	-.14 .27 0.71	- - -	- - -	- - -
Extended family				
Family residence	-1.65* .44 0.19	-1.65* .44 0.19	-1.66* .44 0.19	-1.67* .44 0.19
Patrilocal	-0.41 .05 0.25	-0.40 .05 0.24	-0.40 .05 0.24	-0.39 .04 0.24
Matrilocal	-0.30 .04 0.21	-0.29 .04 0.21	-0.28 .04 0.21	-0.27 .04 0.21
Others				
Family authority	-.73* .24 0.52	-.72* .24 0.49	-.71* .24 0.49	-.73* .24 0.48
Autocratic	-.19 .23 0.93	-.19 .23 0.83	-.19 .23 0.83	-.21 .23 0.81
Syncratic	-.04 .01 0.06	-.04 .02 0.04	-.04 .02 0.04	-.04 .20 0.04
Autonomic	3.86* .69 47.41	3.78* .66 43.64	3.67* .64 39.41	3.53* .59 34.13
Constant	195.94* 21	195.26* 19	194.68* 17	191.91* 16
Omnibus Test for X^2	0.000	0.000	0.000	0.000
-2 log likelihood	1714.51	1715.19	1715.77	1718.54

Notes: Significant at: *p<.01, **p<.05, ***p<0.001; reference category is age-homogamy

It is noteworthy that older men higher SES marry younger women with lower SES for reproductive success or higher family size and greater bargaining power in marital and family life (Buss, 1989; Schoen & Wooldredge, 1989; Shafer & James, 2013). The findings of the study suggest that the couples with medium family size (number of 3-4 live births) than lower (number of 1-2 live births) or higher family size (number of 5+ live births) are the most likely age-heterogamous. Another remarkable finding suggests that patrilocal residence than matrilocal or biolocal residence, and autocratic family authority than syncratic or autonomic family authority are the greatest risks factors to persist age-heterogamous marriages in rural Bangladesh (Author, 2009). According to Buss (1989), the younger females are attracted by older males, because the younger females are capable to reproduce more new generations than older females. Schoen & Wooldredge (1989) explain men with higher socioeconomic resources are the most likely to marry relatively younger women with lower socio-economic resources for greater bargaining power in marital and family situation. The findings on authority pattern are also consistently supported by Blood & Wolfe's (1960) and Pyke & Adams (2010) findings. They found that older men with higher SES resources select younger women with lower SES resources to assert their masculinity and patriarchal power through which men can control women in the families in the traditional, authoritarian societies, including Bangladesh.

LIMITATIONS AND IMPLICATION

This chapter explored that a significant number of age-heterogamous marriages are associated with Muslim ethnicity than Santal ethnicity, differences in couples' SES in the family (e.g., husband's educational is higher than wife, husband income-earner, wife home-maker), middle family income than lower or higher income, arranged marriage than romantic one, middle family size than lower or higher family size, patrilocal family residence than matrilocal residence, and autocratic (authoritarian) family authority than syncratic or autonomic authority in first time marriage. These findings may enrich partially in social evolutionary (Buss, 1988) or social psychological (Schoen & Wooldredge, 1989) hypothesis and fully in sociological hypothesis (Atkinson & Glass, 1985; Casterline, Williams, & McDonald, 1986; Mensch, 1986; Richman, 1977; Pyke & Adams, 2010). Although the findings of the study mainly enhance or enrich family structural sociological hypothesis, future research should control some confounding factors, such as current age or age cohorts, age at first marriage, and duration of marital life of the couples to understand age-heterogamous marriages with the predictor variables.

In spite of the limitations, the findings may be implied with cautions in social policy and practices on background factors related to age-heterogamous marriages and family formation in Bangladesh. Practically, the government of Bangladesh may design appropriate social policy to provide formal and non-formal social support to those Muslim ethnic couples who are age-heterogamous in marriage relation in association with differences gender SES, higher family size norms, patriarchal residence pattern, traditional mate selection and autocratic family authority (Uddin, 2015). To change in the social and family system the government of Bangladesh may also provide social support in informal job skill training to those couples who follow traditional family role. Because past experience has shown that women's educational attainment and occupational role outside the family enhance egalitarian values in family system and its related age-homogenous marriage pattern. Based on the findings social practitioners, especially social workers may work with the couples who suffer from age-heterogeneous marriage relations in connection with Muslim ethnicity, differences in couples' SES in the family, middle family income, arranged marriage, middle family size, patrilocal family residence, and autocratic (authoritarian) family authority in first time marriage in rural Bangladesh. In doing so, family social worker may work with those couples who face negative consequences of age-heterogamous marriages in rural Bangladesh.

CONCLUSION

In this chapter we found that age-heterogamous marriages are associated with ethnicity, dif00ferences in gender SES in the family, middle family income than lower or higher income, arranged marriage than romantic one, middle family size than lower or higher family size, patrilocal family residence than matrilocal residence, and autocratic (authoritarian) family authority than syncratic or autonomic authority in first time marriage. These findings have practical implications in changes age-heterogamous marriages in association with changes in family origins. Although the findings of the study mainly enhance or enrich family structural sociological hypothesis, future researchers should conduct longitudinal research to understand age-heterogamous marriages with the predictor variables across developing societies.

ACKNOWLEDGEMENT

Author acknowledged the respondents who were sincerely consent and actively participated in the study: Predictors of Age-Heterogamy in First Time Marriage in Rural Bangladesh.

REFERENCES

Ahmed, A. U. (1996). Socio-economic determinants of age at first marriage in Bangladesh. *Journal of Biosocial Science*, 18(1), 35–42. DOI: 10.1017/S0021932000006477 PMID: 3944149

Atkinson, M. P., & Glass, B. L. (1985). Marital age heterogamy and homogamy, 1900 to 1980. *Journal of Marriage and Family*, 47(3), 685–691. DOI: 10.2307/352269

Bangladesh Bureau of Statistics. (2010). *Statistical yearbook of Bangladesh*. Statistics Division, Ministry of Planning, Government of the People's Republic of Bangladesh.

Barbieri, M., & Hertrich, V. (2005). Age difference between spouses and contraceptive practice in sub-Saharan Africa. *Population*, 60(5), 617–654. DOI: 10.3917/pope.505.0617

Berardo, F. M., Appel, J., & Berardo, D. H. (1993). Age dissimilar marriages: Review and assessment. *Journal of Aging Studies*, 7(1), 93–106. DOI: 10.1016/0890-4065(93)90026-G

Blood, R., & Wolfe, D. (1960). *Husbands and wives: The dynamics of married living*. Free Press.

Blumberg, R. L., & Coleman, T. M. (1989). A theoretical look at the gender balance of power in the American couple. *Jornal Dos Farmacêuticos*, 10(10), 225–250. DOI: 10.1177/019251389010002005 PMID: 12342284

Bytheway, W. R. (1981). The variation with age of age differences in marriage. *Journal of Marriage and Family*, 43(4), 923–927. DOI: 10.2307/351348

Casterline, J. B., Williams, L., & McDonald, P. (1986). The age difference between spouses: Variations among developing countries. *Population Studies*, 40(3), 353–374. DOI: 10.1080/0032472031000142296

Chen, Y.-H., & Chen, H. (2014). Continuity and changes in the timing and formation of first marriage among postwar birth cohorts in Taiwan. *Journal of Family Issues*, 35(12), 1584–1604. DOI: 10.1177/0192513X14538026

Chowdhury, F. D. (2004). The socio-cultural context of child marriage in a Bangladeshi village. *International Journal of Social Welfare*, 13(4), 244–253. DOI: 10.1111/j.1369-6866.2004.00318.x

Crissey, S. R. (2005). Race/ethnic differences in the marital expectations of adolescents: The role of romantic relationships. *Journal of Marriage and Family*, 67(3), 697–709. DOI: 10.1111/j.1741-3737.2005.00163.x

Dommaraju, P. (2023). Age-gap between spouses in South and Southeast Asia. *Journal of Family Issues*, 45(5), 1242–1260. DOI: 10.1177/0192513X231155662

Glick, J. E., Ruf, S. D., White, M. J., & Goldscheider, F. (2006). Educational engagement and early family formation: Differences by ethnicity and generation. *Social Forces*, 84(3), 1391–1415. DOI: 10.1353/sof.2006.0049

ICDDRB. (2007). *Health and demographic surveillance system- Matlab* (Vol. 39). International Centre for Diarrheal Disease Research, Bangladesh.

Islam, M. N., & Ahmed, A. U. (1998). Age at first marriage and its determinants in Bangladesh. *Asia-Pacific Population Journal*, 13(2), 73–92. DOI: 10.18356/f31b417e-en PMID: 12321742

Kemkes-Grottenthaler, A. (2004). For better or worse, till death do us part: Spousal age gap and differential longevity- evidence from historical demography. *Collegium Antropologicum*, 28, 203–219. PMID: 15571094

Klinger-Vartabedian, L., & Wispe, L. (1989). Age differences in marriage and female longevity. *Journal of Marriage and Family*, 51(1), 195–202. DOI: 10.2307/352380

Komter, A. (1989). Hidden power in marriage. *Gender & Society*, 3(2), 187–216. DOI: 10.1177/089124389003002003

Lloyd, K. M. (2006). Latinas' transition to first marriage: An examination of four theoretical perspectives. *Journal of Marriage and Family*, 68(4), 993–1014. DOI: 10.1111/j.1741-3737.2006.00309.x

Luke, N. (2005). Confronting the 'Sugar Daddy' stereotype: Age and economic asymmetries and risky sexual behavior in urban Kenya. *International Family Planning Perspectives, 31* (1), 6–14. doi:. JSTOR 3649496. PMID 15888404.DOI: 10.1363/3100605

Malhotra, A. (1997). Gender and the timing of marriage: Rural-urban differences in Java. *Journal of Marriage and Family*, 59(2), 434–450. DOI: 10.2307/353481

Malhotra, A., & Tsui, A. O. (1996). Marriage timing in Sri Lanka: The role of modern norms and ideas. *Journal of Marriage and Family*, 58(2), 476–490. DOI: 10.2307/353511

McKenzie, L. (2021). Age-dissimilar couple relationships: 25 years in review. *Journal of Family Theory & Review*, 13(4), 496–514. DOI: 10.1111/jftr.12427

Mensch, B. (1986). Age differences between spouses in first marriage. *Social Biology*, 33, 229–240. PMID: 3563546

Michael, R. T., & Tuma, N. B. (1985). Entry into marriage and parenthood by young men and women: The influence of family background. *Demography*, 22(4), 515–544. DOI: 10.2307/2061586 PMID: 4076482

Mitra, S. N., Ali, M. N., Islam, S., Cross, A. R., & Saha, T. (1994). *Bangladesh demographic and health survey 1993–1994*. Mitra and Associates.

Nam, C. E., & Terrie, E. W. (1981). *Measurement of socioeconomic status: Current issues*. Westview Press.

Parrado, E. A., & Zenteno, R. M. (2002). Gender differences in union formation in Mexico: Evidence from marital search model. *Journal of Marriage and Family*, 64(3), 756–773. DOI: 10.1111/j.1741-3737.2002.00756.x

Presser, H. (1975). Age differences between spouses: Trends, patterns, and social implications. *The American Behavioral Scientist*, 19(2), 190–205. DOI: 10.1177/000276427501900205

Pyke, K., & Adams, M. (2010). What's age got to do with it? A case study analysis of power and gender in husband-older marriages. *Journal of Family Issues*, 31(6), 748–777. DOI: 10.1177/0192513X09357897

Rahaman, S. M. Z. (1995). *Muslim marriage practices in a village of Bangladesh. Rajshahi University Studies* (Vol. 3). Part-C.

Richman, J. (1977). Bargaining for sex and status: the dating service and sex role change. In Stein, P., Richman, J., & Hannon, N. (Eds.), *the family: functions, conflicts, and symbols* (pp. 158–165). Addison Wesley.

Roy, K. T. (2008). Determinants of early marriage in Rajshahi, Bangladesh. *Pakistan Journal of Social Sciences*, 5(6), 606–611.

Schoen, R., Wooldredge, J., & Thomas, B. (1989). Ethnic and educational effects on marriage choice. *Social Science Quarterly*, 70, 617–630.

Schwartz, C. R. (2013). Trends and variation in assortative mating: Causes and consequences. *Annual Review of Sociology*, 39(1), 451–470. DOI: 10.1146/annurev-soc-071312-145544

Shafer, K., & James, S. L. (2013). Gender and socioeconomic status differences in first and scond marriage formation. *Journal of Marriage and Family*, 75(3), 544–564. DOI: 10.1111/jomf.12024

Shehan, C. L., Berardo, F. M., Vera, H., & Carley, S. M. (1991). Women in age-discrepant marriages. *Journal of Family Issues*, 12(3), 291–305. DOI: 10.1177/019251391012003003

Silva, T., & Percheski, C. (2024). Age-heterogamous partnerships: Prevalence and partner differences by marital status and gender composition. *Demographic Research*, 50, 625–642. DOI: 10.4054/DemRes.2024.50.23

South, S. J. (1991). Sociodemographic differentials in mate selection preferences. *Journal of Marriage and Family*, 53(4), 928–940. DOI: 10.2307/352998

Spanier, G., & Glick, P. (1980). Mate selection differentials between whites and blacks in the United States. *Social Forces*, 58(3), 707–735. DOI: 10.2307/2577180

Teachman, J. D., Tedrow, L. M., & Crowder, K. D. (2000). The changing demography of America's families. *Journal of Marriage and Family*, 62(4), 1234–1246. DOI: 10.1111/j.1741-3737.2000.01234.x

Uddin, M. E. (2008). Cross-cultural comparison of family size and composition between Muslim and Santal communities in rural Bangladesh. *World Cultures eJournal, 16*(1), 1-20.

Uddin, M. E. (2009a). Age at first marriage for husband and wife between Muslim and Santal communities in rural Bangladesh. *International Journal of Humanities and Social Science*, 3(4), 318–326.

Uddin, M. E. (2009b). Cross-cultural comparison of marriage relationship between Muslim and Santal communities in a village of Bangladesh. *World Cultures eJournal, 17*(1), 1-17.

Uddin, M. E. (2009c). Correlates of family cultural background and family status and role between Muslim and Santal communities in rural Bangladesh. *Antrocom: Online Journal of Anthropology*, 5(1), 15–27.

Uddin, M. E. (2009d). Family structure between Muslim and Santal communities in rural Bangladesh. *International Journal of Humanities and Social Science*, 5(6), 438–447. DOI: 10.5281/zenodo.1058249

Uddin, M. E. (2009e). Cross-cultural socio-economic status attainment between Muslim and Santal couple in rural Bangladesh. *International Journal of Humanities and Social Science*, 4(11), 779–786. DOI: 10.5281/zenodo.1075058

Uddin, M. E. (2010). *Family structure: A cross-cultural comparison between Muslim and Santal communities in rural Bangladesh*. Saarbruchen: Lambert Academic Publishing.

Uddin, M. E. (2012). Cross-cultural family structure among Muslim, Hindu, Santal and Oraon communities in Bangladesh. *Journal of GLBT Family Studies*, 8(4), 334–360. DOI: 10.1080/1550428X.2012.705620

Uddin, M. E. (2015). Family socio-cultural values affecting early marriage between Muslim and Santal communities in rural Bangladesh. *The International Journal of Sociology and Social Policy*, 35(3/4), 141–164. DOI: 10.1108/IJSSP-06-2014-0046

Uddin, M. E. (2023). Understanding ethnic disparities in family status attainment: Implications for family welfare policy-practice in Bangladesh. In Chandan, H. (Ed.), *Implications of marginalization and critical race theory on social justice* (pp. 197–219). IGI Global. DOI: 10.4018/978-1-6684-3615-8.ch010

Uddin, M. E. (2024). Family socioeconomic inequalities between majorities and minorities across the globe: Implication for policy practice. In Baikady, R. (Eds.), *The Palgrave handbook of Global social problems*. Springer. DOI: 10.1007/978-3-030-68127-2_441-1

Uddin, M. E., & Arefin, M. S. (2007). Family authority pattern and gender dimension of birth control methods adoption in the Santal and Oraon ethnic communities in rural Bangladesh. *International Journal of Humanities and Social Science*, 2(8), 430–437.

United Nations. (1988). *First marriage: Patterns and determinants*. Population Division.

United Nations. (1990). *Patterns of first marriage: Timing and prevalence*. Population Division.

United Nations. (2000). *World marriage patterns*. Population Division.

United Nations Children's Fund (UNICEF). (2001). *Early marriage: child spouses*. UNICEF.

Utomo, A. J. (2014). Marrying up? Trends in age and education gaps among married couples in Indonesia. *Journal of Family Issues*, 35(12), 1683–1706. DOI: 10.1177/0192513X14538023

Vera, H., Berardo, D., & Berardo, F. M. (1985). Age heterogamy in marriage. *Journal of Marriage and Family*, 47(3), 553–566. DOI: 10.2307/352258

Vogler, C., & Pahl, I. (1994). Money, power and inequality in marriage. *The Sociological Review*, 42(2), 263–288. DOI: 10.1111/j.1467-954X.1994.tb00090.x

Wilson, B. (1982). Age differences between spouses and marital instability. Paper presented at the meeting of Population Association of America, San Diego.

Wolfe, D. M. (1959). Power and authority in the family. In D. Cartwright (Ed.): *Studies in social power*. The University of Michigan and an Arbor.

Chapter 2
Family Socio-Cultural Values and Early Marriage Across Ethnic Groups:
The Case of Bangladesh

Emaj Uddin
https://orcid.org/0000-0002-6721-6856
University of Rajshahi, Bangladesh

ABSTRACT

This chapter examines and compares how family socio-cultural values exert effect on early marriage across ethnic groups, focusing on Bangladesh. In doing so, 585 pairs of couples (295 for Muslim and 290 for Santal) were randomly selected from Bangladesh. Data were collected, applying questionnaire method in family setting. Then the collected data were analyzed, using X2 test and binary logistic regression (BLR) technique. The frequency distribution showed that most of the Santal couples compared to the Muslim were married before the minimum legal age in Bangladesh. Results of BLR analysis suggested that early age at first marriage was significantly (p<0.01 & p<0.05) associated with family socio-cultural values studied. It is argued that ethnicity, family pattern, residence pattern, illiteracy and ascriptive occupational status were the risk factors to persist early marriage among the Santal couples than the Muslim ones in rural Bangladesh.

DOI: 10.4018/979-8-3693-3394-5.ch002

INTRODUCTION

Early marriage intended to legitimate sexual relation and reproduction as well as to strengthen child development, mutual social support, and adaptation (Goode, 1963; Murdock, 1960) is a historical and socio-cultural issue across the less-developed societies, including Bangladesh. Family socio-cultural approaches ((Dixon, 1971; Goode, 1963; Murdock, 1960; Smith, 1980; South, 2001; Vygotsky, 1986) rather than bio-psychological developmental (Buss, 1989; Bancroft, 2002), socio-demographic and socio-economic development (Singh & Samara, 1998) indicate that early marriage patterns are deeply rooted in family socio-cultural values and its related practices in the less-developed societies. Purpose of the study is to examine and predict how family socio-cultural values perpetuate early marriage patterns that may vary between Muslim and Santal ethnic groups in rural Bangladesh. The first term "*family socio-cultural values*" refers to the norms, ideas, and preferences of family pattern, residence pattern, ascriptive gender division of family status and role, marital and power arrangement (Aderninto, 1991; Revillard, 2006; Stone, 1994). The second term "*early age at first marriage*" refers to the timing of first marriage, especially before legal marital age prescribed for both man and woman in a given country when the prospective bride and groom are not physically, socially, and psychologically matured enough to bear sexual, reproductive, and social responsibilities to the marital and family life (United Nations Children's Fund, 2001; Uddin, 2009a, 2015b).

Previous comparative studies reveal that early marriage pattern, that may exert negative effects on personal and social life, varies from 70 percent to 5 percent among men and women across the world societies, depending on demographic structure, socio-economic development, religion, region, residence, and social system in which they live (United Nations, 1988, 1990). Continent-wise studies have reported that the rates of early marriage of the adolescents aged 10-18 years are 5 to 20 percent higher in Africa and South Asia than in Central America, Middle East, Latin America and the Caribbean (Singh & Samara, 1998) than in North America, East Asia and Western Europe. United Nations Children's Fund (2001) in the less-developed countries has found that early marriage pattern and its negative social consequences are the most likely to prevail in Niger (77 percent), Chad (71 percent), Bangladesh (65 percent), Mozambique (57 percent), Nicaragua and India (54 percent), and Yemen (48 percent). This marriage pattern also is remarkable among the ethnic groups in the multicultural society. Cross-ethnic studies (Raley et al., 2004; Raley et al., 2009) in the U.S have explored that Mexican American minority people compared to the others (e.g., Asian American, the Whites) are the most likely to marry early.

Over the several decades previous research has shown that early marriage is also a historical and socio-cultural issue in Bangladesh. In order to prevent early marriage and its negative social consequences, legal (e.g., *Child Marriage Restrain Act, 1929* in British period, *Muslim Family Law Ordinance, 1961* in Pakistan regime and *Child Marriage Restrain Act, 1984* in which minimum legal age 18 years for female and 21 years for male was enacted) and social measures (e.g., stipend and food for girls' education, security for girls, occupational quota for women, health and reproductive facilities, and community awareness building) have been taken across the government regimes in this country. Despite legal and social measures taken a great deal of descriptive and analytical studies indicates that early marriage and its negative social consequences are rapidly increasing in the rural poor families, including minority/ethnic groups. Some research reports reveal that rural adolescents with low socio-economic status and traditional social values related to family pattern, patriarchal residence, virginity, dowry system early marriage custom, and ascriptive gender status (Islam & Ahmed, 1998) than the urban adolescents with high socio-economic status and modern/individualistic values (Ahmed, 1996; Roy, 2008; Zahangir et al., 2008) are the most likely to marry at early aged 15 -20 years for male and 10-15 years female. Recent research report has shown 71 percent of the rural people and 62 percent of the urban ones are married at the age when they are just adolescent. Sarker (1997) in a cross-cultural study found that Muslim couples compared to Hindu ones married earlier in rural Bangladesh. Uddin (2009a) in a recent cross-cultural study found that the Santals than the Muslims were more likely to marry early in rural Bangladesh.

The above-mentioned comparative studies reviewed suggest that early marriage and its negative social consequences in this country are increasing among the rural poor families associated with poverty, low socio-economic status and traditional cultural values. This pattern of marriage is also a common phenomenon among the ethnic groups, including Santal, Oraon and Mahali in north-western region of this country. In spite of it, previous research (Chowdhury, 2004; Silva, 1993; Uddin, 2015b; United Nations Population Fund, 2001) has paid little attention on how family socio-cultural values related to the preference of family pattern, residence pattern, ascriptive gender status and role, and positive attitude towards early marriage practices exert independent effects on the differences in early marriage patterns and its related consequences across the ethnic groups in Bangladesh. Based on family socio-cultural theories and its underlying assumptions (Dixon, 1971; Raley et al., 2004; Raley & Sweeney, 2009; Vygotsky, 1986) this chapter investigated the following research questions (RQ) between Muslim and Santal couples in rural Bangladesh: RQ1: Are there significant differences in early marriage patterns associated with family socio-cultural values across countries, including Bangladesh? RQ2: Which factors of the family socio-cultural values are the best predictors to perpetuate early marriage patterns across ethnic groups?

Based on the family socio-cultural frameworks, this chapter examined family socio-cultural values affecting early marriage across ethnic groups, focusing on Bangladesh. This section of the chapter introduces and finds out knowledge gap. The second section presents theoretical background and hypothesis. The third section presents methodology. The fourth section presents the results. The fifth and sixth section interprets the results and draws conclusions.

THEORETICAL FRAMEWORK

Over the decades evolutionary biologist (Buss, 1989; Bancroft, 2002; Ko, Heer & Wu, 1985), social/cultural psychologists (Craig, 1996; Fawcett, 1974; Vygotsky, 1986), economist (Becker, 1973), family demographers (Davis & Blake, 1956; Matras, 1965), sociologists (Dixon, 1971) and anthropologists (Ember & Ember, 1981; Murdock, 1960) have developed several theoretical approaches to study, explain, and manage early marriage and its negative effects on personal, familial, community, and societal life across the world cultures and/or among the sub-cultures within a given society (Pillai, 1985). First of all bio-psychological scientists (Bancroft, 2002; Craig, 1996) explain early age at marriage in relation to puberty and sexual maturity, mediating through natural climate and nutrition. They assume that puberty and sexual maturity mediating through the nutrition and natural climate determine and induce variations in early age at first marriage across the groups. Demographers explain early marriage in connection with fertility, mortality, and migration, influencing socio-economic status in a given society. They argue that people with high fertility and mortality but low socio-economic status and migration marry earlier than its counter-parts.

Socio-economic development theories (Singh & Samara, 1998) contend that men and women with low socio-economic status (e.g., education, occupation, and income) and rural residence than men and women with high socio-economic status and urban residence are more likely to marry early. Becker's (1973) utility approach implies that individuals either marry if they maximize their utilities (viz. companionship, love, number and quality of children, caring, advantage of division of labor, prestige, quality of meals and so on) from the marriage partners or remain single. Fawcett's (1974) psychological framework contends that people decide marrying or not marrying, depending on the "perceived cost and benefits of marriage as was reflected in the utility model. Fawcett argues that these factors in combination interact for the psychological benefits for early marriage but penalties for delaying one.

Family social theories and its related studies suggest that family socio-cultural values and its related practices rather than objective and external factors explained by socio-demographic researchers have deep-seated in and pervasive effects on the early marriage patterns in the traditional societies (Hajnal, 1965; Heaton, 1996; Lee, 1971, 1982; Lewis ed., 1996; Matras, 1965; Morgan & Rindfuss, 1982; Otto, 1979; Pillai, 1985; Silva, 1993; Vygotsky, 1986). Family scientists assert that every child, female or male, is born in a distinct family socio-cultural environment. Through socialization process every child acquires certain family socio-cultural values that have pervasive effects on his or her entire way of life, from birth to early marriage to death. Actually, the children from their birth learn when to marry, whom to marry, where to live, what responsibilities they have to play to the family and community. These socio-cultural values, that are relatively endurable, are transformed into the next generational family formation (Aderinto, 1991; Smith 1980). Dixon's (1971, 1978) sociological framework explains first marriage pattern in association with marriage norms, social expectations, and pressures. Dixon in the model assumes that in different normative systems the same marriage determinants influenced by social expectations and social pressures may have different (even opposite) significant effects on the timing and prevalence of first marriage patterns. Raley et al., (2004) Raley & Sweeney (2009) assume that traditional family values, ascriptive gender status, family responsibility, and early child bearing (familism) compared to liberal family value system are directly related to early age at first marriage.

Reviewing earlier models United Nations (1988, 1990) develop a comprehensive model to study and compare timing of first marriage patterns across the societies and cultures. The main assertion of United Nations' model is that timing of first marriage patterns is the results of interaction of social (socio-economic, cultural and crisis situation), demographic (fertility, mortality, migration, age & sex composition of marriageable population), marriage norms (timing, prevalence and matching), individual (biological & psychological status) and marriage market factors. These studies argue that low socio-economic status and traditional socio-cultural values are responsible to perpetuate early age at first marriage for both men and women in the less-developed region, including Bangladesh. The above-mentioned family socio-cultural approaches rather than biological, demographic, socio-economic/modernization ones, however, may produce fruitful findings related to the root causes (family socio-cultural values and its practices) that perpetuate early marriage pattern over the several decades in less-developed regions, like Bangladesh. Based on family socio-cultural frameworks and its underlying assumptions, we next review literature on sociocultural values and early marriage across countries, focusing on Bangladesh.

SOCIOCULTURAL VALUES AND EARLY MARRIAGE ACROSS COUNTRIES

Ethnicity

Family social-cultural theories and its cross-cultural studies conducted in multi-cultural societies (South & Croder, 2000; Snyder et al., 2004) have hypothesized that men and women who are come from socio-culturally disadvantaged communities, rural residence, non-White ethnic group or traditional families are the most likely to marry early than those from advantaged, modernized, urban residence, and the White families. Based on the hypothesis Raley et al. (2004) and Raley & Sweeney (2009) have found that people with traditional/conservative family values prefer more early age at first marriage, while people with liberal family values relatively prefer medium or late marriage. The hypothesis and its findings are scientifically plausible to compare early age at first marriage in connection with family socio-cultural values and its related practices between Muslim and Santal couples in rural Bangladesh. Actually, family socio-cultural values and its related practices of the Muslim (Alam, 1995) and Santal in Bangladesh (Uddin, 2009b) are embedded in their respective community value system or cultural patterns followed.

Although both the communities are culturally collectivistic live in the same geographical location, and involve in the historical and social processes for their livelihood in the agrarian economy, their fundamental belief systems are completely different. Ethnically, the Muslims are *Sunni*. They speak in *Bengali* language with the mixture of *Arabic-Urdu* preference (Uddin, 2009c). Religiously, they believe in the oneness of God or Monotheism *(Tawhid),* Holy Qur'an as His Devine laws and principles, Muhammad (sm) as His nominated last Prophet and his *Hadith (Sunnah)* as practices of sayings. A man who believes in Monotheism, Qur'an and Hadith is called Muslim. On the other hand, the *Santal* community in this country is the largest tribal group of Aborigines. Racially, they belong to *Proto-Australoid* stocks and speak in *Austric-Mundary*, and sometimes they speak in *Bengali* version with the other *Bengali*-speaking people. They believe in several B*ongas*. A man who believes in several Bongas is called a Santal. The Santal in Bangladesh believe in animism, which includes worships of nature (Ali, 1998; Uddin, 2015a). These fundamental ethnic values/beliefs of the communities shape their respective family socio-cultural values that may differentially exert effects on early age at first marriage in rural Bangladesh. We may derive our first hypothesis from the literature review in the following way:

H1. The ethnicity of the Santal couples compared to the Muslim ones is significantly associated with the more early age at first marriage of the Santal couples than the Muslim ones in rural Bangladesh.

Preference of Family Patterns

The preference of family patterns is one of the aspects of family socio-cultural values and its practices that may affect early marriage pattern across the cultures (Uddin, 2012). Family sociologists and anthropologists broadly classify family pattern into three groups: nuclear, extended, and joint that are the protective or risk factors of age at first marriage in a given culture (Jin et al., 2003; Skinner, 1997). It is protective in the sense every man acquires social values from the family of orientation (a family unit in which someone is born as a son and daughter and is reared), and then he or she forms his own family of procreation (a family unit formed by a newly married couples). It is the risk factor in the sense everybody as a member of many types of family determines early age at marriage, depending on the family types in which she/he lives (Goode, 1963). The theories of family patterns and its research studies (Dixon, 1971; Hajnal, 1982; Skinner, 1997; United Nations, 1988) hypothesize that joint/extended family compared to the nuclear one is related to early age at marriage in a given time and space. Based on the hypothesis previous studies (United Nations, 1990, 2000) have found that while delayed/late age at first marriage ranged from 22 to 28 years for men and 18 to 25 for women is related to nuclear family in the developed cultures, early age at first marriage ranged 20-25 years for men and 17-20 for women is significantly associated with joint/extended family in the developing or less-developed cultures.

In the peasant economy, Muslim culture prefers more joint/extended family (where two or more generations live), because they believe in *familism,* a feeling of subordination of individual goals to the family and belonging to family for co-ordination of family activities to achieve family goals, aid for family members, and maintenance of family continuity, but Santal culture prefer nuclear family type wherein one or two generations live, because of their mass poverty (Uddin, 2012). Sarker (1997) explored that out of 132 families, Muslim nuclear family was 56.8 percent, supplementary nuclear family was 12.1 percent, joint family was 24.9 percent and extended family was 6.2 percent. In a Muslim community Mashreque (1984) found that out of 228 families nuclear family was 54.38 percent, sub-nuclear family was 3.07 percent, supplementary nuclear family was 6.58 percent, joint family was 18.42 percent and complex joint was 17.54 percent. Rahaman (1995) in another Muslim community found that out of 203 family's simple family was 75.37 percent and complex family was 24.63 percent. Siddique (1998) in a study of Santal community found that out of 132 families, nuclear family was 71.97 percent and joint family was 28.03 percent. In another study of Santal Village Kayes (1995) found that of the families included, nuclear family was 67.5 percent and joint family was 31.25 percent. Therefore, we may draw our second hypothesis from the above information and logic in the following way:

H2. The preference of family pattern of the Santal couples compared to the Muslim ones is significantly associated with the more early age at first marriage of the Santal couples than the Muslim ones in rural Bangladesh.

Preference of Residence Patterns

Residence patterns are also the part of family socio-cultural values and its practice for social/group living. Residence refers to the cultural norms by which family members prefer to reside together. Studying family cultural patterns sociologists and anthropologists (Ember & Ember, 1981; Murdock, 1960) conceptualize residential patterns as the *patrilocal* residence refers to the norm of residence by which a married couple lives with the husband's parents' family or husband family, *matrilocal* residence refers to the norm by which a couple lives with the wife's parents' family, *biolocal* residence refers to the norm of residence by which a newly married couple establishes residence with or near the parents of either spouse and *neolocal* residence refers to the norm of residence by which a newly married couple establishes residence separate from both the sides of parents.

Decisions about the place of living typically depend on cultural rules by which family members conform to one of the residence patterns. Family sociological and anthropological studies indicate that these residence patterns are also the protective or risk factors to vary in age at first marriage across the cultures (Synder et al., 2004). Residence patterns are protective in the sense that protects family members from any harmful social threats. For example, People with biolocal and neolocal residence may marry to delay and may protect from its negative consequences, because they consume greater autonomy and freedom in the residence patterns. On the other hand, people with patrilocal and matrilocal residence patterns are the risk factors in which the prospective candidates are in greater pressures of parental authority and extended kin groups for their early marriage (Dixon, 1971; United Nations, 1988, 1990). Several studies (Berthoud, 2000; Caldwell, 1980; Hertrich, 2002; South, 2001) have explored that patrilocal and matrilocal residence compared to the other residential patterns (e.g. biolocal and neolocal) are significantly related to early age at first marriage for both the men and women in less-developed cultures. Although both the Muslim and Santal communities in Bangladesh are patriarchal in nature and prefer patrilocal residence, previous research has shown that the Santal practice more biolocal and neolocal residence pattern than the Muslim (Ali, 1998; Sarker, 1997; Uddin, 2006). In a recent cross-cultural study Uddin (2009) has found that most of the Muslim couples (87.59%) follow patrilocal residence compared to the Santal couples (67.83%). In other residence patterns, such as matrilocal, biolocal, and neolocal percentages of the Santal couples are higher than the Muslim couples.

Regarding this situation our relevant third hypothesis derived from literature review is given below:

H3. The preference of residence pattern of the Santal couples compared to the Muslim ones in the family of orientation is significantly associated with the Santal couples' more early age at first marriage than the Muslim ones in rural Bangladesh.

Ascription of Educational Status

Family socio-cultural values and its related practices in a patriarchal society assign gender norms of educational attainment that may induce variations in early age at first marriage. Educational attainment here refers to the years of formal education/ learning recognized by a given society. Social and cultural theories (Dixon, 1971) and its relevant cross-cultural studies (Hertrich, 2002; South, 2001) have found that timing of formal education in a particular society not only varies between men and women but also varies among the sub-cultures within a given society. These gender variations in educational attainment may exert effect on their timing of first marriage patterns (early marriage and late marriage) among cultural groups in a patriarchal society (United Nations, 1988, 1990). Previous empirical studies (Caldwell et al., 1983; Lee, 1982) hypothesize that education and age at first marriage are positively inter-related. Elaborately, the shorter the times (even no times!) spent in schooling, the earlier the entry into marriage market and the younger the age at entry into first marriage. This plausible hypothesis is also applicable to compare early age at first marriage in relation to gender differences in educational attainment between Muslim and Santal ethnic communities in Bangladesh.

Bangladesh is a patriarchal, patrilineal, and patrilocal society. Previous studies (Sarker, 1997) indicate that the patriarchal norms of this society always prefer men than women across the family, community, and society affairs. By dint of the patriarchal socio-cultural values men than women occupy higher social status and dominate the family, community and society domains. The higher status and dominance of men than women also affect their education attainment and likely early age at first marriage in Bangladesh. Although primary education in this country is universal and obligatory for all male and female children irrespective of religion, region and cultural groups, several research studies have shown that although some parents prefer their son's education than daughter's, but most of the poor and illiterate parents are not interested in their children' formal education (Uddin, 2015c, 2024). Rather than formal education the poor parents according to family social-cultural values teach their children how and when to marry and form a family and manage it. They also teach their male children how to cultivate land and plant on it in traditional agricultural economic system and female ones how to obey parents, elder and even husband; how to rear and care children. Several culture-specific studies

(Ali, 1998) reveal that early age at marriage varies in association with the timing of formal education attainment across the social classes in Bangladesh. Uddin (2006, 2009d) and others have found that average years schooling of Santal couples' are lower than the Muslim couples. Likely average years of early age at first marriage of the Santal couples are lower than the Muslim ones. Our fourth hypothesis derived from the above information and arguments is given below:

H4. The lower ascriptive education attainment of Santal couples compared to the Muslim ones in the family of orientation is significantly associated with the Santal couples' more early age at first marriage than the Muslim ones in rural Bangladesh.

Ascription of Occupational Status

Age at first marriage is also associated with occupational attainment before the marriage. Several studies hypothesize that the lower the status attainment the earlier the age at first marriage and the vice-versa. This hypothesis is consistent in several empirical studies across the societies (United Nations, 1988, 1990). Family sociologist and also anthropologist hypothesize that ascriptive family status and role distributions based on age, sex, gender, and kinship persist early at first marriage for both male and female children to achieve family goals in the traditional agricultural economic system (Smith, 1980; Sheela & Audinarayana, 2000; Udry & Cliquet, 1982). This hypothesis is well-proved in several studies in less-developed cultures and societies.

Relevant cross-cultural family studies (Uddin, 2006, 2009) in rural Bangladesh indicate that although division of labor among the children under the age of 15 years between Muslim and Santal communities is the same (Satter, 1984), there are significant differences in division of labor between men and women after the puberty. Both the Santal adult men and women take part in agriculture and any other fields as manual laborers inside and outside the family. The Santal women work outside the family from dawn to dusk as paid or unpaid laborers, because of the mass poverty and social deprivation (Ali, 1998; Bandyopadhyay, 1999), whereas division of family labor is strictly maintained among the adult Muslim men and women according to sex norms, although many of them are poor. They think adult men are only breadwinner of the family. So the men of the communities should work in agricultural field, involve in petty trade and business, and other formal and informal organizations. Generally, Muslim women do not work on the agricultural field and do not go outside the family alone. Their main functions are to bear and rear children, maintain family chores, serve family members and observe *purdah*, although the lower class women have to work outside the family under economic pressure for maintaining their family (Alam, 1995; Uddin, 2023). However, the findings of the study clearly show that the differences in ascriptive occupational status and role distribution may influence their early age at first marriage between Muslim and Santal couples in rural Bangladesh (Uddin, 2009). Regarding the factor our particular fifth hypothesis drawn from the above cross-cultural evidence and logic is as follows:

H5. The lower ascriptive occupation attainment of Santal couples compared to the Muslim ones in the family of orientation is significantly associated with the Santal couples' more early age at first marriage than the Muslim ones in rural Bangladesh.

Preference of Marital Arrangement

Marital arrangement is an important aspect of family formation. Marriage refers to rules or norms of socially and legally approved relationship between an adult man and woman who expect to have relatively enduring relationship involving economic cooperation, and allowing exclusive sexual relationship leading to child bearing and rearing (Murdock, 1960). Marriage is a rule of incorporating members in the family. By marriage every adult woman becomes a member of her husband or husband's parent's family. This process of family membership is called legal or institutional membership (Uddin, 2009). Family sociologists and anthropologists studying small ethnic community and family cultures broadly classify marital arrangement in mate selection into two categories: *arranged marriage and romantic marriage*. Both the Muslim and Santal communities follow endogamy a marriage norm requiring people to marry someone from their own cultural group, and exogamy a marriage norm requiring people to marry someone from outside the group, rules of marriage (Naher, 1985). Actually, the Muslims and Santal in mate selection are religiously endogamous. The former are both endogamous and exogamous in mojhabs, class, and lineage but the later are tribal endogamous and clan exogamous. That is marriage between a Muslim male and a female may occur in any mojhabs, class, lineage (Rahaman, 1995), but a Santal cannot marry within clan except other eleven classes (Uddin, 2010).

Although both the communities prefer contracted marriage in marital arrangement in which parents or elder members of the family select mates of their son or daughter with or without concerned, the Santal widely practice romantic marriage in marital arrangement in which marital partners fall in love and select themselves as mates for marriage (Ali, 1998; Uddin, 2006) but Muslim cannot prefer romantic marriage. Some culture-specific studies explore that conservative family values related to sexuality and marriage are gradually changing into liberal ones and as a result male and female are being closely connected with each other. As premarital and extramarital sexuality in Bangladesh are strictly prohibited and its outcome is thought wed-locked, so parents and elder members arrange early marriage of those male and female who are fallen in love. Like societal values although both the communities value chastity and preserve virginity of girls, some previous research explores that rates of romantic marriage of the Santal community are higher than the Muslim. Therefore, rates of early age at first marriage occur among the Santal than the Muslim to preserve chastity and virginity. This mate selection and marital arrangement may determine early age at first marriage among the Santal couples than the Muslim couples in rural Bangladesh (Ali, 1998; Uddin, 2006). Therefore, our sixth hypothesis in this respect is the following:

H6. The preference of marital arrangement of the Santal couples compared to the Muslim ones in the family of orientation is significantly associated with the Santal couples' more early age at first marriage than the Muslim ones in rural Bangladesh.

Overview of the social and cultural theories and its related cross-cultural studies reveal that differences in family socio-cultural values related to family pattern, residence pattern, ascriptive educational and occupational attainment (Uddin, 2017), and marital arrangement may persist and induce variations in early age at first marriage patterns between the Muslim and Santal couples in rural Bangladesh. Review of the studies also suggests that the Santal couples compared to the Muslim ones in rural Bangladesh are more affected by early age at first marriage influenced by family socio-cultural values and practices. As the communities' the early age at first marriage patterns are significantly associated with family socio-cultural values, so sixth hypotheses formulated may help to understand the nature, patterns, and trends of relationship between family socio-cultural practices and early age at first marriage patterns. Based on the sixth categorical hypotheses we may formulate a general hypothesis to understand and organize basic ideas (also the best predictors) reflected on the relationships between family socio-cultural values and early age at first marriage patterns between the Muslim and Santal couples in rural Bangladesh. Our general seventh hypothesis is as follows:

General H7. The preferences of family socio-cultural values and its related practices of the Santal couples than the Muslim ones are significantly associated with the earlier age at first marriage patterns among the former (the Santal couples) than the later (Muslim couples) in rural Bangladesh.

DATA AND METHOD

Sample

In order to examine above-mentioned research questions and its related hypotheses field work was conducted from January to June, 2006 in the *Talonda* union of *Tanore Upazila, Rajshahi* district, Bangladesh where Muslim and Santal community was living as neighbors and was widely practiced early marriage for their respective family living. First of all through snow-ball process and checking of marriage documents we carefully identified 598 couples from Muslim and 560 from Santal who were married the first time between 1995 and 2005 years and whose age range was 12 to 48 years for husbands and 10 to 45 years for wives. From the preliminary list, 295 pairs of couples for Muslim (49.33%) and 290 pairs of couples for Santal (51.79%) were randomly selected through cluster sampling. The selected Muslim and Santal couples (e.g., both the husbands and wives) who sincerely informed their consent to actively participate in the study.

Measure

This study analyzes how family socio-cultural values and practices (e.g., preferences of family pattern, residence pattern, ascriptive gender educational and occupational status before marriage, and marital arrangement) induce variations in early age at first marriage patterns between Muslim and Santal couples in rural Bangladesh. The characteristics of family socio-cultural values and its practices in this study were treated as independent variables (IV) and the characteristics of early age at first marriage were used as dependent variables (DV). Both the variables were measured in the following way:

Independent Variables (IV). Family socio-cultural values indicate the infinitive characteristics, such as family pattern, residential pattern, ascriptive/achieved gender status, religion, parental socio-economic status, religious and social custom of marriage, attitudes toward early marriage, motivation, and marital arrangement etc. that may perpetuate early age at first marriage between the communities. Of the family socio-cultural characteristics family pattern, residential pattern, gender educational and occupational attainment, and marital arrangement that were the mostly categorical were included and measured, following from previous research studies (Bharat, 1996; Morgan & Rindfuss, 1982; Uddin, 2006). First of all *community* was nominally measured and coded as 1= Muslim, and 2= Santal. Couples were categorized into two groups and coded as 1= husband and 2= wife. *Family patterns* were nominally measured and coded as 1= nuclear family, 2= joint, and 3= extended family. Residence pattern was measured and coded as 1= patrilocal residence, 2= matrilocal residence, 3= biolocal residence, and 4= neolocal Residence. *Education* attainment of the couples before marriage was numerically measured and accounted for in years. Later the numerical values were categorized into three groups intended to apply Chi-Squire test and coded as 1= Illiterate, 2= Primary, and 3= Secondary and above for both husband and wife. *Ascriptive occupational status* of the couples in their parental home was nominally measured and coded as 1= farming, 2= farming+small business, 3= day laboring for husband and 1= household chores (supporting role for mother and 2= day-Laboring for parental earning and 3= others. Marital arrangement was coded as 1= romantic marriage, and 2= arranged marriage.

Dependent Variable (DV). In measurement of *early age at first marriage* for both husband and wife to access in marital life and form a family, most of the researchers defined the terms as timing norms based on either state's legal or religious or social customary laws and measured in years, applying self-report, interview and survey method to collect reliable and valid data. The present study defined and measured the term *"early age at first marriage"* as the timing norms and measured in years based on the Muslim and Santal community's customary social norms and its practices in rural villages, although the minimum legal age at first marriage for both male (21 years) and female (18 years) in Bangladesh was present. Later the collected data on early age at first marriage for husband were categorized into two groups and coded as 1= early marriage, before legal age at marriage (12-21 years) and 2= late marriage, after legal age at marriage (22+) for husband. Likely, age at first marriage for wife was accounted for and coded as 1= early marriage, before legal age at marriage (10-18 years), and 2= late marriage, after legal age at marriage (19+) for applying Chi-Squire test.

Instrument and Procedure

Study design used in this study was cross-cultural one to examine how different qualitative (subjective) aspects of family socio-cultural values influenced variations in early age at first marriage (early vs. late marriage) between the communities' couples. For this 585 pairs of couples selected were interviewed through semi-structural questionnaire schedule with open-ended and close-ended questions in their family setting, following Uddin (2009) and Mitra's et al. (1994) instruments, and other researches' questionnaires. In order to collect real and valid data through interview method with questionnaire schedule in conservative Muslim and Santal community in rural Bangladesh, several strategies were followed: (1) As both the family socio-cultural values and early age at first marriage were culturally/legally sensitive issues, so we built up rapport with the selected respondents to create consciousness about the research purposes and objectives; (2) we carefully examined and checked official document on the marital age; (3) As Muslim women could not interact with the male interviewer because of observing *purdah*, so one female interviewer, who was trained up on the research issue, worked with the female respondents, and male interviewer (author) with the male respondents.

Data were collected from January to June, 2006. First month of the research period was used to build up rapport with the respondents and second month was worked for preliminary investigation intended to select samples and the next 4 months were used for real data collection. In order to collect data on the DVs and

IVs the interview method with questionnaire schedule was applied. Most of the respondents could not fill up the questionnaire, because of their illiteracy. First of all the simple (background) questions (e.g., age, sex, and ethnicity) were asked and then the questions of the IVs and the DVs designed were presented to them and answers of the questions were written down by the interviewers. Sometimes probing was made when somebody could not understand any question asked. However, the respondents were fully participated in the research and sincerely answered our questions presented to them within one and half hours. By the given procedure the data were collected at afternoon or evening when they were leisured, because most of the respondents as farmers and day laborers would work in the agricultural field from morning to midday and even round the day. In so doing, the author and his collaborate conversed with the respondents in *Bengali* language, because they all did effectively converse in Bengali language (national language), although the Santal would speak in their respective languages, *Santali*. After the completion of each interview, some token money with special thanks was given to each pair of couples if it was necessary again for any errors. The responses on the IVs and DVs given by the respondents were converted into English by author (Brislin, 1980).

Reliability and Accuracy

The responses on early age at first marriage associated with family socio-cultural values were reliable in the sense that we followed some qualitative strategies: the interview technique with the semi-structural questionnaire schedule, appointment of female interviewer, interpersonal trust-building, consideration of socio-cultural status and standard time frame for each interview. Based on the strategies we collected objective data in the family setting (Brislin, 1980; Pareek & Rao, 1980). As the responses on the DVs and IVs were reliable, one-to-one tests of likelihood Chi-squire test were applied to find significant differences in DVs and IVs included. Then Binary Logistic Regression (BLR) analysis, especially Backward Stepwise (Wald) method was applied to predict the DVs (early age at first marriage for both husband and wife in relation to IVs (family socio-cultural values) used. Prediction of accuracy of the tests in step 0 was valid, because we found 60.9% to 59.1% accuracy for husband's age at first marriage across the models and 61.5% to 58.1% for wife's age at first marriage associated with the factors of family socio-cultural values included across the six steps (Uecker & Stokes, 2008). In addition, to fit the model in step-by-step Chi-squire values and its degree of freedom were more or less valid (Morgan & Teachman, 1988).

Data on IVs and DVs were categorical in nature. In order to find out significant differences in early age at first marriage in association with family socio-cultural values and its practices in the selected couples (according to first research question) the collected data on IVs were analyzed, using Spearman's X^2 test (shown in table 1) and on DVs, applying Pearson's X^2 test (shown in table 2). Overall frequency distributions of the X^2 tests, that were normal, revealed that the Santal couples' age at first marriage (e.g., husband, wife) was earlier than the Muslim ones in association with family socio-cultural values practiced. The coefficients of the X^2 tests suggested that family socio-cultural values and early age at first marriage were significantly different (at $p<0.01$ and $p<0.05$ level) between the Muslim and Santal couples in Talonda union of Bangladesh. As the first requirement of data analysis, including distribution, accuracy, and Chi-squire values and its degree of freedom was fulfilled (Morgan & Teachman, 1988), so (according to our second research question and hypotheses formulated) Binary Logistic Regression (BLR) analysis, including Backward Stepwise (Wald) method was applied to predict differences in DVs in relation to IVs used. In doing so, we used coefficients of β, Exponential β, SE, and its 95% confidence intervals (CI) between IVs (family socio-cultural values) and DVs (early age at first marriage). Results of BLR analysis suggested that DVs in relation to IVs were significant at $p<0.01$ for both the husband ($\beta=-.349$, SE= .084), Exp (β) = .706) and the wife ($\beta=-.328$, SE= .084), Exp (β) = .721) between Muslim and Santal communities (Uecker & Stokes, 2008). These findings were consistent with general hypothesis formulated. The results of BLR analysis, in detail, are presented in table 3-4.

RESULTS AND ANALYSIS

Differences in Family Socio-Cultural Values

Table 1 presents comparative data on family socio-cultural values (e.g., family pattern, residence pattern, educational and occupational attainment, and marital arrangement) between Muslim and Santal couples from Spearman's Chi-squire test. The frequency distribution showed that most of the husbands and wives studied would live in nuclear family (80 percent for Muslim and 91 percent for Santal respectively) and the rest of them were in joint (16 percent for Muslim, 4 percent for Santal) and extended family (3 percent for Muslim, 4 percent for Santal) in their early childhood/ family of orientation (X^2= 12.67, df= 9, p= .005 for family pattern). In residence pattern most of the Muslim couples (87.59 percent) in their family of orientation followed patrilocal residence compared to the Santal couples (67.83 percent). In other residence patterns such as Matrilocal, Biolocal and Neolocal percentages of the Santal couples were higher than the Muslim couples (X^2= 16.70, df= 3, p= .002 for residence pattern). Unlike, most of the Santal couples (69 percent for husband and 72 percent for wife) compared to the Muslim ones (30% for husband and 41%

for wife) never went to school, but some of the Santal couples compared to the Muslim completed their primary (22 percent & 24 percent for Santal, 43 percent & 44 percent for Muslim) and secondary education (9 percent & 4 percent for Santal, 26 percent & 14 percent for Muslim) before their marriage (X^2=82.65, df=11, p= .000 for husband's education and X^2=72.29, df=11, p= .000 for wife's education).

Table 1. Results of Spearman's Chi-Squire Test for Frequency of Family Socio-Cultural Values by Muslim (n=295) and Santal (n=290), Talonda, Rajshahi, Bangladesh, 2006

Family Socio-Cultural Values	Muslim%	Santal%	X^2
Education before Marriage in Years For Husbands *Illiterate* *Primary* *Secondary+*	29.65 43.45 26.90	68.53 22.38 9.09	82.65* 0.000
For Wife *Illiterate* *Primary* *Secondary+*	40.69 44.83 14.48	72.02 24.48 3.50	72.29* 0.000
Occupation before Marriage For Husband *Farming* *Farming+Business* *Day-Laboring*	62.76 19.31 17.93	5.59 3.50 90.91	195.05* 0.000
For Wife *Household Chores* *Household Chores+ Day-Laboring*	95.86 4.14	5.59 94.41	249.86* 0.000
Family Pattern before Marriage *Nuclear* *Joint* *Extended*	80.69 15.86 3.45	91.61 4.20 4.20	12.67* 0.005
Residential Patterns *Patrilocal* *Matrilocal* *Biolocal* *Neolocal*	87.59 3.45 5.52 3.45	67.83 9.09 16.78 6.29	16.70* 0.001
Marital Arrangement *Romantic* *Arranged*	25.52 74.48	42.66 57.34	9.42** 0.002

Note: Significant at: * p<0.01, ** p<0.05

That is most of Santal couples compared to the Muslim ones learned social and cultural values from their family life education (informal learning). Likely, although main ascriptive occupation of the respondents was cultivation, most of the Santal husband (91 percent) and wife (94 percent) compared to the Muslim husband (62 percent) before their marriage would work in their parental agricultural field, because their parents were poor or marginal farmers. Others adopted petty trading (19 percent for Muslim and 4 percent for Santal). On the other hand, Muslim women (96 percent) before marriage were exclusively involved in house work and would play supportive role to their mothers and the Santal women (94 percent) were day laborers for parental family earnings as well as would help their mothers in the home (X^2= 195.05, df= 4, p= .000 for husband's ascriptive occupation and X^2= 249.86, df=2, p= .000 for wife's ascriptive occupation). Lastly, most of the Muslim couples (75 percent) were married with parental arrangement, while the Santal couples (43 percent) were married by romantic love (X^2= 9.42, df= 1, p= .002 for marital arrangement).

Differences in Early Marriages

Data of Pearson's X^2 test and its frequency distribution (shown in table 2) suggested that most of the Santal husband (62 percent) and wife (83 percent) compared to the Muslim husband (54 percent) and wife (77 percent) were married before the legal provision of marriage approved by state's marriage laws 1984 enacted (22 years for male and 18 years for female) in Bangladesh. That is 63 percent of Santal husband compared to 55 percent of Muslim ones were married before the legal age ranged 12-21 years. Likely, 84 percent of the wife compared to the Muslim wife (77 percent) was married from 10-17 years (before the legal age 18 years assigned). Average age at first marriage of Muslim couples (mean= 21.12, SD= 3.24 for husband and mean= 15.48, SD = 2.93 for wife) was higher than the Santal couples (mean= 19.69, SD= 3.96 for husband and mean= 14.64, SD= 3.03 wife) in the study area. Results of Pearson's X^2 test also revealed that age at first marriage patterns of husband were significant different at p<0.01 level but wife's at p<0.05 level between the two communities.

Table 2. Results of Pearson Chi-Squire Test for Frequency of Early Age at First Marriage by Muslim (n=295) and Santal Couples (n=290), Talonda, Rajshahi, Bangladesh, 2006

Early Age at First Marriage in Years	Muslim	Santal	X^2
For Husband	54.48	62.24	61.84*
Early marriage (before legal age,12-21)%	45.52	37.78	0.000
Late marriage (after legal age, 22+)%	21.12	19.69	
Mean	3.24	3.96	
SD			
For Wife	77.93	83.22	26.35**
Early marriage (before legal age, 10-18)%	22.07	16.78	0.023
Late marriage (after legal age, 19+)%	15.48	14.64	
Mean	2.93	3.03	
SD			

Note: Significant at: * p<0.01, ** p<0.05

Family Socio-Cultural Predictors of Early Marriages

Husband's Early Marriage

Table 3 presents coefficients of exp β and standard error (SE) from Binary logistic regression analysis (BLR, backward stepwise method) predicting husband's early age at first marriage between Muslim and Santal communities. The overall results of the BLR analysis revealed that the proportions of the Santal husband's early age at first marriage than the Muslim husband's were significantly related to family socio-cultural values (β= -.349, SE= .084), Exp (β) = .706) at $p<0.01$ level. Of the family socio-cultural value indicators analyzed, the first model (shown in column 2 in the table) revealed that nuclear family pattern (β= 1.873, SE=.355, p=0.054), matrilocal residential pattern (β= 2.546, SE= .530, p= 0.053) and educational level [illiteracy (β= 2.021, SE= .298, p= 0.018) & primary (β= 2.541, SE= .350, p= 0.008)] of the Santal husbands that were significant at p<0.05 level were the greatest risks (1 to 2 times) to perpetuate their early age at first marriage practices than the Muslim ones. In addition to these factors our consequent models (shown in column 2, 3 & 4 in the table) suggested that ethnicity (β= 1.421, SE= .172, p= 0.045) of the Muslim husband's than the Santal husband's was also significant at $p<0.01$ and $p<0.05$ level. Our final model (shown in column 5 in the table) indicated that ethnicity (β= 1.428, SE= .171, p= 0.037) of the Muslim and educational level (β= 2.175, SE= .293, p= 0.008) of the Santal husband that were significant at p<0.01 and p<0.05 level were the greatest risks (1 to 2 times) factors to perpetuate their early age at first marriage in the study area of rural Bangladesh. Of the family socio-cultural values the findings of the BLR analysis on ethnicity and husband's educational attainment (illiteracy), however, were consistent with the first and fourth categorical hypotheses formulated for husband's early age at first marriage between the two communities.

Table 3. Coefficients and Standard Error (β, SE) from Binary Logistic Regression Analysis Predicting Husband's Early Age at First Marriage in the Muslim and Santal (n= 585), Talonda, Rajshahi, Bangladesh, 2006

Indicators of Family Socio-Cultural Values	Early Age at First Marriage for Husband				
	Model 1	Model 2	Model 3	Model 4	Model 5
	β (SE)	β (SE)	β (SE)	β(SE)	β (SE)
Ethnicity	1.379	1.412*	1.412*	1.409*	1.428* (.171)
Muslim	(.211)	(.172)	(.172)	(.172)	
Santal	- -	- -			
Family Pattern					
Nuclear	1.873*	1.885*	1.889*	1.970*	
Joint	(.355)	(.355)	(.636)	(.353)	
Extended	2.032	2.048***	2.054***	2.264*	
Residential Pattern	(.431)	(.429)	(.720)	(.423)	
Patrilocal	-	- -			
Matrilocal					
Bilocal	1.688	1.679	1.679		
Neolocal	(.461)	(.461)	(.461)		
Husband's Education	2.546*	2.538*	2.527*		2.175** (.293)
Illiterate	(.530)	(.530)	(.528)		2.647** (.346)
Primary	2.160	2.140	2.151		
Secondary +	(.503)	(.502)	(.500)	2.168**	
Husband's Occupation	- -	- -		(.294)	
Farming only				2.644**	
Farming+business	2.022*	1.022		(.347)	
Day laboring	(.297)	(.199)			
Marital Arrangement	2.551*				
Romantic	(.350)				
Arranged	- -				.285**(.295) 13.37,
Constant					3, 0.004**
Omnibus Test for X²	1.038				
	(.325)				
	1.093				
	(.248)				
	- -		.094**	.151**	
		.093**	(.609)	(.443)	
	1.024	(.609)	22.40, 8,	17.88, 5,	
	(.199)	22.41, 9,	0.004**	0.003**	
	- -	0.008**			
	.092**				
	(.612)				
	22.54, 11,				
	0.021*				

Notes: Significant at: *p>0.05, **p>0.01, ***p>0.001; the figures in the bracket indicate standard error (SE); reference category is late marriage for husband's early age at marriage

Wife's Early Marriage

Table 4 presents coefficients of exp β and standard error (SE) from the same analysis (BLR, backward stepwise method) predicting wife's early age at first marriage between Muslim and Santal communities. The overall results revealed that the proportions of the Santal wife's early age at first marriage than the Muslim ones were significantly related to family socio-cultural values (β= -.328, SE= .084), Exp (β) = .721) at $p<0.01$ level. Of the family socio-cultural value indicators analyzed our first and second step data (shown in model 1 & 2 in the table) revealed that matrilocal residential pattern (β= .412, SE= .502, p= 0.051) and illiteracy (β= 410, SE= .355, p= 0.012) of the Santal wife's, that were significant at $p<0.01$ and $p<0.05$ level, were the greatest risks (1 to 2 times) factors to perpetuate their more earlier age at first marriage practices than the Muslim ones. Our consequent models (shown in column 4-7 in the table) indicated that although other factors of the family socio-cultural values were important, illiteracy (β= .429, SE= .355, p= 0.016 in model 3, β= .416, SE= .349, p= 0.012 in model 4, β= .405, SE= .348, p= 0.019 in model 5 and β= .410, SE= .347, p= 0.010 in model 6) of the Santal wife's than the Muslim ones that were significant at $p<0.01$ and $p<0.05$ level was the greatest risk factor to perpetuate their earlier age at first marriage than the Muslim wife's in the study area of rural Bangladesh. Although the family socio-cultural values, to some extent, contributed to prediction of wife's early marriage the findings of the BLR analysis on wife's educational attainment, especially illiteracy however, was consistent with the fourth categorical hypotheses formulated for wife's early age at first marriage between the two communities.

Table 4. Coefficients and Standard Error (β, SE) from Binary Logistic Regression Analysis Predicting Wife's Early Age at First Marriage in the Muslim and Santal (n= 585), Talonda, Rajshahi, Bangladesh, 2006

Indicators of Family Socio-Cultural Values	Early Age at First Marriage for Wife					
	Model 1	Model 2	Model 3	Model 4	Model 5	Model 6
	β (SE)	β (SE)	β (SE)	β(SE)	β (SE)	β(SE)
Ethnicity	1.204	1.204	1.203	.685 (.317)	.653	.410**
Muslim	(.173)	(.173)	(.173)	1.205	(.316)	(.347)
Santal	- -	- -		(.423)	1.055	.584
Family Pattern					(.392)	(.376)
Nuclear	.682 (.321)	.684 (.320)	.671 (.318)			
Joint	1.261	1.268	1.184			
Extended	(.411)	(.409)	(.404)			
Residential Pattern	-	- -				
Patrilocal						
Matrilocal	.572 (.417)	.572 (.417)				
Bilocal	.412*	.409*		.416**		
Neolocal	(.502)	(.501)		(.349)	.405**	1.533
Wife's Education	.492 (.466)	.496 (.463)		.578 (.378)	(.348)	(.332)
Illiterate	- -	- -			.580	8.73,
Primary			.429**		(.378)	2,0.01**
Secondary +	.410**	.410**	(.351)	1.278		
Wife's Occupation	(.355)	(.355)	.576 (.379)	(.177)		
Housewife only	.539 (.385)	.537 (.384)				
Housewife+Day laboring	- -					
Marital Arrangement			1.274			
Romantic	1.211	1.212	(.177)			
Arranged	(.181)	(.181)		1.782		
Constant	- -			(.459)	2.171	
Omnibus Test for X²				15.25,	(.438)*	
	1.034			df=5,	13.32, 4,	
	(.200)		1.620	0.01**	0.01**	
	- -	3.064**	(.467)			
	3.048*	(.611)	16.40,			
	(.612)	19.99,	df=6,			
	20.02, df=	df=9,	0.01**			
	10, 0.03*	0.02*				

Notes: Significant at: *p>0.05, **p>0.01, ***p>0.001; the figures in the bracket indicate standard error (SE); reference category is late marriage for wife's early age at marriage

DISCUSSION

Based on family socio-cultural framework and its underlying principles we hypothesized family socio-cultural values (e.g., preferences of family patterns, residence patterns, educational and occupational attainment before marriage and marital arrangement) would induce variations in early age at first marriage between Muslim and Santal couples in rural Bangladesh. In order to test the general hypothesis, including 5 categorical hypotheses 585 pairs of first time married couples from both the communities (295 samples for Muslim and 290 samples for Santal) were randomly selected from *Talonda* of *Rajshahi* district, Bangladesh and interview method with structural questionnaire was applied to collect reliable data on the IVs and DVs. Overall frequency distributions of the X^2 tests showed that the Santal couples' age at first marriage (average age 19.69 years for husband and 14.64 years for wife) was earlier than the Muslim ones (average age 21.12 years for husband and 15.48 years for wife) in association with their family socio-cultural values practiced for marriage. The results of the X^2 tests suggested that the indicators of family socio-cultural values and early age at first marriage were significantly different (at $p<0.01$ and $p<0.05$ level) between the Muslim and Santal couples in Talonda union of Bangladesh (Uddin, 2009). In addition, the overall results of Binary Logistic regression (BLR) analysis suggested that the indicators of the family socio-cultural values, that were significant (at $p<0.01$ and $p<0.05$ level) were the best predictors to persist earlier age at first marriage among the Santal couples than the Muslim ones in the study area of Bangladesh. These findings of the study were consistent with the principles of family social and cultural theories (Dixon 1971; United Nations 1988, 1990). These findings were supported by previous cross-cultural studies (Raley et al., 2004; Raley & Sweeney, 2009) conducted in abroad and Bangladesh (Uddin, 2009).

It is interesting to note that of the family socio-cultural values analyzed, husband's education, family pattern, residential pattern and marital practices were the greatest risks to perpetuate earlier age at first marriage practices among the Santal husbands than the Muslim ones. Likely, wife's education, wife's occupation, family pattern, residential pattern and marital practices were the greatest risks factors to perpetuate earlier age at first marriage among the Santal wives than the Muslim ones. United Nations' (1988, 1990) and other cross-cultural studies conducted in developing and under-developed cultures, including Bangladesh found that both male and female who would live in extended/joint family, patrilocal residence and would maintain segregated gender division of labor in the family were more likely to marry early than those who would live in the reverse patterns. Raley et al. (2004) and Raley & Sweeney (2009) found that Mexican American with collectivistic value than the White American and others with individualistic ones would maintain familism and would prefer extended family pattern, patrilocal residence and arranged marriage for mate selection. They would also preserve virginity and ascriptive status and role of both the male and female before marriage that all exerted effects on their early age at first marriage for family formation. Schreck (1998) in the U.S., Silva (1993) in Sri Lanka and Uddin (2009) in their studies also found similar trends across the ethnic groups. Singh & Samara (1998) found that early marriage was related to low socio-economic status, traditional technologies for production, parental positive attitude towards early marriage, especially illiteracy, low life expectancy at birth and child labor or early involvement in livelihood for family maintenance. These findings were also consistent with Becker's (1973, 1974) utility approach and Fawcett's (1974) psychological framework and principles to some extent. Both communities' couples, especially the Santal maximized their utilities (viz. companionship, love, number and quality of children, caring, advantage of division of labor, prestige, quality of meals and so on) from the marriage partners. For these utilities they were prone to marry early than the Muslim couples in rural Bangladesh.

Findings of the study also revealed that husbands in both communities were markedly older than its counter-parts, wife's age at first marriage in the study area of Bangladesh. Based on evolutionary biological perspective Buss found that natural selection produced males and females who attracted each other for reproductive success and resource distribution to protect them and their offspring. According to Buss (1989), the females who were young were attracted by males, whereas the males who possessed sufficient resources (e.g., money, wealth & power) to protect them were attracted by the females. These different strategies used by men and women might be explained sex differences in early age at first marriage between the Muslim and Santal couples in rural Bangladesh. In cross-cultural perspective Buss and others explored that females placed the highest value on cues that indicated a males' resource acquisition (earning, capacity, industriousness, maturity etc.), while males most valued on females' reproductive capacity (youth, health and attractiveness). According to Buss (1989), potential partners seek an equitable "bargain" when they form a relationship. As most societies today are patriarchal, males (especially older males) most likely hold authority to control monetary resources that are traded in the market place to utilizing females' youth and beauty.

CONCLUSION AND IMPLICATION

This chapter examined how family socio-cultural values induced variations in early age at marriage between Muslim and Santal couples in rural Bangladesh. The results of the study suggested that early age at first marriage of the Santal couples compared to Muslim ones was significantly different in association with their family socio-cultural values in Talonda of Bangladesh. Although the indicators of family socio-cultural values consequently contributed to the model developed, it was concluded that ethnicity, family pattern, residence pattern, ascriptive educational (illiteracy) and occupational status were higher risks (2-3 times) factors to predict early age at first marriage among the Santal couples than the Muslim ones in the study area of Bangladesh. These findings were strongly supported by our general hypothesis as well as some categorical hypotheses examined (Dixon 1971; United

Nations 1988, 1990) and were also replicated in some cross-cultural studies (Raley et al., 2004; Raley & Sweeney, 2009) conducted in abroad and Bangladesh (Uddin, 2009).

These cross-cultural findings on the differences in early age at first marriage associated with family socio-cultural values may have practical implications in comparative social policy-practice with the ethnic couples in Bangladesh (Pillai, 1985; Silva, 1993). Practically, the government of Bangladesh may formulate appropriate comparative social policy to provide educational support for consciousness-building to those ethnic couples who are married early in relation to their illiteracy and other socio-cultural values affected (ICDDR, B, 2007b; United Nations Children's Fund, 2001). In addition, the government of Bangladesh may also provide job skill training support to those ethnic couples who are married early in connection with ascriptive occupational status. Because past experience has shown that formal educational attainment and occupational mobility due to job skill training have accelerate changes in traditional family values and its related early marriage pattern (Uddin, 2015a).

Based on the findings social practitioners (e.g., social workers, human rights activists, lawyers) may also work with the ethnic groups or the couples to prevent and combat early age at first marriage to change in their traditional socio-cultural values that perpetuate early marriage in rural Bangladesh (Chowdhury, 2004; United Nations Population Fund, 2001; Uddin, 2023). Although the cross-cultural findings, however, are suggestive to understand differences in early age at first marriage in association with family socio-cultural values between the ethnic couples and contribute to practical social policy implications, there are some limitations on how parental poverty, low socio-economic status, their early marriage history, insecurity for girls, and positive attitudes toward early marriage may affect early marriage in rural Bangladesh (Uddin, 2024). Therefore, further cross-cultural studies should be done on how these socio-psychological factors perpetuate early marriage among the poor ethnic groups in Bangladesh.

REFERENCES

Ahmed, A. U. (1996). Socio-economic determinants of age at first marriage in Bangladesh. *Journal of Biosocial Science*, 18(1), 35–42. DOI: 10.1017/S0021932000006477 PMID: 3944149

Alam, A. Z. M. (1995). *Family values*. Bangladesh Cooperative Society Limited.

Ali, A. (1998). *The Santals of Bangladesh*. The Sabuge Sangah Press.

Arnaldo, C. (2004). Ethnicity and marriage patterns in Mozambique. *African Population Studies*, 19(1), 143–164.

Aziz, K. M. A., & Maloney, C. (1985). Life stages, gender and fertility in Bangladesh. Dhaka, Bangladesh: International Centre for Diarrhoeal Disease research, Bangladesh.

Bancroft, J. (2002). Biological factors in human sexuality. *Journal of Sex Research*, 39(1), 15–21. DOI: 10.1080/00224490209552114 PMID: 12476251

Bandyopadhyay, P. K. (1999). *Tribal situation in Eastern India*. Subarnarekha.

Becker, G. S. (1973). A theory of marriage: Part 1. *Journal of Political Economy*, 81(4), 813–846. DOI: 10.1086/260084

Berthoud, R. (2000). Family Formation in Multi-Cultural Britain: Three Patterns of Diversity. The paper presented to the conference on Social Change and Minority Ethnic Groups organized by the Centre for Research on Elections and Social Trends (CREST). Retrieved from www.iser.essex.ac.uk

Bharat, S. (1996). *Family measurement in India*. Sage Publications Pvt Ltd.

Blossfeld, H. P. (1995). Changes in the process of family formation and women's growing economic independence: a comparison of nine countries. In H. P. Blossfeld, (ed.), *The new role of women: family formation in modern societies* (pp. 3-32). Colorado, US: Boulder.

Brislin, R. W. (1980). Translation and content analysis of oral and written materials. In H. C. Triandis and J. W. Berry (Eds.), *Handbook of cross-cultural psychology, methodology* (pp. 408-410) (Vol.2). Boston: Allyn and Bacon, Inc.

Buss, D. M. (1989). Sex differences in mate preferences: Evolutionary hypotheses tested in 37 cultures. *Behavioral and Brain Sciences*, 12(1), 1–49. DOI: 10.1017/S0140525X00023992

Caldwell, J. C., Reddy, P. H., & Caldwell, P. (1983). The causes of marriage change in South India. *Population Studies*, 37(3), 343–361. DOI: 10.1080/00324728.1983.10408866

Chowdhury, F. D. (2004). The socio-cultural context of child marriage in a Bangladeshi village. *International Journal of Social Welfare*, 13(4), 244–253. DOI: 10.1111/j.1369-6866.2004.00318.x

Craig, G. J. (1996). *Human development*. Prentice Hall Inc.

Davis, K., & Blake, J. (1956). Social structure and fertility: An analytic framework. *Economic Development and Cultural Change*, 4(2), 221–235. DOI: 10.1086/449714

Dixon, R. (1971). Explaining cross-cultural variations in age at marriage and proportions never marrying. *Population Studies*, 32(2), 215–234. DOI: 10.1080/00324728.1971.10405799 PMID: 22070108

Dyer, E. D. (1983). *Courtship, marriage, & family: American style*. The Dorsey Press.

Ember, C. R., & Ember, M. (1981). *Anthropology*. Prentice-Hall, Inc.

Fawcett, J. T. (1974). Psychological determinants of nuptiality. *International Population Conference*, Liege, 1973, vol. 2 (Liege, International Union for the Scientific Study of Population) pp.19-30.

Goldscheider, F., Turcotte, P., & Kopp, A. (2000). Determinants of women's first union formation in the United States, Canada, and Sweden. Paper to be presented at the 2000 Flagship Conference of the Family and Fertility Surveys Project, Brussels, May 29-31, 2000.

Goode, W. J. (1983). *World revolution and family patterns* (2nd ed.). Free Press.

Hajnal, J. (1965). European marriage patterns in perspective. In Glass, D. V., & Everley, D. E. C. (Eds.), *Population in history. Essays in historical demography* (pp. 101–143). Edward Arnold.

Hajnal, J. (1982). Two kinds of preindustrial household formation system. *Population and Development Review*, 8(3), 449–494. DOI: 10.2307/1972376

Harpending, H. (1992). Age differences between mates in Southern African pastoralists. *Behavioral and Brain Sciences*, 15(1), 102–103. DOI: 10.1017/S0140525X00067716

Heaton, T. B. (1996). Socio-economic and familial status of women associated with age at first marriage in three Islamic societies. *Journal of Comparative Family Studies*, 27(1).

Hertrich, V. (2002). Nuptiality and gender relationships in Africa: an overview of first marriage trends over the past 50 years, session on family change in Africa and Latin America. Population Association of America Annual Meeting, Atlanta, 9-11 May.

Hirschman, C., & Rindfuss, R. (1982). The sequence and timing of family formation events in Asia. *American Sociological Review*, 47(5), 660–680. DOI: 10.2307/2095165

ICDDRB. (2007a). *Health and Demographic Surveillance System- Matlab* (Vol. 39). International Centre for Diarrhoeal Disease Research, Bangladesh.

ICDDRB. (2007b). Consequences of early marriage on female schooling in rural Bangladesh. *Health Science Bulletin*, 5(4), 13–18.

Islam, M. N., & Ahmed, A. U. (1998). Age at first marriage and its determinants in Bangladesh. *Asia-Pacific Population Journal*, 13(2), 73–92. DOI: 10.18356/f31b417e-en PMID: 12321742

Jensen, R., & Thornton, R. (2003). Early female marriage in the developing world. In Oxfam, G. B. (Ed.), *In gender, development and Marriage, Caroline Sweetman*. DOI: 10.1080/741954311

Jin, X., Li, S., & Feldman, M. W. (2005). Marriage form and age at first marriage: A comparative study in three counties in contemporary rural China. *Social Biology*, 52(1-2), 18–46.

Kayes, S. (1995). Cultural change of Santal community of Rajshahi district: An anthropological study. M. Phil Dissertation, The Institute of Bangladesh Studies, Rajshahi: University of Rajshahi, Unpublished.

Ko, C. F., Heer, D. M., & Wu, H. Y. (1985). Social and biological determinants of age at first marriage in Taiwan, 1970. *Social Biology*, 32(1-2), 115–128. PMID: 4081802

Lee, H. Y. (1971). A study of changing family values in a Korean middle-town. *International Population Conference*, London, 1969, vol.1, pp. 467-468.

Lee, H. Y. (1982). Age at first marriage in Peninsular Malaysia. *Journal of Marriage and Family*, 44(3), 785–798. DOI: 10.2307/351600

Lewis, J. (Ed.). (1996). Social age for marriage, context: Southeast Asians and other newcomers in California's classrooms, 16(122), 12-23.

Lofstedt, P., Ghilagaber, G., Shusheng, L., & Johansson, A. (2005). Changes in marriage age and first birth interval in Huaning County, Yunnan Province, PR China. *The Southeast Asian Journal of Tropical Medicine and Public Health*, 36(5), 1329–1338. PMID: 16438167

Maitra, P. (2004). Effects of socioeconomic characteristics on age at marriage and total fertility in Nepal. *Journal of Health, Population and Nutrition*, 22(1), 84–96. PMID: 15190816

Maloney, C. T., Aziz, K. M. A., & Sarker, P. C. (1981). *Beliefs and fertility in Bangladesh*. International Centre for Diarrhoeal Disease Research, Bangladesh.

Mashreque, M. S. (1984). The traditional village family in Bangladesh: An anthropological survey. *The Journal of BARD. Comilla*, 13(1/2), 44–72.

Matras, J. (1965). The social strategy of family formation: Some variations in time and space. *Demography*, 2(1), 349–362. DOI: 10.2307/2060123

Mondain, N., Legrand, T., & Sabourin, P. (2007). Changing patterns in men's first marriage among Sereer in rural Senegal. [September.]. *Journal of Comparative Family Studies*, 38(2), 22. DOI: 10.3138/jcfs.38.4.627

Morgan, S. P., & Rindfuss, R. R. (1982). Household structure and tempo of family formation in comparative perspective. Paper presented at the Annual Meetings of the Population Association of America, San diego.

Morgan, S. P., & Teachman, J. D. (1988). Logistic regression: Description, examples, and comparison. *Journal of Marriage and Family*, 50(4), 929–936. DOI: 10.2307/352104

Morrels, S., Matthijs, K., & Leuven, K. U. (2008). The age at first marriage in three Belgian cities: Antwerp, Aalst and Ghent, 1800-1906. Paper presented in the 9th International Conference on Urban history "Comparative History of Urban Cities" Loyn, 27th-30th August 2008.

Murdock, G. P. (1960). *Social structure*. Macmillan Publishing Company.

Naher, M. S. (1985). Marriage pattern: Customs and changes in rural Bangladesh. *The Journal of Social Studies*, 20(30), 121–132.

Nyamongo, I. (2000). Factors influencing education and age at first marriage in an arid region: The case of the Borana of Marsabit district, Kenya. *African Study Monographs*, 21(2), 55–65.

Oppenheimer, V. K. (1988). A theory of marriage timing. *American Journal of Sociology*, 94(3), 563–591. DOI: 10.1086/229030

Otto, L. B. (1979). Antecedents and consequences to marital timing. In Burr, W. R. (Eds.), *contemporary theories about family: research based theories* (Vol. 1, pp. 101–126). Free Press.

Pillai, V. K. (1985). Predicting age at first marriage: A review of recent models. *The Journal of Family Welfare*, 32(1), 41–49.

Quisumbing, A. R., & Hallman, K. (2003). Marriage in transition: Evidence on age, education, and assets from six developing countries. Policy Research Division Working Papers, Population Council, 2003, Retrieved from www.popcouncil.org/publications/wp/prd/rdwplist.html

Rahaman, S. M. Z. (1995). Muslim marriage practices in a village of Bangladesh. *Rajshahi University Studies*, 3, (Part-C), 131-149.

Raley, R. K., Durden, T. E., & Wildsmith, E. (2004). Understanding Mexican American marriage patterns using a life course approach. *Social Science Quarterly*, 85(4), 872–890. DOI: 10.1111/j.0038-4941.2004.00249.x

Reley, R. K., & Sweeney, M. M. (2009). Explaining race and ethnic variation in marriage: Directions for future research. *Race and Social Problems*, 3(3), 132–142. DOI: 10.1007/s12552-009-9013-3

Revillard, A. (2006). Work/family policy in France. *International Journal of Law, Policy and the Family*, 20(2), 133–150. DOI: 10.1093/lawfam/ebl009

Roy, K. T. (2008). Determinants of early marriage in Rajshahi, Bangladesh. *Pakistan Journal of Social Sciences*, 5(6), 606–611.

Sarker, P. C. (1997). *Social structure & fertility behavior: a cross-cultural study*. Dhaka, Bangladesh: Center for development Services.

Sattar, M. A. (1984). A comparison of age and sex patterns of participation in economic activities in Tribal and Non-Tribal communities in Bangladesh. In Qureshi, M. S. (Ed.), *Tribal cultures in Bangladesh*. Institute of Bangladesh Studies.

Schreck, L. (1998). Expectation about marriage and childbearing vary by race and ethnicity among girls in grades 6-8. *Family Planning Perspectives*, 30(5), 252–253. DOI: 10.2307/2991619

Sheela, M. S. J., & Audinarayana, N. (2000). Determinants of female age at first marriage in Tamil Nadu: An analysis of NFHS data. *The Journal of Family Welfare*, 46(2), 25–32.

Siddiquee, M. A. R. (1997). The nature of participation of marginal community in politics: An analysis of Santal Tribe, Unpublished Ph. D. Dissertation, Rajshahi, Bangladesh: University of Rajshahi.

de Silva, W. I. (1993). Family formation: Socio Cultural Differentials in Age at First Marriage in Sri Lanka.

Singh, S., & Samara, R. (1998). Early marriage among women in developing countries. *International Family Planning Perspectives*, 22(4), 148–157. DOI: 10.2307/2950812

Skinner, G. W. (1997). Family systems and demographic processes. In Kertzer, D. I., & Fricke, T. (Eds.), *anthropological demography: toward a new synthesis* (pp. 53–95). University of Chicago Press.

Smith, P. C. (1980). Asian marriage patterns in transition. *Journal of Family History*, 5(1), 58–96. DOI: 10.1177/036319908000500104

Snyder, A. R., Brown, S. L., & Condo, E. P. (2004). Residential differences in family formation: The significance of cohabitation. *Rural Sociology*, 69(2), 255–260. DOI: 10.1526/003601104323087598

South, S. (2001). The variable effects of family background on the timing of first marriage: United States 1969-1993. *Social Science Research*, 30(4), 606–626. DOI: 10.1006/ssre.2001.0714

South, S. J., & Croder, K. D. (2000). The declining significance of neighborhoods? Marital transitions in community context. *Social Forces*, 78(3), 1067–1099. DOI: 10.2307/3005942

Stone, L. (1994). *Family values in a historical perspective*. University of Utah Press.

Uddin, M. E. (2009a). Age at first marriage for husband and wife between Muslim and Santal communities in rural Bangladesh. *International Journal of Humanities and Social Science*, 3(4), 318–326.

Uddin, M. E. (2009b). Cross-cultural comparison of marriage relationship between Muslim and Santal communities in a village of Bangladesh. *World Cultures eJournal, 17*(1), 1-17.

Uddin, M. E. (2009c). Cross-cultural value orientations among the Muslim, Hindu, Santal and Oraon communities in rural Bangladesh. *International Journal of Humanities and Social Science*, 4(10), 754–765.

Uddin, M. E. (2009d). Cross-cultural socio-economic status attainment between Muslim and Santal couple in rural Bangladesh. *International Journal of Humanities and Social Science*, 4(11), 779–786. DOI: 10.5281/zenodo.1075058

Uddin, M. E. (2010). *Family structure: A cross-cultural comparison between Muslim and Santal communities in rural Bangladesh*. Saarbruchen: Lambert Academic Publishing.

Uddin, M. E. (2012). Cross-cultural family structure among Muslim, Hindu, Santal and Oraon communities in Bangladesh. *Journal of GLBT Family Studies*, 8(4), 334–360. DOI: 10.1080/1550428X.2012.705620

Uddin, M. E. (2015a). Exploration and implication of value orientation patterns in social policy-practice with ethnic communities in Bangladesh. *Global Social Welfare : Research, Policy & Practice*, 2(3), 129–138. DOI: 10.1007/s40609-014-0018-5

Uddin, M. E. (2015b). Family socio-cultural values affecting early marriage between Muslim and Santal communities in rural Bangladesh. *The International Journal of Sociology and Social Policy*, 35(3/4), 141–164. DOI: 10.1108/IJSSP-06-2014-0046

Uddin, M. E. (2015c). Ethnic disparity in family socio-economic status in Bangladesh: Implication for family welfare policy-practice. *Global Social Welfare : Research, Policy & Practice*, 2(2), 29–38. DOI: 10.1007/s40609-014-0021-x

Uddin, M. E. (2017). Disparity in family status attainment between majority and minority ethnic groups in Bangladesh. *International Journal of Social Economics*, 44(4), 530–546. DOI: 10.1108/IJSE-07-2015-0187

Uddin, M. E. (2023). Understanding ethnic disparities in family status attainment: Implications for family welfare policy-practice in Bangladesh. In Chandan, H. (Ed.), *Implications of marginalization and critical race theory on social justice* (pp. 197–219). IGI Global. DOI: 10.4018/978-1-6684-3615-8.ch010

Uddin, M. E. (2024). Family socioeconomic inequalities between majorities and minorities across the globe: Implication for policy practice. In Baikady, R. (Eds.), *The Palgrave handbook of Global social problems*. Springer. DOI: 10.1007/978-3-030-68127-2_441-1

Udry, J. R., & Cliquet, R. L. (1982). A cross-cultural examination of the relationship between ages at menarche, marriage, and first birth. *Demography*, 19(1), 53–64. DOI: 10.2307/2061128 PMID: 7067870

Uecker, J. E., & Stokes, C. E. (2008). Early marriage in the United States. *Journal of Marriage and Family*, 70(4), 835–846. DOI: 10.1111/j.1741-3737.2008.00530.x PMID: 20305796

United Nations. (1988). *First marriage: Patterns and determinants*. Population Division.

United Nations. (1990). *Patterns of first marriage: Timing and prevalence*. Population Division.

United Nations. (2000). *World marriage patterns*. Population Division.

United Nations Children's Fund (UNICEF). (2001). *Early marriage: child spouses*. UNICEF.

United Nations Population Fund. (2001). *Socio-cultural aspects of reproductive health*. UNFPA.

Vygotsky, L. S. (1986). *Thought and language*. The MIT Press.

Westoff, C. F. (1992). Age at marriage, age at first birth and fertility in Africa. World Bank Technical Paper # 169. Washington D. C., US: the World Bank.

Chapter 3
Breaking the Chains:
Understanding and Combating Early Marriage-Induced Violence Against Girls

Tripti Bhushan
O.P. Jindal Global University, India

ABSTRACT

Early marriage remains a pervasive issue worldwide, particularly in developing countries, where cultural norms, poverty, and lack of education perpetuate its prevalence. This proposed book chapter aims to delve into the complex dynamics surrounding early marriage-induced violence against girls, examining its root causes, manifestations, and impact on the physical, emotional, and psychological well-being of young brides. Further this book chapter will talk about the mental issues of bride. The chapter will begin by providing an overview of the prevalence of early marriage globally, highlighting the socio-economic and cultural factors that contribute to its persistence. Finally, the chapter will conclude with recommendations for policymakers, practitioners, and activists on effective strategies to combat early marriage-induced violence against girls, emphasizing the importance of multi-sectoral collaboration, empowerment approaches, and holistic support services.

INTRODUCTION

Early marriage remains a pervasive issue, affecting millions of girls worldwide, with profound implications for their physical, emotional, and social well-being (Ahmed & Hossain, 2017; Marphatia, 2016; UNICEF, 2005). This chapter aims to delve into the complex dynamics of early marriage-induced violence against girls,

DOI: 10.4018/979-8-3693-3394-5.ch003

offering insights into its root causes, manifestations, and impacts. By understanding the multifaceted nature of this phenomenon, effective strategies can be developed to combat it and empower affected girls across countries (United Nations, 1966, 1979). A great deal of research shows that early marriage-induced violence against girls is a pervasive human rights violation that continues to plague societies worldwide, disproportionately affecting millions of vulnerable girls each year (Nour, 2006). Defined as marriage before the age of 18, early marriage often results in a myriad of harmful consequences for girls, including physical and psychological abuse, limited educational opportunities, restricted autonomy, and heightened risks of maternal mortality and morbidity (Campbell, 2002; Chaudhury & Banik, 2021). Despite concerted efforts to address this issue, early marriage remains prevalent in many regions, driven by entrenched social norms, poverty, gender inequality, and lack of access to education and resources (Uddin, 2015, United Nations, 2014, 2015).

This chapter seeks to shed light on the complex dynamics of early marriage-induced violence against girls, exploring its root causes, consequences, and implications for gender equality and human rights. Drawing on multidisciplinary perspectives from sociology, psychology, law, and public health, this essay will examine the intersections of early marriage with broader social, cultural, economic, and legal contexts, offering insights into effective strategies to combat this harmful practice.

By contextualizing early marriage within the broader framework of gender-based violence and human rights, this essay aims to deepen understanding of the multifaceted nature of the issue and stimulate dialogue on the urgent need for comprehensive interventions. Through a combination of legislative reforms, community engagement, access to education and empowerment programs, support services for survivors, and multi-sectoral collaboration, stakeholders can work together to dismantle the systems of oppression that perpetuate early marriage-induced violence and create a future where every girl can thrive (West, 2002; Watts & Zimmerman, 2002). In light of the global challenges posed by early marriage-induced violence against girls, this essay calls for collective action and solidarity across sectors and stakeholders to break the chains of oppression and build a world where girls are free to choose their own destinies and realize their full potential.

The objective of this book chapter is to provide a comprehensive understanding of early marriage-induced violence against girls and to explore effective strategies for combating this pervasive human rights violation. By examining the root causes, dynamics, and consequences of early marriage, as well as the socio-cultural, economic, and legal factors that perpetuate it, this chapter aims to raise awareness and inform policymakers, practitioners, and activists about the urgent need for action. Additionally, the chapter seeks to highlight evidence-based prevention and intervention strategies that can empower girls, protect their rights, and create a future where every girl can thrive free from the threat of early marriage-induced violence.

BACKGROUND

"Breaking the Chains: Understanding and Combating Early Marriage-Induced Violence against Girls" addresses a critical issue with profound implications for gender equality, human rights, and social justice. Early marriage, defined as marriage before the age of 18, remains a prevalent practice in many parts of the world, disproportionately affecting girls and perpetuating cycles of poverty, inequality, and violence. Globally, an estimated 12 million girls are married off each year before they reach the age of 18, translating to nearly 23 girls every minute (Save the Children, 2012; United Nations, 2001; UNFPA, 2012, 2020; UNDP, 2016). Despite significant progress in recent years, particularly in reducing child marriage rates, the practice persists due to a complex interplay of socio-cultural, economic, and structural factors.

The phenomenon of early marriage is deeply rooted in patriarchal norms, gender discrimination, and entrenched inequalities that deny girls their rights to education, health, and autonomy (Amin & Amin, 2018; Uddin, 2015). In many communities, girls are viewed as economic burdens, and marriage is seen as a means to alleviate poverty, safeguard family honor, or cement social alliances. However, early marriage often leads to a range of negative consequences for girls, including limited educational opportunities, increased risk of domestic violence, early pregnancy, and adverse health outcomes (Uddin, 2017, 2021). Girls forced into early marriages are deprived of their childhood, robbed of their agency, and subjected to a lifetime of dependence and vulnerability.

Moreover, early marriage-induced violence extends beyond physical harm to encompass psychological trauma, emotional abuse, and economic exploitation. Girls trapped in abusive marriages face immense barriers to seeking help and accessing support services due to social stigma, legal barriers, and lack of awareness (Arthur & Ngugi, 2017; Yount, 2016). Addressing early marriage-induced violence requires a multi-faceted approach that addresses root causes, empowers girls, and mobilizes communities for change. Social and legal interventions such as legislative reforms, access to education and resources, community engagement, and support services for survivors are essential components of comprehensive strategies to combat this pervasive form of gender-based violence (Bhutta et al., 2014; George, 2011; Human Rights Watch, 2013, 2014, 2015). In light of the urgent need to prioritize the rights and well-being of girls, "Breaking the Chains" aims to shed light on the complexities of early marriage-induced violence, raise awareness, and advocate for evidence-based interventions that promote gender equality, empower girls, and create a future free from violence and discrimination (IERW, 2019).

UNDERSTANDING EARLY MARRIAGE

Definition and prevalence of early marriage globally

Early marriage, also known as a child marriage or an underage marriage, refers to the union of individuals below the legal age of marriage, typically 18 years old (Chellaiah, 2019). It is a widespread phenomenon occurring across regions and cultures, with profound implications for individuals' rights, health, and well-being (Uddin, 2015). Globally, an estimated 12 million girls marry before the age of 18 each year, highlighting the magnitude of the issue. While early marriage affects both boys and girls, girls are disproportionately affected, comprising the majority of child brides worldwide (Kusumayati, 2018; UNICEF, 2015, 2018).

Early marriage, also known as child marriage, refers to the union of individuals before the legal age of adulthood, typically before the age of 18. It is a practice deeply rooted in cultural, social, and economic factors, often perpetuated by gender inequality, poverty, and traditional norms. Despite global efforts to eradicate this harmful practice, early marriage remains prevalent in many parts of the world, affecting millions of girls and boys each year. The prevalence of early marriage varies significantly across regions, with higher rates observed in certain parts of Africa, South Asia, and the Middle East (Chellaiah, 2019; International Center for Research on Women, 2014; Kamal et al., 2015; Molla et al., 2018; Uddin, 2015). Approximately 12-15 million girls are married before the age of 18 each year, with more than 650 million women alive today having been married as children (Loaiza et al., 2012; WHO, 2020; United Nations, 2017). Boys are also affected by early marriage, although to a lesser extent compared to girls.

Several factors contribute to the prevalence of early marriage. Poverty plays a significant role, as families living in poverty may see marriage as a way to reduce the financial burden associated with raising a child. In some communities, early marriage is perceived as a means of protecting girls from premarital sex and preserving family honor (ILO, 1999). Gender inequality and discrimination also fuel the practice, with girls often seen as economic burdens or commodities to be traded in marriage (Uddin, 2021). Early marriage has serious consequences for the health, education, and overall well-being of those affected, particularly girls. Child brides are more likely to experience complications during pregnancy and childbirth, including maternal mortality and obstetric fistula. They are also at greater risk of experiencing domestic violence, sexual abuse, and social isolation (Clark et al., 2014; Coker et al., 2002; Crockett & Bingham, 2019; Flood & Pease, 2009). Furthermore, early marriage often results in the interruption of girls' education, limiting their opportunities for personal and economic development. Early marriage is deeply entrenched in cultural norms, social practices, and economic realities, perpetuated by a complex interplay of factors:

Gender Inequality: Patriarchal norms and discriminatory practices devalue girls' rights and agency, often relegating them to subordinate roles within families and communities. Early marriage disproportionately affects girls, subjecting them to increased risks of gender-based violence, restricted autonomy, and limited opportunities for education and economic empowerment.

Poverty: Economic hardship and lack of opportunities drive families to marry off their daughters at a young age, sometimes as a means of economic survival or to alleviate financial burdens.

Social Norms: Prevailing beliefs and customs regarding gender roles, family honor, and chastity contribute to the perpetuation of early marriage as a social norm in many societies.

Education: Limited access to quality education, particularly for girls, reinforces cycles of poverty and perpetuates early marriage, as educated girls are more likely to delay marriage and make informed choices about their futures.

Age: Marrying at a young age exposes individuals to heightened risks of adverse health outcomes, including early pregnancy, maternal mortality, and complications during childbirth.

Socioeconomic Status: Poverty and marginalization intersect with early marriage, perpetuating cycles of inequality and limiting opportunities for social mobility and economic empowerment.

Legal Frameworks and International Conventions Addressing Early Marriage and Child Rights

International human rights instruments, such as the Convention on the Rights of the Child (CRC) and the Convention on the Elimination of All Forms of Discrimination against Women (CEDAW), recognize early marriage as a violation of human rights and child rights (International Women's Rights Action Watch Asia Pacific, 2013; Murphy & Malhotra, 2018). These conventions call for measures to prevent and eliminate early marriage, protect the rights of children, and promote gender equality and women's empowerment (Kabeer, 2020; Lee-Rife, 2010). Additionally, many countries have enacted laws and policies aimed at raising the legal age of marriage, providing support services for at-risk individuals, and promoting education and awareness on the harmful impacts of early marriage (UNFPA, 2018). Efforts to address early marriage require a multi-faceted approach that addresses the underlying drivers of the practice. So, multiple approaches: Legislative reforms, community engagement, access to education and economic opportunities, and support services for survivors are essential components of comprehensive strategies to combat early marriage (United Nations, 2000; 2006). By addressing the root causes of the practice and empowering girls and women, societies can work towards ending early marriage and promoting gender equality and human rights for all.

EFFECTS OF EARLY MARRIAGE ON THE GIRLS

Forms and Dynamics of Violence

Violence manifests in various forms, each with its unique dynamics and consequences, perpetuating cycles of harm and oppression (Johnson, 1995, 2008). Understanding these forms is crucial for addressing violence comprehensively and effectively. Domestic violence refers to violence that occurs within the context of intimate relationships, including spousal abuse, partner violence, and violence against children or elderly family members (Clark et al., 2014; Denner & Kirby, 2019). It can encompass physical, sexual, and psychological forms of abuse and is often characterized by a cycle of violence, with periods of escalating tension followed by explosive episodes of abuse. The dynamics of domestic violence are influenced by factors such as gender roles, cultural norms, and economic dependence (Ellsberg et al., 2008; Ertürk, 2005; Fleming et al., 2015; Meyer, 2016). The following outlines the diverse forms of violence and their underlying dynamics:

a) Physical Violence

✓ Physical abuse encompasses a range of acts, including domestic violence, marital rape, and physical coercion.
✓ Perpetrators may exert physical dominance and control over victims through acts of aggression, assault, or bodily harm.
✓ Power and control dynamics often underpin physical violence, with perpetrators seeking to assert authority and instill fear in their victims.

b) Psychological and Emotional Abuse

Psychological and emotional abuse involves manipulation, intimidation, and degradation, aimed at undermining the victim's sense of self-worth and autonomy.

✓ Tactics may include gaslighting, isolation from support networks, and emotional manipulation to exert control over the victim's thoughts, feelings, and behaviors.

✓ Victims of psychological abuse may experience long-term psychological trauma, including anxiety, depression, and low self-esteem.

c) Sexual Violence

Sexual violence encompasses non-consensual intercourse, sexual coercion, and reproductive coercion, among other forms of sexual abuse.

✓ Perpetrators may use physical force, threats, or manipulation to coerce victims into sexual acts without their consent.
✓ Victims of sexual violence often experience profound psychological and emotional trauma, as well as physical injuries and reproductive health consequences.

d) Socioeconomic Exploitation

Socioeconomic exploitation refers to the exploitation of individuals' economic vulnerability and lack of autonomy (Muthengi & Erulkar, 2016).

✓ Victims may be economically dependent on perpetrators, limiting their ability to leave abusive situations or access resources and support services.
✓ Perpetrators may use financial control, economic abuse, or exploitation to maintain power and control over victims.

e) Intersectional Vulnerabilities

Intersectional vulnerabilities refer to compounding factors that intersect with experiences of violence, exacerbating victims' vulnerabilities and marginalization.

✓ Factors such as ethnicity, disability, socioeconomic status, and displacement can intersect with experiences of violence, shaping victims' access to support, resources, and justice.
✓ Intersectional approaches are essential for understanding and addressing the unique needs and experiences of individuals facing multiple forms of discrimination and violence.
✓ In conclusion, recognizing the diverse forms and dynamics of violence is essential for developing comprehensive strategies to prevent and address violence effectively. By addressing underlying power imbalances, promoting gender equality, and supporting victims' autonomy and agency, stakeholders can work towards creating safer, more equitable communities for all.

Impacts of Early Marriage on Girls' Well-Being

Early marriage, a widespread practice in many parts of the world, has profound impacts on the well-being of girls. Beyond the legal and ethical considerations, early marriage significantly affects various aspects of girls' physical, psychological, and social health (Hamby & Grych, 2013; Jain et al., 2017). This essay explores the multifaceted impacts of early marriage on girls' well-being, encompassing physical health consequences, psychological effects, social isolation and stigma, educational barriers, and economic disenfranchisement (Kasturiangan et al., 2004).

a) **Physical Well-Being:** Early marriage exposes girls to numerous physical health risks, including:
   i) *Injuries*: Young brides are at higher risk of experiencing physical injuries due to sexual and domestic violence within marriage.
   ii) *Reproductive health issues*: Early pregnancy and childbirth pose serious health risks, including complications during labor, maternal mortality, and obstetric fistula.
   iii) *Maternal mortality*: Adolescent mothers face higher rates of maternal mortality compared to adult women, attributed to complications related to childbirth and inadequate access to maternal healthcare services.

b) **Psychological Well-Being:** Early marriage subjects girls to significant psychological distress, including:
   i) *Trauma*: Forced marriage and early pregnancy can traumatize young girls, leading to long-term emotional scars and mental health disorders.
   ii) *Depression and anxiety*: The stress and pressure associated with marital responsibilities at a young age often result in depression, anxiety, and other mood disorders.
   iii) *Post-traumatic stress disorder (PTSD):* Girls forced into early marriage may develop PTSD symptoms, such as flashbacks, nightmares, and emotional numbness, stemming from traumatic experiences.

c) **Social Well-Being:** Early marriage exacerbates social isolation and stigma for girls, manifesting as:
   i) *Ostracism from family and community*: Married girls may face exclusion from social activities, education, and decision-making processes within their families and communities.
   ii) *Limited social support*: Young brides often lack access to support networks, leaving them vulnerable to abuse and neglect without recourse.

d) **Educational Well-Being:** Early marriage disrupts girls' education trajectories, leading to:

i) Dropout rates: Many girls are forced to drop out of school upon marriage, depriving them of educational opportunities and hindering their personal development.
ii) Restricted access to schooling: Cultural norms and familial expectations may prevent married girls from accessing formal education or pursuing higher studies.
iii) Diminished future prospects: Limited education perpetuates cycles of poverty and disempowerment, constraining girls' future prospects and socio-economic mobility.

e) **Economic wellbeing:** Early marriage perpetuates economic dependency and marginalization among girls, resulting in:
  i) *Financial dependency*: Young brides often lack economic autonomy and are financially dependent on their spouses or families, limiting their ability to make independent choices.
  ii) *Limited employment opportunities*: Married girls face barriers to entering the workforce, exacerbating their economic vulnerability and perpetuating gender disparities in employment.
  iii) *Poverty traps*: Early marriage traps girls in cycles of poverty, hindering their ability to escape socio-economic marginalization and achieve financial independence.

The impacts of early marriage on girls' well-being are multifaceted and far-reaching, encompassing physical, psychological, social, educational, and economic dimensions (Lapa et al., 2019; Malhotra et al., 2011). Addressing the root causes of early marriage and implementing comprehensive interventions are essential to safeguarding the rights and well-being of girls, promoting gender equality, and fostering sustainable development (Mandal & Hindin, 2013). Efforts to prevent early marriage must prioritize education, healthcare, social support systems, and economic empowerment to create a positive environment for girls to thrive and reach their full potential.

PREVENTION AND INTERVENTION STRATEGIES

Early marriage, defined as the union of individuals below the legal age of marriage, continues to be a pervasive issue globally, particularly affecting girls. This essay explores various prevention and intervention strategies aimed at addressing early marriage-induced violence against girls. From legislative reforms to community engagement and access to education, a multi-faceted approach is essential to combat this complex issue effectively.

Legislative Reforms: Raising the Minimum Age of Marriage and Enforcing Child Protection Laws

- ✓ Legislative reforms play a crucial role in addressing early marriage by establishing legal frameworks to protect girls' rights and deter harmful practices. Key measures include:
- ✓ Raising the minimum age of marriage: Increasing the legal age of marriage ensures that girls have the opportunity to complete their education, pursue economic opportunities, and make informed decisions about their futures.
- ✓ Enforcing child protection laws: Strengthening laws to prohibit child marriage and penalize perpetrators helps create a deterrent against the practice. This includes strict enforcement mechanisms and sanctions for those who facilitate or engage in early marriage.

Community Engagement and Awareness Campaigns: Challenging Social Norms and Gender Inequality

- ✓ Challenging social norms and promoting gender equality are essential components of preventing early marriage. Community engagement and awareness campaigns can: Challenging deeply ingrained social norms and promoting gender equality are crucial in the global effort to prevent early marriage and combat gender-based violence. Early marriage is not just a cultural practice but is often rooted in patriarchal norms and gender inequality that limit the rights and opportunities of girls. To address this, community engagement and awareness campaigns play a pivotal role by mobilizing collective action, reshaping societal attitudes, and advocating for policy changes. Community engagement and awareness campaigns are critical tools in challenging harmful social norms and promoting gender equality, both of which are necessary for ending early marriage. By involving community leaders, religious figures, and influencers, and by focusing on the importance of girls' education and gender equality, these campaigns can foster lasting change. Engaging men and boys, advocating for legal reforms, and ensuring the sustainability of campaigns further strengthen the efforts to protect girls from early marriage and gender-based violence. Through these multifaceted approaches, communities can begin to dismantle the systems that perpetuate early marriage and gender inequality, paving the way for a more just and equitable future.
- ✓ Challenge harmful traditional practices: By engaging with community leaders, religious figures, and influencers, awareness campaigns can challenge norms that perpetuate early marriage and gender-based violence.

- ✓ Promote gender equality: Education campaigns that emphasize the importance of gender equality and the value of girls' education can shift attitudes and behaviors towards early marriage. Promoting gender equality is fundamental in reducing the incidence of early marriage. When communities start valuing girls' education, health, and autonomy as much as boys', the underlying reasons for early marriage begin to erode. Awareness campaigns that emphasize these points create a foundation for lasting societal change.
- ✓ Education Campaigns on the Importance of Gender Equality:
- ✓ Girls' Education: A key strategy to prevent early marriage is improving access to education for girls. Awareness campaigns can focus on the benefits of education, not just for individual girls but for families and communities as a whole. Educated girls are less likely to marry early, have better health outcomes, and contribute more significantly to the economy. Campaigns can highlight successful role models and data that demonstrate how education delays marriage and improves opportunities for girls.
- ✓ Shifting Attitudes about Gender Roles: Many cultures still view girls as primarily responsible for household duties and child-rearing, while boys are seen as future breadwinners. Campaigns should challenge these stereotypes by promoting the message that girls and boys deserve equal opportunities in all aspects of life, including education, employment, and personal autonomy. Changing these perceptions helps to weaken the rationale for early marriage, as girls are seen as individuals with potential beyond marriage and motherhood.
- ✓ Empowerment Programs for Girls: In addition to advocating for education, awareness campaigns can link with local initiatives that provide girls with life skills, vocational training, and sexual and reproductive health education. These programs can help girls resist early marriage and make informed decisions about their futures. Campaigns that showcase these empowerment programs can inspire other communities to adopt similar initiatives.
- ✓ Engaging Men and Boys: Male Involvement in Gender Equality: While much of the focus on early marriage prevention rightly centers on empowering girls, it's equally important to engage men and boys. Changing the attitudes and behaviors of men—especially fathers, brothers, and future husbands—is crucial to creating a gender-equal society. Awareness campaigns can involve men and boys in discussions about gender equality, challenging the idea that girls should be married off early and raising awareness of their role in preventing violence against women and girls.
- ✓ Breaking the Cycle of Patriarchy: Patriarchal norms, which prioritize male control over female bodies and lives, are deeply ingrained in many societies. Campaigns that target men and boys can foster a more egalitarian view

of gender roles. By promoting values of mutual respect, consent, and partnership in relationships, awareness campaigns can help break down the social structures that support early marriage and other forms of gender-based violence.

- ✓ Promoting Policy Change and Legal Awareness-Awareness campaigns also play a critical role in advocating for stronger laws and policies to prevent early marriage and protect girls from gender-based violence. By raising awareness of existing laws and advocating for legal reforms, campaigns can empower communities to demand accountability from their governments.
- ✓ Legal Awareness Campaigns: Campaigns that focus on legal literacy can inform communities about their rights and the laws surrounding early marriage. In some areas, communities may not be aware that early marriage is illegal, or they may not know how to access justice systems to protect girls. Campaigns can work to increase understanding of the legal age of marriage and the consequences of violating these laws.
- ✓ Human Rights Framework: Awareness campaigns should emphasize that early marriage violates fundamental human rights, including the rights to education, health, and freedom from violence. This global human rights framework provides a strong moral and legal argument against the practice, aligning local campaigns with international efforts to combat early marriage.
- ✓ Advocacy for Policy Changes: Awareness campaigns can push for policy changes that directly address the root causes of early marriage, such as poverty, lack of education, and gender inequality. By organizing grassroots movements, campaigns can advocate for increased investment in girls' education, economic opportunities for families, and access to reproductive health services, all of which contribute to reducing early marriage.
- ✓ Strengthening Child Protection Systems: Campaigns can also advocate for stronger child protection systems and social safety nets for girls at risk of early marriage. This includes improving reporting mechanisms for child marriage cases and ensuring that local authorities are equipped to intervene when girls are at risk.
- ✓ Sustainability of Campaigns: Sustained community engagement is crucial to ensuring long-term change. One-off campaigns may raise awareness, but without continued efforts, harmful practices can persist. Therefore, campaigns need to be part of a broader, sustained effort that includes:
- ✓ Building Local Capacity: Training local activists, community organizers, and leaders ensures that the message continues to be spread long after an initial campaign has ended. Local ownership of anti-child marriage initiatives is key to sustaining change.

- ✓ Monitoring and Evaluation: Successful campaigns should include mechanisms to track their impact, assess progress, and adapt strategies as needed. Ongoing evaluation ensures that campaigns remain relevant and effective.

Access to Education and Empowerment Programs: Enhancing Girls' Agency and Providing Life Skill Training

- ✓ Education is a powerful tool for preventing early marriage and empowering girls to make autonomous decisions about their lives. Strategies include:
- ✓ Enhancing girls' agency: Providing girls with access to education and opportunities for skill-building enhances their agency and decision-making abilities, reducing their vulnerability to early marriage.
- ✓ Life skills training: Equipping girls with life skills, such as critical thinking, communication, and negotiation, helps them navigate challenging situations and assert their rights effectively.

Social Support for Survivors: Shelters, Hotlines, Legal and Psychological Counseling

Providing comprehensive support services for survivors of early marriage-induced violence is essential for their recovery and empowerment. This includes:

i) Shelters and safe spaces: Establishing shelters and safe spaces where survivors can seek refuge from abusive situations and access essential services.
ii) Hotlines: Setting up hotlines and helplines where survivors can seek immediate assistance, including legal advice, counseling, and emergency support.
iii) Legal aid and psychosocial counseling: Offering survivors access to legal aid services for pursuing justice and psychosocial counseling for healing from trauma and rebuilding their lives.

Multi-Sectoral Collaboration

Addressing early marriage requires a coordinated effort involving governments, NGOs, healthcare providers, educators, and law enforcement agencies. Key strategies include:

Policy coordination: Ensuring alignment between policies and programs across sectors, including education, health, social welfare, and justice, to address the root causes of early marriage.

Capacity building: Building the capacity of frontline workers, including teachers, healthcare providers, and social workers, to identify and respond to cases of early marriage effectively.

Data collection and research: Conducting research and data collection to understand the prevalence and drivers of early marriage, inform programmatic interventions, and track progress over time.

Preventing and addressing early marriage-induced violence against girls requires a multi-faceted approach that addresses root causes, strengthens protective measures, and empowers girls to assert their rights and make autonomous decisions about their lives. By implementing legislative reforms, promoting community engagement and awareness, expanding access to education and empowerment programs, providing support services for survivors, and fostering multi-sectoral collaboration, stakeholders can work together to create a world where every girl can thrive free from the threat of early marriage and violence.

LEGAL MEASURES FOR COMBATING EARLY MARRIAGE-INDUCED VIOLENCE AGAINST GIRLS

Raising the Minimum Age of Marriage

Governments should enact and enforce laws which raise the minimum age of marriage to 18 years for both girls and boys, in line with international standards such as the Convention on the Rights of the Child (CRC). This legal measure helps prevent early marriage and protects the rights of girls to education, health, and self-determination. The practice of early marriage remains a pervasive issue worldwide, particularly affecting girls in many regions. Recognizing the detrimental consequences of early marriage on girls' rights, health, and well-being, governments and international organizations have increasingly advocated for raising the minimum age of marriage to 18 years for both girls and boys (Koenig et al., 2003; O'Donnel & Elliott, 2021). This essay explores the significance of enacting and enforcing laws that establish 18 as the minimum age of marriage, in alignment with international standards such as the Convention on the Rights of the Child (CRC).

Raising the minimum age of marriage to 18 is a critical legal measure aimed at preventing early marriage and protecting the rights of girls. Early marriage, often defined as marriage before the age of 18, deprives girls of their childhood and exposes them to numerous risks, including compromised education, increased vulnerability to domestic violence, and adverse reproductive health outcomes (Raj & McDougal, 2017). By setting 18 as the minimum age of marriage, governments affirm their commitment to upholding girls' rights to education, health, and self-determination, as enshrined in international human rights instruments like the CRC (Stanko, 1985; Stark, 2007).

One of the primary rationales for raising the minimum age of marriage is to safeguard girls' access to education. Early marriage often forces girls to drop out of school, limiting their opportunities for personal development and economic empowerment. By delaying marriage until the age of 18, girls are more likely to complete their education, acquire valuable skills, and pursue higher education or vocational training, thereby enhancing their prospects for future employment and economic independence.

Furthermore, raising the minimum age of marriage helps protect girls' health and well-being. Early marriage is associated with increased risks of maternal mortality, child malnutrition, and complications during childbirth, as adolescent girls are often physically and emotionally unprepared for pregnancy and childbirth. By delaying marriage until the age of 18, girls have the opportunity to mature physically and emotionally, reducing the likelihood of negative health outcomes for both themselves and their children.

Moreover, setting 18 as the minimum age of marriage empowers girls to make informed decisions about their lives and futures. Early marriage often deprives girls of autonomy and agency, as they are pressured or coerced into marriage without their consent. By legally recognizing 18 as the age of consent for marriage, governments affirm girls' right to self-determination and protect them from forced or child marriage practices. So, raising the minimum age of marriage to 18 years for both girls and boys is a fundamental legal measure aimed at preventing early marriage and safeguarding girls' rights, health, and well-being. By enacting and enforcing laws that establish 18 as the minimum age of marriage, governments demonstrate their commitment to upholding international human rights standards and promoting gender equality and social justice for all.

Enforcing Child Protection Laws

Strengthening child protection laws is essential for combating early marriage-induced violence against girls. Legislation should criminalize child marriage and impose penalties on those who facilitate, promote, or participate in the practice (Kelly, 1988). Effective enforcement mechanisms such as including law enforcement agencies, judicial systems, and child protection services, are crucial for holding perpetrators accountable and ensuring justice for victims (McDougall et al., 2016).

The practice of early marriage continues to be a significant human rights violation affecting millions of girls worldwide. Enforcing child protection laws is crucial in addressing this issue and safeguarding the rights and well-being of vulnerable girls. Legislation that criminalizes child marriage and imposes penalties on perpetrators is essential in deterring this harmful practice and ensuring accountability. Effective enforcement mechanisms, including law enforcement agencies, judicial systems, and child protection services, play a critical role in holding perpetrators accountable and providing justice for victims (United Nations, 1989).

First and foremost, legislation should explicitly criminalize child marriage and define it as a punishable offense. By criminalizing child marriage, governments send a clear message that this practice is unacceptable and will not be tolerated. Penalties should be imposed not only on those who enter into child marriages but also on individuals who facilitate, promote, or participate in arranging such marriages. This includes parents, guardians, religious leaders, and community members who play a role in perpetuating the practice. Moreover, effective enforcement mechanisms are essential for ensuring that child protection laws are implemented and enforced effectively. Law enforcement agencies, including the police and other relevant authorities, should be trained to identify and respond to cases of child marriage-induced violence promptly. Specialized units or task forces dedicated to addressing child marriage and gender-based violence can help streamline efforts and ensure comprehensive responses (United Nations, 2006).

Furthermore, the judicial system plays a crucial role in holding perpetrators of child marriage accountable and ensuring that justice is served for victims. Courts should prioritize cases related to child marriage and provide swift and fair trials for perpetrators. Judges and legal professionals should receive training on child rights, gender equality, and the legal framework surrounding child marriage to ensure that cases are handled sensitively and in line with international human rights standards. Additionally, child protection services are instrumental in providing support and assistance to victims of early marriage-induced violence. These services should be accessible, responsive, and culturally sensitive to meet the diverse needs of survivors. Support may include counseling, legal aid, shelter, medical care, and educational opportunities to help survivors rebuild their lives and overcome the trauma of early marriage (United Nations, 1966).

Therefore, enforcing child protection laws is paramount in combatting early marriage-induced violence against girls. By criminalizing child marriage, imposing penalties on perpetrators, and implementing effective enforcement mechanisms, governments can send a strong message that child marriage is a human rights violation that will not be tolerated. Through collaboration between law enforcement agencies, judicial systems, and child protection services, perpetrators can be held accountable, and justice can be delivered for victims, ultimately contributing to the eradication of this harmful practice.

Establishing Mandatory Reporting Mechanisms

Governments should establish mandatory reporting mechanisms for cases of child marriage and violence against girls. Healthcare providers, educators, social workers, and other professionals should be required by law to report suspected cases of early marriage or violence to the relevant authorities for intervention and support.

Importance of Mandatory Reporting Mechanisms: Mandatory reporting mechanisms play a critical role in identifying and responding to cases of child marriage and violence against girls. By requiring professionals to report suspected cases to the authorities, these mechanisms ensure timely intervention and support for victims, prevent further harm, and hold perpetrators accountable. Mandatory reporting also helps collect data on the prevalence and patterns of child marriage and violence, enabling governments to develop evidence-based policies and interventions to address these issues effectively.

Benefits of Mandatory Reporting: Early Intervention: Mandatory reporting enables early intervention in cases of child marriage and violence, preventing further harm to girls and facilitating access to support services such as counseling, legal assistance, and shelter.

Protection of Victims: Reporting mechanisms provide a safety net for victims of child marriage and violence, ensuring that they receive the necessary protection and support from government agencies, NGOs, and community-based organizations.

Accountability: Mandatory reporting holds professionals accountable for their role in safeguarding children's rights and well-being. It creates a legal obligation for them to act in the best interests of the child and report any signs of abuse or exploitation promptly.

Data Collection and Monitoring: Reporting mechanisms contribute to data collection and monitoring efforts, allowing governments to track the prevalence and trends of child marriage and violence, identify high-risk areas, and evaluate the effectiveness of interventions over time.

Challenges and Strategies for Implementation

While mandatory reporting mechanisms offer significant benefits, their implementation may face challenges, including:

Lack of Awareness: Professionals may lack awareness of their reporting obligations or the signs of child marriage and violence. Training programs and awareness campaigns can help address this challenge by educating professionals about their legal responsibilities and the importance of early intervention.

Fear of Retaliation: Some professionals may fear retaliation from perpetrators or community members if they report suspected cases of child marriage or violence. Governments should implement measures to protect whistleblowers and provide them with the necessary support and resources.

Resource Constraints: Limited resources, including funding, staff, and infrastructure, may hinder the effective implementation of reporting mechanisms. Governments should allocate sufficient resources to support the establishment and operation of reporting systems, including training, capacity building, and support services for professionals.

Cultural Sensitivities: Cultural norms and attitudes may influence professionals' perceptions of child marriage and violence, making them reluctant to intervene or report cases. Sensitivity training and cultural competency programs can help professionals navigate these challenges and respond appropriately to diverse cultural contexts.

In conclusion, establishing mandatory reporting mechanisms is essential for combatting child marriage and violence against girls. By requiring professionals to report suspected cases to the authorities, governments can ensure early intervention, protect victims, hold perpetrators accountable, and collect data to inform evidence-based policies and interventions. However, successful implementation requires addressing challenges such as lack of awareness, fear of retaliation, resource constraints, and cultural sensitivities through training, support, and resource allocation. Ultimately, mandatory reporting mechanisms play a crucial role in safeguarding children's rights and promoting gender equality and social justice.

Implementing Comprehensive Legal Frameworks

Comprehensive legal frameworks that address multiple dimensions of early marriage-induced violence are essential for protecting girls' rights and promoting gender equality. These frameworks should encompass laws related to child protection, gender-based violence, reproductive rights, education, and social welfare, ensuring a holistic approach to combating early marriage and its harmful consequences (WHO, 2013).

Providing Legal Aid and Support Services: Access to legal aid and support services is crucial for girls who are at risk of or have experienced early marriage-induced violence. Governments should allocate resources to establish legal aid clinics, helplines, and shelters specifically for girls affected by early marriage, providing them with legal assistance, counseling, and protection from further harm. One of the primary reasons for establishing legal aid clinics is to ensure that girls have access to legal assistance when facing issues related to early marriage. These clinics serve as accessible platforms where girls can seek guidance on their legal rights, options, and remedies. Qualified legal professionals can provide girls with information about relevant laws, procedures, and avenues for redressal, empowering them to make informed decisions about their future. Additionally, legal aid clinics can offer representation and advocacy services to girls who require legal intervention to escape abusive or forced marriages (WHO, 2011).

Helplines dedicated to addressing early marriage-induced violence provide girls with confidential and immediate support. Trained counselors and volunteers staff these helplines, offering emotional support, crisis intervention, and referrals to appropriate services. Girls can reach out to helplines for guidance, safety planning, and assistance in accessing legal aid or shelter. Helplines also serve as a vital resource for girls who may feel isolated or powerless in their situations, providing them with a lifeline to support and assistance. Shelters play a critical role in providing safety and protection to girls fleeing early marriage or domestic violence. These shelters offer temporary accommodation, food, clothing, and other essential services to girls in need. Moreover, shelters provide a supportive environment where girls can access counseling, education, vocational training, and healthcare services. By offering comprehensive support, shelters empower girls to rebuild their lives, gain independence, and pursue their aspirations free from violence and coercion (Walker, 1979).

In addition to legal aid clinics, helplines, and shelters, governments should invest in community-based initiatives that raise awareness about early marriage-induced violence and promote girls' rights. Education campaigns, outreach programs, and peer support networks can help challenge harmful norms and attitudes surrounding early marriage, empower girls to assert their rights, and mobilize communities to take action against this form of violence. By fostering a supportive environment and providing holistic support services, governments can effectively address early marriage-induced violence and ensure the well-being and empowerment of girls.

Ratifying and Implementing International Conventions: Governments should ratify and implement international conventions and treaties that protect the rights of children and women, including the CRC, the Convention on the Elimination of All Forms of Discrimination against Women (CEDAW), and the Universal Declaration of Human Rights. Compliance with these international legal instruments strengthens national efforts to combat early marriage and uphold girls' rights.

Promoting Gender-sensitive Legislation and Policies: Legislation and policies should be gender-sensitive and address the root causes of gender inequality and discrimination that perpetuate early marriage-induced violence. Governments should prioritize investments in girls' education, health, and economic empowerment, ensuring equal opportunities and access to resources for all children, regardless of gender. So, legal measures play a crucial role in combating early marriage-induced violence against girls. By enacting and enforcing laws that protect girls' rights, raise awareness, and hold perpetrators accountable, governments can work towards ending the harmful practice of early marriage and ensuring the well-being and empowerment of girls everywhere.

RECOMMENDATIONS AND IMPLICATIONS

Strengthen Legislative Frameworks

- ✓ Raise the minimum age of marriage to 18 for both girls and boys, with no exceptions.
- ✓ Enact and enforce laws specifically targeting early marriage, including penalties for perpetrators and facilitators.
- ✓ Allocate adequate resources for the implementation and enforcement of child protection laws.

Promote Comprehensive Sexuality Education

- ✓ Integrate comprehensive sexuality education into school curricula to empower girls with knowledge about their rights, reproductive health, and relationships.
- ✓ Ensure that sexuality education is age-appropriate, gender-sensitive, and culturally relevant, addressing issues such as consent, gender equality, and healthy relationships.

Invest in Girls' Education and Economic Empowerment

- ✓ Increase access to quality education for girls, including scholarships, stipends, and incentives to keep them in school.
- ✓ Provide vocational training and skills development programs to enhance girls' economic opportunities and financial independence.
- ✓ Address barriers to education, such as poverty, child labor, and cultural norms that prioritize boys' education over girls'.

Engage Communities and Religious Leaders

- ✓ Conduct community-based awareness campaigns to challenge harmful social norms and promote gender equality.
- ✓ Mobilize religious leaders and community influencers to advocate for the prevention of early marriage and the protection of girls' rights.

- ✓ Establish community-led support networks and safe spaces for girls at risk of early marriage, providing them with information, resources, and support.
- ✓ Community-Based Awareness and Engagement
- ✓ Changing societal norms and attitudes towards child marriage requires active community involvement. Strategies to raise awareness and foster engagement include:
- ✓ Community Education Campaigns: Governments and NGOs should collaborate to conduct community outreach programs aimed at educating parents, religious leaders, and local authorities about the harmful effects of early marriage on girls. These campaigns should highlight the physical, psychological, and social consequences of child marriage, including violence and exploitation.
- ✓ Engaging Men and Boys: Efforts to combat early marriage should involve men and boys as allies in challenging harmful gender norms. Workshops, seminars, and educational programs should focus on promoting positive masculinity, respect for women and girls, and the value of delaying marriage for both genders.

Strengthen Support Services for Survivors

- ✓ Expand access to survivor-centered services, including shelters, hotlines, legal aid, and psychosocial counseling.
- ✓ Train frontline workers, including healthcare providers, teachers, and social workers, to identify and respond to cases of early marriage-induced violence sensitively and effectively.
- ✓ Ensure that support services are culturally appropriate, accessible, and responsive to the diverse needs of survivors, including those from marginalized communities.

Foster Multi-Sectoral Collaboration

- ✓ Facilitate coordination and collaboration among government agencies, NGOs, civil society organizations, and grassroots initiatives working to combat early marriage and support survivors.
- ✓ Establish multi-sectoral task forces or working groups to develop and implement comprehensive strategies to address early marriage-induced violence.
- ✓ Prioritize data collection, research, and monitoring and evaluation efforts to track progress, identify gaps, and inform evidence-based interventions.

Empowering Girls as Agents of Change

- ✓ Promote girls' leadership, participation, and decision-making in efforts to prevent early marriage and address gender-based violence.
- ✓ Create opportunities for girls to engage in advocacy, peer support, and community activism, amplifying their voices and agency in shaping policies and programs that affect their lives.
- ✓ Foster mentorship and role modeling initiatives to inspire and empower girls to envision and pursue alternative pathways beyond early marriage.

Research and Data Collection

- ✓ Accurate data on early marriage is essential for shaping effective policies and interventions. Governments and research institutions should:
- ✓ Conduct Surveys and Studies: Comprehensive surveys and studies are necessary to gather data on the prevalence of child marriage and the specific forms of violence it induces. Data collection should focus on both rural and urban areas and highlight regional variations.
- ✓ Monitoring Progress: Establish systems for monitoring and evaluating the effectiveness of laws and programs aimed at combating early marriage. Governments should track progress regularly and make data publicly available to ensure transparency and accountability. Collaboration with Academic Institutions: Governments should collaborate with universities and research centers to explore the underlying causes of early marriage and identify successful interventions. Research findings can inform evidence-based policymaking.

CONCLUSION

Combatting early marriage-induced violence against girls requires a multifaceted approach that engages policymakers, practitioners, activists, communities, and survivors. By strengthening legislative frameworks, promoting comprehensive sexuality education, investing in girls' education and economic empowerment, engaging communities and religious leaders, strengthening support services for survivors, fostering multi-sectoral collaboration, and empowering girls as agents of change, stakeholders can work together to create a world where every girl can realize her full potential free from the threat of early marriage and violence. In conclusion, early marriage-induced violence against girls is a deeply entrenched human rights violation that perpetuates gender inequality, perpetuates cycles of poverty, and undermines the health, well-being, and future prospects of millions of girls worldwide. However, by understanding the root causes and dynamics of early marriage, and implementing comprehensive strategies to address it, we can break the chains of oppression and create a future where every girl can thrive. Throughout this essay, we have explored the multifaceted nature of early marriage-induced violence, examining its social, cultural, economic, and legal dimensions. We have highlighted the devastating impact of early marriage on girls' physical and psychological health, education, and autonomy, underscoring the urgent need for action.

Effective interventions to combat early marriage-induced violence require a holistic approach that engages policymakers, practitioners, activists, communities, and survivors. By raising awareness, challenging harmful social norms, promoting gender equality, providing access to education and economic opportunities, strengthening legislative frameworks, and providing support services for survivors, stakeholders can work together to prevent early marriage, protect girls' rights, and support survivors on their journey to healing and empowerment. Moreover, it is essential to recognize the agency and resilience of girls themselves as key actors in the fight against early marriage-induced violence. By amplifying their voices, empowering them with knowledge and skills, and creating safe spaces for them to express themselves and advocate for change, we can harness the power of girls as agents of change in their own lives and communities.

In closing, combating early marriage-induced violence against girls is not only a moral imperative but also a strategic investment in the future. By breaking the chains of early marriage, we can unlock the full potential of millions of girls, contributing to a more just, equitable, and sustainable world for generations to come. It is time to unite our efforts, stand in solidarity with girls everywhere, and work tirelessly until every girl is free to choose her own path and fulfill her dreams, free from the shackles of early marriage-induced violence.

Moving Forward: A Call to Action

Breaking the chains of early marriage-induced violence requires collective action from governments, civil society, and communities. Legal measures, though vital, must be part of a broader strategy that includes education, community engagement, and economic empowerment. Governments must enforce existing laws, ensure access to justice, and provide comprehensive support services for victims. Simultaneously, efforts to challenge and change harmful social norms that perpetuate early marriage are critical.

Community leaders, educators, and activists play a key role in raising awareness about the dangers of early marriage and advocating for the rights of girls. Empowering girls through education and providing them with opportunities for economic independence is one of the most effective ways to prevent early marriage and combat gender-based violence. It is essential to create a society where girls are valued for their potential, not their marriageability, and where they are free to pursue their dreams without fear of violence or coercion. While progress has been made in combatting early marriage-induced violence, much work remains to be done. By strengthening legal frameworks, enforcing child protection laws, and addressing the root causes of early marriage, we can create a world where girls are empowered to thrive, free from the chains of violence and exploitation. The fight against early marriage-induced violence is not just a legal challenge; it is a moral imperative that demands the collective efforts of all stakeholders to protect the rights, dignity, and future of every girl. Gender-sensitive legislation and policies that address the root causes of early marriage-induced violence are essential for achieving long-term change. Early marriage is often a consequence of deep-rooted gender inequality and discrimination, and efforts to combat this practice must be grounded in a commitment to promoting gender equality. Governments should prioritize investments in girls' education, healthcare, and economic empowerment, ensuring that girls have equal access to opportunities and resources.

Legislation must also be responsive to the specific needs and vulnerabilities of girls affected by early marriage. For example, laws should protect girls' reproductive rights, ensuring they have access to healthcare services, including sexual and reproductive health services, family planning, and maternal care. Additionally, policies should address the economic challenges faced by girls, providing them with opportunities for education, vocational training, and economic empowerment. Mandatory reporting mechanisms are a crucial element of the legal response to early marriage-induced violence. By requiring healthcare providers, educators, social workers, and other professionals to report suspected cases of child marriage or violence, these mechanisms facilitate early intervention, preventing further harm to girls. Reporting mechanisms also play a critical role in collecting data on the prevalence of child marriage and violence, which is essential for developing evidence-based policies and interventions.

However, implementing mandatory reporting mechanisms presents challenges, including a lack of awareness among professionals, fear of retaliation, resource constraints, and cultural sensitivities. Governments must invest in training programs to educate professionals about their reporting obligations and the importance of early intervention. Additionally, protections must be put in place for whistleblowers, ensuring that professionals who report cases of early marriage are safeguarded from retaliation by perpetrators or community members. Adequate resources must be allocated to support the implementation of reporting systems, including the training and capacity-building of professionals, as well as the provision of support services for victims.

REFERENCES

Ahmed, A., & Hossain, S. (2017). Early marriage and intimate partner violence among adolescents in South Asia: Evidence from Bangladesh, India, and Nepal. *Journal of Interpersonal Violence*, 32(8), 1171–1196. PMID: 26021859

Amin, S., & Amin, S. (2018). Understanding early marriage and associated outcomes: An exploratory study in urban slums of Dhaka, Bangladesh. *Journal of Biosocial Science*, 50(5), 632–648. DOI: 10.1017/S002193201700036X

Arnett, J. J. (2019). *Adolescent psychology around the world*. Routledge.

Arthur, M., & Ngugi, E. N. (2017). Legal strategies for addressing early and forced marriage in Africa. *Harvard Law Review*, 130(1), 235–278.

Bhutta, Z. A., Das, J. K., Bahl, R., Lawn, J. E., Salam, R. A., Paul, V. K., & Walker, N. (2014). Can available interventions end preventable deaths in mothers, newborn babies, and stillbirths, and at what cost? *Lancet*, 384(9940), 347–370. DOI: 10.1016/S0140-6736(14)60792-3 PMID: 24853604

Campbell, J. C. (2002). Health consequences of intimate partner violence. *Lancet*, 359(9314), 1331–1336. DOI: 10.1016/S0140-6736(02)08336-8 PMID: 11965295

Chaudhury, R. H., & Banik, R. B. (2021). Socio-economic consequences of child marriage: A study of the Namasudra community of West Bengal. *Child and Youth Services*, 42(2), 127–150. DOI: 10.1080/0145935X.2021.1892552

Chelliah, K. (2019). Understanding early marriage: Perspectives and experiences from Tamil Nadu. *Gender, Technology and Development*, 23(3), 258–278. DOI: 10.1080/09718524.2019.1690249

Clark, C. J., Everson-Rose, S. A., & Suglia, S. F. (2014). Binge drinking and violence against intimate partners in the Americas. *Revista Panamericana de Salud Pública*, 35(5/6), 333–339.

Coker, A. L., Davis, K. E., Arias, I., Desai, S., Sanderson, M., Brandt, H. M., & Smith, P. H. (2002). Physical and mental health effects of intimate partner violence for men and women. *American Journal of Preventive Medicine*, 23(4), 260–268. DOI: 10.1016/S0749-3797(02)00514-7 PMID: 12406480

Crockett, L. J., & Bingham, C. R. (2000). Antecedents and outcomes of abusive romantic relationships: The role of childhood maltreatment. *Journal of Family Violence*, 15(1), 75–88.

Denner, J., & Kirby, D. (2019). Covert use of violence in dating relationships: Development of the coercive control scale. *Aggressive Behavior*, 45(2), 139–154. PMID: 30516286

Ellsberg, M., Jansen, H. A., Heise, L., Watts, C. H., & Garcia-Moreno, C. (2008). Intimate partner violence and women's physical and mental health in the WHO multi-country study on women's health and domestic violence: An observational study. *Lancet*, 371(9619), 1165–1172. DOI: 10.1016/S0140-6736(08)60522-X PMID: 18395577

Ertürk, Y. (2005). Research on violence against women and girls: How are we doing and where do we go from here? *Gender and Development*, 13(1), 11–17.

Fleming, P. J., McCleary-Sills, J., Morton, M., Levtov, R., Heilman, B., & Barker, G. (2015). Risk factors for men's lifetime perpetration of physical violence against intimate partners: Results from the International Men and Gender Equality Survey (IMAGES) in eight countries. *PLoS One*, 10(3), e0118639. DOI: 10.1371/journal.pone.0118639 PMID: 25734544

Flood, M., & Pease, B. (2009). Factors influencing attitudes to violence against women. *Trauma, Violence & Abuse*, 10(2), 125–142. DOI: 10.1177/1524838009334131 PMID: 19383630

George, J. S. (2011). Preventing violence against women: Societal norms and women's economic empowerment. *American Journal of Economics and Sociology*, 70(2), 446–471.

Hamby, S., & Grych, J. H. (2013). *The web of violence: Exploring connections among different forms of interpersonal violence and abuse.* Springer Science & Business Media. DOI: 10.1007/978-94-007-5596-3

Human Rights Watch. (2013). Child marriage: Legal reform needed to protect rights. https://www.hrw.org/news/2013/06/14/child-marriage-legal-reform-needed-protect-rights

Human Rights Watch. (2014). When I grow up, I'll be forced to marry: Child and forced marriage in South Sudan. https://www.hrw.org/report/2014/02/20/when-i-grow-ill-be-forced-marry/child-and-forced-marriage-south-sudan

Human Rights Watch. (2015). Bangladesh: End child marriage. https://www.hrw.org/news/2015/06/08/bangladesh-end-child-marriage

ICRW (International Center for Research on Women). (2019). *Accelerating action to end child marriage: Insights from the Frontline*. ICRW.

International Center for Research on Women. (2014). Too young to wed: The lives, rights, and health of young married girls. https://www.icrw.org/wp-content/uploads/2016/10/Too-Young-to-Wed-Full-Report.pdf

International Labour Organization. (1999). Worst forms of child labour convention, 1999 (No. 182). https://www.ilo.org/dyn/normlex/en/f?p=NORMLEXPUB:12100:0:NO:P12100_ILO_CODE:C182

International Women's Rights Action Watch Asia Pacific. (2013). Child marriage and the law: Legislative reform initiative paper. https://www.iwraw-ap.org/wp-content/uploads/2013/10/IWRAWAP-MY-CM-Legislative-Reform-Initiative-Book.pdf

Jain, S., Gupta, P., & Bhatt, S. (2017). Early marriage and HIV/AIDS: Risk factors among young women aged 15–24 years in India. *Journal of Family Medicine and Primary Care*, 6(4), 703–709. DOI: 10.4103/jfmpc.jfmpc_121_16

Johnson, M. P. (1995). Patriarchal terrorism and common couple violence: Two forms of violence against women. *Journal of Marriage and Family*, 57(2), 283–294. DOI: 10.2307/353683

Johnson, M. P. (2008). *A typology of domestic violence: Intimate terrorism, violent resistance, and situational couple violence.* Northeastern University Press.

Kabeer, N. (2020). Empowering women or pleasing parents? The tension between women's rights and cultural values in the transition to adulthood in Pakistan. *Gender & Society*, 34(1), 74–98. DOI: 10.1177/0891243219899717

Kamal, S. M. M., Hassan, C. H., Alam, G. M., Ying, Y., Sakib, N., & Bhuiya, A. (2015). Child marriage in Bangladesh: Trends and determinants. *Journal of Biosocial Science*, 47(1), 120–139. DOI: 10.1017/S0021932013000746 PMID: 24480489

Kasturirangan, A., Krishnan, S., & Riger, S. (2004). The impact of culture and minority status on women's experience of domestic violence. *Trauma, Violence & Abuse*, 5(4), 318–332. DOI: 10.1177/1524838004269487 PMID: 15361586

Kelly, L. (1988). *Surviving sexual violence.* Polity Press.

Koenig, M. A., Lutalo, T., Zhao, F., Nalugoda, F., Wabwire-Mangen, F., Kiwanuka, N., & Gray, R. (2003). Coercive sex in rural Uganda: Prevalence and associated risk factors. *Social Science & Medicine*, 57(4), 783–797. PMID: 14672593

Kusumayati, A. (2018). Child marriage in Indonesia: Analysis of data from Indonesia Demographic and Health Surveys 2002, 2007 and 2012. *Jurnal Studi Pemuda*, 7(2), 171–185.

Lapa, T. Y., Kozhukhar, N. G., & Kozhukhar, T. V. (2019). Gender-based violence in the family: Theoretical and practical aspects. *Pravo.Zhurnal Vysshei Shkoly Ekonomiki*, 2, 114–135.

Lee-Rife, S. M. (2010). Women's empowerment and reproductive experiences over the lifecourse. *Social Science & Medicine*, 71(3), 634–642. DOI: 10.1016/j.socscimed.2010.04.019 PMID: 20621752

Loaiza, E., & Wong, S. (2012). Marrying too young: End child marriage. *UNFPA Journal*, 3(5), 1–55.

Malhotra, A., Warner, A., McGonagle, A., & Lee-Rife, S. (2011). *Solutions to end child marriage: What the evidence shows*. International Center for Research on Women.

Mandal, M., & Hindin, M. J. (2013). From child marriage to marital rape: The Indian context. *Violence Against Women*, 19(9), 1315–1328.

Marphatia, A. A., Ambale, G. S., & Reid, A. M. (2016). Women's marriage age matters for public health: A review of the broader health and social implications in South Asia. *Frontiers in Public Health*, 4, 1–10. DOI: 10.3389/fpubh.2016.00070 PMID: 29094035

McDougall, J., Toliver, S., & Najmabadi, A. (2016). *Ending child marriage in the Americas: A review of legislative initiatives*. UNICEF.

Meyer, S. (2016). *Domestic violence and vulnerabilities: Intersecting inequalities*. Routledge.

Molla, R. R., Rahman, M. S., Khan, M. M. R., Islam, M. M., Rahman, M. A., Billah, S. M., & Alam, M. M. (2018). Trends, prevalence and determinants of early marriage in Bangladesh: An overview. *Sexual & Reproductive Healthcare : Official Journal of the Swedish Association of Midwives*, 16, 91–99. DOI: 10.1016/j.srhc.2018.02.006

Murphy, M., Pande, R., & Malhotra, A. (2018). *International Child Marriage Laws: Policy and Practice*. Springer.

Muthengi, E., & Erulkar, A. S. (2016). Violence against adolescent girls in lower-income countries: An overview of findings from the violence against children and youth surveys. *The Journal of Adolescent Health*, 59(3), 318–322. PMID: 27320034

Nour, N. M. (2006). Health consequences of child marriage in Africa. *Emerging Infectious Diseases*, 12(11), 1644–1649. DOI: 10.3201/eid1211.060510 PMID: 17283612

O'Donnell, A., & Elliott, K. (2021). *Children, human rights and the law: An introduction*. Routledge.

Raj, A., & McDougal, L. (2017). Sexual violence and girls' vulnerability to child marriage in humanitarian settings. *Reproductive Health Matters*, 25(51), 49–54.

Save the Children. (2012). Ending child marriage: How elevating the status of girls advances U.S. foreign policy objectives. https://www.savethechildren.org/content/dam/usa/reports/advocacy/ending-child-marriage-report-2012.pdf

Stanko, E. A. (1985). *Intimate intrusions: Women's experience of male violence*. Routledge & Kegan Paul.

Stark, E. (2007). *Coercive control: How men entrap women in personal life*. Oxford University Press. DOI: 10.1093/oso/9780195154276.001.0001

Uddin, E. M. (2015). Family socio-cultural values affecting early marriage between Muslim and Santal communities in rural Bangladesh. *The International Journal of Sociology and Social Policy*, 35(3/4), 141–164. DOI: 10.1108/IJSSP-06-2014-0046

Uddin, M. E. (2017). Family demographic mechanisms linking of socioeconomic status to subjective physical health in rural Bangladesh. *Social Indicators Research*, 130(3), 1263–1279. DOI: 10.1007/s11205-015-1209-x

Uddin, M. E. (2021). Teenage marriage and high school dropout among poor girls: A narrative review for family pathways in Bangladesh. *Journal of Research in Social Sciences and Language*, 1(1), 55–76. https://www.jssal.com/index.php/jssal/article/view/15

UNFPA. (2018). Empowering young people to end child marriage and address gender-based violence through the provision of comprehensive sexuality education. https://asiapacific.unfpa.org/en/publications/empowering-young-people-end-child-marriage-and-address-gender-based-violence-through

UNICEF. (2005). Early marriage: A harmful traditional practice. https://www.unicef.org/publications/index_26902.html

UNICEF. (2015). Ending child marriage: Progress and prospects. https://data.unicef.org/resources/ending-child-marriage-progress-and-prospects/

UNICEF. (2018). Progress for every child in the SDG era. https://data.unicef.org/resources/progress-child-sdg-era-2018/

United Nations. (1966). International Covenant on Economic, Social and Cultural Rights. https://www.ohchr.org/en/professionalinterest/pages/cescr.aspx

United Nations. (1979). Convention on the Elimination of All Forms of Discrimination against Women. https://www.un.org/womenwatch/daw/cedaw/

United Nations. (1989). Convention on the Rights of the Child. https://www.ohchr.org/en/professionalinterest/pages/crc.aspx

United Nations. (2000). Optional Protocol to the Convention on the Rights of the Child on the Sale of Children, Child Prostitution and Child Pornography. https://www.ohchr.org/en/professionalinterest/pages/OPSCCRC.aspx

United Nations (2015). The world's women 2015: Trends and statistics.

United Nations. (2017). Child marriage laws around the world. https://www.unwomen.org/en/what-we-do/ending-violence-against-women/facts-and-figures/child-marriage

United Nations Children's Fund. (2014). Ending child marriage: Progress and prospects. https://www.unicef.org/media/files/Child_Marriage_Report_7_17_LR.pdf

United Nations Development Programme. (2016). Ending child marriage: Progress and prospects. https://www.undp.org/content/dam/undp/library/Democratic%20Governance/Women%27s%20Empowerment/Ending-Child-Marriage-Global-Initiative-Progress-and-Prospects-2016.pdf

United Nations Economic and Social Council. (2006). General Comment No. 18: The Right to Non-Discrimination in Economic, Social and Cultural Rights. https://www.refworld.org/docid/4538838d0.html

United Nations General Assembly. (1966). International Covenant on Civil and Political Rights. https://www.ohchr.org/en/professionalinterest/pages/ccpr.aspx

United Nations Human Rights Office of the High Commissioner. (2001). Child marriage. https://www.ohchr.org/Documents/Publications/Factsheet23en.pdf

United Nations Population Fund. (2012). Marrying too young: End child marriage. https://www.unfpa.org/sites/default/files/pub-pdf/MarryingTooYoung.pdf

United Nations Population Fund. (2020). Ending child marriage in Africa: A briefing for journalists. https://www.unfpa.org/sites/default/files/resource-pdf/Ending_child_marriage_in_Africa%2C_a_briefing_for_journalists_EN_LR.pdf

United Nations Population Fund (UNFPA) (2012). "Marrying Too Young: End Child Marriage."

Walker, L. E. A. (1979). *The battered woman*. Harper & Row Publishers.

Watts, C., & Zimmerman, C. (2002). Violence against women: Global scope and magnitude. *Lancet*, 359(9313), 1232–1237. DOI: 10.1016/S0140-6736(02)08221-1 PMID: 11955557

West, C. M. (Ed.). (2002). *Violence in the lives of Black women: Battered, black, and blue*. Haworth Press.

World Bank. (2015). Child marriage: A silent health and human rights issue. https://openknowledge.worldbank.org/bitstream/handle/10986/22788/9781464805007.pdf

World Health Organization. (2011). Global strategy to stop health-care providers from performing female genital mutilation. https://www.who.int/reproductivehealth/publications/fgm/rhr_11_18/en/

World Health Organization. (2020). Child marriage. https://www.who.int/news-room/q-a-detail/child-marriage

World Health Organization (WHO). (2013). *Global and regional estimates of violence against women: Prevalence and health effects of intimate partner violence and non-partner sexual violence*. World Health Organization.

Yount, K. M., Crandall, A., Cheong, Y. F., Osypuk, T. L., Bates, L. M., Naved, R. T., & Schuler, S. R. (2016). Child marriage and intimate partner violence in rural Bangladesh: A longitudinal multilevel analysis. *Demography*, 53(6), 1821–1852. DOI: 10.1007/s13524-016-0520-8 PMID: 27812927

Chapter 4
Child Marriage in Indonesia:
Exploring Social Culture and Gender Inequality

Hari Harjanto Setiawan
0000-0002-4656-9679
Research Center for Social Welfare, Villages and Connectivity, National Research and Innovation Agency (BRIN), Jakarta, Indonesia

Yanuar Farida Wismayanti
Research Center for Public Policy, National Research and Innovation Agency (BRIN), Jakarta, Indonesia

Nyi R. Irmayani
0000-0002-2905-6572
Research Center for Social Welfare, Villages and Connectivity, Research Center for Social Welfare, Villages and Connectivity, National Research and Innovation Agency (BRIN), Jakarta, Indonesia

Adhani Wardianti
Bandung Correctional Center, Ministry of Immigration and Corrections, Bandung, Indonesia

ABSTRACT

Child marriage has become an important issue in recent years, both nationally and globally. This is detrimental to children's growth and development. Many children throughout the world experience problems with child marriage, including in Indonesia. The difficulties they experience include reproductive health, emotional aspects, exploitation, violence and harassment. This paper uses critical discourse

DOI: 10.4018/979-8-3693-3394-5.ch004

analysis methods to explore conceptual and practical gaps. This chapter was written qualitatively, using literature observations and previous research findings on early marriage. The results show that cultural factors and gender equality play a role in the high rate of child marriage in Indonesia. This chapter explains the socio-cultural aspects of early marriage and gender equality based on research in Indonesia. This chapter contributes to the academic and practitioner literature on preventing early marriage in Indonesia. The implication is that child marriage has become a reality in child protection efforts in Indonesia.

INTRODUCTION

The importance of preventing child marriage is because children are in their growth and development period. Children should receive special treatment compared to adults. The goal is for children to achieve optimal growth and development according to their stage of development. Early marriage is a problem for some children. Children's rights say that the state must look after and treat children well. Children who marry too early will psychologically experience problems in their development (Uddin, 2015). Children also receive negative stigma from people in their environment because they are seen as violating social norms. Child marriage has become an important issue in recent years and continues to increase in number. Many children around the world have child marriages, including in Indonesia. Problems that arise as a result of early marriage are reproductive health, emotional aspects, exploitation, violence, and harassment (Yoosefi Lebni et al., 2023).

Child marriage in Indonesia is considered to be a result of the vulnerability of victims, most of whom are girls. This problem is less received by the government, which tends to focus on economic development rather than side issues. The implication is child protection efforts in Indonesia are covering up that information about child marriage. Complexity and weak law enforcement have created challenges in achieving child marriage in Indonesia. The problem of child marriage is examined to violate human rights because it harms both girls and boys. Throughout the world, 14 million children under 19 give birth every year. There are survey results of women aged 20 to 24, and 36% of them married when they were less than 18. Intervention in child marriage is essential in dealing with children's problems. Although many countries have changed their policies and laws, child marriage rates are still very high in those countries with low and middle levels of socioeconomic development (Pourtaheri et al., 2023).

Globally, every country is still struggling to ensure a minimum age due to obstacles and challenges in implementing regulations to prevent children from child marriage (Collin & Talbot, 2023). India, Bangladesh, Philippines and Laos are some of the countries that continue to try to end child marriage. These countries have set the minimum age for marriage at 18 years. The very high Gender Inequality Index (GII) may be the cause of the prevalence of child marriage in these four countries (Uddin, 2015). Thailand and Vietnam have a lower GII than other ASEAN member countries. This condition shows that women have equal access to health services, education and political participation. This means better gender equality can help girls be more empowered, reducing early marriage.

Child marriage is considered a significant issue related to human rights (Huzaimah et al., 2023). This often leads to sexual understanding of men and women. Global data shows that girls marry earlier than boys. All ASEAN member countries state that their laws stipulate a minimum age for marriage. International law, according to the Convention on the Rights of Children, the minimum age for marriage must be the same for men and women (Kusumadewi & Wiswayana, 2024). Member states have a minimum age to consent to marriage based on gender. In Indonesia, legal disagreements also lead to child marriage. According to the Indonesian Child Protection Law 35/2015, a child is someone under 18 years of age. However, Indonesian Marriage Law 1/1974 stipulates that women and men can marry between 16 and 19 years. Children should not give consent in situations like this. Laws, social systems, and cultures differ when it comes to sexual disclosure of children.

Other countries, such as Jordan, have a similar situation. This country sets the lowest age for marriage at eighteen years. To marry off their little daughters, many families perform religious ceremonies. This is because the legal minimum age for girls in some countries, such as Iran and Yemen, is only 15 years old, so many girls are married before they are 18 years old. Dowries are essential for girls in poor areas to earn money—the bride's family through a financial agreement. Children should not give consent in these situations. Cases of child marriage occur in a state of helplessness and are a violation against girls (Eboka, 2023; Uddin, 2021).

According to several studies, child marriage causes emotional and physical trauma, exploitation, physical and sexual violence, dropping out of school, and reproductive health. In addition, children are twice as likely to die during pregnancy as women over twenty years old. Child marriage is a mistake and is dangerous and can lead to poverty (Uddin, 2021). The Indonesian government officially accepts international policies and goals to eliminate child marriage. However, community culture dominates the national discourse on child marriage. Sometimes, marriage is a way to escape poverty (Hartarto & Wibowo, 2023). We tried to find economic conditions to see the characteristics of child marriage.

Various cases of child marriage in Indonesia are determined mainly by socio-cultural and economic factors both within the girl and around her (Baraie et al., 2024). Therefore, policies must focus on how to build an environment that supports children's growth and does not depend on child marriage. Setting the legal age for marriage to someone who is at least 18 years old will prevent child marriage and avoid discrimination against children, especially girls. It is challenging to attain these outcomes in certain countries due to the intricacy of the process and the absence of robust legal enforcement mechanisms. This chapter explains the social culture of early marriage and gender equality based on research in Indonesia. This chapter aims to contribute to the literature on preventing early marriage for academics and practitioners. Specifically, this chapter aims to cover the following:

- To explain case studies in several places in Indonesia.
- To explain the influence of poverty on child marriage
- To explain the social culture of early marriage in Indonesia more broadly.
- To explain gender equality in early marriages that occur in Indonesia.

What is new is that child marriage is influenced by poverty, culture and understanding of gender equality as causes of child marriage. This must be a concern for the country and the world to change this condition so that there are no more child marriages.

METHODOLOGY

The methodology used is a qualitative approach. The research design regarding child marriage is based on collecting and analyzing qualitative data through interviews, observations and documentation studies. In principle, research uses valid primary data because qualitative research positions the researcher as an instrument. A qualitative approach will describe community characteristics, explore community experiences regarding child marriage. This chapter was written qualitatively, using a literature review and previous research findings regarding early marriage in Indonesia. Literature reviews use various data sources, including regulations, literature books, research results, and journals. After being described, the data is studied, analyzed and processed qualitatively. The results of the analysis are described systematically in sentence form, making it easier to summarize the data. Child development theory is used to define children and social culture.

This approach is expected to gain appreciation, knowledge and perception regarding understanding and giving meaning to life (Neuman, 2006). A qualitative approach helps researchers describe the characteristics of society in facing the problem of child marriage because it emphasizes deepening human experience and theoretical observations (Rubin & Babby, 2007). A qualitative approach was chosen to build understanding of the phenomenon of child marriage and develop new theories (Alston & Bowles, 1998). Another opinion states that "the theoretical basis of qualitative research is a phenomenological, symbolic interaction, cultural and ethnomethodological approach" (Moleong, 2018). Researchers observe and interact with research subjects to understand language and their interpretation of nature. Researchers are instruments in data collection (Creswell, 1994).

LITERATURE REVIEW

Definition Of Child Marriage: Complexities Of Laws

The definition of a child is critical for laws, regulations, and child protection services. However, local laws are not agreed between countries. Due to different age limits, laws, and cultures in each country, this definition is complicated, and many other explanations exist for the term child. It is challenging to ensure the legal definition of a child because children's rights must be fulfilled and children protected from violence. The Convention on the Rights of the Child (CRC) defines a child as anyone under 18 unless the age of majority is reached earlier under laws applicable to children. Many countries have ratified this Convention, but they also have guidelines for organizations that keep children safe. In The Covenant on the Rights of the Child in Islam, established in 2004, the Organization of the Islamic Conference (OIC) provides a different definition for children. The general definition is anyone who has not reached maturity according to applicable law (Hashemi, 2017).

Indonesia ratified the CRC in the Child Protection Law of the Republic of Indonesia Number 35 of 2014. A child is anyone under 18 years of age, including infants. However, the Marriage Law of the Republic of Indonesia Number 1 of 1974 stipulates that the minimum age for a man to be married is 19 years. A woman can marry at the age of 16. As evidenced by various laws, there is significant ambiguity regarding the age of consent and marriage, especially for women. The laws of all ASEAN member countries set a minimum age for marriage, except for Myanmar, which does not set a minimum age for marriage. In this context, international law stipulates that the minimum age for marriage must be the same for boys and girls. However, in some member states, sexual consent and the minimum age for marriage are based on gender (Mukharrom & Abdi, 2023).

Many countries have minumun age to marriage due to local context, including in Middle East Countries. For example in Jordan, children under 15 cannot be legally married. However, with special approval from sharia court judges, marriage of children between the ages of 15 and 17 is permitted in exceptional circumstances. The legal age for marriage in Nepal is 18 years; However, boys and girls must have parental permission to do so, and people aged 20 and over can marry without parental consent. However, research results have shown that the law and reality conflict. The minimum age for marriage for men and women in most countries in the Middle East and North Africa differs, ranging from 15 years in Iran to 20 years in Tunisia and Saudi Arabia. This has led many families to carry out their religious ceremonies to marry off their daughters. As a result, this region has a high rate of early marriage.

In addition, the minimum age for marriage in ASEAN member countries is very different. These conditions limit the application of international standards and how child protection organizations can address child marriage (Cameron et al., 2023). There is no worldwide agreement that establishes a legal age for sexual intercourse. Additionally, Indonesian law does not clearly define intent. The Protection Act effectively prohibits actions that are legally considered underhanded. However, Child Protection laws prohibit sexual relations with children under the age of 18. Men who have sex with women under the age of fifteen have three senders. The act is legal and will not be considered an offence if 1) the woman is married to the perpetrator and 2) the perpetrator does not know and cannot suspect that the woman is under fifteen years old.

Child Development in a Social Ecological Perspective Theory

The government must formulate policies that involve parties related to child marriage cases. This article is different from the previous post. The last article looked at children's social environment at a micro level (Setiawan et al., 2020). At the macro level, policies will influence children's development. The social-ecological model is a scope of child development that is external but makes a significant contribution to the child. Bronfenbrenner's ecological model sees children as influenced by the structure of the environment in which they live (Hossain & Uddin, 2023; Uddin, 2017a).

This structure consists of microsystem, mesosystem, ecosystem and macrosystem (Santrock, 2010a). According to the social ecology view, child marriage is caused by the social environment. This article will look at policy from the perspective of the child's environment at the macro level. Child marriage is encouraged by the social environment. In line with this, the individual cannot be separated from the life around him (Zastrow, 2010). The microsystem looks at the child's setting with activities, roles, and interactions with people who have a direct influence. Mesosystem shows the relationship between two or more microsystems. The ecosystem looks directly at the child's social environment but will influence their development. The macrosystem is a system that indirectly influences child development. The chronosystem represents the degree of stability of a child's changes. An ecological perspective will clarify the position of children as "victims".

The descent from infancy to adulthood is an interrelated life span. Children determine the future. Childhood lasts after passing through infancy and reaching the age of two years until adulthood. Boys are thirteen years old, and girls are fourteen years old (Santrock, 2010b). According to this definition, children are cared for by their parents from infancy to adulthood until they can work independently. Many psychoanalytic, cognitive, social, ethological, and ecological theories influence child development (Hossain & Uddin, 2023).

Psychoanalytic Freud argues that early family experiences influence biological determinism in a person's development (Crocker & Baur, 2020). The theory of psychosocial development, developed by Erikson, supports the biological perspective and early family experiences, which are very important (Maree, 2021). Cognitive structures develop thanks to Piaget's cognitive development focus on adaptation and environmental interaction (Lutz et al., 2018). Vygotsky's theory of parenting development is critical because of cultural pressures and childhood influences (Taber, 2020). Early experiences are significant because they can provide information about early changes in a child's growth. According to behavioural and social cognition, it is proven that the environment has a huge impact. Bronfenbrenner's theory is that climate influences children(Adu & Oudshoorn, 2020).

Children must undergo punishment as a consequence of their actions. Children who exhibit antisocial behavior are often called delinquents. As a result, the police had to take action against him because of this incident (Hofmann & Müller, 2018). Included in this category are offences prohibited by criminal law, such as theft, robbery, violence, vandalism, bullying, careless driving, alcohol consumption, promiscuity, and drug use. The two central human rights values are the right to freedom and well-being(Ward & Birgden, 2007). All children have the same right to develop and grow according to age. The 1989 UN Convention recognizes the international rights of children.

The UN established four principles of children's rights: 1) No discrimination, which means the Convention applies to all children; 2) Do good to children. In other words, these principles should be applied to all programs involving children. The Right to Life, given to every child, must be recognized and protected. Respecting Children's Views means that every child's opinion must be considered in decision-making (Correia et al., 2019). This Convention defines a child as someone who is not yet 18 years old. Apart from this understanding, many other things differentiate children from adults.

Child Marriage As a Cultural Patriarchy

Even state institutions such as the Ministry of Religion consider child marriage acceptable in Indonesia. Parents can force their children, both boys and girls, to marry. This happens when a child has intimate relations with his partner before marriage. Parents fear their children will have sex outside of marriage, which is prohibited in Islam. Forcing marriage is the best solution. Minister of Religion Regulation No. 3/1975 allows minors to marry if their parents receive a marriage dispensation permit from the local religious court. Due to economic, cultural, and spiritual factors, the acceptance and practice of child marriage are still high (Kok et al., 2023). In addition to these factors, local beliefs and customs significantly influence how society accepts and permits child marriage. Local customs in several regions of Indonesia require many girls to marry men older than them. Parents often want to marry off their daughters to prevent harm. Still, child marriage can leave their daughters vulnerable to abuse from intimate partners, including sexual, physical, psychological, and emotional violence.

Child marriage is considered a significant human rights issue (Mbamba et al., 2023). This often involves discussions for academics and practitioners regarding underage boys and girls. Research shows that child marriage is still common and is likely to increase. Although child marriage is considered a significant form of violence against girls, it cannot be resolved through the criminal justice system. Indonesia has changed the law regarding child marriage because the previous law was very detrimental to children. Policies and programs based on this law have also been implemented. It is hoped that these programs and policies will reduce child marriage in Indonesia.

In social and ideological construction, patriarchy places men above women, children, and property (Mensah, 2023). This ideology is so strong that they often gain the approval of women they reject. Factors that distinguish patriarchal societal structures include the belief that men are the leaders of the household, men's precedence in paid work, men's dominant sexuality, and cultural institutions led and influenced by men. Indonesia's social system is strongly influenced by patriarchal structures (Mas'udah, 2021). Culture and society shape Indonesia's patriarchal ideology. This patriarchal structure divides the roles of men and women, with men at the top (dominant) and women at the bottom (subordinate). It has become ingrained that men are superior in society, which allows women to live together and internalize feelings of inferiority. The framework for the causes of child marriage can be seen in **Appendix 1**

RESULT AND DISCUSSION

Child Marriage in Indonesia

Discussions about child marriage have once again become the focus of attention in Indonesian society. Child and women's rights observers voiced this case as a social problem that must be addressed immediately (Mady, 2023). Data from the Ministry of PPPA states that in 2019, there were 24 thousand child marriages. Data on the increase can also be seen from data held by the Wonosari Religious Court, Gunung Kidul, which shows that between March and August 2020, 150 requests for marriage-age dispensation were submitted. A research result explains that the rate of child marriage is spread across almost all regions in Indonesia (both rural and urban). A study shows that one in nine children in Indonesia is married before the age of 18. Women are between 20 and 24 years old and married before age 18. There are 1,220,900 cases of child marriage in Indonesia, placing it among the ten countries with the highest number of child marriages in the world.

Practices of sexual violence, such as marital rape, are rarely revealed. In reality, the practice of marital rape occurs almost throughout the world (Aborisade & Olayinka-Aliu, 2023). This happens due to the impact of a culture that tends to be permissive and does not view it as a criminal act. Patriarchal culture makes the practice of marital rape permitted or considered legal so that there are no sanctions for the perpetrators. Currently, marital rape has become a concern for many parties, especially when it is linked to the high number of wives starting to dare to speak out. In an unequal gender relationship, women are vulnerable to exposure from their husbands. This shows how the practice of subordination from patriarchal culture applies in society. One factor is a woman's inability and helplessness as a wife in rejecting their partner. Women are powerless to negotiate the use of condoms when having sexual relations with their husbands.

Child marriage is closely related to women's reproductive health. For example, in terms of maintaining the health of reproductive organs, readiness to have children, and so on. Data on early breastfeeding initiation shows that women aged 20-24 can reach 28.76 percent, while those who marry before 18 are only 18.83 percent. In a review of awareness of giving birth using health services, there are more women aged 20-24 years who married at the age of 18 years and over than women who married before the age of 18 years. In terms of the practice of abortion and miscarriage, it turns out that it occurs more often in first pregnancies and unplanned pregnancies. Low awareness and minimal knowledge about Abortions and miscarriages are motivated by a misunderstanding of sexual and reproductive health rights. The facts about the low rate of early initiation of breastfeeding, access to medical services, and cases of abortion and miscarriage are signs of the importance of strengthening awareness and disseminating knowledge about Sexual and Reproductive Health Rights from an early age (Shukla et al., 2023).

The previous explanation shows that the reasons behind child marriage are very complex. Educational, social, and economic factors and religious and cultural views contribute to the difficulty of resolving cases of child marriage that occur. Indonesia already has several national policies related to child protection and fulfilling children's rights, but they have not been fully implemented according to their objectives. The program to reduce the number of child marriages requires innovative policies that come from local governments as an extension of the central government. For example, a policy in the form of educational scholarships is good practice as a strategy to delay child marriage. How we treat our young generation today determines the nation's future. Child marriage is not a solution but adds to the list of social problems facing our society and country. Of course, we must protect children who are sacrificed in the name of morals and religion (Michel & Tener, 2023).

The Circle of Early Marriage Poverty

Perpetrators of early marriage marry because of poor economic conditions (Michel & Tener, 2023). They dropped out of school because they could not afford school fees. Some informants said they married because they didn't attend school, so no one was busy. Several others stated that they didn't go to school because they didn't have the money to continue their education. Even though they also want to stay in school, their parents' financial situation is very worrying, so they cannot afford to send their children to school. The parents finally decided to marry because they preferred that they go to work helping them in the fields rather than go to school, and they preferred that they not live in school conditions and be unhappy. Early marriage is not only because there are no school fees but also because of the hope of better economic changes with marriage.

Some informants decided to get married for several reasons. One of them is busyness, which prevents them from going to school because they don't have to pay school fees or because their parents don't have a favourable view of school. They hope that by getting married, their living conditions will be better because they will get married, even though the economy is not good. Families with poor economic conditions or below the poverty line often marry early (Dahl, 2010). The child she gave birth to was born to a man who was thought to be able to lighten the burden on his parents.

According to parents, if their daughter proposes and asks to get married, she will become more independent and no longer depend on her parents because a husband is ready to provide for her. However, it is not uncommon for them to marry people with very different economic statuses, which causes new poverty and new problems

(Pope et al., 2023). Some parents see daughters as assets, so those who apply to their parents hope to lighten the family's burden or even improve the status of the family. Apart from that, there is a Sasak Lombok cultural practice where the man gives money to the woman during the marriage process as a bargaining chip. Families often take advantage of the male family because otherwise, the female family would not give their guardians the right to marry their daughters.

One of the essential social problems related to welfare is that teenage girls in families are still superior to boys in terms of fulfilling their nutritional status, namely food adequacy and education level (Mahmuddin et al., 2023). Second, access: Adolescent girls tend to have lower productivity than boys because they have less access to resources. Third, awareness: Adolescent girls still lack knowledge about the health and maturity of their reproductive organs after menstruation. Fourth, parents are still less involved in providing sex education and monitoring girls' behaviour because parents continue to consider information and education about sexuality and behaviour taboo.

The Relation between Child Marriage and Social Culture

Child marriage in Indonesia is influenced by a patriarchal culture that carries conservative views (Arnez & Nisa, 2024; Uddin, 2012, 2015). Symptoms of conservatism are characterized by the emergence of 'moral guardian' groups in the name of religion. This movement targets teenagers, especially women. They also use arguments based on religious views regarding the concept of adulthood, the father's right to coerce the child, and pregnancy out of wedlock as a reason to marry at a young age.

The patriarchal culture that influences religious views often gives rise to gender-biased views and often gives rise to conservative behaviour (Aftab et al., 2023). This means that calls in the name of morals and religion do not show any awareness of the impact of child marriage. When we try to look at the effect, it appears that there is little benefit and more aspects of harm. This is very unfortunate because it has not become an everyday awareness, especially among religious leaders, regarding preventing the practice of child marriage. Furthermore, the practice of child marriage contributes to new problems, namely poverty, underdevelopment, stunting, abortion, low birth weight babies, and domestic violence.

Child marriage does not consider social, economic, educational, or regional status (Aftab et al., 2023). For example, child marriage occurred in one of the districts in South Kalimantan, where polygamy and child marriage are legal and permitted according to custom and religion. In local community culture, child marriage is part of a tradition passed down from generation to generation (Vilán, 2023). Several factors are behind the high child marriage rate in this region. First, there is a culture of honesty, namely the taboo culture of rejecting proposals that come with the stigma or belief that it is difficult to find a partner if you refuse a proposal. In this situation, the woman has no power to reject the proposal that comes to her. Second, the tradition of marrying young is more appreciated. This tradition encourages the practice of marrying under the age of 20. This cultural practice is not a problem for children from wealthy families because they will get economic support from their parents. This is different from families with weak economies. Third, awareness of the importance of education. Most people there still have a low level of understanding of obtaining education.

Moreover, the high cost of education means they have few choices. People believe that the higher the level of education, the more expensive the educational costs that must be incurred given religious conservatism, namely support for regulating adolescent morals through marriage. In studies of gender justice and equality, it is stated that patriarchal culture has positioned girls and women as vulnerable due to discrimination, stigma, and subordination practices in the social structure of society. Not only poverty and underdevelopment, the practice of child marriage also has the potential to cause sexual violence in the household. For example, they forced sexual relations, marital rape, polygamy and so on. Apart from that, child marriage also causes women to experience biological suffering related to the health of their reproductive organs (John et al., 2023).

Gender Equality

Gender norms refer to the characteristics that differentiate boys and girls (Kuhn & Wolter, 2023). Girls in Indonesian families are responsible for care and household work. Girls see society accepting whatever happens to them. It is thought that boys should be raised as physically and emotionally "tough" people, while girls are considered fragile and are supposed to be beneath boys and men. Child marriage is regarded as a violation of rights, and gender inequality, cultural practices, and hierarchies are viewed through the lens of children's rights. However, in many places, it is considered an artistic practice. In Indonesian society, child marriage is still practised and is not considered a violation against children. (Java et al., 2023).

Marriage benefits a family because it has more family members who can help in agriculture. The "Mutual Cooperation" principle says having many children helps the family. Child marriage is still a problem in Indonesia (Kuswanto et al., 2024) because (a) some children start working from an early age, encouraging them to marry with money, (b) parents want to increase the number of family members by marrying their children, and (c) parents enthusiastically accept traditional donations from guests at the wedding party. In circumstances like this, the elimination of child marriage is met with resistance because the change endangers several groups (Green et al., 2022). By "marrying" young children, families believe they act in the interests of the group and the individual.

Customs regulate appropriate ways of acting, from religious ceremonies, everyday social interactions, and marriage agreements to courts dealing with theft or murder. The values of Indonesian Islamic society influence child marriage(Setyanto et al., 2024). In Islam, the relationship between children and parents is considered equal. Children are not obliged to follow their parents' mistakes but may express their opinions. Therefore, it is clear that Indonesia's marriage laws and policies can be linked to Islamic ideology. In addition, child protection models mainly originating from Western countries must be in line with Islamic principles of respecting and protecting children from harm. It protects the mind, beliefs, and physique.

Dowry is often misused in Muslim countries such as North Africa, the Middle East, and others. According to the Koran, a husband or man must give mahr to his partner. Mahr is used widely in all Muslim weddings and is considered a way of providing favours. Dowry is a crucial economic transaction in poor areas. Cases of child marriage occur because of helplessness and the rights of girls who are abused. Child marriage increases the likelihood of sexual disclosure to children in these situations (Morrow et al., 2023). This interpretation states that a girl or boy may refuse to marry if they have not yet reached puberty and cannot understand what they are looking for in their partner.

According to Islamic law, men and women who have reached maturity and whose guardians have consented can marry. A guardian protects the bride's rights-usually the father (Jumarim, 2024). However, the Islamic religion does not prohibit early marriage, and the bride has the right to annul the marriage, referred to as "puberty choice" if she wishes. Religion is often blamed for the increase in child marriage around the world. Child marriage occurs across religions, ethnicities and regions. Although religious beliefs greatly influence child marriage, factors such as poverty and lack of educational opportunities for girls also play a role.

To prevent them from disclosing things of a sexual nature to children, it is essential to discuss broader societal explanations about child marriage in Indonesia. In Indonesia, closed-child marriages are linked to a patriarchal system that displays power, domination, hierarchy, and competition. Additionally, gender norms and gender inequality hinder women's and children's ability to disclose sexual violence. This creates many challenges for the government, stakeholders, and Indonesian society in taking policies to prevent and stop child marriage. Child marriage is still considered a silent issue due to social and cultural problems (Thi et al., 2023). From the discussion above, it is clear that the problem of child marriage in Indonesia stems from patriarchal culture, gender inequality, poverty, religious beliefs and customs.

Issues, Controversies, and Problems

The issue of early marriage is a phenomenon that is currently becoming a severe problem for the Indonesian government and even the world. Early marriage is defined as a marriage between children who have not yet reached legal age. Age limits for groups of children vary by country. This also applies to some international institutions. According to the World Population Fund (UNFPA), early marriage is when both bride and groom are under 18. This concept is in line with the Convention on the Rights of the Child, which stipulates that people under 18 years of age are considered children. Early marriage occurs in almost every corner of the world, especially in developing countries. Various backgrounds or reasons become a solid basis for early marriage. Among them are the culture embedded in society, the mindset of parents, religion, economics, and various other aspects (Uddin, 2015). Early marriage occurs in almost every corner of the world, especially in developing countries.

Some informant parents believed that by marrying their daughters, husbands would be responsible for daily living needs such as food, clothing, and shelter. However, this often does not happen when the economic conditions of women's and men's families are the same (Corno & Voena, 2023). Financial conditions have not changed. They have become worse. Because families are more significant, they face tremendous economic pressure. Additionally, households with lower sources of income face more significant difficulties meeting their daily needs, resulting in a new cycle of poverty. Apart from that, there is no preparation from a financial perspective.

Various backgrounds or reasons become a solid basis for early marriage. Among them are the culture embedded in society, the mindset of parents, religion, economics, and various other aspects. In Indonesia, in some remote areas, early marriage is not something that is rarely found. This is due to the culture of the surrounding community, which believes that women will only remain housewives, so they do not need to go to further or higher school and should marry to produce offspring (Kaplan, 2023). On the other hand, several other reasons are due to pressing economic factors; usually, the victims are Women. Some are based on religions such as Islam, which say quite a lot of those who are dating and doing Jinnah should be married off to avoid unwanted discussions. From the perspective of Islam, early marriage is a marriage that occurs to those who have not reached the age of puberty. Baligh has no specific age standard, although several sources state that puberty is 15. However, the real thing about realizing whether someone has reached puberty or not is producing sperm for men and menstruation for women. Meanwhile, each person's cycle is very different.

CONCLUSION AND IMPLICATIONS

Conclusion

Child marriage is an agreement between husband and wife who still have the status of children. According to civil law, early marriage is when the prospective husband or wife is not yet nineteen years old, and basically marriage is not permitted according to law. However, early civil marriage can be carried out by obtaining permission from both parents and requesting a marriage dispensation from the religious court accompanied by appropriate evidence and conditions. Factors causing the rise of early marriage in Indonesia are poverty, socio-cultural and gender equality.

Indonesia uses various methods to reduce the number of child marriages. These efforts include improving welfare, providing education on the dangers of child marriage, and increasing teenagers' knowledge about gender equality. Preventing child marriage is a shared responsibility between the government, society, families and parents. One way to stop child marriage is to change marriage laws, especially those relating to the age of marriage from 16 years to 19 years, without distinguishing between women and men.

Solution and Recommendation

The Indonesian government issued Law 16/2019 which amends part of Law 1/1974 concerning marriage to reduce the number of child marriages. The minimum age for marriage was raised from 16 to 19 years. At the global and national levels, several policies demonstrate the commitment of stakeholders, especially the Indonesian government, to prevent child marriage. To support this policy, there needs to be a plan that reflects current child marriage practices. Cultural prevention strategies and improving welfare must be implemented to end the practice of child marriage in Indonesia. The hope is that this analysis can become the basis for policy making and strategies to prevent child marriage in Indonesia. The description above produces four main recommendations, namely:

- Strengthen policies and laws to ensure that programs are appropriate in addressing the phenomenon of child marriage.
- One of the factors that encourages child marriage is poverty, so combining child protection strategies with improving welfare is a good strategy. This can increase child care capacity through social protection programs for family economic empowerment.
- Providing gender equality cultural education services to children to break the chain of child marriage, especially for children.

- Social advocacy through social media and seminars on the importance of preventing child marriage.

Future Direction

Further research is to support research that focuses on interventions that have been carried out for married girls, domestic violence that occurs after child marriage, marriage to children in urban areas, and male child marriage, including health (Uddin, 2017b).

ACKNOWLEDGMENT

This chapter does not discuss the receipt of grants from funding agencies. All authors played an essential role in this research, and they collected data by dividing it according to their roles and talking about their findings at each stage of the study.

REFERENCES

Aborisade, R. A., & Olayinka-Aliu, D. A. (2023). Marry your rapist! A phenomenological analysis of the experiences of women forced to marry their assaulters in their childhood. Https://Doi.Org/10.1177/02697580231207652. DOI: 10.1177/02697580231207652

Adu, J., & Oudshoorn, A. (2020). The Deinstitutionalization of psychiatric hospitals in Ghana: An application of Bronfenbrenner's social-ecological model. *Issues in Mental Health Nursing*, 41(4), 306–314. DOI: 10.1080/01612840.2019.1666327 PMID: 31999531

Aftab, J., Abrar, A., & Maroof, L. (2023). Identity construction of Pakistani female entrepreneurs in religious framework: An interplay of sociocultural and religious factors. [JEIEE]. *Journal of Entrepreneurship and Innovation in Emerging Economies*, 9(2), 198–221. DOI: 10.1177/23939575231171003

Arnez, M., & Nisa, E. (2024). *Advocating for change: Cultural and institutional factors of sexual violence in Indonesia*. 21–44. DOI: 10.1007/978-981-99-5659-3_2

Baraie, B., Rezaei, M., Nadrian, H., & Matlabi, H. (2024). What socio-cultural factors encourage child marriage in Sanandaj, Iran? A qualitative study. *Child and Youth Services*, 45(1), 23–44. DOI: 10.1080/0145935X.2023.2167708

Cameron, L., Contreras Suarez, D., & Wieczkiewicz, S. (2023). Child marriage: Using the Indonesian family life survey to examine the lives of women and men who married at an early age. *Review of Economics of the Household*, 21(3), 725–756. DOI: 10.1007/s11150-022-09616-8

Collin, M., & Talbot, T. (2023). Are age-of-marriage laws enforced? Evidence from developing countries. *Journal of Development Economics*, 160, 102950. DOI: 10.1016/j.jdeveco.2022.102950

Corno, L., & Voena, A. (2023). Child marriage as informal insurance: Empirical evidence and policy simulations. *Journal of Development Economics*, 162, 103047. DOI: 10.1016/j.jdeveco.2023.103047

Crocker, M., & Baur, A. (2022). Connecting loose ends: Integrating science into psychoanalytic theory. *Clinical Social Work Journal*, 50(4), 347–357. DOI: 10.1007/s10615-020-00774-9

Dahl, G. B. (2010). Early teen marriage and future poverty. *Demography*, 47(3), 689–718. DOI: 10.1353/dem.0.0120 PMID: 20879684

Eboka, T. (2023). Child marriage: The resilience of the Nigerian woman. *Gendered Perspectives of Restorative Justice, Violence and Resilience: An International Framework*, 107–120. https://doi.org/DOI: 10.1108/978-1-80382-383-620231007/FULL/XML

Green, D. P., Groves, D. W., Manda, C., Montano, B., & Rahmani, B. (2022). A radio drama's effects on attitudes toward early and forced marriage: Results from a field experiment in rural Tanzania. *Comparative Political Studies*, 56(8), 1115–1155. DOI: 10.1177/00104140221139385

Hartarto, R. B., & Wibowo, W. T. (2023). Conditional cash transfer and early marriage: A case study of Mataram City, West Nusa Tenggara. *International Journal of Development Issues*, 22(1), 57–71. DOI: 10.1108/IJDI-08-2022-0171

Hashemi, K. (2017). Religious legal traditions, Muslim states and the convention on the rights of the child: An essay on the relevant UN documentation. *International Law and Islamic Law*, 535–568. https://doi.org/DOI: 10.4324/9781315092515-24/RELIGIOUS-LEGAL-TRADITIONS-MUSLIM-STATES-CONVENTION-RIGHTS-CHILD-ESSAY-RELEVANT-UN-DOCUMENTATION-KAMRAN-HASHEMI

Hofmann, V., & Müller, C. M. (2018). Avoiding antisocial behavior among adolescents: The positive influence of classmates' prosocial behavior. *Journal of Adolescence*, 68(1), 136–145. https://doi.org/https://doi.org/10.1016/j.adolescence.2018.07.013. DOI: 10.1016/j.adolescence.2018.07.013 PMID: 30077085

Hossain, A., & Uddin, E. M. (2023). Physical school environment and infectious diseases: A case of primary school context in Bangladesh. In Azeez, P. A., Nikhil Raj, P. P., & Mohanraj, R. (Eds.), *Ecological and evolutionary perspectives on infections and morbidity* (pp. 126–151). IGI Global. DOI: 10.4018/978-1-7998-9414-8.ch006

Java, W., Yayan, I., Univeristas, S., Negeri, I., Hidayatullah, S., Zezen, J., & Muttaqin, Z. (2023). Child exploitation by parents in early marriage: Case study in Cianjur West Java, Indonesia. *Samarah: Jurnal Hukum Keluarga Dan Hukum Islam*, 7(3), 1921–1942. DOI: 10.22373/sjhk.v7i3.14804

John, N. A., Kapungu, C., Sebany, M., & Tadesse, S. (2023). Do gender-based pathways influence mental health? Examining the linkages between early child marriage, intimate partner violence, and psychological well-being among young Ethiopian women (18–24 years Old). *Youth & Society*, 55(6), 1155–1172. DOI: 10.1177/0044118X221079375

Jumarim, J. (2024). The practice of adoption in the Sasak community and Its implications for marriage law in Indonesia. *Samarah: Jurnal Hukum Keluarga Dan Hukum Islam*, 8(1), 445–467. DOI: 10.22373/sjhk.v8i1.18581

Kaplan, V. (2023). Mental health states of housewives: An evaluation in terms of self-perception and codependency. *International Journal of Mental Health and Addiction*, 21(1), 666–683. DOI: 10.1007/s11469-022-00910-1 PMID: 36091486

Kok, M. C., Kakal, T., Kassegne, A. B., Hidayana, I. M., Munthali, A., Menon, J. A., Pires, P., Gitau, T., & van der Kwaak, A. (2023). Drivers of child marriage in specific settings of Ethiopia, Indonesia, Kenya, Malawi, Mozambique and Zambia – findings from the Yes I Do! baseline study. *BMC Public Health*, 23(1), 1–16. DOI: 10.1186/s12889-023-15697-6 PMID: 36624437

Kuhn, A., & Wolter, S. C. (2023). The strength of gender norms and gender-stereotypical occupational aspirations among adolescents. *Kyklos*, 76(1), 101–124. DOI: 10.1111/kykl.12320

Kusumadewi, H., & Wiswayana, W. M. (2024). Enforcing preventions of child marriage cases in ASEAN member states Within the framework of Sustainable Development Goals. *PROIROFONIC, 1*(1), 407–419. https://proirofonic.upnjatim.ac.id/index.php/proirofonic/article/view/46

Kuswanto, H., Oktaviana, P. P., Efendi, F., Nelwati, N., & Malini, H. (2024). Prevalence of and factors associated with female child marriage in Indonesia. *PLoS One*, 19(7), e0305821. DOI: 10.1371/journal.pone.0305821 PMID: 38968277

Lutz, C., Berges, M., Hafemann, J., & Sticha, C. (2018). In Pozdniakov, S. N., & Dagienė, V. (Eds.), *Piaget's cognitive development in bebras tasks - A descriptive analysis by age groups BT - Informatics in schools. Fundamentals of Computer Science and Software Engineering* (pp. 259–270). Springer International Publishing.

Mady, C. (2023). Women's rights campaigns in Lebanon: A Bakhtinian-Foucauldian approach to voice and visibility. *Feminist Media Studies*, 23(7), 3324–3336. DOI: 10.1080/14680777.2022.2108877

Mahmuddin, M., Mansari, M., & Melayu, H. A. (2023). Community's role in preventing child marriage: An analysis of models and community compliance with village policies. *Gender Equality: International Journal of Child and Gender Studies*, 9(2), 235–244. DOI: 10.22373/equality.v9i2.19673

Maree, J. G. (2021). The psychosocial development theory of Erik Erikson: Critical overview. *Early Child Development and Care*, 191(7–8), 1107–1121. DOI: 10.1080/03004430.2020.1845163

Mas'udah, S. (2021). Power relations of husbands and wives experiencing domestic violence in dual-career families in Indonesia. *Milennial Asia*, 14(1), 5–27. DOI: 10.1177/09763996211039730

Mbamba, C. R., Yeboaa, P. A., Gyimah, C., & Mccarthy, M. (2023). When child marriage and child welfare intersect: Understanding the barriers to education. *Children & Society*, 37(3), 966–978. DOI: 10.1111/chso.12640

Mensah, E. O. (2023). Husband is a priority: Gender roles, patriarchy and the naming of female children in Nigeria. *Gender Issues*, 40(1), 44–64. DOI: 10.1007/s12147-022-09303-z

Michel, M., & Tener, D. (2023). "The problem is that a kibbutz is standing in front of you and you have no name or face for it": Child sexual abuse risk factors and disclosure in the collective kibbutz community. *Children and Youth Services Review*, 148, 106918. DOI: 10.1016/j.childyouth.2023.106918

Morrow, G., Yount, K. M., Bergenfeld, I., Laterra, A., Kalra, S., Khan, Z., & Clark, C. J. (2023). Adolescent boys' and girls' perspectives on social norms surrounding child marriage in Nepal. *Culture, Health & Sexuality*, 25(10), 1277–1294. DOI: 10.1080/13691058.2022.2155705 PMID: 36573269

Mukharrom, T., & Abdi, S. (2023). Harmonizing Islam and human rights through the reconstruction of classical Islamic tradition. *Samarah: Jurnal Hukum Keluarga Dan Hukum Islam*, 7(1), 40–57. DOI: 10.22373/sjhk.v7i1.16436

Pope, D. H., McMullen, H., Baschieri, A., Philipose, A., Udeh, C., Diallo, J., & McCoy, D. (2023). What is the current evidence for the relationship between the climate and environmental crises and child marriage? A scoping review. *Global Public Health: An International Journal for Research, Policy and Practice*, 18(1), 2095655. Advance online publication. DOI: 10.1080/17441692.2022.2095655 PMID: 36403290

Pourtaheri, A., Sany, S. B. T., Aghaee, M. A., Ahangari, H., & Peyman, N. (2023). Prevalence and factors associated with child marriage, a systematic review. *BMC Women's Health*, 23(1), 1–15. DOI: 10.1186/s12905-023-02634-3 PMID: 37817117

Santrock, J. W. (2010a). *Child Development* (13th ed.). McGraw-Hill.

Santrock, J. W. (2010b). *Child Development* (13th ed.). McGraw-Hill.

Setiawan, H. H., Wardianti, A., Yusuf, I., & Asikin, A. (2020). ANAK SEBAGAI PELAKU TERORISME DALAM PERSPEKTIF EKOLOGI SOSIAL. *Sosio Informa : Kajian Permasalahan Sosial Dan Usaha Kesejahteraan Sosial*, 6(3), 252–263. DOI: 10.33007/inf.v6i3.2400

Setyanto, A., Kewuel, H. K., & Zurinani, S. (2024). The phenomenon and impact of early marriage- A case study of Islamic communities in East Java, Indonesia-. *Kurdish Studies*, 12(1), 2297–2307. DOI: 10.58262/ks.v12i1.160

Shukla, S., Ezebuihe, J. A., & Steinert, J. I. (2023). Association between public health emergencies and sexual and reproductive health, gender-based violence, and early marriage among adolescent girls: A rapid review. *BMC Public Health*, 23(1), 1–14. DOI: 10.1186/s12889-023-15054-7 PMID: 36650493

Taber, K. S. (2020). In Akpan, B., & Kennedy, T. J. (Eds.), *Mediated learning leading development—The social development theory of Lev Vygotsky BT - Science education in theory and practice: An introductory gGuide to learning theory* (pp. 277–291). Springer International Publishing., DOI: 10.1007/978-3-030-43620-9_19

Thi, H. D., Huong, T. B. T., Tuyet, M. N. T., & Van, H. M. (2023). Socio-cultural norms and gender equality of ethnic minorities in Vietnam. *Journal of Racial and Ethnic Health Disparities*, 10(5), 2136–2144. DOI: 10.1007/s40615-022-01393-5 PMID: 36006587

Uddin, M. E. (2012). Socio-cultural factors affecting family size between Muslim and Santal communities in rural Bangladesh. *Antrocom: On-Line Journal of Anthropology*, 8(2), 395–410.

Uddin, M. E. (2015). Family socio-cultural values affecting early marriage between Muslim and Santal communities in rural Bangladesh. *The International Journal of Sociology and Social Policy*, 35(3–4), 141–164. DOI: 10.1108/IJSSP-06-2014-0046

Uddin, M. E. (2017a). Ecological framework for primary school attainment in the tri-ethnic communities in rural Bangladesh. *Child Indicators Research*, 10(3), 693–713. DOI: 10.1007/s12187-016-9401-3

Uddin, M. E. (2017b). Family demographic mechanisms linking of socioeconomic status to subjective physical health in rural Bangladesh. *Social Indicators Research*, 130(3), 1263–1279. DOI: 10.1007/s11205-015-1209-x

Uddin, M. E. (2021). Teenage marriage and high school dropout among poor girls: A narrative review for family pathways in Bangladesh. *Journal of Research in Social Sciences and Language*, 1(1), 55–76.

Vilán, A. (2023). The evolution of the global movement to end child marriage. *Human Rights on the Edge*, 110–127. DOI: 10.4324/9781003394464-8

Ward, T., & Birgden, A. (2007). Human rights and correctional cinical prctice. *Aggression and Violent Behavior*, 12(6), 628–643. DOI: 10.1016/j.avb.2007.05.001

Yoosefi Lebni, J., Solhi, M., Ebadi Fard Azar, F., Khalajabadi Farahani, F., & Irandoost, S. F. (2023). Exploring the consequences of early marriage: A conventional content analysis. *Inquiry*, 60, 00469580231159963. Advance online publication. DOI: 10.1177/00469580231159963 PMID: 37073489

Zastrow, C. (2010). *Introduction to social work and social welfare: Empowering people* (10th ed.). Brooks/Cole Cengage Learning.

KEY TERMS AND DEFINITIONS

Child Marriage: marriages carried out formally or informally where one or both parties have not reached the age of 19 years.

Gender Inequality: a set of understandings built on societal perceptions from generation to generation regarding the injustice of roles and authority between men and women. Gender inequality is a condition formed by the social environment in which the individual lives.

Poverty: Low family socioeconomic status is often associated with early marriage. One way for women's families to avoid the problem of poverty is to marry prematurely.

Social Culture: human behavior in society, a habit acquired ritually and cognitively by dominating social groups. Even though social culture is abstract, complex, and broad, its impact is real. The actions of individuals, groups, and societies will all show signs of social behavior.

Chapter 5
Early Marriage and High School Dropout Among Poor Girls Across the Globe:
Family Life Course Perspective

Emaj Uddin
https://orcid.org/0000-0002-6721-6856
University of Rajshahi, Bangladesh

Shara Antara
https://orcid.org/0009-0002-9459-5326
University of Rajshahi, Bangladesh

ABSTRACT

Despite school process-based measures taken, high school dropout (HSD) associated with early marriage (EM) among teenage girls is increasing across countries, including Bangladesh. Based on family life course approach and comprehensive literature review, this chapter explains potential pathways of EM such as early transition to family responsibility, pregnancy, child bearing and rearing and household chores, leading girls to dropout from high school. Based on the FLCA, literature over the past several decades suggests that EM and its subsequent events (e.g., pregnancy, childbearing and rearing, early family role transition) partially explain high school risk behaviors that, in turn, affect girls to drop out from high school. Evidence in this chapter is important for developing effective programs or measures to prevent teenage girls' EM and HSD across developing countries.

DOI: 10.4018/979-8-3693-3394-5.ch005

INTRODUCTION

Preventing high school dropout associated with early marriage is a challenging issue across countries. A great deal of literature over the three decades shows that girls' early marriage associated with family poverty and sociocultural values is significantly linked to high school dropout across the societies and cultures (Dahl, 2010; Klepinger et al., 1999; Lloyd & Mensch, 2006, 2008; Ribar, 1994; UNFPA, 2012, 2013; Uddin 2015). In developed countries, systematic research has shown that girls who marry before their teenage (13-19 years) are 50% more likely to drop out of high school and four times less likely to graduate from college (Klepinger et al., 1999; Ribar, 1994). Although universal primary enrollment policies has improved girls' school enrollment and school participation, there are wide gender gaps in school enrollment and school participation at both primary and secondary school levels due to prevailing social and cultural practice of early marriage and mass family poverty across developing and the least-developed countries, including Bangladesh (Lloyd et al., 2008; UNFPA, 2012, 2013; Uddin, 2021).

Consequently, early marriages and births associated with social and cultural practices, local customs and family poverty are more likely to curtail girls than boys in high school attendance and school exit (Lloyd et al., 2006; Uddin, 2015). Using Demographic and Health Survey Data from the nine Southern and Eastern African countries, Omoeva and Hatch (2014) found that early marriage and its subsequent life events (e.g., school exit and school absence) were the causes of married girls' high school dropout than their counterparts. Using the data from the Nepal Multiple Indicator Cluster Survey 2014, Sekine and Hodgkin (2017) found that the risks of school dropout associated with early marriages heighten after the girls complete their fifth or sixth grade. The risks of dropping out peak in the seventh and eighth grade and remain noteworthy in the ninth and tenth grades. How?

Based on systematic review on theories/approaches and literature, in this chapter we address a fundament problems about family life course pathways to understand how early marriage and subsequent events are more likely to promote high school dropout among poor girls than boys across countries. To attain this aim, first of all, we will define key terms: "Early marriage" and "high school dropout" presented in the second section. Based on systematic literature review, the third section will describe relationships between early marriage (EM) and high school dropout (HSD) across countries. In the fourth section, we will critically review early approaches to high school dropout and find out theoretical knowledge gaps and its limitations for understanding EM and HSD. In the fifth section, we will review family life course approaches and propose a theoretical framework that helps understand pathways by which EM promotes HSD across countries, particularly developing and the least-developed countries. Finally, we will describe limitations the theoretical framework and its applications to improve girls' sociocultural status aimed at preventing EM and HSD.

DEFINING KEY CONCEPTS

Early Marriage

The first term "*early marriage*" used in this chapter refers to the timing of union formation of two adolescents who are joined in marriage, age ranging during 13 through 19 years. In several studies, United Nations (1988, 1990, 2000) and United Nations Children's Fund (2001) have defined early marriage as the timing of first marriage, especially before legal marital age prescribed for girls and boys in a given country when the prospective bride and groom are not physically, socially, and psychologically matured enough to bear sexual, reproductive, and social responsibilities to the marital and family life. In measuring early marriage for both husband and wife to access in marital life and form a family, most of the researchers defined the terms as timing norms based on either state's legal or religious or social customary laws and measured in years, applying self-report, interview and survey method to collect reliable and valid data. Here, we define and measure early marriage as the timing norms and measured in years based on the local community's customary social norms and its practices, although the minimum legal age at first marriage for both male and female are enacted across countries (Uddin, 2015).

High School Dropout

The term "*high school dropout*" defines in many ways (e.g., 'early school leaving', 'not in education, employment or training', 'school completion') and varies in definitions across the countries (Lamb et al., 2011; Uddin, 2021). For example, in the United States and Canada, the term refers to young people who leave school without gaining high school diploma (Lamb et al., 2011). In Australia, dropout means leaving school before year 12 (the final year of secondary school). In United Kingdom and Scotland, there is no concept of school completion or graduation at compulsory school level. When the students reach the end of compulsory school at the age of 16, the duration and content of education vary widely. Actually, there is no standard by which we can judge whether or not a student completes compulsory secondary education (Raffe, 2010).

Snyder (1994) defines a dropout as a person who has not graduated from high school and is not currently enrolled in full-time higher secondary education. In a study, Manlove (1998) defines dropout as excessive absences, indicating as more than

15, 20 or 30 days of unexcused absence. In defining dropout, Barnet et al. (2004) use two methods: (1) they categorizes a student (a girl) as a dropout if her school recodes documented a withdrawal date, and (2) if she was present at school in a given academic year fewer than 20 days of the 180-day school year (e.g., unexcused absence of more than 88% of the school year), she was classified as dropped out. Rumberger (2011) classify dropout into three categories: 1) event dropout rate, 2) status dropout rate, and 3) cohort dropout rate. (1) *The event dropout rate* defines as the percentage of persons or a specified given group (such as students of a particular age enrolled in high school) in a population who drop out of school over a particular time period, which is often a period of single year. (2) *The status dropout rate* defines and measures as the percentage in a population or sub-population who are enrolled in a high school program, but did not pass high school program or do not hold a high school diploma. and (3) The cohort dropout rate refers to the rate of dropping out within an age or grade cohort over a specified period of time, such as the percentage of students in grade 8 who had not attained a high school diploma by the age of 20.

EARLY MARRIAGE AND HIGH SCHOOL DROPOUT

Does teenage marriage relate to high school dropout? Reviewing global marriage and educational trends in the developing countries, Mansory (2007) found that teenage marriage is the vital cause of early school dropout in Afghanistan. Researcher argues that when girls in the traditional conservative society reach puberty, parents consider that it is the proper time for them to be married and tend to arrange marriage and likely they drop out. Holcamp (2009) found that dropout rates of girls than boys in Malawi become higher, as girls leave their parental family after getting married, so parents consider girls' schooling is no benefit for them. LIoyd (2005) also identified that Bangladesh is the only country where early marriage is the most prevalent reason for high school dropout among girls than boys. Studies by Shahidul (2012, 2014) have found that although higher education may give girls better preparation for marriage, parents are reluctant to continue their daughters' education, because higher education raises cost of marriage for girls in India. Emirie (2005) studied early marriage and its effects on girls' primary education in Ethiopia. Using cross-sectional and ethnographic data, the researcher found that practice of early marriage reinforced by economic and social structure and socialization process of girls was the major obstacle of girls' access to formal education. Most of the parents in the rural communities preferred their daughters to arrange marriage early, instead of sending them to schools. Those girls who enrolled in primary school could not continue their education due to their early marriage. The research also found that the effects of early marriage practices on the girls' formal education were mediated through academic performance due to irregular class attendance, lack of time to do school related activities and lack of concentration on their education, high grade repetitions and dropout rates in connection with early marriage practices of girl students. Shahidul (2012) also found that high school dropout of girls with low SES family was significantly associated with early marriage through increasing higher education and dowry in marriage market in Bangladesh. Teenage marriage prohibits girls' education that has most likely to have significant negative consequences for women's health, cognitive development, social maturity, socio-economic status attainment, empowerment, prevention of violence and poverty in later life, including educational attainment. Previous research studies have found that teenage marriage is significantly linked to poor primary attainment and severe high school risks behavior (e.g., late enrollment, school absence, exam exit, lower GPA, school failure, school dropout).

Despite this fact, most of the previous descriptive studies on high school risks and dropout of girls conducted in the developing and under-developed societies, including Bangladesh is based on either socio-cultural approach or functional theoretical framework. For example, following family socio-cultural approach, recent research studies have found that dropout or completion of high school education of female students aged 11-18 years (e.g., enrollment, dropout, performance, and attainment) is associated with individual (health, low motivation, hopelessness, lack of self-efficacy), family (parental poverty, low socio-economic status, negative attitude towards daughter education), school (e.g., school distance, lack of female teacher, poor or lack of toilet facility, school cost, sexual harassment in public place), and community (dowry, gender status, lack of social security and gender-sensitive environment (Amadi, 2013; Sattar et al., 2012; Yaqoob, 2012). For example, using descriptive data Yakoob (2012) explored family socio-cultural constraints (e.g., parent low education, sexual harassment, purdah, distance from school, family permission, son preference over female education, early marriage, gender status, lack of awareness regarding female education) were linked to lower achievement of high school education among girl students than boys students in Mardan District, Khyber, Pakistan.

Using the same approach, Satter et al. (2012) also have found that enrolment ratios of girls than boys at high school level were affected by family and school factors, especially gender discrimination, rigid cultural pattern, poverty, prejudice and stereotyping of girl education, parental low expectation, restricted movement of girl children and lack of female teachers in the school in Southern Punjab, Pakistan. Amadi (2013) examined the effects of family socio-cultural factors (e.g., family background, socio-economic status, parental attitude towards education) on the girl-child education in secondary school in Ihiala of Anambra state, Nigeria and found that almost all factors were responsible for limited access in the education of the girls than boys. Malmberg and Sumra (2001) examined on how socio-cultural factors: parental educational level, gender, age, religion and home language affect high school experience and achievements among students in Morogoro region, Tanzania. The researchers using cross-sectional data found that the girl students with higher parental education, equality in gender status, positive attitude toward education and liberal religion had better achievement in high school than the female students with lower parental education, inequality in gender status, conservative religion, and negative attitude toward girl education in the study area.

Review of literature, however, suggests that although early marriage associated with family background and community values is positively linked to high school dropout among married girls, controlling for family sociodemographic characteristics, little research examines and focuses on how family formation pathways (also mechanisms) of teenage marriage is related to high school dropout among poor girls than rich girls in rural Bangladesh setting. The *first aim* of the study is to analyze relationship between teenage marriage and high school dropout between poor and non-poor girls in rural Bangladesh. *Second*, this study examines how pathways of family formation and its related high school risk behaviors linking of teenage marriage to high school dropout between poor and non-poor married girls (also women) in rural Bangladesh.

Purpose of the study is to explore, compare and analyze how teenage marriage of girls than boys influences their early family formation (e.g., family residence after marriage, early marital sexuality and pregnancy, childbearing and rearing, family responsibility) that may influence their high school risk behavior (e.g., low class participation, examination exit) and early high school dropout in rural Bangladesh. Family life cycle transition and family formation theory rather than socio-cultural, bio-psychological and functional approach suggest that high school risk behavior and high school dropout of female students compared to male students is deeply concerned with early or teenage marriage and its subsequent events, such as early family formation across the developing and under-developed societies, including Bangladesh.

EARLY APPROACHES TO UNDERSTANDING HIGH SCHOOL DROPOUT

Understanding why and how female students drop out of high school is an important avenue for developing effective prevention and intervention programs (Carr, 2009). Early approaches and research studies have focused on multidimensional models to explain several pathways or processes, influencing the students and/or parents' decisions to drop out their sons or daughters from high school instead of descriptions of associations between antecedents and consequences, such as school dropout (Cairns & Cairns, 1994). For example, *Multifaceted Pathways Model* by Ekstrom et al. (1986), *Participation-Identification Model* by Finn (1989), and *Four Possible Pathways Model* by Evans and DiBenedetto (1990) to school dropout are prominent.

Actually, these models suggest that multiple developmental pathways or processes of students lead to early school dropout. First of all, Ekstrom et al.'s (1986) model describes a student's decision to drop out or stay in school. To do so, this model includes demographic factors (e.g., SES, age, sex, religion & ethnicity), family educational support system, school performance and early childhood behavior problems as influences on the student's decision to drop out or stay in school. Using high school data, this model explains that problem behaviors and poor grade points average (GPA) are partially determined by the home educational support system.

Finn's (1989) participation-identification model emphasizes that students' active participation in school, classroom and extra-curriculum activities and feeling of identification with these affect high school completion. Identification with school and its related activities refer to the internalized conception of belonging and valuing high school success. According to this perspective, lack of school engagement is central to the process of school dropout. Engagement is composed of student behavior (e.g., involvement in classroom and school activities) and identification with and feeling of school. The model explains dropout in terms of a behavioral antecedent (lack of identification) and a psychological condition (lack of identification). It portrays dropout as a process of disengagement over time rather than as a phenomenon that occurs in a single day or even a single year. Participation in school environment includes attending school, being prepared to work, and responding to the teachers' directions and questions. Other levels of participation include students' initiative to be involved in the classroom and other school activities, participation in social and extracurricular activities and involvement in decision-making processes. The model, however, emphasizes a developmental process of school participation and engagement that accelerates school success, while school disengagement decelerates dropout of school.

Evans's et al. model (1990) provides four possible pathways that focus on the interaction between individual and school factors that lead early school dropout or withdrawal: (a) unexpected events, (b) long-term underlying problems, (c) early school deficits, and (d) entry problems. They suggest that examining behaviors rather than searching predetermined characteristics of students help better understanding of school dropout. They propose that school dropout may be characterized by snowballing effects, wherein events that occurred early impact on subsequent events. The first pathway of the model emphasizes *unexpected events* (e.g., pregnancy, death of someone) that subsequently influence school enrollment. Such unforeseen events unexpected that may occur in a certain context affect educational support available to the students. The second pathway, *long-term underlying problems*, may not display any psychological difficulties, but over the time the students may engage in deviant behaviors, associating with maladjusted peers which ultimately influence school enrollment. Later this pathway may take time as the students follow a deviant pathway that may ultimately lead to school dropout. The third pathway, *early school (social and cognitive) deficits*, may interact over time and influence school enrollment and continuing reading. For example, a child who grows with reading difficulties may subsequently lack the motivation to continue to struggle with reading. These difficulties in reading affect academic performance over time that ultimately results in early school dropout. The final pathway, *entry problems*, of the model recognizes that some children entry into school with emotional or behavioral problems (e.g., immature & over-active) that lead to problems with classroom behaviors and also with teachers. The students with these behavioral problems dislike school and ultimately decide to withdraw school.

Although above models illustrate numerous pathways or multiple influences that lead to high school dropout, little research has explained family life course pathways of early marriage linking to high school risk behavior and high school dropout over time (Carr, 2009). The following section of the chapter reviews family life course approaches and literature to formulate a process model to understand family life course pathways by which early marriage leads to high school dropout among poor girls.

FAMILY LIFE COURSE APPROACH TO UNDERSTANDING HIGH SCHOOL DROPOUT

Family life course approach (also known as a family life span or family life course perspective) developed in the early 1900s is a popular theoretical framework that emphasizes the timing and sequencing of multiple life event transitions in the family that have positive or negative effects on individual persons (Norton, 1980). Since then, economists, sociologists, psychologists, and demographers have developed their respective models, explaining distinguishable life stages through which all families more or less pass through would be a useful framework for interpreting data on the timing and sequencing of multiple life event transitions across the groups, including age, sex, religion, ethnicity and region (Amato & Kane, 2011; Uddin, 2021).

First of all, Loomis (1936), the main proponent of the family life cycle (FLC) framework, used the construct as a research tool. Later, prominent family researchers, such as Glick (1947, 55, Rodgers (1962), and Duvall (1971) have proposed and used different constructs and schemas on the number of life stages to analyze the FLC. Most of the models devised by the renowned family researchers, however, attempt to identify marriage, divorce, separation, pregnancy, childbearing, childrearing, death of a partner, family role, children present or absent in the family as major transition points within the FLC, life span or life course of a family. Based on the constructs they recognize that different transitions of the life-events have different meanings, predictors, and consequences, depending on when the life events occur (Amato el al., 2011). For example, first marriages at age 12 and age 30 are qualitatively different events that have different consequences on human life. Particularly, early pregnancy, childbearing, childrearing and engagement in family responsibilities than late pregnancy, childbearing, childrearing and engagement in family responsibility have adverse effects on persons' educational, social, economic and political life.

Family life course approach broadly assumes that early transition to marital life has detrimental effects on physical growth, psychological development (e.g., emotional & cognitive), social relations, socioeconomic attainment and involvement in the formal and informal organizations (Amato et al., 2011; Duvall, 1971; Glick, 1947, 1977; Norton, 1980; Rodgers, 1962). Based on the broader assumption, educational researchers contend that early transition to marriages has more negative effects on women's than men's health, cognitive development, social maturity, educational attainment, status attainment, empowerment, violence against women, and poverty in later life. Later, some educational researchers formulate that early marriage is significantly linked to school risk behaviors (e.g., poor class attendance, poor GPA, exam exit) and school dropout (Uddin, 2021). The family life course approach asserts that girls' early transition to marriage is more likely to influence their early family formation and child rearing and engage in family responsibilities and detach from regular schooling such as class attendance, learning, and examination over the months or years. Consequently, they achieve poor GPA or fails in the examination and ultimately dropout from school. Although these pathways of family life course approach are plausible to understand relationship between EM and HSD, few studies has explained the pathways the EM-HSD link.

FAMILY LIFE COURSE PATHWAYS

Early Family Role Transition

Girls' early marriage influences early transition to gender division of family role. Gender division of family role is the aggregations of shared, ordered, and reciprocally expected behavior of men and women who occupy certain statuses within the family (Uddin, 2010, 2015). A central perspective to understand early marriage and school behavior risks and dropout in traditional agricultural society is the *gendered division of family labor* (also specialization & trading), a structural role model formulated by sociologists (Oppenheimer, 1970, 1997, 1988; Parsons, 1954) and new home economists (Becker, 1981). Sociologists and home economists see that highly differentiated gender division of family role has pervasive effect on girls' education than boys' in developing and the least developed countries. The central premise of the structural role model suggests that strict gender specialization of family labor intended to maintain gender inequality and stabilize marriage relationship is more likely to affect girls than boys to disengage in education in the agricultural societies.

According to structural role model, the general tendency for men to specialize in productive works in agriculture, small industry, horticulture etc. and for women in household activities (e.g., household chores, child bearing/caring). These sex-role segregations between men and women within and outside the family, as Parsons argues, lead women to acquire less education than men. Becker (1981) argues that a major benefit of such rigid gender division of labor by sex is mutual dependency: Women depend more on men for their material support and very existence, but men on women for household chores and child bearing or caring. A female with her economic dependency selects relatively older male as a marital partner, because at older age her male partner is able to provide economic support and social security. Oppenheimer (1988) further argues that the greater the economic reliance of wife on husband's income indicates that women than men need not to get more education rather they should train up to household responsibilities. Based on the gender division of family role theory, several empirical studies have found that sex role segregation between men and women in the agricultural societies is more likely to influence girls' early marriage than boys' and likely their early transition to family responsibilities that, in turn, affect high school education. Research shows that girls after marriage are more likely to face high school risk behaviors (e.g., poor class attendance, practice lessons, exam exit, and grade failure) and ultimately dropout from high school (Uddin, 2009a, 2021).

Teenage Pregnancy

Early marriage is linked to early pregnancy. Early/teen pregnancy, also known as an adolescent pregnancy associated with teen marriage and unprotected sexual intercourse is pregnancy in females under the age of 20. A female becomes pregnant from unprotected sexual intercourse after she has begun to ovulate, which can be before her first menstrual period (menarche), but it usually occurs after the onset of her periods in well-nourished females, menarche usually takes place around the age of 12 or 13 (World Health Organization, WHO, 2004; Uddin, 2007). Pregnant teens face many problems related to pregnancy than women at later ages. Under the age of 15 they are less likely to physically mature enough to sustain healthy pregnancy or to give birth (Mayor, 2004). Other studies show that teenagers also face high risks of low birth weight, premature labor, anemia, and preeclampsia due to their immature biological age (Abalkhail, 1995). Despite these risks and other preventive measures (e. g. educational intervention, birth control), a million of teen females becomes pregnant within and outside marital bonds across countries. World-wide data show that teenage pregnancy rates[1] range from 143 per 1000 in sub-Saharan African countries to 2.9 per 1000 in South Korea. According to UNFPA, in each region of the world girls who are come from poor, poorly educated families, or living in urban slums, or rural areas are at greater risk of becoming pregnant than those who are come from wealthier, well-educated and urban families. The report also shows that 95% of the world's births of adolescents aged 15-19 occur in developing countries. Save the Children found that annually, 13 million children are born to women under aged 20 worldwide, more than 90% in developing countries (UNFPA, 2013). Another account shows that in developing countries 7.3 million females under the age of 18 give birth each year (Mayor, 2004).

Systematic research over the last two decades shows that teen girls who become pregnant are less likely to complete high school or college across countries. For those who manage to stay in school, teenage pregnancy raises major obstacles to academic achievement and substantially exacerbates the challenges of completing high school and going to college. Children born to teen mothers are more likely to become teen mothers themselves (Hoffman, 2006; Maynard, 1996). Based on family life cycle and its sister's theory of family formation (FF), a comprehensive literature reviewed suggests that high school risk behaviors (e.g., school absence, exam exit, poor class performance) and HSD are significantly associated with teenage pregnancy or repeated teen pregnancy with short duration and its related time duration and complexity (Hoffman, 2006; Levine & Painter, 2003; Manlove, 1998). Eloundou-Enyegue and Strokes (2004) found that teenage pregnancy of girls is related to high school dropout that is a major cause of gender differences in high school attainment. This study argues that as teenage girls than boys face pregnancy and its related complications at this age, their school absence, exam exit, and dropout rates are higher than the teen boys. In some settings, schoolgirl pregnancy has been found to be common cause of school dropout. Eloundou-Enyegue (2004) found that pregnancy accounted for 13% of girls' dropout in grade 6 (last year of primary school, and 33% of dropout in grade 7 (first year of secondary school in Cameroon. But using Demographic and Health Survey Data from five francophone West African countries, Lloyd and Mensch (2008) found that teenage marriage and pregnancy together explained up to 20% of school dropout. Schoolgirl pregnancy accounted for only 5% to 10% of girls' departures from school. Using instrumental variables to account for endogeneity of schooling and pregnancy Kruger, Berthelon and Navia

(2009) found that about 24-37% of teenage mothers did not attend to school and complete high school in Chile. Studying adolescents living in the Kibera slums in Nairobi Erulkar and Matheka (2007) found that among girls who were out of school, 14% of the girls reported that they left school due to early marriage and 9% of the girls reported that they left school due to pregnancy. Basch (2011) investigated the relationship between teenage pregnancy and achievement gap among urban minority youths in the US. Using secondary data and literature review, Basch found that birth rates of non-Hispanic Black women aged 15-17 years were more than three times (36.1 per 1000 women) higher than that in the non-Hispanic White women (11.8 per 1000 women). Compared with women who delay marriage and childbearing until age 30, teen mothers' education was estimated 2 years shorter. They were less likely to complete high school and had 14-29% lower odds of attending college. The findings from southern Malawi by Kelly, Chalasani, Mensch, & Soler-Hampejsek (2014) indicate that as much as one quarter of high school dropout may be due to early pregnancy.

Increased risks of high school behaviors and its dropout are perhaps the several paths by which early marriage and its subsequent event such as teenage pregnancy is more likely to affect teenage girls than boys in high school education, including HSD. Although the high school dropout problem are influenced by school, family and community factors, the National Education Longitudinal Study by Levine and Painter (1988) has found that about one half of the observed effects of teenage pregnancy on dropout remain after statistical adjustment of environmental disadvantages (e.g., poverty, negative attitude toward education, less social support). Manlove (1998) also found similar effects of teenage pregnancy on HSD. Of the 433,000 teen births of unmarried teens, only one half of the school dropout was significantly related to teenage pregnancy and its related complexities remained a very important contributor to reduced levels of high school attainment. Using cross-sectional data from high school 4768 girls in Nigeria, Ea et. al. (2016) found that about 46% of the girls were forced into marriage by their parents and 20.3% of the girls who got married at early ages, because they had no money to go to school. Most of the respondents who married early became pregnant after short duration of their marriages and about 54.4% of them experienced a complication during pregnancy, excessive bleeding (14%) and anemia (13%) during delivery and obstructed/prolonged labor (10%). About 82.4% of the girls studied were absent from school associated with their pregnancy and its related complicacies were ultimately dropout from high school.

Teenage Childbearing

Assuming from family life course approach several research studies have found that EM and its subsequent life events, such as pregnancy and childbearing are also linked to school absence, poor grades and HSD among married girls than unmarried girls across across countries (Barnet et al., 2004; Moore & Waite, 1977; Mott & Marsiglio, 1985). Although relationship between early pregnancy and childbearing and high school risk behavior are well-documented in the previous research, there is surprisingly little research on how early pregnancy and frequent childbearing after marriage mediate the relationship between EM and high school absence, low GPA and HSD. For example, Card and Wise (1978) found that teenage mothers ultimately obtain less education than do women have late pregnancy and delay childbearing. In a longitudinal survey study, Mott and Marsiglio (1985) selected 4,696 women aged 20-26 and repeatedly interviewed the respondents over the years (from 1979 to 1987) and found that teenagers who became early pregnant and gave birth while in high school or soon after leaving school were far less likely to eventually graduate from high school than women who delayed pregnancy and childbearing until their 20s.

Using data of National Survey of Families and Households, Glass and Jacobs (2005) found that a pattern of earlier marriage and childbearing among women raised in conservative religious households had detrimental effects on high school educational attainment. They found that the women who were truncated their educational attainment in order to facilitate early family formation, the same pattern of lower educational attainment would be found, given the incompatibility of full-time school attendance with supporting an independent household and/or raising children. Using nationally representative data, Fitzgerald and Glass (2008) assess whether the timing of life course transitions (e.g., marriage, pregnancy, childbirth etc.) can explain the lower educational attainment of women rose in conservative Protestant (CP) households. They found that early family formation affects educational attainment of the women in the CP households, after adjustment for control variables. Studies by Kiernan (1986) and Kalmuss and Namerow (1994) have found that women who marry in their teens tend to have more children earlier than those who marry later. Especially, Kiernan (1986) found that about 23% of women who married in their teens gave birth to five or more children, while 8% of those who married later in life.

Kalmuss and Namerow (1994) found that married teen mothers were 40% more likely to have a second birth within 24 months of their first birth compared with unmarried teen mothers. Berglas, Brindis & Cohen (2003) observed that poor school performance was the vital cause of HSD. According to them, young women who became teen parents tended to have lower GPA, more school absences, and more difficulties with school work. Most studies have concluded that early childbearing of high school-going girls compared to delay childbearing of the girls does increase high school risk behavior, including dropout. Using modified status attainment model incorporating a life-course perspective, Upchurch and McCarthy (1990) examined the relationship between the timing of a first birth, high school dropout and high school completion in the US. Using data from National Longitudinal Youth Survey 1979-1986 and data analyzing with event-history techniques, they found that having a baby did not predict dropping out of high school. The women who had a baby while still enrolling and remaining in school were more likely to graduate as women did not. Among high school dropouts, however, having a baby reduced the chances of eventual graduation.

There are, of course, many background factors such as family poverty, low SES, family structure, disadvantaged neighborhood, school quality, future aspirations and educational motivation that lead to EM and its subsequent risks such as teenage pregnancy, teenage childbearing and HSD (Hofferth & Moore, 1979; Marini, 1984). Some research (see, Ashcraft & Lang, 2006; Fletcher & Wolfe, 2008; Lee, 2010) suggests that differences in high school risk behaviors (e.g., poor class attendance, poor grade, lack of homework completion, exam exit, high school dropout) between those who do and don't have teenage births are attributable to teenage pregnancy and childbearing. Several studies (Covington, Peters, Sabia & Price, 2011; Fletcher & Wolfe, 2012), using extensive statistical controls for differences in both observed and unobserved characteristics between teen girls who do and don't have a birth or births still find a statistically significant associations between teenage childbearing and HSD. Likely, recent literature focusing on the outcomes for teenage fatherhood finds that teen childbearing has a significant, negative influence on their high school educational attainment.

Teenage Child Caring and Raring

Early birth and parenting can be a life-altering experience. Regardless sociodemographic status early motherhood uniformly places demands on teen mothers that are not existent prior to the birth of a child (Uddin, 2009b). When school-aged girls become mothers, new responsibilities related to child care can be overwhelming. The teen mothers who lack supports from their husband's parents or her own parents, their child care and schooling responsibilities may be challenging at a time. Relevant literature suggests that teenage students with dependent children drop out from high school, because of heavy burdens of child care responsibility when children are under five years old. Studying representative sample, Brosh et al. (2007) found that only 10% of the mothers between the ages of 15-17 graduated from high school on time, but 67% of the mothers never graduated from high school. Using data from the National Education Longitudinal Study, Melhado (2007) found that teen parents had a total of 11.9 years of education compared to those who had on average 13.9 years of education without children. Melhado argues that having access to appropriate resources can reduce this educational gap between parents with or without children.

Family Responsibility

Family life course and gender division of family labor perspective draws attentions to the ways in which past life events (such as marriage, pregnancy & child-bearing) and its sequences shape women's family role transitions, especially family responsibility (Sweet & Moen, 2006; Uddin, 2010, 2021). Although boys' decision to continue high schooling or returning to schooling shapes by family cultural tradition (masculine role, especially income earner role), teenage girls' to continue schooling after marriage and its subsequent events are closely tied to family demands and responsibility, including household chores, husband's parental care and child rearing (Bem, 1993; Bay, 1999; Carr & Sheridan, 2001; Pascall & Cox, 1993). For example, Maynard and Pearsall (1994) found that women were more likely to negotiate with their entire family to continue or postpone their current education and further to enroll in the next class, depending on their current age, developmental needs of their dependent children and family responsibility assigned on them.

Gorard et al. (2001) described that women decide to postpone their further education because of their "enforced altruism." Likely, Mohney and Anderson (1988) have found that women compared to men postpone to schooling because of external factors, especially family responsibilities and less likely to personal motivational factors. Further research suggests that women than men to continue their schooling face family conflicts in meeting familial responsibilities (Ballmer & Cozby, 1981; Gilbert, Manning, & Ponder, 1980; Home, 1998; Scala, 1996). For example, Scala found that a higher percentage of women than men encountered problems with family or time pressures when they continued their education to return to education. In their comparative study, Gilbert et al. (1980) found that more women than men after marriage faced family demands (as the source of the role conflict while attending school, whereas more men than women attributed role conflict to self-beliefs and interpersonal dissatisfactions. Although men with traditional family responsibilities may experience particular pressure to fulfill the traditional expectations of the masculine gender role, women with their traditional family responsibilities may face heavy burdens that affect not only high school risk behavior but also dropping out from high school.

LIMITATIONS AND IMPLICATIONS

Literature review shows that EM negatively influences HSD across countries, Including Bangladesh. Based on family life course approach and comprehensive literature review, this chapter explains potential pathways of EM such as early transition to pregnancy, child bearing and rearing and household chores. These family life course pathways partially explain underlying the relationship between EM and HSD across countries. But association between early or teenage marriage, pregnancy, childbearing, childrearing and family responsibility and high school risk behavior (e.g., poor attendance, exam exit, poor GPA & dropout) does not equate causation.

Although the strength of relationship is one of the criteria to make overall judgment about a causal relationship, data from cross-sectional survey do not indicate causality (Ward, 2009). It needs the direction of influences of predictors on subsequent events such as life course pathways and HSD over the time. Are girls pulled out from high school to be married or are they married at a young age because they dropout from high school. The causality between teenage marriage and high school dropout may go both ways. The pathways of the life events, from decision of teenage marriage to high school leaving, are complex and multifaceted. Nguyen and Wodon (2014) argue that educational prospects of teenage girls in the African context depend on their parents' decision whether to stay in high school or get married. That means decisions by parents or guardians about the early marriage and timing of leaving high school are often concomitant. This makes it technically difficult to elucidate the causal order of teen marriage of girls and high school dropout. Although the link between EM and HSD deserves greater attention, there is little empirical evidence on the pathways of family formation process that increase the risks of high dropout process. Future longitudinal studies should focus on the limitations to understand the link between EM and HSD via family life course pathways.

Despite these limitations, evidence in FLCA and literature may have implications to prevent EM and HSD across societies. In developing and the least developed countries, the stakeholders such as legal enforcement agencies, development workers, social media workers, social activists, policy-makers, and voluntary organizations should take actions and programs to prevent EM and HSD among poor and disadvantaged girls at local, national and international level. Particularly, national and international social Medias should take programs for consciousness-building about the negative consequences of EM. Law enforcement agencies should take actions to prevent EM at local level. Social policy-makers should design policy programs in which they provide economic and educational supports to the poor girls to stay them at school.

CONCLUSION

Despite school process-based measures taken, high school dropout (HSD) associated with early marriage (EM) among teenage girls is increasing across countries, including Bangladesh. Based on family life course approach and comprehensive literature review, this chapter explains potential pathways of EM such as early transition to family responsibility, pregnancy, child bearing and rearing and household chores, leading girls to dropout from high school. Based on the FLCA and literature over the past several decades suggests that EM and its subsequent events (e.g., pregnancy, childbearing and rearing, early family role transition) partially explain high school risk behaviors (e.g., late enrollment, frequently class absence, poor reading practice, exam exit, poor GPA) that, in turn, affect girls than boys from HSD. Evidence in this chapter is important for developing effective programs or measures to prevent teenage girls' EM and HSD across developing countries.

REFERENCES

Abalkhail, B. A. (1995). Adolescent pregnancy: Are there biological barriers for pregnancy outcomes? *The Journal of the Egyptian Public Health Association*, 70(5-6), 609–625. PMID: 17214178

Amadi, E. C. (2013). Socio-cultural factors on the girl-child education in secondary schools Ihiala local government area of Anambra state, Nigeria. *International Journal of Education, Learning and Development*, 1(1), 71–74.

Amato, P. R., & Kane, J. B. (2011). Life-course pathways and the psychosocial adjustment of young adult women. *Journal of Marriage and Family*, 73(1), 279–295. DOI: 10.1111/j.1741-3737.2010.00804.x PMID: 23188928

Ashcraft, A., & Lang, K. (2006). The consequences of teenage childbearing (Working Paper No. 12485). Cambridge, MA: National Bureau of Economic Research.

Ballmer, H., & Cozby, P. C. (1981). Family environment of women who return to college. *Sex Roles*, 7(10), 1019–1026. DOI: 10.1007/BF00288502

Barnet, B., Arroyo, C., Devoe, M., & Duggan, A. K. (2004). Reduced school dropout rates among adolescent mothers receiving school-based prenatal care. *Archives of Pediatrics & Adolescent Medicine*, 158(3), 262–268. DOI: 10.1001/archpedi.158.3.262 PMID: 14993086

Basch, C. E. (2011). Teen pregnancy and the achievement gap among urban minority youth. *The Journal of School Health*, 81(10), 614–618. DOI: 10.1111/j.1746-1561.2011.00635.x PMID: 21923873

Bay, L. (1999). Twists, turns and returns: Returning adult students. *Teaching English in the Two-Year College*, 26(3), 305–312. DOI: 10.58680/tetyc19991834

Becker, G. S. (1981). *A treatise on the family*. University of Chicago Press.

Bem, S. L. (1993). *The lenses of gender: Transforming the debate on sexual inequality*. Yale university Press.

Berglas, N., Brindis, C., & Cohen, J. (2003). *Adolescent pregnancy and childbearing in California. The Prepared at the Request of Senator Dede Alpert with Funding Provided by The David and Lucile Packard Foundation*. California Research Bureau.

Brosh, J., Weigel, D., & Evans, W. (2007). Pregnant and parenting adolescents' perception of sources and supports in relation to educational goals. *Child & Adolescent Social Work Journal*, 24(6), 565–578. DOI: 10.1007/s10560-007-0107-8

Cairns, R., & Cairns, B. (1994). *Lifelines & risks: Pathways of youth in our time.* Cambridge University Press.

Card, J. J., & Wise, L. L. (1978). Teenage mothers and teenage fathers: The impact of early childbearing on the parents' personal and professional lives. *Family Planning Perspectives*, 17(5), 234–237. DOI: 10.2307/2134267 PMID: 567590

Carr, D. (Ed.). (2009). Encyclopedia of the life course and human development: Vol. 1. *Childhood & adolescence.* Macmillan Reference USA.

Carr, D., & Sheridan, J. (2001). Family turning-points and career transitions at midlife. In Marshall, V. W., Heinz, W. R., Kruger, H., & Verma, A. (Eds.), *Restructuring work and the life course* (pp. 201–227). University of Toronto Press. DOI: 10.3138/9781442679290-014

Convington, R., Peters, H. E., Sabia, J. J., & Price, J. P. (2011). Teen fatherhood and educational attainment: Evidence from three cohorts of youth (Working Paper, October, 2011).

Dahl, G. B. (2010). Early teen marriage and future poverty. *Demography*, 47(3), 689–718. DOI: 10.1353/dem.0.0120 PMID: 20879684

Duvall, E. M. (1988). Family development's first forty years. *Family Relations*, 37(2), 127–134. DOI: 10.2307/584309

Ea, E., Umaru, R. J., No, I., Ia, O., Eo, O., & Zoakah, A. I. (2016). Determinants and effect of girl child marriage: A cross-sectional study of school girls in Plateau State, Nigeria. *International Journal of Medicine*, 5(3), 122–128.

Ekstrom, R., Goertz, M., Pollack, J., & Rock, D. (1986). Who drops out of high school and why? Findings from a national longitudinal study. *Teachers College Record*, 87(3), 356–373. DOI: 10.1177/016146818608700308

Eloundou-Enyegue, P. M. (2004). Pregnancy-related dropouts and gender inequality in education: A life table approach and application to Cameroon. *Demography*, 41(3), 509–528. DOI: 10.1353/dem.2004.0021 PMID: 15461012

Eloundou-Enyegue, P. M., & Strokes, C. S. (2004). Teen pregnancy and gender inequality in education: A contextual hypothesis. *Demographic Research*, 11, 305–322. DOI: 10.4054/DemRes.2004.11.11

Emirie, G. (2005). Early marriage and its effects on girls' education rural Ethiopia: The case of Mecha Woreda in West Gojjam, North-Western Ethiopia. Ph. D Dissertation, Georg-August University of Goettingen, Goettingen, Ethiopia.

Erulkar, A., & Matheka, J. (2007). *Adolescence in the Kibera slums of Nairobi Kenya*. Population Council.

Evans, I., & DiBenedetto, A. (1990). Pathways to school dropout: A conceptual model for early prevention. *Special Services in the Schools*, 6(1-2), 63–80. DOI: 10.1300/J008v06n01_04

Finn, J. (1989). Withdrawing from school. *Review of Educational Research*, 59(2), 117–142. DOI: 10.3102/00346543059002117

Fitzgerald, S. T., & Glass, J. (2008). Can early family formation explain the lower educational attainment of U. S. conservative Protestants? *Sociological Spectrum*, 28(5), 556–577. DOI: 10.1080/02732170802206203

Fletcher, J. M., & Wolfe, B. L. (2012). The effects of teenage fatherhood on young adult outcomes. *Economic Inquiry*, 50(1), 182–201. DOI: 10.1111/j.1465-7295.2011.00372.x PMID: 22329053

Gilbert, L. A., Manning, L., & Ponder, M. (1980). Conflicts with the student role: A comparison of female and male reentry students. *Journal of the National Association for Women Deans, Administrators & Counselors*, 44(1), 26–32.

Glass, J., & Jacobs, J. (2005). Childhood religious conservatism and adult attainment among black and white women. *Social Forces*, 94(1), 555–579. DOI: 10.1353/sof.2005.0098

Glick, P. C. (1947). The family cycle. *American Sociological Review*, 12(2), 164–174. DOI: 10.2307/2086982

Glick, P. C. (1955). The cycle of the family. *Marriage and Family Living*, 17(1), 3–9. DOI: 10.2307/346771

Gorard, S., Rees, G., Fevre, R., & Welland, T. (2001). Learning trajectories: Some voices of those in transit"? *International Journal of Lifelong Education*, 20, 167–187.

Hofferth, S. L., & Moore, K. A. (1979). Early childbearing and later economic well-being. *American Sociological Review*, 44(5), 784–815. DOI: 10.2307/2094528 PMID: 533035

Hoffman, S. D. (2006). *By the numbers: The public costs of adolescent childbearing*. National Campaign to Reduce Teen Pregnancy.

Holcamp, G. (2009). Researching the girls' dropout rate in Malawi. Why girls dropout of primary schools and in what way this rate can be reduced. Master Thesis Special Education.

Home, A. M. (1998). Predicting role conflict, overload and contagion in adult women university students with family and jobs. *Adult Education Quarterly*, 48(2), 85–97. DOI: 10.1177/074171369804800204

Kalmuss, D., & Namerow, P. (1994). Subsequent childbearing among teenage mothers: The determinants of a closely spaced second birth. *Family Planning Perspectives*, 26(4), 149–153. DOI: 10.2307/2136238 PMID: 7957815

Kelly, C. A., Chalasani, S., Mensch, B. S., & Soler-Hampejsek, E. (2014). Adolescent pregnancy and education trajectories in Malawi. Paper presented at 2013 27th IUSSP International Population Conference. Busan, Republic of Korea, 28 August.

Kiernan, K. (1986). Teenage marriage and marital breakdown: A longitudinal study. *Population Studies*, 40(1), 35–54. DOI: 10.1080/0032472031000141826

Klepinger, D., Lundberg, S., & Plotnick, R. (1999). How does adolescent fertility affect the human capital and wages of young women. *The Journal of Human Resources*, 34(3), 421–448. DOI: 10.2307/146375

Kruger, D. I., Berthelon, M., & Navia, R. (2009). Adolescent motherhood and secondary schooling in Chile. Institute for the Study of Labor (IZA) Discussion Paper No. 4552. Bonn, Germany: November.

Lamb, S., Markussen, E., Teese, R., Sandberg, N., & Polesel, J. (Eds.). (2011). *School dropout and completion: International comparative studies in theory and practice*. Springer Publishing Company. DOI: 10.1007/978-90-481-9763-7

Lee, D. (2010). The early socioeconomic effects of teenage childbearing: A propensity score matching approach. *Demographic Research*, 23, 697–736. DOI: 10.4054/DemRes.2010.23.25

Levine, D. L., & Painter, G. (2003). The schooling costs of teenage out-of-wedlock childbearing: Analysis with a within-school propensity score-matching estimator. *The Review of Economics and Statistics*, 85(4), 884–900. DOI: 10.1162/003465303772815790

LIoyd. C. (2005). Growing up global: The changing traditions to adulthood in developing countries. Panel on transitions to adulthood in developing countries. Committee on Population, National Research Council and Institute of Medicine. Washington, D. C.: The National Academic Press.

Lioyd, C. B., & Mensch, B. S. (2008). Marriage and childbirth as factors in dropping out from school: An analysis of DHS data from sub-Saharan Africa. *Population Studies*, 62(1), 1–13. DOI: 10.1080/00324720701810840 PMID: 18278669

Lloyd, C. B., & Mensch, B. S. (2006). *Marriage and childbirth as factors in school exit: An analysis of DHS data from sub-Saharan Africa* (Population council Working Paper No.219). New York: Population Council.

Loomis, C. P. (1936). The study of the life cycle of families. *Rural Sociology*, 1, 180–199.

Malmberg, L.-E., & Sumra, S. (2001). Socio-cultural factors and Tanzanian primary school students' achievements and school experience. [New Series]. *Utafiti*, 4(Special Issue), 207–219.

Manlove, J. (1998). The influence of high school dropout and school disengagement on the risk of school-age pregnancy. *Journal of Research on Adolescence*, 8(2), 187–220. DOI: 10.1207/s15327795jra0802_2 PMID: 12294323

Mansory, A. (2007). *Dropout study in basic education level of schools in Afghanistan*. Swedish Committee for Afghanistan.

Marini, M. M. (1984). Age and sequencing norms in the transition to adulthood. *Social Forces*, 63(1), 229–244. DOI: 10.2307/2578867

Maynard, E. M., & Pearsall, S. J. (1994). What about male mature students? A comparison of the experiences of men and women students. *Journal of Access Studies*, 9, 229–240.

Maynard, R. A. (1996). *Kids having kids: Economic costs and social consequences on teen pregnancy*. National Campaign to Reduce Teen Pregnancy.

Mayor, S. (2004). Pregnancy and childbirth are leading causes of death in teenage girls in developing countries. *BMJ (Clinical Research Ed.)*, 328(7449), 328. DOI: 10.1136/bmj.328.7449.1152-a PMID: 15142897

Melhado, L. (2008). Teenage parents' educational attainment is affected more by available resources than by parenthood. *Perspectives on Sexual and Reproductive Health*, 39, 184–185.

Mohney, C., & Anderson, W. (1988). The effect of life events and relationships on adult women's decisions to enroll in college. *Journal of Counseling and Development*, 66(6), 271–274. DOI: 10.1002/j.1556-6676.1988.tb00866.x

Moore, K. A., & Waite, L. J. (1977). Early childbearing and educational attainment. *Family Planning Perspectives*, 9(5), 220–225. DOI: 10.2307/2134432 PMID: 902716

Mott, F. L., & Marsiglio, W. (1976). Early childbearing and completion of high school. *Family Planning Perspectives*, 17(5), 234–237. DOI: 10.2307/2135098 PMID: 3842664

Mott, F. L., & Marsiglio, W. (1985). Child bearing and completion of high school. *Family Planning Perspectives*, 17(5), 234–237. DOI: 10.2307/2135098 PMID: 3842664

Nguyen, M. C., & Wodon, Q. (2014). Impact of child marriage on literacy and education attainment in Africa. Available from http://allinschool.org/wp-content/uploads/2015/02/OOSC-2014-QW-Child-Marriage-final.pdf

Norton, A. J. (1980). Family life cycle: 1980. *Journal of Marriage and Family*, 45(2), 267–275. DOI: 10.2307/351506

Omoeva, C., & Hatch, R. (2014). *Teenage, married, and out of school: Effects of early marriage and childbirth on school dropout*. Education Policy and Data Center Working Paper.

Oppenheimer, V. K. (1970). *The female labor force in the United States: Demographic and economic factors determining its growth and changing composition*. Population Monograph Series, N. 5, Institute of International Studies. Berkeley: University of California.

Oppenheimer, V. K. (1988). A theory of marriage timing. *American Journal of Sociology*, 94(3), 563–591. DOI: 10.1086/229030

Oppenheimer, V. K. (1997). Women's employment and the gain to marriage. The specialization and trading model. *Annual Review of Sociology*, 23(1), 431–453. DOI: 10.1146/annurev.soc.23.1.431 PMID: 12348280

Parsons, T. (1954). *Essays in sociological theory*. Free Press.

Pascall, G., & Cox, R. (1993). Education and domesticity. *Gender and Education*, 5(1), 17–35. DOI: 10.1080/0954025930050102

Raffe, D. (2010). Scotland: System of education. In Baker, E., Peterson, P., & McGaw, B. (Eds.), *The international encyclopedia of education* (3rd ed., Vol. 5, pp. 770–775). Elsevier. DOI: 10.1016/B978-0-08-044894-7.01429-9

Ribar, D. (1994). Teen fertility and high school completion. *The Review of Economics and Statistics*, 76(3), 413–424. DOI: 10.2307/2109967

Rodgers, R. H. (1964). Toward a theory of family development. *Journal of Marriage and Family*, 26(3), 262–270. DOI: 10.2307/349456

Rumberger, R. W. (2011). High school dropout in the United States. Lamb, S., Markussen, E., Teese, R., Sandberg, N., & Polesel, J. Editors, *School dropout and completion: International comparative studies in theory and practice* (pp. 275-294). London: Springer Publishing Company. DOI: 10.1007/978-90-481-9763-7_16

Sattar, T., Yasin, G., & Afzal, S. (2012). Socio-cultural and economic impediments of inequality in provision of educational rights to female: A case of Southern Punjab (Pakistan). *International Journal of Human Resource Studies*, 2(1), 122–138. DOI: 10.5296/ijhrs.v2i1.1210

Scala, M. A. (1996). Going back to school: Participation motives and experiences of older adults in an undergraduate classroom. *Educational Gerontology*, 22(8), 747–773. DOI: 10.1080/0360127960220804

Sekine, K., & Hodgkin, M. E. (2017). Effect of child marriage on girls' school dropout in Nepal: Analysis of data from the multiple indicator cluster survey 2014. *PLoS One*, 20(7), 1–13. DOI: 10.1371/journal.pone.0180176 PMID: 28727793

Shahidul, S. M. (2012). Marriage market and an effect on girls' school dropout in Bangladesh. *Journal of Alternative Perspectives in the Social Sciences*, 4(2), 552–564.

Shahidul, S. M. (2014). Parents' class background and hypergamy in the marriage market of Bangladesh: Does the dowry affect school dropout among girls? *The Asia-Pacific Education Researcher*, 23(3), 709–715. DOI: 10.1007/s40299-013-0142-5

Snyder, T. (1994). [IES: The National Center for Education Statistics.]. *Digest of Educational Statistics*, •••, 1994.

Sweet, S., & Moen, P. (2006). Advancing a career focus on work and family: Insights from the life course perspective. In Pitt-Catsouphes, M., Kossek, E. E., & Sweet, S. (Eds.), *The work and family handbook: Multidisciplinary perspectives, methods, and approaches* (pp. 189–208). Erlbaum.

Uddin, E. M. (2015). Family socio-cultural values affecting early marriage between Muslim and Santal communities in rural Bangladesh. *The International Journal of Sociology and Social Policy*, 35(3/4), 141–164. DOI: 10.1108/IJSSP-06-2014-0046

Uddin, M. E. (2007). Marital duration and sexual frequency among the Muslim and Santal couples in rural Bangladesh: A cross-cultural Perspective. *International Journal of Humanities and Social Science*, 2(8), 444–453.

Uddin, M. E. (2009a). Age at first marriage for husband and wife between Muslim and Santal communities in rural Bangladesh. *International Journal of Humanities and Social Science*, 3(4), 318–326.

Uddin, M. E. (2009b). Cross-cultural comparison of marriage relationship between Muslim and Santal communities in a village of Bangladesh. *World Cultures eJournal, 17*(1), 1-17.

Uddin, M. E. (2010). *Family structure: A cross-cultural comparison between Muslim and Santal communities in rural Bangladesh. Saarbruchen*. Lambert Academic Publishing.

Uddin, M. E. (2021). Teenage marriage and high school dropout among poor girls: A narrative review for family pathways in Bangladesh. *Journal of Research in Social Sciences and Language*, 1(1), 55–76. https://www.jssal.com/index.php/jssal/article/view/15

UNFPA (2012). *Marrying too young: Ending child marriage*. New York: United Nations Population fund.

UNFPA. (2013). *Adolescent pregnancy*. United Nations Population Fund.

United Nations. (1988). *First marriage: Patterns and determinants*. Population Division.

United Nations. (1990). *Patterns of first marriage: Timing and prevalence*. Population Division.

United Nations. (2000). *World marriage patterns*. Population Division.

United Nations Population Fund. (2001). *Socio-cultural aspects of reproductive health*. UNFPA.

Upchurch, D. M., & McCarthy, J. (1990). The timing of a first birth and high school completion. *American Sociological Review*, 55(2), 224–234. DOI: 10.2307/2095628

Ward, A. C. (2009). The role of causal criteria in causal inferences: Bradford Hill's aspects of association. *Epidemiologic Perspectives & Innovations*, 6(1), 2. DOI: 10.1186/1742-5573-6-2 PMID: 19534788

WHO. (2004). *Adolescent pregnancy*. World Health Organization.

Yakoob, T. (2012). Socio-cultural constraints faced by girls regarding access to their secondary education in Mardan, Khyber Pakhtunkhuwa. *International Journal of Management Sciences and Business Research*, 1(12), 11–19.

ENDNOTE

[1] In reporting teenage pregnancy rates, the number of pregnancies per 1000 females aged 15 to 19 when the pregnancy ends are generally used.

Chapter 6
Early Marriage and Mental Health in India:
A Socio-Ecological Approach

Lalhriatpuii Fanai
https://orcid.org/0000-0001-8319-9921
Christ University, India

Vaishnavi Jeyachandran
https://orcid.org/0000-0002-3910-956X
Christ University, India

Deepthi Jose Maliakkal
https://orcid.org/0000-0001-8968-9198
Christ University, India

ABSTRACT

Child marriage constitutes an extreme breach of the United Nations Convention on the Rights of the Child. It is estimated that the total number of women who get married before reaching the age of 18 will surpass 60 million. Out of these women, more than one-third live in South Asia. India has experienced the most rapid decrease in early marriage (EM) at a rate of 3.8%. However, the eradication of EM will not happen at the current pace until there are advancements in girls' education, an increase in marital household wealth, and a deeper understanding of the negative repercussions of child marriage. Consequently, it is crucial to implement comprehensive and cross-sectoral initiatives to decrease the occurrence of EM. This study utilized the socio-ecological approach to comprehensively explore the intricate phenomenon of EM in the Indian context.

DOI: 10.4018/979-8-3693-3394-5.ch006

1. INTRODUCTION

Early marriage in India severely impacts the mental health of young women, disrupting their education, limiting personal growth, and increasing their vulnerability to abuse, which often leads to depression, anxiety, low self-esteem, and even suicidal thoughts (UNICEF 2012, 2019). This chapter explores the intricate relationship between cultural norms and the prevalence of early marriage globally. It further examines how cultural beliefs, traditions, and social structures contribute to normalizing and perpetuating this harmful practice. The primary objective of this discussion is to examine the psychosocial factors that give rise to the occurrence of child marriage, as well as society's tendency to perceive it as a normal practice. According to the United Nations' fifth Sustainable Development Goal (SDG-5), which aims to ensure gender equality and empower all women and girls, one in five (19%) young women get married before turning eighteen. The United Nations' Sustainable Development Goals include Target 5.3, which aims to eliminate child marriage by 2030. However, given our current rate of progress, it would take 300 years to fulfil this goal. Although child marriage rates decreased in 2016, the emergence of the pandemic posed a threat to this decline, putting more girls in danger of being forced into child marriage. Along with the cultural differences, the impact of geographic location and its influence will also be highlighted (UNICEF, 2020).

2. THEORETICAL FRAMEWORK

Several sociocultural factors deeply influence the custom of early marriage (Uddin, 2015). To comprehend and tackle these varying determinants effectively, it is crucial to consider the interconnected nature of these various elements within the community. The socio-ecological framework encompasses factors across varying levels: Individuals, Interpersonal, Organizations, Communities, Policy, and Societal (Erickson et al., 2024). It becomes essential to emphasize the necessity for coordination and collaboration across these diverse levels to address early marriage effectively (Reupert, 2017). This approach serves as a potent tool for uncovering the underlying factors contributing to early marriage in diverse contexts and levels (Pourtaheri et al., 2024). Prior research underscores the complex interactions and numerous risk factors across different tiers (Putri et al., 2022). Embracing a multi-level approach is pivotal for grasping the systemic effects of health-related issues and identifying areas for intervention (Pourtaheri et al., 2024).

A comprehensive literature review was implemented using databases such as Google Scholar, ScienceDirect, and Springer. Studies on child marriage, especially in India and other collectivistic Asian and African countries were the main focus of the search. The key terms mentioned are early marriage, child marriage, well-being, impact, reports, and reviews. Out of the initial pool of eighty papers, forty-five were chosen based on their relevance to the Indian context, collectivistic practices, and medical issues related to child/early marriage. An integrative review (Souzma et al., 2010) facilitated a synthesized review of literature on the effects of early marriage on mental health through the socio-ecological lens. The results of the review are presented in the next section (see, Fig. 1).

3. THE EFFECTS OF EARLY MARRIAGE ON MENTAL HEALTH

3.1 Individual Factors

In the discussion about early marriage, it is essential to emphasize the well-being of the girl child. It is necessary to give prominence to both physical and emotional well-being. The relevance of social well-being and financial dependency, on the other hand, needs to be brought to the forefront because they contribute to both physical and emotional well-being.

Education

There is an association between the early marriage of girls and the early dropout from school or constraints in higher study. Girls eventually come to accept it because it has become accepted as normal, even though they wish not to jeopardize their future or education (Uddin, 2021). Education is what enables women to do more in a developing nation like India, and having secure employment is what makes it easier to reach financial independence. Marriage at a young age makes it more difficult to complete one's high school education (Bhabha & Kelly, 2013; UNICEF, 2019). Even in the event that they were to graduate from high school, would not be encouraged to continue their education at a college or vocational school, nor would they be permitted to find any employment. Not only does it restrict their educational opportunities, but it also restricts their ability to become financially independent in the future. It causes them to become dependent on their husbands and families, which in turn leads to a cycle of poverty (Singh & Vennam, 2016). They are rendered helpless and easily susceptible to being abused as a result.

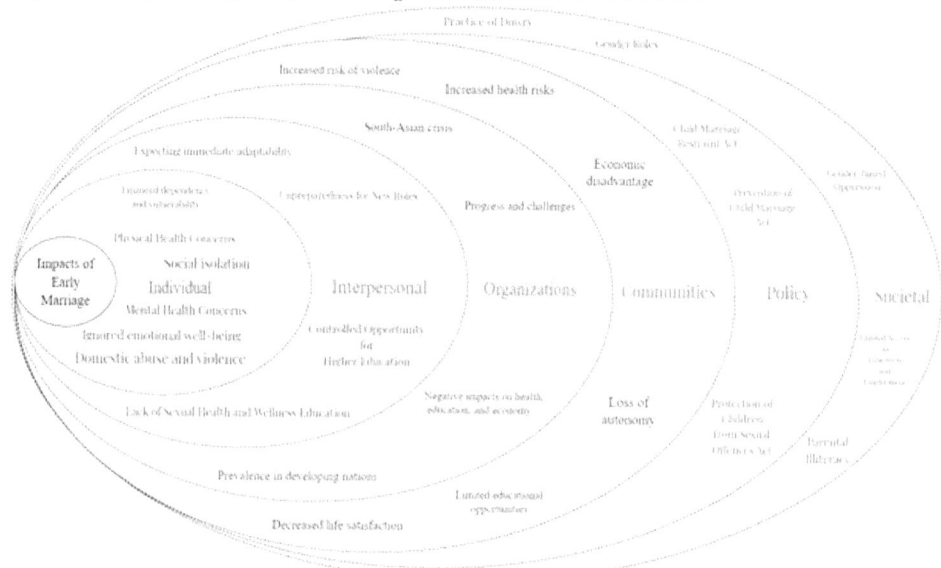

Figure 1. Impacts of early marriage on mental health in India

Socialization and Social Support

In the case of young girls, getting married at a young age significantly restricts their avenues for socializing (Nour, 2006). There are many instances in which social isolation occurs, particularly in the case of girls who were subjected to abuse at the hands of their in-laws (Goli, 2016). These girls may not even be aware that their in-laws have socially isolated them. The young brides were frequently victims of family abuse, sexual violence, assault, neglect, and exploitation (EP & Poonia, 2015). On the other hand, it is either considered to be a common occurrence within the community, or the society is turning a blind eye to the girl's situation, or the society refuses to believe the accusations of a young girl.

Emotional Health Concerns

It was still considered a stigma in many underdeveloped nations, including India, to seek support from mental health professionals. Women have a difficult time obtaining professional care, particularly in rural areas where mental health is regarded as being subject to a significant taboo and where the practice of early marriage is prevalent (Kumar, 2011). Additionally, the likelihood of availability is quite low. In light of this, it is essential to have a comprehensive understanding of the immediate and long-term impact that early marriage has on young girls (Goli, 2016).

Short-Term Impact

When a teenage girl gets married, she goes through many transitions. Changes in one's life, such as location, roles, and responsibilities, as well as the incapacity to continue living the same life, may perhaps cause grief. The girl, who had previously lived with her parents and other family members, might experience both grief and stress as a result of her relocation with people her family has never met (Patowari et al., 2019). The majority of the time, they are neither emotionally ready for marital complexities and obligations nor prepared for marriage. This results in feelings of worry and anxiety.

Post-traumatic stress disorder (PTSD) is a condition that can develop in a person if the marriage was forced upon them, if there was sexual abuse or violent sexual acts committed by the spouse after the marriage, or if the marriage was carried out against their will (Singh & Vennam, 2016). The unexpected changes in their lives affect their control over personal and social situations in which they grow and live. The presence of abuse in their marital relationship or from their in-laws (Patowari et al., 2019) could all contribute to feelings of anxiety and depression (Nour, 2006). Not only can early marriage result in a limitation on education, but it also has the potential to lead to social isolation (Bhabha & Kelly, 2013; Nour, 2006). As a result of the fact that their lives after marriage may sometimes revolve around their spouse, their in-laws, and the new role that they have as wives, they have very little time for themselves and are rarely able to do what they want. There is a possibility that it will result in low self-esteem and a sense of worthlessness (Patowari et al., 2019).

Long-Term Impact

Living under constant pressure to fulfil the roles, occasionally having fewer resources and assistance, and the potential for abuse are all factors that could contribute to chronic stress. Both the mental and physical well-being of a person could be impacted. Early marriage is associated with lower emotional maturity. It is possible that it would be a barrier that prevents establishing a good connection with the spouse, the in-laws, and, in many cases, the children that would be born in the future (Fan & Koski, 2022). Some women may turn to alcohol or drugs as a means of coping with the emotional demands they are managing (Berg et al., 2010), although the intake of alcohol and drugs by women is frowned upon in Indian society. Similarly, the chance of them becoming a victim of domestic abuse due to their partner's alcoholism also should not be ignored (Goli, 2016).

In exceptional circumstances, a person who is always under pressure, experiencing stress, and feeling hopeless, as well as who does not receive support from their family and who does not have control over their own life, may develop feelings of resentment not only toward their family but also toward themselves (Goli, 2016). As a result, this may result in thoughts of self-harm and attempts to act on it. It can be challenging for young mothers to raise their children when they have not had adequate support and find themselves struggling with mental health issues as a result of early marriage (UNICEF, 2019). Sometimes, they repeat the pattern of what happened to them—early marriage to their children—which results in the cycle of intergenerational trauma that continues to be passed down from generation to generation (Raj, 2010; Singh & Vennam, 2016).

Physical Health Concerns

Young women and adolescents are particularly susceptible to the physical health risks that early marriage and early sexual activity might bring about because their bodies are still developing. It is necessary to examine the concerns of physical well-being from two distinct perspectives: the immediate impact and the long-term impact, as both are important (Uddin, 2017).

Short-Term Impact

A correlation can be seen between early marriage and malnutrition since the young girl was expected to take on the new tasks and obligations that were assigned to her (Roest, 2016). Girls frequently tend to ignore their own needs, which can manifest in a variety of ways, including skipping meals, eating whatever is left over, eating less, or eating nothing at all, all depending on the family situation. It resulted in a situation of malnutrition. If the young bride becomes pregnant, malnutrition may have a negative impact on both the young bride's growth and the growth of the fetus (Ghosh & Kar, 2010).

The young bride was frequently tasked with performing various duties around the house (Atim, 2017). Some of these responsibilities involve working and remaining in the same posture for an extended period of time, which affects physical health (Goli, 2016), including restricting blood circulation and lifting heavy objects, such as carrying water or gas cylinders. Muscle tension, muscle injury, and joint discomfort are all potential outcomes of this situation. If the condition is not addressed or managed, it may result in chronic pain.

Many young people were refused access to sexual health and well-being services when they required them because it was still considered a taboo topic (Tripathi & Sekher, 2013). Having less control over the intimate relationship that exists inside a marriage and a lack of sexual education could both increase the likelihood of sexually transmitted illnesses (Osakinle & Tayo-Olajubutu, 2017).

Regardless of the bride's age, the bride is sometimes subjected to pressure from both society and their families to have children once they have tied the knot. Since her body is still developing, the young girl who becomes pregnant poses a significant number of risks to both the mother and the child (Goli, 2016; UNICEF, 2019). There is a possibility of abortion, the child being born prematurely, the infant being malnourished, the child having a low birth weight, the young mother receiving injuries during childbirth, and, in the worst-case scenario, the possibility of both the mother and the child or one of them passing away during the process of childbirth (Raj, 2010).

Long-term Impact

Both malnutrition (EP & Poonia, 2015) and stress, as well as injuries that are either neglected or poorly treated, have the potential to have a long-term impact on one's physical health. It can result in diabetes, high blood pressure, cardiovascular disease, and obesity in later years of life (Datta, 2022).

Due to the sexual relationship and stress, young girls suffer from physical illness (Goli, 2016), including headaches, stomach aches, and a weakened immune system. Their physical conditions were rarely treated in a timely manner. Sometimes they develop psychosomatic conditions, but they are neither identified nor treated. Young girls who were married at a young age frequently do not have access to healthcare for a variety of reasons, including living in poverty, being subject to restrictions from their families and communities, and not being aware of the resources and services that are freely available to them (Goli, 2016). This situation also has an impact on prenatal care (Goli, 2016; Roest, 2016).

The disease known as fistula, which is caused by both obstructed and prolonged labour, was frequently seen in child marriages (Goli, 2016). Infections might occur as a result of the hole that is created during childbirth between the vaginal canal and the bladder or rectum. On top of causing discomfort and irritation to the skin, it can also spread. Even though it is not a life-threatening condition, if it is not treated, it could result in complications such as sepsis, which is an infection of the blood, or peritonitis, which is inflammation of the abdominal lining (Osakinle & Tayo-Olajubutu, 2017). Cervical cancer was high in child brides (Goli, 2016) due to sexual activity at a young age, having multiple conceptions, and miscarriages. In the majority of cases, the diagnosis was made at a very late stage for many women, leading to life risks (Osakinle & Tayo-Olajubutu, 2017).

3.2 Interpersonal Factors

The little girl turns into a young bride and a wife. The position of a wife involves not only the role of the wife but also the role of the daughter-in-law, and it is not long before everyone in society anticipates that she will eventually become a mother. Being a young/child bride meant not only that one's autonomy, childhood and/or adolescent years, and possibly even educations, as well as the opportunity to pursue aspirations and social support were all compromised, but it also meant that these things were restricted.

Readiness as Wife and Daughter-in-Law

Young women were not adequately prepared to engage in a marriage relationship and to take on the responsibilities that come with being married. The readiness to take on the role of wife and daughter-in-law was theoretically taught to a young girl who was not practically prepared for it at times or emotionally unprepared most of the time (Atim, 2017). Their in-laws frequently disregarded their preparedness and readiness, and the fact that their maternal family also suggests that they should adapt more quickly is another factor. There was an expectation that they would take on the role of wife swiftly and carry it out to the perfect standard. The young girls who were not adequately prepared for it are put in an adverse situation due to these expectations.

Especially in a collectivistic country like India, the challenge is the same as it is to fulfill the expected duty of a daughter-in-law as well as a wife. The daughter-in-law was expected to fulfill the responsibilities of caring for her in-laws, performing all of the household chores, including cooking for the entire family, cleaning and maintaining the house to perfection, and catering to the needs of every member of the family (Singh et al., 2023). This was the case even though the daughter-in-law was a young little girl by any stretch of the imagination. The delicate shoulder is the one that bears the duty of leading the family, even if the girl was not prepared for it or did not want to take on the position (Goli, 2016; UNICEF, 2019). Even though some families allow the female child to adjust to the situation over a period of time, there are many instances in which the girl child is expected to be ready for it immediately.

Preparedness for Intimacy

Lack of preparation and readiness might extend beyond domestic tasks. Intimate connection expectations and demands could not be overlooked. Similarly, young girls are expected to fulfill their marital responsibilities to their husbands, including engaging in sexual activity, regardless of the age gap between them, even if the husband is too old or the child bride is too young (Roest, 2016). Many times, girls are not physically or emotionally ready to be physically intimate with someone. It is critical to note that many schools do not provide sexual and reproductive health education, despite its importance. Some state governments, including Gujarat, Madhya Pradesh, Maharashtra, Karnataka, Kerala, Rajasthan, Chhattisgarh, and Goa, have banned sex education (Tripathi & Sekher, 2013). It was still regarded as a taboo topic, with the misconception that it contradicted cultural and societal values (Goli, 2016). Even in most Indian families, parents do not educate their children—both young girls and young boys—about sexual and reproductive health. As a result, they were clueless about sexual relationships, reproductive hygiene, and safe sex (Goli, 2016; UNICEF, 2019).

A lack of awareness may raise the likelihood of experiencing health concerns, as well as the possibility of being exploited, abused, or subjected to violence (Raj, 2010). The absence of sex education may result in teenage pregnancy and childbirth at a younger age. It is not uncommon for family members to offer assistance during pregnancy and the first few weeks or months following childbirth, but, in the long run, it is not possible to completely depend on the support of family members (Roest, 2016).

Possibility of Higher Education

Young brides were very rarely sent to higher education institutions, and their right to education was denied (Goli, 2016; Roest, 2016; UNICEF, 2019). In rare instances, if they were sent for higher education, they were still obligated to fulfill their other commitments, including to take care of her spouse, in-laws, and family elder, do the domestic responsibilities, and focus on her education (Goli, 2016). If the young bride also became a teen mother, it was required of her to take care of the child while also making sure that she fulfilled all of her other obligations (Goli, 2016; Roest, 2016; UNICEF, 2019). Or, she was expected to give up her schooling in most instances to nurture the pregnancy and then later take care of the child.

Child brides were not given the opportunity to adjust, but they were pushed to adapt soon. In reality, the little girl's dreams were ripped away, and she was frequently forced to leave home in the name of marriage, only to fulfill her family obligations by taking care of the in-law's house. She was denied the right to agree in all parts of her life, and her individuality was dismissed at every turn (Goli, 2016).

3.3 Organizational Factors

There is a growing awareness on a global scale regarding the need to eradicate the prevalence of early marriage, even though it continues to be a deeply ingrained custom in certain places, particularly in India. According to Gausman et al. (2024), it is estimated that more than 33 percent of girls in developing countries will get married before they reach the age of 18, and 11 percent of girls will get married before they turn 15 years old. This is despite the fact that there is widespread dedication to eliminating child marriage, and around 14.2 million women worldwide are married every year, with up to 39,000 young women being married every day.

The practice of child marriage is still widespread in South Asia, where more than half of girls and women (46 percent) report having been married before reaching the age of 18 (Subramanee et al., 2022). The highest rates of child marriage are found in Niger and Chad, with 75% and 72% of girls being married off, respectively. Whereas the overall incidence in South Asia is 46%, which is greater than the rate of 37% in Sub-Saharan Africa, South Asia has a higher overall incidence. Furthermore, India has the largest number of child brides among all nations in the world (United Nations Fund for Population Activities, 2012). This is despite the fact that Bangladesh has a greater rate of early marriage, which is 66 percent, compared to India's 47 percent. For this reason, various stakeholders must work together with communities and organizations to achieve the goal of preventing child marriage. It is possible to accomplish this by ensuring that cases of child marriage that require protection are identified and referred to appropriate authorities promptly. In the absence of the implementation of a comprehensive strategy to address the repeated practices listed above, girls will continue to be excluded from the development agenda promoted by a multitude of organizations, and they will be unable to attain their full potential.

While it is acknowledged that altering long-standing standards can be difficult and gradual, there have been observable indications of incremental improvements aimed at enhancing girls' lives (Gausman et al., 2024). To fully address this topic, it is vital to implement a cooperative strategy that includes the engagement of communities, governments, medical professionals, non-governmental organizations (NGOs), and families. This participation is necessary to adequately address this matter. The enhancement of educational opportunities for girls, the empowerment of families through the implementation of economic aid programs, and the dissemination of information regarding the negative impacts of child marriage are all potential steps in this direction. By working together, these important participants have the potential to create an environment that is conducive to the protection of the rights and welfare of girls in India as well as the advancement of gender parity (Murphy-Graham & Lloyd, 2015; Porter, 2016).

3.4 Community Factors

In India, the practice of marrying girls at an early age, generally before they reach the age of 18, is commonly attributed to the rigorous societal norms that are prevalent in the country. As a result of the widespread stigma that is attached to engaging in sexual behavior outside of marriage (Gopal, 2021), the likelihood of being unmarried is increased. According to UNFPA-UNICEF (2022), India is responsible for thirty percent of all early marriages worldwide. As published by IIPS and ICF (2022), the average age of first marriage in India has climbed from 17.4 to 19 years between 2005-2006 and 2015-2016. This represents a significant increase from the previous age of 17.4 years.

Due to the ever-increasing costs involved with dowries, parents who have a lower socioeconomic level are more likely to arrange early marriages for their daughters (Paul, 2020). This is another reason why early marriages are more common among their daughters. According to the most recent National Family Health Survey 5 (UNFPA-UNICEF, 2022) the rate of early marriage among those aged 20 to 24 has dramatically fallen, going from 47 percent in 2005 to 23 percent in 2019-2021. This represents a significant decline. Despite the fact that the rate of early marriage is decreasing, it is still rather high, especially among those who are economically disadvantaged, those who are in the lowest income bracket, rural areas, and those who are experiencing population expansion (Wodon et al., 2017).

In a survey conducted by the National Family Health (2021), it became apparent that girls who married at a young age saw a gradual decrease in their overall level of contentment with their lives. This reduction was observable even before they were married and persisted until they reached the age of 22. However, there was no evidence to suggest that being married at a young age has a direct negative impact on the total level of satisfaction one experiences. Patterns of deprivation that began in early childhood were tied to the complex relationship between early marriage and life satisfaction. The intricate relationship between early marriage and patterns of deprivation has significant implications for the health of young women, as evidenced by research conducted by Gausman et al. (2024) and the National Family Health Survey (2021). This study also found that early marriage had a negative impact on women's subjective health and academic educational achievement.

The prevalence of child marriage is driven by deeply rooted patriarchal traditions as well as gender imbalances in society (Lobenstine, 2015). Within the context of these standards, the interests of men are typically accorded a higher level of importance than those of women and girls. The pattern of child marriage is perpetuated by the influence of traditional practices and societal norms regarding marriage, gender roles, and family reputation. Therefore, these factors have an effect on the standards that are passed down from generation to generation. Intergenerational norms that are related to child marriage are significantly impacted by social norms, which are of utmost importance. It is common for these cultural practices to be passed down from one generation to the next in communities where child marriage is prevalent. This can lead to a lack of informed decision-making and the normalization of early marriage as a societal norm (Seth et al., 2018).

Following customary marital customs, such as paying dowries, helps parents and their kids avoid social disapproval (Parsons et al., 2015; Singh & Vennam, 2016). According to Santhya et al. (2010), a meagre dowry might lessen a girl's prestige, which in turn can further diminish a girl's authority over resources because early marriage and dowry systems are intimately related to one another. Studies have also demonstrated that early marriage can further exacerbate the already elevated risk of violence against women (Fan & Koski, 2022; Speizer & Pearson, 2011; Yount, Krause & Miedema, 2017). Hence, there is a direct connection between the two, as getting married at a younger age is connected with an increased risk of experiencing physical violence.

3.5. Policy Factors

In India, a considerable proportion of girls are subjected to marriage before the age of 18 years. According to UNICEF (2020), one in five girls is married before she reaches 18 years, leaving them ill-equipped to handle the challenges of married life and depriving them of opportunities for growth and development. To address this issue, it is critical to focus on education, awareness, and combating gender discrimination.

Several societal factors, such as poverty, are likely to contribute to early marriage and its impact on mental health. A review by Burgess et al. (2022) states that the mental health consequences of child marriage include depression, psychological distress, stress, suicidality, substance misuse, and other mental disorders and symptoms. Children of early marriage are likely to exhibit depressive symptoms, suicidal thoughts, and attempts (Aggarwal et al., 2023). The possibility of experiencing abuse, sexual violence, and intimate partner violence can worsen one's mental health. While physical and sexual violence perpetrated among married women is closely linked to depressive disorders and attempted suicide, the risks are likely greater for young girls, given the limited resources (Aggarwal et al., 2023).

The recently published fifth edition of the National Family Health Survey (2019-2021) reveals a decline in the prevalence of child marriage from 26.8% in 2015-16 to 23.3% in 2019-21. The Sustainable Development Goals (SDG) of the United Nations aim to eliminate harmful practices such as child labour, early and forced marriage, and genital mutilation by 2030. To this end, 193 countries have pledged to end child marriages by that year. However, the SDG's objective of eliminating child marriage by 2030 seems unlikely without determined efforts by government, stakeholders, and society. Urgent action is therefore necessary to achieve this goal.

Current Policies and Initiatives

In International Law, according to Article 1 of the Convention on the Rights of the Child, 1989, a child is defined as an individual below the age of 18 years. The Convention on the Elimination of All Forms of Discrimination Against Women (CEDAW), 1979, has established explicit provisions to combat child marriage. It is noteworthy that India has entered reservations on Article 5, which concerns cultural and traditional practices that unjustly discriminate against women, and Article 16 of the CEDAW, which governs the marriages of a child and the mandatory registration of marriages.

The Child Marriage Restraint Act (CMRA) was introduced in 1929 and later replaced by the Prohibition of Child Marriage Act in 2006 in India to put an end to the customary practice of child marriage. Over the years, the Act has undergone several changes, mainly aimed at the increasing age of minors. The minimum age limit for males and females has increased to 21 years and 18 years, respectively. Subsequent amendments have been made to the Hindu Marriage Act of 1955 and the Indian Christian Marriage Restraint Act of 1872 (Bhat et al., 2005, p. 195-196).

The Act primarily emphasises the minor or child category and outlines the punishment for parties involved in child marriage practices. However, it fails to address several concerns faced by children (Banerjee & Sharma, 2022; Goli, 2016; Bhat et al., 2005). There have also been instances of using child marriage as a facade for trafficking for prostitution, as documented in places like Andhra Pradesh (Bhat et al., 2005). The vagueness of the Act leaves the police feeling helpless, either not having the power to prevent such marriages from happening or not being able to file such cases under the CMRA. It is unfortunate that the penalisation for child marriage, as prescribed by this Act, is only three months (Bhat et al., 2005, p. 41-42). While the steps taken by this Act are noteworthy, several concerns still need to be addressed to eradicate the practice of child marriage in India.

The Prevention of Child Marriage Act (2006) was enacted to address the loopholes of the CMRA and prevent the solemnisation of child marriages. The Act deals with all matters related to child marriage, such as increasing the age for men and women to 21 years and 18 years, respectively. This amendment brings clarity to instances where a child marriage will be void, the maintenance provided to the women/wives, the custody and maintenance of the children of these child marriages, the Power of the District Court to modify orders, punishment if males consenting to marry a child and for those who solemnise the child marriage, and the assignment of Child Marriage Prevention Officers (Bhat et al., 2005, p, 241 - 249). The Protection of Children from Sexual Offences (POCSO) Act, 2012, was implemented to protect children from all forms of sexual offences. The change in the minimum age of marriage ensures that it can no longer be used as an excuse for any form of sexual activity.

3.6 Societal Factors

India is a country of diverse cultures, customs, and rituals, and as such, it plays a significant role in the practice of child marriage. Although the practice of child marriages dates back to the 19th century, it is still prevalent in modern India, influenced by various social, cultural, and economic factors. In a region that has witnessed a high incidence of female infanticide, the birth of a girl child often did not receive the same allocades as that of a boy child (Aggarwal et al., 2023). In many cases, girl children were viewed as a financial burden on their families, as parents were required to pay a dowry to the groom's family when their daughter married (Banerjee & Sharma, 2022). This often resulted in families spending most of their savings on dowry payments, perpetuating a vicious cycle of poverty. On the other hand, male children were seen as an asset that would bring in more revenue and offer hope of saving the family from dowry and poverty.

India's status as a developing country means that most households fall within the low and middle-income categories. This leaves them with limited resources and opportunities to invest in alternative options for girls. Consequently, parents may view their daughters as an economic burden, leading them to assess the costs and benefits of marriage and decide to marry their daughters early (Banerjee & Sharma, 2022). This is one of the leading causes of early marriage, which occurs before the legal age of 18 years.

The practice of child marriage, which is still prevalent in some parts of India, dictated that the younger the child, the less dowry would be paid. This resulted in early marriage for girls, often before they reached puberty, to reduce dowry payments. Girls who were educated or older were expected to bring more dowry, leading to the practice of marrying them off at a young age to avoid paying a higher dowry (Banerjee & Sharma, 2022). This led to a situation where girls were deprived of education, work, and the opportunity to marry at an age that coincides with the onset of emotional and sexual development (Paul, 2020).

Marriage during adolescence can be life-altering and overwhelming, placing girls in the roles and responsibilities of a married woman, which can be challenging to handle. Being thrust into the duties of a wife, daughter-in-law, and often, a mother can have severe repercussions on the mother and the child's mental health. Studies have shown that adolescents who marry early are more likely to exhibit symptoms of depression and more likely to attempt suicide (Aggarwal et al., 2023) and have an increased possibility of experiencing some form of gender-based oppression, such as spousal or family violence (Raj, 2010). It can be challenging for these child brides to address the needs of their own children, given that they are still children themselves.

The practice of early marriage deprives girls of opportunities, perpetuating dependency and the lack of self-sufficiency, leading to a situation where girls turn to early marriages to survive poor conditions (Raj, 2010). It creates a vicious cycle difficult to break without access to education and employment opportunities. Higher levels of education are associated with lower rates of child marriage. However, girls in India have limited access to education and employment opportunities, making it challenging to break the cycle of early marriage (Banerjee & Sharma, 2022). Parental illiteracy and lack of awareness also promote child marriage, as parents with low levels of education may be unaware of the negative consequences of child marriage on their daughters (Paul, 2020).

Child marriage is prevalent in rural India, where 75% of all married children come from, with 57% being young girls (Child Rights and You, 2020). Some communities view child marriage as a social tradition or significant custom, which perpetuates the practice. Factors include the ease of finding a groom when girls are young (66%), their adaptability to marital life when younger (57%), requiring less dowry when younger (57%) and requiring less dowry when younger and less educated (50%) contribute to the continuation of early marriage. Another contributing factor is the peer and relative pressure for marriage (41%) (Child Rights and You, 2020, pg. 38). It becomes evident that the issue of child marriage in India is a complex one that is influenced by various factors. Addressing these factors requires a multifaceted approach that addresses the economic, social, and cultural issues behind the practice of child marriage.

4. FUTURE IMPLICATION

It is essential to address the intricate and multifaceted factors that contribute to early child marriage. For the various influences that perpetuate this practice, solutions must be comprehensive and tailored to address the concerns on both individual and societal levels. Effective awareness campaigns targeted at educating parents about the negative consequences of child marriage are essential. Besides the consequences, people must be aware of the existing policies and schemes that aim to reduce the prevalence of early marriage, reduce education costs, and encourage children to stay in school. Community-based interventions to address the factors that enable poor mental health and early marriage need to be further explored (Burgess et al., 2022). In addition, promoting awareness of government initiatives that support education and employment opportunities may help reduce child marriage rates. While initiatives and policies are valuable, it would be beneficial to involve the community, law enforcement, and even religious leaders to educate others about the consequences of this practice (Raj, 2010). Ensuring that girls remain in school and have access to education is also a viable strategy to prevent child marriage. Efforts aimed at reducing poverty and social inequality are also vital to eliminating child marriages.

Improving child protection mechanisms in rural areas is crucial to preventing child marriage. Encouraging discussions and imparting education about sexual and reproductive health at the village level can also be effective in this regard. We must protect informants who report such cases to tackle the underreporting of early marriages. The mentality towards girl children and early marriage has shifted significantly over the last few decades. Advocacy for change and efforts to educate the masses on the ill effects of early marriage on girls and their children have contributed to the realization that a girl is also an asset. Providing girls access to education and employment opportunities has facilitated society's development by utilizing their skills and resources, reducing poverty, and improving the quality of life for all.

5. CONCLUSION

India is still plagued by the issue of child marriage, which is a widespread problem that persists due to societal standards, financial restrictions, and a complex link with dowry systems. As a result of the fact that rigid societal rules typically give preference to the welfare of males, the custom of early marriage for females is still maintained. As a result, families from lower socioeconomic backgrounds are more likely to arrange early marriage for their daughters, in addition to the financial pressure dowries place on them. Even though there has been a little increase in the average age at which girls get married, this trend has a stronger impact on girls who live in areas that are economically disadvantaged and rural. In addition, it has significant repercussions for the lives of young women, and it has a negative impact on their academic performance, their personal well-being, and their general level of pleasure. Furthermore, some data implies a correlation between getting married at a young age and an increased chance of violence against women.

In conclusion, child marriage is a significant concern, with approximately one in five girls being forced into such unions, as per UNICEF's 2020 report. The likelihood of adolescent girls becoming parents is high, which can have harmful effects on a child's well-being and girls' health. Achieving Target 5.3 of the Sustainable Development Goals (SDGs) and eliminating child marriage by 2030 necessitates identifying and addressing the factors that enable this practice to prevail in our communities. It is evident that the rates of child marriage have reduced over time, and this reduction is due to the policies and social norms in place; however, there is still a collective responsibility to ensure further decline and ultimately eradicate this harmful practice.

REFERENCES

Aggarwal, S., Francis, K. L., Dashti, G. S., & Patton, G. (2023). Child marriage and the mental health of adolescent girls: A longitudinal cohort study from Uttar Pradesh and Bihar, India. *The Lancet Regional Health. Southeast Asia*, 8, 100102. Advance online publication. DOI: 10.1016/j.lansea.2022.100102 PMID: 37384140

Atim, G. (2017). Girls not brides: ending child marriage in Nigeria. *Journal of Gender, Information and Development in Africa (JGIDA)*, 6(1-2), 73-94. https://www.proquest.com/openview/ba3526799a9961e3b8243b1200c96759/1?pq-origsite=gscholar&cbl=2044835

Banerjee, S., & Sharma, G. (2022). The Status of Child Marriage in India: A Guide for NGOs and CSOs on Using the Law to End Child Marriages in India*. Girls Not Brides. https://www.girlsnotbrides.org/documents/1783/Child_marriage_in_India_law_guide_and_directory.pdf

Berg, M. J., Kremelberg, D., Dwivedi, P., Verma, S., Schensul, J. J., Gupta, K., Chandran, D., & Singh, S. K. (2010). The effects of husband's alcohol consumption on married women in three low-income areas of greater Mumbai. *AIDS and Behavior*, 14(S1), 126–135. DOI: 10.1007/s10461-010-9735-7 PMID: 20544380

Bhabha, J., & Kelly, O. (2013). Child marriage and the right to education: evidence from India. Evidence submitted to the Office of High Commission of Human Rights. University of Harvard, 72-80. https://www.ohchr.org/sites/default/files/Documents/Issues/Women/WRGS/ForcedMarriage/NGO/HavardUniversityFXB3.pdf

Bhat, A., Sen, A., & Pradhan, U. (2005). *Child marriages and the law in India*. Human Rights Law Network.

Burgess, R. A., Jeffery, M., Odero, S. A., Rose-Clarke, K., & Devakumar, D. (2022). Overlooked and unaddressed: A narrative review of mental health consequences of child marriages. *PLOS Global Public Health*, 2(1), 1–21. DOI: 10.1371/journal.pgph.0000131 PMID: 36962120

Child Rights You. (2020). Status and Decadal Trends of Child Marriage in India. New Delhi: Child Rights and You. https://www.cry.org/downloads/safety-and-protection/Status-of-Child-Marriage-In-The-Last-Decade.pdf

Datta, B., Tiwari, A., & Glenn, L. (2022). Stolen childhood taking a toll at young adulthood: The higher risk of high blood pressure and high blood glucose comorbidity among child brides. *PLOS Global Public Health*, 2(6), e0000638. DOI: 10.1371/journal.pgph.0000638 PMID: 36962354

EP. A. A., & Poonia, A. (2015). Determinants, attitudes and practices on child marriage: Evidences from rural Rajasthan. *Social Work Chronicle, 4*(1). https://www.proquest.com/docview/1738729327?pq-origsite=gscholar&fromopenview=true&sourcetype=Scholarly%20Journals

Erickson, P. J., Cermak, A., Michaels, C., Blake, L., Lynn, A., Greylord, T., & Benning, S. (2024). Mental health and well-being ecological model. Center for Leadership Education in Maternal & Child Public Health, University of Minnesota–Twin Cities. https://mch.umn.edu/resources/mhecomodel

Fan, S., & Koski, A. (2022). The health consequences of child marriage: A systematic review of the evidence. *BMC Public Health*, 22(1), 309. DOI: 10.1186/s12889-022-12707-x PMID: 35164724

Gausman, J., Kim, R., Kumar, A., Ravi, S., & Subramanian, S. V. (2024). Prevalence of girl and boy child marriage across states and Union Territories in India, 1993–2021: A repeated cross-sectional study. *The Lancet. Global Health*, 12(2), e271–e281. DOI: 10.1016/S2214-109X(23)00470-9 PMID: 38109909

Ghosh, B., & Kar, A. M. (2010). Child marriage in rural West Bengal: Status and challenges. *Indian Journal of Development Research and Social Action*, 6(1-2), 1–23. https://www.researchgate.net/profile/Biswajit-Ghosh-3/publication/235624523_Child_marriage_in_Rural_West_Bengal_Status_and_Challenges%27/links/00b7d51be61ac1ef82000000/Child-marriage-in-Rural-West-Bengal-Status-and-Challenges.pdf

Goli, S. (2016). Eliminating child marriages in India: Progress and prospects. https://api.research-repository.uwa.edu.au/ws/portalfiles/portal/58285434/EliminatingChildMarriageReport_e_Book.pdf

Gopal, M. (2021). Early and child marriage in India: A framework to achieve SDGs. In *Encyclopedia of the UN sustainable development goals* (pp. 183–191). DOI: 10.1007/978-3-319-95687-9_109

IIPS and ICF. (2022). *India National Family Health Survey NFHS-5 (2019-21)*. Mumbai, India: IIPS and ICF. Retrieved from https://www.dhsprogram.com/pubs/pdf/FR375/FR375.pdf

Kumar, A. (2011). Mental health services in rural India: Challenges and prospects. *Health (Irvine, Calif.)*, 3(12), 757–761. https://papers.ssrn.com/sol3/papers.cfm?abstract_id=1978314. DOI: 10.4236/health.2011.312126

Lobenstine, D. (Ed.). (2015). *Early and Child Marriage in India: A Landscape Analysis*. Nirantar Trust.

Murphy-Graham, E., & Lloyd, C. (2015). Empowering adolescent girls in developing countries: The potential role of education. *Policy Futures in Education*, 14(5), 556–577. DOI: 10.1177/1478210315610257

Nour, N. M. (2006). Health consequences of child marriage in Africa. *Emerging Infectious Diseases*, 12(11), 1644–1649. DOI: 10.3201/eid1211.060510 PMID: 17283612

Osakinle, E., & Tayo-Olajubutu, O. (2017). Child marriage and health consequences in Nigeria. *American Scientific Research Journal for Engineering, Technology, and Sciences (ASRJETS)*, 30(1), 351-356. https://core.ac.uk/download/pdf/235050181.pdf

Parsons, J., Edmeades, J. D., Kes, A., Petroni, S., Sexton, M. W., & Wodon, Q. (2015). Economic Impacts of Child Marriage: A Review of the Literature. *The Review of Faith & International Affairs*, 13(3), 12–22. DOI: 10.1080/15570274.2015.1075757

Patowari, P., Huirem, R., & Loganathan, K. (2019). The Paradoxical Problem of Child Marriage in India. *Department of Social Work, 10*(1), 117. http://www.aus.ac.in/social-work-department/wp-content/uploads/sites/15/2021/02/Vol-10_No-1_Social-Work-Journal.pdf#page=118

Paul, P. (2020). Child Marriage Among Girls in India: Prevalence, Trends and Socio-Economic Correlates. *Indian Journal of Human Development*, 14(2), 304–319. DOI: 10.1177/0973703020950263

Paul, P., & Mondal, D. (2020). Child marriage in India: A human rights violation during the COVID-19 pandemic. *Asia-Pacific Journal of Public Health*, 33(1), 162–163. DOI: 10.1177/1010539520975292 PMID: 33233942

Porter, S. A. (2016). Girls' education, development and social change. *Policy Futures in Education*, 14(5), 517–538. DOI: 10.1177/1478210315625904

Pourtaheri, A., Mahdizadeh, M., Tehrani, H., Jamali, J., & Peyman, N. (2024). Socio-ecological factors of girl child marriage: A meta-synthesis of qualitative research. *BMC Public Health*, 24(428), 1–23. DOI: 10.1186/s12889-023-17626-z PMID: 38341573

Putri, U. F. W., Prasetyo, B., & Salim, L. A. (2022). Causes of Early Marriage on Socio-Ecological Levels. *Budapest International Research and Critics Institute-Journal*, 5(3), 18869–18876. DOI: 10.33258/birci.v5i3.5884

Raj, A. (2010). When the mother is a child: The impact of child marriage on the health and human rights of girls. *Archives of Disease in Childhood*, 95(11), 931–935. DOI: 10.1136/adc.2009.178707 PMID: 20930011

Reupert, A. (2017). A socio-ecological framework for mental health and well-being. *Advances in Mental Health Promotion. Advances in Mental Health*, 15(2), 105–107. DOI: 10.1080/18387357.2017.1342902

Roest, J. (2016). Child marriage and early child-bearing in India: Risk factors and policy implications. *Young Lives Policy Paper, 10*, 12-34. https://www.younglives-india.org/sites/default/files/syndicated/YL-PolicyPaper-10-Sep16_0.pdf

Santhya, K. G., Ram, U., Acharya, R., Jejeebhoy, S. J., Ram, F., & Singh, A. (2010). Associations between early marriage and young women's marital and reproductive health outcomes: Evidence from India. *International Perspectives on Sexual and Reproductive Health*, 36(3), 132–139. DOI: 10.1363/3613210 PMID: 20880798

Seth, R., Bose, V., Qaiyum, Y., Chandrashekhar, R., Kansal, S., Taneja, I., & Seth, T. (2018). Social determinants of child marriage in rural India. *the Ochsner Journal, 18*(4), 390–394. DOI: 10.31486/toj.18.0104

Singh, P., Pattanaik, F., & Singh, A. (2023). Beyond the Clock: Exploring the Complexities of Women's Domestic Roles in India Through the Lenses of Daughters and Daughters-in-Law. *The Indian Journal of Labour Economics : the Quarterly Journal of the Indian Society of Labour Economics*, 66(2), 535–559. DOI: 10.1007/s41027-023-00441-w

Singh, R., & Vennam, U. (2016). Factors shaping trajectories to child and early marriage: Evidence from Young Lives in India. https://ora.ox.ac.uk/objects/uuid:14005c76-8e23-4817-b74f-64578861af18/download_file?safe_filename=YL-WP149-Trajectories%2Bto%2Bearly%2BMarriage.pdf&file_format=application%2Fpdf&type_of_work=General+item

Souza, M. T. D., Silva, M. D. D., & Carvalho, R. D. (2010). Integrative review: What is it? How to do it? *Einstein (Sao Paulo, Brazil)*, 8(1), 102–106. DOI: 10.1590/s1679-45082010rw1134 PMID: 26761761

Speizer, I. S., & Pearson, E. (2011). Association between early marriage and intimate partner violence in India: A focus on youth from Bihar and Rajasthan. *Journal of Interpersonal Violence*, 26(10), 1963–1981. DOI: 10.1177/0886260510372947 PMID: 20587462

Subramanee, S. D., Agho, K., Lakshmi, J., Huda, M. N., Joshi, R., & Akombi-Inyang, B. (2022). Child Marriage in South Asia: A Systematic review. *International Journal of Environmental Research and Public Health*, 19(22), 15138. DOI: 10.3390/ijerph192215138 PMID: 36429857

Tripathi, N., & Sekher, T. V. (2013). Youth in India ready for sex education? Emerging evidence from national surveys. *PLoS One*, 8(8), e71584. DOI: 10.1371/journal.pone.0071584 PMID: 23951197

Uddin, M. E. (2015). Family socio-cultural values affecting early marriage between Muslim and Santal communities in rural Bangladesh. *The International Journal of Sociology and Social Policy*, 35(3/4), 141–164. DOI: 10.1108/IJSSP-06-2014-0046

Uddin, M. E. (2017). Family demographic mechanisms linking of socioeconomic status to subjective physical health in rural Bangladesh. *Social Indicators Research*, 130(3), 1263–1279. DOI: 10.1007/s11205-015-1209-x

Uddin, M. E. (2021). Teenage marriage and high school dropout among poor girls: A narrative review for family pathways in Bangladesh. *Journal of Research in Social Sciences and Language*, 1(1), 55–76.

UNFPA. (2022). *Taking the Field Forward: Investing in Knowledge to End Child Marriage*. UNFPA-UNICEF. Retrieved May 7, 2024 from https://www.unicef.org/documents/child-marriage-publication-catalogue-2020-2021

UNICEF. (2012). *Latest trends and future prospects Child Marriage*. UNICEF.

UNICEF. (2019). Child Marriage IN South Asia: An Evidence Review. New York: UNICEF. Downloaded from http://digitalrepository.fccollege.edu.pk/bitstream/123456789/949/1/Child%20marriage%20in%20south%20asia%20An%20Evidence%20Review.pdf

UNICEF. (2020). Child Marriage. New York: UNICEF. Downloaded from https://www.unicef.org/protection/child-marriage

United Nations Fund for Population Activities. (2012). Marrying too young: end child marriage. UNFPA. Retrieved on May 6, 2024, from https://www.unfpa.org/publications/marrying-too-young

Wodon, Q., Malé, C., Nayihouba, K. A., Onagoruwa, A. O., Savadogo, A., Yedan, A., Edmeades, J., Kes, A., John, N., Murithi, L., Steinhaus, M., & Petroni, S. (2017). Economic impacts of child marriage: global synthesis report. *MINISTERIO DE EDUCACIÓN*, 1–99.

Yount, K. M., Krause, K. H., & Miedema, S. S. (2017). Preventing gender-based violence victimization in adolescent girls in lower-income countries: Systematic review of reviews. *Social science & medicine (1982)*, *192*, 1–13. DOI: 10.1016/j.socscimed.2017.08.038

Chapter 7
Mental Health Impact of Early Marriage:
Exploring the Psychological Consequences of Early Marriage

Mohit Yadav
https://orcid.org/0000-0002-9341-2527
O.P. Jindal Global University, India

Ajay Chandel
https://orcid.org/0000-0002-4585-6406
Lovely Professional University, India

Ta Huy Hung
https://orcid.org/0009-0008-6835-3036
Vietnam National University, Hanoi, Vietnam

ABSTRACT

Early marriage poses significant psychological and societal challenges, impacting both individuals and communities worldwide. This abstract examines the mental health consequences of early marriage, including depression, anxiety, and PTSD. It explores the cultural and societal contexts that perpetuate early marriage, emphasizing the roles of traditional norms, gender inequality, and societal pressures. The intergenerational impact of early marriage is also highlighted, revealing how it affects children of young mothers and strains community resources. Effective interventions and support mechanisms, including preventive measures, psychological support, and successful case studies, are discussed. The need for comprehensive approaches that integrate education, empowerment, and policy reforms is emphasized. This analysis underscores the importance of addressing early marriage's root

DOI: 10.4018/979-8-3693-3394-5.ch007

Copyright © 2025, IGI Global Scientific Publishing. Copying or distributing in print or electronic forms without written permission of IGI Global is prohibited.

causes and implementing tailored strategies to mitigate its psychological impact.

INTRODUCTION

Early marriage, generally defined as the timing of formal or informal marital arrangement usually before the age of 18, is a global issue with very deep roots intertwined with cultural, social heritage and economic factors (Amin & Amin, 2018; Uddin, 2015). Despite social and legal measures to prevent this marriage, it is widely practiced and prevalent in many regions, particularly in South Asia, Sub-Saharan Africa, and parts of the Middle East. This common practice is justified through cultural tradition, economic reason and gender norms, as it prioritizes control over the sexuality and labor of young girls (Naghizadeh et al., 2021).

There are several global reports outlining key insights into the consequences of early marriage and then going to look at some effective interventions that will address these effects.

In a report: *Child marriage: A review of the evidence*, UNICEF (2014) and UNDP (2016) presents a thorough analysis of the prevalence and implications of child marriage, with the main focus area being its substantial impacts on mental health. It emanates that early marriage often results in increased levels of depression and anxiety among young brides through an abrupt transition from childhood to adult responsibilities, leading to social and economic pressures. UNICEF underscored the need for multi-sectoral approaches, which ranged from increased opportunities for education to increased community engagement in the fight against early marriage and for support for those who are affected. In similar vein, World Bank (2017) investigated the economic and social mental health costs of this vice. It posits that child marriage translates to less education and economic investments for the girl children, with sizeable consequences on long-term psychological and socio-economic well-being. It further calls for investments in girls' education and health services that would, in fact, help address and mitigate the impacts mentioned.

The Girls Not Brides report (2019), *Child marriage and its impact on mental health*, focuses that early marriage worsens the state of psychological distress, PTSD, and depression and the need for tailor-made interventions to support mental state. It does call for comprehensive mental health support, educational programs, and community-based initiatives of the young brides. Thus, the International Center for Research on Women (ICRW, 2014), *Child marriage and its impact on young women and girls: An evidence review*, reviews the broader consequences of early matrimony as a health, economic, and psychological outcome. In the report, it strongly contends that early marriage often heralds different mental health issues, especially anxiety and low self-esteem, and called for integrative methods that include legal frameworks, support services, and community engagement (Vettriselvan & Rajan, 2019a).

According to the World Health Organization (WHO, 2017), *Early marriage and its impact on adolescent health*, the negative health consequences of early marriage may lead to adverse mental disorders. This report states that early marriage is a risk factor for mental health disorders such as PTSD and depression and provides strong health systems with comprehensive care for affected brides. But the early marriage that has become a societal problem deprives many young people, especially girls, of their rights and choices. Among others, this problem is highlighted in the UNFPA's State of world population report, 2016: *Young people, rights and choices* (UNFPA, 2005, 2015, 2018). According to the report, early marriage practices are harmful for mental health and suggest increased options for education, health services, and legal protections for young people (Vettriselvan et al., 2019b). Taken together, all these reports point out the dire impact of early marriage on mental health and address the need for comprehensive, culturally sensitive strategies for its prevention globally.

Although a great deal of research has focused on the physical risks of early marriages, such as early pregnancy complications, childbearing, and childbirth, few studies have explained its psychological risks. This chapter explains how early marriage causes a mental health impact by contributing to the development of different psychological disorders and specifically depression, anxiety, and post-traumatic stress disorder (John et al., 2019, 2022). A standing consequence for many young girls who enter into early marriage is the abrupt ending of their childhood and initiation into adult life with grown-up responsibilities, mostly in settings where they have little resources, skills and power. This early transition to marriages can leave a heavy mental toll and may serve to provoke feelings of isolation, hopelessness, and fear. These emotional struggles are compounded by pressures of domestic duties, possible abuse, and loss of educational and social opportunities (Uecker, 2012; Uddin, 2021).

Based on narrative approach for literature review, in the chapter we attempt to deliberate on the mental health effects of early marriage—direct or indirect—contributing to depression, anxiety, and PTSD. In doing so, it also looks into the general societal and cultural contexts that continue to foster early marriage and further compound the psychological effects. This chapter also will discuss the intergenerational impact of early marriage and the mental health of the children born to these young mothers, highlighting targeted interventions and support mechanisms that could break the cycle (Taplak & Yılmaz, 2022; John et al., 2019). Understanding the impact of early marriage on mental health will help in advocating comprehensive strategies for its prevention and the provision of support to the girls affected. This chapter, however, contributes to the growing body of research that discusses these manifold challenges created by early marriage and the implications for mental health in the long run (John et al., 2019).

THEORETICAL FRAMEWORK

Developmental Theory

Developmental theory focuses on the aspect of human development and how experiences early in life set the pace for psychological development. According to Erik Erikson's theory of psychosocial development by Munley (1975), early marriage disrupts this normal developmental trajectory during childhood through adolescence. This period is a very critical phase of identity formation and establishment of autonomy. Such an early assumption into adult responsibilities may disturb emotional and cognitive development at this stage, resulting in problems such as low self-esteem and problems of identity confusion that lead to mental illnesses (Uddin, 2015, 2024). Early marriage frequently pushes young people into roles for which they are not psychologically ready and, thus, affects their healthy development and well-being.

Social Learning Theory

Albert Bandura's Social Learning Theory (2011) highlights observational learning, imitation, and modeling as the described features of behavior acquisition. The theory postulates, from an early marriage approach, that a young person might internalize and replicate the behaviors and attitudes viewed in his or her family or community. If a society or community does require early marriage as normal practices, adolescents or youths may just view the path as one that is acceptable or inevitable (McLeod, 2011). In this way, one can see how an intergenerational cycle of early marriage is reinforced. Social learning theory stresses how changing attitudes within a society and providing alternative role models can alter the extent of the practices of early marriage.

Feminist Theory

Feminist theory articulates how gender inequalities and patriarchal structures lead to early marriage practices. According to this theory, early marriage is an expression of gender power imbalance, whereby girls are seen as a property or a sure way to retain family or economic gains. The feminist view brings out how early marriage is perpetuated at the junction between gender, culture, and socio-economic factors in a community. In trying to combat gender inequality and fighting for women's rights, the feminist theory offers a framework through which we question and alter/change the systemic factors that sustain early marriage in the society.

Ecological Systems Theory

Urie Bronfenbrenner (1995) and his associates (Bronfenbrenner & Ceci, 1994; Bronfenbrenner & Evans, 2000) develops ecological systems theory to understand human development. According to Urie Bronfenbrenner's Ecological Systems Theory (1995), human development is considered as to their existence within multiple environmental systems: family, community, and societal influences. The theory postulates that early marriage is determined by interactions between individual, familial, and societal factors (Hossain & Uddin, 2023). For instance, economic pressures, cultural norms, and family dynamics all result in early marriage. The ecological systems theory calls for multi-level interventions that address factors, ranging from the individual level of support to broader societal changes (Hertler et al., 2018; Uddin, 2017).

Stress and Coping Theory

Stress and coping theory developed by R. Lazarus and S. Folkman (1984) and later S. Folkman and R. S. Lazarus (2013), describes the reactions of individuals to stress and their modes of coping. Early marriage is usually attended by heavy doses of stressors, such as financial stress, low education, and social isolation. According to this theory, the variance in abilities to cope with these stressors is contingent upon the available resources, social support, and personal resilience (Uddin, 2011). It will, therefore, be important to note the coping strategies that are currently employed by young brides, pointing out the barriers to effective coping and supportive interventions. These support systems can be designed to mitigate the psychological impact of early marriage on young girls in a particular context.

Human Rights Framework

The human rights framework spotlights core entitlements and liberties that every human being should enjoy. In consideration these, this framework adds a dimension to the analysis of early marriage with respect to children and women as a violation of rights, especially education, health, and protection from coercion (Uddin, 2021). In this view, framing early marriage as relevant to human rights means this perspective urges legal reforms, protective mechanisms, and international conventions that protect and implement the rights of early marriage-affected individuals.

Theory of Intersectionality

The theory of intersectionality, as introduced by Kimberl Crenshaw (1991), analyzes the ways in which the different social identities of a person, such as gender, class, and ethnicity, overlap to form life experiences and structural inequalities. This is an important theory toward understanding how early marriage affects an individual, because of their intersectional identities. For example, the practices and experiences of early marriage would vary across socio-economic classes or among ethnic groups. The intersectionality theory emphasizes the importance of nuanced approaches in the design of effective interventions and support systems, given all these many intersecting factors (Nishat et al., 2023).

Behavioral Economics Theory

Behavioral economics theory considers how psychological factors and cognitive biases influence decision-making and economic behavior. The theory can help explain why early marriage might be chosen by the individual or family in the face of its long-term consequences. These could be immediate economic gains, social pressures, or simply a lack of information. This will increase the fire for decisions, leading toward early marriage. The theory of behavioral economics has, therefore, put this into perspective: Through the correction of cognitive biases or the introduction of incentives and support in line with long-term well-being (Burgess et al., 2022).

The review of the frameworks provides the basis for theory that can be used to gain an in-depth understanding of causality and consequences in early marriage. Integrating insights from developmental theory, social learning theory, feminist theory, ecological theory, stress and coping theory, human rights theory, intersectionality theory, and behavioral economics theory help us understand to handle the complexities of early marriage and design more effective strategies for prevention and support. These theoretical approaches have also emphasized the necessity of multi-dimensional and culturally sensitive interventions to address and mitigate the psychological and social impacts of early marriage (Strat et al., 2011; Williams, 2003). Based on the theoretical orientations, we next explain the psychological consequences of early marriage across societies and cultures.

PSYCHOLOGICAL CONSEQUENCES OF EARLY MARRIAGE

Early marriage, mostly taking place at the adolescent stage or even before, tends to have very serious psychological impacts, which in many cases affect their mental health. An abrupt shift from child roles to adult ones, coupled with the coercively enforced nature of such marriages through culture, can only worsen the continued rise of various mental health problems. In this regard, the section will delve into three main psychological impacts of early marriage: depression, anxiety, and post-traumatic stress disorder (PTSD) (Nishat et al., 2023).

Depression

One of the most common psychological consequences of early marriage is depression characterized by being almost always sad, hopeless, and losing interest in many daily activities. The following risk factors to such depression emanating from early marriage may include:

- *Childhood loss:* Early marriage is too often an untimely end to childhood, taking off the years of formation from the individual. This transition, from schoolgirl to wife and mother, can give a sense of loss and disorientation. So, depressive symptoms can be caused (Nurfieni, 2023).
- *Social Isolation:* Social isolation experienced by a young bride not only severs connections with the peer groups but also from other known support groups. This also may lead to feelings of loneliness and can add depressive symptoms (Nishat et al., 2023).
- *Lack of Support:* Most of the time, young brides do not get the required amount of emotional and psychological support to sustain their new roles. Isolation from family support and limited access to mental health can fasten their depressive attitudes.
- *Economic Stress:* Most of the early marriages are marked by financial insecurities, which may create more stress and striking feelings of inadequacy and hopelessness. Wanting to contribute economically while maintaining home life can sometimes be an overwhelming burden of stressors (Nishat et al., 2023).
- *Case Studies and Statistical Evidence:* It has been found that the age of marriage is significantly associated with depression level. A study conducted in India reveals that young brides have significantly higher levels of depressive symptom than their age group who get married at an older age (Nurfieni, 2023).

Anxiety

Anxiety disorder is another psychological impact of early marriage. The following are the factors that create more anxiety among young brides:

- *Uncertainty about the Future:* Early marriage can bring with it many unknowns about the future, concerning fiscal stability, career growth, and personal well-being. This is an attribute that may be significantly responsible for anxiety (Handayani et al., 2021).
- *Fear of Failure*: An array of responsibilities is thrust on them at a very tender age that should make them behave like adults, which can instil the fear of failures. A young bride may experience fears concerning the successful performance of her roles as a wife and family member in the eyes of her husband and her family respectively (Nishat et al., 2023). This situation creates a fear of failure in the family life.
- *Marital Pressures:* Young brides in marriage relationships feel burdened to perform as wives and mothers. These expectations, in addition to compliance with traditional gender roles and meeting family expectations raise and elevate the level of anxiety at individual level (Itebiye, 2016).
- *Inability to Cope:* Adolescents have less developed coping mechanisms through which they are unable to adapt and adjust to the stressors of early marriage. This lack of coping skills can make it very hard for them to handle their anxiety effectively.
- *Affecting Daily Life:* Anxiety badly affects the daily life routine of a young bride. For this reason, she cannot take part in social events, perform housework, and maintain personal relationships. This can turn them into a vicious cycle of increased stress and lower levels of well-being.
- *Coping Mechanisms and Lack Thereof:* The absence of healthy coping mechanisms and support systems induces high anxiety. The reason many young brides have limited access to mental health resources and support networks is that they lack the tools to help them overcome their anxiety (Itebiye, 2016).

Post-Traumatic Stress Disorder (PTSD)

PTSD could manifest after traumatization or witnessing such traumatizing events, which early marriage is often associated with. The following are some of the facets that may lead to PTSD due to early marriage:

- *Traumatic Experiences:* Early marriages, especially forced or vastly abusive, can be traumatizing. Sexual violence, domestic abuse and coerced experiences can lead to the development of PTSD in marital relationships (Nishat et al., 2023).
- *Symptoms of PTSD:* They can be found in the form of intrusive thoughts, flashbacks, nightmares, hypervigilance, alarms, and avoid reminders of the

traumatic event. These symptoms due to early marriage can hugely and deeply impair the mental health and functioning very severely of a young bride.
- *Long term effects:* Untreated PTSD can lead to chronic anxiety, depression, and difficulty in establishing healthy relations.
- *Lack of Treatment:* Young brides, especially from low-resource settings, often lack access to mental health services and trauma-informed care. The lack of appropriate treatment can perpetuate the effects of PTSD and hinder recovery (Nurfieni, 2023).
- *Case Studies and Evidence:* A history of forced or abusive early marriage has shown to increase the risk for PTSD through studies. For example, studies have found high levels of PTSD in young girls who were exposed to early and forced marriage across the world in conflict zones.

The psychological effects of early marriage mentioned are severe and complicated; they cause depression, anxiety, and PTSD. All these are linked to sudden loss of childhood, social isolation, a lack of a support system, and the trauma one goes through. These are very crucial aspects that should be realized in the search for effective interventions and support mechanisms for such patients. An all-inclusive approach to the mental health implications of early marriage would require prevention through education added to the provision of mental health services (Handayani et al., 2021).

EARLY MARRIAGE AND MENTAL HEALTH IN SOCIETAL AND CULTURAL CONTEXTS

The psychological effects of early marriage can somehow not be understood without considering the larger societal and cultural contexts that keep such practice going and on the other hand normalizes it. These broader contexts widely produce mental health outcomes in an early marriage. The following section explains the cultural norms, gender inequalities, societal pressures, and others that lead to the prevalence of early marriage and contribute to aggravating the psychological impact of the early marriage (Nurfieni, 2023; Uddin, 2015).

Cultural Norms and Expectations

Also, cultural norms and traditions boost the early marriage phenomenon quite strongly. Often it will be a particular age that this involves and therefore expectations that should be levied on younger brides (Uddin, 2015). Early marriage viewed as an issue of cultural tradition and thus goes unchallenged in most societies and cultures.

There are cultural beliefs that are put on considerations on the age at which marriage should start and the role of the woman. In some communities, early marriage is perceived as the only way to keep the bloodline of the family intact and continue culture (Liang & Chikritzhs, 2011; Uddin, 2008, 2009).

- *Social Acceptance:* As social acceptance of early marriage starts taking prevalence, there is a Mexican wave in the perception that little or no need for reform. With normalization of these marriages, it becomes quite impossible for one to want to seek help or even speak about the impacts of the same. The feeling of everyone doing it and, therefore, the 'I should conform for acceptance' will easily shut up any campaigner for change (Itebiye, 2016).
- *Mental Health Impact:* Cultural norms often exert so much pressure that they trigger severe mental health stress. The mental pressure between following one's desires and those dictated by society may lead to one's feelings of guilt, anxiety, and depressive emotions. Even young brides can suffer severe mental health problems if there are, in other cultural settings, no other alternatives to overcome or no other role to offer for them (Iustitiani & Ajisuksmo, 2018).
- *Gender Inequality*: Gender-based inconsistencies form the very core of the rationale behind early marriages and play a pivotal role in the alarming mental health conditions faced by young brides (Uddin et al., 2019). This imbalance of gendered power and resource distribution are inherently meant to take various forms, which, in the long run, impact how the psychological state of common people is catered to, particularly young girls.
- *Power Dynamics:* Child marriage often upholds patriarchal structures of power in which the young brides are subject to the authority and control them by their husbands and in-laws. Such power dynamics can trigger their feelings of helplessness and low esteem, which can actually fester into mental health issues such as depression and anxiety among the young brides (Handayani et al., 2021).
- *Limited Autonomy:* Women who marry at an extremely early ages often have very little autonomy and decisional power. Losing control over life and decisions can quickly lead to frustration and feelings of powerlessness. This could result in a limitation of personal agency that has serious psychological implications, such as anxiety and depressive symptoms (Nishat et al., 2023).
- *Gender-Based Violence:* Child marriage is often tied to increased gender-based violence, which can include not only domestic violence but also sexual abuse. This can also play a vital role in potentially causing PTSD and other psychological conditions. Violence that is normalized under certain cultural and social contexts complicates addressing and treating the potential psychological aftermath of pervasive exposure among young girls (Nurfieni, 2023).

- *Educational and Economic Disparities:* Gender inequality associated with early marriage is often the cause of lower education and economic dependency on men for young brides. The poor educational attainment and financial dependency is linked to a life of poverty and mental suffering among young brides (Uddin, 2021). Such disparities might enhance a feeling of helplessness and contribute to long-term mental health problems.
- *Social Pressure to Conform:* Societal pressure in trying to conform to traditional practices and roles could bring a sense of obligation in an individual, thus limiting their freedom to make decisions on a personal basis. It is a very pressure that can bring about the stress, anxiety, and feelings of inadequacy in young brides if they fail to meet the societal expectations across cultures (Itebiye, 2016).
- *Stigma and Shame:* Stigma and shame related to early marriage and its psychological consequences might be potential barriers to seeking help among young brides. There is a fear of being judged or shamed, deterring these young brides from talking about their mental health problems or seeking help for its improvements. This stigma could also have an impact on the readiness of communities to react and talk freely about the bad psychological impacts of early marriage across cultures (Iustitiani & Ajisuksmo, 2018).
- *Community Support Systems:* Community support systems for the affected girls may be weak in many cultures. There is a sense of isolation from social networks for the girls affected, which is further exacerbated by the lack of these social networks. In such situations, mental health problems of the girls increase. The absence of community-driven interventions and support also inhibits treatment of their severe mental health conditions.

The societal and cultural contexts described above are central to early marriage and its psychological implications. Cultural norms, gender inequality, and societal pressures account for the high prevalence of early marriage and its related mental health challenges faced by these young brides. These contextual issues can only be achieved through a comprehensive approach that is coupled with cultural sensitivity, gender justice, and community support. Addressing the broader societal drivers of early marriage is one of the preventive measures to ensure that the adverse psychological impact is acted upon and that the interventions are better handled for everyone involved (Nurfieni, 2023).

INTERGENERATIONAL IMPACT

Early marriage and its consequential mental health problems transmit over generations. Research shows that the psychological impacts of early marriage are not only restricted to psychological impacts that young brides undergo but also highly resonate in the subsequent generations. Intergenerational impacts of early marriage include the mental health of children born to young mothers and broader community repercussions. The next section considers these intergenerational impacts in detail (Nishat et al., 2023).

Impact on Children of Young Mothers

Children born to young mothers are usually exposed to a myriad of problems that may weigh down their minds and consequently hinder their healthy growth and development over time (Hynek et al., 2022). Based on theory and relevant literature, we found the following impact of early marriage on children.

- *Increased Health Risks:* There is an elevated risk on a baby born to young mothers, going through physical and mental health problems. Early marriage may elevate the risk of low birth weight, prematurity, and delayed development. All these health challenges can affect the emotional and psychological well-being of a child from an early stage of his or her life and have lasting effects on their psychosocial and emotional development (Itebiye, 2016).
- *Psychosocial Development*: The sociocultural contexts in which young mothers raise their children determine their children's psychosocial development over time. Given their experiences with inadequate resources, poor parenting skills, and increased stress of young parents, their children may be affected in their emotional and psychological development. Any signs of stress and instability in a young mother, therefore, lead to less support and an uninformed environment for the children (Iustitiani & Ajisuksmo, 2018).
- *Educational and Economic Disadvantages:* Educational and economic disadvantages often affect children when their mothers become very young. Usually, young mothers have little or no education or financial resources to support children to development. These poor psychosocial resources are passed on to the children in terms of access to education and social and economic advancement opportunities. In turn, this forms a cycle of disadvantages and poverty, in thus way affecting children's mental health and its related psychological problems (John et al., 2022).
- *Intergenerational Trauma:* The life struggles and its emotional stress (including depression and anxiety) in which young mothers are engaged could poten-

tially be transferred to the next generations (such as children) via mechanisms (e.g., parenting behaviors and emotional availability) that affect children's mental health, including stress, anxiety and depression. Particularly, young children are prone to internalizing the stress and ebbs and flows of emotions from their mothers, thereby beginning the groundwork for children's mental health struggles (Nurfieni, 2023).

Broader Community Mental Health

The effects of early marriage on young mothers and their children also have broader implications for community health and well-being (Hynek et al., 2022).

- *Cycle of Poverty*: Early marriage often takes place in a vicious cycle of poverty that breaks the economic backbone of communities. It can make young brides and their children to suffer from economic hardship, hence limiting access to social needs, including crucial educational services and medical care. Further, this poor economic condition can contribute to one of the circles that communities are associated with the cricial issues of mass poverty that may affect health and well-being (Iustitiani & Ajisuksmo, 2018).
- *Impact on Community Resources:* Early marriages can stretch community resources, like healthcare systems, educational institutions, and social services. High rates of early marriage can make it hard to provide adequate service for young brides and their children while services and support are relevant to their needs, hence affecting the health of the community at large (Itebiye, 2016).
- *Social and Economic Development:* High rates of early marriage also hamper the achievements in social and economic development of the community, because of the result of early marriage faced by a considerable proportion of the populations, in terms of low educational potential and economic instability. These, in turn, limit the community to move forward and develop (Hynek et al., 2022).
- *Intergenerational Effect on Community Values:* The continued practice of early marriage in communities serves to solidify and reinforce socially constructed norms of masculinity and femininity and stereotypical expectations in a society. It creates the backdrop for early marriage to thrive and continue it in a cyclical process, with future consequences for the community's set of values and attitude on gender equality and the rights of women (Nurfieni, 2023).

Strategies for Breaking the Cycle

Interventions and support mechanisms to address the intergenerational effect of early marriage must be targeted. The following factors are important.

- *Education and Empowerment:* The chain of early marriage over generations can only be broken by affording mechanisms of education and empowerment to young girls and women. Of the factors, education can play an important role to promote a delayed marriage, enhance opportunities for economic development, and increase well-being among young girls. Educational attainment also helps the young women to be more empowered with skills and leadership programs for realizing a more secure future for them and their children (John et al., 2022).
- *Support Services for Young Mothers:* Support services should be given to young mothers to help minimize the impact of early marriage on their children. Proper provision should be made for parenting education, mental health support, and economic assistance. Providing proper resources and support may improve their quality of life and mental health (Itebiye, 2016).
- *Community-Based Programs:* As cultural and societal factors foster and perpetuate early marriage, community-based programs will be required to change and provide supports for the girls to be sustainable in social life. Leaders in communities, in couples, families, and organizations are important social and political forces to struggle against cultural tradition and foster new strategies by which early marriage decline and mental health improve among young bridges and their children (Iustitiani & Ajisuksmo, 2018).
- *Policy and Legal Frameworks:* Strengthening policy and legal frameworks vis-à-vis the protection of young girls and women from early marriage and mental health consequences is of essence. Effective implementation of laws for prohibiting early marriage and enhancing access to comprehensive support services may promote late marriages and minimize their effects on mental health (Nurfieni, 2023).

The intergenerational effects of early marriage tell us that this problem requires a multi-sectoral approach (Vettriselvan & Arunkumar, 2018a; Vettriselvan et al., 2019b). This, hence, calls for proper resources and empowering support to the young mothers and children and the wider community who carry the burdens as a result of their vulnerability. Investing in education, empowerment measures, community-based interventions, and good policy frameworks may improve early marriages and its intergenerational effects, addressing the trajectory of progressively building dignified, healthy, and equitable societies (John et al., 2022).

INTERVENTIONS AND SUPPORT MECHANISMS

Medical, psychological, and social impacts of early marriages suggest an inclusive approach to avert preventive measures, support systems, and interventions that work effectively. This section presents different strategies and mechanisms that intend to protect, assist, and prevent future occurrences in relation to early marriages that tend to traumatize a society (Arthur & Ngugi, 2017; Liang & Chikritzhs, 2011).

Preventive Measures

Preventing early marriage involves wholesomeness of remedies in regard to negating the possible impact on individuals and society. Effective preventive measures include:

- *Education and Awareness Campaigns:* Awareness of the ill impacts should be given to the general public, explaining why this practice can be harmful and what advantages should result from delayed marriage. The campaigns could focus on communities, schools, and families with the intent of changing the norm to regard young girls' education and consider personal development as important (Nurfieni, 2023).
- *Community Engagement and Advocacy:* Community leaders, church leaders, and organizations can be brought on board to help influence cultural norms that are the main drivers of child marriage. Community-based programs should bring in leaders who shall dialogue on issues around gender equality and delayed marriage (Itebiye, 2016).
- *Youth Empowerment Programs:* Expanding youth's education, skills development, and strong leadership can arm his or her voice with a stand on taking informed decisions concerning their respective futures. It also builds self-confidence, critical thinking, and decision-making skills, helping them to avoid pressures of early marriage (Carlson, 2012; John et al., 2022).
- *Legislative and Policy Reforms*: Laws should be put in place and implemented that fix the minimum legal age for marriage and protect against forced marriage. Governments have the solemn duty to further strengthen legal frameworks, ensure proper enforcement, and provide resources for the recovery of victims of early marriage such as young mothers and children (Iustitiani & Ajisuksmo, 2018).
- *Economic Incentives:* The government and non-government agencies should provide economic incentives such as scholarships for the girls to continue their education and financial support to the families. Economic stability can

reduce this need that is felt for early marriage as a source of security (Nurfieni, 2023).

Psychological Support and Counselling

Access to mental health services and counseling is critical to supporting individuals who have gone through or are at risk for early marriage. They include:

- *Mental Health Services:* There is a need to offer mental health services that would meet the needs of survivors of early marriage. The services should include counseling, psychotherapy, and support groups necessary in containing depression, anxiety, and PTSD (Lebni et al., 2023; Bozorgi-Saran & Koolaee, 2022; Solhi et al., 2021).
- *Trauma-Informed Care:* The efficacy of mental health support may be further increased by providing trauma-informed care that recognizes and addresses the unique experiences of survivors of early marriage. This would involve understanding the impact of trauma and providing a safe and supportive environment for healing (Itebiye, 2016).
- *Crises Intervention Services:* Establish crises intervention services for those who are in immediate danger or are severely challenged by their mental health. These can be emergency services that provide support and then link them to long-term resources for the cure.
- *Family Counseling and Support:* Providing family counseling may be of help in solving the issues that concern relations and reconnection of major family ties. This family support may improve the general environment and offer a more conducive setting in which the young people affected by an early marriage grow up (Naghizadeh et al., 2021; Sulistiawati, 2021).

Effective Intervention or Program Case Studies

As far as identification of learning from the case studies of an effective intervention or program in addressing early marriage and associated consequences is concerned, it can be very helpful in many a way. Following are some:

- *Educational Programs:* "Girls Not Brides", for instance, is an initiative aimed at ending the phenomenon of child marriage. It has a logic of preventive action: education and community engagement. These programs, by promoting the education of girls and providing support through community-based interfacing, have shown success in arresting downward marriage (Iustitiani & Ajisuksmo, 2018).

- *Health and Well Being Programs:* For instance, in the country, Better Life Program in several countries carries sensitization, vocational training, and psychological support concerning the young brides. The programs have proved promising in improving the well-being and economic opportunities for young women (Itebiye, 2016).
- *Legal and Policy Initiatives:* Legal reformation and community-based interventions, such as in Bangladesh, have succeeded in reducing the prevalence of early marriage. They include the "Child Marriage Restraint Act" and local advocacy campaigns, which have helped in curbing the prevalence of early marriages and in helping those who are already into it (Obeisat, 2021).
- *Community-Led Approaches:* Community-led approaches to early marriage involve peer-to-peer education and advocacy groups at the local level, which can be considered to have recorded significant success in community-based initiatives aimed at finding sustainable solutions (John et al., 2022; John et al., 2022; Hegazy & Elsadek, 2019).

Way Forward for Future Research and Policy

Future research and policy recommendations are all targeted at strengthening efforts to end early marriage and bring support to those already affected. These include the following:

- *Further research:* The effectiveness of interventions and support mechanisms needs more targeted studies for establishing best practices and adapting strategies as need be. It is relevant at this point that research conducted addresses quantitative, as it does qualitative data for the best understanding of the impact of early marriage (Itebiye, 2016).
- *Policy Formulation:* Detailed policies pertaining to each diversified aspect of early marriage—inclusive of education, health, and economic support—can bring much-needed integration into tackling the issue. Such policies should be devised by the policymakers in coordination with NGOs, community organizations, and international bodies, which have to be effective and implemented (Bozorgi-Saran & Koolaee, 2022; Noor et al., 2021; Ahmed et al., 2014).
- *Strengthening Partnerships:* Government, NGOs, community organizations, and international agencies can devise partnerships that help in the strengthening of interventions. At the same time, collaboration provides a framework within which one can mobilize resources, tap into expertise, and use networks to mount a more coordinated response to early marriage (John et al., 2019).

- *Monitoring and Evaluation:* The presence of robust mechanisms for monitoring and evaluation is required to establish the effects of interventions and programmes. This involves periodic reviews of the successes and challenges of efforts in ensuring that they remain effective and responsive to the needs of the affected population (Taplak & Yılmaz, 2022).

Any effect of early marriage calls for a wholesome package of preventive measures, psychological guidance, and effective interventions. Focusing on education, community engagement, and specially designed support services, we could work together to reduce the prevalence of early marriage and, consequently, mitigate their psychic effects. Successful case studies and current research provide valuable lessons in strategies that work. Recommendations for the future will turn out to be useful guidelines for these continued efforts toward helping and empowering the victims of early marriage (Itebiye, 2016; Hadi, 2016).

CONCLUSION

The psychological and social repercussions of child marriage are deep and long term. The effects of child marriage do not affect the individual but also their families and community. They mostly lead to acute mental health problems, such as depression, anxiety, and PTSD, propelled by conditions such as sudden responsibility from childhood, isolation, economic pressure, and cultural norms that sometimes hide or normalize the effects. These are again intertwined with the social and cultural environments that further sustain early marriage practices, which include traditions, gender inequalities, and social pressures. In addition, intergenerational effects of early marriage underscore the issue, reflecting on the health and development of children born to young mothers, and straining community resources and development (WHO, 2011, 2013).

The situation has to be addressed through multidimensional approaches involving preventive measures, legal reforms, and strong support systems. Educational awareness and creating awareness about the importance of deferring marriage are challenging to cultural norms. Training girls while at a young age can enable them to fight for their rights, avoid Early Marriage, and have better lives in the future. Setting up specific psychological support and counseling is of essence since many young brides face mental health problems. Successful intervention programs and activities bring to light effective strategies, pointing to culturally sensitive approaches and community engagement (WHO, 2020).

In the future, this should be supported by reinforcement in support systems and research, and policy development has to go on in the face of changing issues related to early marriage. This will be accomplished by a mix of prevention, support, and cultural change: reducing early marriage's prevalence and mitigating its psychological and societal repercussions. Only an all-dimensional and compassionate approach can help break the cycle of early marriage to ultimately have a world with healthier and more equitable communities, and a brighter future for all.

REFERENCES

Aggarwal, S., Francis, K. L., Dashti, S. G., & Patton, G. (2022). Child marriage and mental health of adolescent girls: A longitudinal study from Uttar Pradesh and Bihar, India. *The Lancet Regional Health. Southeast Asia*, 16(8), 100102. DOI: 10.1016/j.lamsea.2022.100102 PMID: 37384140

Ahmed, S., Khan, A., Khan, S., & Noushad, S. (2014). Early marriage: A root of current physiological and psychosocial health burdens. *International Journal of Endorsing Health Science Research*, 2(1), 50. DOI: 10.29052/IJEHSR.v2.i1.2014.50-53

Amin, S., & Amin, S. (2018). Understanding early marriage and associated outcomes: An exploratory study in urban slums of Dhaka, Bangladesh. *Journal of Biosocial Science*, 50(5), 632–648. DOI: 10.1017/S002193201700036X

Arthur, M., & Ngugi, E. N. (2017). Legal strategies for addressing early and forced marriage in Africa. *Harvard Law Review*, 130(1), 235–278.

Bandura, A. (2011). The social and policy impact of social cognitive theory. In M. M. Mark, S. I. Donaldson, & B. Campbell (Eds.), *Social psychology and evaluation* (pp. 31–71). The Guilford Press.

Bozorgi-Saran, S., & Koolaee, A. (2022). Child bride, a story that never ends: A look at experiences of Iranian women. *International Social Work*, 66(5), 1497–1512. DOI: 10.1177/00208728211066830

Bronfenbrenner, U. (1995). *Developmental ecology through space and time: A future perspective.*

Bronfenbrenner, U., & Ceci, S. J. (1994). Nature-nurture reconceptualized: A bio-ecological model. *Psychological Review*, 10(4), 568–586. DOI: 10.1037/0033-295X.101.4.568 PMID: 7984707

Bronfenbrenner, U., & Evans, G. W. (2000). Developmental science in the 21st century: Emerging questions, theoretical models, research designs and empirical findings. *Social Development*, 9(1), 115–125. DOI: 10.1111/1467-9507.00114

Burgess, R., Jeffery, M., Odero, S., Rose-Clarke, K., & Devakumar, D. (2022). Overlooked and unaddressed: A narrative review of mental health consequences of child marriages. *PLOS Global Public Health*, 2(1), e0000131. DOI: 10.1371/journal.pgph.0000131 PMID: 36962120

Carlson, D. (2012). Deviations from desired age at marriage: Mental health differences across marital status. *Journal of Marriage and Family*, 74(4), 743–758. DOI: 10.1111/j.1741-3737.2012.00995.x

Crenshaw, K. (1991). Mapping the margins: Intersectionality, identity politics, and violence against women of color. *Stanford Law Review*, 43(6), 1241–1299. DOI: 10.2307/1229039

Elnakib, S., Elsallab, M., Wanis, M. A., Elshiwy, S., Krishnapalan, N. P., & Naja, N. A. (2022). Understanding the impacts of child marriage on the health and well-being of adolescent girls and young women residing in urban areas in Egypt. *Reproductive Health*, 19(8), 8. Advance online publication. DOI: 10.1186/s12978-021-01315-4 PMID: 35033114

Folkman, S., & Lazarus, R. S. (2013). Stress and coping theory applied to the investigation of mass industrial psychogenic illness. In *Mass psychogenic illness* (pp. 237–255). Routledge.

Girls Not Brides. (2019). Mental health consequences of child marriages. Retrieved from https://www.girlsnotbrides.org

Hadi, A. (2016). Social perspectives on the relationship between early marriage, fertility and infertility in Tambour town, Central Sudan. *International Journal of Sociology and Anthropology*, 8(4), 27–35. DOI: 10.5897/IJSA2016.0655

Handayani, P. W., Moeis, F. R., & Ayuningtyas, D. (2021). Comparing Indonesian men's health-seeking behavior and likelihood to suffer from illness across sociodemographic factors. *The Journal of Men's Health*. Advance online publication. DOI: 10.31083/jomh.2021.078

Hegazy, M., & Elsadek, A. (2019). Early marriage and associated health consequences among female children in giza governorate. *Egyptian Journal of Health Care*, 10(1), 420–435. DOI: 10.21608/ejhc.2019.213861

Hertler, S. C., Figueredo, A. J., Peñaherrera-Aguirre, M., Fernandes, H. B., Woodley of Menie, M. A., Hertler, S. C., ... & Woodley of Menie, M. A. (2018). Urie Bronfenbrenner: Toward an evolutionary ecological systems theory. *Life history evolution: A biological Meta-theory for the social sciences*, 323-339.

Hossain, A., & Uddin, E. M. (2023). Physical school environment and infectious diseases: A case of primary school context in Bangladesh. In Azeez, P. A., Nikhil Raj, P. P., & Mohanraj, R. (Eds.), *Ecological and evolutionary perspectives on infections and morbidity* (pp. 126–151). IGI Global. DOI: 10.4018/978-1-7998-9414-8.ch006

Hynek, K., Abebe, D., Liefbroer, A., Hauge, L., & Straiton, M. (2022). The association between early marriage and mental disorder among young migrant and non-migrant women: A norwegian register-based study. *BMC Women's Health*, 22(1), 258. Advance online publication. DOI: 10.1186/s12905-022-01836-5 PMID: 35761261

International Center for Research on Women. (2014). Too young to wed: The lives, rights, and health of young married girls. https://www.icrw.org/wp-content/uploads/2016/10/Too-Young-to-Wed-Full-Report.pdf

Itebiye, B. (2016). Forced and early marriages: Moral failures vs religious nuances. *European Scientific Journal*, 12(17), 305. DOI: 10.19044/esj.2016.v12n17p305

Iustitiani, N., & Ajisuksmo, C. (2018). Supporting factors and consequences of child marriage. *Anima Indonesian Psychological Journal*, 33(2), 100–111. DOI: 10.24123/aipj.v33i2.1581

John, N., Edmeades, J., & Murithi, L. (2019). Child marriage and psychological well-being in Niger and Ethiopia. *BMC Public Health*, 19(1), 1029. Advance online publication. DOI: 10.1186/s12889-019-7314-z PMID: 31370825

John, N., Kapungu, C., Sebany, M., & Tadesse, S. (2022). Do gender-based pathways influence mental health? Examining the linkages between early child marriage, intimate partner violence, and psychological well-being among young Ethiopian women (18–24 years old). *Youth & Society*, 55(6), 1155–1172. DOI: 10.1177/0044118X221079375

Lazarus, R. S., & Folkman, S. (1984). *Stress, appraisal, and coping*. Springer Publishing company.

Lebni, J., Solhi, M., Azar, F., Farahani, F., & Irandoost, S. (2023). Exploring the consequences of early marriage: A conventional content analysis. *Inquiry*, 60, 004695802311599. DOI: 10.1177/00469580231159963

Liang, W., & Chikritzhs, T. (2011). Brief report: Marital status and alcohol consumption behaviours. *Journal of Substance Use*, 17(1), 84–90. DOI: 10.3109/14659891.2010.538463

McLeod, S. (2011). *Albert Bandura's social learning theory*. Simply Psychology.

Munley, P. H. (1975). Erik Erikson's theory of psychosocial development and vocational behavior. *Journal of Counseling Psychology*, 22(4), 314–319. DOI: 10.1037/h0076749

Naghizadeh, S., Mirghafourvand, M., Mohammadi, A., Azizi, M., Taghizadeh-Milani, S., & Ganbari, H. (2021). Knowledge and viewpoint of adolescent girls regarding child marriage, its causes and consequences. *BMC Women's Health*, 21(1), 351. Advance online publication. DOI: 10.1186/s12905-021-01497-w PMID: 34615510

Nishat, J., Shovo, T., Ahammed, B., Islam, M., Rahman, M., & Hossain, M. (2023). Mental health status of early married girls during the covid-19 pandemic: A study in the southwestern region of bangladesh. *Frontiers in Psychiatry*, 13, 1074208. Advance online publication. DOI: 10.3389/fpsyt.2022.1074208 PMID: 36683997

Noor, M., Fatimah, H., Rahman, F., Laily, N., & Yulidasari, F. (2021). The impact of physical and psychological health of early married behaviors in adolescents. *Journal Berkala Kesehatan*, 7(1), 16. DOI: 10.20527/jbk.v7i1.9618

Nurfieni, A. (2023). The impact of law number 16 of 2019 marriage dispensation and child marriage gap. *Indonesian Journal of Law and Islamic Law (Ijlil)*, 5(2), 50–61. DOI: 10.35719/ijlil.v5i2.330

Obeisat, S. (2021). The lived experience of early marriage in jordan: The perspective of adolescent girls and young women. *SAGE Open*, 11(3), 215824402110488. DOI: 10.1177/21582440211048895

Solhi, M., Azar, F., Farahani, F., & Lebni, J. (2021). Exploring the consequences of early marriage among Kurdish women: a qualitative study in western Iran. https://doi.org/DOI: 10.21203/rs.3.rs-55314/v2

Strat, Y., Dubertret, C., & Foll, B. (2011). Child marriage in the united states and its association with mental health in women. *Pediatrics*, 128(3), 524–530. DOI: 10.1542/peds.2011-0961 PMID: 21873691

Sulistiawati, I., & Pratiwi, C. S. (2021). Psychological disorders found on the early-age married teenagers who are under 18. *International Journal of Health Science and Technology*, 2(3), 177–189. DOI: 10.31101/ijhst.v2i3.1969

Taplak, A., & Yılmaz, F. (2022). Adolescent marriage and motherhood in turkey: A qualitative study exploring determinants, impacts and opinions about preventive strategies. *Journal of Advanced Nursing*, 78(8), 2537–2547. DOI: 10.1111/jan.15211 PMID: 35285542

Uddin, J., Pulok, M. H., Johnson, R. B., Rana, J., & Baker, E. (2019). Association between child marriage and institutional delivery care services use in Bangladesh: Intersections between education and place of residence. *Public Health*, 171, 6–14. DOI: 10.1016/j.puhe.2019.03.014 PMID: 31071578

Uddin, M. E. (2008). Cross-cultural comparison of family size and composition between Muslim and Santal communities in rural Bangladesh. *World Cultures eJournal, 16*(1), 1-18.

Uddin, M. E. (2009). Age at first marriage for husband and wife between Muslim and Santal communities in rural Bangladesh. *International Journal of Humanities and Social Science*, 3(4), 318–326.

Uddin, M. E. (2011). Cross-cultural social stress among Muslim, Hindu, Santal and Oraon communities in Rasulpur of Bangladesh. *The International Journal of Sociology and Social Policy*, 31(5/6), 361–388. DOI: 10.1108/01443331111141318

Uddin, M. E. (2015). Family socio-cultural values affecting early marriage between Muslim and Santal communities in rural Bangladesh. *The International Journal of Sociology and Social Policy*, 35(3/4), 141–164. DOI: 10.1108/IJSSP-06-2014-0046

Uddin, M. E. (2017). Family demographic mechanisms linking of socioeconomic status to subjective physical health in rural Bangladesh. *Social Indicators Research*, 130(3), 1263–1279. DOI: 10.1007/s11205-015-1209-x

Uddin, M. E. (2021). Teenage marriage and high school dropout among poor girls: A narrative review for family pathways in Bangladesh. *Journal of Research in Social Sciences and Language*, 1(1), 55–76.

Uddin, M. E. (2024). Human development pathways for understanding sustainable use of neighborhood resources and successful aging in a world of crises. In Baikady, R. (Eds.), *The Palgrave handbook of Global social problems* (pp. 1–21). Springer.

Uecker, J. (2012). Marriage and mental health among young adults. *Journal of Health and Social Behavior*, 53(1), 67–83. DOI: 10.1177/0022146511419206 PMID: 22328171

UNFPA. (2018). Empowering young people to end child marriage and address gender-based violence through the provision of comprehensive sexuality education. https://asiapacific.unfpa.org/en/publications/empowering-young-people-end-child-marriage-and-address-gender-based-violence-through

UNICEF. (2005). Early marriage: A harmful traditional practice. https://www.unicef.org/publications/index_26902.html

UNICEF. (2015). Ending child marriage: Progress and prospects. https://data.unicef.org/resources/ending-child-marriage-progress-and-prospects/

UNICEF. (2023). Child marriage data and statistics. Retrieved from https://www.unicef.org/reports/child-marriage-data-and-statistics

United Nations Children's Fund. (2014). Ending child marriage: Progress and prospects. https://www.unicef.org/media/files/Child_Marriage_Report_7_17_LR.pdf

United Nations Development Programme. (2016). Ending child marriage: Progress and prospects. https://www.undp.org/content/dam/undp/library/Democratic%20Governance/Women%27s%20Empowerment/Ending-Child-Marriage-Global-Initiative-Progress-and-Prospects-2016.pdf

Vettriselvan, R., Anto, R., & Rajan, F. S. A. (2018b). Pathetic Health Status and Working Condition of Zambian Women. *Indian Journal of Public Health Research & Development*, 9(9), 259–264. DOI: 10.5958/0976-5506.2018.01006.9

Vettriselvan, R., & Arunkumar, N. (2018a). Child labour in unorganized mechanical engineering industries of Tamil Nadu: A situation analysis. *International Journal of Mechanical Engineering and Technology*, 9(10), 809–819.

Vettriselvan, R., Rajan, F. S. A., & Arunkumar, N. (2019a). Occupational Health Issues Faced by Women in Spinners. *Indian Journal of Public Health Research & Development*, 10(1), 500–512. DOI: 10.5958/0976-5506.2019.00098.6

Vettriselvan, R., Rengamani, J., James, F. A., Srinivasan, R., & Poongavanam, S. (2019b). Issues and Challenges of Women Employees in Indian Technical Industries. *International Journal of Engineering and Advanced Technology*, 8(2S2), 404-409.

WHO. (2011). Global strategy to stop health-care providers from performing female genital mutilation. https://www.who.int/reproductivehealth/publications/fgm/rhr_11_18/en/

WHO. (2013). *Global and regional estimates of violence against women: Prevalence and health effects of intimate partner violence and non-partner sexual violence*. World Health Organization.

WHO. (2017). *Mental health of adolescents*. Geneva: World Health Organization. Retrieved from https://www.who.int/

WHO. (2020). Child marriage. https://www.who.int/news-room/q-a-detail/child-marriage

WHO. (2022). *Adolescent pregnancy: Overview*. Geneva: World Health Organization. Retrieved from https://www.who.int/news-room/fact-sheets/detail/adolescent-pregnancy

Williams, K. (2003). Has the future of marriage arrived? a contemporary examination of gender, marriage, and psychological well-being. *Journal of Health and Social Behavior*, 44(4), 470. DOI: 10.2307/1519794 PMID: 15038144

World Bank. (2015). Child marriage: A silent health and human rights issue. https://openknowledge.worldbank.org/bitstream/handle/10986/22788/9781464805007.pdf

World Bank. (2017). *Economic impacts of child marriage: Global synthesis report*. World Bank.

Chapter 8
Health Consequences of Early Marriage:
Examining Morbidity and Long-Term Wellbeing

R. Vettriselvan
https://orcid.org/0000-0002-1324-136X
Academy of Maritime Education and Training, India

A. Deepan
https://orcid.org/0009-0002-2806-9686
Sambhram University, Uzbekistan

Geetanjali Jaiswani
Saraswathi Institute of Medical Sciences, Hapur, India

A. Balakrishnan
Gandhigram Rural Institute, India

R. Sakthivel
https://orcid.org/0000-0001-9518-0064
DMI-St. Eugene University, Zambia

ABSTRACT

Early marriage, defined as marriage occurring before the age of 18, has significant health implications that affect individuals throughout their lives. Based on life course approach, this chapter investigates the health risks associated with early marriage, emphasizing both immediate and long-term consequences. It highlights increased vulnerability to various health issues, such as higher rates of maternal and infant complications, chronic illnesses, and mental health disorders. Additionally, the

DOI: 10.4018/979-8-3693-3394-5.ch008

chapter explores the interplay between socio-economic factors and health outcomes, revealing how these factors exacerbate existing disparities and restrict access to healthcare services. Through an examination of current research and case studies, this chapter provides a comprehensive overview of the health challenges associated with early marriage and offers recommendations for strategies to mitigate these risks. By addressing these issues, the chapter seeks to contribute to a deeper understanding of the broader implications of early marriage on individual and public health.

INTRODUCTION

Early marriage, typically defined as a union occurring before the age of 18, remains a significant global concern with far-reaching implications for health and wellbeing (Fan & Koski, 2022; Uddin, 2015). This practice, prevalent in various cultures and regions, has been linked to numerous adverse health outcomes for both individuals and their offspring. Despite international efforts to address and curb early marriage, the phenomenon persists, influenced by a complex interplay of socio-cultural, economic, and legal factors (Uddin, 2015). Globally, an estimated 12 million girls are married before the age of 18 each year, with the highest rates found in sub-Saharan Africa, South Asia, and parts of Latin America (UNICEF, 2023). Early marriage is not merely a matter of cultural practice but is deeply intertwined with issues of gender inequality, poverty, and lack of education. The implications of early marriage extend well beyond the immediate context of the marriage itself, affecting long-term health outcomes for both young brides and their children (Miller & Roca, 2022). One of the most pressing health concerns associated with early marriage is its impact on maternal and infant health.

Life course theories suggest that girls' early transition to marriages leads to subsequent advance health effects and socioeconomic inequality in later life (Uddin, 2021). Theories and research shows that early marriage often leads to early pregnancies, which are associated with a range of health risks (Uddin, 2021). Adolescents whose bodies are still developing face higher risks of complications during pregnancy and childbirth compared to young women. Studies have consistently shown that girls who give birth at a young age are more likely to experience complications such as eclampsia, postpartum hemorrhage, and obstructed labor, which can lead to increased maternal and infant mortality (Delprato & Akyeampong, 2017; Kok, 2021). The World Health Organization (2022) reported that complications from pregnancy and childbirth are among the leading causes of death for adolescent girls aged 15-19 years. In addition to the physical health risks, early marriage and early pregnancies are linked to a range of chronic health conditions. Early marriage often results in prolonged exposure to poverty and limited access to healthcare services, which exacerbates the risk of chronic diseases such as low-weight, malnutrition, anaemia, hypertension and diabetes. Moreover, the nutritional deficits commonly associated with early pregnancies can lead to long-term health issues for both the mother and child (Godha et al., 2013, 2016).

Mental health is another critical area affected by early marriage. Adolescents who marry early often face significant psychological stress, including anxiety, depression, and low self-esteem (Lim & Raymo, 2016). The transition from childhood to adolescence is already a challenging period, and early marriage can compound these difficulties, leading to adverse mental health outcomes (Uddin, 2021). Research has indicated that young brides frequently experience feelings of isolation, lack of autonomy, and pressure to conform to traditional roles, which can significantly impact their mental wellbeing (Singh, 2020).

The socio-economic implications of early marriage further complicate the health landscape (Uddin, 2017). Early marriage often curtails educational and economic opportunities, trapping individuals in cycles of poverty and limiting their access to healthcare. Girls who marry early are less likely to complete their education and are more likely to face economic dependency, which perpetuates the cycle of disadvantage over time (Hassan & Nader, 2021; Uddin, 2017). The lack of education and economic opportunities not only affects their immediate health but also leads to their long-term poor health outcomes and quality of life.

Addressing the health consequences of early marriage requires a multifaceted approach that includes improving access to education, healthcare, and economic opportunities. Interventions must also consider the socio-cultural factors that perpetuate early marriage. Effective strategies include community-based programs that promote the benefits of delaying marriage and empowering girls through education and economic opportunities (Rashid & Karim, 2022). Additionally, policy changes at the national and international levels can play a crucial role in combating early marriage and improving health outcomes. Early marriage poses significant health risks, particularly for young girls and their children. The implications of early marriage extend beyond immediate health concerns, affecting long-term physical and mental health, as well as socio-economic attainment. To effectively address these challenges, a comprehensive understanding of the issue and targeted interventions are essential. This chapter aims to explore comprehensive health consequences, drawing on current research and case studies to provide a thorough examination of the impact of early marriage on health and to offer recommendations for mitigating these risks. To attain this aim of the chapter, we define key concepts presented in the second section. In the third section, we describe early marriage and health (mental and physical) consequences. In the fourth section, we analyse socioeconomic status and health outcomes in association with early marriage. In the fifth section we present case studies to illustrate the health consequences of early marriage and its mitigating strategies across countries. The sixth section describes intervention and policy practice to improve health consequences of early marriage. Finally, we describe concluding remarks.

DEFINITION AND SCOPE

Constitutes Early Marriage

Early marriage is broadly defined as the timing of forming marital union where one or both partners are under the age of 18 (Uddin, 2021). This age threshold is set by international standards, including those established by the United Nations and various human rights organizations, to ensure that individuals are sufficiently mature to make informed decisions about marriage and family life (UNICEF, 2023). The practice of early marriage can involve a range of age differences, but the focus is primarily on unions where at least one party is a minor, typically between 15 and 17 years old. The significance of the age threshold stems from developmental, legal, and social considerations. Adolescents under 18 are still undergoing physical and psychological development, which can be compromised by early marriage and associated responsibilities (Uddin, 2021). Early marriage often involves complexities that can hinder the development and rights of young individuals, impacting their educational opportunities, economic stability, and overall health (Kok, 2021).

Global and Regional Statistics

Globally, early marriage remains a significant issue, with varying prevalence across regions. According to UNICEF (2023), approximately 12 million girls are married before the age of 18 each year. The prevalence of early marriage is not uniform; it varies significantly by region, socio-economic status, and cultural norms. In sub-Saharan Africa, early marriage rates are particularly high. Countries such as Niger, Chad, and the Central African Republic have some of the highest rates of child marriage, with nearly half of girls married before reaching adulthood (UNICEF, 2023). In these regions, early marriage is often driven by poverty, gender inequality, and cultural practices that prioritize early unions for girls as a means of securing family alliances or economic stability. South Asia also experiences high rates of early marriage, although the situation is somewhat more variable. In countries like Bangladesh, India, and Nepal, significant numbers of girls are married before 18, influenced by traditional practices and socio-economic factors. However, efforts in some areas have led to reductions in these rates due to increased awareness and educational initiatives (Miller & Roca, 2022). In contrast, early marriage rates are lower in many parts of Latin America and the Caribbean, though significant pockets of early marriage still exist. For instance, in some rural areas of countries like Guatemala and Honduras, early marriage remains prevalent, often influenced by cultural traditions and economic conditions (Hassan & Nader, 2021).

Table 1. Definition of the key concepts

Concept	Description of definition
Early Marriage:	A marriage that occurs before the legal age of adulthood, typically under the age of 18. Early marriage is often associated with cultural, economic, and social pressures.
Morbidity:	Refers to the presence of disease or health complications within a population. In the context of early marriage, morbidity may encompass physical, mental, and reproductive health issues that affect young brides.
Long-Term Wellbeing:	A holistic measure of an individual's overall quality of life, including physical health, mental health, social relationships, and economic stability. Early marriage can significantly impact these dimensions over a person's lifetime.
Reproductive Health:	A state of complete physical, mental, and social well-being in all matters relating to the reproductive system. Early marriage can lead to early pregnancies, increasing risks for reproductive health issues.
Social Implications:	The effects of early marriage on social structures and relationships, including gender dynamics, family roles, and community interactions. These implications often contribute to the perpetuation of early marriage practices.
Economic Consequences:	The financial impacts of early marriage on individuals and families, including reduced educational and employment opportunities, which can lead to poverty and limited economic mobility.
Psychosocial Effects:	The psychological and social factors that influence mental health and emotional well-being. Early marriage can lead to stress, anxiety, and depression due to the challenges faced by young brides.
Childbearing Risks:	The health risks associated with early pregnancy and childbirth, which can include complications such as obstetric fistula, maternal mortality, and adverse neonatal outcomes.
Cultural Norms:	The shared beliefs and practices within a community that influence behaviors, including the acceptance of early marriage. Cultural norms can perpetuate cycles of early marriage and its associated health consequences.
Education Access:	The availability and ability of young individuals, particularly girls, to pursue education. Early marriage often results in the withdrawal of girls from school, affecting their long-term educational and economic prospects.
Gender Inequality:	The unequal treatment and opportunities afforded to individuals based on their gender. Early marriage is often rooted in and contributes to ongoing gender inequality, limiting women's rights and autonomy.
Public Health Interventions:	Programs and policies aimed at improving health outcomes and reducing the risks associated with early marriage. These may include education, advocacy, and access to health services.
Community Awareness:	The level of understanding and knowledge within a community regarding the implications of early marriage. Increasing community awareness can be crucial for changing attitudes and practices surrounding early marriage.

continued on following page

Table 1. Continued

Concept	Description of definition
Legal Framework:	The laws and regulations governing the legal age of marriage and protections against child marriage. Effective legal frameworks can help to combat early marriage and its negative health impacts.
Empowerment Programs:	Initiatives designed to increase the autonomy and decision-making power of young women. Empowerment programs can mitigate the factors leading to early marriage and improve health outcomes.
Mental Health Outcomes:	The psychological effects resulting from early marriage, which can include stress, depression, and anxiety. These outcomes can have long-lasting implications for overall health and well-being.
Health Education:	Informational programs aimed at improving individuals' understanding of health issues, including reproductive health and the consequences of early marriage. Health education is vital for informed decision-making.
Advocacy:	The efforts to promote policy changes and raise awareness about the issues related to early marriage and its health consequences. Advocacy plays a critical role in challenging norms and implementing change.

The Legal and Cultural Dimensions of Early Marriage

The legal frameworks surrounding early marriage vary widely around the world. Many countries have established legal minimum ages for marriage, typically set at 18, in line with international human rights standards. However, there are often exceptions that permit marriage at younger ages with parental consent or judicial approval. These legal provisions can create loopholes that undermine efforts to prevent early marriage (Rashid & Karim, 2022). For example, in the United States, while the legal age for marriage without parental consent is 18, many states allow individuals as young as 16 or even younger to marry with parental consent or judicial approval. This legal flexibility can contribute to cases where minors enter into marriage without adequate protection or consideration of their developmental needs (Singh, 2020).

Cultural norms and traditions play a crucial role in perpetuating early marriage. In many societies, early marriage is seen as a traditional practice or a means of securing family honor. For instance, in some communities in sub-Saharan Africa and South Asia, early marriage is linked to social customs that value early unions as a way to ensure social status or economic stability. Similarly, in certain communities in Latin America, cultural expectations around gender roles and family structure can support the practice of early marriage (Uddin et al., 2019). These cultural practices are often reinforced by economic factors, such as poverty and lack of access to education. Families may view early marriage as a way to alleviate economic burdens or secure financial stability, particularly in impoverished areas where educational and economic opportunities are limited. In such contexts, early marriage is not only a cultural norm but also a pragmatic response to economic challenges. Efforts to address early marriage must consider both legal reforms and cultural contexts.

Legal frameworks can be strengthened to ensure stricter enforcement of minimum marriage ages and eliminate exceptions that allow for early marriage. Simultaneously, cultural norms and practices need to be addressed through community-based education and outreach programs that promote the benefits of delaying marriage and advancing educational and economic opportunities for girls (Rashid & Karim, 2022). Early marriage is defined as a union involving individual less than 18 years of age, with significant variations in prevalence across different regions. The practice is influenced by a complex interplay of legal standards, cultural norms, and socio-economic factors. Understanding these dimensions is crucial for developing effective strategies to combat early marriage and its associated health and social impacts.

EARLY MARRIAGE AND HEALTH RISKS

Maternal Health

Early marriage is closely associated with several adverse health outcomes, particularly for young mothers. Adolescents who marry early are at a heightened risk of pregnancy-related complications due to their physical and developmental immaturity. Early pregnancy often leads to increased rates of complications such as preeclampsia, postpartum hemorrhage, and obstructed labor (World Health Organization, 2022). These complications can be life-threatening for both the mother and the child, reflecting the physiological vulnerabilities of young adolescents whose bodies are not fully developed to handle the stresses of childbirth. Research indicates that adolescent girls face a much higher risk of death during childbirth compared to older women. Studies have shown that girls aged 15-19 experience higher rates of severe complications during childbirth due to underdeveloped pelvic structures and increased susceptibility to pregnancy-related complications (Kok, 2021). This heightened risk is often exacerbated by inadequate access to prenatal care and health education, which are crucial for preventing and managing complications. Moreover, early marriage and subsequent early pregnancies can have long-term impacts on maternal health. Young mothers are more likely to suffer from chronic health issues related to their reproductive systems and overall health. For instance, recurrent pregnancies at a young age can lead to conditions such as uterine prolapse, which has been observed in regions with high rates of early marriage (Hassan & Nader, 2021; Santhya et al., 2010). These chronic conditions can severely impact the quality of life and health of young women, making early marriage a significant concern from a health perspective.

Infant Health

The health of infants born to young mothers is also a critical concern. Infants who are born to adolescent mothers face higher risks of mortality and health issues compared to those born to young mothers. Infants of young mothers are more likely to be born prematurely, have low birth weights, and suffer from complications such as neonatal infections and respiratory problems. These health risks are often due to inadequate prenatal care, poor maternal nutrition, and the general physical health of young mothers (Lebni et al., 2023). Additionally, early maternal age negatively impacts child development. The physical and emotional stress experienced by young mothers can influence their ability to provide adequate care and nutrition, which is essential for the healthy development of their children. Children born to young mothers are at higher risk for developmental delays, cognitive impairments, and behavioral issues. This impact extends beyond infancy, affecting educational outcomes and long-term health as these children grow (Miller & Roca, 2022).

Chronic Diseases

Early marriage and subsequent early pregnancies contribute to the prevalence of chronic health conditions among young women. The long-term exposure to poverty, inadequate nutrition, and limited access to healthcare often associated with early marriage exacerbates the risk of developing chronic diseases. Early-married individuals frequently experience higher rates of chronic conditions such as hypertension, diabetes, and anaemia (Ahmed et al., 2014; Hassan & Nader, 2021). Nutritional deficits associated with early pregnancies can lead to chronic health issues that persist throughout life, affecting overall wellbeing. The prevalence of chronic diseases among early-married women is also influenced by socio-economic factors. Limited access to healthcare services and preventive care often means that chronic conditions are not managed effectively, leading to worsening health over time (Miller & Roca, 2022; Vikram et al., 2023). For instance, early-married women who experience complications from pregnancy may not receive appropriate follow-up care, increasing their risk of developing long-term health issues.

Mental Health

The psychological effects of early marriage are profound and multifaceted. Early marriage often leads to significant psychological stress and mental health disorders. Young brides frequently experience feelings of isolation, depression, and anxiety due to the abrupt transition from adolescence to adult responsibilities, often without adequate support systems (Singh, 2020). The lack of autonomy and control over their lives, coupled with societal pressures and expectations, can contribute to severe mental health issues. Research indicates that early marriage can exacerbate mental health problems, leading to chronic conditions such as depression and anxiety. The psychological burden of early marriage is often compounded by the challenges of balancing familial responsibilities with limited personal freedom and opportunities. This stress can have lasting effects on emotional wellbeing, impacting the quality of life and overall mental health of young women (Marphatia et al., 2017; Hassan & Nader, 2021). Furthermore, the impact of early marriage on emotional wellbeing extends beyond the individual to affect family dynamics and relationships. Young brides may struggle with feelings of inadequacy and low self-esteem, which can strain marital relationships and impact their ability to provide emotional support to their families (Hassan & Nader, 2021).

This emotional strain can create a cycle of psychological distress, affecting both the individual and their immediate family. Early marriage is associated with a range of significant health risks, including increased maternal and infant health complications, prevalence of chronic diseases, and severe mental health issues. The physical and psychological challenges faced by early-married individuals highlight the need for targeted interventions and comprehensive support systems to address these health risks (Kalamar et al., 2016). Addressing early marriage requires not only legal and policy reforms but also community-based programs that promote education, healthcare access, and mental health support for young individuals. By understanding and addressing the multifaceted health risks associated with early marriage, it is possible to mitigate its adverse effects and improve the wellbeing of those affected.

SOCIOECONOMIC STATUS AND HEALTH OUTCOMES

The Effect of Socio-Economic Status on Health Risks

Socio-economic status (SES) profoundly influences health outcomes, particularly in the context of early marriage. SES encompasses factors such as income, education, occupation, and living conditions, which collectively impact access to resources and opportunities that are crucial for maintaining good health (Rashid & Karim, 2022). Early marriage often correlates with lower SES, which exacerbates health risks for both young brides and their children. Research indicates that individuals from lower socio-economic backgrounds face higher risks of poor health due to several interconnected factors. Poor socio-economic conditions can limit access to essential health services, increase exposure to environmental hazards, and restrict opportunities for health education (Miller & Roca, 2022). For young girls who marry early, these conditions are often magnified, leading to poorer health outcomes. Low SES is frequently associated with higher rates of maternal and infant mortality, increased incidence of chronic diseases, and poorer mental health (Kok, 2021). For example, families in lower socio-economic brackets might prioritize immediate financial gains over long-term health, leading to decisions such as early marriage. This practice often results in diminished health outcomes due to insufficient prenatal care, inadequate nutrition, and limited access to emergency medical services. The cycle of poverty and poor health perpetuates, making it difficult for affected individuals to break out of socio-economic constraints (Hassan & Nader, 2021).

Access to Healthcare and Its Limitations

Access to healthcare is a critical determinant of health outcomes, and limitations in this access can significantly impact individuals who marry early. Healthcare access issues are often exacerbated by socio-economic factors, including low income, lack of insurance and limited availability of services in underserved areas (Rashid & Karim, 2022). For early-married individuals, these barriers can be particularly severe. In many low-income settings, healthcare infrastructure is inadequate, leading to insufficient prenatal and postnatal care. Young mothers in such environments may not receive the necessary medical attention to manage pregnancy-related complications or to address their own health issues effectively. Limited access to healthcare services also means that preventive care, such as vaccinations and health screenings, may be neglected, increasing the risk of preventable diseases and complications (World Health Organization, 2022). Additionally, the financial burden of healthcare costs can deter families from seeking necessary medical care. Early-married individuals, who often come from socio-economically disadvantaged backgrounds, may struggle with the costs of medical services, leading to delayed or inadequate treatment. This lack of access can result in poorer health outcomes and contribute to the perpetuation of health disparities (Miller & Roca, 2022).

Educational and Economic Opportunities and Health

Educational attainment and economic opportunities play a significant role in shaping health outcomes. In many cases, early marriage leads to the truncation of educational and economic opportunities, which in turn impacts health. The interruption of education often limits individuals' knowledge about health and access to better job opportunities, perpetuating cycles of poverty and poor health (Singh, 2020). For young girls, early marriage frequently results in the end of formal education. Education is closely linked with improved health outcomes, as it equips individuals with knowledge about health, nutrition, and preventive care. Additionally, higher educational attainment is associated with better job prospects and increased earning potential, which can improve access to health services and overall living conditions (Uddin, 2017). Without education, young brides may lack the skills needed to secure stable employment and achieve economic independence, further entrenching them in poverty. Economic opportunities are equally important. Limited economic prospects can restrict access to quality healthcare, nutritious food, and safe living conditions. Early-married individuals, who may lack financial stability and job security, often struggle to afford basic needs and healthcare services. This economic disadvantage can exacerbate health issues, leading to poorer outcomes for both individuals and their families (Rashid & Karim, 2022). Socio-economic factors have a profound impact on health outcomes, particularly for individuals who marry early. Low socio-economic status often leads to increased health risks due to limited access to healthcare, inadequate living conditions, and restricted educational and economic opportunities. Addressing these issues requires a comprehensive approach that includes improving access to healthcare, enhancing educational opportunities, and providing economic support (Uddin, 2017). By addressing the socio-economic determinants of health, it is possible to improve the wellbeing of young individuals and mitigate the adverse effects associated with early marriage.

CASE STUDIES AND EMPIRICAL EVIDENCE

Review of Studies from Various Regions

A comprehensive understanding of the health impacts of early marriage requires examining empirical evidence and case studies from different regions. This approach provides insights into the varying health outcomes associated with early marriage across diverse socio-economic and cultural contexts. In sub-Saharan Africa, early marriage is prevalent, and several studies highlight its detrimental health effects. For instance, a study in Niger, one of the countries with the highest rates of child marriage, found that adolescent mothers face significantly higher rates of maternal mortality and morbidity compared to older women. The research showed that young mothers in Niger are at increased risk of obstructed labor and preeclampsia, conditions that are exacerbated by limited access to healthcare services (Hassan & Nader, 2021). This situation is compounded by the high prevalence of poverty, which limits access to prenatal care and contributes to poor health outcomes for both mothers and infants. Similarly, in South Asia, particularly in India and Bangladesh, early marriage has been linked to adverse health outcomes.

A study conducted in rural areas of Bangladesh revealed that girls married before the age of 18 have higher rates of neonatal and infant mortality compared to those born to older mothers (Miller & Roca, 2022). The study attributed these outcomes to inadequate maternal nutrition, limited access to healthcare, and the physical immaturity of young mothers. Additionally, the research highlighted that early marriage often leads to interrupted education and limited economic opportunities, which further exacerbate health disparities. In Latin America, early marriage is less prevalent but still significant in certain areas. For example, research conducted in rural Guatemala found that early marriage is associated with higher rates of maternal and infant health issues, including preterm births and low birth weight (Uddin, 2017). The study emphasized that socio-economic factors such as low income and lack of education contribute to these adverse health outcomes, as they limit access to adequate prenatal care and nutrition.

Analysis of Health Outcomes in Different Socio-Economic Contexts

The impact of early marriage on health outcomes varies significantly across different socio-economic contexts. Studies have shown that socio-economic factors play a crucial role in determining the extent of health risks associated with early marriage. In lower socio-economic settings, the health outcomes of early marriage are generally more severe due to a combination of factors such as limited access to healthcare, inadequate living conditions, and poor nutrition (Uddin, 2017). For instance, in many low-income countries, early marriage is often accompanied by poverty, which exacerbates health risks. Research indicates that young brides from low-income families are more likely to experience complications during pregnancy and childbirth, and their infants are at higher risk of mortality and poor health outcomes (World Health Organization, 2022). Limited financial resources and lack of access to healthcare services contribute to these adverse outcomes, highlighting the need for targeted interventions in these settings. Conversely, in higher socio-economic contexts, early marriage may still present health risks but with relatively less severe outcomes. For example, in urban areas of middle-income countries, early marriage is often less common, and there may be better access to healthcare services and educational opportunities. However, even in these contexts, early marriage can still lead to significant health challenges, particularly if it is associated with lower socio-economic status and limited access to resources (Singh, 2020).

Success Stories and Lessons Learned from Interventions

Despite the challenges posed by early marriage, there have been several successful interventions that offer valuable lessons for addressing this issue. These interventions often focus on improving access to education, healthcare, and economic opportunities for young girls and their families. One notable success story is the community-based programs implemented in Ethiopia, where efforts have been made to reduce early marriage through education and empowerment initiatives. Programs such as the "Girl Hub" initiative focus on increasing educational opportunities for girls, raising awareness about the negative effects of early marriage, and providing support for girls to remain in school (Hassan & Nader, 2021). These efforts have led to a noticeable decline in early marriage rates and improved health outcomes for young girls in the region.

In India, the "Beti Bachao Beti Padhao" (Save the Daughter, Educate the Daughter) scheme has been successful in promoting female education and reducing the incidence of early marriage. By providing financial incentives for families to keep their daughters in school and delaying marriage, the program has contributed to improved educational attainment and better health outcomes for young women (Miller & Roca, 2022). The success of this program underscores the importance of integrating educational and economic incentives into efforts to combat early marriage. Another example is the "Youth Empowerment Program" in Kenya, which focuses on providing comprehensive health education and services to adolescents. The program includes components such as sexual and reproductive health education, access to healthcare services, and economic support for young women. The positive impact of this program on reducing early marriage and improving health outcomes highlights the effectiveness of multi-faceted interventions that address both educational and health needs (Kalamar et al., 2016). Empirical evidence and case studies from various regions underscore the significant health risks associated with early marriage. The impact of early marriage on health outcomes varies across different socio-economic contexts, with lower socio-economic settings often experiencing more severe health challenges. However, successful interventions demonstrate that targeted efforts in education, healthcare, and economic empowerment can effectively address these issues and improve health outcomes for young individuals. Lessons learned from these interventions highlight the importance of comprehensive approaches that integrate multiple facets of support to combat early marriage and its associated health risks.

Remedial Measures

Addressing the health consequences of early marriage requires a comprehensive strategy that considers both the immediate and long-term impacts on young women. Based on current research, several remedial measures can be proposed to mitigate the adverse effects and improve overall well-being. These measures integrate findings from various studies on occupational health and working conditions of women in different sectors.

Enhancing Healthcare Access and Reproductive Education

Improving healthcare access is crucial for addressing the health issues associated with early marriage. Women in vulnerable situations, such as those described by Vettriselvan et al. (2018b), face significant health risks due to inadequate healthcare services. Expanding access to health facilities through mobile clinics and community health programs can ensure that these women receive necessary medical care. Additionally, comprehensive reproductive health education should be provided to empower young women with knowledge about family planning and sexual health, helping them make informed decisions and reduce health complications related to early pregnancies.

Improving Working Conditions and Safety Standards

Women working in hazardous environments often face severe health risks, as highlighted by Vettriselvan et al. (2018b) in their study of construction workers in Theni District. Implementing and enforcing strict occupational health and safety regulations can significantly improve working conditions. Providing adequate protective equipment and ensuring regular health check-ups are essential measures. In industries such as spinning mills, where women experience considerable occupational health issues (Vettriselvan & Rajan, 2019a), enhancing ergonomic practices and health management strategies can help mitigate these risks.

Strengthening Legal Frameworks and Enforcement

Robust legal protections are vital for safeguarding women's rights and improving their working conditions. The study by Vettriselvan and Arunkumar (2018a) underscores the need for stricter enforcement of labor laws to combat child labor and ensure fair working conditions. Strengthening legal measures to prevent early marriage and protect young girls from exploitation is critical. Effective monitoring and enforcement of these laws can help create safer environments and prevent health-related issues associated with early marriage.

Promoting Skill Development and Economic Empowerment

Economic empowerment through skill development can significantly impact women's health and employment opportunities. Providing vocational training and career development programs can help women transition from hazardous jobs to safer, more stable employment. Vettriselvan and Arunkumar (2018a) highlight the importance of such measures in improving job security and working conditions. Supporting entrepreneurship and offering access to financial resources can further enhance economic independence and reduce vulnerabilities associated with early marriage.

Fostering Community Support and Engagement

Community-based interventions are essential for addressing the root causes of early marriage and its associated health impacts. Engaging local leaders, educators, and health workers in community programs can create a supportive environment for young women. Establishing peer support groups and providing counselling services can offer emotional and psychological support, helping individuals cope with the challenges related to early marriage (Vettriselvan et al., 2018b). Promoting community awareness and involvement can also drive collective efforts to address and prevent early marriage.

Encouraging Ongoing Research and Policy Development

Continuous research and evidence-based policy development are crucial for addressing the evolving challenges faced by women. The findings from Vettriselvan et al. (2019b) provide valuable insights into specific health and occupational issues. Collaborating with academic institutions and non-governmental organizations to conduct further research can help identify emerging problems and develop effective strategies. Policies informed by ongoing research can better address the complexities of health consequences related to early marriage and improve long-term well-being.

INTERVENTION AND POLICY RECOMMENDATIONS

Effective Strategies for Mitigating Health Risks

Addressing the health risks associated with early marriage requires a multi-faceted approach that combines education, healthcare access, and community engagement. Interventions and effective strategies for mitigating these risks include (Marphatia et al., 2017):

1. ***Educational Initiatives***: Increasing educational opportunities for girls is a fundamental strategy for combating early marriage and its associated health risks. Programs that keep girls in school and provide comprehensive sex education have been shown to delay marriage and improve health outcomes. For example, interventions that offer scholarships, school supplies, and financial incentives for families to keep their daughters in school have proven effective. In Ethiopia, the "Girl Hub" initiative has successfully reduced early marriage rates by providing girls with educational resources and support (Hassan & Nader, 2021).

2. ***Healthcare Access and Services***: Improving access to healthcare services is crucial for managing the health risks associated with early marriage. This includes providing comprehensive prenatal and postnatal care, family planning services, and reproductive health education. Mobile health clinics and community health workers can extend services to remote areas where early marriage is prevalent. In Kenya, the "Youth Empowerment Program" offers sexual and reproductive health education and access to healthcare services, significantly improving health outcomes for young mothers (Godha et al., 2013).

3. ***Community Engagement and Awareness***: Raising awareness about the negative consequences of early marriage and promoting community-based interventions can help change social norms. Community engagement initiatives that involve local leaders, religious figures, and families can challenge and transform harmful practices. For instance, community-based programs in India have successfully reduced early marriage by involving local leaders and providing education about the health risks and legal implications of early marriage (Miller & Roca, 2022).

4. *Economic Support and Empowerment*: Economic empowerment programs can provide financial stability and reduce the economic pressures that often drive early marriage. Initiatives that offer vocational training, microloans, and income-generating activities can help families improve their economic situation and reduce the incidence of early marriage. Programs that support young women in achieving economic independence have shown promise in mitigating the health risks associated with early marriage (Rashid & Karim, 2022).

Role of Healthcare Systems and Community Support

Healthcare systems and community support play a critical role in addressing the health risks associated with early marriage. Effective healthcare systems can provide essential services and support for early-married individuals, while community support can help create an environment conducive to positive change.

1. *Strengthening Healthcare Systems*: Robust healthcare systems are essential for managing the health risks of early marriage. This involves ensuring that healthcare facilities are adequately equipped, healthcare workers are trained, and services are accessible to all individuals, particularly those in underserved areas. Integrating reproductive health services into primary healthcare systems can ensure that young mothers receive the care they need before, during, and after pregnancy (World Health Organization, 2022).
2. *Training Healthcare Providers*: Training healthcare providers to address the specific needs of young mothers is crucial. Healthcare professionals should be equipped with the knowledge and skills to manage the complications associated with early pregnancy and provide appropriate counselling and support. This includes training on adolescent health issues, communication skills, and culturally sensitive care (Singh, 2020).
3. **Community-Based Support Systems**: Community support systems can help address the social and cultural factors that contribute to early marriage. Support networks, including family, peers, and community organizations, can provide emotional support and practical assistance to young married individuals. Programs that involve community members in promoting health education and supporting young mothers can create a supportive environment and help reduce stigma (Hassan & Nader, 2021).
4. **Advocacy and Awareness Campaigns**: Advocacy and awareness campaigns can drive public support for policies and programs aimed at reducing early marriage and improving health outcomes. Campaigns that educate the public about the risks of early marriage and promote the benefits of delaying marriage can influence social norms and encourage families to prioritize education and health (Miller & Roca, 2022).

Policy Recommendations to Address Early Marriage and Improve Health Outcomes

To effectively address early marriage and its associated health risks, comprehensive policy recommendations are needed. These policies should focus on legal, educational, and health aspects to create a supportive framework for preventing early marriage and improving health outcomes.

1. ***Strengthen Legal Frameworks***: Implementing and enforcing laws that set the minimum age for marriage and protect the rights of young individuals is crucial. Governments should ensure that legal frameworks are robust and effectively enforced to prevent child marriage. This includes establishing clear legal penalties for those who violate marriage laws and providing mechanisms for reporting and addressing cases of early marriage (Hassan & Nader, 2021).
2. ***Promote Universal Education***: Policies that promote universal education, particularly for girls, can help delay marriage and improve health outcomes. Governments should invest in educational infrastructure, provide financial support for families to keep their daughters in school, and ensure that educational opportunities are accessible to all children, regardless of socio-economic status. Programs that offer incentives for school attendance and academic achievement can further support this goal (Rashid & Karim, 2022).
3. ***Enhance Access to Reproductive Health Services***: Policies should ensure that reproductive health services are accessible to young individuals, including those in rural and underserved areas. This includes expanding family planning services, providing comprehensive sexual education, and integrating reproductive health services into primary healthcare systems. Governments should also support programs that provide education and resources for young mothers to manage their health effectively (World Health Organization, 2022).
4. ***Support Economic Empowerment Programs***: Economic empowerment policies can help reduce the financial pressures that contribute to early marriage. Governments should support programs that provide vocational training, microloans, and income-generating opportunities for families and young individuals. By improving economic stability, these programs can reduce the incidence of early marriage and enhance overall health outcomes (Miller & Roca, 2022).
5. **Invest in Community-Based Interventions**: Policies should support community-based interventions that address the social and cultural factors contributing to early marriage. This includes funding for community education programs, support networks for young mothers, and initiatives that involve local leaders in promoting health and education. Investing in community-based approaches

can create a supportive environment for reducing early marriage and improving health outcomes (Singh, 2020).

Addressing the health risks associated with early marriage requires a multifaceted approach that includes effective strategies, robust healthcare systems, and comprehensive policy recommendations. By focusing on education, healthcare access, community support, and economic empowerment, it is possible to mitigate the adverse health effects of early marriage and improve the wellbeing of young individuals. Implementing these strategies and policies will require coordinated efforts from governments, healthcare providers, communities, and individuals to create a supportive framework for preventing early marriage and promoting better health outcomes.

CONCLUSION AND IMPLICATIONS

This chapter has provided a comprehensive exploration of the health risks associated with early marriage, highlighting the significant implications for both individuals and communities. The evidence gathered from various regions and socio-economic contexts underscores the multifaceted nature of early marriage and its impact on health. Early marriage is closely linked to a range of adverse health outcomes. For young brides, the risks associated with pregnancy and childbirths are notably higher compared to older women. Maternal health complications such as obstructed labor, preeclampsia, and postpartum hemorrhage are prevalent among those who marry early, largely due to their physical immaturity and inadequate access to healthcare services (Hassan & Nader, 2021). Additionally, the elevated rates of maternal mortality and morbidity highlight the urgent need for targeted healthcare interventions. Infant health is also adversely affected by early marriage. Children who are born to young mothers face higher risks of neonatal and infant mortality. Research indicates that early maternal age can lead to health issues such as preterm births and low birth weight, which have long-term implications for child development (Miller & Roca, 2022). The intersection of inadequate maternal nutrition, limited healthcare access, and socio-economic factors contributes to these negative outcomes. The prevalence of chronic diseases and mental health disorders among early-married individuals further compounds the health challenges. Chronic conditions such as diabetes and hypertension are more common in those who marry early, partly due to the cumulative impact of early pregnancies and socio-economic stress (Uddin, 2017). Additionally, mental health issues, including anxiety and depression, are prevalent, reflecting the psychological strain associated with early marriage and its associated socio-economic pressures (Singh, 2020).

Implications for Future Research and Practice

The findings from this chapter highlight several areas that warrant further research and practice improvement. Future research should focus on the longitudinal impact of early marriage on health outcomes to better understand the long-term consequences for both mothers and children. Studies that track health indicators over time could provide valuable insights into how early marriage influences chronic disease prevalence and mental health over the life course. Additionally, research should explore the effectiveness of various interventions aimed at mitigating the health risks of early marriage. Comparative studies evaluating the success of different programs—such as educational initiatives, healthcare access improvements, and economic empowerment strategies—can inform best practices and guide the development of more effective interventions (Rashid & Karim, 2022). Investigating the role of community-based approaches in changing social norms and reducing early marriage rates can also offer practical insights for future program development. From a practical perspective, it is essential to integrate findings into policy and practice. Healthcare systems need to be strengthened to better address the needs of young mothers. This includes ensuring comprehensive prenatal and postnatal care, training healthcare providers in adolescent health issues, and expanding access to reproductive health services. Community-based programs should be scaled up to provide education and support that challenges harmful social norms and promotes the benefits of delaying marriage (World Health Organization, 2022).

Implications for Social Practice

Addressing the health risks associated with early marriage requires concerted action from a range of stakeholders, including governments, non-governmental organizations (NGOs), healthcare providers, and community leaders. The *governments* should prioritize the implementation and enforcement of laws that set the minimum age for marriage and protect the rights of young individuals. Developing and funding policies that promote universal education and improve healthcare access are critical steps. Governments should also support initiatives that empower girls economically and socially, which can help reduce the incidence of early marriage and its associated health risks (Hassan & Nader, 2021). The *NGOs* and international organizations play a crucial role in advocating for and implementing interventions that address early marriage. They should focus on supporting educational programs, providing healthcare services, and raising awareness about the consequences of early marriage. Collaborations with local organizations can enhance the effectiveness of interventions and ensure that they are culturally sensitive and contextually appropriate (Miller & Roca, 2022). *Healthcare providers* need to be equipped with the knowledge and skills to address the specific health needs of young mothers. Training programs should emphasize the importance of adolescent health and provide practical guidance on managing pregnancy-related complications. Additionally, healthcare providers should work closely with community organizations to ensure that young mothers receive the support and resources they need (Lee & Smith, 2023). *Community leaders and local organizations* are instrumental in driving cultural change and challenging social norms that perpetuate early marriage. By engaging with communities, raising awareness about the benefits of delaying marriage, and promoting educational and economic opportunities for girls, community leaders can help shift attitudes and practices related to early marriage (Singh, 2020).

In conclusion, early marriage poses significant health risks that impact individuals and communities worldwide. The evidence presented underscores the need for comprehensive strategies to address these risks, including improvements in education, healthcare access, and economic empowerment. Future research should focus on evaluating the effectiveness of interventions and exploring the long-term health outcomes of early marriage. Stakeholders must work together to implement and support policies and programs that promote the well-being of young individuals and reduce the incidence of early marriage. By addressing these issues collaboratively, it is possible to mitigate the health risks associated with early marriage and create a healthier, more equitable future for all.

REFERENCES

Ahmed, S., Khan, A., Khan, S., & Noushad, S. (2014). Early marriage: A root of current physiological and psychological health burdens. *International Journal of Endorsing Health Science Research*, 2(1), 50–53. DOI: 10.29052/IJEHSR.v2.i1.2014.50-53

Delprato, M., & Akyeampong, K. (2017). The effect of early marriage timing on women's and children's health in sub-Saharan Africa and Southwest Asia. *Annals of Global Health*, 83(3-4), 557–567. DOI: 10.1016/j.aogh.2017.10.005 PMID: 29221529

Fan, S., & Koski, A. (2022). The health consequences of child marriage: A systematic review of the evidence. *BMC Public Health*, 22(1), 309. DOI: 10.1186/s12889-022-12707-x PMID: 35164724

Godha, D., Gage, A. J., Hotchkiss, D. R., & Cappa, C. (2016). Predicting maternal health care use by age at marriage in multiple countries. *The Journal of Adolescent Health*, 58(5), 504–511. DOI: 10.1016/j.jadohealth.2016.01.001 PMID: 26984836

Godha, D., Hotchkiss, D. R., & Gage, A. J. (2013). Association between child marriage and reproductive health outcomes and service utilization: A multi-country study from South Asia. *The Journal of Adolescent Health*, 52(5), 552–558. DOI: 10.1016/j.jadohealth.2013.01.021 PMID: 23608719

Hassan, S., & Nader, R. (2021). Socio-economic implications of early marriage in low-income countries. *Journal of Global Health*, 11(2), 345–359. DOI: 10.7189/jogh.11.02001

Kalamar, A. M., Lee-Rife, S., & Hindin, M. J. (2016). Interventions to prevent child marriage among people in low- and middle-income countries: A systematic review of the published and gray literature. *The Journal of Adolescent Health*, 59(3), 16–21. DOI: 10.1016/j.jadohealth.2016.06.015 PMID: 27562449

Kok, M. (2021). Adolescent pregnancy and health outcomes: A global perspective. *International Journal of Women's Health*, 13, 111–124. DOI: 10.2147/IJWH.S296773

Lebni, J. Y., Solhi, M., Azar, F. E. F., Farahani, F. K., & Irandoost, S. F. (2023). Exploring the consequences of early marriage: A conventional content analysis. *Inquiry: The Journal of Health Care Organization, Provision, and Financing*, 60, 1–14.

Lim, S., & Raymo, J. M. (2016). Marriage and women's health in Japan. *Journal of Marriage and Family*, 78(3), 780–796. DOI: 10.1111/jomf.12298 PMID: 30774150

Marphatia, A. A., Ambale, G. S., & Reid, A. M. (2017). Women's marriage age matters for public health: A review of the broader health and social implications in South Asia. *frontiers in Public Health, 5*:269. DOI: 10.3389/fpubh.2017.00269

Miller, E., & Roca, M. (2022). The intersection of early marriage and health: A review of current research. *Health Policy and Planning, 37*(4), 529–540. DOI: 10.1093/heapol/czac021

Rashid, T., & Karim, M. (2022). Empowering girls through education and economic opportunities: Strategies to delay early marriage. *Development Studies Research, 9*(3), 234–249. DOI: 10.1080/21665095.2022.2117739

Santhya, K. G., Ram, U., Acharya, R., Jejeebhoy, S. J., Ram, F., & Singh, A. (2010). Associations between early marriage and young women's marital and reproductive health outcomes: Evidence from India. *International Perspectives on Sexual and Reproductive Health, 36*(3), 132–139. DOI: 10.1363/3613210 PMID: 20880798

Singh, A. (2020). Psychological impacts of early marriage on adolescent girls: A literature review. *The Journal of Adolescent Health, 67*(5), 654–661. DOI: 10.1016/j.jadohealth.2020.06.025

Uddin, E. M. (2015). Family socio-cultural values affecting early marriage between Muslim and Santal communities in rural Bangladesh. *The International Journal of Sociology and Social Policy, 35*(3/4), 141–164. DOI: 10.1108/IJSSP-06-2014-0046

Uddin, J., Pulok, M. H., Johnson, R. B., Rana, J., & Baker, E. (2019). Association between child marriage and institutional delivery care services use in Bangladesh: Intersections between education and place of residence. *Public Health, 171*, 6–14. DOI: 10.1016/j.puhe.2019.03.014 PMID: 31071578

Uddin, M. E. (2017). Family demographic mechanisms linking of socioeconomic status to subjective physical health in rural Bangladesh. *Social Indicators Research, 130*(3), 1263–1279. DOI: 10.1007/s11205-015-1209-x

Uddin, M. E. (2021). Teenage marriage and high school dropout among poor girls: A narrative review for family pathways in Bangladesh. *Journal of Research in Social Sciences and Language, 1*(1), 55–76. https://www.jssal.com/index.php/jssal/article/view/15

UNICEF. (2023). Child marriage data and statistics. Retrieved from https://www.unicef.org/reports/child-marriage-data-and-statistics

Vettriselvan, R., Anto, R., & Jesu Rajan, F. S. A. (2018b). Pathetic health status and working condition of Zambian women. *Indian Journal of Public Health Research & Development, 9*(9), 259. DOI: 10.5958/0976-5506.2018.01006.9

Vettriselvan, R., & Arunkumar, N. (2018a). Child labour in unorganized mechanical engineering industries of Tamil Nadu: A situation analysis. *International Journal of Mechanical Engineering and Technology*, 9(10), 809–819.

Vettriselvan, R., Rajan, A. J., & Arunkumar, N. (2019). Occupational health issues faced by women in spinners. *Indian Journal of Public Health Research & Development*, 10(1), 500. DOI: 10.5958/0976-5506.2019.00098.6

Vettriselvan, R., Rengamani, J., James, F. A., Srinivasan, R., & Poongavanam, S. (2019). Issues and challenges of women employees in Indian technical industries. *International Journal of Engineering and Advanced Technology,* 8(2S2), 2019.

Vikram, K., Visaria, A., & Ganguly, D. (2023). Child marriage as a risk factor for non-communicable diseases among women in India. *International Journal of Epidemiology*, 52(5), 1303–1315. DOI: 10.1093/ije/dyad051 PMID: 37159526

World Health Organization. (2022). Adolescent pregnancy: Overview. Retrieved from https://www.who.int/news-room/fact-sheets/detail/adolescent-pregnancy

Chapter 9
Early Marriage From a Health Perspective:
Risks and Intervention Strategies

Sevinç Sütlü
https://orcid.org/0000-0001-6847-1798
Burdur Mehmet Akif Ersoy University, Turkey

Özge Kutlu
https://orcid.org/0000-0002-4774-7326
Burdur Mehmet Akif Ersoy University, Turkey

ABSTRACT

Early marriage is one of the most significant global issues created by traditional and patriarchal cultures, particularly impacting girls and women and hindering societal development. Mostly prevalent in impoverished and rural areas of underdeveloped and developing countries, early marriages are now recognized as a violation of women's and girls' human rights. Early marriage has various adverse effects on individuals' health. It increases the likelihood of fertility-related health risks such as pregnancy and childbirth complications, particularly for young people who haven't completed their physical and emotional development. The health implications of early marriage are extensive and diverse, emphasizing the importance for youth to comprehend its risks and consequences for a healthy and secure future. Hence, it's imperative to develop comprehensive strategies and supportive policies to prevent early marriages and safeguard young people's health rights.

DOI: 10.4018/979-8-3693-3394-5.ch009

INTRODUCTION

Early marriage is a formal, unofficial or traditional marriage that is included in a socially or officially accepted marriage contract, but where at least one of the spouses is a "child", before the girl or boy is psychologically and physiologically ready for marriage and having children (Ackerman & Abay, 2013; Kıran, 2017; Parsons et al., 2015; UNFPA-UNICEF, 2023; Wodon, 2016). Early marriage is one of the most important global problems created by traditional and patriarchal culture, which negatively affects especially girls and women and stands as an obstacle to the development of societies. Although it is seen all over the world, early marriages, which mostly occur in poor and rural areas of underdeveloped and developing countries, are today considered a violation of the human rights of women and girls.

Early marriage is a phenomenon that has various negative effects on the health of individuals. Early marriage increases the individual's likelihood of facing fertility-related health risks, such as pregnancy and birth complications (Sezgin&Punamaki, 2019; St-Germain, Kirby, Urquia, 2022). Young people who have not yet completed their physical and emotional development may have a harder time coping with such risks. Early marriage causes the spread of sexual health problems such as sexually transmitted infections (Irani& Roudsari, 2019; Hallett et al., 2007). However, the education and income levels of young people who marry at an early age are generally low, limiting their access to health services. Early marriage also causes emotional and psychological problems among young people. The health implications of early marriage are profound and diverse. It is an important priority for societies for young people to understand the risks and consequences of early marriage for a healthy and safe future. Therefore, it is necessary to develop comprehensive strategies and supportive policies to prevent early marriages and secure young people's health rights.

Current situation in the world

According to United Nations data, the rate of marriage under the age of 15 is 5% and the rate of marriage under the age of 18 is 19% worldwide. However, the data contains large differences between countries and regions. While the rate of marriages under the age of 15 is highest in the West and Central Africa region with 12%, it has the lowest rate with 1% in Eastern Europe and Central Asia and East Asia and the Pacific Regions. While the rate of marriage under the age of 18 is 37% in underdeveloped countries and West and Central Africa regions, it is 7% in East Asia and the Pacific Region. In the Eastern Europe and Central Asia Region, where Turkey is located, the rate of marriage under the age of 15 and under the age of 18 is 1% and 10%, respectively (Figure 1) (UNICEF, 2023).

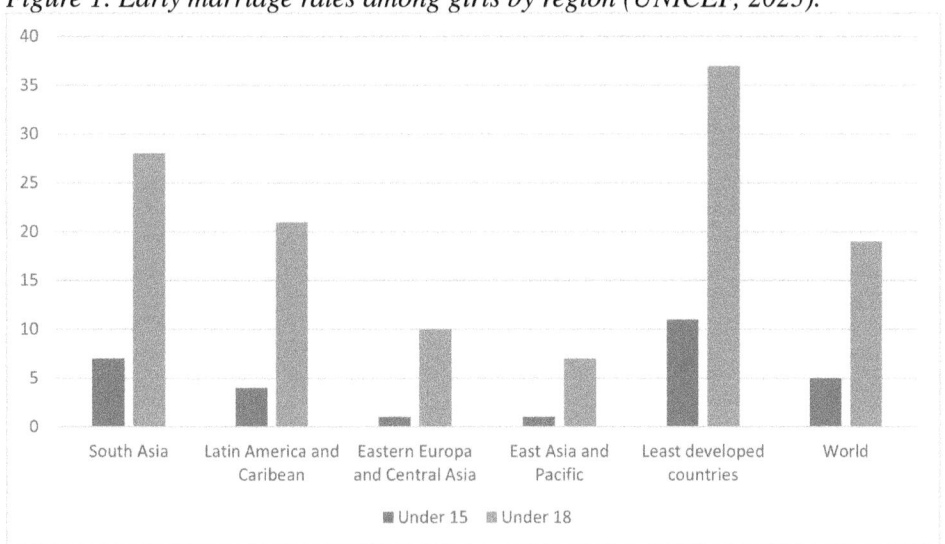

Figure 1. Early marriage rates among girls by region (UNICEF, 2023).

Reference: *UNICEF. (2023). Child-marriage global Database. Retrieved from https://data.unicef.org/topic/child-protection/child-marriage/*

At the global level, the number of child grooms is considerably lower than child brides. However, it is a very common human rights violation in some parts of the world (Figure 2).

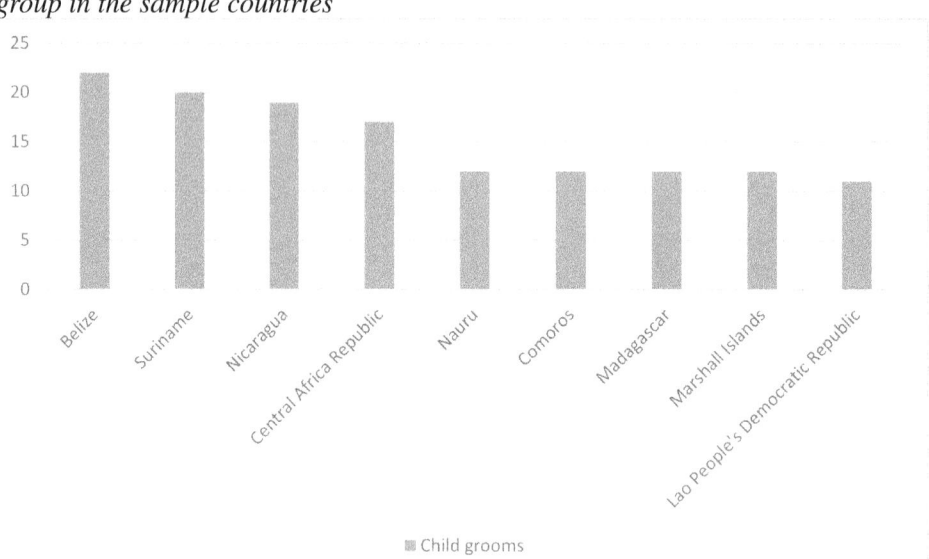

Figure 2. Rate of those married under the age of 18 among men in the 20-24 age group in the sample countries

Reference: *UNICEF. (2023). Child-marriage global Database. Retrieved from https://data.unicef.org/topic/child-protection/child-marriage/*

Current situation in Turkey

According to UNICEF data, among married women between the ages of 20-24, marriages under the age of 15 are 2% and marriages under the age of 18 are 18% (UNICEF, 2023). The most comprehensive data on early marriages in Turkey were obtained from the analyses of the 1993-TNHS, 1998-TNHS, 2003-TNHS, 2008-TNHS, 2013-TNHS and 2018-TNHS, which were conducted at five-year intervals between 1993 and 2018 within the scope of the Turkish Population Health Surveys (TSNA). Among married women between the ages of 20-24, marriages under the age of 15 are 2.0% and marriages under the age of 18 are 14.7%. This rate is higher among women in the 20-49 age group, 3.6% and 19.9%, respectively. There are differences in early marriage rates by region (Figure 3) (UNFPA, 2020).

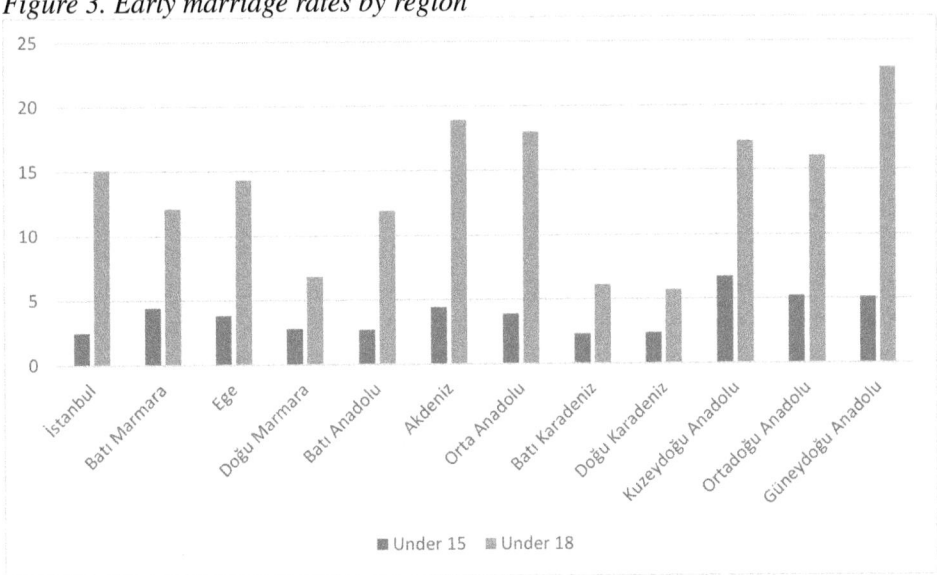

Figure 3. Early marriage rates by region

Reference: *UNFPA. (2020). Türkiye'de Çocuk Yaşta Erken ve Zorla Evlilikler: 1993-2018 Türkiye Nüfus ve Sağlık Araştırmaları Veri Analizi. Retrieved from https://turkiye.unfpa.org/sites/default/files/pub-pdf/turkce_web _son_pdf.pdf*

Conceptual Framework

While the biological definition of male or female is unique and undisputed in all societies, it is not possible to say the same for their counterparts in society. The genetic, physiological and biological characteristics of a person as male or female are called "sex". Gender refers to the socially determined roles and responsibilities of men and women. Gender is a concept not related to biological differences, but to how society sees us as men and women, how it perceives us, how it thinks and how it expects us to behave. Gender refers to the socially constructed characteristics of women, men, girls and boys. It includes the norms, behaviors, roles and relationships with each other regarding being a woman, man, girl or boy. Unlike biological sex, gender difference occurs as a result of social construction and can change/change over time (WHO, 2024). According to social scientists, gender is seen as a process and refers to all the tools that society uses to turn baby boys and girls into men and women (Tong, 2012).

Ideas about how men or women should be and behave are called gender norms (Pearse&Connell, 2016; Xing et al., 2022). These ideas are taught and internalized as "rules" from the early stages of life. Gender norms are the expectations and generally observed standards regarding gender identity within a certain period of time in a society, culture or community. In social norms theory, gender norms complete the missing perspective on how gender-related roles are included in institutions and how they are reproduced through daily interactions. Gender norms are norms that specifically relate to gender differences.

Within the scope of gender norms, it includes the qualities deemed appropriate by society for men and women, apart from their biological characteristics. For example, qualities such as courage, self-confidence, and strength are attributed to men, while qualities such as sacrifice, obedience, softness, and shyness are attributed to women. Although the roles assigned to men and women according to gender vary from society to society and culture to culture, it is common for men to be given the responsibility of providing for the household and to be strong alone through all difficulties, and for women to be given the responsibility of motherhood and taking care of daily household chores (Sütlü, 2022).

Social constructions of gender can create hierarchies. The inability of women to benefit from gender equality and equity in almost every society throughout history has led to the emergence of the concept of women's rights. Many of the rights that women demand are not privileged rights specific to women, but rights that every human being, male or female, should have from birth, that is, human rights. As a matter of fact, UNESCO states that gender equality is a fundamental human right and that gender equality is one of the necessary conditions for the success of internationally approved development goals (UNESCO(b), 2014). Due to gender, women face inequalities in many areas, especially education, health, employment and participation in politics, and they may be exposed to violence because they are women or girls. Girls and women may face different health-based discrimination at different developmental stages of the life cycle. During adolescence, girls may experience problems such as virginity control, sexual abuse, violence, as well as early and forced marriages and early pregnancies. Child, early and forced marriages are also a form of gender-based violence. Early marriages pose an obstacle to the exercise of rights such as the right to education, the right to participate in business life, and sexual and reproductive health rights.

Gender and early marriages

Early marriages, which disproportionately affect girls, are rooted in gender inequalities. Although there are boys who are married at an early age, proportionally, girls are 6 times more likely to be married than boys (UNFPA-UNICEF, 2023). According to data obtained from 82 countries covering 51% of the global male population, only 4.5% of young men aged 20-24 were married before the age of 18. This rate varies significantly between countries and varies between 0.1% and 27.9% (Gastón et al., 2019). The legal marriage age for girls and boys varies by country.

According to World Bank 2017 data, the legal marriage age for boys is higher than for girls in 17 countries. In Mali, it is 16 for girls and 18 for boys; In Iran, it is 13 for girls and 15 for boys; In India, the legal age for marriage is 18 for girls and 21 for boys (Lekanova, 2020). Statistics show that early marriages especially affect girls. Child marriages violate girls' rights to education, health and economic opportunity. In patriarchal structures where gender norms are dominant, girls do not have the right to choose whether, when and to whom they will marry. It is reported that girls from poor families, excluded groups or living in rural areas are at greater risk. Girls who marry at an early age leave school earlier than those who do not marry, are exposed to social isolation, and have limited access to health services (Yoosefi Lebni et al., 2023).

Definitions

In this section, terms that can often be used interchangeably but have different meanings are explained in the light of the definitions made by the Gender Equality Glossary of Terms and Concepts' (UNICEF, 2017) and the Glossary of Terms and Concepts (Capper, 2022).

Age-disparate marriage: In population and health research, it is the expression of the age difference between a woman and her husband in whole years. It is generally classified as less than five years, 5-9 years and 10 years or more. In arranged or forced marriages, the age difference is likely to be large. Power differences based on age put married women at a disadvantage in areas such as violence, health and economy.

Child marriage: Marriage of girls or boys before the age of 18 is called child marriage. It includes both formal and informal partnerships. Marriages can be made within the scope of civil law, religious law, customs and traditions. It may be referred to as "child, early and forced marriage" in United Nations resolutions.

Early marriage: It has largely the same meaning as child marriage and defines marriages in which one or both spouses are under 18 years of age. It is generally used to describe marriages at younger ages than those legally allowed to marry under the country's laws. However, it also includes situations where one or both spouses are over the age of 18 but are not ready to give consent due to lack of knowledge about their physical, emotional, sexual or psychological development levels and life preferences.

Forced marriage: It describes marriages in which one or both spouses, regardless of age, do not give full, free consent without informed and prior consent. It is also used to describe unions in which one or both spouses are unable to end or leave an existing marriage. Many countries consider all child marriages as forced marriages because they do not recognize that children can consent. However, there are also examples where adolescents under the age of 18 marry voluntarily. It is stated that the reasons why girls consent to marriage should be evaluated (Efevbera & Bhabha, 2020).

Inbreeding: It describes marriages between teenagers or children where there is little or no age difference between the spouses. Inbreeding can occur by force or voluntarily.

Self-initiated marriage: It describes marriages in which both spouses choose to marry each other. It may be preferred to escape from abuse or forced marriages. It provides a way for young people to become sexually active in societies where sex and pregnancy are only legitimized within the socially sanctioned institution of marriage. It can also be a way of establishing a separate household from their parents and declaring their independence, as a reflection of brain development, peer relationships and the desire for independence during adolescence.

Early Marriages and Sustainable Development Goals

In 2015, United Nations member states determined the Sustainable Development Goals, global development priorities that are expected to be achieved by 2030. Ending poverty and hunger, healthy and quality living, quality education, gender equality, clean water and sanitation, accessible and clean energy, decent work and economic growth, industry, innovation and infrastructure, reducing inequalities, sustainable cities and communities, 17 goals were determined and signed, including responsible production and consumption, climate action, life under water, life on land, peace, justice and partnership for strong institutions and purposes. The fifth of the Sustainable Development Goals, the 3rd of the 9 subheadings determined to ensure gender equality, is "Eliminating all harmful practices such as child marriage, early forced marriage and female circumcision" (Sampedro, 2021). In addition, goals such as ensuring that girls and boys continue to secondary education under the heading of education, preventing preventable maternal deaths under the heading of healthy and quality life and informing about reproductive health are directly related to early marriages.

Child marriage is primarily a human rights violation. It threatens girls' quality of life, health and career prospects. Early marriages cause early pregnancies, and pregnancy and birth complications are more common in this group. These complications are one of the main causes of death in girls aged 15-19 in developing countries. As a result of studies aimed at preventing early pregnancies, the rate has been reduced from 60% to 45% in the past 6 decades. It is stated that 160 years are needed to prevent child pregnancies if the current rate of progress continues (UNFPA&UNICEF, 2023). Married children are at greater risk of sexually transmitted diseases. Early marriage mostly occurs due to interruption of education. Interruption of education is career expectation It is the most important obstacle to participation in economic life. Failure to prevent child marriage will result in failure to achieve more than one of the sustainable development goals (UNICEF & UNFPA, 2010). Child marriages can lead to interruption of education, economic inadequacy, violation of laws, age fraud, unofficial marriages, problems in registering newborn babies, psychological problems, restriction of freedoms and reproductive health problems (Iustitiani & Ajisuksmo, 2018a).

Effects of Early Marriages on Women's Health

Due to gender, there are many health risks that women face at every stage of their life cycle, starting from the intrauterine period. Health-based practices for adolescence;

1. Social pressure
2. Virginity control
3. Gender-based violence
4. Sexual harassment/abuse
5. Paid sex
6. Nutritional disorders
7. Substance addictions
8. Mental problems due to social life restrictions and pressure
9. Sexually transmitted infections
10. Intentional and unhealthy abortions
11. Unintended pregnancies
12. Early and forced marriage
13. They are listed as so-called honor killings.

90% of early pregnancies occur within the framework of marriage (Chantler, 2023). Pregnancy and birth-related complications are among the leading causes of death, especially for girls in the 15-19 age group (Say et al., 2014). Girls who marry before the age of fifteen are 50% more likely to experience violence from their partners than those who are older.

Early marriages cause children to encounter sex at a time when they do not have sufficient knowledge about reproductive health and rights and are not physically and spiritually ready. Early pregnancies, which pose many health risks, occur due to child marriages. Being married to men who are older and sexually active increases the risk of contracting sexually transmitted diseases. Additionally, the risk of experiencing gender-based sexual violence increases. In some cases, there are associations between genital mutation, which is a human rights violation, and early marriages. Burkina Faso, the Central African Republic, Ethiopia, Guinea, Liberia, Mali, Mauritania, Nigeria and Somalia are among the 20 countries where both early marriages and genital mutation are most common (Henrion, 2003).

The Impact of Early Marriages on Women's Education

Education is the most important element in eliminating gender inequality. It strengthens girls by increasing their knowledge and power to oppose discriminatory practices. Girls who want to be married leave school. Therefore, one of the most effective ways to delay early marriages is to keep girls in school. Each year of secondary education reduces the risk of early marriage by 6%. In addition to adolescent pregnancies, there are obstacles such as social roles given to married girls and concerns about stigma (Quentin et al., 2018). The effect of access to education on time to marriage is greater than the effect of marriage on access to education (UNICEF, 2021). It is almost impossible for a girl whose education was left unfinished and married to return to her education life.

Early Marriages and Child Pregnancies

The World Health Organization uses the term adolescent pregnancy to describe pregnancies occurring between the ages of 10 and 19 (Adolescent Pregnancy, 2004). Adolescent pregnancies and early marriages are closely related child rights violations. Social environment, geography and structural inequalities cause some children to reach adulthood at greater risk than their peers. Young girls in the poorest fifth of the population face four times the risk of becoming pregnant than those in the richest fifth. The onset of fertility at an early age may lead to an increase in the number of births and a decrease in the birth interval (WHO, 2011).

Key determinants of child pregnancies include early marriages, sexual repression, and lack of knowledge about access to and use of birth control. Most early pregnancies occur within the framework of marriage (Diabelková et al., 2023). In a study conducted by UNFPA in developing countries, covering 96% of the 20-24 age group, it was reported that one in every 3 young women gave birth during adolescence (Diabelková et al., 2023). Nearly half of these births (45%) took place at the age of 17 or younger. Child mothers continue to give birth as child mothers in the following periods. Early pregnancy has low access to quality prenatal, delivery and postpartum care. Therefore, the risks of pregnancy and birth complications and mortality and morbidity due to unsafe abortion practices are high (Chandra-Mouli et al., 2013). It has been reported that adolescent mothers whose age at birth is 10-19 have a higher risk of pre-eclampsia and eclampsia than mothers in the 20-24 age group, and endometritis and systemic infections are more common (Chandra-Mouli et al., 2013). Not receiving adequate prenatal care during pregnancy, anemia, nutritional deficiencies, miscarriage, stillbirth and excessive bleeding are other health risks of this period (Şen & Kavlak, 2011).

The fact that the child's body is not physically ready for pregnancy and birth causes negativities for the mother and the baby. The development of the pelvic bone, which has a critical place in normal birth, is completed between the ages of 20-22. For this reason, difficult birth is common in early pregnancies, and the risk of operational intervention increases (Şen & Kavlak, 2011; Suveren & Turan, 2022). Obstetric fistulas that cause urinary and fecal incontinence occur more frequently after birth. Problems related to the incomplete cognitive and psychological development of the child and mother are also common. They become women who are alone at home, unhappy, insecure, and exposed to more domestic violence (Trickett, Noll, Putnam, 2011; Toso, Cock, Leavey, 2020). Impairment of the mother's psychological health negatively affects the child's development (Boran et al., 2013; Malhotra et al., 2011).

If the mother is under 20 years of age, it also negatively affects the health of the newborn baby. Babies face low birth weight, premature birth and related complications (Chandra-Mouli et al., 2013). Maternal mortality rate at birth and increased infant mortality rate with low birth weight babies are common in premature births. Child deaths are occurring more frequently. Early pregnancies increase the economic burden of men and cause them to be deprived of education.

Risk Factors for Early Marriages

Family structure, socioeconomic factors, religious and cultural factors may be effective in early marriages. Religious and cultural factors hinder girls' rights to make their own choices due to their gender roles. There is a lot of evidence showing that poverty and lack of education are risk factors. Poverty and low educational attainment are both causes and consequences of child marriages. It has been reported that girls from poor families are twice as likely to marry early as those from high-income families. Especially in cultures where bride price is common, the marriage of a daughter is considered a source of economic income. In cultures where girls are paid as a "dowry" when marrying, early marriages are preferred because the amount of dowry to be given increases in proportion to the girl's age (Klugman et al., 2014). The probability of early marriage has been found to be highest among those with less education and the lowest economic status (Parsons & McCleary-Sills, 2014; Raj, 2010).

Unwanted pregnancies, families' concerns about facing slander or inappropriate behavior, and environmental attitudes are among the reasons for child marriages (Iustitiani & Ajisuksmo, 2018b). In studies conducted in Turkey, poverty, low education level, deficiencies in legal regulations, violence and abuse, traditions and gender inequalities, and migration have been identified as the reasons for child marriages (Anık & Barlin, 2017; Kahraman, 2018; Gök, 2016).

Studies conducted in Bangladesh and Sub-Saharan Africa found that the literacy level of women who married early was 5% lower and the level of secondary education was 8% lower (Nguyen & Wodon, 2014). In a study covering 18 of the 20 countries where child marriages are highest, it was determined that uneducated girls are 8 times more likely to marry early than girls who have completed secondary education (International Center for Research on Women, 2005).

In Indonesia, Rumble et al. (2018), Grijns and Horii (2018), and Marshan et al. (2013) education, family income level, number of children, religion, and access to social media were determined as risk factors for child marriages (Grijns & Horii, 2018; Natanael& Fajar, 2013; Rumble et al., 2018) . In the research conducted in Tanzania, religion, poverty, gender-based economic inequalities, lack of access to education and unemployment were identified as important determinants of child marriages (Stark, 2018). In studies conducted on child marriages; Poverty and economic conditions, lack of education, gender inequalities, cultural norms and traditions, gender-based violence, and conflict and crisis environments have been reported as common reasons (Sarah et al., 2019).

Method

Within the scope of the research, field studies conducted in Burdur province in Turkey in 5 different years to evaluate the prenatal care services routinely provided to pregnant women registered in family medicine units were retrospectively examined in terms of early marriage. Interviews with a total of 3598 pregnant women were included in the study. Women's age at marriage, age at first pregnancy, utilization of prenatal care services, and sociodemographic characteristics were described. The aim of the study was to determine whether there is a difference between the fertility characteristics and sociodemographic characteristics of women who marry early and those who do not.

Statistical analysis

It was performed using IBM SPSS version 23.0 (IBM Corp., Armonk, NY). Number and percentage values were used as descriptive statistics. Analysis of the data was done using the chi-square test. $P<0.05$ was taken as the limit value for statistical significance. In order to determine the situations affected by early marriages, binary logistic regression analysis was performed by creating a model with the variables found to be significant in univariate analyses.

Results

Within the scope of prenatal care, 3598 pregnant women between the ages of 13-45 were interviewed. 3.0% of the total marriages (108 people) were under the age of 15, and 19.1% (687 people) were under the age of 18. 0.7% (26 people) of pregnant women in the 20-24 age group were married under the age of 15, and 6% (217 people) were married under the age of 18. 59.2% (407) of women who married under the age of 18 had their first pregnancy under the age of 18. Those whose marriage age was under 18 years old and those aged 18 years and above were compared in terms of education, employment, income level, number of people living at home, type of marriage and pregnancy history. Considering the fertility characteristics, it was observed that there was a statistically significant difference between the two groups in terms of the number of children dying under the age of 5, birth intervals being less than 2 years, and the number of pregnancies being more than 3. It has been observed that women who get married early do not want their current pregnancies. It has also been determined that early marriages are mostly arranged and child brides live in large families (more than 4 people). It has been observed that the education period of men and women who marry early remains below 8 years, the man cannot have a job that will earn a regular income and household income is insufficient ($p<0.05$) (Table 1).

Table 1. Distribution of sociodemographic and pregnancy-related characteristics by age at marriage

	Marriage age under 18 n (%)	Marriage age 18 years and above n (%)	X^2	p
Pregnancy interval* (Among those without first pregnancy)				
2 years and under	217 (18,6)	950 (81,4)	7,158	**0.007**
More than 2 years	386 (22,7)	1313 (77,3)		
Number of pregnancies				
2 and under	396 (16,1)	2062 (83,9)	45,718	**0.000**
3+	290 (25,9)	830 (74,1)		
State of wanting pregnancy				
Wanted	509 (17,8)	2358 (82,2)	15,999	**0.000**
Didn't want to	177 (24,4)	547 (75,6)		
Death of children under five years of age				

continued on following page

Table 1. Continued

	Marriage age under 18 n (%)	Marriage age 18 years and above n (%)	X²	p
There is	23 (32,4)	48 (67,6)	4,867	**0.027**
None	582 (21,0)	2192 (79,0)		
Received prenatal care for the first time				
14 weeks and below	598 (18,9)	2576 (81,1)	0,772	
More than 15 weeks	87 (20,7)	334 (79,3)		0.380
Number of prenatal care				
4 and above	476 (19,4)	1977 (80,6)	0,490	0.484
Less than 4	210 (18,4)	930 (81,6)		
Kinship with spouse				
Yes	58 (21,2)	216 (78,8)		
No	629 (19,0)	2690 (81,0)	0,785	0.376
Civil marriage				
Yes	653 (18,6)	2862 (81,4)	22,272	**0.00**
No	34 (41,5)	48 (58,5)		
Arranged marriage				
Yes	356 (21,3)	1316 (78,7)		**0.002**
No	331 (17,2)	1591 (82,8)	9,560	
Female education status				
8 years and under	617 (30,6)	1401 (69,4)		**0.000**
More than 8 years	56 (3,7)	1473 (96,3)	481,468	
Spouse educational status				
8 years and under	493 (28,1)	1263 (71,9)		
More than 8 years	188 (10,3)	1635 (89,7)	188,208	**0.000**
Women's working status				
Not working	644 (21,3)	2380 (78,7)	86,772	
Working	27 (5,5)	466 (94,5)		**0.000**
Spouse's employment status				
Doesn't have a regular job	221 (25,6)	641 (74,4)	30,058	**0.000**
Has a regular job	465 (17,0)	2269 (83,0)		
Sufficient household income				
Sufficient	125 (14,0)	767 (86,0)		
Barely /insufficient income	160 (21,3)	592 (78,7)	14,970	**0.000**

continued on following page

Table 1. Continued

	Marriage age under 18 n (%)	Marriage age 18 years and above n (%)	X²	p
Number of people living in the house				
4 and under	539 (17,1)	2619 (82,9)	60,923	
More than 4	148 (33,7)	291 (66,3)		0.000
Total	687 (19,1)	2911 (80,9)	3598	

Parameters found to be statistically significant in the chi-square test were included in the logistic regression analysis. Binary logistic regression analysis is required to model the effect of two-way independent variables on the dependent variable. (Table 2).

Table 2. Binary Logistic Regression Analysis

Dependent Variable: Marriage age under 18 or not							
Independent variables		B	SE.	Wald	Odds Ratio	%95 CI (EK-EB value)	p
Educational status of the woman	8 years and under	2.179	0.294	54.9	8.838	4.966-15.728	0.000
	More than 8 years	Referans				
Spouse's education level	8 years and under	0.549	0.188	8.493	1.732	1.197-2.505	0.004
	More than 8 years	Reference					
Arranged marriage situation	Yes	0.437	0.173	6.336	0.646	0.460-0.908	0.012
	No	Referans					

With logistic regression analysis, it was determined that marriages under the age of 18 pose a risk for interrupting the education of men and women and for arranged marriages. For those who marry early, the risk of interruption of education after the primary level is 8.8 (CI: 4.966-15.728) times higher for girls and 1.7 (1.197-2.505) times higher for boys. The rate of arranged marriages is high (OR: 0.65; CI: 0.460-0.908) (Table 2).

DISCUSSION

Preventing early marriages is among the Sustainable Development Goals. Early marriages pose significant challenges to the health, education, and economic prospects of girls, often perpetuating cycles of poverty and inequality (Marphatia, Ambale, Reid, 2017). According to the analysis results of the Turkey Population Health Survey, the rates of women married under the age of 18 and 15 among women in the 20-24 age group in Turkey in 2018 were reported to be 2.0% and 14.7%, respectively. In the Mediterranean Region, where Burdur province is located, the rate of marriage under the age of 18 is 19% (UNFPA, 2020). In our study, 3.0% (108 people) of marriages in all age groups were under the age of 15, and 19.1% (687 people) were under the age of 18. 0.7% (26 people) of pregnant women in the 20-24 age group were married under the age of 15, and 6% (217 people) were married under the age of 18. Our findings show that the level of early marriage in Burdur province is below the Türkiye and World average. When we look at the data of all age groups and the 20-24 age group, it is seen that early marriages have decreased over the years but have not been reset. 59.2% (407) of women who married under the age of 18 had their first pregnancy under the age of 18. According to TNSA 2018 data, 54% of women in the 20-24 age group had their first birth at the age of 18-19, and 33% of them gave birth between the ages of 15-17. It is seen that early marriages result in early pregnancies.

In our study, it was determined by logistic regression analysis that marriages under the age of 18 pose a risk for interrupting the education of men and women and for arranged marriages.

Consistent with the literature, in our study, the education level of men and women of 8 years or less was determined to be an important risk factor for early pregnancy. According to TDHS data, 11% of child brides are uneducated or below primary school; 30% are primary school; 52% are secondary school graduates and 7% are high school graduates. Being a secondary school graduate does not prevent girls from getting married. In the Mediterranean region, where the research data were collected, 18.9% of women aged 20-24 were married under the age of 18. In the same region, the rate of marriage before the age of 15 among women in the 20-49 age group was reported as 4.4%, while the rate of marriage under the age of 18 was reported as 22.4%. In a study conducted in South Asia, lack of education was identified as a risk factor for early marriages. It has been reported that the increased risk is not only among those with the least and highest education, but also between those with 6-9 years of education and those with 10 years or more of education (Scott et al., 2021). A study conducted in Iran reported that education plays a key role in early marriages. Illiterate women who got married between the ages of 10-14 are 3 times more likely than literate ones (4.52% versus 1.26%). While

9% of men who got married between the ages of 15-19 are illiterate, this rate is 2% among literate men. It was determined as 13 (Asna-ashary et al., 2021). In a study covering Ethiopia, India, Peru and Vietnam, dropping out of school was reported as a risk factor for early marriage (Bhan et al., 2019). Hossain et al. (2016), Islam et al. (2016) and Kamal et al. (2015) in Bangladesh, the education level of the husband was found to be a risk factor for early marriages (Hossain et al., 2016; Islam, 2016; Kalamar et al., 2016).

In our study, arranged marriage was identified as a risk factor for early marriage. The way of meeting your spouse was questioned in the TDHS 2018 study. 69% of women who got married early stated that their method of marriage was arranged. Among all married women, this rate drops to 55%. In other words, childhood marriages were planned mostly through family and parents. Poverty, the lack of deterrent legal regulations to prevent early marriages, the patriarchal family structure, and the fact that early marriages are normal and common in the environment are considered as factors affecting the family's guiding role in early marriages (Çay Padalıhasanoğlu & Yaman, 2022). Many studies talk about early marriage of girls as a method of coping with financial problems. For this purpose, girls are forced into marriage, especially by their fathers (Anık & Barlin, 2017; Kara, 2015). Marriage of girls at an early age, especially to earn income from bride price, is a human/woman trafficking problem. Forced marriages in the United Nations Joint Program to prevent child, early and forced marriages; It is defined as "human trafficking, traditional arranged marriages, kidnappings, marriages for the purpose of obtaining citizenship, and marriages in which the victim lacks the capacity to give full and informed consent" (UNFPA, 2019). Early marriages, which are considered to occur voluntarily, can be seen as a way to escape from the abusive environment and start a family, especially for children who were physically and sexually abused during their childhood (McNiss et al., 2021; Pallitto & Murillo, 2008).

CONCLUSION

The steps to be taken within the scope of the action plan implemented in cooperation with UNFPA and UNICEF to end child marriages have been determined (UNFPA-UNICEF, 2023). Girls' education should be improved by removing the physical, social and economic barriers to girls' inclusion in education. Adolescents need to be encouraged and empowered to make their voices heard in order to build their social, cognitive and economic gains. Sexual and reproductive health and rights should be improved to ensure access to services and information. Gender inequality must be combated at structural, relational and individual levels. Changing attitudes, norms and behaviors about gender roles and adolescent sexuality should be encouraged.

Early marriages are a concrete example of gender inequality, especially for girls. It is a significant obstacle to the exercise of fundamental rights such as education, health, business and participation in social life. In some parts of the world, this also poses a problem for boys. By giving the son the responsibility of supporting the household, it paves the way for child labor and poverty. Legal regulations that include deterrent penalties against child marriages should be made, and the sanctions in the law should be applied without exception. Although progress has been made in preventing early marriages, it seems that we are far from the goal of completely eliminating it within the scope of the Sustainable Development Goals. The common point of studies in this field is that schooling problems, especially for girls but also for boys, are the main risk factor. It is seen that being literate alone is not enough, and the education level should be increased to high school level for both genders. It is clear that poverty must be eliminated so that girls are not seen as a source of income through bride price or as an expense item that requires dowry.

REFERENCES

Ackerman, X., & Abay, N. A. (2013). Improving Learning Opportunities and Outcomes for Girls in Africa. *Center for Universaal Education at Brookings, December*.

Anık, M., & Barlin, R. (2017). Türkiye'de Çocuk Gelinler Sorunu : Balıkesir Örneği. *Insan ve Topllum Bilimleri Araştırmaları Dergisi, 6*(3).

Asna-Ashary, M., Farzanegan, M. R., Feizi, M., & Gholipour, H. F. (2021). Socio-Economic Determinants of Child Marriage: Evidence from the Iranian Provinces. SSRN *Electronic Journal*. DOI: 10.2139/ssrn.3535283

Bhan, N., Gautsch, L., McDougal, L., Lapsansky, C., Obregon, R., & Raj, A. (2019). Effects of Parent–Child Relationships on Child Marriage of Girls in Ethiopia, India, Peru, and Vietnam: Evidence From a Prospective Cohort. *The Journal of Adolescent Health, 65*(4), 498–506. Advance online publication. DOI: 10.1016/j.jadohealth.2019.05.002 PMID: 31279722

Boran, P., & Gökçay, G., Deveciòglu, E., & Eren, T. (2013). Çocuk gelinler Child brides. *Marmara Medical Journal*, ●●●, 26.

Capper, D. (2022). Glossary of Terms and Concepts. In *Roaming Free Like a Deer*. DOI: 10.7591/cornell/9781501759574.002.0007

Chandra-Mouli, V., Camacho, A. V., & Michaud, P. A. (2013). WHO guidelines on preventing early pregnancy and poor reproductive outcomes among adolescents in developing countries. In *Journal of Adolescent Health* (Vol. 52, Issue 5). DOI: 10.1016/j.jadohealth.2013.03.002

Chantler, K. (2023). Forced Marriage. In *Gender-Based Violence: A Comprehensive Guide*. DOI: 10.1007/978-3-031-05640-6_5

Diabelková, J., Rimárová, K., Dorko, E., Urdzík, P., Houžvičková, A., & Argalášová, Ľ. (2023). Adolescent Pregnancy Outcomes and Risk Factors. *International Journal of Environmental Research and Public Health, 20*(5), 4113. Advance online publication. DOI: 10.3390/ijerph20054113 PMID: 36901128

Efevbera, Y., & Bhabha, J. (2020). Defining and deconstructing girl child marriage and applications to global public health. *BMC Public Health, 20*(1), 1547. DOI: 10.1186/s12889-020-09545-0 PMID: 33054856

Gastón, C. M., Misunas, C., & Cappa, C. (2019). Child marriage among boys: A global overview of available data. *Vulnerable Children and Youth Studies, 14*(3), 219–228. DOI: 10.1080/17450128.2019.1566584

Gök, M. (2016). Child marriages in Turkey with different aspects. *International Journal of Human Sciences*, 13(1), 2222. DOI: 10.14687/ijhs.v13i1.3795

Grijns, M., & Horii, H. (2018). Child Marriage in a Village in West Java (Indonesia): Compromises between Legal Obligations and Religious Concerns. *Asian Journal of Law and Society*, 5(2), 453–466. Advance online publication. DOI: 10.1017/als.2018.9

Hallett, T., Lewis, J., Lopman, B., Nyamukapa, C., Mushati, P., Wambe, M., Garnett, G., & Gregson, S. (2007). Age at first sex and HIV infection in rural Zimbabwe. *Studies in Family Planning*, 38(1), 1–10. DOI: 10.1111/j.1728-4465.2007.00111.x PMID: 17385378

Henrion, R. (2003). Mutilations génitales féminines, mariages forcés et grossesses précoces. *Bulletin de l'Académie Nationale de Médecine*, 187(6), 1051–1066. DOI: 10.1016/S0001-4079(19)33937-8 PMID: 14978867

Hossain, M. G., Mahumud, R. A., & Saw, A. (2016). Prevalence of child marriage among Bangladeshi women and trend of change over time. *Journal of Biosocial Science*, 48(4), 530–538. Advance online publication. DOI: 10.1017/S0021932015000279 PMID: 26286142

International Center for Research on Women. (2005). *Too Young To Wed: Education & Action Toward Ending Child Marriage*. The International Center for Research on Women.

Irani, M., & Roudsari, R. (2019). Reproductive and Sexual Health Consequences of Child Marriage: A Review of literature. *Journal of Midwifery & Reproductive Health*, 7, 1584–1590. DOI: 10.22038/JMRH.2018.31627.1342

Islam, A. (2016). Prevalence and Determinants of Contraceptive use among Employed and Unemployed Women in Bangladesh. [IJMA]. *International Journal of MCH and AIDS*, 5(2). Advance online publication. DOI: 10.21106/ijma.83 PMID: 28058196

Iustitiani, N. S. D., & Ajisuksmo, C. R. P. (2018a). Supporting Factors and Consequences of Child Marriage. *ANIMA Indonesian Psychological Journal*, 33(2), 100–111. DOI: 10.24123/aipj.v33i2.1581

Iustitiani, N. S. D., & Ajisuksmo, C. R. P. (2018b). Supporting Factors and Consequences of Child Marriage. *ANIMA Indonesian Psychological Journal*, 33(2), 100–111. DOI: 10.24123/aipj.v33i2.1581

Kahraman, A. B., & Şenateş, T. (2020). Çocuk gelinler (Siverek örneği). *Journal of Social Sciences*, 29(29), 380–392.

Kalamar, A. M., Lee-Rife, S., & Hindin, M. J. (2016). Interventions to Prevent Child Marriage Among Young People in Low- and Middle-Income Countries: A Systematic Review of the Published and Gray Literature. In *Journal of Adolescent Health* (Vol. 59, Issue 3). DOI: 10.1016/j.jadohealth.2016.06.015

Kara, B. (2015). Değişen Aile Dinamikleri Açisindan Erken Yaşta Evlilikler Sorunu ve Toplumsal Önemi. *Süleyman Demirel Üniversitesi İktisadi ve İdari Bilimler Fakültesi Dergisi*, 20(2), 59–72.

Kıran, E. (2017). Toplumsal cinsiyet rolleri bağlaminda türkiye'de çocuk gelinler. Balkan Sosyal Bilimler Dergisi, (ICOMEP 2017 Özel Sayısı), 1-8.

Klugman, J., Hanmer, L., Twigg, S., Hasan, T., McCleary-Sills, J., & Santamaria, J. (2014). Voice and Agency: Empowering Women and Girls for Shared Prosperity. In *Voice and Agency: Empowering Women and Girls for Shared Prosperity*. DOI: 10.1596/978-1-4648-0359-8

Lekanova, E. E. (2020). Legal Regulation of the Minimum Marriage Age: The Past and the Present. *Actual Problems of Russian Law*, 15(8), 84–95. Advance online publication. DOI: 10.17803/1994-1471.2020.117.8.084-095

Malhotra, A., Warner, A., Mcgonagle, A., & Lee-Rife, S. (2011). *WHAT THE EVIDENCE SHOWS Solutions to End Child Marriage Solutions to End Child Marriage*. International Center for Research on Women.

Marphatia, A., Ambale, G., & Reid, A. (2017). Women's Marriage Age Matters for Public Health: A Review of the Broader Health and Social Implications in South Asia. *Frontiers in Public Health*, 5, 269. Advance online publication. DOI: 10.3389/fpubh.2017.00269 PMID: 29094035

McNiss, C., Kalarchian, M., & Laurent, J. (2021). Factors associated with childhood sexual abuse and adolescent pregnancy. *Child Abuse & Neglect*, 120, 105183. Advance online publication. DOI: 10.1016/j.chiabu.2021.105183 PMID: 34245975

Natanael, M. J., & Fajar, M. R., and M. R. (2013). Prevalence of Child Marriage and Its Determinants among Young Women in Indonesia. *Child Poverty and Social Protection Conference*.

Nguyen, M. C., & Wodon, Q. (2014). Impact of child marriage on literacy and education attainment in Africa. *Global Partnership for Education, September*.

Padalıhasanoğlu, E. Ç., & Yaman, Ö. M. (2022). Gayriresmî Erken Evlilikler: 18 Yaş Altı Evlilik Yapan Kadınların Evlilik Öncesi Aile Yaşantılarının İncelenmesi. Turkish Studies-Social Sciences, 17(5).

Pallitto, C. C., & Murillo, V. (2008). Childhood Abuse as a Risk Factor for Adolescent Pregnancy in El Salvador. *The Journal of Adolescent Health*, 42(6), 580–586. Advance online publication. DOI: 10.1016/j.jadohealth.2007.11.148 PMID: 18486867

Parsons, J., Edmeades, J., Kes, A., Petroni, S., Sexton, M., & Wodon, Q. (2015). Economic Impacts of Child Marriage: A Review of the Literature. *The Review of Faith & International Affairs*, 13(3), 12–22. Advance online publication. DOI: 10.1080/15570274.2015.1075757

Parsons, J., & McCleary-Sills, J. (2014). *Preventing Child Marriage*. EnGender Impact.

Pearse, R., & Connell, R. (2016). Gender Norms and the Economy: Insights from Social Research. *Feminist Economics*, 22(1), 30–53. DOI: 10.1080/13545701.2015.1078485

Quentin, W., Montenegro, C., Nguyen, H., & Onagoruwa, A. (2018). Missed opportunities: the high cost of not educating girls. In *World Bank*. Issue July.

Raj, A. (2010). When the mother is a child: The impact of child marriage on the health and human rights of girls. In *Archives of Disease in Childhood* (Vol. 95, Issue 11). DOI: 10.1136/adc.2009.178707

Rumble, L., Peterman, A., Irdiana, N., Triyana, M., & Minnick, E. (2018). An empirical exploration of female child marriage determinants in Indonesia. *BMC Public Health*, 18(1), 407. Advance online publication. DOI: 10.1186/s12889-018-5313-0 PMID: 29587705

Sampedro, R. (2021). The Sustainable Development Goals (SDG). *Carreteras*, 4(232), 253–257. Advance online publication. DOI: 10.4324/9780429282348-52

Sarah, D., Media, G., & Hough-Stewart, L. (2019). *The State of Girls' rights in the UK 2019-2020*. Lecturer in Social Anthropology.

Say, L., Chou, D., Gemmill, A., Tunçalp, Ö., Moller, A. B., Daniels, J., Gülmezoglu, A. M., Temmerman, M., & Alkema, L. (2014). Global causes of maternal death: A WHO systematic analysis. *The Lancet. Global Health*, 2(6), e323–e333. Advance online publication. DOI: 10.1016/S2214-109X(14)70227-X PMID: 25103301

Scott, S., Nguyen, P. H., Neupane, S., Pramanik, P., Nanda, P., Bhutta, Z. A., Afsana, K., & Menon, P. (2021). Early marriage and early childbearing in South Asia: Trends, inequalities, and drivers from 2005 to 2018. *Annals of the New York Academy of Sciences*, 1491(1), 60–73. DOI: 10.1111/nyas.14531 PMID: 33258141

Şen, S., & Kavlak, O. (2011). Çocuk Gelinler: Erken Yaş Evlilikleri ve Adölesan Gebeliklere Yaklaşım. *Journal of Social Policy Studies*, 7(25).

Sezgin, A., & Punamäki, R. (2019). Impacts of early marriage and adolescent pregnancy on mental and somatic health: The role of partner violence. *Archives of Women's Mental Health*, 23(2), 155–166. DOI: 10.1007/s00737-019-00960-w PMID: 30955087

St-Germain, A., Kirby, R., & Urquia, M. (2022). Reproductive health among married and unmarried mothers aged less than 18, 18–19, and 20–24 years in the United States, 2014–2019: A population-based cross-sectional study. *PLoS Medicine*, 19(3), e1003929. Advance online publication. DOI: 10.1371/journal.pmed.1003929 PMID: 35271581

Stark, L. (2018). Early marriage and cultural constructions of adulthood in two slums in Dar es Salaam. *Culture, Health & Sexuality*, 20(8), 888–901. Advance online publication. DOI: 10.1080/13691058.2017.1390162 PMID: 29111880

Sütlü, S. (2022). Polıcıes On Gender Equalıty. In Sütlü, S., & Say Şahin, D. (Eds.), *Dısadvantaged Groups: A Socıal Polıcy Perspectıve* (pp. 17–28). Nobel Publishing.

Suveren, Y., & Turan, Z. (2022). Erken Evlilik Sorunu ve Kadın Sağlığı: Güncel Bir Değerlendirme. *Universal Journal of History and Culture*, 4(1), 78–99. DOI: 10.52613/ujhc.1010759

Tong, R. (2012). Gender Roles. In *Encyclopedia of Applied Ethics* (pp. 399–406). Elsevier., DOI: 10.1016/B978-0-12-373932-2.00307-0

Toso, K., Cock, P., & Leavey, G. (2020). Maternal exposure to violence and offspring neurodevelopment: A systematic review. *Paediatric and Perinatal Epidemiology*, 34(2), 190–203. Advance online publication. DOI: 10.1111/ppe.12651 PMID: 32026500

Trickett, P., Noll, J., & Putnam, F. (2011). The impact of sexual abuse on female development: Lessons from a multigenerational, longitudinal research study. *Development and Psychopathology*, 23(2), 453–476. DOI: 10.1017/S0954579411000174 PMID: 23786689

UNESCO. (b). (2014). UNESCO Priority Gender Equality Action Plan for 2014-2021. *United Nations Educational, Scientific and Cultural Organization*.

UNFPA. (2019). *Çocuk Yaşta, Erken ve Zorla Evliliklerin Önlenmesine Yönelik Birleşmiş Milletler Ortak Programı*. https://www.cocukyastaevliligeson.org/#/?id=ba%c5%9flarken

UNFPA. (2020). *Türkiye'de Çocuk Yaşta Erken ve Zorla Evlilikler: 1993-2018 Türkiye Nüfus ve Sağlık Araştırmaları Veri Analizi*. https://turkiye.unfpa.org/sites/default/files/pub-pdf/turkce_web_son_pdf.pdf

UNFPA-UNICEF. (2023). UNFPA-UNICEF Global Programme to Accelerate Action to End Child Marriage. *Unfpa, January*.

UNICEF, & UNFPA. (2010). Marrying Too Young. In *United Nations Population Fund UNFPA* (Vol. 11, Issue 1).

UNICEF. (2017). Gender and Equality: Glossary Of Terms And Concepts. In *The Qur an, Morality and Critical Reason* (Issue November).

UNICEF. (2021). *Evolution in the evidence base on child marriage (2000-2019)*. https://www.unicef.org/media/91991/file/Child-marriage-evidence-report-2021.pdf

UNICEF. (2023). *Child-marriage global Database*. https://data.unicef.org/topic/child-protection/child-marriage/

WHO. (2004). *Adolescent pregnancy*. Retrieved from: (https://apps.who.int/iris/bitstream/handle/10665/42903/9241591455_eng.pdf;jsessionid=4EE656F1D73E523CA32062208E4D280C? Sequence WHO. (2011). *Preventing Early Pregnancy and Poor Reproductive Outcomes Among Adolescents in Developing Countries*. Retrieved from https://iris.who.int/bitstream/handle/10665/44691/9789241502214_eng.pdf

WHO. (2024). *Gender and health*. https://www.who.int/health-topics/gender#tab=tab_1

Wodon, Q. (2016). Early Childhood Development in the Context of the Family: The Case of Child Marriage. *Journal of Human Development and Capabilities*, 17(4), 590–598. Advance online publication. DOI: 10.1080/19452829.2016.1245277

Xing, C., Betancor, V., Chas, A., & Rodríguez-Pérez, A. (2022). Gender inequality in incivility: Everyone should be polite, but it is fine for some of us to be impolite. *Frontiers in Psychology*, 13, 966045. Advance online publication. DOI: 10.3389/fpsyg.2022.966045 PMID: 36225692

Yoosefi Lebni, J., Solhi, M., Ebadi Fard Azar, F., Khalajabadi Farahani, F., & Irandoost, S. F. (2023). Exploring the Consequences of Early Marriage: A Conventional Content Analysis. *Inquiry*, 60, 00469580231159963. Advance online publication. DOI: 10.1177/00469580231159963 PMID: 37073489

Chapter 10
Enormities of Early Marriages of Girls Lensing Physical–Mental Health Impairments:
Projecting Socio–Legal Implications in Global Context

Bhupinder Singh
https://orcid.org/0009-0006-4779-2553
Sharda University, India

ABSTRACT

Early marriages have long been a source of worry because of the possible negative impacts on one's physical and mental health, especially when they involve females. Child marriage continues to be a common practice in many places, affecting millions of girls globally, despite global attempts to abolish it. Gender inequality, socio-economic circumstances and cultural expectations are some of the main causes of early marriages. The physiological immaturity of young brides poses risks during pregnancy and childbirth, leading to higher rates of maternal and infant mortality. Legislation and enforcement play a pivotal role in preventing and combating child marriages. This chapter explores existing legal frameworks globally and highlights the importance of stringent laws, effective implementation and awareness campaigns to curb this harmful practice via- Policy Recommendations; Education and Awareness: Support Systems; Community Engagement because early marriages can have profound effects on the physical health of girls.

DOI: 10.4018/979-8-3693-3394-5.ch010

INTRODUCTION

Early marriage and sexual activity is widely remarkable across societies and cultures, including India. Research shows that early marriage and its related sexual activity influences teenage girls to their reproductive health challenges, including a higher susceptibility to the risks of reproductive health and sexually transmitted infections. The early marriage of girls is one of the most pressing global concerns, especially in areas where cultural and social pressures coupled with economic forces result in young children being forced into marriages as soon as they can be delivered a groom (Alghamdi, 2024; Uddin, 2015). The harms associated with such practices transcend their immediate health (e.g., physical and mental) and social consequences, for these young girls experience a far-reaching encumbrance on both psycho-social and physical health that transcends into long-term outcomes related to general well-being and quality of life (Alnasser et al., 2024; Uddin, 2017).

Early marriage is physically harmful for the girl and the most important repercussions are that these young brides deal with early pregnancies and miscarriages, which are harmful both to them and their growing babies. Based on health perspective, research shows that early pregnancies during adolescence result several health complicacies such as obstetric fistula preeclampsia to even maternal or infant death (Altwaijri et al., 2023; Uddin, 2021). They are exposed to a greater degree of these risks due to little or no access to suitable healthcare and family planning. Power imbalances in relationships and insufficient knowledge of sexual reproductive health also make young girls at risk to suffer from sexually transmitted infections (STIs). In addition, early marriage has devastating psychological outcomes (Alsmeheen, 2023). Based on psychosocial perspective, research indicates that 20-40% of the young girls are acting as "little mothers," with grave consequences such as forced sexual activity, early motherhood, and the stress from early adult responsibilities for which they have no training or personal resources or skills (Almadani & Alwesmi, 2023). These early characteristics predispose child brides to increased levels of depression, anxiety and post-traumatic stress disorder (PTSD). Additionally, early marriage limits educational and social opportunities that can reinforce girls to a sense of worthlessness regarding control over her personal life (Banda, 2023; Boveda et al., 2023). It leads to the internalization of a deep sense of personal impotency and inferiority, with despair attaching itself chronically onto their mental landscape (Strungaru, 2024; Uddin et al., 2019).

Early marriage has not only devastating physical and mental effects on young girls, but also further entrenches their poverty, gender inequities, and health disparities. Preventing these adverse outcomes with a three-pronged approach, encompassing education, law enforcement reform and access to health service is crucial in order to secure the safety of at-risk girls and advance their welfare. The psychological toll of early marriages on girls is a critical aspect that deserves attention. The abrupt transition from childhood to marital responsibilities can contribute to heightened stress, anxiety and depression (Novianti et al., 2023; Uddin, 2021). Comprehending the extensive ramifications of these partnerships is vital in order to build efficacious remedies and legal structures. The girls who are forced into early marriages often struggle with limited autonomy, restricted educational opportunities and increased vulnerability to domestic violence which further exacerbate their mental health challenges (Asaoui et al., 2023; Alonzo & Zubarroglu-Ioannides, 2023).

In this chapter, we address a number of early marriage-related topics while concentrating on the problems with physical and mental health that frequently result from this practice. This chapter examines the socio-legal ramifications and talk about the actions governments and non-governmental organizations (NGOs) have made to address early marriage. The objective is to investigate the underlying factors that lead to early marriage, the effects it has on girls' health, and how well-functioning the current legal systems are in combating this sociocultural practice (Nurmila & Winddiana, 2023; Uddin, 2015). Addressing the issue of early marriages requires a comprehensive approach that includes socio-legal considerations. This chapter explores the prevalence of early marriages and their effects on girl's physical and mental health with the goal of illuminating the socio-legal aspects of this widespread problem. Early marriage which is defined as being married before turning 18 remains a serious issue in many parts of the world, including India. Families may choose to marry off their girls at a young age due to cultural customs and financial constraints, even in nations where early marriage is illegal (McKinley, 2023; Uddin, 2015, 2021). This practice has adverse effects on young girls' health, education, and general well-being, which, in turn, restrict their future prospects and prevent their significant contributions to a society.

Figure 1. The landscapes of introduction split

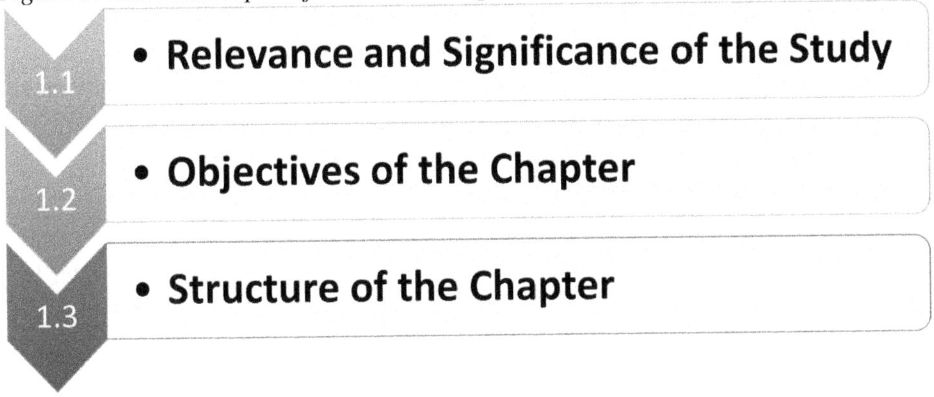

- 1.1 • **Relevance and Significance of the Study**
- 1.2 • **Objectives of the Chapter**
- 1.3 • **Structure of the Chapter**

Relevance and Significance of the Study

An early marriage essentially ends a girl's youth and has terrible effects on her life. A teenage girl is forced into an early maturity before she is emotionally and physically ready. The rights of child brides to personal safety, education, health care, and social interaction are frequently violated through early marriage (Danquah, 2023). In addition, girls are usually compelled to marry considerably older men in arranged marriages, which can result in their age difference in marital relationships (Murewanhema, et al., 2023). Young brides have a far lower likelihood of finishing their school, which has long-term negative effects on their social and financial positions in the family. They don't have much flexibility and frequently experience social isolation. They have a greater chance of experiencing physical and/or sexual abuse when they get married early (Inkane & Petkar, 2023). In addition, there is a higher chance of HIV/AIDS infection, domestic abuse, and hazardous problems during pregnancy and delivery period. Research shows that each year almost 17 million girls give a number of births. When a girl's body isn't physiologically mature enough for a safe birth, forced pregnancies and early childbearing often brought on by child marriage which occur, and can cause major health and social issues (Phiri et al., 2023).

Worldwide, the primary cause of mortality for females between the ages of 15 and 19 is complications related to pregnancy and delivery. Adolescent mothers who bear and care children have significantly elevated risks of maternal mortality, as well as a greater probability of low birth weight, malnourishment, and developmental problems. In addition, young mothers are far less likely to attend school and earn money, which frequently leads them to financial difficulties in later life.

Objectives of the Chapter

The early marriages of 'young girls' have the significant effects on their physical and mental health (Zaky et al., 2024). These marriages often have adverse outcomes that affect not only the young brides but also the broader society. This study sheds light on the dire consequences of early marriage around the world, focusing on the health harms experienced by young brides and examining the socio-legal impacts (Manohar et al., 2023). Through a comprehensive analysis of existing studies, case reports, and legal frameworks, this chapter aims to highlight the need for robust policies and social support systems to address this critical issue. This chapter has the following objectives:

1. To explore the global trends in early marriages, with a particular emphasis on how common they are across various geographies, cultural contexts, and socioeconomic classes. Investigating the main causes of early marriages, such as poverty, gender disparity, cultural customs, and legal loopholes, is part of this.
2. To assess the negative effects of early marriage on health, with a special emphasis on the damage that young marriage does to a girl's physical and emotional well-being. Analyzing the risks of adolescent pregnancies, difficult deliveries, mental health conditions, and heightened susceptibility to abuse and violence is another aspect of this chapter.
3. To look into the socio-legal effects of early marriages, including how it impacts young girls' rights and chances and what legal frameworks and enforcement issues are now in place. This goal also includes suggesting legislative changes, social initiatives, and policy changes that can lessen the negative effects of early marriage and improve the health and wellbeing of young females.

Figure 2. The Objectives of the Chapter

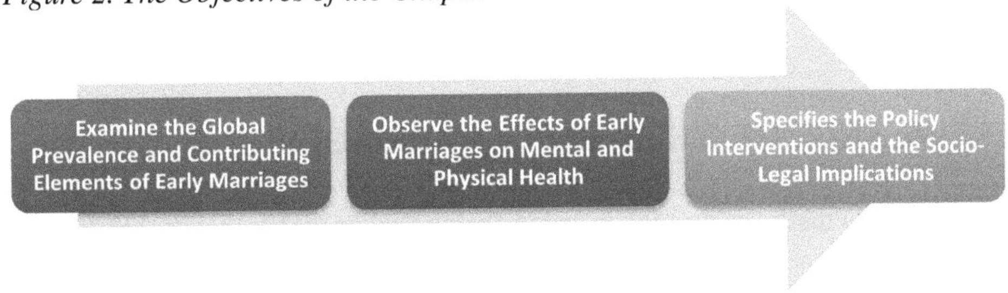

| Examine the Global Prevalence and Contributing Elements of Early Marriages | Observe the Effects of Early Marriages on Mental and Physical Health | Specifies the Policy Interventions and the Socio-Legal Implications |

Structure of the Chapter

Based on multiple approaches this chapter comprehensively explores the magnitudes of early marriages of girls lensing physical-mental health impairments: Projecting socio-legal Implications in global context. Section 2 elaborates the prevalence of early marriages. Section 3 discusses the early marriages and health: risks to physical and mental health. Section 4 highlights the social and legal consequences of early marriages. Section 5 lays down the suggestions and interventions in policy. Section 6 concludes the chapter with direction for future research.

Figure 3. The Flow of this Chapter (Source- Original)

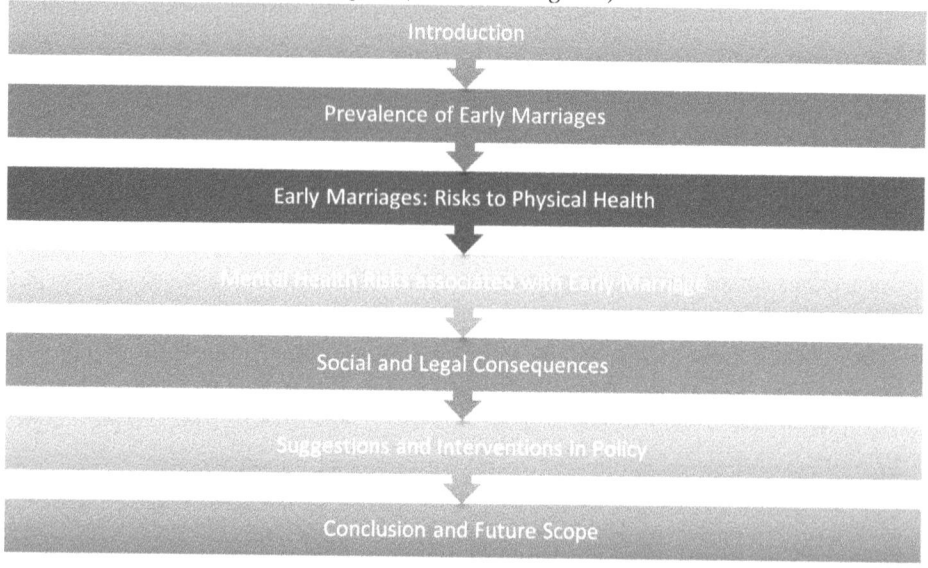

- Introduction
- Prevalence of Early Marriages
- Early Marriages: Risks to Physical Health
- Mental Health Risks associated with Early Marriage
- Social and Legal Consequences
- Suggestions and Interventions in Policy
- Conclusion and Future Scope

PREVALENCE OF GIRLS' EARLY MARRIAGES

Girls' early marriage usually occurred during teen ages (13-18 years) is a global problem. This type of marriage is remarkable throughout the world, including nations, cultures, religions, and ethnic groups. Previous studies reveal that girls' early marriage, that may exert negative effects on personal and social life, varies from 70 percent to 5 percent across the countries, depending on demographic structure, socio-economic development, religion, region, residence, and social system in which they live (United Nations, 1988, 1990; 2000). Continent-wise data reveal that the rates of early marriage of the adolescents aged 10-18 years are 5 to 20 percent higher in Africa and South Asia than in Central America, Middle East, Latin America and the Caribbean (Singh & Samara, 1998) than in North America, East Asia and Western Europe. United Nations Children's Fund, UNICEF (2001, 2023) in the less-developed countries has found that early marriage pattern and its negative social consequences are the most likely to prevail in Niger (77 percent), Chad (71 percent), Bangladesh (65 percent), Mozambique (57 percent), Nicaragua and India (54 percent), and Yemen (48 percent). This marriage pattern also is remarkable among the ethnic groups in the multicultural society. Cross-ethnic studies (Raley et al., 2004; Raley et al., 2009) in the U.S have explored that Mexican American minority people compared to the others (e.g., Asian American, the Whites) are the most likely to marry early.

A great deal of research has found that early marriage is increased by a number of important variables, including poverty, especially in rural regions, lack of enforcement of the law, and poor legal frameworks (Alnasser et al., 2024; Danquah, 2023). The idea that marriage offers "protection," customary or religious regulations, and gender inequity are further contributing factors. Early marriage is more prevalent in areas with high rates of poverty, restricted educational opportunities, and deeply ingrained patriarchal customs. Global research shows that about 12 million girls under the age of 18 are married each year (UNICEF, 2001b, 2023). Most of the girls' early marriage occurs in developing and the least-developed countries.

Sub-Saharan Africa and South Asia have the greatest rates of early marriage worldwide, with Bangladesh, Niger, and Chad having some of the highest rates. With asking about the number of children born before using contraception and the overall amount of contraceptive usage, the use of contraception prior to the first delivery was assessed. If a woman had ever used contraception of any kind, it was assumed that she had done so before to giving birth to her first kid (Evendia et al., 2023). On the other hand, if a woman said she had never used contraception before giving birth to her first child, she was considered to have never used it.

Based on a single inquiry on the length of marriage prior to the first childbirth, early fertility was determined by determining if childbirth took place within the first year of marriage. It was assumed that women who had not given birth had not had a child within their first year of marriage. A person's lifetime fertility was assessed by counting all of their offspring as boys and girls and using that amount to define high fertility based on the median split having three or more children was considered high fertility (Yuliastuti et al., 2024). The one way to determine low lifetime fertility control was to inquire how many months had passed between consecutive deliveries, since this was indicative of a history of fast repeat delivery. Using the usual definition of rapid repeat pregnancy, fast repeat delivery was defined as having a kid fewer than 24 months after a prior birth (Skandro et al., 2024; UNICEF, 2001a).

A significant number of girls admitted that their husbands should have accompanied them to doctor's appointments and public health centers during their pregnancy (96.7% said their husbands were usually with them) and 94.0 percent said they felt safe and taken care of during their pregnancy. 34.0% of the women, however, said that their husbands did not help out or take up household duties while they were pregnant. Early in marriage, the division of labor often reflects gender norms. Even while 66.0% of respondents said their husbands assisted with some household duties when their wives were pregnant, 34.0% of respondents said they didn't receive any help, which suggests that many men still don't help out around the house, even when their wives are expecting.

Sociocultural Factors Influencing Girls' Early Marriage

Cultural Practices: Early marriage is viewed in many cultures as a means of preserving a girl's virginity, defending family honor, or cementing family bonds via alliances (Alsmeheen, 2023; United Nations, 2000; Uddin, 2015). In Bangladesh, Uddin (2015) found that social values and attitudes were significantly associated with early marriage.

Economic Pressures: Poor families frequently see early marriage as a means of securing a bride price or dowry, as well as easing the financial strain of raising a daughter (Sanu, 2023). Numerous studies have found that poverty and economic uncertainties are the drivers of early marriage in developing and the least-developed countries, including Africa, Latin America and South Asia (United Nations, 2000; UNICEF, 2001a, 2001b). In India, Kumari and Shekhar (2023) found that poor wealth index was significantly associated with early marriage.

Lack of Education: Girls who are married off at a young age are more likely to be denied access to education or to drop out of school. Global report shows that illiteracy and low-educational levels of parents are important factors, influencing girls to marry during their teen ages (United Nations, 2000; UNICEF, 2001a, 2001b). In India, Kumari and Shekhar (2023) found that parents' illiteracy was the sole factor, influencing early marriage.

Figure 4. Sociocultural factors

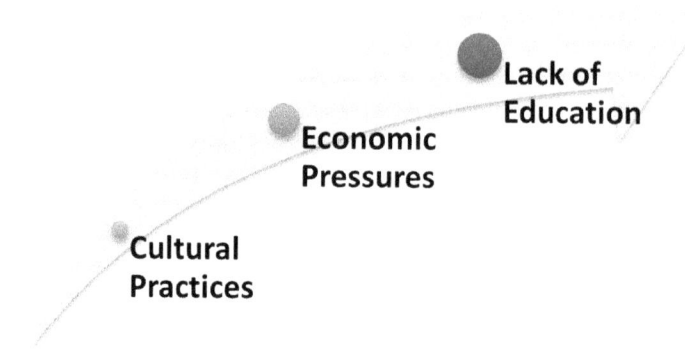

GIRLS' EARLY MARRIAGES AND HEALTH

Physical Health Risks of Early Marriages

Girls who are not emotionally or physically ready for sexual activity may be forced into child marriage, especially if they are unaware of their own rights and health about sex and reproduction (SRHR) (Salim et al., 2024). In addition to increasing the risk of sexually transmitted illnesses and gender-based violence, child marriage is a major contributing factor to teenage pregnancy, which entails serious physical health hazards (GBV) (Bravo-Queipo-de-Llano et al., 2024). Child marriage is sometimes intimately linked to female genital mutilation/cutting (FGM/C), a human rights violation that is detrimental to the physical and emotional health of girls (Datta & Tiwari, 2022; Tammary & Manasi, 2023). Millions of girls and women's health, as well as the health of their offspring, can be greatly enhanced by reducing child marriage. Young women face serious hazards to their physical health when they get married early and among these dangers are:

Early Pregnancy and Difficulties with Childbirth: Young married girls are more likely to become pregnant early in life, which increases the risk of difficulties during childbirth. According to the World Health Organization (WHO), females between the ages of 15 and 19 are more likely to experience maternal morbidity and death (KV et al., 2023). In Nepal, Seta (2023) found that about 41% of girls were married off in association with sociocultural pressures during their teen ages and consequently they suffered from early pregnancies, delivery complicacies and immature child births, affecting their physical health.

In India, Vikram et al. (2023) studied girls' child marriage and their non-communicable diseases and reproductive health and found that child marriage was associated with hypertension [adjusted odds ratio 1.20 (95% CI: 1.17–1.24)], diabetes [1.29 (1.22–1.37)], heart disease [1.27 (1.18–1.36)], asthma [1.19 (1.11–1.28)] and thyroid disorder [1.10 (1.02–1.18)]. Early motherhood also increased the risk of NCDs among young mothers. The findings of the study emerged as a pathway linking child marriage with hypertension, diabetes and heart disease; however, it provided a partial explanation for the disadvantage associated with child marriages. Using the most recent nationally representative data from India, Datta and Tiwari (2022) separately assessed the odds in favor of having the two chronic conditions for women who were married during early (10–14 years), middle (15–17 years), and late (18–19 years) adolescence. They found that an earlier age at marriage during adolescence was associated with a higher risk of chronic conditions later in life. Women who were married during early adolescence were respectively 1.29 and 1.23 times more likely ($p < 0.001$) to have high blood pressure and high blood glucose compared to women who were married in their youth. These findings highlight the importance of preventing underage marriage among adolescent females to address the risk of downstream chronic health consequences as adults.

Sexually Transmitted Infections (STIs): Child marriage is a key driver of adolescent pregnancy – which carries serious health risks – and can increase the risk of contracting sexually transmitted infections and experiencing gender-based violence (GBV). Unprotected sexual activity is a common aspect of early marriage, which raises the risk of STIs, including HIV/AIDS (Bramhankar et al., 2023). In India, Santhya and Jejeebhoy (2007) studied available programmatic sexual and reproductive health initiatives focusing disproportionately on the unmarried and on premarital sexual activity. They found that married young people received little attention as a vulnerable group with distinct needs because marriage was assumed to be safe and because married adolescents and young people were assumed to face none of the stigma that their unmarried counterparts experienced in accessing sexual and reproductive health services. Emerging evidence highlighted that neither of these assumptions were tenable. Within the sub-population of young people, married young women constituted a group with distinct risks of human immunodeficiency virus and faced a host of obstacles in making informed sexual and reproductive health decisions.

Domestic Violence: Young brides are particularly vulnerable to this type of abuse, which can cause trauma and long-term physical health problems. In India, Speizer and Pearson (2011) explored the relationship between intimate partner violence (IPV) and early marriage using the 2005-2006 India National Family Health Survey (NFHS-3). The NFHS-3 collected data from a representative sample of women and men in India with a large enough sample size to have a representative sample at the state level. The focus is on youth from Bihar and Rajasthan, two states with high IPV and early marriage. Multivariate logistic regression analyses demonstrate that women ages 20-24 who married before age eighteen, the legal age at marriage in India, are more likely to have ever experienced IPV in their lifetime and recently experienced IPV (in the last 12 months) than their counterparts who married later. The results were significant in Rajasthan but not in Bihar. To reduce IPV, targeted efforts must be made to decrease the proportion of India's girls who are married under the legal age of marriage.

Heath Care: Child marriage also affects girls to take health care across countries. In India, Datta et al. (2022) examined relationships child marriage and health care among young mothers. Using data on 496,283 married women aged 18 to 49 years from the India National Family and Health Survey 2015–2016, we developed an 11-point composite score (ranging from 0 to 10) outlining the extent of problems accessing healthcare, as follows: (i) no/little problem (score 0 to 2), (ii) some problems (score 3 to 6), and (iii) big problems (score 7 to 10). The differences between child brides and their peers married as adults were assessed by the relative risk ratios obtained from multinomial logistic regressions. The adjusted risk of having "some problems" and "big problems" accessing healthcare relative to "no/little problem" for child brides was found to be 1.22 (95% CI: 1.20–1.25) and 1.26 (95% CI: 1.22–1.29) times that of those married as adults, respectively. These findings highlight the disproportionate barriers to healthcare access faced by women married as children compared to women married as adults and the need for further research to inform policies regarding effective public health interventions to improve healthcare access. Santhya et al. (2010) focused disproportionately on the unmarried and on premarital sexual activity. According to them, married young people have received little attention as a vulnerable group with distinct needs because marriage is assumed to be safe and because married adolescents and young people are assumed to face none of the stigma that their unmarried counterparts experience in accessing sexual and reproductive health services. Emerging evidence highlights that neither of these assumptions are tenable. Within the sub-population of young people, married young women constitute a group with distinct risks of human immunodeficiency virus and face a host of obstacles in making informed sexual and reproductive health decisions.

Figure 5. Serious Physical Health Hazards

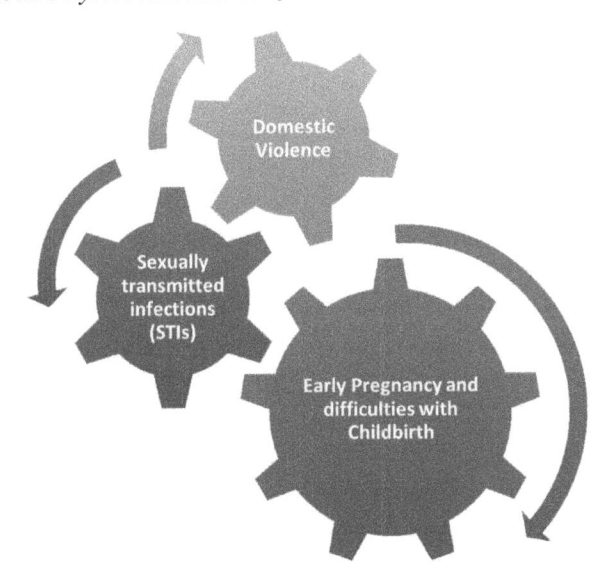

Making consenting teenage sexual behavior illegal may drive child marriage underground (Banda, 2023). In order to avoid being discovered, a teenage girl who falls pregnant in such an environment is unlikely to register her baby's birth or go to prenatal checkups. Girls frequently experience intense pressure from society to demonstrate their fertility after they get married (Semaan et al., 2023). They may find it very difficult to negotiate safe sexual practices and the use of contraception, or to exercise control over whether or not to become pregnant. Girls find it more difficult to manage or space out pregnancies when they seek safe abortion options and contraception. These hurdles include physical ones, such as distance and restricted mobility, which make it challenging to go to clinics, as well as criticism from medical professionals. Teenage girls who are pregnant frequently turn to unlicensed, covert abortion providers, endangering their health and lives, especially in areas with high incidence of unwanted pregnancies and tight abortion regulations. An estimated 8–11% of maternal fatalities are attributed to unsafe abortion, with adolescent girls being more likely than older women to seek care from these providers (Saleh et al., 2024). There is evidence of greater suicide rates among girls who are unable to obtain safe abortion services in Central America, a region with some of the harshest abortion regulations in the world (Nevangga et al., 2023).

Mental Health Risks of Early Marriages

Early marriage typically has negative effects on a couple's and their child's mental, emotional, and psychological well-being in addition to their physical health. Domestic violence can result from young females marrying into emotionally unstable relationships. Emotional maturity is largely influenced by age, with puberty marking the beginning of the shift from infancy to adulthood. This phase includes both emotional and physical development. With the conclusion of her teenage years, or between the ages of 17 to 22, a girl is deemed emotionally mature if she can control her emotions, have a critical understanding of herself and weigh her options before acting. Any official or informal union involving a kid under the age of eighteen and an adult or another child is known as child marriage. Despite a slow decline over the past 10 years, this harmful practice is still common, with around one in five girls globally getting married when still very young (Altwaijri et al., 2023). Equally troubling are the effects of early marriage on mental health as the young brides frequently encounter as follows:

1. **Sadness and Anxiety**: Young brides may experience sadness and anxiety as a result of the stresses of marriage, childbearing, and household duties.
2. **Isolation and Lack of Social Support**: early females who marry early are frequently cut off from their friends and social networks, which exacerbate feelings of insecurity and loneliness (Prisco, 2023).
3. **Restricted Autonomy and Self-Worth**: Young brides may have long-term mental health issues as a result of the social expectations that undermine their feeling of autonomy and self-worth (Gupta & Anitha, 2024).

Girls lose their youth and their wellbeing when they marry as children. Before turning 18, girls are more likely to become victims of domestic abuse and are also less likely to complete their education. Compared to their single counterparts, they frequently have lower health and economic results, which can be inherited by their own children and put further strain on the nation's health and educational systems (Tinago et al., 2024). Deeply ingrained gender inequity commonly leads to child marriage, with girls suffering the most from it. Boys' rates of underage marriage are just one-sixth those of girls' worldwide (Mishra et al., 2023). Adolescent brides frequently become pregnant around this time, when there is an increased chance of difficulties with pregnancy and childbirth (Hemegan et al., 2024). Also, the social isolation from friends and family as a result of this practice might have a serious negative effect on their mental health. However, in young marriages, there's a greater chance of conflict, divorce, and domestic violence since both females and their spouses frequently haven't acquired this degree of emotional maturity. Girls' prospects may suffer as a result of trauma or divorce brought on by domestic abuse. Children may experience psychological harm from divorce and domestic abuse, which can make them feel unloved and uneasy in their families (Asraoui et al., 2023). In India, Kanji et al. (2024) examined an association of early marriage with life satisfaction, education and subjective health. The researchers found that women who married early experience a trajectory of lower life satisfaction which is in evidence before marriage, even at age 12, persisting until the latest survey at age 22. There is no evidence of a causal negative effect of early marriage on life satisfaction; the relationship is more complicated, linked to trajectories of deprivation which commence from a very young age. In contrast, early marriage negatively affects women's self-reported health and educational attainment by age 22.

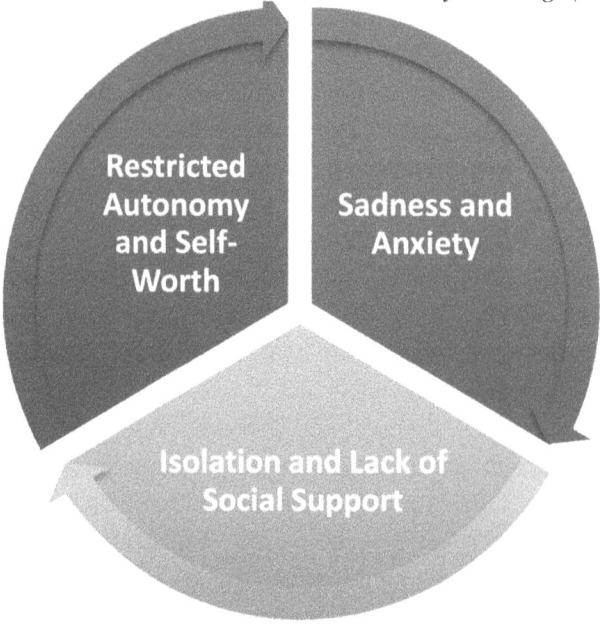

Figure 6. The Mental Health Risks associated with Early Marriage (Source- Original)

SOCIAL AND LEGAL CONSEQUENCES OF EARLY MARRIAGES

There are significant social and legal ramifications to young marriage for combating child marriage necessitates an understanding of the factors that sustain it (Gupta, 2023). Although the origins of this practice differ across nations and cultures, it is often perpetuated by poverty, a lack of educational opportunities, and limited access to healthcare. Some families arrange their daughters' marriages to ease financial strain or generate income. Others may do so under the belief that marriage will secure their daughters' futures or shield them from harm. Compared to those who marry later, child brides are more likely to become pregnant early and have more children overall, which raises the possibility of difficulties during pregnancy and delivery (Trivedi et al., 2023). Younger moms are more at risk for long-term health problems or even death as a result of these difficulties. Children of child brides are also more likely to experience health issues such as low birth weight, premature delivery, and serious neonatal disorders. Throughout their childhood, they are also at a higher risk of suffering from malnutrition and stunted growth (Odeleye, 2023).

Traditional gender roles and stereotypes, along with the socio-economic risks associated with out-of-wedlock pregnancies, also contribute to the persistence of child marriage. Young girls' physical immaturity has a role in the region's high rates of maternal and newborn death as well as other unfavorable health outcomes (Defar et al., 2023). In sub-Saharan Africa in 2004, maternal diseases ranked as the second most common cause of mortality for teenagers. A number of maternal health conditions, including as obesity, anemia, malaria, STDs, mental illness, and obstetric fistula, are associated with early childbearing (Khoei et al., 2023). The majority of women who have obstetric fistulas experienced severe physical and social consequences when they were adolescents. Adolescent moms' babies are also impacted negatively by early pregnancies' detrimental effects on their health. Early marriage is nevertheless commonplace despite international agreements that support the preservation of children's rights, such as the Convention on the Rights of the Child (CRC) and the Convention on the Elimination of All Forms of Discrimination Against Women (CEDAW) (Nsahlai et al., 2023).

Enforcement and Legal Frameworks

1. **International and National Laws**: Marriage before the age of eighteen is illegal in many nations, but cultural opposition and corruption make it difficult to execute the law.
2. **Legal Loopholes**: Some nations provide for marriages requiring court or parental approval. These exceptions might be used to justify early marriages (Veronese et al., 2023).
3. **Lack of Legal Awareness**: Communities in many areas continue to violate the law because they are unaware of the prohibitions against early marriage.

Figure 7. illuminates the Factors for Enforcement and Legal Frameworks (Source-Original)

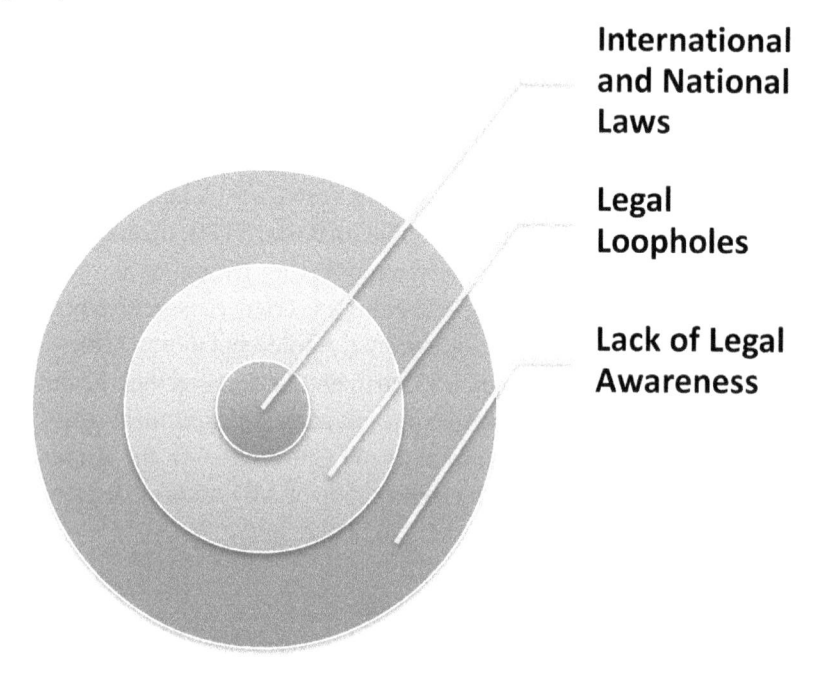

- International and National Laws
- Legal Loopholes
- Lack of Legal Awareness

Gender Inequality and Social Consequences

1. **Gender Disparity**: With restricting women's access to higher education and career prospects and by reinforcing conventional roles for them, early marriage contributes to gender disparity (Rahman et al., 2024).
2. **Intergenerational Cycle**: Since young brides are less likely to seek further education or careers, early marriage adds to a cycle of poverty and limited prospects.

INTERVENTION AND IMPLICATIONS IN POLICY

Girls who marry before the age of 18, when people are usually able to give informed consent, have a 50% higher chance of experiencing intimate partner violence, a 23% higher risk of cancer, heart disease, diabetes, stroke, a higher risk of HIV and other STDs (Sharma & Lakwal, 2023). Child brides are also more likely to suffer from serious mental illnesses, such as major depressive disorder, antisocial personality disorder, and certain phobias (Ibrahim, 2023). These illnesses frequently lead to drug and alcohol addiction as well as nicotine addiction. Child marriage is a serious worldwide health concern and the following suggestions are put up to address the problem of early marriage and the related health and social-legal ramifications are as follows:

1. **Increasing the Strict Enforcement of the Law**: Laws that forbid early marriage should be strictly enforced by governments, and any legal loopholes that permit exceptions should be closed (Almadani & Alwesmi, 2023).
2. **Education and Awareness Campaigns**: Public awareness campaigns may support the advantages of education for females and work to alter cultural attitudes on early marriage.
3. **Social Support Services**: Helping young brides with counseling, medical care, and educational opportunities is one way to lessen the negative consequences of being married young (Gani et al., 2023).
4. **Community Engagement**: Changing cultural behaviors related to early marriage can be accomplished via involving religious and community leaders.

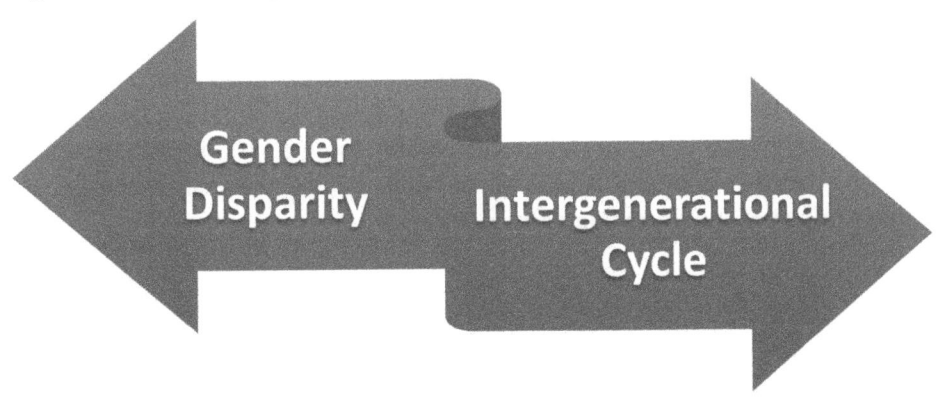

Figure 8. shares the Suggestions and Interventions in Policy (Source- Original)

Girls throughout the world are disproportionately affected by early marriage, which violates their human rights and deprives them of the opportunity to live free from violence (Boveda et al., 2023). Early marriage is any marriage in which at least one of the parties is under the age of eighteen, according to the Office of the United Nations High Commissioner for Human Rights. Many fundamental rights are violated by early marriage, such as the freedom from violence, the freedom of movement, the right to marry by mutual agreement, the right to an education and career, the right to procreate, and the right to obtain sexual and reproductive health care (Alghamdi, 2024). Early marriage also limits girls' full involvement in the political, social, and economic realms by making them more susceptible to abuse, prejudice, and violence (Heyman et al., 2024).

CONCLUSION AND DIRECTION FOR FUTURE RESEARCH

Early marriage poses significant physical and mental health risks for young girls, along with broader social-legal implications. Addressing this issue requires a multifaceted approach, involving legal reform, education, and community engagement. Many individuals do not automatically associate child marriage with poor health consequences. Instead, they emphasize the other horrendous effects of pressuring a kid into an early marriage, such as acute poverty, the loss of potential, the sudden end of childhood, and the chance that the child will never finish or pursue their education. Above all, though, child marriage has detrimental effects on the child bride's health since it nearly exclusively affects females. Adolescent pregnancies result from child marriage, which in turn causes underage sexual activity and child marriage, which can lead to a number of detrimental health effects, including maternal and fetal death. In reality, among the main causes of mortality for females between the ages of 15 and 19 are issues related to pregnancy and delivery. With understanding the root causes of early marriage and its impact on young girls' health, policymakers and stakeholders can work toward creating a more equitable and supportive environment for all children, especially those at risk of early marriage. Through concerted efforts, it is possible to break the cycle of early marriage and ensure a brighter future for young girls worldwide.

REFERENCES

Ahmed, S., Khan, A., Khan, S., & Noushad, S. (2014). Early marriage: A root of current physiological and psychological health burdens. *International Journal of Endorsing Health Science Research*, 2(1), 50–53. DOI: 10.29052/IJEHSR.v2.i1.2014.50-53

Alghamdi, N. A. A. (2024). Gender and intersectionality: understanding and addressing women's mental health within the cultural context of Saudi Arabia. Unpublished PhD Dissertation, Glasgow: University of Glasgow.

Almadani, N. A., & Alwesmi, M. B. (2023). The Relationship between Happiness and Mental Health among Saudi Women. *Brain Sciences*, 13(4), 526. DOI: 10.3390/brainsci13040526 PMID: 37190491

Alnasser, L. A., Moro, M. F., Naseem, M. T., Bilal, L., Akkad, M., Almeghim, R., Al-Habeeb, A., Al-Subaie, A. S., & Altwaijri, Y. A. (2024). Social determinants of anxiety and mood disorders in a nationally-representative sample–Results from the Saudi National Mental Health Survey (SNMHS). *The International Journal of Social Psychiatry*, 70(1), 166–181. DOI: 10.1177/00207640231197944 PMID: 37740657

Alonzo, D., & Zubaroglu-Ioannides, P. (2023). Suicide and Violence against Women in Azerbaijan: Risk Factors and Barriers for Seeking Mental Healthcare. *J Ment Health Soc Behav*, 5(1), 179.

Alsmeheen, F. A. (2023). Psychological Adjustment And Its Relationship With Some Variables Among Married Minors In The Southern Region In Jordan. *Journal of Namibian Studies: History Politics Culture*, 36, 626–643.

Altwaijri, Y., Al-Habeeb, A., Al-Subaie, A., Bruffaerts, R., Bilal, L., Hyder, S., Naseem, M. T., & Alghanim, A. J. (2023). Dual burden of chronic physical conditions and mental disorders: Findings from the Saudi National Mental Health Survey. *Frontiers in Public Health*, 11, 1238326. DOI: 10.3389/fpubh.2023.1238326 PMID: 38089017

Asraoui, A., Khassouani, C. E., & Soulaymani, A. (2023). Prevalence, sociodemographic and economic determinants of violence against ever-married women in Morocco. *Eastern Mediterranean Health Journal*, 29(12), 944–953. DOI: 10.26719/emhj.23.122 PMID: 38279863

Banda, P. (2023). Lost amidst the chaos: The impact of Covid-19 on girls' education in Malawi.

Boveda, M., Reyes, G., & Aronson, B. (2023). Disciplined to access the general education curriculum: Girls of color, disabilities, and specialized education programming. In *Disability as Meta Curriculum* (pp. 49–69). Routledge. DOI: 10.4324/9781003252313-4

Bramhankar, M., Kundu, S., Pandey, M., Mishra, N. L., & Adarsh, A. (2023). An assessment of self-rated life satisfaction and its correlates with physical, mental and social health status among older adults in India. *Scientific Reports*, 13(1), 9117. DOI: 10.1038/s41598-023-36041-3 PMID: 37277415

Danquah, F. (2023). *Child Marriage in Ghana: Assessing the Legal Implementation of Child Rights Standards* (Doctoral dissertation, University of Manitoba).

Datta, B., Pandey, A., & Tiwari, A. (2022). Child marriage and problems accessing healthcare in adulthood: Evidence from India. *Health Care*, 10(10), 1994. DOI: 10.3390/healthcare10101994 PMID: 36292439

Datta, B., & Tiwari, A. (2022). Early marriage in adolescence and risk of high blood pressure and high blood glucose in adulthood: Evidence from India. *Women*, 2(3), 189–203. DOI: 10.3390/women2030020

Delprato, M., & Akyeampong, K. (2017). The effect of early marriage timing on women's and children's health in sub-Saharan Africa and Southwest Asia. *Annals of Global Health*, 83(3-4), 557–567. DOI: 10.1016/j.aogh.2017.10.005 PMID: 29221529

Evendia, M., & Firmansyah, A. A. (2023). KENVORM legal protection for prevention of child marriage in a decentralization. *Progressive Law Review*, 5(02), 141–155.

Fan, S., & Koski, A. (2022). The health consequences of child marriage: A systematic review of the evidence. *BMC Public Health*, 22(1), 309. DOI: 10.1186/s12889-022-12707-x PMID: 35164724

Godha, D., Gage, A. J., Hotchkiss, D. R., & Cappa, C. (2016). Predicting maternal health care use by age at marriage in multiple countries. *The Journal of Adolescent Health*, 58(5), 504–511. DOI: 10.1016/j.jadohealth.2016.01.001 PMID: 26984836

Godha, D., Hotchkiss, D. R., & Gage, A. J. (2013). Association between child marriage and reproductive health outcomes and service utilization: A multi-country study from South Asia. *The Journal of Adolescent Health*, 52(5), 552–558. DOI: 10.1016/j.jadohealth.2013.01.021 PMID: 23608719

Hassan, S., & Nader, R. (2021). Socio-economic implications of early marriage in low-income countries. *Journal of Global Health*, 11(2), 345–359. DOI: 10.7189/jogh.11.02001

Kalamar, A. M., Lee-Rife, S., & Hindin, M. J. (2016). Interventions to prevent child marriage among people in low- and middle-income countries: A systematic review of the published and gray literature. *The Journal of Adolescent Health*, 59(3), 16–21. DOI: 10.1016/j.jadohealth.2016.06.015 PMID: 27562449

Kanji, S., Carmichael, F., Darco, C., Egyei, R., & Vasilakos, N. (2024). The impact of early marriage on the life satisfaction, education and subjective health of young women in India: A longitudinal analysis. *The Journal of Development Studies*, 60(5), 705–723. DOI: 10.1080/00220388.2023.2284678

Kok, M. (2021). Adolescent pregnancy and health outcomes: A global perspective. *International Journal of Women's Health*, 13, 111–124. DOI: 10.2147/IJWH.S296773

Kumari, N., & Shekhar, C. (2023). Trend and determinants of early marriage in Rajasthan: Evidence from the national family health survey. *Children and Youth Services Review*, 145, 106746. DOI: 10.1016/j.childyouth.2022.106746

Lebni, J. Y., Solhi, M., Azar, F. E. F., Farahani, F. K., & Irandoost, S. F. (2023). Exploring the consequences of early marriage: A conventional content analysis. *Inquiry: The Journal of Health Care Organization, Provision, and Financing*, 60, 1–14.

Lim, S., & Raymo, J. M. (2016). Marriage and women's health in Japan. *Journal of Marriage and Family*, 78(3), 780–796. DOI: 10.1111/jomf.12298 PMID: 30774150

Marphatia, A. A., Ambale, G. S., & Reid, A. M. (2017). Women's marriage age matters for public health: A review of the broader health and social implications in South Asia. *frontiers in Public Health,* 5:269. DOI: 10.3389/fpubh.2017.00269

Miller, E., & Roca, M. (2022). The intersection of early marriage and health: A review of current research. *Health Policy and Planning*, 37(4), 529–540. DOI: 10.1093/heapol/czac021

Nevangga, R. P., Ardlianawati, N., Wicaksono, D., Arisyna, A., & Sasmita, N. S. (2023, November). Situational analysis of the mental health of referral COVID-19 hospital staff. In *AIP Conference Proceedings* (Vol. 2739, No. 1). AIP Publishing. DOI: 10.1063/5.0126737

Novianti, D., Fatonah, S., Abadi, M. T. D., Haq, M. F., & Sagita, V. A. (2023). Social Media and Early Marriage During the Covid-19 Pandemic in Indonesia. *Journal of Social and Political Sciences*, 6(4), 35–46. DOI: 10.31014/aior.1991.06.04.443

Nurmila, N., & Windiana, W. (2023). Understanding the Complexities of Child Marriage and Promoting Education to Prevent Child Marriage in Indramayu, West Java. *Ulumuna*, 27(2), 823–853. DOI: 10.20414/ujis.v27i2.680

Phiri, M., Namayawa, S., Sianyeuka, B., Sikanyiti, P., & Lemba, M. (2023). Determinants of spousal physical violence against women in Zambia: A multilevel analysis. *BMC Public Health*, 23(1), 934. DOI: 10.1186/s12889-023-15927-x PMID: 37221522

Prisco, G. (2023). "Girls giving birth to babies". A pedagogical perspective for the self-determination and existential planning of young mothers. *Women &Education*, (2), 088-093.

Rahman, M. A., Tohan, M. M., Zaman, S., Islam, M. A., Rahman, M. S., Howlader, M. H., & Kundu, S. (2024). A structural equation modelling to explore the determinants of mental health disorders among reproductive-aged women in Nepal: A nation-wide cross-sectional survey.

Raley, R. K., Durden, T. E., & Wildsmith, E. (2004). Understanding Mexican American marriage patterns using a life course approach. *Social Science Quarterly*, 85(4), 872–890. DOI: 10.1111/j.0038-4941.2004.00249.x

Rashid, T., & Karim, M. (2022). Empowering girls through education and economic opportunities: Strategies to delay early marriage. *Development Studies Research*, 9(3), 234–249. DOI: 10.1080/21665095.2022.2117739

Reley, R. K., & Sweeney, M. M. (2009). Explaining race and ethnic variation in marriage: Directions for future research. *Race and Social Problems*, 3(3), 132–142. DOI: 10.1007/s12552-009-9013-3

Santhya, K. G., & Jejeebhoy, S. J. (2007). Early marriage and HIV/AIDS risk factors among young women in India. *Economic and Political Weekly*, 42(14), 1229–1297.

Santhya, K. G., Ram, U., Acharya, R., Jejeebhoy, S. J., Ram, F., & Singh, A. (2010). Associations between early marriage and young women's marital and reproductive health outcomes: Evidence from India. *International Perspectives on Sexual and Reproductive Health*, 36(3), 132–139. DOI: 10.1363/3613210 PMID: 20880798

Semaan, S., Haddad, C., Awad, E., Sacre, H., Hallit, R., Akel, M., Salameh, P., Obeid, S., & Hallit, S. (2023). Caring for a mentally ill patient at home, mental health, religiosity, and spirituality and their association with family caregivers' quality of life in Lebanon. *The Primary Care Companion for CNS Disorders*, 25(4), 47977. DOI: 10.4088/PCC.22m03333 PMID: 37471477

Seta, R. (2023). Child marriage and its impact on health: A study of perceptions and attitudes in Nepal. *Journal of Global Health Reports*, 7, e2023073. DOI: 10.29392/001c.88951

Speizer, I. S., & Pearson, E. P. (2011). Association between early marriage and intimate partner violence in India: A focus on youth from Bihar and Rajasthan. *Journal of Interpersonal Violence*, 26(10), 1963–1981. DOI: 10.1177/0886260510372947 PMID: 20587462

Strungaru, S. (2024). Understanding Child Marriage: Law and Practice. In *The Hidden Child Brides of the Syrian Civil War: Vulnerable and Voiceless in Human Rights Law and Practice* (pp. 13–33). Springer Nature Singapore. DOI: 10.1007/978-981-97-2159-7_2

Tinago, C. B., Frongillo, E. A., Warren, A. M., Chitiyo, V., Jackson, T. N., Cifarelli, A. K., Fyalkowski, S., & Pauline, V. (2024). Testing the effectiveness of a community-based peer support intervention to mitigate social isolation and stigma of adolescent motherhood in Zimbabwe. *Maternal and Child Health Journal*, 28(4), 657–666. DOI: 10.1007/s10995-023-03821-2 PMID: 37957412

Uddin, E. M. (2015). Family socio-cultural values affecting early marriage between Muslim and Santal communities in rural Bangladesh. *The International Journal of Sociology and Social Policy*, 35(3/4), 141–164. DOI: 10.1108/IJSSP-06-2014-0046

Uddin, J., Pulok, M. H., Johnson, R. B., Rana, J., & Baker, E. (2019). Association between child marriage and institutional delivery care services use in Bangladesh: Intersections between education and place of residence. *Public Health*, 171, 6–14. DOI: 10.1016/j.puhe.2019.03.014 PMID: 31071578

Uddin, M. E. (2017). Family demographic mechanisms linking of socioeconomic status to subjective physical health in rural Bangladesh. *Social Indicators Research*, 130(3), 1263–1279. DOI: 10.1007/s11205-015-1209-x

Uddin, M. E. (2021). Teenage marriage and high school dropout among poor girls: A narrative review for family pathways in Bangladesh. *Journal of Research in Social Sciences and Language*, 1(1), 55–76. https://www.jssal.com/index.php/jssal/article/view/15

UNICEF. (2023). Child marriage data and statistics. Retrieved from https://www.unicef.org/reports/child-marriage-data-and-statistics

United Nations. (1988). *First marriage: Patterns and determinants*. Population Division.

United Nations. (1990). *Patterns of first marriage: Timing and prevalence*. Population Division.

United Nations. (2000). *World marriage patterns*. Population Division.

United Nations Children's Fund (UNICEF). (2001b). *Early marriage: child spouses.* UNICEF.

United Nations Population Fund. (2001a). *Socio-cultural aspects of reproductive health.* UNFPA.

Veronese, G., Mahmid, F. A., & Bdier, D. (2023). Gender-based violence, subjective quality of life, and mental health outcomes among Palestinian women: The mediating role of social support and agency. *Violence Against Women*, 29(5), 925–948. DOI: 10.1177/10778012221099988 PMID: 36042012

Vettriselvan, R., Anto, R., & Jesu Rajan, F. S. A. (2018b). Pathetic health status and working condition of Zambian women. *Indian Journal of Public Health Research & Development*, 9(9), 259. DOI: 10.5958/0976-5506.2018.01006.9

Vettriselvan, R., & Arunkumar, N. (2018a). Child labour in unorganized mechanical engineering industries of Tamil Nadu: A situation analysis. *International Journal of Mechanical Engineering and Technology*, 9(10), 809–819.

Vettriselvan, R., Rajan, A. J., & Arunkumar, N. (2019). Occupational health issues faced by women in spinners. *Indian Journal of Public Health Research & Development*, 10(1), 500. DOI: 10.5958/0976-5506.2019.00098.6

Vettriselvan, R., Rengamani, J., James, F. A., Srinivasan, R., & Poongavanam, S. (2019). Issues and challenges of women employees in Indian technical industries. *International Journal of Engineering and Advanced Technology, 8*(2S2), 2019.

Vikram, K., Visaria, A., & Ganguly, D. (2023). Child marriage as a risk factor for non-communicable diseases among women in India. *International Journal of Epidemiology*, 52(5), 1303–1315. DOI: 10.1093/ije/dyad051 PMID: 37159526

World Health Organization. (2022). Adolescent pregnancy: Overview. Retrieved from https://www.who.int/news-room/fact-sheets/detail/adolescent-pregnancy

Yuliastuti, A., Mubin, M. F., Ernawati, E., & Pranata, S. (2024). Bibliometric Analysis of the Impact of Early Marriage on Adolescents. *Indonesian Journal of Global Health Research*, 6(2), 759–770.

Chapter 11
Social and Economic Consequences of Early Marriage on Women's Education and Workforce Participation

Ajay Chandel
 https://orcid.org/0000-0002-4585-6406
Lovely Professional University, India

Mohit Yadav
 https://orcid.org/0000-0002-9341-2527
O.P. Jindal Global University, India

Ta Huy Hung
 https://orcid.org/0009-0008-6835-3036
Vietnam National University, Hanoi, Vietnam

ABSTRACT

This chapter explores and explains the effects of the significant social and economic consequences of early marriage on women's education and workforce participation. Early marriage, often driven by cultural, religious, and economic factors, disrupts educational opportunities for young girls, leading to lower education attainment and limited access to formal employment. These poor socioeconomic attainments perpetuate the cycles of poverty and reinforce gender inequality, trapping women in economic dependency and social marginalization. The chapter employs theoretical frameworks such as social reproduction theory, human capital theory, and intersec-

DOI: 10.4018/979-8-3693-3394-5.ch011

tionality to analyze how early marriage sustains these inequalities. It also examines the historical, cultural, and legal contexts that underpin the practice, highlighting the need for targeted, culturally sensitive interventions. The findings underscore the importance of comprehensive strategies to empower women, challenge patriarchal norms, and promote education and economic participation.

INTRODUCTION

Early marriage is still widely practiced today, partly due to a combination of cultural, religious, and socio-economic factors in various parts of the world. Early marriage refers to marriage between two parties before the age of 18 (Uddin, 2015, 2021). Despite the global efforts to reduce the practice, it still affects millions of young girls; often their future is at stake (Lowe et al., 1989). This chapter will consider the complex and intertwining social and economic implications of early marriage for women, especially girls' access to educational opportunities and women's participation in the workforce. The importance of the topic can hardly be exaggerated; apart from abrogating or at best, substantially reducing the opportunity for receipt of education, early marriage remains a potent force in bequeathing cycles of poverty and lack of gender equality. There needs to be an additional layer of understanding about the challenges young women face such as historical context, cultural underpinnings, and legal frameworks that still sustain early marriage across the countries (Kartika et al., 2021).

This chapter will further detail the way early marriage disrupts education, leading to an increase in lost attainment levels and often prompting the girl to drop out of school. This presents a very direct link between education disruption and employment prospects, since limited education brings about less access to the formal job markets and related lower incomes, and thus economic dependency. Moreover, this chapter also discusses social implications such as health consequences, social isolation, underpinning the reinforcement of adverse gender inequality (Naghizadeh et al., 2021).

A myriad of case studies, policy analysis, and personal narratives have been used to understand of how early marriages affect the women folk in various ways. The chapter will start by creating an introduction that will form a base that probably will critically justify the reason as to why such an analysis is important in making reforms and interventions in policy implication, needing to curb such occurrences and ensuring greater opportunities for women in education and workforce (Hajihasani & Sim, 2018).

THEORETICAL FRAMEWORK

Social Reproduction Theory

The social reproduction theory postulates that social classes are sociocultural constructed in every society; it is, therefore, not an individual's creating but rather a product of history, a division that comes about from social stratification. The theory of social reproduction must be taken into account in considering how early marriage makes these social inequalities and transfers them from one generation to another. Rooted in sociologists' thoughts like Bourdieu and Passeron (1990), this theory postulates that the social structures of family, education, and cultural norms are at the very core of reproducing pre-existing social hierarchies. Therefore, early marriage is a mechanism for the retention of women's bodies, labor, and futures within patriarchy and economic systems to ensure the perpetuation of power relations between men and women. The social reproduction theory explains why early marriages still persist in specific cultures today despite legal prohibitions and an increase in the levels of education. It also draws out the dimensions to which early marriage cuts short women's participation in education and workforce by engaging them in the cycles of dependency and marginalization in the social and cultural processes (Kamal et al., 2014).

Human Capital Theory

Human capital theory developed by economists, Gary Becker (2009) presents an economic lens through which we view the adverse consequences of early marriage in education and workforce participation. This theory posits that people invest in their own schooling and skills to enhance productivity and earnings in the labor market. Early marriage interrupts this process of human capital accumulation because girls are forced out of school into domestic roles, thereby reducing their possibility of acquiring the necessary skills and knowledge to participate successfully in labor markets. This does not only hold back an individual's earning capability but also has broader economic ripples in the sense that it reduces total productivity and, hence, economic growth of a society. Application of human capital theory will help us to elicit more of the economic costs of early marriage for individuals in particular and societies in general (Opesemowo & Odumosu, 2023).

Gender and Development Theory

The gender and development (GAD) theory, which evolved as a critique to earlier development theories (Parpart et al., 2000), focuses on gender relations in development. It is of the views that development policies and programs have regard for the different needs and experiences of men and women, and the gender inequalities that may stand in the way of larger development issues. From the GAD perspective, early marriage emerges as an issue originating from and causing gender inequality. It reflects and deeply ingrains patriarchal beliefs in the devaluation of women's education and independence and their economic dependence on men. Application of the GAD theory helps highlight the significance of gender-sensitive policies and interventions that empower women and work to overcome the obstacles of social structures and perpetrating early marriages in a given society (Rumble et al., 2018).

The Theory of Intersectionality

The concept of intersectionality postulated by Kimberlé Crenshaw (2019) gives a critical framework within which we understand the formation of experiences at the intersection of several axes of discriminatory relations in the case of early marriage women bound by gender, race, class, and religion (Uddin, 2015). Consequently, the theory becomes very helpful in understanding how people find benefits and suffer from early marriages in appreciably distinct ways. For example, girls from poor, rural, or minority groups are much more likely to experience early marriage and its negative consequences than their peers from more privileged groups. The later will show that early marriage intersects with other social determinants to create unique challenges for women to attain education and participate in the workforce. This perspective also highlights the need for targeted women's interventions and addresses the needs of specific groups afflicted by early marriages.

Rights-Based Approach

Early marriage, following a rights-based approach founded on the international human rights laws is placed in the axis of basic human rights violations like violation of the right to education, work, and to live in free from any discrimination and violence. This legal strategy is, therefore, based on important international instruments, namely the Convention on the Rights of the Child and the Convention on the Elimination of All Forms of Discrimination against Women, which set out the legal and moral commitments of the state in protecting children and women from all harmful practices, including early marriage (Paul, 2020). Based on the rights-based framework, we argue that early marriage should not only be made sense of as a social or even economic issue but also it should be canvassed as a critical human rights issue. This view also underlines the legal and policy frameworks designed to prevent early marriage against the full enjoyment of rights of the women and girls to education and barely economic participation in the labor force.

Social Norms Theory

The social norms theory is imperative in understanding how community beliefs and practices become the very fabric that sustains early marriage (Uddin, 2017). The theory espouses that individual behavior is controlled by shared expectations within the community. In many societies, early marriage is backed up by social norms that lay family honor and control over female sexuality and economic security in the name of rights and well-being of the girls. These norms are usually maintained by the leaders in a community and also the heads of religion, and in some cases also by the family head of the girls (Zegeye et al., 2021). The social norms theory helps explain why it can be challenging to change an entrenched practice, including early marriage. It also brings out the significance of societies and the education it impacts on the chance of eradicating early marriages as well as explains why legal measures will in most cases fail to eliminate early marriages without a change in social norms.

HISTORICAL CONTEXTS

Origins and Evolution of Early Marriage Practices

Early marriage, as defined as a union of two persons below the age of 18, has its very roots in ancient history. Within many societies, it has been a long-standing tradition, often viewed as a required and accepted part of a social life (Uddin, 2021). The historical nature of early marriage has social and economic dimensions. In agrarian societies, where families depend on the labor of all members to procure sustenance, marrying off daughters early ensures that they can attach to the economic unit of another family, hence lightening the burden on the natal family. Early marriage is also often associated with the transfer of wealth in the form of dowries or bride prices in such a way of exchanges typically bound alliances between certain families and communities (Saleheen et al., 2021).

Early marriage is deep rooted in some of the ancient civilizations. In some ancient Roman culture and Greece, girls were mostly wedded when they were in their early teens, sometimes even below their teenage years; it was a means of forming alliances and would ensure the restraint of long family lines. Similarly, in Asia, Africa, and the Middle East, early age of marriage practice deemed and seen to be mostly driven by the pressures of local culture and tradition favors the platinum of family honor and social integrity over the desires and volition of the brides or grooms (Elengemoke & Susuman, 2020).

Cultural and Religious Influences

Early age at marriage gets promoted by different cultures and religious sectors of the world. In most cultures, a marriage is considered a rite of maturity: from childhood to adulthood. This is especially the case in societies where the value of a girl is attached to her being a wife and mother. The cultural stance about female purity, combined with the cultural management of women's sexuality, on many occasions inculcates the practice of early marriage as seen to secure girl's virginity. It, in turn, is considered very critical to the reputation and rank of the family (Abalos, 2014).

Religious teachings in principles also have been manning factors that propagate and legalize early marriage. In most religious traditions, marriage is viewed as a sacred duty, and early marriage would encourage or be part of the teachings of our religion. For instance, under various interpretations of Islamic law, marriage age is associated with the onset of puberty, and such views have been used to justify the marriage of very young girls. In other communities, interpretation of religious texts and teaching has gone to lengths to support the practice of early marriage in communities of Christians, Hindus, and Jews. These religious influences have often been deeply intertwined with local customs, making it problematic to challenge or change the practice (Fatmawati et al., 2023).

Legal Frameworks and Age of Consent

More widely divergent legal frameworks on marriages and the age of consent would not have been possible for different historical periods and across the cultures. In many pre-modern societies, there were few legal restrictions imposed on early marriages, and decisions about marriage were normally made by families or local communities on the basis of social and economic considerations. However, here too, the laws regulating matrimonial age began to emerge as nation-states evolved more formal legal systems.

During the colonial experience, different Europeans imposed their legal systems on people's territories, which were often at variance with local customs and traditions. Sometimes, they have tried to do that; however, with their setting the lowest ages for marriage at European standards, most of the natives in those countries would resist the move, considering it an attack on their cultural and religious practices. In other cases, local customs continued to be exercised with the consent of the colonial administrations, and this practice resulted in the existence of a dual system where the laws differed for different people based on religion or ethnicity. This legacy of legal pluralism lives on in many countries where, to this day, customary and religious laws run parallel with national legal frameworks, especially in matters of marriage (Alfiana et al., 2022).

During the 20th century, the international trend toward universal standards regarding age at marriage began to gain ground, especially after the 1948 adoption of the Universal Declaration of Human Rights and subsequent international human rights treaties, including the Convention on the Rights of the Child and the Convention on the Elimination of all Forms of Discrimination against Women. These conventions are focused on safeguarding children's rights and removing discrimination against women, and hence, they necessitate the fixing of a minimum age for marriage. Even so, these international thresholds have not been able to see their realization or practice uniformly, and several countries have continued to make exceptions for religious or cultural rationales (Alem et al., 2020).

Economic Drivers and Social Structures

Early marriage has often represented a way to ensure economic security and social status. Many observers argue that in all societies, marriage was, and in some, remains a transaction that involves the exchange of goods, services, or money between families. Dowries, bride prices and other forms of economic exchange are among the most commonplace ways marriages are cemented and the young bride becomes part of this exchange. When occurring in poor societies, early marriage is considered a survival strategy, with disposal of daughters through early marriage removing the economic burden of the family and ensuring the girl a future in the absence of alternative opportunities (Muharry et al., 2018).

However, this form of early marriage is also associated with class outcomes in a society, and at times even with social structures that favor the inheritance of land or any other property. For example, in a patrilineal society, the inheritance of property may be through the male line: in such a case, marrying off girls at an early age ensures that they are married into the appropriate community, thus keeping the property and wealth within the same family or clan. That has been especially common in societies relating to agriculture, where land ownership has always been a paramount determinant of social and economic power (Raymo & Iwasawa, 2005).

Influences of the Colonial and Post-Colonial Periods

The colonial period introduced massive change in marriage practices in most parts of the world. Indeed, many European colonial powers made attempts at imposing their cultural and legal norms upon colonized societies, including marriage.

The outcomes of this process were extremely varied, depending on the context. In some cases, colonial powers actually discouraged marriage at too early an age and encouraged education for females; in others, they were actively complicit in reinforcing current practices by siding with local elites who believed in maintaining social order through early marriage (Manandhar & Joshi, 2020).

In some cases, the government has tried to revise its marriage law so as to increase the minimum marriage age and also save the rights of young girls, but such kinds of reforms have been highly resisted by traditional groups which argue that these reforms work against their cultures and religions. Accordingly, this legacy of colonialism remains embedded in the marriage laws of many countries, in which debates about the proper balance that should be struck between the honoring of cultural traditions and the rights and welfare of the girl are continuous (Abalos, 2014).

Changes in Modernization and Globalization

Substantial changes have affected the practice of early marriage during the 20th and 21st centuries, driven by processes of modernization and globalization. The classic economic and social structures that supported early marriage began to break down as societies urbanized and their economies shifted from an agricultural to a non-agricultural base. In many parts of the world, education has emerged as a way to achieve economic stability and social mobility. Rates of early marriage are thus lower (Fatmawati, 2023).

Even so, the waves of modernization and globalization have not uniformly affected the societies, some communities already showing swift change, while others are deeply bound by tradition. The essay argues that in many cases, early marriage remains a common phenomenon in rural or marginalized areas where education, healthcare, and economic opportunity remain low. Globalization has also meant increased exposure to the harms of early marriage, with international organizations, NGOs, and grassroots movements advocating for girls' rights and promoting legal and social reforms for ending the practice (Alfiana et al., 2022).

Current Trends and Continuing Challenges

Despite that there has been quite a reasonable drop in the rates of early marriage. This practice remains an enormous challenge across large parts of the world. Trends are mixed, with important declines in some countries but very high rates in others. Poverty, gender inequality, lack of education access, and other major drivers of early marriage persist in far too many communities today. This comes at a time when awareness and global advocacy efforts have increased more than ever before (Fatmawati, 2023).

EDUCATIONAL CONSEQUENCES

Disruption of Education: Drop Outs and Attainment Levels

Early marriage is among the leading causes for girls to drop out of school, especially in countries where the practice is common. Taking up their roles as wives and mothers immediately after marriage means that girls often discontinue school. The responsibilities of household chores, rearing children, and meeting the expectations of the husband make it almost impossible for young brides to continue their education (Manandhar & Joshi, 2020). In many cases, girls are pulled out of school before they even reach secondary education, thus their academic careers are brought to a premature close, or the opportunities available for them in the future are drastically reduced.

The disruption has a profound impact. Girls who are out of school miss that very critical time of learning, particularly affecting literacy, numeracy, and overall scholastic achievement. In the long run, this diminishes their future chances of finding employment with a decent wage or establishing economic independence. Moreover, lower educational attainment resulting from early marriage among girls is related to the cycle of poverty and gender inequality since these women will less likely have the aptitude and qualifications that would bring them out of poverty (Saleh et al., 2022).

Social Stigma and Family Obligations: Barriers to Re-Enrolment

Even when early married girls express interest in returning to school, they have significant barriers to re-enrolment. Probably the most pervasive challenge is social stigma. This is deeply held in many communities: a girl's marriage signifies the end of schooling, and going back to school is seen as inappropriate or shameful. A married girl, especially one who has become a mother, may be socially excluded by peers and discriminated against by teachers and school administrators. This stigma creates an unfriendly environment that deters them from re-enrolling for more education (Alem et al., 2020).

Responsibilities to the family are also another critical factor that can inhibit re-enrolment. A married girl is expected to take up her wife and mother roles as opposed to pursuing her personal development. Running a home, raising the children, among other spousal duties, leaves very little time and energy for academics. A girl returning to school after getting married is not supported in most families, either because they do not see a need for it or because they have become dependent upon the girl's contributions to household work. The lack of available, inexpensive childcare and flexible schooling options exacerbates these challenges, in which the draining-off of young mothers is needed to properly balance their duties with their education (Saleh et al., 2022).

Psychological Impact and Loss of Motivation

The other critical factor, probably most neglected, is the psychological impact of early marriage on education. Early marriage may lead to a loss of motivation and self-confidence as girls start to internalize beliefs that their major role in life is to be a wife and mother, not a student or professional. Added to these pressures of marital life are the possible traumas that come as a result of early marriage: forced unions, domestic violence, or early pregnancy. Such experiences can lead to anxiety, depression, and a lower sense of self-esteem. These psychological burdens further undermine the ability of a girl to focus on education; therefore, making it harder for her to succeed even when she does go back to school (Wahyudi et al., 2019).

Long-Term Economic Consequences of Educational Disruption

The economic consequences of disruption to education, caused by an early marriage, stretch into the long term in these girls and further into the families and communities of which they form part. Education is a prime determinant of earning capability, so girls not completing school are unlikely to secure a better-paid position within the formal economy. Far more often, they will be relegated to low-wage, informal labor or to unpaid home jobs, with their cycle of poverty and economic dependence intensified (Alfiana et al., 2022).

The economic impact of early marriage extends beyond the individual to community and national levels. Where thousands of girls do not complete their education, the overall level of human capital in a society is reduced. Lower productivity of labor forces and fewer chances of catching up on economic development follow. In large part, countries with high early marriage rates miss the mark on many sustainable development goals—most notably, those related to gender equity, poverty reduction, and education (Wahyudi et al., 2019).

Intergenerational Impact on Education

Early marriage consequences in terms of education extend beyond one generation. Early marriage and low education for women result in children who have less chance of receiving adequate education. Studies have shown that mothers' education is one of the strongest predictors for children's success in education. In the event that mothers are uneducated or poorly educated, they are less able to support the learning of their children at home and in manifold ways in succeeding in the education system. This produces a cycle of educational disadvantage that is hard to break because each generation faces similar barriers to getting access to and completing education (Sarkar, 2021).

Case Studies: Regional Variations and Personal Narratives

The impact of early marriage on education is varied across all regions and communities. Cultural norms, socio-economic conditions, and legal frameworks work together to mediate the extent to which early marriage compromises the education of girls. Early marriage is so deeply ingrained in the social fabric of some regions that the possibility of continued education for married girls is almost non-existent. Whereas in some cases, other areas might provide an opportunity for married girls to continue education, such cases are usually an exception rather than the rule (Mukherjee & Agarwal, 2023).

Due to the variety of experiences undergone by girls affected by early marriage, personal stories or even case studies develop useful insight into these issues. These stories provide nuanced approaches in understanding the complex interplay of factors that lead to educational disruption, challenges, and opportunities for married girls. For example, in several communities, innovative programs and interventions have built up experience supporting married girls in staying at school, which provides hope and inspiration for broader actions to address the issue (Sarkar, 2021).

Broader Implications for Gender Equality and Development

Education represents one of the most empowering ways for women to make informed choices and take part in decision-making, as well as bringing about economic and social development in society. If girls withdraw from school or are not allowed to stay in school, that is equivalent to depriving this empowerment; it reinforces gender inequality and hence diminishes the potential for women to become full contributors to society (Mukherjee & Agarwal, 2023).

This has a ripple effect on development outcomes from the loss of educational opportunities for girls. Informed women have brighter chances of forming small, healthy families, investing in the education of their children, and participating in the labor force. Early marriage reduces the chances of education attainment for large numbers of girls, hence undermining efforts at improving health, reducing poverty, and promoting sustainable development. The impact of early marriage on education thus becomes an individual rights issue and an urgent problem in the development and well-being of entire societies (Sarkar, 2021).

ECONOMIC CONSEQUENCES

Job Prospects

Early marriage has one of its most direct economic consequences in the great restriction it places upon women's access to the job market. Most of the girls who enter into early marriage are made to drop out from school compulsorily and never continue further. Lack of education or training puts them in a lower position as regards qualification and skill acquisition. These young women lack the sort of education and training that places them at a distinct disadvantage in the labor market. They are confined mostly to low-paying, less skilled jobs or, in many cases, entirely outside formal employment education (Alem et al., 2020).

Early marriage in women largely pushes them into traditional wives and mothers' roles, hence further constraining their chance to work in paid employment. Taking care of the house, children, and observing spousal roles are duties that normally supplant economic participation. In many societies, it is expected that married women, especially young ones, should undertake family commitments at the expense of other personal or professional ambitions (Bezie & Addisu, 2019). This societal pressure, coupled with a lack of support systems, such as childcare or flexible working conditions or even spousal support contribute to making entry into, or continuation within, the workforce almost impossible for young married women (Wahyudi et al., 2019).

Income Disparity: Wage Gaps and Economic Dependence

This educational disruption directly creates income disparity between them and others, since early girls cannot go to school to the levels of education attained by their age mates who either marry late or remain single, which usually means earning differential rates. There is a considerable wage difference between women marrying early and those not, which simply means that those early married earn considerably less over their lifetime. This wage gap is further continued by the fact that women who marry early are more likely to be engaged in low wage work, or no work at all, and less likely to have opportunity for promotions (Rahayu & Wahyuni, 2020).

Yet another critical impact of early marriage is a woman's economic dependence on her husband or her family. As most of the women getting married at an early age are not adequately educated or employed, they tend to be dependent on their husbands. This may weaken their bargaining position within the household and hence make them more vulnerable to economic exploitation or abuse. Women who are unable to support themselves may stay in abusive or unhappy marriages. The economic dependency which early marriage creates does harm to women's well-being not only in the present time but also has long-lasting impacts on their ability to invest in health, education, and the well-being of their children (Bajracharya & Amin, 2012).

Intergenerational Poverty and Its Implication on Families' Economic Life in the Long Run

The economic effects of early marriage do not end with the individual and frequently continue with a whole family and society. In most cases, very early marriages lead to intergenerational cycles of poverty. Women who start marriage early and have very few years of schooling and limited working experience are more prone to have children who are poor and have little access to a proper level of education. This often leads to a cycle of poverty and lack of opportunity in one generation after another (Abalos, 2014).

Children born to young married mothers are likely to grow up in poor households with low financial resources and, in all probabilities, to have impaired access to education, health care, and nutrition. Because of the economic stress these families endure, children — especially girls — stop schooling prematurely to either contribute to family earnings or get married early themselves, thus falling into the cycle of poverty. For such children, the implications are lower education, and hence economic opportunities implying fewer job opportunities, low wages, and therefore, resulting in higher poverty in their adulthood—thus a cycle of poor economic status.

Intergenerational poverty from child marriage also extends to other stakeholders in development, such as the communities in a nation. Communities with a high prevalence of child marriage usually face harder times in realizing sustainable economic development and growth. As under-education and underemployment of large numbers of women constitute a loss of human capital, the factor of reducing productivity sets a limit on the possible economic innovations and diversification. In many instances, these communities get trapped in such cycles of poverty and underdevelopment, with little opportunity to break out of the same cycle unless there are considerable extraneous inputs through intervention or systemic changes (Mukherjee & Agarwal, 2023).

Health Costs and Economic Burden

Another major economic implication of early marriage is the escalation of health expenditure and economic burden resulting from early childbirth. This is because women who are married earlier in life also tend to commence childbirth early in life, which comes with its health-related risks and complications. These health-related risks increase medical costs for families and communities, resulting in losses of productivity owing to illnesses or disabilities (Abalos, 2014).

Early marriage also puts a strain on the economy by contributing to the poor health of women in their old age. Women who marry early and bear children are likely, in their mature age, to suffer from serious health complications, the consequences of chronic conditions resulting from early and frequent pregnancies. These can be potentially expensive, both to individual systems and health care systems, especially poor communities with no accessibility to quality health care.

Broader Economic Implications: Impact on National and Global Development

Early marriage poses serious economic implications with regard to developmental issues of national and global concern. Among these, at a national level, high rates of early marriage decrease the potential for economic growth when the capabilities of a huge proportion of potential factor input are shackled. If women cannot contribute fully to the economy owing to early marriage, the economic contributions that those women could make by completing their education and having jobs are lost (Abalos, 2014).

The economic impact of child marriage extends to global development efforts. Early marriage is deeply linked with many of the key challenges identified in the United Nations' Sustainable Development Goals: poverty reduction, gender equality, and access to quality education. Tackling early marriage becomes key, in this respect, to meet the goals of sustainable development and let everyone reach their full potential (Abalos, 2014). Instability at this level will not stop at the community; it flows upwards to affect national security and global stability (Rahayu & Wahyuni, 2020).

Economic Interventions and Policy Responses

This makes targeted economic interventions and policy responses very critical to handling the situation of early marriage. This may involve interventions geared toward improving access to education and skills training among girls at risk of early marriage, and economic support to families in a way that decreases financial pressures causing early marriage (Mukherjee & Agarwal, 2023). Women who have already been married off early also benefit greatly from economic empowerment programs that offer microfinance, entrepreneurship training, and job placement services to aid young women married off to be independent and increase their economic value. Policies that promote gender equality at the workplace such as the legislation for the payment of equal wages and parental leave are very important in narrowing the wide economic gap brought about by marriage at an early age (Manandhar & Joshi, 2020).

SOCIAL IMPLICATIONS

Health Implications: Physiological and Psychological Health

A social implication that is so critical pertaining to early marriage is its impact on mental and physical health. Early marriage commonly culminates in that early pregnancy, which is quite risky health-wise for both a mother and a child. A teenager's body is not properly developed to bear children, hence it is prone to complications in pregnancy and dangers at birth, like obstructed labor, preeclampsia, and severe bleeding. These complications may further result in long-term health problems, disability, or death. In fact, early pregnancy is the leading cause of maternal death among adolescents in low-income countries (Mukherjee & Agarwal, 2023).

Apart from the health risks mentioned, early marriage poses far-reaching effects on mental health. The stresses get too much to be handled since running a marriage, taking care of the household, and, at most times, being a mother at a very tender age is too much for the young girls, thus resulting in depression, anxiety, and other mental conditions. A lot of young brides feel rather isolated, more so if they got into a marriage with a man way above their age or if they were shipped off to other parts of the country without their family. Lack of social support and the expectation that she conforms to traditional gender roles have the ability to feed into these feelings of isolation and helplessness. Moreover, in the event of an early marriage having been forced or coerced, the girls are likely to experience traumatic situations, more so if they are at the receiving end of incidences of physical abuse or rape in that marriage (Manandhar & Joshi, 2020).

Social Isolation: Impact on Social Networks and Mobility

Early marriage frequently causes girls who have become brides to be significantly isolated from their peer environment, family, and community networks. When married, if young girls get not only married, they are often taken out of the social context that has been familiar to them so far and placed in the husband's household, over which they will not have much control, and they will also be restricted in their contact with others. This is particularly the case for a girl who has been married off to some far away land, a land far away from her family or community (Mukherjee & Agarwal, 2023).

The social seclusion of young brides will have long-term effects on their ability to move on socially and form supportive network. Consequently, these girls usually get cut off from their peers and their chances of education. In most cases, they are not able to establish any social ties that often drive personal and professional development. Without social capital, opportunities and resources cannot be reached. Moreover, such perceptions of the role of married women—all inward—centric onto the household—foster isolation and do more to ensure that they have narrow possibilities for engagement in broader social and civic life (Mukherjee & Agarwal, 2023).

Perpetuation of Patriarchy and Gender Inequality

Early marriage is both an outcome and a reinforcer of gender inequality and patriarchal norms. In many cultures, the motivation behind early marriage lies in the belief that a girl's primary role is to be a wife and mother and that her value is attached to her marital status and to her ability to bear children (Muharry et al., 2018). These norms undervalue girls' education and autonomy, making stronger the idea that their purpose is to please and serve their husbands and families.

Another aspect in which early marriage practices reinforce such gendered expectations is through the practice itself: early marriage for girls often denies them education or skills that would have enabled them to achieve economic independence. This economic dependence reinforces their subordinate position within the household and hinders their capacity to challenge or change the power dynamics in their marriage. Inability to access education or become economically empowered also means these women will always be powerless to fight for their own rights or those of their children to advance gender inequality (Mukherjee & Agarwal, 2023).

Effects on Children and Family Structure

The social consequences of early marriage go as far as to touch the children born to young mothers and the family in general. The children of such mothers are more likely to be at a serial disadvantage, characterized by low levels of education, poor health status, and high rates of impoverishment. The cycle of disadvantage caused by early marriage usually perpetuates from one generation to the next. For example, children of young mothers are more likely to drop out of school themselves and to marry young, continuing the cycle of poverty and limited opportunity (Sarkar, 2021).

Moreover, having to start childbearing soon after a young bride is married places additional strain on family resources, resulting in increased poverty, particularly in the most concentrated areas of child marriage. Large families with little access to resources may not be able to provide adequate care for their children, leading to poverty in education, health care access, and provision of nutrition. This damages the children's well-being and development of their futures, further binding them into cycles of disadvantage and chance for upward social mobility (Muharry et al., 2018).

Contribution to Population Growth and Social Services Strain

Early marriage contributes to higher fertility rates, in which, girls who marry early are more likely to start childbearing at an early age and have many children throughout their lifetime. This can bring about an accelerated population growth in a community, in which early marriage is extremely common, thus, straining already limited social services and facilities. More so in many low-income countries where most of the early marriages occur have the high population growth that tends to overstretch governments' and organizations' call to provide services such as health, education, and social, among others to meet the high demand (Sarkar, 2021).

High population growth tends to stretch social services and it has social implications that a number of them are harmful. For instance, schools that tend to be crowded can be of poor quality, since resources are spread thin and teachers are not able to attend to students in the right way. Increased demand for maternal and child health services will result in longer waiting times, lower quality care, and higher rates of maternal and child mortality. As will be shown below, yet, failure of such social services to rise up to the growth is most likely to aggravate social inequalities since the least resourceful individuals are the ones in whom these challenges bite (Muharry et al., 2018).

High population growth can create more competition for resource-constrained environments; land, water, employment, among others, that might lead to social strains and sometimes even conflicts. In addition, the pressure on social services may restrain efforts to increase social indicators for education and health outcomes, thus making it hard for countries to achieve their sustainable development goals to improve the well-being of their populations (Rahayu & Wahyuni, 2020).

Normative Influence on Younger Generations

The practice of early marriage has strong normative influence down the generations, setting in place expectations and aspirations for the young girl. In communities where early marriages are practiced, young girls usually grow up expecting that they too would get married early, and the opportunities to visualize any other kind of futures for themselves may be poor. Such normalization further creates a scenario where the practice is perpetuated, as the girl child grows up with the understanding that her main duty is to be a wife and mother, as opposed to going to school or getting a career (Bezie & Addisu, 2019).

This normative influence applies to the boy child, where he is brought up believing that he should get married to young girls whose primary place is in the home. By doing so, they fail to deal with the actual possibilities of girls and boys interacting with diverse identities and roles; therefore, they further solidify strict traditional gender roles and discourage social development. Normative influence also fosters early marriage; this makes social change in attitudes and behavior even more challenging because each new generation reinforces the expectations passed on from the previous generation (Sarkar, 2021).

Community Cohesion and Social Stability

Whereas early marriage might confer at times a strengthening of family relationships, hence guaranteeing some kind of social cohesion, there is, in other cases, an opposite effect. Where the rights of women and girls become more recognized by communities, or economic pressures make early marriage less viable, it is causing tensions between traditional practice and modern values. Hence, the tension is riddled with the risk of social division, wherein some members of the community are for change while others remain attached to their traditional norms. This may further lead to conflict within families, communities, and broader social instability (Rahayu & Wahyuni, 2020).

Moreover, as is the global trend in the movement for gender equality, communities continuing the practice are bound to be under pressure from international organizations, governments, and NGOs to alter their practices. This pressure can subsequently give way to resistance and backlash, thus further complicating early marriage and social change efforts. One of the major issues for those concerned with the social effects of early marriage is how to balance respect for cultural traditions with protection of the rights and well-being of girls and women (Bezie & Addisu, 2019).

Globalization and Change in Social Norms

Globalization has involved significant social change, particularly in regard to gender equity and the rights of women. Although these changes have been insinuating themselves only slowly into perceptions of early marriage with increased exposure to global media, education, and human rights campaigns touting new ideas and values, they have nonetheless altered social norms in these communities. Such global influences have witnessed a high proliferation of the importance of girls' education and raising awareness about the dangers of early marriage.

The impacts of globalization on changing social norms with respect to early marriage, however, are complex and varied. Sometimes, there is value conflict when globalization challenges traditional communities that strongly resist the imposition of foreign ideas and therefore try to conserve their cultural practices. This resistance can manifest itself in different ways, such as local customs being strongly upheld or its influence being totally rejected. However, globalization of gender equality norms has also empowered local activists and organizations that tend to agree with early marriage and provide incentives for change from within (Rahayu & Wahyuni, 2020). The shifts in social norms regarding early marriage resulting from globalization are not uniform, with the pace different across regions and communities. While the social norms are changing at a rapid pace in some areas, in other places, early marriage remains very deep-seated. These uneven effects of globalization on social norms underline the fact that early marriage requires context-specific approaches, taking into account the unique cultural, social, and economic factors that influence this practice in different communities.

POLICY RESPONSES AND INTERVENTIONS

Legal Reforms: Raising the Legal Age of Marriage

Probably the most direct policy response related to early marriage is the enactment and enforcement of minimum age legislation, typically setting 18 years as the legal age of marriage. Rising the legal age for marriage has a great bearing on protecting young girls from very early marriages and ensuring that they complete their education and attain some level of maturity before taking on the responsibilities of marriage and motherhood (Saleh et al., 2022).

Legal reforms in many countries raise the minimum age of marriage and bring national laws into line with these and other international human rights instruments, including the Convention on the Rights of the Child (CRC) and the Convention on the Elimination of All Forms of Discrimination Against Women (CEDAW). For instance, Malawi and Zimbabwe are among the countries that, in the past few years, have raised the minimum age of marriage to 18 years, recognizing how early marriage damages the rights and development of girls. Still, while these legal reforms may be one of the pillars in this battle against early marriage, more often than not, they turn out to be inadequate on their own. dual legal systems—in which customary or religious laws work side by side with national laws—are present in many countries and may undermine the effectiveness of legal reforms (Bezie & Addisu, 2019).

Most of such customary and religious practices make exceptions to the legal age of marriage, particularly based on grounds of parental consent or a judicial ruling. Secondly, the weak enforcement of marriage laws—predominantly in rural or remote areas—may mean that the practice of early marriage continues despite being illegal. The challenges of addressing these call for more than strengthening legal frameworks; they call for laws to be effectively enforced and for communities to be educated on the legal age of marriage and the rights of the girl child (Abalos, 2014).

Education Initiatives: Keeping Girls in School

Education is a strong means by which early marriage can be avoided and girls are empowered to make informed decisions about their lives. Policies and interventions keeping girls at school are important in delaying marriage and hence improving future economic opportunities available for girls. Governments and non-governmental organizations have done many initiatives in education to increase school attendance, reduce dropouts, and provide a good atmosphere that would enable girls to keep on learning (Mukherjee & Agarwal, 2023). This has been credited with causing a drastic drop in early marriage rates and an increase in the number of girls attending secondary schools in this country (Saleh et al., 2022).

This will call for financial incentives and policies targeting problems in girls' education, including a lack of safe transportation facilities to and from school, appropriate school facilities, and access to sanitary products. On such measures, girl-friendly school environments free from violence, harassment, and discrimination will make sure that girls are safeguarded throughout their educational journey. Furthermore, providing comprehensive sexuality education (CSE) will serve to empower girls with knowledge and skills for making informed decisions on matters concerning sexual and reproductive health, resisting pressures to marry early, and knowing the rights available (Abalos, 2014).

Programs on Economic Empowerment: Improving Livelihood Opportunities

These economic empowerment programs are part of the struggle against early marriage within communities in which poverty and economic insecurity prevail as drivers. Through this program, the objective is to enhance the economic prospects of girls and young women by making relevant vocational and skills training available, along with entrepreneurship opportunities, to reduce financial pressures that lead them toward early marriages (Raymo & Iwasawa, 2005).

These include the microfinance initiatives, savings groups, and income-generating activities, which have been shown to work in various contexts. For example, life-skills training is combined with vocational-skill development in the BRAC Empowerment and Livelihood for Adolescents (ELA) program in Uganda to offer a platform for girls to begin businesses or generate income. The evidence shows that the potential for early marriage reduces with increased financial independence for girls (Mukherjee & Agarwal, 2023).

Community Engagement and Behavior Change Initiatives

Community engagement and behaviour change initiatives are the key to addressing the cultural and social norms that perpetuate the practice of early marriage. This is where one works directly with communities to increase awareness about the negative consequences of early marriage, promote gender equality, and support girls' and women's rights (Saleh et al., 2022). Programs that mobilize community leaders, religious authorities, parents, and young people are very effective in changing attitudes and behavior towards early marriage. For example, in Ethiopia, the Berhane Hewan program works through community leaders and elders to generate discourse regarding the harms of early marriage and to develop community-led interventions that protect girls. This includes secondary mentorship, education, and economic support to girls and their families, which no doubt drastically reduced the rate of early marriage in participating communities (Manandhar & Joshi, 2020).

Behavior change initiatives may apply a variety of methods to reach different segments of the population, including community dialogues, mass media campaigns, and peer education. Indeed, mass media campaigns are able to challenge harmful gender norms and increase awareness. An illustrative example of such campaigns includes radio, television, and social media messages detailing the advantages of delaying marriage and investing in girls' education (Saleh et al., 2022). Besides behavior change, most community engagement initiatives are bound to have the core features of strengthening local institutions-including schools, health services, and child protection systems-so that they can be effectively responsive to girls at greatest risk from early marriage. Such programs can build capacity in these institutions and provide high community ownership of the issue, hence a supportive environment for girls and change that can last (Raymo & Iwasawa, 2005).

Health Interventions to Support Reproductive Health and Rights

Health interventions are, therefore, very instrumental in mitigating the effects of early marriage and in promoting the reproductive health and rights of young brides. Early marriage usually goes with early pregnancy, posing serious health hazards to girls at adolescence and their children. Hence, health interventions play a very important role in minimizing risks to health, which are associated with early marriage, by improving access to reproductive health services such as family planning, maternal health care, and sexual health education (Fatmawati, 2023).

Family planning programs can also support early and unplanned pregnancies by providing contraceptives to young women and offering information about their right to reproductive choice. This would enable the young brides to have better control over their reproductive lives. For example, in India, the government envisions delayed pregnancy in the first instance and spacing of birth in its For example, in India, the government's Reproductive, Maternal, Newborn, Child, and Adolescent Health (RMNCH+A) program, which is very important for adolescent girls who marry early (Manandhar & Joshi, 2020).

Apart from family planning, there is a need for health interventions dealing with the general health status of the young bride. These involve access to antenatal care, skilled birth attendance, postnatal care, and reducing risks due to pregnancy and childbirth. Such programs also introduce mental health support, particularly to girls who have gone through forced or compelled marriage, to deal with the mental ramifications of early marriage (Rahayu & Wahyuni, 2020).

International and Regional Initiatives: Global Advocacy and Cooperation

International and regional initiatives are an integral part of the global drive towards ending early marriage because they provide a platform for advocacy, coordination, and resource mobilization. International and regional initiatives involve partnerships between governments, international organizations, NGOs, and civil society organizations that have combined to advance girls' and women's rights and implement strategies geared toward prevention (Sarkar, 2021).

The United Nations Sustainable Development Goals (SDGs) act as one of the major international frameworks, particularly goal 5, with the vision of 'Achieving gender equality and empowering all women and girls.' Target 5.3 particularly calls for the elimination of all harmful practices, including child marriage, early marriage, and forced marriage. SDGs will therefore contribute to a global benchmark of progress and will spur countries towards formulation and implementation of action plans on early marriage (Rahayu & Wahyuni, 2020).

These regional initiatives—the African Union Campaign to End Child Marriage in Africa and the South Asia Initiative to End Violence against Children (SAIEVAC) have been very instrumental in raising awareness and driving action at the regional level. This entails cross-border cooperation, knowledge sharing, and development of regional strategies on how to end early marriage and related challenges (Muharry et al., 2018).

The organizations, such as Girls Not Brides, that have engaged in international advocacy are very instrumental in mobilizing the world's attention and resources toward addressing early marriage. These organizations influence policy, support movements at the grassroots level, and hold governments accountable for their commitment to ending early marriage. Global advocacy campaigns, like the International Day of the Girl Child, are also very instrumental in raising awareness and mobilizing political will toward addressing the situation (Sarkar, 2021).

Monitoring and Evaluation: Measuring Impact and Improving Interventions

Robust monitoring and evaluation (M&E) systems let effectual policy responses and interventions ensure the impact is effectively measured, best practices are identified, and programs are executed towards achieving their purpose. Through M&E, it will be possible to understand what works, what does not, and why, hence enabling policymakers and practitioners to refine and improve their approaches towards combating early marriage (Fatmawati, 2023).

In general, M&E systems involve collection and analysis of data on key indicators, including rates of early marriage, school enrollment and completion rates, access to health services, and economic outcomes of girls and women (Vettriselvan et al., 2018). Such data would be used to understand efficiency in terms of specific interventions, lapses in execution, or progress toward broader goals set out by national action plans or international frameworks, such as the SDGs (Muharry et al., 2018).

It is in learning from the lived experiences of girls and women regarding early marriage and capturing the social and cultural dynamics sustaining the practice that qualitative research methods—such as in-depth interviews, focus groups, and case studies—assume a very significant role in the collection of quantitative data. This kind of research would be able to provide important insights on barriers and enablers of change and ensure that interventions are culturally relevant and responsive to the target population (Sarkar, 2021).

Furthermore, M&E systems should be designed in a participatory manner. This involves the communities and persons most affected by early marriage in the evaluation and improvement of the interventions. The participatory approach ensures that local ownership of issues can be built, ensuring that interventions are linked to the realities of the communities they aim to serve, which in turn increases accountability and transparency (Raymo & Iwasawa, 2005).

Challenges and Barriers to Effective Policy Implementation

While there has been significant progress in the development and implementation of policies and interventions to address early marriage, several challenges and barriers remain (Uddin et al., 2019). First, one of the major problems is that early marriage and other traditional practices are underpinned by deeply entrenched social and cultural norms. These will take time to change, with firsts being directed at all levels, from the grass roots of community engagement to reform of national policy (Muharry et al., 2018).

Another critical challenge in implementation relates to the insufficient resources and capacity for efficient policy delivery and enforcement. Very few low-income countries have adequate funding, infrastructure, and human resources of the government and organizations involved, thereby reducing the scope of interventions that can be implemented and their penetration. It is very important to ensure that adequate resourcing of policies happens, with capacity assured for effective implementation and enforcement if meaningful change is to be realized (Wahyudi et al., 2019).

Furthermore, early marriage is one of the complex problems that may partly be in, or linked to, various sectors—including education, health, justice, and social protection—all of which require an effective response to such linkages through coordination and collaboration, which generally eludes practice. Greater coordination and stronger integration of policies and programs, ensuring consistency and mutual reinforcement, would be more fitting to respond effectively to meet the multi-sectoral nature of the challenge of early marriage (Raymo & Iwasawa, 2005).

CONCLUSION

Early marriage has deep, multi-dimensional effects in women's education and labour-force participation, while continuing cycles of poverty, dependency, and gender inequality. It disrupts education and reduces subsequent economic opportunities, further enhancing social hierarchies that reduce the potential of women. While international legal frameworks for action exist, cultural and religious norms perpetuating early marriage have been difficult to change. Such an approach would include the comprehensive treatment of the problem in all its dimensions: legal reform, education, economic opportunities, and social change through community engagement. This is very important; ending child marriage will open up opportunities for the full participation and realization of their potential for every girl and woman.

REFERENCES

Abalos, J. B. (2014). Trends and determinants of age at union of men and women in the philippines. *Journal of Family Issues*, 35(12), 1624–1641. DOI: 10.1177/0192513X14538024

Alem, A. Z., Yeshaw, Y., Kebede, S. A., Liyew, A. M., Tesema, G. A., Agegnehu, C. D., & Teshale, A. B. (2020). Spatial distribution and determinants of early marriage among married women in ethiopia: A spatial and multilevel analysis. *BMC Women's Health*, 20(1), 207. Advance online publication. DOI: 10.1186/s12905-020-01070-x PMID: 32933491

Alfiana, R. D., Yulyani, L., Subarto, C. B., Mulyaningsih, S., & Zuliyati, I. C. (2022). The impact of early marriage on women of reasonable age in the special region of yogyakarta. *Indonesian Journal of Nursing and Midwifery*, 10(1), 89. DOI: 10.21927/jnki.2022.10(1).89-101

Bajracharya, A., & Amin, S. (2012). Poverty, marriage timing, and transitions to adulthood in Nepal. *Studies in Family Planning*, 43(2), 79–92. DOI: 10.1111/j.1728-4465.2012.00307.x PMID: 23175948

Becker, G. S. (2009). *Human capital: A theoretical and empirical analysis, with special reference to education*. University of Chicago press.

Bezie, M., & Addisu, D. (2019). Determinants of early marriage among married women in Injibara town, northwest Ethiopia: Community-based cross-sectional study. *BMC Women's Health*, 19(1), 134. Advance online publication. DOI: 10.1186/s12905-019-0832-0 PMID: 31703577

Bourdieu, P., & Passeron, J. (1990). *Reproduction in education, society and culture*. SAGE Publications.

Crenshaw, K. (2019). 'Difference' through intersectionality 1. In *Dalit Feminist Theory* (pp. 139–149). Routledge India. DOI: 10.4324/9780429298110-15

Elengemoke, J., & Susuman, A. (2020). Early marriage and correlates among young women in sub-Saharan African countries. *Journal of Asian and African Studies*, 56(6), 1345–1368. DOI: 10.1177/0021909620966778

Fatmawati, F., Yantina, Y., & Susilawati, S. (2023). Factors causing early marriage from sociocultural view in the working area of ketapang health center of south sungkai regency, north Lampung district in 2023. *MAHESA: Malahayati Health Student Journal*, 3(12), 3953–3971. DOI: 10.33024/mahesa.v3i12.11891

Hajihasani, M., & Sim, T. (2018). Marital satisfaction among girls with early marriage in Iran: Emotional intelligence and religious orientation. *International Journal of Adolescence and Youth*, 24(3), 297–306. DOI: 10.1080/02673843.2018.1528167

Kamal, S., Hassan, C., Alam, G., & Yang, Y. (2014). Child marriage in Bangladesh: Trends and determinants. *Journal of Biosocial Science*, 47(1), 120–139. DOI: 10.1017/S0021932013000746 PMID: 24480489

Kartika, N. Y., Efendi, M., Normelani, E., Heru, H., & Sopyan, S. (2021). The influence of education, welfare and residential area on adolescent marriages. *Journal of Anthropologic: Isu-Isu Sosial Budaya*, 23(1), 18. DOI: 10.25077/jantro.v23.n1.p18-26.2021

Lowe, G., Hughes, D., & Witt, D. (1989). Changes in the influence of early marriage on the educational attainment of men and women. *Sociological Spectrum*, 9(2), 163–173. DOI: 10.1080/02732173.1989.9981881

Manandhar, N., & Joshi, S. (2020). Health co-morbidities and early marriage in women of a rural area of nepal: A descriptive cross-sectional study. *JNMA; Journal of the Nepal Medical Association*, 58(230). Advance online publication. DOI: 10.31729/jnma.5205 PMID: 34504369

Muharry, A., Hakimi, M., & Wahyuni, B. (2018). Family structure and early marriage on women in indramayu regency. *Journal of Kesehatan Masyarakat*, 13(3), 314–322. DOI: 10.15294/kemas.v13i3.8946

Mukherjee, P. and Agarwal, M. (2023). Factors influencing female workforce participation in urban India: A case study. *International Journal of Indian Economic Light*, 1-7. https://doi.org/DOI: 10.36713/epra12849

Naghizadeh, S., Mirghafourvand, M., Mohammadi, A., Azizi, M., Taghizadeh-Milani, S., & Ganbari, H. (2021). Knowledge and viewpoint of adolescent girls regarding child marriage, its causes and consequences. *BMC Women's Health*, 21(1), 351. Advance online publication. DOI: 10.1186/s12905-021-01497-w PMID: 34615510

Opesemowo, O. A., & Odumosu, E. T. (2023). The sway of early marriage on the girl child education among some ethnic groups in Lagos state, Nigeria. *Journal of Culture and Values in Education*, 6(3), 26–41. DOI: 10.46303/jcve.2023.18

Parpart, J. L., Connelly, P., & Barriteau, E. (Eds.). (2000). *Theoretical perspectives on gender and development*. IDRC.

Paul, P. (2019). Child marriage and its association with morbidity and mortality of children under 5 years old: Evidence from India. *Journal of Public Health (Berlin)*, 28(3), 331–338. DOI: 10.1007/s10389-019-01038-8

Rahayu, W., & Wahyuni, H. (2020). The influence of early marriage on monetary poverty in Indonesia. *Journal of Indonesian Economy and Business*, 35(1). Advance online publication. DOI: 10.22146/jieb.42405

Raymo, J., & Iwasawa, M. (2005). Marriage market mismatches in japan: An alternative view of the relationship between women's education and marriage. *American Sociological Review*, 70(5), 801–822. DOI: 10.1177/000312240507000504

Rumble, L., Peterman, A., Irdiana, N., Triyana, M., & Minnick, E. (2018). An empirical exploration of female child marriage determinants in Indonesia. *BMC Public Health*, 18(1), 407. Advance online publication. DOI: 10.1186/s12889-018-5313-0 PMID: 29587705

Saleh, A., Othman, S., Ismail, K., & Shabila, N. (2022). Exploring Iraqi people's perception about early marriage: A qualitative study. *BMC Women's Health*, 22(1), 393. Advance online publication. DOI: 10.1186/s12905-022-01980-y PMID: 36175884

Saleheen, A., Afrin, S., Kabir, S., Habib, M., Zinnia, M., Hossain, M., Haq, I., & Talukder, A. (2021). Sociodemographic factors and early marriage among women in Bangladesh, ghana and iraq: An illustration from multiple indicator cluster survey. *Heliyon*, 7(5), e07111. DOI: 10.1016/j.heliyon.2021.e07111 PMID: 34095593

Sarkar, S. (2021). Local crime and early marriage: evidence from India. WIDER Working Paper. https://doi.org/DOI: 10.35188/UNU-WIDER/2021/975-4

Uddin, J., Pulok, M. H., Johnson, R. B., Rana, J., & Baker, E. (2019). Association between child marriage and institutional delivery care services use in Bangladesh: Intersections between education and place of residence. *Public Health*, 171, 6–14. DOI: 10.1016/j.puhe.2019.03.014 PMID: 31071578

Uddin, M. E. (2015). Family socio-cultural values affecting early marriage between Muslim and Santal communities in rural Bangladesh. *The International Journal of Sociology and Social Policy*, 35(3/4), 141–164. DOI: 10.1108/IJSSP-06-2014-0046

Uddin, M. E. (2017). Family demographic mechanisms linking of socioeconomic status to subjective physical health in rural Bangladesh. *Social Indicators Research*, 130(3), 1263–1279. DOI: 10.1007/s11205-015-1209-x

Uddin, M. E. (2021). Teenage marriage and high school dropout among poor girls: A narrative review for family pathways in Bangladesh. *Journal of Research in Social Sciences and Language*, 1(1), 55–76.

Wahyudi, T., Hasanbasri, M., Kusnanto, H., & Hakimi, M. (2019). Social determinants of health of child marriage (analysis of ifls 2000, 2007, 2014). *Journal of Kesehatan Masyarakat*, 15(1), 62–68. DOI: 10.15294/kemas.v15i1.16514

Zegeye, B., Keetile, M., Ahinkorah, B. O., Ameyaw, E. K., Seidu, A., & Yaya, S. (2021). Utilization of deworming medication and its associated factors among pregnant married women in 26 sub-Saharan African countries: A multi-country analysis. *Tropical Medicine and Health*, 49(1), 53. Advance online publication. DOI: 10.1186/s41182-021-00343-x PMID: 34193313

Chapter 12
Early Marriage as a Model of Child Trafficking:
Exploring the Legal Safeguards to Victims

Ramy El-Kady
https://orcid.org/0000-0003-2208-7576
Police Academy, Egypt

ABSTRACT

The chapter deals with the issue of early marriage as one of the most prominent issues plaguing societies. The family is the entity of society, and women are the cornerstones of the family. There is no doubt that forming a family requires the availability of several conditions, the most important of which is the woman's ability to manage family affairs, as practical reality has resulted in the spread of the phenomenon of underage marriage. As one of the reflections resulting from poverty, the spread of ignorance, and adherence to some customs and traditions. This chapter aims to shed light on the psychological, health, and social aspects of early marriage and explain why it has become more and more common in society. It also aims to explain the legal framework that governs its confrontation as one of the most prominent forms of child trafficking. The study concluded that the need for an integrated community confrontation plan or strategy depends on enforcing laws and adopting large-scale mass media campaigns to spread public awareness of this issue and establish emergency lines.

DOI: 10.4018/979-8-3693-3394-5.ch012

INTRODUCTION

Early marriage, also referred to as child marriage, is an issue that many countries are aware of. It is categorized as a type of human trafficking, or more specifically, child trafficking. The whole community has noticed this phenomenon, and numerous international bodies and organizations are now concerned about it. *"Marriage in which one or both parties are under the age of 18 or have not reached the age of majority specified in the country"* is the definition of early marriage (El-Kady, 2024).

Since one or both parties lack full autonomy to consent or fail to express explicit permission to marriage because they are unable to choose a suitable mate for them, early marriage is regarded as a form of forced marriage. They are particularly considering that each person's incapacity to give consent may stem from a variety of circumstances, such as the pace of one's own physical, psychological, sexual, or emotional development or the fact that one of the parties does not have the necessary life experiences to make the right choice (Mazurana & Marshak, 2019).

Young girls are frequently the ones most impacted by the early marriage phenomena, as some families force the girl to choose her future life partner from the moment of her birth. She is immediately married off when she reaches the legal age of parenthood (Sezgin & Punamäki, 2020).

The importance of the study is highlighted in light of the violation of children's human rights that this dangerous social phenomenon represents, as well as the various negative repercussions that fall upon girls as a result of this marriage, especially the health, psychological, and social effects of early marriage on the girl and her newborn (El-Kady, 2024).

In addition to highlighting the most significant legal protections afforded to victims in this context, this study aims to shed light on the psychological, health, and social aspects of early marriage and explain why it has become more and more common in society. It also aims to explain the legal framework that governs its confrontation as one of the most prominent forms of child trafficking.

Additionally, International estimates indicate that sexual jihad, which is known by some terrorist organizations such as ISIS, is considered human trafficking, as this practice is used by Organizations to victimize women and girls to entice young people to join these organizations and according to the Global Report on the Situation of Human Trafficking for 2020, armed groups and terrorists traffic women and children to generate money and recruit new members by enticing them into sexual jihad or marrying minors, which will undoubtedly lead to an increase in the number of victims of human trafficking, which at the same time, it constitutes a severe violation of human rights (El-Kady, 2024).

The USA 2023 Trafficking in Persons Report in Syria reveals that Syrian children are at risk of coerced early marriages, often to individuals affiliated with terrorist organizations like ISIS, leading to sexual enslavement and forced labor. Displaced children also endure forced labor from organized begging networks. Armed factions, community members, and criminal syndicates in Syria exploit women, girls, and boys, particularly vulnerable groups like internally displaced persons and persons with disabilities, through sex trafficking in exchange for food or compensation (El-Kady, 2024).

Despite ISIS' territorial defeat in 2019, the group continues to coerce Syrian girls and women into marriages with its militants, subjecting them to forced marriages, domestic servitude, systematic rape, sexual slavery, and other forms of sexual violence. ISIS has publicly documented its ideology and methods of oppression, including a system of organized sexual slavery and forced marriage (*Syria - United States Department of State*, 2023).

The study hypothesizes that victims of early marriage suffer from many psychological, social, and legal problems, which requires the need to provide integrated societal protection, especially legal protection, in the face of trafficked persons. The victim faces many different difficulties that require the need to provide integrated health and social care for her and her children. This chapter will explore the topic through three parts: the first part will define the concept of early marriage, the second part will discuss human trafficking as an encompassing criminal framework that encompasses child trafficking, and the third part will examine the legal protections provided for victims of human trafficking, including those affected by early marriage, in Egyptian and Arab laws.

LITERATURE REVIEW

Early marriage, often involving underage individuals, is often viewed as a form of child trafficking due to its coercive nature, exploitation, and infringement on children's rights. This practice, often involving money transactions, often leads to psychological repercussions and hinders child growth, similar to trafficking. Enhanced legislative frameworks and more effective enforcement are crucial to address these abuses and safeguard the rights of children. Early marriages frequently entail coercion, when youngsters are compelled into relationships without their agreement, akin to those who fall victim to sex and forced labor trafficking. Forced child marriages exhibit slave-like traits akin to child trafficking since children are compelled into these relationships and obliged to participate in activities akin to those of victims of sex and labor trafficking (Warria, 2017).

Some scholars see that early marriage may be regarded as a manifestation of child trafficking because of its detrimental effects on society, such as the coerced acquisition or resale of underage females, sexual servitude, and exploitation (Raval & Bharad, 2021). On the other hand, other researchers argue that these weddings can be seen as a type of economic exploitation since they frequently entail money transactions that benefit the adult individuals entering the marriage.

Meanwhile, others see that compulsory early marriage (CEFM) can be considered a type of sexual abuse and exploitation of minors, as well as commercial exploitation, because adult parties benefit financially from entering into a partnership (Er et al., 2015). Child marriage is classified as a type of trafficking involving girls and hence violates international agreements about the rights of children and the practice of forced labor (Warner, 2011).

Some researchers argue that youngsters tied up in early marriages are often vulnerable to sexual exploitation and abuse, similar to the ordeals faced by trafficked children (Warria, 2017). Otherwise, others see that exposure to marriage, pregnancy, and sexual abuse during childhood before the age of 16 is linked to a higher likelihood of female sex workers being victims of child sex trafficking (Boyce et al., 2018). Furthermore, Other scholars see these marriages as encompassing coerced labor, in which the child is compelled to carry out domestic or other arduous duties under oppressive circumstances (Warria, 2017).

Meanwhile, other researchers argue that early marriages often entail financial transactions in which the bride's family receives monetary compensation, therefore constituting a type of bride trafficking (Raval & Bharad, 2021). This practice is widespread in economically disadvantaged areas where families sell their daughters to relieve financial hardships (Raval & Bharad, 2021).

In parallel, some scholars argue that early marriages result in significant psychosocial repercussions, such as depression, post-traumatic stress disorder, and social isolation, which are prevalent among juvenile victims of trafficking. These marriages impede the child's growth, education, and prospects, paralleling the consequences of trafficking. Early marriage isolates children from their relatives and peers, exposes them to marital abuse, and can result in psychological issues like despair and attrition (zimova & Universiteti, 2021).

Otherwise, some academics argue that despite the existence of international and national laws that prohibit child marriage and trafficking, the implementation of these laws is still inadequate, and the practices persist, particularly in poor nations (Warria, 2017). While several academics argue that early marriage is linked to a higher likelihood of intimate partner violence (IPV), later age at marriage is related to reduced chances of physical and emotional IPV. The consensus was that more robust legislative frameworks and improved implementation are necessary to safeguard children from these exploitative behaviors (Hayes & Protas, 2021).

Furthermore, some argue that early marriage can be seen as a manifestation of child trafficking, driven by economic motives, religious beliefs, and parental control, resulting in youngsters being selfless and blindly obeying their parents' desires (Sopyan et al., 2023). Furthermore, several researchers argue that early marriage in Turkey is linked to variables such as female gender, school dropout, low socioeconomic status of the family, and fractured family presence (Yüksel & Koçtürk, 2021). Indeed, it is widely acknowledged that Child and Early Forced Marriage (CEFM) constitutes a type of child abuse and a severe violation of the human rights of both girls and boys (Campbell et al., 2020).

METHODOLOGY

The study will use the comparative descriptive-analytical method, suitable for studying the phenomenon of early marriage in all aspects, with a review of the comparative experiences organized for this topic. The descriptive-analytical method is defined as: "the study of the phenomenon as it exists in reality, describing it closely and expressing it qualitatively or quantitatively in order to reach conclusions that contribute to understanding and developing this reality" (Crootof, 2019); this approach aims to research and analyze the phenomenon of Earley Marriage from its criminal legal aspects by reviewing the legal guarantees that the law provides to victims of early marriage, as it is a form of human trafficking.

Early Marriage – Definition, Reasons, and Consequences

Definition of Early marriage

Early marriage or Child marriage can be defined as a *marital union in which at least one of the individuals is below 18*. Early marriage is different from forced marriage, which is defined as a *marital union in which one or both partners have not independently and entirely given their permission to the union. Considering that one or both parties have not given complete, voluntary, and informed permission*, child marriage is classified as a type of forced marriage (El-Kady, 2024).

Reasons for Early Marriage

Early marriage is a complex issue that is influenced by various social, economic, cultural, and religious factors, especially the legal aspects of human traffickers in various countries. For Early marriage reasons, there are numerous justifications for early marriage, and they might be outlined as follows: Insufficient level of education, in which the girl's lack of access to secure transportation, poor quality of education, and limited educational possibilities have resulted in her being unable to attend school. Consequently, she is more likely to be inclined towards early marriage. After receiving ten years of education, the rate of marriage for girls under 18 reduces by a factor of six (Gastón et al., 2019).

Inadequate compliance with legal regulations and their enforcement, in which Inadequate dissemination of comprehensive information, particularly regarding the Law Prohibiting Early Marriage enacted in 2006, along with its application procedures and the repercussions of non-compliance, has resulted in ineffective enforcement. Society lacks faith in the institutions responsible for administering this rule, primarily due to the prevailing belief that traditions and conventions hold more sway than the law and institutions. This perception is reinforced by the low number of documented incidents of early marriage (Mahato, 2016).

Poor economic situation: Approximately 40% of girls who were married at a young age come from the most impoverished families globally. One reason families in poverty support early marriage is the belief that the dowry payment can help alleviate their financial struggles by providing for the family's needs, paying off debts, and resolving economic difficulties.

These households also take into account the marriage of their daughters. They minimized family expenditures while ensuring she would be provided with sustenance, attire, and a suitable education following her marriage. However, in certain nations where the responsibility of providing a bridal dowry lies with the wife's family, there is a tendency to marry her off at a young age. This is because the financial burden is lower when the bride is young and lacks education. (Lee-Rife et al., 2012).

Social traditions in which numerous cultures perceive a girl who has reached the age of puberty as suitable for marriage, and it is customary for her to acquire the roles of a wife and mother through marriage (Ahmed et al., 2014). The vulnerability and proliferation of crises in communities where girls are subjected to peril, Harassment, and acts of physical or sexual assault. Parents often arrange marriages for their daughters to safeguard them and ensure their well-being. Areas afflicted by humanitarian crises and natural catastrophes, as well as those plagued by widespread violence and poverty, experience elevated rates of early marriages. Of the ten countries experiencing crises in various forms, nine have a significant prevalence of early marriage. (Ahmed et al., 2013). (see Figure 1)

Figure 1. Reasons for Early Marriage

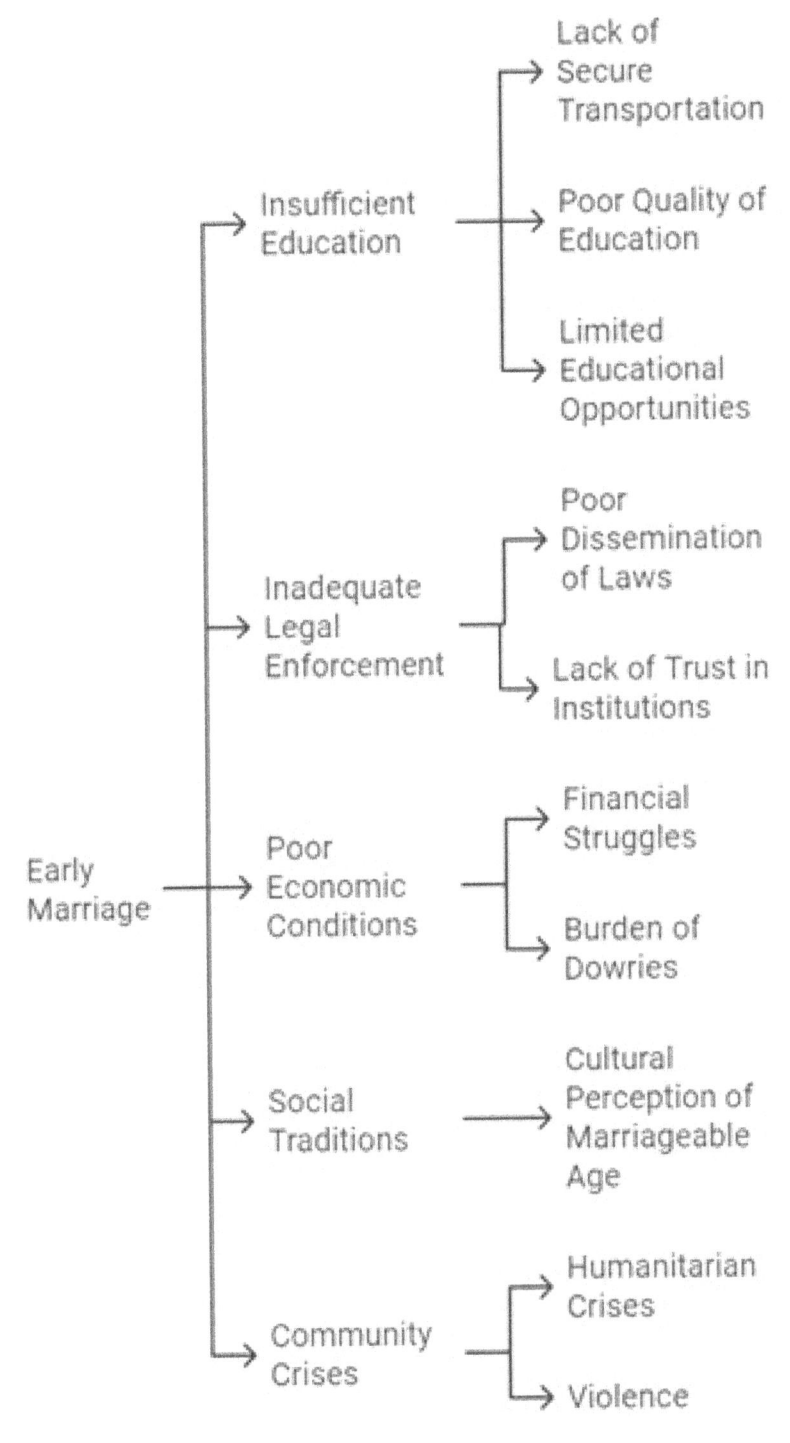

- Early Marriage
  - Insufficient Education
    - Lack of Secure Transportation
    - Poor Quality of Education
    - Limited Educational Opportunities
  - Inadequate Legal Enforcement
    - Poor Dissemination of Laws
    - Lack of Trust in Institutions
  - Poor Economic Conditions
    - Financial Struggles
    - Burden of Dowries
  - Social Traditions
    - Cultural Perception of Marriageable Age
  - Community Crises
    - Humanitarian Crises
    - Violence

Early Marriage Consequences

Early marriage is prevalent in certain countries, particularly among male children. However, the rate of early marriage is more than twice as high for girls compared to boys. The consequences of early marriage affect both genders, but they are more pronounced in girls. Both boys and girls face various risks and effects due to early marriage, which are influenced by their biological and social differences. It is important to note that all of these effects are considered a violation of children's rights, regardless of their gender (Parsons et al., 2015).

A child who enters into marriage at a young age has social alienation, being separated from their family, friends, and individuals who support them. Furthermore, she encounters challenges in acquiring an education and securing a job. For instance, in Malawi, over two-thirds of women lacking formal education are married as children, with just a mere 5% of them managing to transition to adulthood. Post-secondary and tertiary education. These girls are also incapable of handling marital issues, as they are more susceptible to sexually transmitted infections—for example, the AIDS virus (Mpilambo et al., 2017).

Early pregnancy is a consequence of social pressure on child brides. In Nepal, over 33% of women aged 20 to 24 who were married before the age of fifteen have three or more children, while only 1% of women who married after reaching puberty have the same number of children. However, these women do not receive adequate medical care during pregnancy (Hayes & Protas, 2022). In countries like Bangladesh, Ethiopia, Nepal, and Niger, women who marry during puberty are twice as likely to receive adequate healthcare during childbirth compared to women who marry before the age of fifteen, despite their bodies being insufficiently developed to give birth safely. This situation poses significant risks to mothers and their children (Desai et al., 2018).

The impact of early marriage on males in which an adverse consequence of early marriage on male children is the imposition of significant responsibilities for which they lack the necessary qualifications. Assuming the parental role at a young age also results in financial burdens that may hinder the married child's ability to pursue education and acquire the necessary skills to secure suitable employment (Gastón et al., 2019).

The physical and mental consequences of marrying at a young age for girls in which female fertility begins at the onset of puberty, enabling women to conceive. However, pregnancies occurring before the age of fifteen are associated with numerous adverse outcomes. Conditions such as anemia, maternal hypertension, and fetal macrosomia (enlarged head size compared to the mother's pelvis) (Dangal, 2008). Adolescent moms aged 10 to 19 years have an increased risk of developing preeclampsia, postpartum endometriosis, and reproductive system infections compared to mothers aged 20 to 24 years (Leftwich & Alves, 2017).

Furthermore, around 3.9 million severe miscarriages occur among adolescent girls aged 15 to 19 years each year, often resulting in fatalities or long-term health complications. The emotional, psychological, and social care needs of pregnant teenage moms surpass their other needs. Elderly females (Elfenbein & Felice, 2003). Adolescent mothers have a higher likelihood of experiencing postpartum depression compared to older mothers. They may exhibit symptoms such as mood swings, anxiety, melancholy, and difficulties with concentration, appetite, and sleep, which can last for a period of one to two weeks. There is also a possibility of an elevated risk of depression. The likelihood of an increase is higher if the mother gives birth before the completion of nine months.

Other symptoms that might occur alongside postpartum depression include Challenges in forming a positive maternal bond between the child and the mother. Severe exhaustion. Feelings of fear, panic, and anxiety attacks. The mother contemplates self-harm or damage to the child. The girl no longer finds pleasure in activities that used to bring her joy (Samsuddin et al., 2019).

Early marriage has significant psychological consequences for girls, stemming from the loss of parental affection and the denial of a childhood filled with joy and freedom. The multiple responsibilities of married life expose these young girls to immense pressure, as they lack an understanding of the complexities of marital relationships. Consequently, various psychological effects manifest in them. Instances of marital discord caused by fear can often necessitate medical intervention (Wardani, 2022).

The spouse may also display symptoms of despair and anxiety due to the numerous marital issues stemming from a lack of mutual comprehension. During pregnancy and postpartum, the likelihood of experiencing personality disorders, hysteria, and schizophrenia may increase. This is because the duties of motherhood place additional stress on women, potentially leading to the development of psychiatric problems. Furthermore, the husband's and relatives' expectations must also be considered (Ahmed et al., 2014).

It puts the girl and her child at risk. The health consequences of early marriage on young girls are apparent, as indicated by the fivefold increase in mortality rates for females married before the age of 15 compared to those married at the age of 20. Additionally, these young girls are more susceptible to experiencing bleeding and difficulties after childbirth (Stoyanova, 2016).

According to Save The Children's 2004 annual report, children born to females who marry before reaching puberty are twice as likely to die during the first year of their lives compared to children born to girls who marry at the age of twenty. However, if they manage to live, they are more prone to experiencing inadequate healthcare and malnutrition due to their moms' suboptimal feeding practices, in contrast to older mothers (Kakar, 2020).

The ramifications of early marriage on children's health and psychological well-being are that adolescent women have a higher likelihood of delivering premature infants that experience low birth weight. This is attributed to inadequate time for fetal development within the mother's womb, resulting in low birth weight. A kid with low birth weight typically weighs between 1,500 and 2,500 grams; in severe situations, their weight may drop below 1,500 grams. In this scenario, the child requires medical assistance in the neonatal intensive care unit of the hospital, including the potential use of a respirator to assist with breathing if needed (Males, 2010).

The health consequences on the fetus might manifest in several ways, such as Exposure to asphyxiation within the mother's womb. Premature birth can result in inadequate blood circulation, which can lead to various dangers for the infant, such as underdeveloped lungs and harm to the digestive system. The child may also experience delayed physiological and cognitive growth, and an elevated risk of having cerebral palsy, visual impairment, or auditory impairment, or the youngster may succumb to many sorts of infections (Wardani, 2022).

The child's psychological well-being is impacted by the sense of deprivation resulting from the underage mother's incapacity to fulfill her parental responsibilities. This leads to the development of psychological abnormalities that might persist into adulthood and manifest as psychological illnesses. Conditions such as schizophrenia and depression, along with inadequate educational support, result in a kid experiencing delayed mental development. Consequently, the occurrence of early marriage contributes to the proliferation of diseases and psychological disorders among both the family and society, resulting in a heightened financial strain on the healthcare system (Pocuca & Krstinic, 2023).

Early marriage produces several social consequences. For instance, premature divorce may occur when the partners realize they are unprepared to have a prosperous family. This is because of their youth and inadequate understanding of family formation (Wardani, 2022). Early marriage has several social consequences, including the proliferation of domestic violence. The prevalence of spousal sexual assault among married adolescent girls aged 15 to 19 is 13%; in contrast, Older and more educated women are at a higher risk of experiencing violence, abuse, and contracting HIV (Fan & Koski, 2022).

Early marriage usually arises between two parties with a large gap resulting from the significant age difference, which causes a crisis in the marital relationship, and domestic violence occurs, as 50% of girls who are married under the age of 18 are exposed to violence by their partner during the period of marriage (Parsons et al., 2015). The spread of poverty: Early marriage is widespread among the poorest groups around the world, and early marriage is an obstacle to achieving higher levels of education and financial stability for both parties, whether male or female. Therefore, poverty and early marriage are interconnected problems (El-Kady, 2024). Early marriage hinders a girl's educational pursuits due to societal disapproval of married or engaged girls attending school, potential opposition from the husband, domestic responsibilities such as housework and childcare, and potential complications. Pregnancy impedes a girl's ability to attend school and pursue education (Parsons et al., 2015). (see Figure 1)

Figure 2. Consequences of Early Marriage

Consequences of Early Marriage

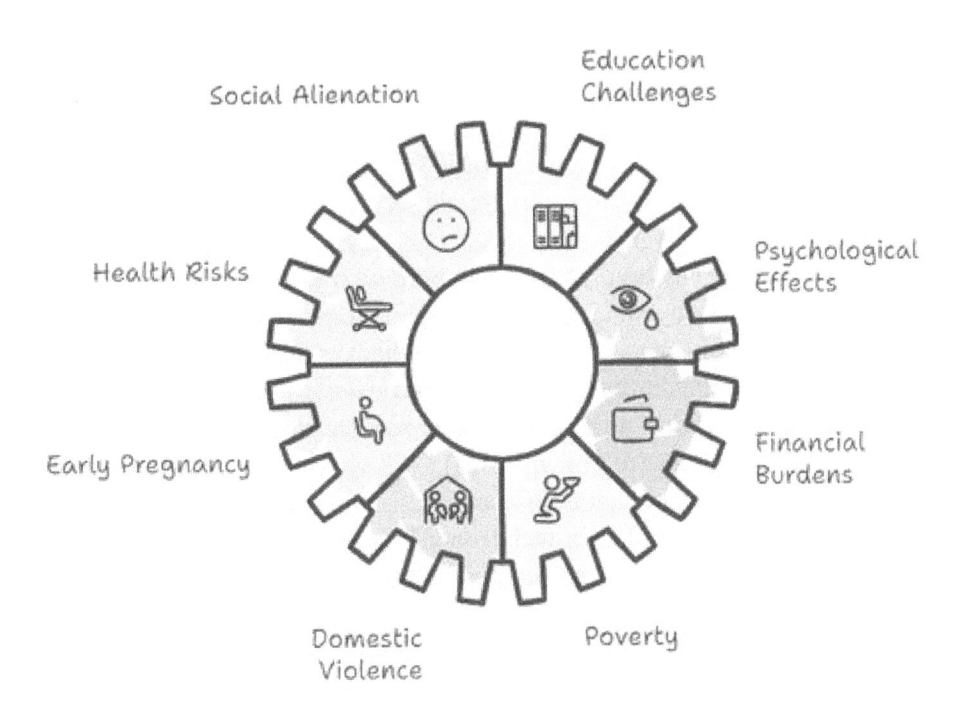

- Social Alienation
- Education Challenges
- Psychological Effects
- Health Risks
- Financial Burdens
- Early Pregnancy
- Domestic Violence
- Poverty

Psychological Effects of Early Marriage on Children

Early marriage, the practice of marrying individuals under 18, can lead to significant psychological issues such as depression, anxiety, post-traumatic stress disorder, emotional distress, and diminished well-being. These consequences are exacerbated by social seclusion, domestic abuse, and economic and educational inequities.

Comprehensive treatments involving psychological, social, and structural support are needed to mitigate these adverse outcomes. Studies show a correlation between early marriage and increased sadness and anxiety (zimova & Universiteti, 2021).

Meanwhile, others see that marriage occurring at a very young age is inversely correlated with psychological well-being, depression, anxiety, positive well-being, vitality, and general health in both Niger and Ethiopia (John et al., 2019). Furthermore, others see that the practice of child marriage is associated with considerable psychological anguish, particularly mental health disorders, and adverse overall welfare, with depression being the most often reported mental illness (Burgess et al., 2021).

The previous studies confirmed that child brides frequently encounter substantial emotional anguish, encompassing sadness, anxiety, and other psychological disturbances such as post-traumatic stress disorder (PTSD) and suicide inclinations (zimova & Universiteti, 2021). However, other individuals perceive that early marriage adversely affects several dimensions of psychological well-being, such as energy, positive well-being, and overall physiological health (Burgess et al., 2021). Meanwhile, many observe that early marriage frequently results in social isolation and heightened vulnerability to domestic abuse, hence intensifying psychiatric problems (zimova & Universiteti, 2021).

Simultaneously, it has been shown that those who enter into early marriages typically lack the maturity and experience required for successful parenting. This can result in the adoption of harsh or negligent methods of raising children, therefore contributing to a continuous cycle of psychological suffering. Early marriage can result in parents subjecting their children to severe treatment, harsh reprimands, shouting, or undue indulgence (Salam, 2023).

Meanwhile, many argue that early marriage is associated with decreased educational achievement and diminished economic stability, both of which lead to prolonged psychological strain and diminished overall societal welfare. Engaging in early marriage results in inferior maternal and newborn health and less economic resilience compared to marriage throughout adulthood (Ernawati et al., 2023).

Furthermore, a study demonstrates that marrying during early or late adolescence is linked to a 12%/6% greater probability of being in the lowest wealth quintile in later life and a 29%/20% higher probability of not finishing elementary education (Sagalova et al., 2021).

Moreover, studies indicate that parental divorce is linked to an increased likelihood of children acquiring a range of mental health disorders, including depression, anxiety, and distress (Auersperg et al., 2019). At the same time, others observe that a considerable proportion of youngsters endure long-term psychological and social challenges linked to ongoing and new pressures within the family after divorce (Wallerstein, 1991).

Meanwhile, previous studies indicate that parental separation does not influence children's psychological development but rather is associated with variables such as income, education, ethnicity, child-rearing attitudes, depressive symptoms, and behavior of the mothers (Clarke-Stewart et al., 2000). Ultimately, several studies demonstrate that the enduring consequences of divorce on children's views of their relationships with parents, especially their fathers, are somewhat unfavorable. However, these negative impacts can be alleviated by maintaining a secure family life before the divorce and achieving successful adaptation. (see Figure 3)

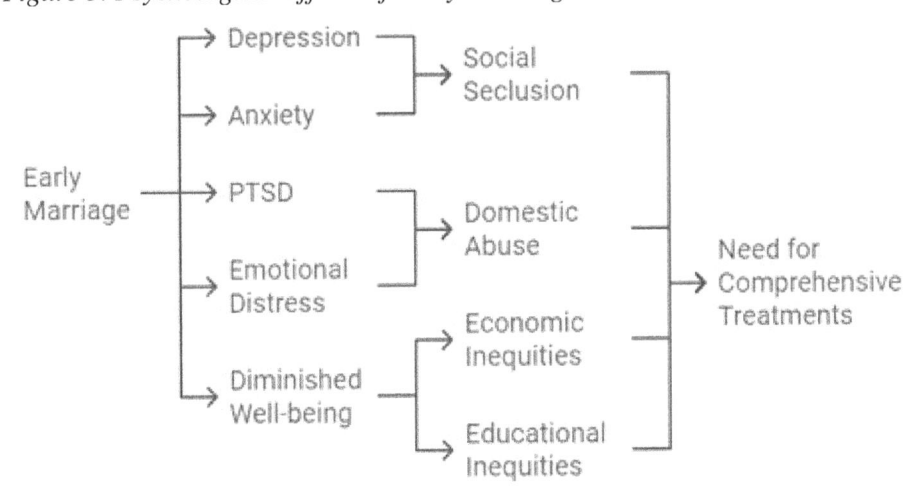

Figure 3. Psychological Effects of Early Marriage on Children

Global Rates and Geographical Distribution of Early Marriage

Rural locations exhibit a higher prevalence of early marriage compared to metropolitan areas. However, there is a disparity in early marriage between sectarian and tribal populations. Research has revealed that specific tribal communities have a lower incidence of child marriage compared to other groups (Hayes & Protas, 2022). Sub-Saharan African nations have the highest rate of early marriage, with 40% of young women getting married before the age of 18. South Asian countries follow closely behind, with 30% of young women getting married before 18.

The prevalence of early marriage in Latin America and the Caribbean stood at 25%. In comparison, in the Middle East and North Africa, it was 18%, and in Eastern Europe and Central Asia, it reached 11%. There is a geographical distinction between countries where the marriage of girls is prevalent and countries where early child marriage is prevalent (Hayes & Protas, 2022). (see Figure 4)

Figure 4. Global Prevalence of Early Marriage by Region

Region	Percentage of Young Women Married Before 18
Sub-Saharan Africa	40
South Asia	30
Latin America and Caribbean	
Middle East and North Africa	18
Eastern Europe and Central Asia	11

Global Prevalence of Early Marriage by Region

UNICEF recorded 765 million cases in 2019, encompassing both males and females who were married before the age of 18. This figure also includes the number of boys and men who had previously married before reaching 18. The Central African Republic has the highest rate of male child marriage, with 28% of cases, followed by Nicaragua with 19%, and finally Madagascar with 13% out of a total of 115 million cases (Whitley, 2021).

Early marriage transcends socioeconomic boundaries. Empirical evidence demonstrates that early marriage is a pervasive occurrence that has permeated all continents, cultures, religions, and economic strata, encompassing both impoverished and affluent nations. However, it is prevalent to a greater extent in developing countries, as poverty is one of the primary factors contributing to its occurrence. Approximately one-third of girls in the developing world are married before age 18. Most of these marriages, accounting for 82%, occur before 18. Annually, a staggering 12 million girls are wedded prior to reaching puberty, lacking any form of physical or emotional readiness (Gastón et al., 2019).

The prevalence of early marriage in Southeast Asian nations has experienced a substantial decline in the last decade, with the rate decreasing from 50% to 30%. Notably, India has played a pivotal role in this progress, primarily attributed to implementing practical strategies by the Indian government, particularly in enhancing educational opportunities. To address the issue of child marriage among girls, it is essential to focus on expanding investments specifically aimed at teenage girls. Additionally, it is crucial to broadcast awareness messages at the national level that condemn the legitimacy of child marriage and provide clear information about the magnitude of its negative consequences (Wardlaw et al., 2014). (see Figure 5)

Figure 5. Global Trends in Early Marriage

Global Trends in Early Marriage

2019
UNICEF records 765 million child marriages

2022
Research reveals lower child marriage rates in specific tribal communities

2022
Geographical distinction between countries with prevalent girl marriage and child marriage

2014
Southeast Asia sees a decline in early marriage rates

2019
12 million girls are married before puberty annually

2021
Central African Republic has the highest rate of male child marriage

2022
Sub-Saharan Africa has the highest rate of early marriage for young women

2022
South Asian countries have the second highest rate of early marriage for young women

2022
Latin America and the Caribbean have a 25% rate of early marriage

2022
Middle East and North Africa have an 18% rate of early marriage

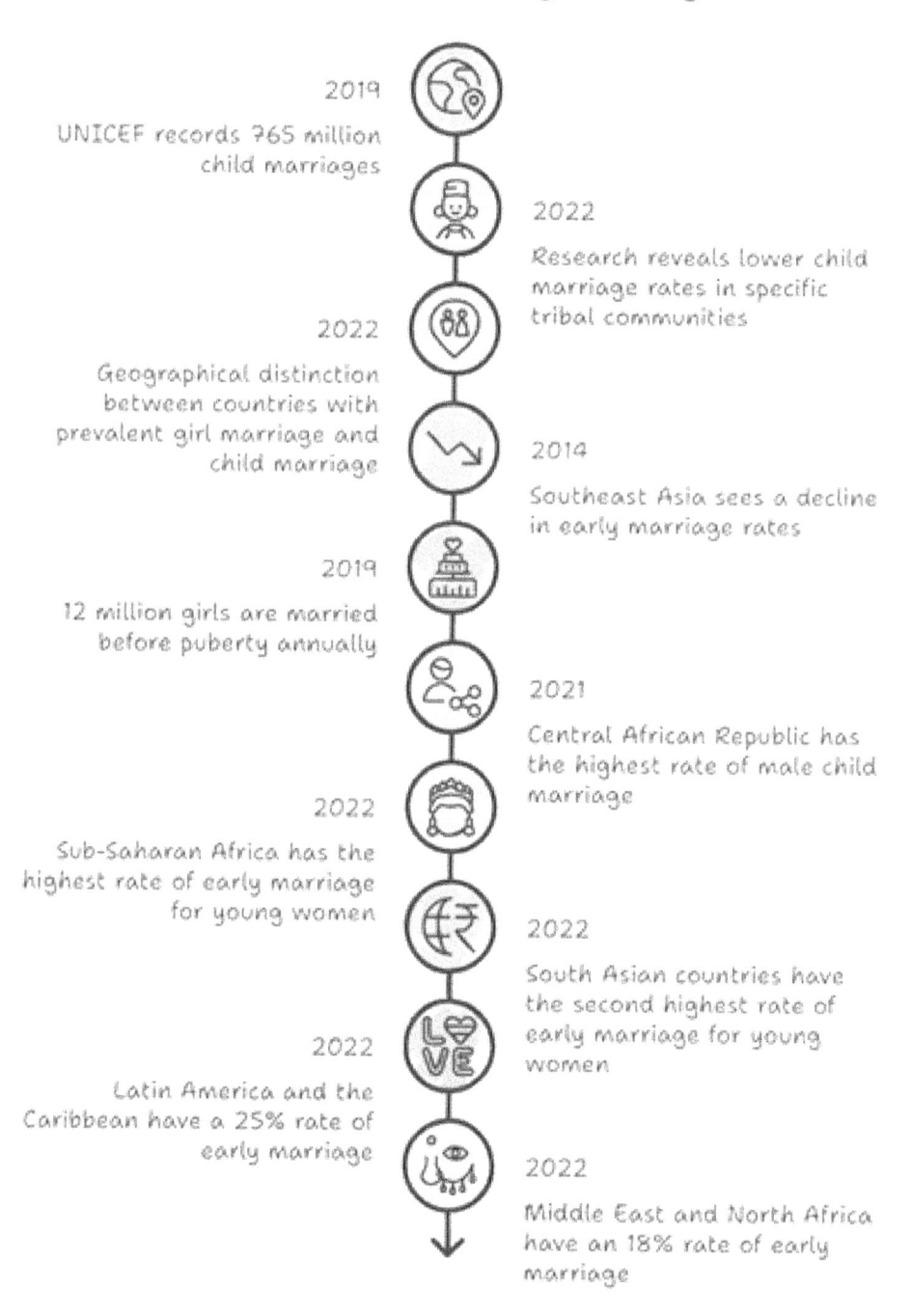

Integrated Community Confrontation of Early Marriage

Confronting early marriage requires an integrated societal response that includes many appropriate mechanisms to deal with this phenomenon, the most prominent of which is spreading awareness. The United Nations Population Fund (UNFPA) has established the "Action for Adolescent Girls" program, which includes 12 countries in Asia, Africa, and Latin America; it aims to teach girls their rights, which include the right to education, health, the right to live in a safe place free of violence, the right to dignity, and the right to choose a life partner like any adult (El-Kady, 2024).

Girls also receive programs related to reproductive health and training that includes life skills. Such as the skill of negotiation that can help convince parents to abandon the matter of engagement for a certain period or even reject it; these girls have become role models in their communities who express the educated teenage girl, hoping that this will be the normal situation for all girls of the same age (Lee-Rife et al., 2012).

Although most countries of the world have issued strict laws against child marriage and imposed the necessary penalties for violating these laws, parents fear for their daughters weakened these laws somewhat, so the matter called for finding solutions to the roots of the phenomenon of early marriage by promoting gender equality and ending the problem of poverty by building a social safety net that protects girls and their families, increasing education opportunities, providing health services, and providing job opportunities (Parsons et al., 2015).

Creating mass campaigns by attracting the attention of the world's population and global rulers, where the consequences of early marriage that many young people suffer from were disseminated through global campaigns, and calling for placing the issue of child marriage among a priority at the international level. In 2015, the General Assembly called for the United Nations to show support and reject early marriage on social media. Establishing emergency lines provides the necessary assistance to those suffering from the effects of early or forced marriage by providing legal assistance through receiving protection, legal separation, divorce, or deciding on custody in the case of the presence of children. Services can also be provided for social services or safe housing in emergencies (Nour, 2009).

Besides, establishing awareness centers for those about to marry, as these centers target young people in the pre-marriage stage, with the support of local community organizations, to find solutions to the problems of young people in their teenage years, Such as helping to find suitable job opportunities for them, and providing pre-marital rehabilitation courses that care about the family, explain its importance, how to deal with and respect the wife, and ways to secure livelihoods in the future.

For young girls, these centers provide comprehensive awareness on how to shoulder the responsibilities of marriage, respect for the husband, effective parenting methods, and other educational, health, psychological, and social matters. This holistic approach ensures that all aspects of a young girl's life are considered, providing a solid foundation for her future (Wodon, 2017). Finally, the importance of family cohesion cannot be overstated. By fostering an integrated, understanding family environment, the number of girls married early can be significantly reduced (El-Kady, 2024). (see Figure 6)

Figure 6. Integrated Strategies to combat Early marriage

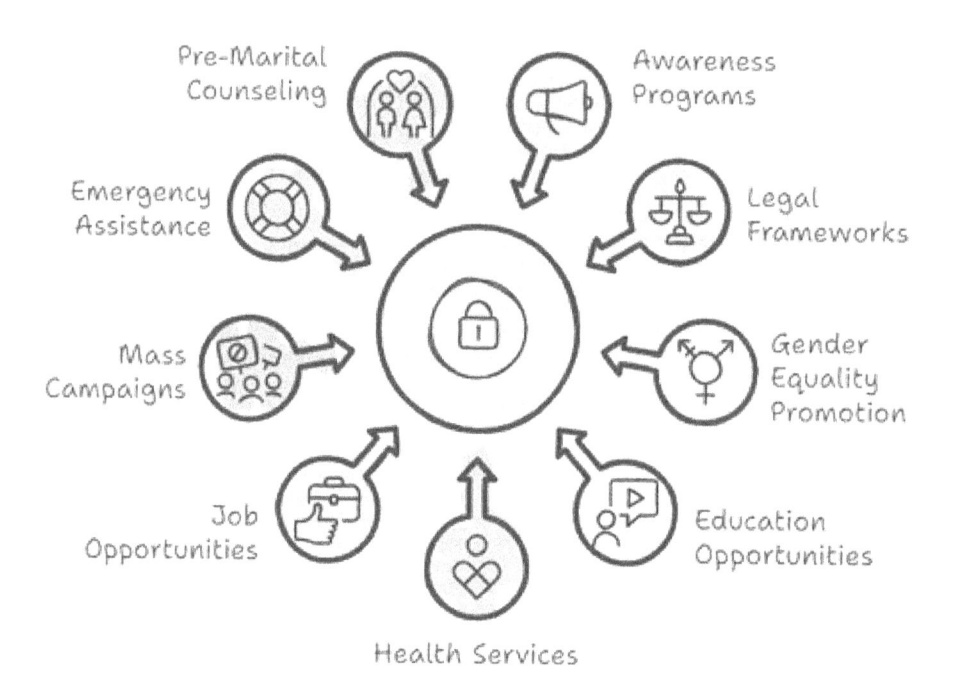

Integrated Strategies to Combat Early Marriage

- Pre-Marital Counseling
- Awareness Programs
- Emergency Assistance
- Legal Frameworks
- Mass Campaigns
- Gender Equality Promotion
- Job Opportunities
- Education Opportunities
- Health Services

Legal Protection of Children against Early Marriage and Child Trafficking in the International Convention

1. Convention on the Rights of the Child (CRC)

The United Nations Convention on the Rights of the Child (UNCRC) is a multilateral treaty that protects the rights of all children, regardless of their ethnicity, religion, or capabilities. It mandates governments to fulfill children's fundamental needs and ensure their maximum capabilities. The UNCRC includes rights such as life, survival, development, protection from violence, and education. In 2000, it introduced optional protocols to ensure the exclusion of children below 18 from military conscription and ban child prostitution, pornography, and slavery. Since its adoption in 1989, the UNCRC has been adopted by 196 countries.

2. Convention on the Elimination of All Forms of Discrimination against Women (CEDAW)

The Convention on the Elimination of All Forms of Discrimination Against Women (CEDAW) is a global legal agreement aimed at eliminating discrimination against women and girls. It is a vital part of the Global Bill of Rights for Women and is a crucial tool for UN Women's efforts towards gender equality and empowering women and girls worldwide.

Early Marriage in Egypt

Early marriage in Egypt is a pressing issue that violates children's laws and violates international human rights. The government has imposed severe penalties for supporting minor marriages but circumvents these laws. Early marriage is linked to wealthy Gulf men buying temporary marriages with underage Egyptian women, causing problems for both parties. The issue affects women's social and economic status, fertility, and population growth. According to the 2017 Egypt Census, approximately one out of every twenty girls aged 15-17 is married or was previously married, with a significant difference between rural and urban areas. The United Nations Population Fund warns of the worsening of this phenomenon, with the number of early marriages expected to reach over 15 million girls worldwide by 2030. The President of the Arab Republic of Egypt has directed the President to issue a law preventing early marriage that explicitly stipulates the legal age for marriage, emphasizing girls' rights and their role in society. Despite the enactment of laws, child marriage continues to be a prevalent problem in specific areas of the country (El-Kady, 2024).

Criminal Confrontation of Early Marriage in Egyptian Legislation

The Egyptian Penal Code penalizes individuals who express false statements or submit incorrect papers to a marriage court, leading to imprisonment or fines. The penalty has also been increased for circumventing the law by contracting minors into common-law marriages until they reach legal age. The Children's Law No. 126 of 2008 increases the minimum penalty for crimes committed by adults against children, parents, guardians, or servants, and those involved in pornographic works involving children or sexual exploitation. Tools and funds used in these crimes are confiscated, and the crime sites are closed for six months (El-Kady, 2024).

Human Trafficking as a Legal Model to Confront Early Marriage

Early marriage is punishable in Egyptian Law under the legal model of Human Trafficking, which defines human trafficking as any act of exploitation of a natural person, including prostitution, sexual exploitation, child exploitation, pornography, forced labor, slavery, or begging. The Egyptian judiciary has been hesitant to consider parental authority as a form of abuse of power in human trafficking cases, as it is often used to obtain financial sums without considering the psychological and physiological harm caused to the victims (El-Kady, 2022).

In one case, the Criminal Court acquitted the guardians of the victimized girls based on their lack of criminal intent, claiming they resorted to a legitimate means of marrying well-off people. However, the Court of Cassation ruled that the contested ruling did not prove the validity of the ruling and that the appellants were innocent. The author agrees with the Court of Cassation's decision, as it refutes the presumption upon which the Criminal Court relied in acquitting the defendants who were guardians of the victims. The author also agrees with the Court of Cassation's decision to overturn the Criminal Court's ruling, stating that a preponderance of suspicion in the place of certainty does not defend the charges (El-Kady, 2024).

Legal Protections Provided for Victims in Arabic Legislation

In Egyptian and Qatari legislation, victims of human trafficking are defined as natural persons who have suffered material or moral harm, including bodily, psychological, or mental harm or economic loss, directly caused by one of the crimes stipulated in the law. International conventions and Arab legislation prohibit the use of victim consent in human trafficking crimes, regardless of age or coercive means. The Palermo Protocol states that a victim's consent to exploitation is irrelevant if any of the methods mentioned in subparagraph (a) have been used. Egyptian law also stipulates that the victim is not held criminally or civilly responsible for human trafficking crimes as long as the crime occurred or was directly related to being a victim. The United Nations Convention against Organized Crime and the European Convention for Action against Trafficking in Human Beings have approved this principle (Bahlbi, 2016).

Egyptian and Qatari legislation guarantees victims' rights, including physical, psychological, and mental safety, identity protection, access to relevant administrative, legal, and judicial procedures, and the right to be heard and their views considered during criminal proceedings without prejudice to defense rights. Qatari law follows the Egyptian legislator's path, ensuring victims are protected from exploitation and can seek legal assistance. (El-Kady, 2024).

Figure 7. Legal protections for Human Trafficking Victims

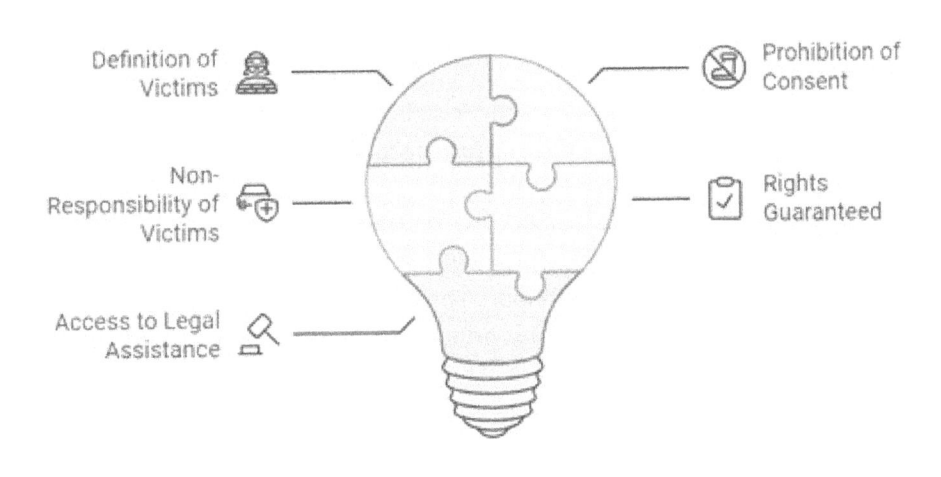

(A) The Right to Health and Social Care

Article (22) of the Anti-Human Trafficking Law guarantees the protection of victims and ensures their health, psychological, educational, and social care. It also aims to rehabilitate and integrate victims into society within a freedom and dignity framework. The law also allows for the swift return of victims, whether foreigners or permanent residents, following rules and procedures set by the Council of Ministers.

The Palermo Protocol and the European Convention on Action against Trafficking in Human Beings (Merkouris et al., 2020) play a significant role in shaping the legal framework for human trafficking victims' protection. Article 6/3 of the Palermo Protocol, for instance, stipulates that: "Each State Party shall consider implementing measures to enable the physical, psychological and social recovery of victims of trafficking in persons, including, in cases where this is necessary, cooperation with non-governmental organizations and other relevant organizations and others." The European Convention, in Article (16/5), also mandates States Parties to adopt legislative measures and procedures and develop resettlement programs involving relevant international institutions or non-governmental organizations to avoid repeated harm to the victim.

Qatari, Kuwaiti, and Syrian laws stand out for their comprehensive protection of victims' health and social care rights. Qatari law, for instance, guarantees protection, provides health, education, and social care, and ensures rehabilitation and integration into society. It also ensures victims' return to their country of origin or residence, especially for expatriates or non-permanent residents. Kuwaiti law provides medical and psychological care to victims, and Omani law provides specialist doctor services. With their broad scope, these laws aim to ensure victims' swift and safe return to their country of origin or residence (El-Kady, 2024).

(b) The Right to Be Protected from the Exposure of Others

Egyptian law emphasizes the importance of protecting victims and identifying them to prevent their exploitation. This principle is also reflected in the Protocol Palermo. Arab legislations, such as Emirati law and Qatari law, establish confidentiality in human trafficking cases. UAE law requires competent authorities to maintain the confidentiality of information obtained and disclose it only when necessary. Qatari law requires authorities to adhere to confidentiality of information related to crimes and only disclose it as necessary. Syrian law also upholds this principle, ensuring that victims are protected and their identities are not shared with perpetrators. These laws provide legal protection for victims in human trafficking cases (El-Kady, 2024).

(c) The Right to Physical, Psychological, and Moral Integrity

Article (23/a) of the Egyptian law stipulates the right of the victim to physical, psychological, and moral integrity, which is also indicated in Article (6/5) of the Palermo Protocol that: "Everyone shall strive to A State Party shall provide for the physical safety of victims of trafficking in persons while they are within its territory."

(d) The Right to Preserve Her Sanctity and Identity

As per Article (23/b) and the Palermo Protocol and European Convention, Egyptian law guarantees the victim's right to protect their sanctity and identity. State parties are required to preserve the personal privacy and identity of trafficking victims, including making legal procedures confidential. The European Convention also requires the protection of victims' private lives and identities, particularly personal data, under international agreements. Qatari law, among Arab legislation, also supports the right of victims to preserve their sanctity and identity, as stated in Article 20/1.

€ The Right to Participate in the Procedures

The Egyptian law, particularly Article (23/c), ensures victims' rights. It guarantees their right to be informed about administrative, legal, and judicial procedures and obtain relevant information. Paragraph (d) also guarantees their right to be heard and their opinions considered in all criminal proceedings without prejudice to defense rights. This aligns with Article (6/2) of the Palermo Protocol, which requires each state party to ensure its internal legal or administrative system provides victims with the necessary information and assistance to present their opinions and concerns in criminal proceedings. The importance of stipulating victim participation lies in allowing them to present their perspective on facts and provide necessary information. Arab legislation, such as Qatari, Kuwaiti, and Omani laws, also support this right. The aim is to ensure that victims have the opportunity to present their viewpoints and provide the necessary information (El-Kady, 2022).

(f) The Right to Legal Assistance

Article (23/e) of Egyptian law stipulates the victim's right to legal aid, particularly seeking help from a lawyer during the investigation and trial stages. If he has not chosen a lawyer, the public prosecution or court must, according to the circumstances, require that a lawyer be appointed for him by the rules stipulated in the Code of Criminal Procedure regarding assigning a lawyer for the accused. This ensures the fairness of the legal system, instilling confidence in the audience. Some scholars have criticized the legislator's approach, arguing that the legislator had mixed up the rights of the accused in criminal procedures with the rights of the victim (El-Kady, 2024).

However, this criticism can be answered by saying that the victim of human trafficking crimes may be the subject of accusation in other offenses related to trafficking. Therefore, he needs someone to defend him. In this context, the assistance of a lawyer, which is a right of the accused, becomes a guarantee for the victim, consistent with the legislator's approach to protecting victims.

Article (16/6) of the European Convention underscores the importance of enacting legislative measures that empower victims to collaborate with any state that can aid them within the country or their homeland. This includes law enforcement agencies, non-governmental organizations, and professional entities capable of providing legal and social care and counseling. Notably, Arab legislations such as Qatari law (Article 20/4), Kuwaiti law (Article 12), Omani law (Article 5), and Syrian law all uphold the right of the victim to seek assistance from a lawyer, further reinforcing the protective measures in place.

(g) The Right not to be Influenced

Article (23/f) of the Egyptian law stipulates that: "In all cases, the competent court shall take measures to ensure the provision of protection for the victim and witnesses and not to influence them, and whatever this may require of not disclosing Their identity, all without prejudice to the right of defense and the requirements of the principle of confrontation between adversaries."

(h) Care, Education, Rehabilitation, and Training of Victims

Article (26) of Egyptian law stipulates that: "The competent authorities shall provide care, education, training and rehabilitation programs for Egyptian victims, whether through governmental or non-governmental institutions."

(i) Exemption from Civil Lawsuit Fees

In addition to the previous guarantees, Omani law stipulates that the victim of a human trafficking crime is exempted from paying the fees related to the civil lawsuit that he files to claim compensation for the damage resulting from his exploitation in the crime (see Article 17 of the Omani Human Trafficking Law). (see Figure 8)

Figure 8. Comprehensive Protections for Human Trafficking Victims

Comprehensive Protections for Human Trafficking Victims

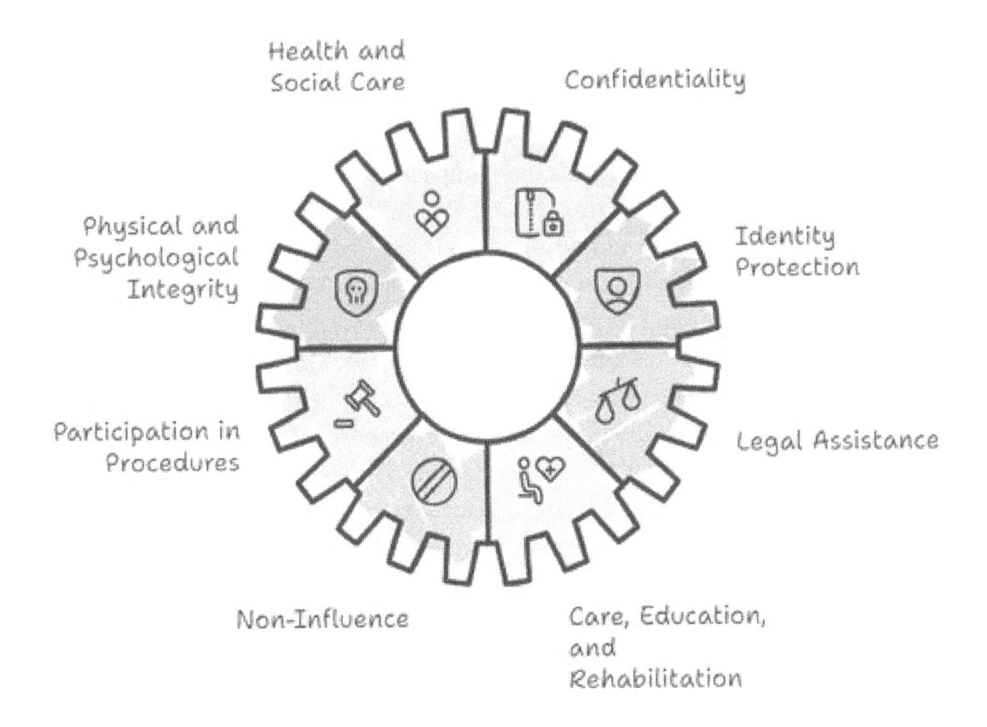

- Health and Social Care
- Confidentiality
- Identity Protection
- Legal Assistance
- Care, Education, and Rehabilitation
- Non-Influence
- Participation in Procedures
- Physical and Psychological Integrity

Forms of Legal Protection Assigned to Victims

Egyptian law provides victims with a comprehensive array of legal protections, encompassing criminal, social, and security protection. This robust legal framework safeguards victims from exposure to danger, contact with perpetrators, misinformation about their rights, or any threat to their physical, psychological, or mental well-being, with severe penalties for violators. Social protection ensures the safety of victims and creates conducive conditions for assistance, health, education, social care, rehabilitation, and social integration. The state is mandated to prioritize the protection of the victim and their assistance and consider their fundamental interests in all decisions and procedures, regardless of the entity issuing or undertaking them. The Council of Ministers is responsible for determining these rules and procedures. The state must also ensure victims' swift and safe return to their homeland, guaranteeing their freedom and human dignity (El-Kady, 2024). This comprehensive legal framework should reassure you about the safety and protection of victims.

Effective Interventions to Prevent Early Marriage and Child Trafficking

Research shows that initiatives promoting girls' education, community involvement, empowerment programs, and awareness campaigns are effective in deterring early marriage and child trafficking. These practices, particularly in poor and moderate-income countries, significantly impact adolescent females' well-being, education, and economic prospects. Practical solutions include educational assistance, life skills training, community mobilization, and empowerment initiatives. Single-component interventions are more scalable and sustainable while promoting community involvement and transforming societal conventions are crucial.

Experts acknowledge that interventions that provide financial or non-financial assistance to girls for their education are very successful in reducing child marriage. Several studies indicate that interventions that provide financial or non-financial assistance to girls for their education and create competitive employment opportunities demonstrate the most evident pattern of effectiveness in reducing child marriage (Malhotra & Elnakib, 2021).

Evidence demonstrates that six high-quality interventions have shown favorable outcomes in reducing the percentage of individuals married or raising the age at which marriage occurs, hence preventing child marriage in low—and middle-income countries (Kalamar et al., 2016). Furthermore, there is a scarcity of high-caliber impact assessments on interventions aimed at preventing child marriage in Africa. The predominant approaches in these evaluations are health, empowerment, education, legislation, and policies (Greene et al., 2023).

Nevertheless, some argue that Conditional cash transfers, which necessitate postponing marriage, yield inconsistent outcomes. Conversely, unconditional cash transfers aimed at alleviating poverty typically have no impact. Conversely, programs that offer life skills and livelihood training consistently demonstrate favorable outcomes in delaying marriage (Malhotra & Elnakib, 2021). Programs that provide incentives and empower girls can effectively prevent child marriage and facilitate relatively rapid transformation (Lee-Rife et al., 2012).

Moreover, community mobilization and engagement initiatives, like those carried out in Bangladesh, are known to greatly enhance understanding and attitudes towards child marriage, thereby contributing to its prevention. The awareness initiative implemented by Shornokishoree Network successfully enhanced the understanding of child marriage among teenagers, therefore making a significant contribution to the prevention of child marriage (Brownia & Habibb, 2023). Interventions characterized by community involvement, skill development to improve voice and agency, and growth of social networks show the potential to mitigate violence against adolescent girls and young women aged 10-24 (Yount et al., 2017).

Alternatively, advocates argue that community conversations and systematic community involvement are successful in mitigating child marriage and teenage pregnancy in sub-Saharan Africa. The provision of scholarships and the systematic implementation of community discussions have been consistently successful interventions in reducing child marriage and teenage pregnancy in sub-Saharan Africa (Feyissa et al., 2023). Meanwhile, many believe that empowerment programs aimed at improving the human capital and chances of girls are successful in reducing cases of child marriage (Malhotra & Elnakib, 2021).

Moreover, some demonstrate that Interventions targeting the modification of societal norms and gender attitudes have the potential to mitigate violence against women and girls, including the issue of child marriage (Yount et al., 2017). Nevertheless, other studies indicate that programs targeting dating violence in schools, community-based interventions, and parenting interventions have the potential to reduce adolescent intimate partner violence and sexual violence (Lundgren & Amin, 2015). Conversely, contrasting evidence suggests that multi-component interventions often exhibit poorer success rates, scale-up, and sustainability than single-component interventions (Malhotra & Elnakib, 2021).

Furthermore, other studies demonstrate that CARE's Tipping Point Program in Nepal significantly enhanced knowledge and behavioral modifications among participants with higher levels of involvement and pre-programmed variables, indicating a reduced likelihood of child marriage (Clark et al., 2023). In addition, research suggests that individuals who have experienced child marriage in the past may have more challenges in obtaining favorable outcomes from programs aimed at reducing intimate partner violence (Falb et al., 2015). (see Figure 9)

Figure 9. Reducing Child Marriage: Effective Interventions and Outcomes

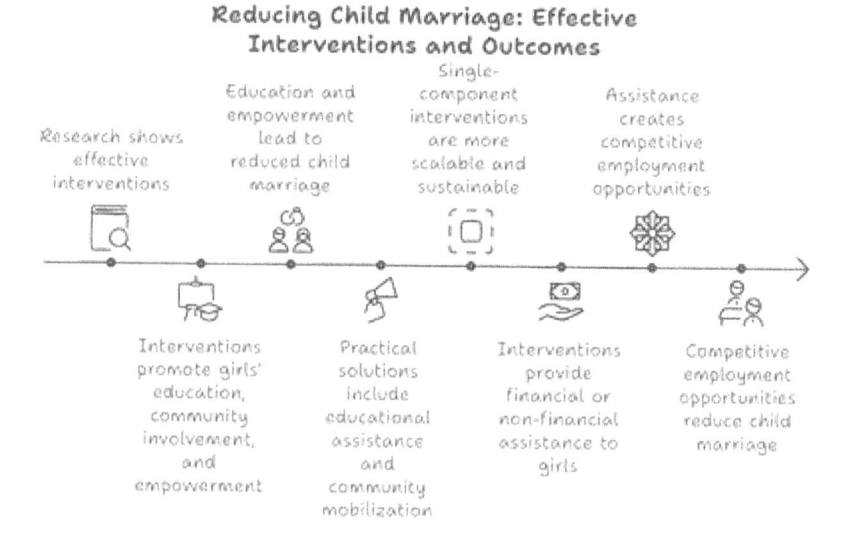

POLICY RESPONSE TO END CHILD MARRIAGE IN EGYPT

Egypt's National Strategic Plan (NSP) aims to reduce child marriage prevalence by 50% within five years. The National Council for Childhood and Motherhood (NCCM) is working to eradicate the practice through reporting procedures and other government organizations. System strengthening is necessary, including enhancing reporting systems, fortifying local prevention and response systems, and improving legal reporting systems. A cohesive framework is also needed to coordinate the efforts of various stakeholders.

Imposing criminal sanctions on child marriage and enhancing legal enforcement is crucial for successful eradication. Access to quality services is essential, and investments in education and school facilities are needed to empower girls. Strategies should involve active parental involvement and foster ownership in schools.

Social and behavioral change is crucial, including involving men in mobilizing communities and media to modify long-standing conventions. Addressing the convictions and behaviors of influencers and religious leaders can help change the way community members view child marriage. Further research is needed to understand the financial implications of child marriage prevention and response measures, understand the origins and consequences of child marriage, and examine the social and health impacts to provide a more comprehensive understanding of child rights. (see Figure 10)

Figure 10. Eradicating Child Marriage in Egypt: A Comprehensive Strategy

Eradicating Child Marriage in Egypt: A Comprehensive Strategy

- Strengthening Systems
- Enhancing Access to Services
- Promoting Social Change
- Implementing Comprehensive Prevention Strategies
- Imposing Legal Sanctions
- Investing in Education
- Conducting Research

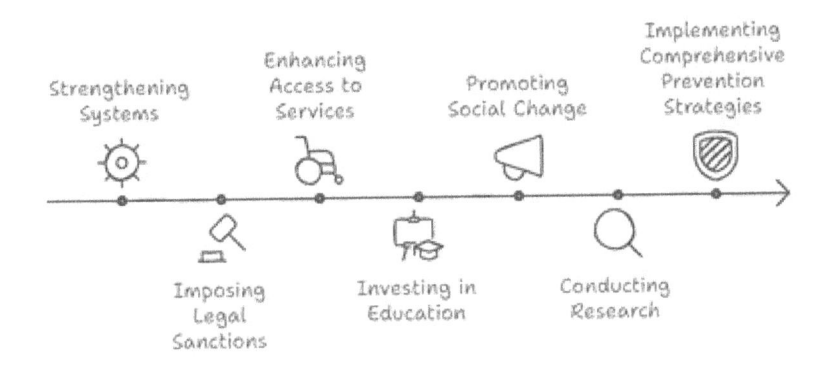

CONCLUSION

The study addressed the widespread problem of early marriage in many societies and its most prominent causes, repercussions, and negative repercussions on the individual and society. It also addressed the legal framework for confronting it in the context of human trafficking and reviewed the judiciary's direction towards early marriage issues. The study also reviewed the most prominent legal guarantees established for victims of human trafficking, including Early marriage victims.

The study concluded with many results, the most prominent of which is the spread of early marriage in many societies, including many countries in the continents of Asia, Africa, and some Arab countries, resulting from some established social and cultural customs and beliefs in those countries.

The legal view of early marriage has developed as it constitutes a form of child trafficking. Through this legal perspective, great attention must be paid to the victims of young girls who fall victim to their families' exploitation of their state of weakness and need for them, which leads them to marry them in what is known as transactional marriage, which constitutes a grave violation of their fundamental rights.

The study confirmed the need for an Integrated Community confrontation plan or strategy depends on enforcing laws and adopting large-scale mass media campaigns to spread public awareness of the seriousness of this issue and establishing emergency lines and awareness centers for those about to get married, Finally, issuing a law preventing early marriage that explicitly stipulates the legal age for marriage, as an independent law that guarantees girls' rights, stressing respect for women's rights and the importance of their role in society.

REFERENCES

zimova, S., & Universiteti, A. (2021). Psychosocial consequences of early marriages. *Sprachwissenschaft*, 15(3), 83–86. DOI: 10.36719/2663-4619/64/83-86

Ahmed1&2, S., Khan, A. K. S., & Noushad, S. (2014). Early marriage is the root of current physiological and psychosocial health burdens.

Ahmed1&2, S., Khan, A. K. S., & Noushad, S. (2013). Psychological impact evaluation of early marriages. *International Journal of Endorsing Health Science Research, 1*(2), 84-86.

Auersperg, F., Vlasak, T., Ponocny, I., & Barth, A. (2019). Long-term effects of parental divorce on mental health - A meta-analysis. *Journal of Psychiatric Research*, 119, 107–115. DOI: 10.1016/j.jpsychires.2019.09.011 PMID: 31622869

Bahlbi, Y. M. (2016). Human Trafficking and Human Smuggling to and from Eastern Sudan: Intended and Unintended Consequences of States' Policies. https://core.ac.uk/download/228570950.pdf

Boyce, S., Brouwer, K., Triplett, D., Servin, A., Magis-Rodríguez, C., & Silverman, J. (2018). Childhood Experiences of Sexual Violence, Pregnancy, and Marriage Associated With Child Sex Trafficking Among Female Sex Workers in Two US-Mexico Border Cities. *American Journal of Public Health*, 108(8), 1049–1054. DOI: 10.2105/AJPH.2018.304455 PMID: 29927652

Brownia, F., & Habibb, S. (2023). The Effectiveness of Community Mobilization Intervention in Creating Awareness Regarding Early Marriage among Adolescents in Bangladesh: The Case of Shornokishoree Network. *Journal of Social Behavior and Community Health*. https://doi.org/.DOI: 10.18502/jsbch.v7i1.12796

Burgess, R., Jeffery, M., Odero, S., Rose-Clarke, K., & Devakumar, D. (2021). Overlooked and unaddressed: A narrative review of mental health consequences of child marriages. *PLOS Global Public Health*, 2(1), e0000131. Advance online publication. DOI: 10.1371/journal.pgph.0000131 PMID: 36962120

Campbell, G., Roberts, K., & Sarkaria, N. (2020). Child and Early Forced Marriage., 79-89. https://doi.org/.DOI: 10.1057/978-1-137-53312-8_5

Clark, C., Jashinsky, K., Renz, E., Bergenfeld, I., Durr, R., Cheong, Y., Kalra, S., Laterra, A., & Yount, K. (2023). Qualitative endline results of the tipping point project to prevent child, early and forced marriage in Nepal. *Global Public Health: An International Journal for Research, Policy and Practice*, 18(1), 2287606. Advance online publication. DOI: 10.1080/17441692.2023.2287606 PMID: 38054604

Clarke-Stewart, K., Vandell, D., Mccartney, K., Owen, M., & Booth, C. (2000). Effects of parental separation and divorce on very young children. *Journal of Family Psychology: JFP: Journal of the Division of Family Psychology of the American Psychological Association*, 14(2), 304–326. DOI: 10.1037/0893-3200.14.2.304 PMID: 10870296

Crootof, R. (2019). The internet of torts: Expanding civil liability standards to address corporate remote interference. *Duke Law Journal*, 69, 583.

Dangal, G. (2008). Teenage pregnancy: Complexities and challenges. *Middle East*, 56, 1000.

Desai, M., Goel, S., Desai, M., & Goel, S. (2018). Child Rights to Prevention of Child Marriage. *Child Rights Education for Inclusion and Protection: Primary Prevention*, 299-322.

El-Kady, R. (2024). The Complex Landscape of Human Trafficking: A Comprehensive Exploration with Emphasis on Legal Safeguards for Victims in Egyptian and Arab Legislation. In Borges, G., Guerreiro, A., & Pina, M. (Eds.), *Modern Insights and Strategies in Victimology* (pp. 118–140). IGI Global., DOI: 10.4018/979-8-3693-2201-7.ch006

El-Kady, R. M. (2022). The crime of human trafficking in Egyptian legislation in light of the opinions of jurisprudence and jurisprudence. *National Criminal Review*, 65(2), 93–148.

Elfenbein, D. S., & Felice, M. E. (2003). Adolescent pregnancy. *Pediatric Clinics*, 50(4), 781–800. PMID: 12964694

Er, C., Wodon, Q., Petroni, S., Malé, C., Onagoruwa, A., Savadogo, A., Edmeades, J., Kes, A., John, N., Yarrow, E., Apland, K., Anderson, K., Hamilton, C., Darroch, J.,, W., Bankole, A., Ls, A., Myers, J., & Gt, L. (2015). Thematic report: Unrecognised sexual abuse and exploitation of children in child early and forced marriage... https://doi.org/.DOI: 10.1163/2210-7975_HRD-9926-2015003

Ernawati, H., Mas'udah, A., Setiawan, F., & Isroin, L. (2023). Health, psychology, economic resilience, and wellbeing: Long-term effects on family welfare of an early marriage. *F1000Research*. https://doi.org/DOI: 10.12688/f1000research.128719.1

Falb, K., Annan, J., Kpebo, D., Cole, H., Willie, T., Xuan, Z., Raj, A., & Gupta, J. (2015). Differential Impacts of an Intimate Partner Violence Prevention Program Based on Child Marriage Status in Rural Côte d'Ivoire.. *The Journal of adolescent health: official publication of the Society for Adolescent Medicine*, 57 5, 553-8 . https://doi.org/.DOI: 10.1016/j.jadohealth.2015.08.001

Fan, S., & Koski, A. (2022). The health consequences of child marriage: A systematic review of the evidence. *BMC Public Health*, 22(1), 309. DOI: 10.1186/s12889-022-12707-x PMID: 35164724

Feyissa, G., Tolu, L., Soboka, M., & Ezeh, A. (2023). Effectiveness of interventions to reduce child marriage and teen pregnancy in sub-Saharan Africa: A systematic review of quantitative evidence. *Frontiers in Reproductive Health*, 5, 1105390. Advance online publication. DOI: 10.3389/frph.2023.1105390 PMID: 37064827

Gastón, C. M., Misunas, C., & Cappa, C. (2019). Child marriage among boys: A global overview of available data. *Vulnerable Children and Youth Studies*, 14(3), 219–228. DOI: 10.1080/17450128.2019.1566584

Greene, M., Siddiqi, M., & Abularrage, T. (2023). Systematic scoping review of interventions to prevent and respond to child marriage across Africa: Progress, gaps and priorities. *BMJ Open*, 13(5), e061315. Advance online publication. DOI: 10.1136/bmjopen-2022-061315 PMID: 37130688

Hayes, B., & Protas, M. (2021). Child Marriage and Intimate Partner Violence: An Examination of Individual, Community, and National Factors. *Journal of Interpersonal Violence*, 37(21-22), NP19664–NP19687. DOI: 10.1177/08862605211042602 PMID: 34476987

Hayes, B. E., & Protas, M. E. (2022). Child marriage and intimate partner violence: An examination of individual, community, and national factors. *Journal of Interpersonal Violence*, 37(21-22), NP19664–NP19687. DOI: 10.1177/08862605211042602 PMID: 34476987

John, N., Edmeades, J., & Murithi, L. (2019). Child marriage and psychological well-being in Niger and Ethiopia. *BMC Public Health*, 19(1), 1029. Advance online publication. DOI: 10.1186/s12889-019-7314-z PMID: 31370825

Kakar, S. (2020). Child/forced/servile marriages⇌ Human trafficking. *The Palgrave international handbook of human trafficking*, 503–519.

Kalamar, A., Lee-Rife, S., & Hindin, M. (2016). Interventions to Prevent Child Marriage Among Young People in Low- and Middle-Income Countries: A Systematic Review of the Published and Gray Literature.. *The Journal of adolescent health: official publication of the Society for Adolescent Medicine*, 59 3 Suppl, S16-21 . https://doi.org/.DOI: 10.1016/j.jadohealth.2016.06.015

Lee-Rife, S., Malhotra, A., Warner, A., & Glinski, A. M. (2012). What works to prevent child marriage: A review of the evidence. *Studies in Family Planning*, 43(4), 287–303. DOI: 10.1111/j.1728-4465.2012.00327.x PMID: 23239248

Leftwich, H. K., & Alves, M. V. O. (2017). Adolescent pregnancy. *Pediatric Clinics*, 64(2), 381–388. PMID: 28292453

Lundgren, R., & Amin, A. (2015). Addressing intimate partner violence and sexual violence among adolescents: emerging evidence of effectiveness.. *The Journal of adolescent health: official publication of the Society for Adolescent Medicine*, 56 1 Suppl, S42-50 . https://doi.org/.DOI: 10.1016/j.jadohealth.2014.08.012

Mahato, S. K. (2016). Causes and consequences of child marriage: A perspective. *International Journal of Scientific and Engineering Research*, 7(7), 697–702. DOI: 10.14299/ijser.2016.07.002

Males, M. A. (2010). *Teenage sex and pregnancy: Modern myths, unsexy realities.* Bloomsbury Publishing USA. DOI: 10.5040/9798216023890

Malhotra, A., & Elnakib, S. (2021). 20 Years of the Evidence Base on What Works to Prevent Child Marriage: A Systematic Review.. *The Journal of adolescent health: official publication of the Society for Adolescent Medicine.* https://doi.org/.DOI: 10.1016/j.jadohealth.2020.11.017

Mazurana, D., & Marshak, A. (2019). Addressing data gaps on child, early, and forced marriage in humanitarian settings. *Save the Children, White Paper and Discussion Draft December.*

Mpilambo, J. E., Appunni, S. S., Kanayo, O., & Stiegler, N. (2017). Determinants of early marriage among young women in Democratic Republic of Congo. *Journal of Social Sciences*, 52(1-3), 82–91. DOI: 10.1080/09718923.2017.1322393

Nour, N. M. (2009). Child marriage: A silent health and human rights issue. *Reviews in Obstetrics & Gynecology*, 2(1), 51. PMID: 19399295

Parsons, J., Edmeades, J., Kes, A., Petroni, S., Sexton, M., & Wodon, Q. (2015). Economic impacts of child marriage: A review of the literature. *The Review of Faith & International Affairs*, 13(3), 12–22. DOI: 10.1080/15570274.2015.1075757

Pocuca, M. B., Krstinic, D. M., & Šarkić, N. (2023). Prohibition of Minor Marriages. *Kultura Polisa*, 20(2), 101–129. DOI: 10.51738/Kpolisa2023.20.2r.101pks

Raval, D., & Bharad, B. (2021). EARLY MARRIAGE: NEGLECTED FORM OF CHILD ABUSE. *GAP GYAN -. Global Journal of Social Sciences*, 4(4), 58–62. Advance online publication. DOI: 10.47968/gapgyan.440011

Sagalova, V., Nanama, S., Zagré, N., & Vollmer, S. (2021). Long-term consequences of early marriage and maternity in West and Central Africa: Wealth, education, and fertility. *Journal of Global Health*, 11, 13004. Advance online publication. DOI: 10.7189/jogh.11.13004 PMID: 34484711

Salam, A. (2023). *Analysis of The Impact of Early Marriage On Children's Parenting Patterns*. Journal Transnational Universal Studies., DOI: 10.58631/jtus.v1i1.1

Samsuddin, S. N. A., Masroom, M. N., & Wan Mohd Yunus, W. M. A. (2019). Mental Health of Muslim Unwed Pregnant Teenagers. *Malaysian Journal of Medicine & Health Sciences, 15*.

Sezgin, A. U., & Punamäki, R. L. (2020). Impacts of early marriage and adolescent pregnancy on mental and somatic health: The role of partner violence. *Archives of Women's Mental Health*, 23(2), 155–166. DOI: 10.1007/s00737-019-00960-w PMID: 30955087

Sopyan, Y., Muttaqin, Z., Solihat, C., & Aripin, J. (2023). Child Exploitation by Parents in Early Marriage: Case Study in Cianjur West Java, Indonesia. *Samarah: Jurnal Hukum Keluarga dan Hukum Islam*. https://doi.org/.DOI: 10.22373/sjhk.v7i3.14804

Stoyanova, V. (2016). United Nations against slavery: Unravelling concepts, institutions, and obligations. *Mich. J. Int'l L.*, 38, 359.

Syria - United States Department of State. (2023, December 7). United States Department of State. https://www.state.gov/reports/2023-trafficking-in-persons-report/syria/

Wallerstein, J. (1991). The long-term effects of divorce on children: A review. *Journal of the American Academy of Child and Adolescent Psychiatry*, 30(3), 349–360. DOI: 10.1097/00004583-199105000-00001 PMID: 1810276

Wardani, I. H. (2022, December). Legal Protection of Underage Women in Early Marriage. In *Proceeding International Seminar and Conference on Islamic Studies (ISCIS)* (Vol. 1, No. 1).

Wardlaw, T., You, D., Hug, L., Amouzou, A., & Newby, H. (2014). UNICEF Report: Enormous progress in child survival, but more significant focus on newborns urgently needed. *Reproductive Health*, 11(1), 1–4. DOI: 10.1186/1742-4755-11-82

Warner, E. (2011). Behind the Wedding Veil: Child Marriage as a Form of Trafficking in Girls. *The American University Journal of Gender, Social Policy & the Law*, 12, 1.

Warria, A. (2017). Forced child marriages as a form of child trafficking. *Children and Youth Services Review*, 79, 274–279. DOI: 10.1016/j.childyouth.2017.06.024

Whitley, R., & Whitley, R. (2021). Family ties: marriage, divorce, and the mental health of men and boys. *Men's Issues and Mental Health: An Introductory Primer*, 207-234.

Wodon, Q., Male, C., Nayihouba, A., Onagoruwa, A., Savadogo, A., Yedan, A., ... & Petroni, S. (2017). Economic impacts of child marriage: global synthesis report.

Yount, K., Krause, K., & Miedema, S. (2017). Preventing gender-based violence victimization in adolescent girls in lower-income countries: Systematic review of reviews. *Social Science & Medicine*, 192, 1–13. DOI: 10.1016/j.socscimed.2017.08.038 PMID: 28941786

Yüksel, F., & Koçtürk, N. (2021). Investigation of Factors Associated with the Child Marriage in Turkey. *Journal of Child Sexual Abuse*, 30(6), 653–666. DOI: 10.1080/10538712.2021.1956664 PMID: 34323160

Chapter 13
Teenage Pregnancy and Health Implications

Shafia Jan
University of Kashmir, Srinagar, India

Bilal Ahmad Bhat
Sher-e-Kashmir University of Agricultural Sciences and Technology, India

ABSTRACT

Adolescent pregnancy and parenthood have emerged as major social issues in recent years, which is an issue of life and death to the teenagers. Poverty and ignorance magnifies this problem to a greater extent. According to National Family Health Survey-3, the incidence of teenage pregnancy in India was 16%, with majority of them occurring in uneducated rural population (Saloi, 2017). Teenage mothers face numerous health complications, both physical and mental. Pregnancy-induced hypertension and preeclampsia are more common in teenage pregnancies, posing significant health risks. Additionally, obstructed labour is a frequent issue due to immature pelvic structures, often necessitating caesarean sections. Maternal mortality rates are also higher among teenage mothers compared to older women, underscoring the severe risks involved.. Efforts can be made to empower teenagers to make informed decisions about their sexual health and reduce the incidence of teenage pregnancy.

INTRODUCTION

Teenage pregnancy refers to pregnancies occurring in young women aged 13-19 years. It is a complex issue with multifaceted implications on health, mental wellbeing, social standing and economic stability (Uddin, 2017). It is a significant

DOI: 10.4018/979-8-3693-3394-5.ch013

public health issue due to its prevalence and associated complications. Teenage pregnancy can have profound effects and consequences on the teenage mother, the father, and their babies. These impacts span across various aspects, including health, economic, social, and psychological dimensions. The rates of teenage pregnancy vary widely around the world, with higher incidences in low- and middle-income countries. According to the World Health Organization (WHO), approximately 16 million girls aged 15 to 19 and around 1 million girls under 15 give birth each year, primarily in low- and middle-income nations. This high prevalence highlights the need for targeted interventions to address the health and social challenges associated with teenage pregnancy (Uddin, 2015). Addressing teenage pregnancy involves various health implementations aimed at prevention, care, and support (Uddin, 2021).

FACTORS INFLUENCING PREGNANCY AND HEALTH

Teenage pregnancy is influenced by a complex interplay of various risk factors, which can be categorized into several key areas:

1. Cultural and Societal Influences

Cultural Norms and Attitudes-Cultural factors also significantly impact teenage pregnancy rates. In some cultures, early marriages and societal norms promote teenage pregnancies, often limiting girls' ability to make informed choices about their reproductive health (Uddin, 2015). Rates of teenage pregnancies are higher in societies where it is traditional for girls to marry young and where they are encouraged to bear children as soon as they are able. Many teenagers are not taught about methods of birth control and how to deal with peers who pressure them into having sex before they are ready (Uddin, 2008, 2009). Many pregnant teenagers do not have any cognition of the central facts of sexuality. Cultural beliefs and norms regarding sexuality, gender roles, and family expectations can shape teenagers' perceptions and behaviors related to sexual activity and contraception. Religious teachings and community values may influence attitudes towards premarital sex and contraception use.

2. Behavioral and Psychological Influence

Early Initiation of Sexual Activity-Most males experience sexual intercourse for the first time before their 20th birthday. Teens who initiate sexual activity at a younger age are at higher risk of unintended pregnancies due to less experience with contraception and decision-making. Factors such as curiosity, exploration, and lack of future orientation can contribute to early sexual debut. Several polls have indicated peer pressure as a factor in encouraging both girls and boys to have sex. The increased sexual activity among adolescents is manifested in increased teenage pregnancies and an increase in sexually transmitted diseases.

Substance Use and Risky Behaviors-Alcohol and drug use can impair judgment and increase risky sexual behaviors, including unprotected sex. Teens who engage in risky behaviors are more likely to have unintended pregnancies and face related consequences. Inhibition-reducing drugs and alcohol may possibly encourage unintended sexual activity. The drugs with the strongest evidence linking them to teenage pregnancy are alcohol, cannabis, "ecstasy" and other substituted amphetamines.

Early Puberty-Girls who mature early (precocious puberty) are more likely to engage in sexual intercourse at a younger age, which in turn puts them at greater risk of teenage pregnancy.

Lack of Contraception-Adolescents may lack knowledge of, or access to, conventional methods of preventing pregnancy, as they may be too embarrassed or frightened to seek such information. Inconsistent or incorrect use of contraceptives, including condoms and hormonal methods, increases the risk of unintended pregnancies among sexually active teenagers. Misinformation or misconceptions about contraceptive methods can lead to ineffective use.

Young women often think of contraception either as 'the pill' or condoms and have little knowledge about other methods. Over concern about side-effects, for example weight gain and acne, often affect choice.

3. Sexual Abuse

Sexual abuse can significantly increase the risk of teenage pregnancy. Here are some ways in which sexual abuse can be a risk factor:

Early Sexual Initiation-Victims of sexual abuse may be more likely to engage in sexual activity including unprotected sex at a younger age than their peers who have not experienced abuse. This early initiation of sexual activity increases the risk of unintended pregnancy.

Limited Control over Sexual Choices-Victims of sexual abuse may struggle with asserting control over their sexual decisions and may be coerced or manipulated into risky sexual behaviors, including unprotected sex.

Psychological Impact-Sexual abuse can lead to psychological issues such as low self-esteem, depression, and anxiety. These psychological factors may contribute to engaging in risky sexual behaviors that increase the likelihood of pregnancy.

Substance Abuse-Survivors of sexual abuse may turn to substance abuse as a coping mechanism, which can impair judgment and increase the likelihood of engaging in unprotected sex and thus pregnancy.

Lack of Support Networks-Victims of sexual abuse may lack supportive relationships or adults they can trust, which can limit access to accurate information about contraception and reproductive health.

Reproductive Coercion-In some cases, perpetrators of sexual abuse may exert reproductive coercion by sabotaging contraception or pressuring the victim not to use birth control, which increases the risk of pregnancy.

Repeat Victimization-Unfortunately, victims of sexual abuse may be at higher risk of experiencing subsequent abuse, which can further perpetuate the cycle of risky sexual behaviors and unintended pregnancies.

4. Socioeconomic Factors

Teenage pregnancy has been defined predominantly within the research field and among social agencies as a social problem. Socioeconomic factors play a crucial role, with poverty often correlating with higher rates of teenage pregnancy. Limited educational and employment opportunities further exacerbate this issue, as girls in these settings may see fewer alternatives to early motherhood.

Poverty- Poverty is associated with increased rates of teenage pregnancy. Teens from low-income households often have limited access to educational opportunities and healthcare services, including reproductive health care. Economic pressures may contribute to early sexual activity and lower contraceptive use.

Educational Attainment- Teens with lower educational aspirations or achievement levels may be at higher risk due to limited awareness about contraception and reproductive health. Lack of comprehensive sex education in schools can further exacerbate this risk.

5. Family and Social Factors

Parental Influence- Lack of parental supervision, support, or communication about sexual health and contraception can increase the likelihood of teenage pregnancy. Family instability, including single-parent households or parental conflict, may also contribute.

Peer Influence-Pressure from peers to engage in sexual activity or to conform to social norms regarding sexuality can influence teenagers' behaviors. Teens may face challenges in making informed decisions about contraception due to peer influences.

Media influence-Adolescents who were more exposed to sexuality in the media were also more likely to engage in sexual activity themselves. According to Time, "teens exposed to the most sexual content on TV are twice as likely as teens watching less of this material to become pregnant before they reach age 20".

HEALTH IMPLICATION

Teenage mothers face numerous health complications, both physical and mental. Physically, they are at increased risk for anaemia due to inadequate nutrition during pregnancy. Pregnancy-induced hypertension and preeclampsia are more common in teenage pregnancies, posing significant health risks (WHO, 2020). Additionally, obstructed labour is a frequent issue due to immature pelvic structures, often necessitating caesarean sections. Maternal mortality rates are also higher among teenage mothers compared to older women, underscoring the severe risks involved (WHO, 2011). The socioeconomic impact on teenage mothers is profound. Educational disruption is a significant consequence, with many teenage mothers dropping out of school. This educational interruption limits their future job opportunities and increases their dependence on social support systems. The economic strain is considerable, as these young mothers often lack the financial resources to support themselves and their children. This situation perpetuates intergenerational cycles of poverty and teenage pregnancy, with the children of teenage mothers more likely to experience similar issues.

Teenage pregnancy can significantly increase the risk of various health complications for both the mother and the baby due to the biological, social, and economic challenges faced by pregnant teenagers. Teenage bodies, especially in younger teens, are often not fully developed, leading to a higher risk of complications during pregnancy and childbirth. - Teenage mothers often come from socioeconomically disadvantaged backgrounds, which can limit their access to quality healthcare, nutritious food, and stable housing. Teenagers may not seek or have access to comprehensive prenatal care, which is crucial for monitoring the health of both the mother and the baby and managing complications (WHO, 2017). The stress associated with an unplanned pregnancy, societal stigma, and the demands of balancing education, work, and childcare can contribute to physical health problems. Addressing these issues through comprehensive sex education, accessible prenatal care, nutritional support, and emotional counselling can help mitigate the health risks associated with teenage pregnancy.

Here's how teenage pregnancy can lead to specific health issues:

1. Pregnancy Hypertension and Pre-Eclampsia

Immature Vascular System: Teenagers' bodies, especially if they are very young, may not be fully matured, leading to an increased risk of hypertension and pre-eclampsia. Teenagers may not seek or have access to adequate prenatal care, which is crucial for monitoring and managing blood pressure.

Anaemia: Anaemia is fairly common in teenage mothers due to various factors

Nutritional Deficiencies: Teenagers might not have a balanced diet, leading to iron deficiency anaemia.

Increased Nutritional Needs: Pregnancy increases the demand for iron, and teenagers might struggle to meet these increased needs due to poor dietary habits.

2. Obstructive Labour
   - **Pelvic Immaturity:** Younger teenagers may have smaller, less developed pelvises increasing the risk of obstructed labor.
   - **Inadequate Prenatal Care:** Lack of adequate prenatal care can mean potential complications aren't identified and managed in time.
   - **Preterm Birth:** Teenage mothers often give birth to pre term babies which can be due to following factors.
   - **Physical Immaturity:** The body of a teenager might not be fully prepared to carry a pregnancy to term.
   - **Socioeconomic Stress:** Teenagers often face significant stress due to economic and social pressures, contributing to premature labor.
3. **Birth Defects:** Birth defects in the babies are fairly common due to following reasons
   - **Inadequate Nutrition and Care:** Poor prenatal nutrition and inadequate medical care can lead to an increased risk of birth defects.
   - **Lack of Education and Resources:** Teenagers may lack knowledge about necessary prenatal supplements and healthcare practices.
4. **Stillbirth:** Rates of still birth are high among teenage mothers due to:
   - **Medical Complications:** Conditions like pre-eclampsia, anaemia, and obstructive labor increase the risk of stillbirth.
   - **Infections and Lifestyle Factors:** Teenagers are more susceptible to infections and may engage in high-risk behaviors like smoking and substance abuse.

Mental Issues

Mentally, teenage mothers are more susceptible to postpartum depression, exacerbated by the stress and lack of support often experienced during this period. Anxiety and low self-esteem are common due to societal stigma and personal challenges. These mental health issues can lead to substance abuse as a coping mechanism, further complicating the health outcomes for these young mothers. Teenage pregnancy can lead to various mental health issues such as depression, anxiety, and stress. These mental health challenges arise due to several factors including:

1. Stigma and social isolation: Pregnant teenagers often face stigma from their peers, family, and community. The stigma can lead to social isolation, which exacerbates feelings of loneliness and depression.
2. Unplanned and unwanted pregnancies: Many teenage pregnancies are unplanned, which can cause significant stress and anxiety about the future. Teenagers may feel unprepared to handle the responsibilities of parenthood.
3. Educational disruption: Pregnant teenagers often face disruption in their education, which lead to feelings of inadequacy and hopelessness about their future prospects.
4. Relationship strain: teenage pregnancy can strain relationships with partner, family, and friends. The lack of support from significant others can lead to increased stress and mental health issues.

Other effects of teenage pregnancy

Social impact

The social impact of teenage pregnancy is profound and multifaceted. it affects not only the teenage mothers but also their families and communities:

1. Educational attainment: Teenage mothers are less likely to complete their education, which affects their future employment opportunities and earning potential. This educational disruption can perpetuate a cycle of poverty.
2. Economic burden: Teenage pregnancies often result in increased economic burden on families and social services. Young mothers may rely on government assistance to support their children.
3. Intergenerational effects: Children of teenage mothers are more likely to face social and economic challenges, including lower educational attainment and higher rates of teenage pregnancy themselves.
4. Health inequalities: Teenage mothers and their children are more likely to experience health inequalities. These include higher rates of preterm, low birthweight and infant mortality.

Financial Effects

Teenage pregnancy often results in significant financial challenges for the young mother and her family:

1. Limited Earning Potential: Due to educational disruption, teenage mothers often have limited job prospects and earning potential. This can lead to long-term financial instability.
2. Increased Healthcare Costs: Pregnant teenagers and their children often require additional healthcare services, which can be a financial strain.
3. Childcare Costs: The cost of childcare can be prohibitive for teenage mothers who wish to continue their education or enter the workforce.
4. Government Assistance: Many teenage mothers rely on government assistance programs to support their children, which can contribute to the economic burden on society.

Long-Term Effects

The long-term effects of teenage pregnancy can be profound and far-reaching:

1. Economic Stability: Teenage mothers are more likely to experience long-term economic instability. They often face barriers to education and employment, which can limit their financial independence.
2. Health Outcomes: Both teenage mothers and their children are at higher risk for poor health outcomes. Children of teenage mothers are more likely to experience developmental delays, behavioral problems, and chronic health issues.
3. Social Mobility: Teenage pregnancy can limit social mobility for both the mother and the child. The educational and economic disadvantages associated with teenage pregnancy can be passed down to future generations.
4. Relationship Dynamics: Teenage mothers may face challenges in forming stable and supportive relationships. The stress and responsibilities of early parenthood can strain romantic relationships and affect future family dynamics.

Effects of Termination of Pregnancy

The effects of terminating a teenage pregnancy can vary widely and depend on several factors, including the individual's personal beliefs, the circumstances surrounding the pregnancy:

1. Emotional and psychological effects: Terminating a pregnancy can lead to a range of emotional responses, including relief, sadness, guilt, and grief. Some teenagers may experience depression and anxiety after an abortion.
2. Social Stigma: In many societies, abortion is stigmatized, which can lead to feelings of shame and social isolation for teenagers who terminate their pregnancies.

3. Health Risks: While legal and medically supervised abortions are generally safe, there can be physical health risks associated with the procedure, such as infection or complications from the surgery.
4. Future Fertility: Generally, safe and legal abortions do not affect future fertility. However, complications from unsafe abortions can lead to fertility issues.

Effects and Consequences on the Teenage Father

1. **Educational and Career Impact:** Like teenage mothers, teenage fathers are more likely to drop out of school. They may take on low-paying jobs to support their child, limiting their career growth.
2. **Financial Strain:** Teenage fathers often face financial difficulties, as they are usually unprepared for the economic responsibilities of parenthood.
3. **Emotional and Social Impact:** Teenage fathers can experience stress and anxiety due to the sudden responsibilities. They might face social stigma and challenges in balancing work, education, and parenting duties.

Effects and Consequences on the Babies:

Babies born to teenage mothers are at higher risk for several health complications. Premature birth is a common issue, increasing the likelihood of low birth weight and associated health problems. Neonatal and infant mortality rates are higher in this group, with a significant risk of death in the first year of life. Developmental issues are more prevalent among these infants, with long-term health and developmental problems being common. Behavioural and cognitive outcomes are also affected, with these children facing greater risks of lower academic achievement and behavioural issues later in life. These challenges highlight the need for comprehensive healthcare and support services for both teenage mothers and their babies.

1. **Health Risks:** Babies born to teenage mothers are at a higher risk of being born prematurely or with low birth weight, leading to long-term health issues. They are also more susceptible to infant mortality and developmental delays.
2. **Developmental and Behavioral Issues:** These children might face cognitive and behavioral problems due to the challenging environments they often grow up in.
3. **Educational Outcomes:** Children of teenage parents are more likely to struggle academically and drop out of school.
4. **Economic and Social Disadvantages:** They often grow up in lower-income households, which can limit their access to resources and opportunities.

Preventive Measures and Interventions

Medical diagnosis of teenage pregnancy is confirmed through pregnancy tests and prenatal visits. Early identification is crucial for timely intervention and care, ensuring better health outcomes for both the mother and the baby. Preventive measures and interventions are critical in addressing teenage pregnancy and its complications. Screening for complications such as hypertension, anaemia, and gestational diabetes is an essential part of prenatal care for teenage mothers, helping to manage and mitigate potential health risks. Following factors can prove to be beneficial:

1. **Education and Awareness:** Comprehensive sexual education programs are essential, providing accurate information about contraception and reproductive health. These programs should also educate young people about the consequences of teenage pregnancy, helping them make informed decisions. Comprehensive sex education can reduce the incidence of teenage pregnancy. Programs that focus on goal-setting and future planning can help teenagers understand the consequences of early parenthood.
2. **Support Systems:** Access to healthcare, childcare, and educational support can help teenage parents manage their responsibilities. Healthcare services need to be accessible and comprehensive, offering prenatal, maternal, and postnatal care. Counselling and mental health supports for teenage mothers are also crucial, helping them cope with the challenges they face and improving their overall well-being. Counselling services can provide emotional support to both parents.
3. **Community and Policy Initiatives:** Empowerment programs focusing on girls' education and economic opportunities are also effective in preventing teenage pregnancies. These initiatives help build self-esteem and life skills, providing young women with alternatives to early motherhood. Community programs that provide mentoring and support can be beneficial. Policies that support maternity and paternity leave for teenage parents can help them balance their responsibilities.

Besides these, ensuring access to contraception is another vital measure. This involves making contraceptives available and affordable for teenagers, and promoting their use through education and counselling. Community and parental involvement play a crucial role in prevention efforts. Encouraging open communication about sexual health and reproductive rights, and providing parental guidance and support, can significantly reduce the rates of teenage pregnancy.

By addressing these issues through education, support systems, and community initiatives, the negative impacts of teenage pregnancy can be mitigated, leading to better outcomes for the teenage parents and their children.

CONCLUSION

Addressing the risk factors associated with teenage pregnancy requires a multi-faceted approach that includes comprehensive sex education, accessible reproductive healthcare services, supportive family environments, and targeted interventions aimed at reducing socioeconomic disparities. By understanding and addressing these factors, efforts can be made to empower teenagers to make informed decisions about their sexual health and reduce the incidence of teenage pregnancy.

REFERENCES

Basch, C. E. (2011). Teenage pregnancy and the health of urban young women. *Journal of Urban Health*, 88(1), 61–73.

Charles, V. E., Polis, C. B., Sridhara, S. K., & Blum, R. W. (2008). Abortion and long-term mental health outcomes: A systematic review of the evidence. *Contraception*, 78(6), 436–450. DOI: 10.1016/j.contraception.2008.07.005 PMID: 19014789

Harden, A., Brunton, G., Fletcher, A., & Oakley, A. (2009). Teenage pregnancy and social disadvantage: Systematic review integrating controlled trials and qualitative studies. *BMJ (Clinical Research Ed.)*, 339(nov12 1), b4254. DOI: 10.1136/bmj.b4254 PMID: 19910400

Hoffman, S. D., & Maynard, R. A. (2008). *Kids Having Kids: Economic Costs and Social Consequences of Teen Pregnancy*. Urban Institute Press.

Major, B., Appelbaum, M., Beckman, L., Dutton, M. A., Russo, N. F., & West, C. (2009). Abortion and mental health: Evaluating the evidence. *The American Psychologist*, 64(9), 863–890. DOI: 10.1037/a0017497 PMID: 19968372

Manlove, J., Terry-Humen, E., Ikramullah, E., & Moore, K. A. (2006). The role of parent religiosity in teens' transitions to sex and contraception. *The Journal of Adolescent Health*, 39(4), 578–587. DOI: 10.1016/j.jadohealth.2006.03.008 PMID: 16982394

Osofsky, J. D., & Osofsky, H. J. (2001). The psychological effects of war and violence on children. *Paediatrics*, 108(2), 301–309.

Roberts, T. A., Auinger, P., & Klein, J. D. (2005). Emotional problems among adolescents and young adults and their association with sexual behavior. *Paediatrics*, 115(6), 1727–1734.

Sawhill, I. V. (2006). *Teenage Pregnancy Prevention: Welfare Reform's Missing Component*. Brookings Institution.

SmithBattle, L.SmithBattle. (2007). Legacies of advantage and disadvantage: The case of teen mothers. *Public Health Nursing (Boston, Mass.)*, 24(5), 409–420. DOI: 10.1111/j.1525-1446.2007.00651.x PMID: 17714225

Uddin, M. E. (2008). Cross-cultural comparison of family size and composition between Muslim and Santal communities in rural Bangladesh. *World Cultures eJournal*, 16(1), 1-18.

Uddin, M. E. (2009). Age at first marriage for husband and wife between Muslim and Santal communities in rural Bangladesh. *International Journal of Humanities and Social Science*, 3(4), 318–326.

Uddin, M. E. (2011). Cross-cultural social stress among Muslim, Hindu, Santal and Oraon communities in Rasulpur of Bangladesh. *The International Journal of Sociology and Social Policy*, 31(5/6), 361–388. DOI: 10.1108/01443331111141318

Uddin, M. E. (2015). Family socio-cultural values affecting early marriage between Muslim and Santal communities in rural Bangladesh. *The International Journal of Sociology and Social Policy*, 35(3/4), 141–164. DOI: 10.1108/IJSSP-06-2014-0046

Uddin, M. E. (2017). Family demographic mechanisms linking of socioeconomic status to subjective physical health in rural Bangladesh. *Social Indicators Research*, 130(3), 1263–1279. DOI: 10.1007/s11205-015-1209-x

Uddin, M. E. (2021). Teenage marriage and high school dropout among poor girls: A narrative review for family pathways in Bangladesh. *Journal of Research in Social Sciences and Language*, 1(1), 55–76.

WHO. (2011). Global strategy to stop health-care providers from performing female genital mutilation. https://www.who.int/reproductivehealth/publications/fgm/rhr_11_18/en/

WHO. (2017). *Mental health of adolescents*. Geneva: World Health Organization. Retrieved from https://www.who.int/

WHO. (2020). Child marriage. https://www.who.int/news-room/q-a-detail/child-marriage

Chapter 14
Causes, Effects, and Remedies of Early Marriage:
Social Work Implication

Iranna Ronad
https://orcid.org/0000-0002-8801-9501
Shree Sangameshwar Arts and Commerce College, Chadchan, Karnataka, India

ABSTRACT

Abstract Despite the fact that marriage has a unique character, variety, and significance in all communities on the planet, sociologists contend that early marriage has had a number of detrimental effects. There is a wide range of views and attitudes in society about early marriage. While some believe that it is highly advantageous for the family, others think that getting married young is not a good idea and that it will only cause troubles and negative outcomes. Even though it is against the law, early weddings are never less common in many civilizations throughout the world. These types of marriages involve girls under the age of eighteen for various reasons. Many low-income parents wed their daughters before the age of eighteen. Due to their lack of resources, high expectations of their children, and intense feelings, many poor people complete their responsibility by marrying off their daughters at the young age of eighteen or younger.

INTRODUCTION

Purpose

Child marriage, also known as early marriage, is the marriage of a person below the age of 18 (United Nations Children's Fund, 2012). In addition to being illegal and discriminatory against women, child marriage violates the rights of minors and can have serious negative effects on one's physical, mental, social, political, and economic well-being. There will be negative effects on both sexes from this. Early marriage can occur for a variety of reasons, including social, cultural, and economic ones. Girls experience emotional, mental, and physical issues, as well as issues with health education, during this time because they are still developing physically and psychologically. This is exploitation and a violation of human rights. Early marriage causes girls to drop out of school (Uddin, 2021). Not only does she suffer bad effects from these, but her family and community also suffer unfavorable effects.

Early marriage causes girls to drop out of school. In addition, it creates problems for their community. Numerous studies indicate that she is more likely to be the victim of abuse and exploitation within the family. Her accomplishments and independence diminish, and her economic productivity stops. Mortality rate of the new born can increase if the mother's body and mental state are immature enough to give birth to a child. She also passes away from latent illness and diseases like HIV and AIDS. In the past, females were married off before the age of eighteen and were the victims of social conventions and superstitions. There was also a high percentage of illiteracy in the village. Girls used to get slapped by the boy, and their parents showed up back then because they lacked the guts to confront them or because of their decency, but things have changed since then. The girl's parents are also getting educated (Uddin, 2017). Girls have the ability to make independent judgments regarding their personal lives, jobs, and partners in all societies. Early marriage has become a significant societal issue that is linked to culture and social standards. The following are the aims of this chapter:

- To determine the causes and repercussions of early marriage from a social work perspective.
- To raise awareness of the negative impacts of early marriage among teenage girls.
- Preventing teenage girls from getting married too young everywhere and spreading knowledge about the negative effects of this practice.
- Advising the general population and caregivers of the immediate and long-term consequences and ultimately

- How to mobilize other family members and community members, including girls and parents, to eradicate the problem of child marriage and mitigate its effects through social work interventions

Conceptual Understanding and Background

One of the most important and hotly debated social concerns in Indian society is child marriage. Child marriage can be defined as a marriage that occurs before a certain age. The practice of marrying young children is upheld by tradition and social norms. The issue of Child marriage is such a reality in many countries that it was not questioned for years together and was accepted as the norm (Ahmed, 2015). The Prohibition of Child Marriage Act, 2006, describes that a male must be 21 years old to marry, and a female must be 18 years old. The government said the increase in the minimum age of marriage for women to 21, as provided in the Prohibition of Child Marriage Amendment Act, 2021, will come into effect two years after the bill is notified after it is passed in Parliament (The Hindu, https://www.thehindu.com). The Child Marriage Restraint Act of 1929 suggests that if a man marries a child between the ages of 18 and 21, it includes a jail term of 15 days and a fine of one thousand rupees; a man above 21 years of age faces a jail term of up to three months and a possible fine. For anyone who conducts a child marriage, if the marriage they have made is not proven to be a child marriage, it includes a jail term of up to three months and a possible fine. In villages throughout several Indian states, child marriage is a common practice even with these legal or regulated laws.

Child marriage is a crucial issue in contemporary India. Many other developing countries are facing the problem of child marriage (Fernandes, 2023). It is especially common in many villages as well as in some tribal communities and tribes where there is a lack of knowledge and awareness. Parents tend to avoid educating their daughters too much, fearing it will make finding a suitable husband more challenging. As a result, girls often handle household chores alongside their mothers and are not allowed to object to child marriage (Kumar, 2023). Early marriages have long-lasting impacts on the young generation of the country as they constrain the different indicators and dimensions of human and social development (Azeez & Poonia, 2015). There are many negative effects of marrying girls when they are not sexually, mentally, or emotionally dominant. These include violations of human rights, domestic abuse, assaults, beatings, physical and psychological injuries, early pregnancy, population growth, and an increase in maternal and infant mortality, restrictions on education, a decline in women's status, malnutrition, and more.

Review of Literature

Using different keywords in Google Scholar and Research Gate, a technical literature collection of the suggested content was completed. Terms like child marriage, early marriage, the effects of early marriage, social work, child protection, etc. were used in the literature search. An analysis was conducted on the impact of early marriage on several aspects, such as education, health, economics, and society. Approximately 1,000 relevant items were found using this search method. The definition of "child" differs throughout the laws. For instance, under the Juvenile Justice Act of 2000, a child was any person under the age of eighteen, regardless of gender, as defined under child labor laws. A boy or girl is considered a kid if they are younger than 14 years old, according to the Prohibition and Regulation Act of 1986. Still, the legal minimum age of marriage is established by the Prohibition of Child Marriage Act (PCMA), 2006. Boys are 21 years old, and girls are 18. Child marriage is rooted in socio-cultural practices and religious beliefs in many communities, but beyond stylized facts, the relationships between faith and child marriage are complex and change depending on the community (Gemignani & Wodon, 2015). The problems include soaring birth rates, grinding poverty and malnutrition, high illiteracy and infant mortality, and low life expectancy, especially among rural women (Burns, 1998).

The term 'adolescent' refers to any person aged between 10 and 19 years old, as per the definition used by the United Nations. The period of adolescence can be separated into three stages: early (10–13 years of age), middle (14–16), and late (17–19). The status of women in Indian society has not significantly improved despite India's rapid growth. In 2015, India was placed in the lowest group of the United Nations Gender Development Index, which indicates a deviation of more than 10 percent from gender parity in the Human Development Index (UNDP, 2016). A UNICEF report published in 2020 describes that India contributes the highest number of child marriages in the world, with 223 million child brides accounting for one-third of the global percentage. Kidman (2017) found that "child marriage also places adolescents at elevated risk for intimate partner violence (IPV), which is in turn linked to adverse physical and mental health outcomes. Raj (2010) observes that early birth is associated with maternal and infant mortality or morbidity and intimate partner violence in adolescence, as well as inter-generational poverty, poor health, and being incapable for married women and their children. Lal (2015) found that child marriage profiling is also characteristic of oppressed women. Burns (1998) observes that child marriage is a big issue in modern society. These are issues of poverty, hunger, illiteracy, and infant mortality and are particularly prominent among rural women. Tembo (2021) suggests that "child marriage" is a vice that has destroyed a number of young girls and boys dreams. Their future has been emptied even before they even become conscious of themselves. Early marriage is defined by the United Nations Convention on the Rights of the Child as "the marriage of individuals under the age of 18, while every early marriage' involves individuals under 16 years." Gill & Harvey (2016) found that child and adolescent marriages can be described as forced marriages, as minors are not deemed capable of providing [suitable] informed consent.

Recent Statistics

(UNICEF, 2014) reports that globally, more than 700 million women were married before reaching age 18 years, and more than one in three (about 250 million) entered into nuptial union before completing 15 years of age. The Indian Ministry of Statistics reports that the country's sex ratio is 108.176, or 924 females for every 1000 males. The world's largest percentage of child brides is found in India. Approximately 47% of the girls marry before turning 18.91% of women were married by the time they were 25 years old, according to 2011 census data, with a frightening 30.2% of girls getting married before turning 18 (Lal, 2021). India is home to one in three child brides worldwide. This suggests that child marriages are increasing. Childline India reports that in June and July 2020, the number of distress calls regarding girls being married off as children increased by 17% over the previous year (Sheth, 2021).

India has the highest absolute number of child brides in the world, which accounts for nearly one-third of the global total. In India, there are 223 million brides who have been married in childhood, i.e., before attaining the age of 18. In other words, approximately one in every four young women was married or in a union before their 18th birthday (Kishore, 2023). India is called as a home to the highest number of child brides in the world, with over 47% of girls in India married before attaining marriageable age. States like Bihar and Rajasthan, 69% and 65% respectively, of young girls are forced into marriage (Dahiya, 2019).

Karnataka had the most cases filed under the PCM Act among all Indian states and union territories. 849 cases between 2011 and 2021 make up more than 19% of all cases that were recorded. While Assam recorded 596 instances, Tamil Nadu (649) and West Bengal (619) had the second and third highest numbers of cases, respectively. Together, these four states were responsible for over 59% of all cases that were reported during that time (Kumar, 2023).

CAUSES OF EARLY MARRIAGE: SOCIO-ECONOMIC AND CULTURAL

Child marriage is encouraged by current social and cultural norms, practices, and attitudes. Customs and cultural practices, poverty, traditional customs and cultural beliefs, gender inequality, low educational attainment, abuse and violence in the home, etc., are major contributors to the continuation of child marriage. Social, Cultural, and Religious Practices

The practice of child marriage has been somewhat impacted by religious underpinnings and considerations. For instance, females are married off right before puberty or right after their first menstruation in certain religious communities. It is among the numerous societal problems that women still encounter. According to society, women must marry and continue the family tradition because these things are ingrained in the culture. This idea of getting married young has led to generations of women avoiding their likes and preferences in a variety of ways (Pampapathi, 2018; Uddin, 2015). Child marriages are further encouraged by beliefs that early marriage is a way to ensure the girl's chastity and virginity because children may not listen to their parents as they grow up, and so on. It was also created to fully fulfil the desires of the family's elders and aging or ill parents. Child marriage is also a result of a lack of scientific and secular education that would help people reject their irrational beliefs and customs (Pampapathi, 2018).

Social Origins and Social Norms

In rural and tribal societies, child marriage is more common among Scheduled Castes and Scheduled Tribes. Social norms are standards of conduct that people are expected to follow. These are scale assumptions of some sort. In India, people are following certain social norms from ancient times that are still prevailing in society due to a lack of education, advocacy, and awareness (Kumar, 2023). In general, rural girls experience child marriage at a higher rate than urban girls. One could argue that societal and cultural influences have a strong hold on this determinant activity. Child marriage is encouraged by long-standing social norms and practices. These traditions and rituals are mandatory for girls to follow.

Traditional Practices

Traditional views support child marriage as a social norm. The older members of the family, in particular, have instilled the conviction in their children that they should marry young and that, by doing so, they will inherit wealth and progeny and have better lives. The conservative outlook of the rural people and religious mystifications usually contribute to worsening the situation (Kishore, 2023). Girls want to work and study, but they marry for the excuse of fewer responsibilities. In child marriages, one or both parties, the child is under the age of 18, and the marriage is not formal but usually religious or traditional (Yağmur, 2023).

Social Pressure

India is a nation where gender-based violence is pervasive. Many parents see marriage as a means of giving their daughters stability. Parents of young girls are concerned that allowing them to attend school and work while single could indicate to predatory men that they are available for marriage; according to police records from investigations into local child weddings (Patankar, 2021). According to a study, peer pressure and child marriages are closely related since many teenagers are pressured into unwelcome weddings by their peers in their communities. Everyone in society talks about not getting married just yet if there are older girls at home. The girls and their parents experience some social insecurity as a result of this. Stigma eventually results from this emotion. For instance, if an adult girl (18 years old) is at home, parents in Nepal dread social disgrace. Environments of many peers have made an early marriage; women also do an early marriage (Ela et al. 2014). But there are differences in the influence of friends between teenagers who get married early and unmarried teenagers (Wijayati & Soemanto, 2017).

The Dowry System

The beliefs that girls who marry while they are young receive a smaller dowry that the expense of marriage rises with age, and that dowries become larger are some of the beliefs that encourage child marriage in certain societies. Dowry plays a major role in child marriage. In the event that the girl's family is required to pay dowry, it can be less if she is young and illiterate. Because there are lucrative prospects and privileges, the demand for girls increases with their age. The girl's parents can then extend an invitation to the groom's family to pay a smaller payment.

In difficult financial circumstances, it will be more practical for middle-class and lower-class families to pay a smaller dowry and use the leftover funds to cover all of the marriage's costs. As families faced financial instability due to job losses and economic downturns, marrying off daughters became a way to reduce the economic burden. The dowry typically expected for younger girls is often lower, which can also incentivize families to arrange marriages earlier than they might have otherwise (Youvan, 2024).

Security and Care for Young Girls

Mothers and fathers in families are always willing to protect and look after their daughters. After marriage their daughter gets more protection and care from her partner and their family, they get their daughter married at an early age with the hope that the daughter will have a trouble-free and safe life in her husband's house.

Gender Disparity

One significant Social issue influencing child marriage is gender disparity. Girls are not encouraged to make decisions of any type, both inside and outside the home, in patriarchal households. Compared to boys, girls are not afforded the same freedom or support. Even in this day and age, girls' parents still make all of the decisions about their education, careers, marriage, and other aspects of their lives. This even happens after they are married and move in with their husbands. Girls are sometimes viewed as a financial and social burden in these cultures, and they are not granted the same prestige and respect as boys. They receive no incentives in the form of a job, school, or other concerns. The belief that their responsibilities end when they are married and that her husband and his family have more obligations is what drives child marriage.

Lack of Education

A person can manage their demands and issues in life and support themselves financially by obtaining an education. Girls who have an education are able to comprehend the drawbacks of underage marriage. However, the majority of households in rural areas send their girls to secondary school before forcing them into child marriage. Child marriage is more likely to occur when women, in particular, have limited access to education. Parents who lack literacy may not see the value of educating daughters and may place a higher priority on getting married young.

Poverty and Religious Beliefs

Because of their poverty, the parents in the family are unable to provide for the needs and desires of their children. The conditions of poverty are regarded as an important factor that encourages child marriage. When the individuals are residing in conditions of poverty, then their per capita income is stated to be insufficient to meet the needs and requirements of all family members (Kapur, 2019). Among household-level factors, households' lower standard of living, which is a proxy of households' poor economic status, plays an important role in perpetuating early marriage. A strong and positive association has been established between poverty and low age at marriage, the inability to pay for education, and economic insecurity arising out of lack of livelihood options, in general, and for women, in particular (Sakshamaa: Initiative for Catalyzing Change, 2020).

Restricted Economic Position in Household

Women's economic roles are restricted. They are unable to work, and the job they do is useless. In patriarchal households, girls are seen as a financial burden in order to minimize large wedding costs. Parents believe that we can save more money as their daughter gets married at an early age. There are theories that claim marrying girls into a boy's household would provide more help and unpaid labor for economic activities.

Control over Female Sexuality

Early marriage is seen as a way to control girls' sexuality and protect them from a perceived threat of sexual violence, which can potentially damage a family's status, pride, and honor. (Sakshamaa: Initiative for Catalyzing Change, 2020). The factor of trend of sexuality is also responsible for child marriage in many parts of India. It has been found that sexuality encourages people to participate in the process of child marriage (Anwaruzzaman, & Khan, 2021). Female sexuality and reproductive choices are restricted by patriarchal institutions, or systems ruled by males, which place a premium on virginity in girls. This may entail dictating a girl's behavior, appearance, where she goes, who she sees, and whether, with whom, and when she gets married. Control over women's sexuality is central to a society that is both patriarchal and divided by class and caste. These boundaries are kept in place by restricting women's sexuality and ability to procreate in order to limit inheritance of wealth and maintain caste purity (Nirantar Trust, 2015).

EFFECTS OF EARLY MARRIAGE

Illiteracy

Numerous studies indicate that underage marriage is a direct contributor to illiteracy. Even continuing education and jobs for women is their aspiration, but after getting married at a young age, her aspiration of education and employment is still just that—a dream. Marriage at an early, young age and sooner childbearing after marriage can lead women to school dropout, disturb their career development, and stop many other activities that they need to accomplish in their life (Shrestha & Khanal, 2024). She is unable to pursue higher education, and her mother-in-law and husband make this decision as well. Girls' education is hindered by the belief that "education is a waste for girls." As a result, they are unable to pursue higher education or gain professional skills (Uddin, 2021).

Domestic Violence

Approximately one in three women and girls will at some point in their lives encounter physical or sexual abuse. One example of this violence is child marriage, which increases the likelihood that women and girls may experience sexual, physical, and psychological abuse throughout their lives, as well as associated consequences including poor health and depression. Numerous studies suggest that the prevalence of domestic violence rises with child marriage. The little girl has been abused physically, psychologically, and sexually; rape has also occurred frequently.

Accepting Accountability for one's Family Life/ Too Busy with Household Chores.

In patriarchal households, the mother is the one who handles all of the family's tasks, but the father typically carries the brunt of them. Every family activity, including taking care of the kids, performing all the housework, and providing support, affection, and love to each other, must eventually be managed well." Family conflict may result from the married girl's utter incapacity to handle all of these duties, both mentally and physically.

Curse of the World

These repercussions affect the girl personally, as well as her family and community. A young lady who gets married is more likely to drop out of school, not make money, and not give back to the community. She has a higher risk of contracting HIV/AIDS and experiencing domestic abuse. The growth of the boy and girl involved in the marriage, as well as the family, community, and nation, are all negatively impacted by child marriage, impeding progress. Additionally, neither males nor girls can make any kind of educational, social, economic or other contribution to their family, society, or nation.

Social Isolation

Child marriage causes social isolation for many girls. They have to leave their parents, brothers, sisters, relatives, and friends behind when they marry young, and this is a very terrible life for them to live alone in their husband's home at a time when they should be eating, playing, and growing up. According to numerous studies, child marriage is the primary reason for divorce.

Violation of Child Rights

Human rights abuses include the exploitation of minors, child marriage, education, liberty, health, and life rights, as well as the right to be free from exploitation. Child marriage, also referred to as early marriage, is a serious human rights violation and detrimental practice that exposes children to increased risk of violence, exploitation, and abuse. It requires serious deliberation and action (Subramanee et al., 2022).

Child marriage is not only a custom but a social evil that takes away the basic rights from the children and takes away their childhood away from them. Child marriage was practiced in India from time immemorial, and it is still present in India after having a number of laws (Singh & Kaur, 2024). Child marriage is a flagrant breach of human rights that results in lifelong physical, psychological, and emotional trauma. Children have all the rights to enjoy their freedom and not lose their childhood in the backdrop of the social condition of early marriages. Either male or female, marriage before legal age affects them physically, mentally, intellectually, psychologically, and emotionally (Gautam & Shekhar, 2018).

Early Motherhood

Young ladies who marry are not yet emotionally, psychologically, or physically mature. They are too young to get married and start a family. Studies have demonstrated that miscarriage rates, maternal mortality rates, and infant mortality rates rise as a result of this. A sizeable proportion of children born low birth weight are born to mothers less than 20 years of age. Improvement in intrauterine growth could reduce the probability of low birth weight, and while maternal age in itself is not an independent determinant of intrauterine growth or gestational period, it still has indirect causal effects like access to nutrition and rest, health services, etc. that affect the intrauterine growth. Early motherhood can be detrimental to one's physical, mental, and emotional well-being (Chatterjee, 2015). This results in their precarious pregnancy and it's after effects, including bodily ailments, depression, HIV/AIDS, cancer, and delivery.

Education and Career

India has witnessed a dramatic expansion of higher education, and women have emerged as noteworthy winners in the process (Vikram, 2023). Early marriage requires them to drop out of school completely. Their education is consequently limited, which prevents them from learning more and becoming more knowledgeable. They are unable to support their family, society, or nation as a result. They retaliated in a professional manner as well. She needs her mother-in-law and husband's approval before she can go outside and work after marriage in order to get money. It is impossible to make money and achieve financial independence without going to work.

Physical and Mental Health Issues

The health of women is adversely affected by child marriage. Numerous studies have found that girls are disproportionately affected by physical, mental, and emotional stress, as well as depressive disorders. Premature conception is another of these. Sexual activity typically begins shortly after marriage, and early pregnancy and childbirth can increase the risk of both maternal and newborn death. There are numerous detrimental impacts of child marriage on a girl's physical, mental, and emotional well-being. The primary outcome of this is adolescent pregnancy. Females are 2-3 times more at risk of HIV infection from just one unprotected sex session compared to males. In addition, the highest prevalence rate of relationships between child marriage and variables of pregnancy termination, surgical sterilization and contraceptive consumption before the first child delivery, several unwanted pregnancies, re-pregnancy at less than two-year intervals, and a high fertility rate (Irani & Roudsari, 2019).

APPLICATION OF PRINCIPLES OF SOCIAL WORK

The social work profession places a high value on professional principles. How ought a social worker to proceed? And what should one avoid doing? The principles provide insight into that. Many issues, including child marriage, can be avoided by effectively applying these principles and concepts.

Principle of Acceptance

It's critical to accept the individual, family, and/or community that has had or is now experiencing child marriage. Acceptance is not limited to the individual with the issue; it also extends to the community. Not only should the individual with the issue be accepted, but the social worker should also be accepted by the individual, family, and community. As a result, in social work, the acceptance principle is crucial.

Principle of Individualization

This principle states that every person (male or female) facing child marriage is unique and significant and should be treated as such. Because the problem is just as important to us as the individual is. According to this idea, each individual is distinct and distinctive. This idea forbids social workers from making assumptions about them or making predictions about them based on clients or issues. Since everyone deserves respect and dignity, girls who are facing child marriage receive the same treatment. This idea will enable people to overcome obstacles and accomplish their goals in life. Recognizing and appreciating the distinctive characteristics of each client dealing with the issue of child marriage, and using a range of ideas and strategies to assist in improving their lives' compatibility. The boy or girl has the right to be acknowledged as distinct persons with special qualities in addition to being acknowledged as human beings.

Principles of Communication

Miscommunication or a lack of communication can lead to a number of issues. Effective communication is the foundation on which social workers work with their clients, families and communities. Social workers will establish appropriate written and verbal communication channels with their clients, families, communities, and organizations to eliminating or preventing child marriage. Thus, it is possible to permitting the unrestricted articulation of thoughts, emotions, and historical information pertaining to the resolution of the issue of child marriage

Principle of Confidentiality

In social work, confidentiality or privacy is a fundamental and significant principle. The clients and their families are instilled with confidence by the assumption that personal and family information acquired from them during the handling of child marriage cases cannot be left behind or revealed to third parties.

Principle of Self-Determination

This idea represents a crucial individual right. This one rule helps the client (boys and girls and their families) make decisions about their own lives in situations like child marriage because only they are aware of their own issues, strengths, and weaknesses. Here, Social workers give them options in order to encourage them to take charge of their own lives and solve their own problems.

Principles of Non-Judgmental Attitude

This idea assists clients in avoiding judging themselves according to certain standards of what constitutes good or terrible, or polite or impolite, in situations involving child marriage.

Principles of Relationships

In situations of child marriage, this idea aids in the development of deep and professional relationships with clients (boy, girl or their family, and community). Because improving our relationship with they will enable us to address the issue of child marriage as a whole and find a solution.

Principle of Controlled Emotional Involvement

The three elements of controlled emotional involvement are as follows: sensitivity to sentiments that are expressed or not expressed, comprehension of human behavior based on knowledge, and a purpose-driven, knowledgeable response.

Principles of Utilization of Recourses

Social workers are able to collect resources from the environment and society and use them at different stages of problems in order to regulate and address major social issues like child marriage.

APPLICATION OF METHODS OF SOCIAL WORK

Social Case Work

Social workers employ individual social work as a crucial technique to help clients overcome challenges related to social adjustment. People come to social workers with issues such as child marriage, child labor, alcoholism, drug addiction, unemployment, and poverty in the community because they don't know how to solve them on their own or how to overcome them. Individual social work takes a methodical approach to addressing the issues with child dispute marriage. Individual social work assists us in methodically handling the challenges of marriage and child disputes. Complex societal concerns, including child marriage, can occasionally clash with the law. In this instance, we get to deal with such problems subtly by utilizing particular social work principles, strategies, and talents as tools. Therefore, individual social work's applicability and relatedness make it ideal for appropriately and methodically treating situations like child marriage or pre-marriage. The goal of family social work is to assist and support families. This assistance could take the form of keeping an eye on things at home to make sure they're safe or offering assistance in a classroom by dealing with behavioral issues.

Social Group Work

In the field of education, school social workers frequently combine individual social work with social group work. Through group formation, it is a crucial primary way of social work that facilitates both internal and external changes in the cadres, ultimately leading to social development and transformation. Community groups are developed to provide adequate awareness and education in order to address important societal problems like child marriage. Social group work can be used more successfully in school settings because many children there are susceptible to the issues associated with child marriage at a young age. To forming girl or adolescent girl groups in schools, educating and enlightening them about a range of personal and social issues that impact them, such as child marriage in the community, and offering recreational and facilitating resources. To conduct the group's growth by offering facilitation services, recreational opportunities, and other amenities to its members, as well as education and understanding on a range of personal and social issues that impact them, such as child marriage.

1. Purposeful group formation

    Experience sharing, resources developed inside the groups, Girls collaborate freely in groups to foster the development of their social skills and to share resources, experiences, and talents with one another.

2. To offer relevant programs for the management and elimination of child marriage

    Groups help girls build a social network with other girls and prevent them from feeling alone and isolated.

3. Provides the means to handle decisions that can alter one's life, like getting married and having children.

Community Organization

One fundamental and significant approach to social work with communities is community organizing. Collaborates with communities by bringing together members to address a range of challenges and making sure they are integrated and involved at every turn. To date, the majority of child marriage incidents in India have been documented in tribal and rural communities. The social worker uses this technique. With this approach, the social worker facilitates community development by organizing and carrying out a range of community programs and projects, inspiring community members to get involved in community organization, resource mobilization and distribution, education and awareness-raising, and more.

Social Action

"Collective solutions to collective problems" is how social action is defined. Eliminating social facts or practices, such as child marriage, requires a strong emphasis on social action approaches. Social workers can effectively avoid and manage social problems, including child marriage, by organizing people against these issues, obtaining the necessary resources, and employing this strategy in society. By employing this strategy in society, social workers can successfully avoid and manage social issues like child marriage, mobilize people against these issues, and battle the government to obtain enough facilities.

Social Work Research

The research approach of social work is used to investigate social facts or issues that are common in society and to identify solutions. (For example, issues related to dowries, domestic abuse, alcohol and drug addiction, child labor, child marriage, poverty, unemployment, and housing issues). Social workers use this secondary approach very efficiently to do in-depth research on social and serious problems, such as early marriage, assess the causes and effects of these problems, and create projects or programs aimed at remediation.

THE SCOPE OF SOCIAL WORK INTERVENTION

In order to support and promote children's future health, education, and positive culture in communities and families, social work intervention is essential and required. This chapter discusses early marriage from the standpoint of social work (causes, influences, and solutions), and how might social work interventions prevent child marriage or early marriage, which are common in some developing communities around the world? Or restricted? It focuses on social work viewpoints on how people in the community, including girls and parents, can be mobilized to deal with this particular issue.

Addressing violations of children's rights and shielding them from abuse, exploitation, neglect, and violence are two main goals of child protection. Eliminating child marriage requires achieving gender equality. We put forth great effort to combat the damaging gender norms and stereotypes that support this practice. Our goal is to establish a culture where girls and boys are respected equally through awareness initiatives and community involvement. The ICRW identified five evidence-based interventions to delay or prevent child marriage, which are highlighted in this policy brief: 1) Equip girls with knowledge, abilities, and support systems; 2) offer financial assistance and incentives to girls and their families; 3) Inform and mobilize community members and parents; 4) Strengthen girls5. Avoiding future hostilities is a crucial goal.

1. Preventing Child Marriage

In order to lower the rate of child marriage in India, more needs to be done to advance gender equality, enhance access to education, and reduce poverty. Girls and their families in the community need to be made aware of the need to end child marriage. Women's empowerment and education should be prioritized. It is important to give girls the freedom to think for themselves and make decisions about their marriage, education, and careers. To put a stop to this societal issue, individuals, families, communities, social workers, the police, political elites, social groups, and the government should collaborate.

2. Spreading Awareness

Among the strategies discussed at a recent meeting to reduce the widespread prevalence of child marriages in some areas of the country were the launch of awareness programs and campaigns through the media, the Integrated Child Development Services (ICDS), and involving the panchayats as well as legal services authorities. Studies indicate that one of the best strategies to stop child marriage is to keep females in school. For every year a female attends secondary school, her likelihood of being married before turning 18 decreases by half.. In order to lower the rate of child marriage in India, more needs to be done to advance gender equality, enhance access to education, and reduce poverty.

3. Marriage Counseling

By examining and resolving emotional needs, closeness, and affection, marriage counselors assist couples in reestablishing their emotional connection. The intention is to establish a more intimate and emotionally satisfying relationship. Social workers assist families in strengthening their bonds and navigating challenging circumstances like divorce, illness, or death. They assist families in identifying issues, setting objectives, and resolving conflicts as they move through the counseling process. Counseling is one-on-one assistance meant to help someone with an issue they are unable to resolve on their own.

4. Child Guidance Clinics and Counselling

The main focus of a child's development is the behavioural changes that occur as they mature. It addresses qualitative shifts that might either improve or worsen and eventually contribute to a higher standard of living (Choudhary, 2021). Children deal with a variety of issues. These comprise issues related to children's mental health, psychology, psychopathology, social and educational. The foundation of child guidance clinic operations is teamwork. When it comes to treating and repairing children from physical, mental, emotional, and psychotic traumas, child guidance and counselling centres are crucial. These facilities are beneficial in that they help children receive better guidance and counselling and offer treatment or palliation for mental, physical, and emotional trauma resulting from child marriage, including rape, psychological abuse, physical assault, and sexual harassment.

Child guidance and counselling facilities are crucial in offering therapy and rehabilitation for children who have experienced physical, mental, emotional, or psychotic traumas. These centres enable children to receive better supervision and counselling, as well as treatment or palliation for mental, physical, and emotional traumas (such as rape, psychological abuse, physical assault, and sexual harassment) brought on by child marriage.

5. Child Protection Role

Social workers connect individuals with relevant social structures and resources in an effort to prevent and lessen this disequilibrium. They gain proficiency in fostering dialogue and establishing connections. Some kids require assistance because they face difficulties on a daily basis. The obligation to care for children is a shared duty and responsibility between the community, parents, and the government. All parties must synergize and contribute according to their respective abilities in order to achieve maximum child protection (Mansari & Melayu, 2023).

6. Assisting Families and Girls

Counselling, life skills instruction, and house-to-house campaigns to inform parents of girls' rights and the detrimental effects of girl weddings are some of the interventions used with girls. Research validates the importance of assisting girls and their families in avoiding girl marriage.

THE ROLE OF SOCIAL WORKSERS IN MITIGATING CHILD MARRIAGES

The current chapter aims to explore the causes and basic aspects of child marriage. In light of the determinant effects of child marriage, social workers now have a number of responsibilities in communities where child marriage is regarded as a significant and serious problem. In order to address the issue of child marriage and raise awareness among the local population, social workers are essential. To rising community awareness of drafting laws and other measures to prevent child marriage, carrying out numerous duties, and holding positions in many departments that are related to each other. Community education and counseling are crucial among these. Numerous studies have demonstrated the value of micro- and macro-approaches in preventing child marriage. Social workers will increase the degree of social comprehension in the process. In order to address the issue of child marriage, social workers must provide a suitable framework (backed by the government, law enforcement, and police) and develop different strategies based on micro- and macro-level studies. One of the most significant ways to stop child marriage is to plan intervention strategies with girls. Social workers especially plan these interventions for the families in the communities where they reside. Social workers educate girls about the gravity of the determinant effects of underage marriage. Ensuring that their rights are not restricted and that atrocities against them are avoided is its primary objective. Making them a human asset and teaching them to have a human appearance are the most important things. It is crucial to help families become capable of making their own decisions in situations where child marriage occurs.

Social workers collaborate with the community to teach them about the negative impacts of child marriage. They do this by upholding workshops, awareness component campaigns, social media, and education campaigns. Children's rights will be upheld, and they will also be able to pursue a better future for themselves. Social workers can play different roles in averting further tragedies by fighting in the end in these difficult situations with the help of the relevant government departments and authorities, as well as the Act and other laws. Although it could seem difficult to avoid ongoing marriage, for the time being, social workers find joy in defending the girl's right to marriage and safeguarding the future of the child.

In order to avoid early marriage, social workers hold community meetings, workshops, street plays, awareness campaigns, and encounters with the public to inform people about the negative effects of issues like child marriage. It operates by implementing successful interventions at different phases of child marriage. Early marriage is linked to a number of systems, including families, laws, governments, the police, the judicial system, and the community through its mediation. They play an important role by mediating. Several studies have demonstrated that girls who are forced into child marriage typically become victims of domestic abuse and have negative social, economic, health, and educational consequences. To reduce the rate of early marriage or child marriage, the social workers concentrate on the following points:

- Child protection
- Quality education or family education
- Empowerment
- Promotion of women's human rights
- Research, legislation, and policy
- Advocate for girls and parents.
- Interventions
- Gender equality
- Risk mitigation and crisis intervention

Social workers are specialists in a variety of social work approaches, tenets, theories, and models. They contribute significantly to the prevention of major societal problems like child marriage by employing their talents, the arts, etc. They utilize three primary systems.

1. Families and communities
2. The judicial system and the formulation of policies
3. Education or empowerment of women

In order to reduce the number of girl marriages, social workers should address the larger social, economic, and cultural circumstances that contribute to the practice. They should also mobilize role players, such as girls who may be at risk, to jointly address the reasons for girl marriage in order to advance social justice. Social workers use a variety of strategies to prevent and control child marriage. They address the many factors listed above that contribute to child marriage. Social workers primarily play the role of protectors, working to end harmful and immoral practices like child marriage, safeguard vulnerable groups, and uphold children's rights.

Early marriages as well as early childbearing are harmful to the health of both mother and child. The bodies of mothers who conceive at a young age are still developing, and there is competition for growth and development between the mothers and the foetuses (Acharya, 2010). This contains a higher chance of girls being victimized. Social workers are crucial in preventing child marriage, which primarily involves promoting child rights and social justice for the protection of children. To decrease abuse, prejudice, violence, and inequality, the practice of child marriage is widely spread. It is currently practiced in Indian society. This is a significant societal phenomenon where young girls marrying adults are involved. Typically, married girls at this age may experience additional health concerns such as HIV, early sexual problems, obstetric disorders, new-born mortality, and mother fatalities. Child marriage can result from social and economic disadvantages as well as traditions and customs. Social workers are assisting with important community initiatives.

A significant role for counselling plays in the delicate procedures of social work. It is a crucial method for problem-solving and for clients to acquire a variety of skills. Social workers encourage girls to face challenges with confidence and assist them in managing their child marriage issues in a methodical manner. For instance, stress, depression, annoyance, loneliness, etc. To keep girls from getting married when they are still unsure of what marriage means and to reinforce the roles that their parents place in their lives in their capacity. As counsellors and social workers, we help women learn about how to handle various life's circumstances and assist them in acquiring the necessary skills. Collaborating with local communities Social workers constantly collaborate with local communities to raise awareness of a range of issues among the population of girls and their families in communities about the determinental impacts of child marriage through interactions, talks, workshops, and consultation. Child marriage is a significant social problem that requires community-based treatment to address the grave implications of child marriage. Arranging and distributing different mass media programs and initiatives based on their determinant consequences. Social workers and community members try their hardest to prevent female marriages. It is necessary to alter public perceptions of this immoral behaviour. This can be achieved through rising community awareness, which is something in which local residents' involvement is crucial. Programs to stop child marriage can be implemented by social workers, educators, and the relevant departments. They also include life skills development and provide guidance on how to handle favourable outcomes.

Community members are encouraged to participate at all levels, according to social workers. The prevention of child marriage has proven extremely challenging in the absence of active community involvement. Open social engagement contributes to the community's structural transformation. Dealing with the issues that girls face in the community can benefit from direct connection with them.

DISCUSSION AND CONCLUSION

Based on the above chapter, we can conclude that child marriage is a significant social issue that impedes the growth of the person, the family, and the community. Child marriage is a human rights violation. Despite laws against it, the practice remains widespread, mainly because of persistent poverty and gender inequality. It has an extremely deleterious effect on the health and well-being of the child (Zeejin & Kumar, 2020). Statistics show that one in five girls worldwide gets married before turning eighteen. In many Indian communities, this practice is common for socio-cultural and economic reasons. Human rights are allegedly being violated by this. The effects of this harmful practice are unevenly felt by women and girls worldwide. In these situations, girls could feel pressured to abstain from marriage and take their own lives.

It is possible to raise awareness of the determinant impacts of child marriage among teams and their families in appropriate and efficient ways. Regarding the issues that surface in their lives following child marriage, it is feasible to learn from the difficulties they face at every turn. Intimate and psychological treatment will be more beneficial at certain points. This appears to be made feasible by a number of interventions that assist teenagers in gaining the abilities they will need throughout their lives. Taking the required judgments and acting well, building procedures that control and reduce negative effects, reducing difficulties related to child marriage, and developing effective and acceptable solutions. It is imperative that young girls and their families be made aware of the determinant effects of child marriage using appropriate and practical measures. At every stage of the problems that emerge, their difficulties can be lessened. Counselling, advice, and direction eventually become more beneficial. In order to help teenagers develop the skills they need for their daily lives and strive toward making the right decisions, different interventions have been developed. Establishing procedures to control and suppress harmful consequences. To raise their knowledge and address issues such as unintended pregnancies, abuse of both physical and mental health, and cleanliness. Children that marry young are prone to losing their youth. It negatively affects not just their lives but also their rights.

There is a reduction in rights, including protection, health, and education. It is a nasty habit that negatively impacts girls. They are unable to lead a violent, free life like everyone else. It is during this time that girls in particular lack the physical, mental, and emotional maturity necessary to solve problems that may develop in their lives. Their job options are thus limited. Further, they struggle to make the necessary adjustments in their lives and deal with the challenges that crop up in their personal lives. Studies have shown that women who become pregnant in marriages under the age of fifteen have an increased risk of dying during childbirth. Young girls who marry have an increased risk of contracting HIV and other infectious diseases. Child marriage sets women on a negative health trajectory, resulting in a heightened risk of chronic diseases in India (Vikram et al. 2023). This is due to the fact that men typically have multiple sexual partners, and as a result of their carelessness and ignorance about sex, they might transmit HIV and other diseases to their partners. Child marriage has been identified as a major obstacle to development and progress from various perspectives, including social, economic, political, and personal ones. It is common in some developing countries and has determinant effects on the individual, family, and community. Some of the problems associated with child marriage include dowry, violence, low social status, limited opportunities, and the end of an independent life.

REFERENCES

Acharya, A. K. (2010). *The influence of female age in marriage on fertility and child loss in India*. Trayectorias.

Ahmed, T. (2015). Child marriage: A discussion paper. *Bangladesh Journal of Bioethics*, 6(2), 8–14. DOI: 10.3329/bioethics.v6i2.25740

Akter, A., & Ashadujjaman, M. The Impact of Child Marriage on Socioeconomic Aspects in Bangladesh.

Anwaruzzaman, K. M., & Khan, S. (2017). Early marriage of girls in India: A regional perspective. In Saha, G. (Ed.), *Child marriage: The root of social maladies*. Levant Books.

Azeez, A., & Poonia, E.P., A. (2015). Determinants, attitudes, and practices on child marriage: Evidence from rural Rajasthan. *Social Work Chronicle*, 4(2), 1–15.

Castill, C. (2018). Political role models and child marriage in India. *Review of Development Economics*, 22(4), 1409–1431. DOI: 10.1111/rode.12513

Chatterjee, K. (2015). What could work to prevent child marriages and delay pregnancy during adolescence in India: A systematic review of evidence from low and middle income countries? *European Academic Research*, 8(2), 1458–1490.

Choudhary, S. (2021). Social work intervention and child development in India. [TOJQI]. *Turkish Online Journal of Qualitative Inquiry*, 12(10), 5295–5306.

Dahiya, P. (2019). The child marriage: A curse in India. *JETIR*, 6(6), 441–449.

Fernandes, M. (2023). Child marriage in India: A sociological review. *Integrated Journal for Research in Arts and Humanities*, 3(5), 171–176. DOI: 10.55544/ijrah.3.5.15

Gautam, A., & Shekhar, R. (2018). Child marriage in India: A spatio-temporal Analysis. *Śodha Pravāha*, 8(2), 224-230.

Ghosh, B. (2011). Child marriage, society, and the law: A study in a rural context in West Bengal, India. *International Journal of Law, Policy and the Family*, 25(2), 199–219. DOI: 10.1093/lawfam/ebr002

Irani, M., & Roudsari, R. L. (2019). Reproductive and sexual health consequences of child marriage: A review of literature. *Journal of Midwifery & Reproductive Health*, 7(1), 1584–1590. DOI: 10.22038/jmrh.2018.31627.1342

Kapur, R. (2019). Understanding the societal problem of child marriage. Downloaded from https://researchgate.net.>civil law < marriage

Kishore, P. (2023). Child marriages: A curse for humanity. Downloaded from http://www.brighterkashmir.com › child-marriages-a-cur... Kumar, S. (2023). Exploring the socioeconomic factors behind girl-child marriage in India. *Indian Journal of Health, Sexuality, and Culture, 9*(1), 142-151.

Kumar, V. (2022). The socio-cultural changes in Indian society: A sociological perspective. In Thanavathi, C., & Ramya, S. (Eds.), *Women education in India* (pp. 18–26). Island Publishers.

Lal, B. S. (2015). Child marriage in India: Factors and problems. [IJSR]. *International Journal of Scientific Research, 4*(4), 2993–2998.

Livesey, L. (2017). *A literature review on early marriage.* University of Gloucestershire. Downloaded from https://eprints.glos.ac.uk › Research › Research Repository

Mahmuddin, M., Mansari, M., & Melayu, H. A. (2023). Community's role in preventing child marriage: An analysis of models and community compliance with village policies. *Gender Equality: International Journal of Child and Gender Studies, 9*(2), 235. DOI: 10.22373/equality.v9i2.19673

Nabila, R., Roswiyani, R., & Satyadi, H. (2022). A literature review of factors influencing early marriage decisions in Indonesia. *Advances in Social Science, Education and Humanities Research,* 655, 1392–1402. DOI: 10.2991/assehr.k.220404.223

Naruka, R., Kumar, V., Singh, H., & Kaushik, T. K. (2023). Domestic child adoption in India: The problem and prospectives. *Tuijin Jishu Journal of Propulsion Technology, 44*(6), 1162–1174.

Nirantar Trust. (2015). *Early and child marriages in India: A landscape analysis.* Drishti Printers.

Pampapathi, N. L. (2018). Child marriages in India: Causes and consequences. *IJCRT, 6*(1), 1436–1439.

Parsons, J., Edmeades, J., Kes, A., Petroni, S., Sexton, M., & Wodon, Q. (2015). Economic impacts of child marriage: A review of the literature. *The Review of Faith & International Affairs, 13*(3), 12–22. DOI: 10.1080/15570274.2015.1075757

Parvez, N., & Gauhar, F. R. (2024). Child in conflict with law in India: Changing concerns and constraints. *Sprin Journal of Arts, Humanities, and Social Sciences,* 3(7), 1–6. DOI: 10.55559/sjahss.v3i7.367

Patankar, S. (2021). Fighting social acceptance of child marriage in India. Downloaded from https://borgenproject.org › The Blog

Rasmussen, B., Maharaj, N., Kumnick, M., & Sheehan, P. (2021). Evaluating interventions to reduce child marriage in India. *Journal of Global Health Reports*, 5, e2021044. DOI: 10.29392/001c.23619

Roest, J. (2016). Child Marriage and Early Childbearing in India: Risk Factors and Policy Implications. The final version is available online from Young Lives at: https://www.younglives.org.uk/content/child-marriage-and-early-child-bearing-india-risk-factors-and-policy-implications

Sagade, J. (2005). *Child marriage in India: Socio-legal and human rights dimensions*. OUP India Publishers.

Sen, S., & Ghosh, A. (Eds.). (2021). *Love, labour, and law: Early and child marriage in India*. SAGE Publications Pvt. Ltd.

Seth, R., Bose, V., Qaiyum, Y., Chandrashekhar, R., Kansal, S., Taneja, I., & Seth, T. (2018). Social determinants of child marriage in rural India. *The Ochsner Journal*, 18(4), 390–394. DOI: 10.31486/toj.18.0104 PMID: 30559625

Sheth, C. (2021). A community-based approach to preventing child marriage. *India Development Review*. https://idronline.org › a-community-based-approach-to-...
Shrestha. I. K., & Khanal S. P. (2024). Factors associated with time to first birth after marriage: A systematic review. *BIBECHANA 21*(2), 180-194.

Singh, S., & Kaur, M. (2024). Child marriage in India: The chains of tradition. *Educational Administration: Theory and Practice*, 30(1), 1425–1434.

Subramanee, S. D., Agho, K., Lakshmi, J., Huda, M. N., Joshi, R., & Akombi-Inyang, B. (2022). Child marriage in South Asia: A systematic review. *International Journal of Environmental Research and Public Health*, 19(22), 15138. DOI: 10.3390/ijerph192215138 PMID: 36429857

Tembo, G. (2021). *Causes and effects of early marriages in Zambia*: A case study of the University of Zambia.

Uddin, E. M. (2015). Family socio-cultural values affecting early marriage between Muslim and Santal communities in rural Bangladesh. *The International Journal of Sociology and Social Policy*, 35(3/4), 141–164. DOI: 10.1108/IJSSP-06-2014-0046

Uddin, M. E. (2017). Family demographic mechanisms linking of socioeconomic status to subjective physical health in rural Bangladesh. *Social Indicators Research*, 130(3), 1263–1279. DOI: 10.1007/s11205-015-1209-x

Uddin, M. E. (2021). Teenage marriage and high school dropout among poor girls: A narrative review for family pathways in Bangladesh. *Journal of Research in Social Sciences and Language*, 1(1), 55–76. https://www.jssal.com/index.php/jssal/article/view/15

Vikram, K. (2023). Modern marriage in a traditional society: The influence of college education on marriage in India. *Journal of Family Issues*, 45(5), 1116–1141. DOI: 10.1177/0192513X231155591

Vikram, K., Visaria, A., & Ganguly, D. (2023). Child marriage as a risk factor for non-communicable diseases among women in India. *International Journal of Epidemiology*, 52(5), 1303–1315. DOI: 10.1093/ije/dyad051 PMID: 37159526

Wijayati, N. A., & Soemanto, R. B. (2017). Socioeconomic and cultural determinants of early marriage in Ngawi, East Java: Application of the PRECEDE-PROCEED Model. *Journal of Health Promotion and Behavior*, 2(4), 302–312. DOI: 10.26911/thejhpb.2016.02.04.02

Yadav, K. P. (2006). *Child marriage in India*. Adhyayan Publishers.

Yağmur, S. K. (2023). Early and forced marriages, child brides. *International Journal of Arts, Humanities, and Social Sciences*, 4(7), 26–30. DOI: 10.56734/ijahss.v4n7a4

Youvan, D. C. (2024). Child marriage and legal paradoxes: India's battle with tradition and child protection laws. DOI:DOI: 10.13140/RG.2.2.10715.17446

Zeejin, V. M., & Kumar, G. S. (2020). A study on child marriage in a multilateral approach with special reference to Gudiyatham, Vellore district, Tamil Nadu. *Mukt Shabd Journal*, 9(4), 2557–2578.

Chapter 15
The Role of International Mechanisms in Preventing Early Marriage:
Empowering Asylum Seekers Through International Protection in Türkiye

Bekir Güzel
Recep Tayyip Erdoğan University, Turkey

Sema Nur Beserek
Independent Researcher, Turkey

ABSTRACT

Early marriage is an increasing global problem all over the world. International mechanisms play a critical role in combating this problem, which is even more prevalent in underdeveloped or developing countries. These mechanisms make important contributions in many areas from raising awareness to creating a legal framework, from developing programmes/interventions to providing funds. Türkiye has the largest population of asylum seekers in the 21st century. [..] The Ministry of Family and Social Services is the primary ministry authorised for child protection in Türkiye. These institutions (NGOs and MFSS) in Türkiye implement different empowerment-based practice models in the field. These include information and advocacy on judicial processes and legal procedures, medical intervention, psychosocial support, education and counselling as well as protective-preventive and

DOI: 10.4018/979-8-3693-3394-5.ch015

empowering activities. This chapter indicates that international mechanisms play an important global role in ending early marriage.

INTRODUCTION

The world is witnessing increasing and diversifying migration movements every day. Hundreds of thousands, perhaps even millions, of people are mobilised every day from one place to another, regardless of young, old, women, children and disabled people. Today, the world, with its vast geographies, has become the intersection point of social, cultural, economic and political dynamics. Migration is not only the physical movement of individuals; it also involves processes of interaction, adaptation and transformation between different societies. As many researchers agree (Bhagat, 2020; De Haas et al., 2019; Rozelle et al., 1999), migration brings opportunities and challenges. Particularly in the case of women, children, elderly or disabled individuals, who are already disadvantaged, the intersectionality adds another layer of disadvantage. This chapter will focus on the intersectional disadvantage of individuals involved in migration movements, especially children and youth, as a result of early marriage.

Early Marriage: What Kind of Phenomenon?

Various definitions of early marriage can be seen. According to UNICEF (2024), early marriage or child marriage refers to "any formal marriage or informal union between a child under the age of 18 and an adult or another child." Another definition by the European Institute for Gender Equality (2024) is that "marriage for individuals whose physical, emotional, sexual and psychosocial development level is such that they cannot freely and fully consent to marriage."

Early marriage[1] is a widespread social problem that has profound effects on public health and social welfare. According to studies, the rate of early marriage is five times higher among girls than boys worldwide[2] (Anık and Barlin, 2017; Duman & Coşkun, 2019; Uddin, 2015). As a matter of fact, as stated by Marphatia et al. (2017), early marriage is closely related to complex factors such as women's social status, education level and archaic/cultural norms towards women (Uddin, 2021). These factors can have significant impacts on the health of individuals and communities. Early marriage is associated with serious and negative consequences such as forced marriage, sexual exploitation and trafficking, especially in settings affected by armed conflict (McAlpine et al., 2016). In such environments, children are often vulnerable and families may force their children to marry at an early age under economic or social pressures. Similar situations are also in question, especially for families who have undergone forced migration (Mourtada et al., 2017; Öztürk et al., 2021).

Today, despite social changes and developments, there are still a considerable number of people who marry at an early age. Moreover, this situation is independent of the level of development of countries. In other words, when we talk about early marriage, we are talking about a widespread social problem that is visible from developed to undeveloped countries (Uddin, 2015). As stated by Uecker and Stokes (2008), who researched this issue through the American society, the prevalence of early marriage reveals the need for continuous research and intervention. In this context, more information and strategies are required to identify, cope with and prevent early marriage. This need serves as the main motivation of this study.

As can be clearly seen in the table above, there is a decline in the rates of early marriage all over the world. These drops are remarkable in some regions, such as in South Asia. Nevertheless, it is still open to debate whether there has been a sufficient decline. The fact that there has been only a 7% decline in the last 25 years worldwide clearly indicates that national and international organisations (especially the UN) need to improve their struggling mechanisms.

There are various factors (social norms, violence against women, barriers to educational opportunities, humanitarian crises, etc.) that cause early marriage, as well as multidimensional effects of early marriage such as violence, oppression, health problems, lack of access to education and employment, etc. (Muhith et al., 2018; Sezgin & Punamäki, 2020; Saleheen et al., 2021; Udgiri, 2017). For instance, firstly; early marriage can lead to serious health problems. Young girls who are not physically developed are at greater risk during pregnancy and childbirth. In addition, early marriage may result in the spread of health problems such as sexually transmitted infections and HIV (Uddin, 2017). Secondly, early marriage often limits educational opportunities. These individuals are less likely to attend school, which limits the future career and economic opportunities of the individuals (Uddin, 2021). Moreover, this situation is not limited to individual impacts, as it can affect the overall development and well-being of society.

Table 1. Percentage of Women Married the Before Age of 18 (Between 20-24 Age Group)

Region	25 Years Ago	10 Years Ago	Today
South Asia	60%	49%	31%
West and Central Africa	49%	45%	43%
Eastern and Southern Africa	45%	42%	35%
Middle East and North Africa	34%	24%	19%

continued on following page

Table 1. Continued

Region	25 Years Ago	10 Years Ago	Today
Latin America and the Caribbean	24%	26%	25%
Eastern Europe and Central Asia	17%	16%	12%
East Asia and Pacific	9%	8%	6%
World * All percentages are given as approximate values.	28%	27%	21%

Source: UNICEF, 2018

INTERNATIONAL MECHANISMS IN PREVENTING EARLY MARRIAGE

Today, early marriage is internationally recognised as a violation of human rights (children's rights) and a different type of violence against women. In this context, early marriages are considered as a violation of human rights in international conventions due to the fact that individuals do not have the right to marry with their own free and full consent. Within the framework of international legislation on this issue, there are a number of important documents that emphasise human rights.

Firstly, Article 16 of the Universal Declaration of Human Rights adopted in 1948 emphasises the right to marry and protects the right of individuals to marry freely and with full consent. The Convention on the Rights of the Child (1989), on the other hand, focuses on the fundamental rights of children and protects them by setting age restrictions on marriage. The Convention on the Elimination of All Forms of Discrimination against Women (CEDAW-1979) emphasises women's equal right to marry and to found a family in Article 16. Moreover, the Convention on Consent to Marriage, Minimum Age of Marriage and Postponement of Marriage (1964), the International Covenant on Economic, Social and Cultural Rights (1979), the International Covenant on Civil and Political Rights (1976), the International Convention on the Political Rights of Women (1976) and the Council of Europe Convention on Preventing and Combating Violence against Women (Istanbul Convention-2014) contain detailed provisions on marriage, equality and combating violence. These conventions reflect the commitments of the international community on early marriage, marriage rights, gender equality and combating gender-based violence. Briefly, when the international legislation on early marriage is analysed in detail, it is understood that international law is in a common effort to prohibit early marriage based on various human rights conventions. The relevant legislation builds its struggle on four main issues: consent, minimum age, children's rights and women's rights. Among these notions, "consent" is particularly important, since the other three have a more legal or public connotation. However, consent essentially corresponds to an individual context and therefore to an individual right. Consent is a fundamental condition for marriage and both parties must give their free and full consent for the marriage to be valid. Therefore, legal measures can be taken in relation to other concepts; it is also necessary to provide information and awareness-raising for individuals on consent rather than these measures.

In addition to the aforementioned legislation, various academic disciplines have developed different perspectives and methods for combating early marriage. In this chapter, the problem of early marriage will be addressed through the empowerment approach of the social work discipline based on human rights and social justice principles. Social work stands out as an applied discipline and profession with the aim of improving and empowering the lives of individuals and communities. This approach aims to empower individuals, support them to discover their own potential and sustain their lives in a healthier way (Thompson, 2006). Social work plays an effective role in combating social problems such as early marriage. The empowerment-based approach aims to enable individuals and communities to find their own resources and solution strategies against such problems (Adams, 2017). For combating early marriage, social work professionals play an important role in raising awareness in communities and encouraging young people to cope with such risky situations through education and support services. In this way, social work contributes to societies to deal with social problems more effectively with its empowerment-based approach (Solomon, 1987). Likewise, many countries are preparing action plans for the prevention of early marriage and the coordination between state institutions, NGOs and international organisations is getting stronger. Especially in the case of asylum-seeking children, the effects and consequences of early marriage are more severe and heavy due to the intersectionality of disadvantage. The importance of a multi-stakeholder approach based on co-operation increases at this point.

In Türkiye, international organisations such as the United Nations High Commissioner for Refugees (UNHCR), United Nations Children's Fund (UNICEF), United Nation Women (UN WOMAN), United Nations Population Fund (UNFPA), Amnesty International, International Catholic Migration Commission (ICMC), International Red Cross and Red Crescent Movement (IFRC), GOAL Global, Save The Children, Doctors of the World, Association for Solidarity with Asylum Seekers and Migrants (SGDD-ASAM) are actively working in this field. National organisations such as Red Crescent Community Centre, Life Support Association, Social and Cultural Life Development Association (SCLDA), Human Resources Development Foundation (HRDF), Development Foundation of Türkiye (DFT), International Blue Crescent Relief and Development Foundation (IBC), Refugees Association, Mazlumder, International Association for Migration and Solidarity (IAMS) are also active in the area.

These organisations also carry out important activities for migrants, asylum seekers, refugees, individuals under temporary protection or international protection status in Türkiye. These organisations carry out important activities in cooperation with different institutions and organisations for individuals/groups that have experienced migration in connection with early marriage. As a solution, empowering children with a migration background through education is among the most preventive strategies. Financial assistance provided to families and scholarships provided to children play an important role in this combat. Enrolment of children in formal education, support for school enrolment processes, activities carried out to improve children's life skills during the time they are out of school are among the important steps taken to prevent children from early marriage.

Measures taken for the empowerment of children, raising awareness of children about their rights, and activities for the participation of children are also among the important activities in order to cope with early marriage. Among community-based activities; trainings provided to communities, committees for sexual and reproductive health, information activities carried out on social platforms, messages conveyed by leaders who have the power to influence the society, counselling services such as social, legal, health and education provided by state institutions and NGOs are considered as examples of good practices. However, the empowering activities in this regard cannot be fully realised due to the status of persons under international protection in Türkiye, which does not correspond to the national legislation. For this reason, permanent and sustainable solutions cannot be produced despite the effective combat with this problem.

WAYS OF INTERNATIONAL PROTECTION

Although the first international conceptualisations of refugees are generally dated to the establishment of the United Nations and the 1951 Geneva Convention, there is a history tracing back to the Treaty of Westphalia in 1648. After the establishment of the League of Nations, the first international refugee organisation was established in 1921 under the leadership of Fridthof Nansen (Çingir and Erdağ, 2017). However, the most significant developments took place in the aftermath of World War II. Founded in 1945, the United Nations established the United Nations High Commissioner for Refugees (UNHCR) in 1950.

The UNHCR, whose main objective was to help millions of Europeans who had fled or lost their homes after World War II, later acquired a mission outside the European continent. In fact, a similar situation is also valid for the Geneva Convention adopted in 1951. The Convention was first opened for signature to respond to asylum requests within the European continent. Türkiye was among the first signatory countries of this convention. Nonetheless, when this "geographical limitation" on the European continent was abolished after the meeting in New York in 1967, Türkiye preferred to continue the convention with a "geographical limitation". This was justified and even rationalised by its geopolitical position between the Middle East and Eurasia. Therefore, today Türkiye still does not recognise asylum-seekers from outside the European continent as "refugees". In fact, since its foundation, the Republic of Türkiye has traditionally adopted a policy of "temporariness" migration with the aim of directing migrants or asylum-seekers without ancestry (ethnic) ties to safe third countries or encouraging their voluntary return to their home countries. One of the reasons why Türkiye has maintained the geographical limitation in the 1951 Geneva Convention stems from this policy approach (Çingir and Erdağ, 2017).

Law on Foreigners and International Protection (No. 6458), adopted in 2013 sets the framework for Türkiye's responses to asylum requests and the international protection regime. According to this law (Article 61/1) *"A person who as a result of events occurring in European countries and owing to well-founded fear of being persecuted for reasons of race, religion, nationality, membership of a particular social group or political opinion, is outside the country of his citizenship and is unable or, owing to such fear, is unwilling to avail himself or herself of the protection of that country; or who, not having a nationality and being outside the country of his former residence as a result of such events, is unable or, owing to such fear, is unwilling to return to it, shall be granted refugee status upon completion of the refugee status determination process."*

Therefore, due to Türkiye's "geographical limitation" to the 1951 Geneva Convention Relating to the Status of Refugees, asylum seekers from outside the borders of Europe are not granted refugee status even if they meet the requirements for refugee status. In accordance with the Law on Foreigners and International Protection (2013), these people are named as "conditional refugees" (Article 62/1) and are allowed to stay in Türkiye until they are resettled in a third country. As for conditional refugees, the term "until they are resettled in a third country" can be considered as a reflection of the previously mentioned policy of "temporariness". Besides these types of international protection, there are two other statuses in Türkiye: subsidiary protection and temporary protection.

Subsidiary protection (Article 63/1) is defined as "A foreigner or a stateless person, who neither could be qualified as a refugee nor as a conditional refugee, shall nevertheless be granted subsidiary protection upon the status determination because if returned to the country of origin or country of [former] habitual residence would: a) be sentenced to death or face the execution of the death penalty; b) face torture or inhuman or degrading treatment or punishment; c) face serious threat to himself or herself by reason of indiscriminate violence in situations of international or nationwide armed conflict; and therefore is unable or for the reason of such threat is unwilling, to avail himself or herself of the protection of his country of origin or country of [former] habitual residence." The inclusiveness of this status and the number of asylum-seekers to whom it is granted is highly controversial. Unlike other types of status (in particular temporary protection status), it is not possible to obtain clear data and information on subsidiary protection. The last status in the Law is the temporary protection status for Syrians who come to the Turkish border and seek asylum as a result of the events in their country. The Law (Article 91/1) states that temporary protection status can be granted to "foreigners" who have been forced to leave their country cannot return to the country that they have left, and have arrived at or crossed the borders of Türkiye in a mass influx situation seeking immediate and temporary protection." This status is concrete evidence that Türkiye's migration policy, which has traditionally been based on "temporariness" continues in this way.

All these status differences cause the international protection of asylum-seekers to be complex, difficult and delayed. This situation indirectly affects the national/international support and services to be provided to asylum seekers. The process of struggle against early marriage of asylum-seeking children, which is at the centre of this study, is inevitably affected by this situation and conditions in some way.

EMPOWERING ASYLUM SEEKERS THROUGH INTERNATIONAL MECHANISMS/PROTECTION AND CIVIL SOCIETY (NGOS)

Empowerment, which has entered the agenda of social work in the last half century, is one of the most dominant approaches widely used today. Notably since the 1970s, it has been brought to attention as an alternative to the medical model that has been effective until that time. Empowerment approach can be defined as a concept that is essentially built on the concept of "power". Initially, the concept of power was handled in a more micro level individual context beyond the power or authority relations in the macro structure. However, later it started to be addressed in different dimensions.

In light of this, power can generally be analysed from three different perspectives. Firstly, *personal power* is important, which refers to the individual's ability to achieve desired goals by utilising his or her own potential or skills. Secondly, *hierarchical or authoritarian power* is based on a certain pattern of inequality or dominance in relationships. Finally, *egalitarian social power* refers to a structure in which people relate to each other as equal partners and develop relationships based on mutual respect and value (Erbay, 2019; Neath & Schriner, 1998). In his book *Power and Empowerment*, Neil Thompson (2006) discussed power in four different dimensions: "*power over, power with, power to* and *power from within*". Although it was emphasised here that each power dimension had an effect on individuals, it is useful to highlight the concept of power from within. Indeed, the empowerment approach was mainly based on power from within, even though other types of power were also involved. So, what exactly does empowerment and empowerment approach refer to?

The concept of empowerment can be defined as the ability of individuals, groups and communities to control their own lives, achieve their goals and make efforts to improve their quality of life. This concept also refers to the ability of people to realise their potential and play an active role in situations that can affect them (Adams, 2003). The empowerment approach, which is shaped on this concept, considers the client as an active and participatory individual with potential power. The empowerment approach aims to provide qualities such as critical thinking, being strong against oppressive practices and policies, self-confidence and being the defender of their rights in this direction. The aim is to contribute to the creation of strong individuals who can stand on their own feet. This approach is firmly based on the principle of self-determination. The social worker is a facilitator in this approach. The client is the person who can make the right decisions about the situation he/she is in. However, social workers are professionals who emphasise the strengths of the process and support the client in this way. The aim of the social worker is to ensure that the client takes responsibility for his/her own situation and to make him/her the main actor of change. In the intervention process, the client is not an object of the practice, but an active and responsible subject of the practice directly (Erbay, 2019).

The concept of empowerment has its origins in the efforts of professionals working with socially disadvantaged population groups. In the following phase of this study, empowerment is focussed on asylum seekers who were forced to marry at an early age. It is observed that non-governmental organisations[3] (NGOs) are particularly active in solving the problem of early marriage among asylum seekers in Türkiye. As it is known, civil society, operating at local, national and international level, has an important role in the development of children's rights, raising awareness, improving laws and services and ensuring the well-being of children. Civil society activities, also playing an important role in the historical development of social work, are of great importance in the development of children's rights to life, health, development, protection and participation on the basis of equality (Buz & Afyonoğlu, 2021).

The Ministry of Family and Social Services is the primary ministry authorised for child protection in Türkiye. While the Ministry is the main state institution responsible for prevention and intervention in cases of early marriage, it is necessary to involve multiple actors from multiple sectors in the processes of identifying and meeting the needs of a child who has been married at an early age. Therefore, inter-institutional cooperation and coordination is of great importance (UNICEF, 2017). Considering the activities of NGOs serving in the field; it is apparent that they play an active role in carrying out the notification and follow-up processes with the local units of the Ministry of Family and Social Services in cases of early marriages. As seen in many cases, experienced field teams of NGOs are at the forefront in identifying and reporting children at risk. At this point, NGOs cooperate with local units (such as schools, mukhtars, health centres). Meetings are held with teachers, school administrations, mukhtars, health professionals, representatives of the Provincial Directorate of National Education, Provincial Directorate of Family and Social Services, Provincial Directorate of Youth and Sports, Public Education Centres in order to strengthen relations with local stakeholders and make services more inclusive.

Besides, most of the NGOs in Türkiye carry out their services with the funds and programmes of international organisations affiliated to the United Nations. These organisations carry out important activities for foreign nationals (asylum seekers, refugees and temporary protection holders or migrants) in Türkiye. Many of the NGOs providing services in the field of child welfare carry out activities with the justice system on the right to protection of children, especially for children who are exposed to neglect and abusement or who are at risk. They also play an important role in the determination, notification and case management of early marriages. When a child who has been married at an early age or who is at risk of being married is identified, the child is interviewed alone in a private place. First, the child is informed about the services of the organisation, professional roles and responsibilities, children's rights, risks and safety requirements. Secondly, the child is informed about what can be done for him/her together with the organisation and his/her opinions and wishes are taken. Finally, the child's immediate needs and, if any, other protection needs (exposure to violence, disability, pregnancy, neglect, separation from family, being unaccompanied, exposure to human trafficking, child labour, violation of the right to education, etc.) are assessed.

According to UNHCR's Best Interests Assessment Procedures, the assessment should be based on four main rights groups: "the views of the child and those close to the child, safe environment, family and close relationships, development and identity needs". (UNHCR, 2021). Following the assessment of the best interests of the child, the case planning and implementation stages are initiated. It is known that the NGOs in Türkiye implement different empowerment-based practice models in the field. These include information and advocacy on judicial processes and legal procedures, medical intervention, psychosocial support, education and counselling as well as protective-preventive and empowering activities. In the following section, these studies will be briefly mentioned and the practices in the context of Türkiye will be discussed.

Information and advocacy on judicial processes and legal procedures

Law on Child Protection (No. 5395), Law on Protection of the Family and the Prevention of Violence Against Women (No. 6284) and the Turkish Penal Code have introduced certain obligations regarding the notification of early marriage and risk situations. According to Article 6 of the Law on Child Protection (2005); *"Judicial and administrative authorities, law enforcement officers, health and education institutions, non-governmental organisations are obliged to report children in need of protection to the Social Services and Child Protection Agency"*. As per Article 278 of the Turkish Penal Code (2004) entitled *Failure to Report a Crime*; *"A person who has not reported a crime in progress to the competent authorities shall be sentenced to imprisonment for up to one year"*. Also, according to Article (7/1) of the Law on Protection of the Family and the Prevention of Violence Against Women (2012); *"In case of violence or threat of violence, anyone can report this situation to the official authorities or bodies"*.

As per the relevant laws, all children in need of protection, married or at risk of marriage are reported by NGOs to the Provincial Directorate of the Ministry of Family and Social Services (PDMFSS), police/gendarmerie and prosecutor's office. When a child is reported to have been subjected to sexual abuse, the process is carried out in coordination. In such cases, if there is a Child Monitoring Centre (CMC) in the province where the sexual abuse took place, law enforcement officers are required to notify the CMC and the CMC is required to notify the Republic Prosecutor. In order to prevent the child victim of abuse from being traumatised in judicial processes and legal procedures, the child's statement regarding the abuse is recorded in the most appropriate environment possible, by an expert on the subject. Following these processes; necessary cautionary decisions listed in the Child Protection Law such as counselling, education, care, health and shelter are taken. Meanwhile, if the abuse has not been experienced in or around the family, protective and supportive cautionary decisions aiming to protect the child in the family environment are implemented (UNICEF, 2017). Upon reporting an early marriage, social service centres affiliated to PDMFSS are contacted and the status of this notification (whether it is taken into consideration and whether the necessary controls are carried out), the actions to be taken and the follow-up of the court process are monitored by the expert assigned with the case in NGOs.

Medical intervention

Individuals marrying at an early age often face problems related to general health and sexual or reproductive health. These problems may result in preventable deaths, various diseases and disabilities. Unfortunately, early marriages reduce the quality of healthy life of children. Various health problems and risks occur as a result of adolescent pregnancies, including maternal and infant mortality, difficult and/or premature birth, miscarriage, growth retardation in the baby during pregnancy, severe bleeding, rupture, exposure to sexually transmitted infections and postnatal problems (Köseli & Çelik, 2020). Necessary tests, tools and information should be provided by health professionals to children who have been married at an early age on the risk of sexually transmitted infections, treatment, prevention and termination of unwanted pregnancies. NGOs undertake important tasks in the field on issues related to health and birth processes. Health trainers working in NGOs provide the necessary health counselling and refer to state hospitals for medical intervention by paying attention to the principles of confidentiality, non-discrimination, privacy and ensuring the safety of the child.

Psychosocial support

The fact that children are married off before completing both their physical and psychosocial development prevents them from overcoming responsibilities such as having a family, managing a home and being a parent. Children who are removed from their families and social environment at an early age may feel excluded, isolated from social life and unhappy. It is commonly accepted that such situations are at the root of mental problems of individuals. Moreover, early marriages cause deep physiological and psychological damages on children (Demir et al., 2022). In the report titled "A multi-sectoral approach to the health risks and consequences of child, early and forced marriages" published by the United Nations Population Fund (2020), the fact that individuals are married off at an early age while they are still in the identity formation period, and that the social environment in which they live imposes burdens on them that they cannot carry, constitute an obstacle to their progress towards becoming a healthy individual (Köseli & Çelik, 2020).

In Türkiye, NGOs carry out a case-specific planning and psychosocial needs analysis before psychosocial support interventions in cases of early marriage. Professionals assigned or appointed to the case explain to the child and parents (or caregivers) the purpose of the questions they will ask during the assessment phase, and the strengths of the child within his/her family and social environment are assessed. After the first interviews and preliminary assessments, due to the specialised nature of the psychosocial support process, children are either referred to state/public institutions or psychosocial support is provided by professionals working in NGOs.

Education

Children's participation in social life, the development of their socio-economic status and access to the right to education are of great importance in terms of preventing early marriages. In the field, it is observed that children who have been married at an early age or who are at risk of being married are more likely to be out of school. Under these circumstances, it becomes critical to ensure children's continuity in education. Regarding the work of NGOs, especially within the scope of UNICEF projects developed with a focus on education, the activities carried out to identify out-of-school children, the reasons behind their out-of-school stay and the detection/prevention of early marriages support children's participation in the right to education. Activities are carried out to ensure children's access to the right to education by directing them to appropriate educational opportunities according to their special needs.

Accordingly, efforts to overcome the obstacles to schooling of children are carried out such as improving the knowledge and awareness of families and children about education, informing the relevant institutions, solving the problems encountered in educational institutions, carrying out joint studies at schools, supporting children's school enrolment processes, ensuring the integration of the child into the education system in Türkiye, providing extracurricular activities. As one of the biggest obstacles to children's access to education is economic deprivation, information and guidance services are provided for families and children on access to Conditional Cash Transfer for Education (CCTE) funded by the EU, Norway and the USA. In addition, depending on the grant status of the projects carried out jointly with international organisations in the field, education kit support is also provided and guidance is provided within the scholarship opportunities of international organisations.

Child / Family Counselling Service

Case assessment, service planning and counselling services are provided in coordination within the scope of case management in NGOs. It can be stated that the clients (children) face various problems in accessing services due to lack of rights and information, negative attitudes of service providers or discrimination and bullying. Social workers working in NGOs provide services for individuals to access basic rights and services. Actions are taken with the empowerment approach of social work, and importance is attached to informing the child at every stage, observing his/her best interests and ensuring his/her participation. With a focus on child protection, services are provided in areas such as social counselling, legal information, health counselling, combating bullying, individual and environmental awareness and social cohesion. The clients are informed about the services provided by NGOs and/or public institutions, and they are directed to the relevant institutions and organisations in line with their needs. Social workers carry out activities to solve the problems encountered by individuals with the role of advocacy and networking (Buz & Afyonoğlu, 2021).

Guiding principles for the best interests of the child developed by UNHCR are also considered as the basis for child protection activities and case management processes (UNHCR, 2021). In practice, a family and community-based approach is developed, taking into account that the best environment for the child's growth, well-being and protection is the family environment. Firstly, the urgency of early marriage cases is assessed, as the protection and care of children is always a priority. Such an approach aims to identify the specific needs and capacities of children so that their rights are protected in a non-discriminatory and inclusive manner. There are a number of indicators for social workers or other service providers to identify a child who is at risk of being married or who has been married. These can be listed as follows:

- Disenrollment of the child from school or prolonged absenteeism from school;
- Absence in previously participated activities (such as sports, social activities);
- Seeing the child as a caregiver in family;
- Early marriages among older brothers/sisters or other relatives in the child's neighbourhood;
- Increasing number of domestic violence acts;
- Signing or indications of sexual violence;
- Facing sexual and reproductive health problems;
- A suspicion that the child will leave home and be sent elsewhere;
- Developing some psychological problems in the child.

In case of the above-mentioned symptoms, it is considered that the child has been married or is about to be married and is approached more carefully (UNICEF, 2017). Social workers and other professionals working in the field take into account the family, culture and social environment in which the child grows up, and ensure the participation of children in solutions with the principle of non-harm. In this process, responsible and ethical planning is the main criterion. In order to better assess the current situation and sensitivity of the child, household visits are planned and individual interviews are conducted with family members. During the best interest of the child assessment and counselling phase, professionals working in

NGOs also receive case management support from their supervisors. Supervisory support positively affects the process of avoiding deficiencies that may occur in case management, resolving the difficulties encountered and taking the necessary actions, and ensures an effective intervention. Depending on the current risks and sensitivity of the child, follow-up interviews are held at certain periods. Furthermore; security, health, psychosocial support and judicial processes are also monitored. Cases are terminated by acknowledging of the supervisors according to the well-being of the child and the achievement of the determined goals. Before that, the child and family are informed about where they can continue to receive services and/or where they can apply.

CONCLUSION AND RECOMMENDATIONS

In Türkiye, it is observed that international mechanisms and NGOs have important functions in preventing early marriages among asylum-seeking children, protecting children's rights and improving their well-being by considering the best interests of children. It could be indicated that early marriages are common among asylum-seeking families in Türkiye due to reasons such as socio-cultural structure, poverty, lack of education and information (especially lack of information about the laws in Türkiye). With early marriage, children who have not yet completed their biological/physiological and psychosocial development are expected to take on new roles, especially through unofficial religious marriages and becoming parents at early ages. This affects psychology of the children badly.

Moreover, it is revealed that particularly girls are out of school due to gender-related roles attributed to children (a girl cannot attend high school, a married child cannot attend school, a woman must take care of children at home, a married woman cannot go out without her husband, etc.). When the activities of NGOs at micro, meso and macro levels are analysed, it is evident that each child is considered as a unique individual within his/her social environment and family structure. Detection and reporting of early marriages and awareness raising activities on children's rights help to break the gender-based perception in families. Although it is not possible to say that the cultural cycle in families and society has been broken within the scope of the activities carried out by NGOs, it could be claimed that families are more cautious about early marriages due to the activities carried out and the legal enforcement of this issue.

In addition, the efforts of NGOs are mostly insufficient in reaching the macro dimension (politicians and legislators). However, it can be argued that it is very crucial to increase activities such as research and data collection with all institutions (national or international) working in the field of child protection. As a result, it is suggested that NGOs should improve their cooperation with all institutions working in the field of child protection without making any distinction between public, private, civilian, national or international. Within this framework, a number of specific recommendations can be developed for all actors to be more effective in the multi-stakeholder struggle against early marriage:

Strengthening social awareness campaigns: This study focuses on the problem of early marriage for asylum seekers. However, in developing countries like Türkiye, especially in rural and disadvantaged areas, campaigns to raise public awareness about the risks and harms of early marriage are vital. These campaigns can reach wider audiences with the support of cultural and religious leaders, teachers, local authorities and the media. International organisations and local NGOs can contribute by funding these campaigns and providing content, materials and human resources.

Improving educational opportunities and increasing girls' access to education: Education plays a key role in preventing early marriage. In developing countries such as Türkiye, increasing girls' access to education and ensuring that they remain in education can be an effective strategy in solving this problem. In this sense, international mechanisms can strengthen local efforts by providing support in areas such as scholarships, educational programmes and improving school infrastructure.

Financial empowerment programmes: Considering the economic reasons underlying early marriages, financial empowerment of families is of critical importance in solving this problem. Financial empowerment activities such as micro-credit programmes, entrepreneurship training and vocational skills training projects for women can contribute to the prevention of early marriages. International organisations can ensure the sustainability of local initiatives by providing financial and technical support to such programmes.

Strengthening legal and institutional capacities: An effective legal framework and its implementation are crucial to combating early marriage. In countries such as Türkiye, the support of international mechanisms can ensure that local legal frameworks are strengthened, existing laws are effectively implemented and early marriage is subject to criminal penalties and even increased. In addition, the expansion of legal support and counselling services can facilitate victims' access to justice.

Building and improving international co-operation: As discussed in this chapter, international mechanisms can have a major impact on early marriage. Developing countries such as Türkiye can develop examples of good practices or transfer practices from other countries through deeper and multidimensional co-operation with international mechanisms. In furtherance, building local capacity with technical support from international NGOs and the UN can contribute to the development of sustainable solutions in the long term.

Finally, it can be emphasised that combating early marriage requires a comprehensive and multidimensional approach. The activities of NGOs at the local level can be strengthened with the support of international mechanisms and preventive strategies such as ensuring social cohesion, increasing educational opportunities and expanding financial empowerment programmes can be implemented. Such integrated approaches will be effective in minimising the problem of early marriage in Türkiye and similar developing countries.

REFERENCES

Adams, R. (2003). *Social work and empowerment*. (3rd ed.) British Association of Social Workers / Palgrave Macmillan.

Adams, R. (2017). *Empowerment, participation and social work*. Bloomsbury Publishing.

Anık, M., & Barlin, R. (2017). Türkiye'de çocuk gelinler sorunu: Balıkesir örneği. *İnsan ve Toplum Bilimleri Araştırmaları Dergisi*, 6(3), 1827-1841.

Bhagat, N. K. (2020). Socio-environmental Hurdles and Difficulties in the Seasonal Migration of Bakarwal: A Case study of Mahore Region of Reasi District of J&K. *Vidhyayana-An International Multidisciplinary Peer-Reviewed E-Journal*-ISSN 2454-8596, 5(5).

Buz, S., & Afyonoğlu, M. F. (2021). *Sivil Toplum Örgütleri ve Sosyal Hizmet*. Nobel Yayıncılık.

Çingir, Ö. F., & Erdağ, R. (2017). Türkiye'de biyopolitika ve göç: Iraklı mülteciler örneği. *Ege Academic Review*, 17(4), 517–525. DOI: 10.21121/eab.2017431300

De Haas, H., Castles, S., & Miller, M. J. (2019). *The age of migration: International population movements in the modern world* (6th ed.). Bloomsbury Publishing.

Demir, Y., Özel, C., & Sütçü, S. (2022). Erken yaşta evliliklerin bireysel ve toplumsal sonuçları. *Disiplinlerarası Çocuk Hakları Araştırmaları Dergisi*, 2(3), 49–62.

Duman, N., & Coşkun, B. N. (2019). "Çocuk yaşta evlilik" ya da "çocuk gelin" olgusuna psikososyal bir bakış. [IBAD]. *Uluslararası Bilimsel Araştırmalar Dergisi*, 4(2), 267–276. DOI: 10.21733/ibad.536029

Erbay, E. (2019). Güç ve Güçlendirme Kavramları Bağlamında Sosyal Hizmet Uygulaması. *Sosyal Politika Çalışmaları Dergisi*, 19(42), 41–64. DOI: 10.21560/spcd.vi.546674

European Institute for Gender Equality. (2024). Early marriage, https://eige.europa.eu/publications-resources/thesaurus/terms/1173?language_content_entity=en (16.03.2024)

Köseli, A., & Çelik, K. (2020). *Çocuk Yaşta, Erken ve Zorla Evliliklerin Sağlık Riskleri ve Sonuçlarına Çok Sektörlü Yaklaşım*. UNFPA, Birleşmiş Milletler Nüfus Fonu.

Law on Child Protection. (No. 5395). (2005). https://www.mevzuat.gov.tr/MevzuatMetin/1.5.5395.pdf (24.03.2024)

Law on Foreigners and International Protection-LFIP. (No. 6458) (2013). resmigazete.gov.tr/eskiler/2013/04/20130411-2.htm (20.03.2024).

Law on Protection of the Family and the Prevention of Violence against Women (No. 6284) (2012). https://www.mevzuat.gov.tr/File/GeneratePdf?mevzuatNo=17030&mevzuatTur=KurumVeKurulusYonetmeligi&mevzuatTertip=5 (24.03.2024)

Marphatia, A., Ambale, G., & Reid, A. (2017). Women's marriage age matters for public health: A review of the broader health and social implications in south Asia. *Frontiers in Public Health*, 5, 269. Advance online publication. DOI: 10.3389/fpubh.2017.00269 PMID: 29094035

McAlpine, A., Hossain, M., & Zimmerman, C. (2016). Sex trafficking and sexual exploitation in settings affected by armed conflicts in africa, asia and the middle east: Systematic review. *BMC International Health and Human Rights*, 16(1), 34. Advance online publication. DOI: 10.1186/s12914-016-0107-x PMID: 28031024

Mourtada, R., Schlecht, J., & DeJong, J. (2017). A qualitative study exploring child marriage practices among Syrian conflict-affected populations in Lebanon. *Conflict and Health*, 11(S1, Suppl 1), 27. DOI: 10.1186/s13031-017-0131-z PMID: 29167699

Muhith, A., Fardiansyah, A., Saputra, M. H., & Nurmiyati, . (2018). Analysis of causes and impacts of early marriage on madurese sumenep East Java Indonesia. *Indian Journal of Public Health Research & Development*, 9(8), 1495–1499. DOI: 10.5958/0976-5506.2018.00944.0

Neath, J., & Schriner, K. (1998). Power to people with disabilities: Empowerment issues in employment programming. *Disability & Society*, 13(2), 217–228. DOI: 10.1080/09687599826795

Öztürk, A. B., Albayrak, H., Karataş, K., & Aslan, H. (2021). Dynamics of Child Marriages among Syrian and Afghan Refugees in Turkey. *Atatürk Üniversitesi Sosyal Bilimler Enstitüsü Dergisi*, 25(1), 251–269.

Rozelle, S., Guo, L., Shen, M., Hughart, A., & Giles, J. (1999). Leaving China's farms: Survey results of new paths and remaining hurdles to rural migration. *The China Quarterly*, 158, 367–393. DOI: 10.1017/S0305741000005816

Saleheen, A. A. S., Afrin, S., Kabir, S., Habib, M. J., Zinnia, M. A., Hossain, M. I., Haq, I., & Talukder, A. (2021). Sociodemographic factors and early marriage among women in Bangladesh, Ghana and Iraq: An illustration from Multiple Indicator Cluster Survey. *Heliyon*, 7(5), e07111. DOI: 10.1016/j.heliyon.2021.e07111 PMID: 34095593

Sezgin, A. U., & Punamäki, R. L. (2020). Impacts of early marriage and adolescent pregnancy on mental and somatic health: The role of partner violence. *Archives of Women's Mental Health*, 23(2), 155–166. DOI: 10.1007/s00737-019-00960-w PMID: 30955087

Solomon, B. B. (1987). Empowerment: Social work in oppressed communities. *Journal of Social Work Practice*, 2(4), 79–91. DOI: 10.1080/02650538708414984

Thompson, N. (2006). *Power and Empowerment*. Russell House Publishing Ltd.

Turkish Penal Code. (2004). https://www.mevzuat.gov.tr/mevzuat?MevzuatNo=5237&MevzuatTur=1&MevzuatTertip=5 (23.03.2024)

Uddin, E. M. (2015). Family socio-cultural values affecting early marriage between Muslim and Santal communities in rural Bangladesh. *The International Journal of Sociology and Social Policy*, 35(3/4), 141–164. DOI: 10.1108/IJSSP-06-2014-0046

Uddin, M. E. (2017). Family demographic mechanisms linking of socioeconomic status to subjective physical health in rural Bangladesh. *Social Indicators Research*, 130(3), 1263–1279. DOI: 10.1007/s11205-015-1209-x

Uddin, M. E. (2021). Teenage marriage and high school dropout among poor girls: A narrative review for family pathways in Bangladesh. *Journal of Research in Social Sciences and Language*, 1(1), 55–76. https://www.jssal.com/index.php/jssal/article/view/15

Udgiri, R. (2017). Socio-demographic factors for early marriage and early pregnancy - A community based study. *Journal of Comprehensive Health*, 5(2), 59–66. DOI: 10.53553/JCH.v05i02.009

UNHCR. (2021). Yüksek Yarar Prosedürü Kılavuz İlkeleri: Çocuğun Yüksek Yararının Değerlendirilmesi ve Belirlenmesi. Birleşmiş Milletler Mülteciler Yüksek Komiserliği (BMMYK). https://www.unhcr.org/sites/default/files/2024-04/guidelines-on-supervised-independent-living-for-unaccompanied-children-turkish.pdf (22.03.2024)

UNICEF. (2017). *Çocuk Yaşta Evliliklerin Önlenmesi Hizmet Sağlayıcılar için Uygulama Rehberi*. UNICEF.

UNICEF. (2018). A Profile of Child Marriage in the Middle East and North Africa, UNICEF, New York. https://www.unicef.org/mena/media/2641/file/MENA-ChildMarriageReport.pdf.pdf (21.03.2024)

UNICEF. (2024). Child marriage, https://www.unicef.org/protection/child-marriage (20.03.2024)

ENDNOTES

[1] This phenomenon is also commonly referred to "child marriage". However, in this chapter, the term "early marriage" is preferred for consistency within the chapter.

[2] However, this should not be interpreted as boys do not experience this situation.

[3] Some of these NGOs have been mentioned in the previous sections.

APPENDIX 1

A case study of early marriage

Maryam (40 years old), a single parent of Syrian nationality, lost her husband during the war in Syria. Maryam migrated to Türkiye with her two children, Fatıma (16 years old) and Abdullah (9 years old). Abdullah is diagnosed with developmental delay and speech disorder. However, he did not apply for health services in Türkiye. Other family members do not have any serious health problems. Maryam does not work because she provides childcare and does not speak Turkish. Their only source of income is 2400 TL per month from ESSN assistance. It was found out that her daughter Fatıma had a religious marriage with the 30 years old son of a family they knew from Syria and was subjected to violence by her husband. It was also learnt that the children (Fatıma and Abdullah) do not continue their education. Maryam applied to the organisation for financial support and to help her daughter Fatıma.

Engagement

During the interview with Maryam, information was obtained about Fatıma's history of violence, neglect and abuse, and it was decided that she was at risk. It was determined that the family was in need of in-kind and cash assistance, social, legal, educational and health counselling services. Considering Fatıma's biopsychosocial needs, a face-to-face individual interview was planned. The mother was also informed that the organisation was under the obligation to notify/report Fatıma as a child at risk.

Assessment

A detailed interview was conducted with Fatıma in order to assess the best interests of the child and to present an appropriate case plan. During the interview, Fatıma's thoughts, wishes and feelings were tried to be learnt by taking her age and maturity level into consideration. A security risk assessment was made by obtaining information about the house she lives in, the frequency of harms, the types and main causes of the violence she was exposed to. Information was obtained about Fatıma's family, her husband, her husband's family and her relationships in her social environment. In addition to these, Fatıma's developmental and identity needs such as her physical and mental health status, educational needs were evaluated. According to the interview, Fatıma usually spends time at home during the day, she takes care of all the household chores, her husband takes care of her younger siblings and she feels tired most of the time and has trouble sleeping. Fatıma stated that she wanted to separate from her husband; however, she was afraid of harming herself and her family members and that her mother did not have the economic resources to take care of her and her siblings.

Planning

Fatıma's psychological, biological and economic problems were identified and the problems were prioritised according to their urgency. What can be done for Fatıma at the micro level, what can be done for her mother and siblings at the meso level, and what can/should be done in terms of early child marriage at the macro level were planned. First of all, due to Fatıma's safety risk, a notification was made to Konya Provincial Directorate of Family and Social Services (KPDFSS). With the KPDFSS notification, it was planned to take action in accordance with the Law on Child Protection (No. 5395) and Law on Protection of the Family and Prevention of Violence against Women (No. 6284). It is planned to contact the Social Service Centre (SSC) to follow up on the actions to be taken and prevention processes. Intervention objectives have been determined in the areas of strengthening Fatıma's social life skills, improving her Turkish language skills, benefiting from her right to education, ensuring her access to economic support, raising awareness on gender inequality and preventing gender-based violence. In addition to KPDFSS, Fatıma and her family members were targeted to access the services of Konya Provincial Directorate of Health, Provincial Directorate General of Migration Management, Provincial Directorate of National Education and Konya Metropolitan Municipality.

Implementation

In this phase, within the scope of the case management objectives, as a result of the interviews with Fatıma, the planning made with her was tried to be realised. Following the KPDFSS notification, a home investigation was organised by the SSC officials to the residence address and her mother's house. Following the interviews with Fatıma and other family members, education, counselling and health cautionary decisions were implemented for the child. Fatıma was taken to a child psychiatrist working at the State Hospital and started to receive psychological support from the clinical psychologist working at the institution. Fatıma's brother also received psychiatry/psychological support for his speech disorder. In addition, Abdullah (9 years old) was provided with a health report for developmental delay and regular health check-ups. In cooperation with Konya Directorate of National Education, Fatıma's school enrolment process was completed and she was able to continue her formal education. Konya Youth and Sports District Directorate was contacted and it was ensured that Fatıma was enrolled in sports clubs planned to be opened in the summer period. To improve the Turkish language skills of the family, their participation in Turkish speaking courses organised by the organisation was ensured. A connection was established with the Konya branch of the Turkish Employment Agency and the mother was placed in a hotel as a housekeeper. Financial and rental assistance was provided to the family until the mother found a job with the help of international funds by the organisation. Regular professional meetings were held with Fatıma by the psychologist and social worker of the organisation and counselling services were provided on the laws and her rights. Fatıma participated in activities and sessions held within the organisation to develop and strengthen her skills to cope with difficulties by improving her social, mental, emotional and physical abilities, and to adapt to daily life and increase her abilities. Also family members participated in awareness raising trainings on issues such as gender inequality and violence.

Evaluation, Termination and Follow-up

Necessary evaluations were made as a result of the implementation with Fatıma. Fatıma and her family were counselled about their rights and laws in Türkiye and regular interviews were conducted with them. Fatıma separated from her husband and started to live with her mother, a protection order was issued against her husband and it was learnt that she was not currently exposed to any threats. Fatıma reported that her mother and brother were more understanding and empathetic towards her.

Within the scope of health and counselling measures, meetings with the child psychiatry department of the state hospital and the Provincial Directorate of Family and Social Services continue. Fatıma continues to participate in activities within the organisation to improve her life skills. During the implementation process, it was also observed that she improved her Turkish language level. It was informed that her mother continues to work and they are able to meet their basic needs. It is noted that Fatıma continues formal education and her brother continues special education, and educational follow-up is also provided.

As a result of the interview with the specialist working at the SSC and following the case, it was decided to carry out a monitoring and interview process with Fatıma once every two weeks for the first six months and once a month in the following period. The family was informed that they could reach the institution at any time and the contact number of the organisation was given in case of any emergency.

Compilation of References

Abalkhail, B. A. (1995). Adolescent pregnancy: Are there biological barriers for pregnancy outcomes? *The Journal of the Egyptian Public Health Association*, 70(5-6), 609–625. PMID: 17214178

Abalos, J. B. (2014). Trends and determinants of age at union of men and women in the philippines. *Journal of Family Issues*, 35(12), 1624–1641. DOI: 10.1177/0192513X14538024

Aborisade, R. A., & Olayinka-Aliu, D. A. (2023). Marry your rapist! A phenomenological analysis of the experiences of women forced to marry their assaulters in their childhood. Https://Doi.Org/10.1177/02697580231207652. DOI: 10.1177/02697580231207652

Acharya, A. K. (2010). *The influence of female age in marriage on fertility and child loss in India*. Trayectorias.

Ackerman, X., & Abay, N. A. (2013). Improving Learning Opportunities and Outcomes for Girls in Africa. *Center for Universaal Education at Brookings, December*.

Adams, R. (2003). *Social work and empowerment*. (3rd ed.) British Association of Social Workers / Palgrave Macmillan.

Adams, R. (2017). *Empowerment, participation and social work*. Bloomsbury Publishing.

Adu, J., & Oudshoorn, A. (2020). The Deinstitutionalization of psychiatric hospitals in Ghana: An application of Bronfenbrenner's social-ecological model. *Issues in Mental Health Nursing*, 41(4), 306–314. DOI: 10.1080/01612840.2019.1666327 PMID: 31999531

Aftab, J., Abrar, A., & Maroof, L. (2023). Identity construction of Pakistani female entrepreneurs in religious framework: An interplay of sociocultural and religious factors. [JEIEE]. *Journal of Entrepreneurship and Innovation in Emerging Economies*, 9(2), 198–221. DOI: 10.1177/23939575231171003

Aggarwal, S., Francis, K. L., Dashti, G. S., & Patton, G. (2023). Child marriage and the mental health of adolescent girls: A longitudinal cohort study from Uttar Pradesh and Bihar, India. *The Lancet Regional Health. Southeast Asia*, 8, 100102. Advance online publication. DOI: 10.1016/j.lansea.2022.100102 PMID: 37384140

Aggarwal, S., Francis, K. L., Dashti, S. G., & Patton, G. (2022). Child marriage and mental health of adolescent girls: A longitudinal study from Uttar Pradesh and Bihar, India. *The Lancet Regional Health. Southeast Asia*, 16(8), 100102. DOI: 10.1016/j.lamsea.2022.100102 PMID: 37384140

Ahmed1&2, S., Khan, A. K. S., & Noushad, S. (2013). Psychological impact evaluation of early marriages. *International Journal of Endorsing Health Science Research*, 1(2), 84-86.

Ahmed1&2, S., Khan, A. K. S., & Noushad, S. (2014). Early marriage is the root of current physiological and psychosocial health burdens.

Ahmed, A. U. (1996). Socio-economic determinants of age at first marriage in Bangladesh. *Journal of Biosocial Science*, 18(1), 35–42. DOI: 10.1017/S0021932000006477 PMID: 3944149

Ahmed, A., & Hossain, S. (2017). Early marriage and intimate partner violence among adolescents in South Asia: Evidence from Bangladesh, India, and Nepal. *Journal of Interpersonal Violence*, 32(8), 1171–1196. PMID: 26021859

Ahmed, S., Khan, A., Khan, S., & Noushad, S. (2014). Early marriage: A root of current physiological and psychosocial health burdens. *International Journal of Endorsing Health Science Research*, 2(1), 50. DOI: 10.29052/IJEHSR.v2.i1.2014.50-53

Ahmed, T. (2015). Child marriage: A discussion paper. *Bangladesh Journal of Bioethics*, 6(2), 8–14. DOI: 10.3329/bioethics.v6i2.25740

Akter, A., & Ashadujjaman, M. The Impact of Child Marriage on Socioeconomic Aspects in Bangladesh.

Alam, A. Z. M. (1995). *Family values*. Bangladesh Cooperative Society Limited.

Alem, A. Z., Yeshaw, Y., Kebede, S. A., Liyew, A. M., Tesema, G. A., Agegnehu, C. D., & Teshale, A. B. (2020). Spatial distribution and determinants of early marriage among married women in ethiopia: A spatial and multilevel analysis. *BMC Women's Health*, 20(1), 207. Advance online publication. DOI: 10.1186/s12905-020-01070-x PMID: 32933491

Alfiana, R. D., Yulyani, L., Subarto, C. B., Mulyaningsih, S., & Zuliyati, I. C. (2022). The impact of early marriage on women of reasonable age in the special region of yogyakarta. *Indonesian Journal of Nursing and Midwifery*, 10(1), 89. DOI: 10.21927/jnki.2022.10(1).89-101

Alghamdi, N. A. A. (2024). Gender and intersectionality: understanding and addressing women's mental health within the cultural context of Saudi Arabia. Unpublished PhD Dissertation, Glasgow: University of Glasgow.

Ali, A. (1998). *The Santals of Bangladesh*. The Sabuge Sangah Press.

Almadani, N. A., & Alwesmi, M. B. (2023). The Relationship between Happiness and Mental Health among Saudi Women. *Brain Sciences*, 13(4), 526. DOI: 10.3390/brainsci13040526 PMID: 37190491

Alnasser, L. A., Moro, M. F., Naseem, M. T., Bilal, L., Akkad, M., Almeghim, R., Al-Habeeb, A., Al-Subaie, A. S., & Altwaijri, Y. A. (2024). Social determinants of anxiety and mood disorders in a nationally-representative sample–Results from the Saudi National Mental Health Survey (SNMHS). *The International Journal of Social Psychiatry*, 70(1), 166–181. DOI: 10.1177/00207640231197944 PMID: 37740657

Alonzo, D., & Zubaroglu-Ioannides, P. (2023). Suicide and Violence against Women in Azerbaijan: Risk Factors and Barriers for Seeking Mental Healthcare. *J Ment Health Soc Behav*, 5(1), 179.

Alsmeheen, F. A. (2023). Psychological Adjustment And Its Relationship With Some Variables Among Married Minors In The Southern Region In Jordan. *Journal of Namibian Studies: History Politics Culture*, 36, 626–643.

Altwaijri, Y., Al-Habeeb, A., Al-Subaie, A., Bruffaerts, R., Bilal, L., Hyder, S., Naseem, M. T., & Alghanim, A. J. (2023). Dual burden of chronic physical conditions and mental disorders: Findings from the Saudi National Mental Health Survey. *Frontiers in Public Health*, 11, 1238326. DOI: 10.3389/fpubh.2023.1238326 PMID: 38089017

Amadi, E. C. (2013). Socio-cultural factors on the girl-child education in secondary schools Ihiala local government area of Anambra state, Nigeria. *International Journal of Education, Learning and Development*, 1(1), 71–74.

Amato, P. R., & Kane, J. B. (2011). Life-course pathways and the psychosocial adjustment of young adult women. *Journal of Marriage and Family*, 73(1), 279–295. DOI: 10.1111/j.1741-3737.2010.00804.x PMID: 23188928

Amin, S., & Amin, S. (2018). Understanding early marriage and associated outcomes: An exploratory study in urban slums of Dhaka, Bangladesh. *Journal of Biosocial Science*, 50(5), 632–648. DOI: 10.1017/S002193201700036X

Anık, M., & Barlin, R. (2017). Türkiye'de Çocuk Gelinler Sorunu : Balıkesir Örneği. *Insan ve Topllum Bilimleri Araştırmaları Dergisi, 6*(3).

Anık, M., & Barlin, R. (2017). Türkiye'de çocuk gelinler sorunu: Balıkesir örneği. *İnsan ve Toplum Bilimleri Araştırmaları Dergisi*, 6(3), 1827-1841.

Anwaruzzaman, K. M., & Khan, S. (2017). Early marriage of girls in India: A regional perspective. In Saha, G. (Ed.), *Child marriage: The root of social maladies*. Levant Books.

Arnaldo, C. (2004). Ethnicity and marriage patterns in Mozambique. *African Population Studies*, 19(1), 143–164.

Arnett, J. J. (2019). *Adolescent psychology around the world*. Routledge.

Arnez, M., & Nisa, E. (2024). *Advocating for change: Cultural and institutional factors of sexual violence in Indonesia*. 21–44. DOI: 10.1007/978-981-99-5659-3_2

Arthur, M., & Ngugi, E. N. (2017). Legal strategies for addressing early and forced marriage in Africa. *Harvard Law Review*, 130(1), 235–278.

Ashcraft, A., & Lang, K. (2006). The consequences of teenage childbearing (Working Paper No. 12485). Cambridge, MA: National Bureau of Economic Research.

Asna-Ashary, M., Farzanegan, M. R., Feizi, M., & Gholipour, H. F. (2021). Socio-Economic Determinants of Child Marriage: Evidence from the Iranian Provinces. SSRN *Electronic Journal*. DOI: 10.2139/ssrn.3535283

Asraoui, A., Khassouani, C. E., & Soulaymani, A. (2023). Prevalence, sociodemographic and economic determinants of violence against ever-married women in Morocco. *Eastern Mediterranean Health Journal*, 29(12), 944–953. DOI: 10.26719/emhj.23.122 PMID: 38279863

Atim, G. (2017). Girls not brides: ending child marriage in Nigeria. *Journal of Gender, Information and Development in Africa (JGIDA), 6*(1-2), 73-94. https://www.proquest.com/openview/ba3526799a9961e3b8243b1200c96759/1?pq-origsite=gscholar&cbl=2044835

Atkinson, M. P., & Glass, B. L. (1985). Marital age heterogamy and homogamy, 1900 to 1980. *Journal of Marriage and Family*, 47(3), 685–691. DOI: 10.2307/352269

Auersperg, F., Vlasak, T., Ponocny, I., & Barth, A. (2019). Long-term effects of parental divorce on mental health - A meta-analysis. *Journal of Psychiatric Research*, 119, 107–115. DOI: 10.1016/j.jpsychires.2019.09.011 PMID: 31622869

Azeez, A., & Poonia, E.P., A. (2015). Determinants, attitudes, and practices on child marriage: Evidence from rural Rajasthan. *Social Work Chronicle*, 4(2), 1–15.

Aziz, K. M. A., & Maloney, C. (1985). Life stages, gender and fertility in Bangladesh. Dhaka, Bangladesh: International Centre for Diarrhoeal Disease research, Bangladesh.

Bahlbi, Y. M. (2016). Human Trafficking and Human Smuggling to and from Eastern Sudan: Intended and Unintended Consequences of States' Policies. https://core.ac.uk/download/228570950.pdf

Bajracharya, A., & Amin, S. (2012). Poverty, marriage timing, and transitions to adulthood in Nepal. *Studies in Family Planning*, 43(2), 79–92. DOI: 10.1111/j.1728-4465.2012.00307.x PMID: 23175948

Ballmer, H., & Cozby, P. C. (1981). Family environment of women who return to college. *Sex Roles*, 7(10), 1019–1026. DOI: 10.1007/BF00288502

Bancroft, J. (2002). Biological factors in human sexuality. *Journal of Sex Research*, 39(1), 15–21. DOI: 10.1080/00224490209552114 PMID: 12476251

Banda, P. (2023). Lost amidst the chaos: The impact of Covid-19 on girls' education in Malawi.

Bandura, A. (2011). The social and policy impact of social cognitive theory. In M. M. Mark, S. I. Donaldson, & B. Campbell (Eds.), *Social psychology and evaluation* (pp. 31–71). The Guilford Press.

Bandyopadhyay, P. K. (1999). *Tribal situation in Eastern India*. Subarnarekha.

Banerjee, S., & Sharma, G. (2022). The Status of Child Marriage in India: A Guide for NGOs and CSOs on Using the Law to End Child Marriages in India*. Girls Not Brides. https://www.girlsnotbrides.org/documents/1783/Child_marriage_in_India_law_guide_and_directory.pdf

Bangladesh Bureau of Statistics. (2010). *Statistical yearbook of Bangladesh*. Statistics Division, Ministry of Planning, Government of the People's Republic of Bangladesh.

Baraie, B., Rezaei, M., Nadrian, H., & Matlabi, H. (2024). What socio-cultural factors encourage child marriage in Sanandaj, Iran? A qualitative study. *Child and Youth Services*, 45(1), 23–44. DOI: 10.1080/0145935X.2023.2167708

Barbieri, M., & Hertrich, V. (2005). Age difference between spouses and contraceptive practice in sub-Saharan Africa. *Population*, 60(5), 617–654. DOI: 10.3917/pope.505.0617

Barnet, B., Arroyo, C., Devoe, M., & Duggan, A. K. (2004). Reduced school dropout rates among adolescent mothers receiving school-based prenatal care. *Archives of Pediatrics & Adolescent Medicine*, 158(3), 262–268. DOI: 10.1001/archpedi.158.3.262 PMID: 14993086

Basch, C. E. (2011). Teen pregnancy and the achievement gap among urban minority youth. *The Journal of School Health*, 81(10), 614–618. DOI: 10.1111/j.1746-1561.2011.00635.x PMID: 21923873

Basch, C. E. (2011). Teenage pregnancy and the health of urban young women. *Journal of Urban Health*, 88(1), 61–73.

Bay, L. (1999). Twists, turns and returns: Returning adult students. *Teaching English in the Two-Year College*, 26(3), 305–312. DOI: 10.58680/tetyc19991834

Becker, G. S. (1973). A theory of marriage: Part 1. *Journal of Political Economy*, 81(4), 813–846. DOI: 10.1086/260084

Becker, G. S. (1981). *A treatise on the family*. University of Chicago Press.

Becker, G. S. (2009). *Human capital: A theoretical and empirical analysis, with special reference to education*. University of Chicago press.

Bem, S. L. (1993). *The lenses of gender: Transforming the debate on sexual inequality*. Yale university Press.

Berardo, F. M., Appel, J., & Berardo, D. H. (1993). Age dissimilar marriages: Review and assessment. *Journal of Aging Studies*, 7(1), 93–106. DOI: 10.1016/0890-4065(93)90026-G

Berglas, N., Brindis, C., & Cohen, J. (2003). *Adolescent pregnancy and childbearing in California. The Prepared at the Request of Senator Dede Alpert with Funding Provided by The David and Lucile Packard Foundation*. California Research Bureau.

Berg, M. J., Kremelberg, D., Dwivedi, P., Verma, S., Schensul, J. J., Gupta, K., Chandran, D., & Singh, S. K. (2010). The effects of husband's alcohol consumption on married women in three low-income areas of greater Mumbai. *AIDS and Behavior*, 14(S1), 126–135. DOI: 10.1007/s10461-010-9735-7 PMID: 20544380

Berthoud, R. (2000). Family Formation in Multi-Cultural Britain: Three Patterns of Diversity. The paper presented to the conference on Social Change and Minority Ethnic Groups organized by the Centre for Research on Elections and Social Trends (CREST). Retrieved from www.iser.essex.ac.uk

Bezie, M., & Addisu, D. (2019). Determinants of early marriage among married women in Injibara town, northwest Ethiopia: Community-based cross-sectional study. *BMC Women's Health*, 19(1), 134. Advance online publication. DOI: 10.1186/s12905-019-0832-0 PMID: 31703577

Bhabha, J., & Kelly, O. (2013). Child marriage and the right to education: evidence from India. Evidence submitted to the Office of High Commission of Human Rights. University of Harvard, 72-80. https://www.ohchr.org/sites/default/files/Documents/Issues/Women/WRGS/ForcedMarriage/NGO/HavardUniversityFXB3.pdf

Bhagat, N. K. (2020). Socio-environmental Hurdles and Difficulties in the Seasonal Migration of Bakarwal: A Case study of Mahore Region of Reasi District of J&K. *Vidhyayana-An International Multidisciplinary Peer-Reviewed E-Journal*-ISSN 2454-8596, 5(5).

Bhan, N., Gautsch, L., McDougal, L., Lapsansky, C., Obregon, R., & Raj, A. (2019). Effects of Parent–Child Relationships on Child Marriage of Girls in Ethiopia, India, Peru, and Vietnam: Evidence From a Prospective Cohort. *The Journal of Adolescent Health*, 65(4), 498–506. Advance online publication. DOI: 10.1016/j.jadohealth.2019.05.002 PMID: 31279722

Bharat, S. (1996). *Family measurement in India*. Sage Publications Pvt Ltd.

Bhat, A., Sen, A., & Pradhan, U. (2005). *Child marriages and the law in India*. Human Rights Law Network.

Bhutta, Z. A., Das, J. K., Bahl, R., Lawn, J. E., Salam, R. A., Paul, V. K., & Walker, N. (2014). Can available interventions end preventable deaths in mothers, newborn babies, and stillbirths, and at what cost? *Lancet*, 384(9940), 347–370. DOI: 10.1016/S0140-6736(14)60792-3 PMID: 24853604

Blood, R., & Wolfe, D. (1960). *Husbands and wives: The dynamics of married living*. Free Press.

Blossfeld, H. P. (1995). Changes in the process of family formation and women's growing economic independence: a comparison of nine countries. In H. P. Blossfeld, (ed.), *The new role of women: family formation in modern societies* (pp. 3-32). Colorado, US: Boulder.

Blumberg, R. L., & Coleman, T. M. (1989). A theoretical look at the gender balance of power in the American couple. *Jornal Dos Farmacêuticos*, 10(10), 225–250. DOI: 10.1177/019251389010002005 PMID: 12342284

Boran, P., & Gökçay, G., Deveciİoğlu, E., & Eren, T. (2013). Çocuk gelinler Child brides. *Marmara Medical Journal*, •••, 26.

Bourdieu, P., & Passeron, J. (1990). *Reproduction in education, society and culture.* SAGE Publications.

Boveda, M., Reyes, G., & Aronson, B. (2023). Disciplined to access the general education curriculum: Girls of color, disabilities, and specialized education programming. In *Disability as Meta Curriculum* (pp. 49–69). Routledge. DOI: 10.4324/9781003252313-4

Boyce, S., Brouwer, K., Triplett, D., Servin, A., Magis-Rodríguez, C., & Silverman, J. (2018). Childhood Experiences of Sexual Violence, Pregnancy, and Marriage Associated With Child Sex Trafficking Among Female Sex Workers in Two US-Mexico Border Cities. *American Journal of Public Health*, 108(8), 1049–1054. DOI: 10.2105/AJPH.2018.304455 PMID: 29927652

Bozorgi-Saran, S., & Koolaee, A. (2022). Child bride, a story that never ends: A look at experiences of Iranian women. *International Social Work*, 66(5), 1497–1512. DOI: 10.1177/00208728211066830

Bramhankar, M., Kundu, S., Pandey, M., Mishra, N. L., & Adarsh, A. (2023). An assessment of self-rated life satisfaction and its correlates with physical, mental and social health status among older adults in India. *Scientific Reports*, 13(1), 9117. DOI: 10.1038/s41598-023-36041-3 PMID: 37277415

Brislin, R. W. (1980). Translation and content analysis of oral and written materials. In H. C. Triandis and J. W. Berry (Eds.), *Handbook of cross-cultural psychology, methodology* (pp. 408-410) (Vol.2). Boston: Allyn and Bacon, Inc.

Bronfenbrenner, U. (1995). *Developmental ecology through space and time: A future perspective.*

Bronfenbrenner, U., & Ceci, S. J. (1994). Nature-nurture reconceptualized: A bio-ecological model. *Psychological Review*, 10(4), 568–586. DOI: 10.1037/0033-295X.101.4.568 PMID: 7984707

Bronfenbrenner, U., & Evans, G. W. (2000). Developmental science in the 21st century: Emerging questions, theoretical models, research designs and empirical findings. *Social Development*, 9(1), 115–125. DOI: 10.1111/1467-9507.00114

Brosh, J., Weigel, D., & Evans, W. (2007). Pregnant and parenting adolescents' perception of sources and supports in relation to educational goals. *Child & Adolescent Social Work Journal*, 24(6), 565–578. DOI: 10.1007/s10560-007-0107-8

Brownia, F., & Habibb, S. (2023). The Effectiveness of Community Mobilization Intervention in Creating Awareness Regarding Early Marriage among Adolescents in Bangladesh: The Case of Shornokishoree Network. *Journal of Social Behavior and Community Health*. https://doi.org/.DOI: 10.18502/jsbch.v7i1.12796

Burgess, R. A., Jeffery, M., Odero, S. A., Rose-Clarke, K., & Devakumar, D. (2022). Overlooked and unaddressed: A narrative review of mental health consequences of child marriages. *PLOS Global Public Health*, 2(1), 1–21. DOI: 10.1371/journal.pgph.0000131 PMID: 36962120

Buss, D. M. (1989). Sex differences in mate preferences: Evolutionary hypotheses tested in 37 cultures. *Behavioral and Brain Sciences*, 12(1), 1–49. DOI: 10.1017/S0140525X00023992

Buz, S., & Afyonoğlu, M. F. (2021). *Sivil Toplum Örgütleri ve Sosyal Hizmet*. Nobel Yayıncılık.

Bytheway, W. R. (1981). The variation with age of age differences in marriage. *Journal of Marriage and Family*, 43(4), 923–927. DOI: 10.2307/351348

Cairns, R., & Cairns, B. (1994). *Lifelines & risks: Pathways of youth in our time*. Cambridge University Press.

Caldwell, J. C., Reddy, P. H., & Caldwell, P. (1983). The causes of marriage change in South India. *Population Studies*, 37(3), 343–361. DOI: 10.1080/00324728.1983.10408866

Cameron, L., Contreras Suarez, D., & Wieczkiewicz, S. (2023). Child marriage: Using the Indonesian family life survey to examine the lives of women and men who married at an early age. *Review of Economics of the Household*, 21(3), 725–756. DOI: 10.1007/s11150-022-09616-8

Campbell, G., Roberts, K., & Sarkaria, N. (2020). Child and Early Forced Marriage., 79-89. https://doi.org/.DOI: 10.1057/978-1-137-53312-8_5

Campbell, J. C. (2002). Health consequences of intimate partner violence. *Lancet*, 359(9314), 1331–1336. DOI: 10.1016/S0140-6736(02)08336-8 PMID: 11965295

Capper, D. (2022). Glossary of Terms and Concepts. In *Roaming Free Like a Deer*. DOI: 10.7591/cornell/9781501759574.002.0007

Card, J. J., & Wise, L. L. (1978). Teenage mothers and teenage fathers: The impact of early childbearing on the parents' personal and professional lives. *Family Planning Perspectives*, 17(5), 234–237. DOI: 10.2307/2134267 PMID: 567590

Carlson, D. (2012). Deviations from desired age at marriage: Mental health differences across marital status. *Journal of Marriage and Family*, 74(4), 743–758. DOI: 10.1111/j.1741-3737.2012.00995.x

Carr, D. (Ed.). (2009). Encyclopedia of the life course and human development: Vol. 1. *Childhood & adolescence*. Macmillan Reference USA.

Carr, D., & Sheridan, J. (2001). Family turning-points and career transitions at midlife. In Marshall, V. W., Heinz, W. R., Kruger, H., & Verma, A. (Eds.), *Restructuring work and the life course* (pp. 201–227). University of Toronto Press. DOI: 10.3138/9781442679290-014

Casterline, J. B., Williams, L., & McDonald, P. (1986). The age difference between spouses: Variations among developing countries. *Population Studies*, 40(3), 353–374. DOI: 10.1080/0032472031000142296

Castill, C. (2018). Political role models and child marriage in India. *Review of Development Economics*, 22(4), 1409–1431. DOI: 10.1111/rode.12513

Chandra-Mouli, V., Camacho, A. V., & Michaud, P. A. (2013). WHO guidelines on preventing early pregnancy and poor reproductive outcomes among adolescents in developing countries. In *Journal of Adolescent Health* (Vol. 52, Issue 5). DOI: 10.1016/j.jadohealth.2013.03.002

Chantler, K. (2023). Forced Marriage. In *Gender-Based Violence: A Comprehensive Guide*. DOI: 10.1007/978-3-031-05640-6_5

Charles, V. E., Polis, C. B., Sridhara, S. K., & Blum, R. W. (2008). Abortion and long-term mental health outcomes: A systematic review of the evidence. *Contraception*, 78(6), 436–450. DOI: 10.1016/j.contraception.2008.07.005 PMID: 19014789

Chatterjee, K. (2015). What could work to prevent child marriages and delay pregnancy during adolescence in India: A systematic review of evidence from low and middle income countries? *European Academic Research*, 8(2), 1458–1490.

Chaudhury, R. H., & Banik, R. B. (2021). Socio-economic consequences of child marriage: A study of the Namasudra community of West Bengal. *Child and Youth Services*, 42(2), 127–150. DOI: 10.1080/0145935X.2021.1892552

Chelliah, K. (2019). Understanding early marriage: Perspectives and experiences from Tamil Nadu. *Gender, Technology and Development*, 23(3), 258–278. DOI: 10.1080/09718524.2019.1690249

Chen, Y.-H., & Chen, H. (2014). Continuity and changes in the timing and formation of first marriage among postwar birth cohorts in Taiwan. *Journal of Family Issues*, 35(12), 1584–1604. DOI: 10.1177/0192513X14538026

Child Rights You. (2020). Status and Decadal Trends of Child Marriage in India. New Delhi: Child Rights and You. https://www.cry.org/downloads/safety-and-protection/Status-of-Child-Marriage-In-The-Last-Decade.pdf

Choudhary, S. (2021). Social work intervention and child development in India. [TOJQI]. *Turkish Online Journal of Qualitative Inquiry*, 12(10), 5295–5306.

Chowdhury, F. D. (2004). The socio-cultural context of child marriage in a Bangladeshi village. *International Journal of Social Welfare*, 13(4), 244–253. DOI: 10.1111/j.1369-6866.2004.00318.x

Çingir, Ö. F., & Erdağ, R. (2017). Türkiye'de biyopolitika ve göç: Iraklı mülteciler örneği. *Ege Academic Review*, 17(4), 517–525. DOI: 10.21121/eab.2017431300

Clark, C. J., Everson-Rose, S. A., & Suglia, S. F. (2014). Binge drinking and violence against intimate partners in the Americas. *Revista Panamericana de Salud Pública*, 35(5/6), 333–339.

Clark, C., Jashinsky, K., Renz, E., Bergenfeld, I., Durr, R., Cheong, Y., Kalra, S., Laterra, A., & Yount, K. (2023). Qualitative endline results of the tipping point project to prevent child, early and forced marriage in Nepal. *Global Public Health: An International Journal for Research, Policy and Practice*, 18(1), 2287606. Advance online publication. DOI: 10.1080/17441692.2023.2287606 PMID: 38054604

Clarke-Stewart, K., Vandell, D., Mccartney, K., Owen, M., & Booth, C. (2000). Effects of parental separation and divorce on very young children. *Journal of Family Psychology: JFP: Journal of the Division of Family Psychology of the American Psychological Association*, 14(2), 304–326. DOI: 10.1037/0893-3200.14.2.304 PMID: 10870296

Coker, A. L., Davis, K. E., Arias, I., Desai, S., Sanderson, M., Brandt, H. M., & Smith, P. H. (2002). Physical and mental health effects of intimate partner violence for men and women. *American Journal of Preventive Medicine*, 23(4), 260–268. DOI: 10.1016/S0749-3797(02)00514-7 PMID: 12406480

Collin, M., & Talbot, T. (2023). Are age-of-marriage laws enforced? Evidence from developing countries. *Journal of Development Economics*, 160, 102950. DOI: 10.1016/j.jdeveco.2022.102950

Convington, R., Peters, H. E., Sabia, J. J., & Price, J. P. (2011). Teen fatherhood and educational attainment: Evidence from three cohorts of youth (Working Paper, October, 2011).

Corno, L., & Voena, A. (2023). Child marriage as informal insurance: Empirical evidence and policy simulations. *Journal of Development Economics*, 162, 103047. DOI: 10.1016/j.jdeveco.2023.103047

Craig, G. J. (1996). *Human development*. Prentice Hall Inc.

Crenshaw, K. (1991). Mapping the margins: Intersectionality, identity politics, and violence against women of color. *Stanford Law Review*, 43(6), 1241–1299. DOI: 10.2307/1229039

Crenshaw, K. (2019). 'Difference' through intersectionality 1. In *Dalit Feminist Theory* (pp. 139–149). Routledge India. DOI: 10.4324/9780429298110-15

Crissey, S. R. (2005). Race/ethnic differences in the marital expectations of adolescents: The role of romantic relationships. *Journal of Marriage and Family*, 67(3), 697–709. DOI: 10.1111/j.1741-3737.2005.00163.x

Crocker, M., & Baur, A. (2022). Connecting loose ends: Integrating science into psychoanalytic theory. *Clinical Social Work Journal*, 50(4), 347–357. DOI: 10.1007/s10615-020-00774-9

Crockett, L. J., & Bingham, C. R. (2000). Antecedents and outcomes of abusive romantic relationships: The role of childhood maltreatment. *Journal of Family Violence*, 15(1), 75–88.

Crootof, R. (2019). The internet of torts: Expanding civil liability standards to address corporate remote interference. *Duke Law Journal*, 69, 583.

Dahiya, P. (2019). The child marriage: A curse in India. *JETIR*, 6(6), 441–449.

Dahl, G. B. (2010). Early teen marriage and future poverty. *Demography*, 47(3), 689–718. DOI: 10.1353/dem.0.0120 PMID: 20879684

Dangal, G. (2008). Teenage pregnancy: Complexities and challenges. *Middle East*, 56, 1000.

Danquah, F. (2023). *Child Marriage in Ghana: Assessing the Legal Implementation of Child Rights Standards* (Doctoral dissertation, University of Manitoba).

Datta, B., Pandey, A., & Tiwari, A. (2022). Child marriage and problems accessing healthcare in adulthood: Evidence from India. *Health Care*, 10(10), 1994. DOI: 10.3390/healthcare10101994 PMID: 36292439

Datta, B., & Tiwari, A. (2022). Early marriage in adolescence and risk of high blood pressure and high blood glucose in adulthood: Evidence from India. *Women*, 2(3), 189–203. DOI: 10.3390/women2030020

Datta, B., Tiwari, A., & Glenn, L. (2022). Stolen childhood taking a toll at young adulthood: The higher risk of high blood pressure and high blood glucose comorbidity among child brides. *PLOS Global Public Health*, 2(6), e0000638. DOI: 10.1371/journal.pgph.0000638 PMID: 36962354

Davis, K., & Blake, J. (1956). Social structure and fertility: An analytic framework. *Economic Development and Cultural Change*, 4(2), 221–235. DOI: 10.1086/449714

De Haas, H., Castles, S., & Miller, M. J. (2019). *The age of migration: International population movements in the modern world* (6th ed.). Bloomsbury Publishing.

de Silva, W. I. (1993). Family formation: Socio Cultural Differentials in Age at First Marriage in Sri Lanka.

Delprato, M., & Akyeampong, K. (2017). The effect of early marriage timing on women's and children's health in sub-Saharan Africa and Southwest Asia. *Annals of Global Health*, 83(3-4), 557–567. DOI: 10.1016/j.aogh.2017.10.005 PMID: 29221529

Demir, Y., Özel, C., & Sütçü, S. (2022). Erken yaşta evliliklerin bireysel ve toplumsal sonuçları. *Disiplinlerarası Çocuk Hakları Araştırmaları Dergisi*, 2(3), 49–62.

Denner, J., & Kirby, D. (2019). Covert use of violence in dating relationships: Development of the coercive control scale. *Aggressive Behavior*, 45(2), 139–154. PMID: 30516286

Desai, M., Goel, S., Desai, M., & Goel, S. (2018). Child Rights to Prevention of Child Marriage. *Child Rights Education for Inclusion and Protection: Primary Prevention*, 299-322.

Diabelková, J., Rimárová, K., Dorko, E., Urdzík, P., Houžvičková, A., & Argalášová, Ľ. (2023). Adolescent Pregnancy Outcomes and Risk Factors. *International Journal of Environmental Research and Public Health*, 20(5), 4113. Advance online publication. DOI: 10.3390/ijerph20054113 PMID: 36901128

Dixon, R. (1971). Explaining cross-cultural variations in age at marriage and proportions never marrying. *Population Studies*, 32(2), 215–234. DOI: 10.1080/00324728.1971.10405799 PMID: 22070108

Dommaraju, P. (2023). Age-gap between spouses in South and Southeast Asia. *Journal of Family Issues*, 45(5), 1242–1260. DOI: 10.1177/0192513X231155662

Duman, N., & Coşkun, B. N. (2019). "Çocuk yaşta evlilik" ya da "çocuk gelin" olgusuna psikososyal bir bakış. [IBAD]. *Uluslararası Bilimsel Araştırmalar Dergisi*, 4(2), 267–276. DOI: 10.21733/ibad.536029

Duvall, E. M. (1988). Family development's first forty years. *Family Relations*, 37(2), 127–134. DOI: 10.2307/584309

Dyer, E. D. (1983). *Courtship, marriage, & family: American style*. The Dorsey Press.

Ea, E., Umaru, R. J., No, I., Ia, O., Eo, O., & Zoakah, A. I. (2016). Determinants and effect of girl child marriage: A cross-sectional study of school girls in Plateau State, Nigeria. *International Journal of Medicine*, 5(3), 122–128.

Eboka, T. (2023). Child marriage: The resilience of the Nigerian woman. *Gendered Perspectives of Restorative Justice, Violence and Resilience: An International Framework*, 107–120. https://doi.org/DOI: 10.1108/978-1-80382-383-620231007/FULL/XML

Efevbera, Y., & Bhabha, J. (2020). Defining and deconstructing girl child marriage and applications to global public health. *BMC Public Health*, 20(1), 1547. DOI: 10.1186/s12889-020-09545-0 PMID: 33054856

Ekstrom, R., Goertz, M., Pollack, J., & Rock, D. (1986). Who drops out of high school and why? Findings from a national longitudinal study. *Teachers College Record*, 87(3), 356–373. DOI: 10.1177/016146818608700308

Elengemoke, J., & Susuman, A. (2020). Early marriage and correlates among young women in sub-Saharan African countries. *Journal of Asian and African Studies*, 56(6), 1345–1368. DOI: 10.1177/0021909620966778

Elfenbein, D. S., & Felice, M. E. (2003). Adolescent pregnancy. *Pediatric Clinics*, 50(4), 781–800. PMID: 12964694

El-Kady, R. (2024). The Complex Landscape of Human Trafficking: A Comprehensive Exploration with Emphasis on Legal Safeguards for Victims in Egyptian and Arab Legislation. In Borges, G., Guerreiro, A., & Pina, M. (Eds.), *Modern Insights and Strategies in Victimology* (pp. 118–140). IGI Global., DOI: 10.4018/979-8-3693-2201-7.ch006

El-Kady, R. M. (2022). The crime of human trafficking in Egyptian legislation in light of the opinions of jurisprudence and jurisprudence. *National Criminal Review*, 65(2), 93–148.

Ellsberg, M., Jansen, H. A., Heise, L., Watts, C. H., & Garcia-Moreno, C. (2008). Intimate partner violence and women's physical and mental health in the WHO multi-country study on women's health and domestic violence: An observational study. *Lancet*, 371(9619), 1165–1172. DOI: 10.1016/S0140-6736(08)60522-X PMID: 18395577

Elnakib, S., Elsallab, M., Wanis, M. A., Elshiwy, S., Krishnapalan, N. P., & Naja, N. A. (2022). Understanding the impacts of child marriage on the health and well-being of adolescent girls and young women residing in urban areas in Egypt. *Reproductive Health*, 19(8), 8. Advance online publication. DOI: 10.1186/s12978-021-01315-4 PMID: 35033114

Eloundou-Enyegue, P. M. (2004). Pregnancy-related dropouts and gender inequality in education: A life table approach and application to Cameroon. *Demography*, 41(3), 509–528. DOI: 10.1353/dem.2004.0021 PMID: 15461012

Eloundou-Enyegue, P. M., & Strokes, C. S. (2004). Teen pregnancy and gender inequality in education: A contextual hypothesis. *Demographic Research*, 11, 305–322. DOI: 10.4054/DemRes.2004.11.11

Ember, C. R., & Ember, M. (1981). *Anthropology*. Prentice-Hall, Inc.

Emirie, G. (2005). Early marriage and its effects on girls' education rural Ethiopia: The case of Mecha Woreda in West Gojjam, North-Western Ethiopia. Ph. D Dissertation, Georg-August University of Goettingen, Goettingen, Ethiopia.

EP. A. A., & Poonia, A. (2015). Determinants, attitudes and practices on child marriage: Evidences from rural Rajasthan. *Social Work Chronicle, 4*(1). https://www.proquest.com/docview/1738729327?pq-origsite=gscholar&fromopenview=true&sourcetype=Scholarly%20Journals

Er, C., Wodon, Q., Petroni, S., Malé, C., Onagoruwa, A., Savadogo, A., Edmeades, J., Kes, A., John, N., Yarrow, E., Apland, K., Anderson, K., Hamilton, C., Darroch, J.,, W., Bankole, A., Ls, A., Myers, J., & Gt, L. (2015). Thematic report: Unrecognised sexual abuse and exploitation of children in child early and forced marriage... https://doi.org/.DOI: 10.1163/2210-7975_HRD-9926-2015003

Erbay, E. (2019). Güç ve Güçlendirme Kavramları Bağlamında Sosyal Hizmet Uygulaması. *Sosyal Politika Çalışmaları Dergisi*, 19(42), 41–64. DOI: 10.21560/spcd.vi.546674

Erickson, P. J., Cermak, A., Michaels, C., Blake, L., Lynn, A., Greylord, T., & Benning, S. (2024). Mental health and well-being ecological model. Center for Leadership Education in Maternal & Child Public Health, University of Minnesota–Twin Cities. https://mch.umn.edu/resources/mhecomodel

Ernawati, H., Mas'udah, A., Setiawan, F., & Isroin, L. (2023). Health, psychology, economic resilience, and wellbeing: Long-term effects on family welfare of an early marriage. *F1000Research*. https://doi.org/DOI: 10.12688/f1000research.128719.1

Ertürk, Y. (2005). Research on violence against women and girls: How are we doing and where do we go from here? *Gender and Development*, 13(1), 11–17.

Erulkar, A., & Matheka, J. (2007). *Adolescence in the Kibera slums of Nairobi Kenya*. Population Council.

European Institute for Gender Equality. (2024). Early marriage, https://eige.europa.eu/publications-resources/thesaurus/terms/1173?language_content_entity=en (16.03.2024)

Evans, I., & DiBenedetto, A. (1990). Pathways to school dropout: A conceptual model for early prevention. *Special Services in the Schools*, 6(1-2), 63–80. DOI: 10.1300/J008v06n01_04

Evendia, M., & Firmansyah, A. A. (2023). KENVORM legal protection for prevention of child marriage in a decentralization. *Progressive Law Review*, 5(02), 141–155.

zimova, S., & Universiteti, A. (2021). Psychosocial consequences of early marriages. *Sprachwissenschaft*, 15(3), 83–86. DOI: 10.36719/2663-4619/64/83-86

Falb, K., Annan, J., Kpebo, D., Cole, H., Willie, T., Xuan, Z., Raj, A., & Gupta, J. (2015). Differential Impacts of an Intimate Partner Violence Prevention Program Based on Child Marriage Status in Rural Côte d'Ivoire.. *The Journal of adolescent health: official publication of the Society for Adolescent Medicine*, 57 5, 553-8. https://doi.org/.DOI: 10.1016/j.jadohealth.2015.08.001

Fan, S., & Koski, A. (2022). The health consequences of child marriage: A systematic review of the evidence. *BMC Public Health*, 22(1), 309. DOI: 10.1186/s12889-022-12707-x PMID: 35164724

Fatmawati, F., Yantina, Y., & Susilawati, S. (2023). Factors causing early marriage from sociocultural view in the working area of ketapang health center of south sungkai regency, north Lampung district in 2023. *MAHESA: Malahayati Health Student Journal*, 3(12), 3953–3971. DOI: 10.33024/mahesa.v3i12.11891

Fawcett, J. T. (1974). Psychological determinants of nuptiality. *International Population Conference*, Liege, 1973, vol. 2 (Liege, International Union for the Scientific Study of Population) pp.19-30.

Fernandes, M. (2023). Child marriage in India: A sociological review. *Integrated Journal for Research in Arts and Humanities*, 3(5), 171–176. DOI: 10.55544/ijrah.3.5.15

Feyissa, G., Tolu, L., Soboka, M., & Ezeh, A. (2023). Effectiveness of interventions to reduce child marriage and teen pregnancy in sub-Saharan Africa: A systematic review of quantitative evidence. *Frontiers in Reproductive Health*, 5, 1105390. Advance online publication. DOI: 10.3389/frph.2023.1105390 PMID: 37064827

Finn, J. (1989). Withdrawing from school. *Review of Educational Research*, 59(2), 117–142. DOI: 10.3102/00346543059002117

Fitzgerald, S. T., & Glass, J. (2008). Can early family formation explain the lower educational attainment of U. S. conservative Protestants? *Sociological Spectrum*, 28(5), 556–577. DOI: 10.1080/02732170802206203

Fleming, P. J., McCleary-Sills, J., Morton, M., Levtov, R., Heilman, B., & Barker, G. (2015). Risk factors for men's lifetime perpetration of physical violence against intimate partners: Results from the International Men and Gender Equality Survey (IMAGES) in eight countries. *PLoS One*, 10(3), e0118639. DOI: 10.1371/journal.pone.0118639 PMID: 25734544

Fletcher, J. M., & Wolfe, B. L. (2012). The effects of teenage fatherhood on young adult outcomes. *Economic Inquiry*, 50(1), 182–201. DOI: 10.1111/j.1465-7295.2011.00372.x PMID: 22329053

Flood, M., & Pease, B. (2009). Factors influencing attitudes to violence against women. *Trauma, Violence & Abuse*, 10(2), 125–142. DOI: 10.1177/1524838009334131 PMID: 19383630

Folkman, S., & Lazarus, R. S. (2013). Stress and coping theory applied to the investigation of mass industrial psychogenic illness. In *Mass psychogenic illness* (pp. 237–255). Routledge.

Gastón, C. M., Misunas, C., & Cappa, C. (2019). Child marriage among boys: A global overview of available data. *Vulnerable Children and Youth Studies*, 14(3), 219–228. DOI: 10.1080/17450128.2019.1566584

Gausman, J., Kim, R., Kumar, A., Ravi, S., & Subramanian, S. V. (2024). Prevalence of girl and boy child marriage across states and Union Territories in India, 1993–2021: A repeated cross-sectional study. *The Lancet. Global Health*, 12(2), e271–e281. DOI: 10.1016/S2214-109X(23)00470-9 PMID: 38109909

Gautam, A., & Shekhar, R. (2018). Child marriage in India: A spatio-temporal Analysis. *Śodha Pravāha,* 8(2), 224-230.

George, J. S. (2011). Preventing violence against women: Societal norms and women's economic empowerment. *American Journal of Economics and Sociology*, 70(2), 446–471.

Ghosh, B. (2011). Child marriage, society, and the law: A study in a rural context in West Bengal, India. *International Journal of Law, Policy and the Family*, 25(2), 199–219. DOI: 10.1093/lawfam/ebr002

Ghosh, B., & Kar, A. M. (2010). Child marriage in rural West Bengal: Status and challenges. *Indian Journal of Development Research and Social Action*, 6(1-2), 1–23. https://www.researchgate.net/profile/Biswajit-Ghosh-3/publication/235624523_Child_marriage_in_Rural_West_Bengal_Status_and_Challenges%27/links/00b7d51be61ac1ef82000000/Child-marriage-in-Rural-West-Bengal-Status-and-Challenges.pdf

Gilbert, L. A., Manning, L., & Ponder, M. (1980). Conflicts with the student role: A comparison of female and male reentry students. *Journal of the National Association for Women Deans, Administrators & Counselors*, 44(1), 26–32.

Girls Not Brides. (2019). Mental health consequences of child marriages. Retrieved from https://www.girlsnotbrides.org

Glass, J., & Jacobs, J. (2005). Childhood religious conservatism and adult attainment among black and white women. *Social Forces*, 94(1), 555–579. DOI: 10.1353/sof.2005.0098

Glick, J. E., Ruf, S. D., White, M. J., & Goldscheider, F. (2006). Educational engagement and early family formation: Differences by ethnicity and generation. *Social Forces*, 84(3), 1391–1415. DOI: 10.1353/sof.2006.0049

Glick, P. C. (1947). The family cycle. *American Sociological Review*, 12(2), 164–174. DOI: 10.2307/2086982

Glick, P. C. (1955). The cycle of the family. *Marriage and Family Living*, 17(1), 3–9. DOI: 10.2307/346771

Godha, D., Gage, A. J., Hotchkiss, D. R., & Cappa, C. (2016). Predicting maternal health care use by age at marriage in multiple countries. *The Journal of Adolescent Health*, 58(5), 504–511. DOI: 10.1016/j.jadohealth.2016.01.001 PMID: 26984836

Godha, D., Hotchkiss, D. R., & Gage, A. J. (2013). Association between child marriage and reproductive health outcomes and service utilization: A multi-country study from South Asia. *The Journal of Adolescent Health*, 52(5), 552–558. DOI: 10.1016/j.jadohealth.2013.01.021 PMID: 23608719

Gök, M. (2016). Child marriages in Turkey with different aspects. *International Journal of Human Sciences*, 13(1), 2222. DOI: 10.14687/ijhs.v13i1.3795

Goldscheider, F., Turcotte, P., & Kopp, A. (2000). Determinants of women's first union formation in the United States, Canada, and Sweden. Paper to be presented at the 2000 Flagship Conference of the Family and Fertility Surveys Project, Brussels, May 29-31, 2000.

Goli, S. (2016). Eliminating child marriages in India: Progress and prospects. https://api.research-repository.uwa.edu.au/ws/portalfiles/portal/58285434/EliminatingChildMarriageReport_e_Book.pdf

Goode, W. J. (1983). *World revolution and family patterns* (2nd ed.). Free Press.

Gopal, M. (2021). Early and child marriage in India: A framework to achieve SDGs. In *Encyclopedia of the UN sustainable development goals* (pp. 183–191). DOI: 10.1007/978-3-319-95687-9_109

Gorard, S., Rees, G., Fevre, R., & Welland, T. (2001). Learning trajectories: Some voices of those in transit"? *International Journal of Lifelong Education*, 20, 167–187.

Green, D. P., Groves, D. W., Manda, C., Montano, B., & Rahmani, B. (2022). A radio drama's effects on attitudes toward early and forced marriage: Results from a field experiment in rural Tanzania. *Comparative Political Studies*, 56(8), 1115–1155. DOI: 10.1177/00104140221139385

Greene, M., Siddiqi, M., & Abularrage, T. (2023). Systematic scoping review of interventions to prevent and respond to child marriage across Africa: Progress, gaps and priorities. *BMJ Open*, 13(5), e061315. Advance online publication. DOI: 10.1136/bmjopen-2022-061315 PMID: 37130688

Grijns, M., & Horii, H. (2018). Child Marriage in a Village in West Java (Indonesia): Compromises between Legal Obligations and Religious Concerns. *Asian Journal of Law and Society*, 5(2), 453–466. Advance online publication. DOI: 10.1017/als.2018.9

Hadi, A. (2016). Social perspectives on the relationship between early marriage, fertility and infertility in Tambour town, Central Sudan. *International Journal of Sociology and Anthropology*, 8(4), 27–35. DOI: 10.5897/IJSA2016.0655

Hajihasani, M., & Sim, T. (2018). Marital satisfaction among girls with early marriage in Iran: Emotional intelligence and religious orientation. *International Journal of Adolescence and Youth*, 24(3), 297–306. DOI: 10.1080/02673843.2018.1528167

Hajnal, J. (1965). European marriage patterns in perspective. In Glass, D. V., & Everley, D. E. C. (Eds.), *Population in history. Essays in historical demography* (pp. 101–143). Edward Arnold.

Hajnal, J. (1982). Two kinds of preindustrial household formation system. *Population and Development Review*, 8(3), 449–494. DOI: 10.2307/1972376

Hallett, T., Lewis, J., Lopman, B., Nyamukapa, C., Mushati, P., Wambe, M., Garnett, G., & Gregson, S. (2007). Age at first sex and HIV infection in rural Zimbabwe. *Studies in Family Planning*, 38(1), 1–10. DOI: 10.1111/j.1728-4465.2007.00111.x PMID: 17385378

Hamby, S., & Grych, J. H. (2013). *The web of violence: Exploring connections among different forms of interpersonal violence and abuse.* Springer Science & Business Media. DOI: 10.1007/978-94-007-5596-3

Handayani, P. W., Moeis, F. R., & Ayuningtyas, D. (2021). Comparing Indonesian men's health-seeking behavior and likelihood to suffer from illness across sociodemographic factors. *The Journal of Men's Health*. Advance online publication. DOI: 10.31083/jomh.2021.078

Harden, A., Brunton, G., Fletcher, A., & Oakley, A. (2009). Teenage pregnancy and social disadvantage: Systematic review integrating controlled trials and qualitative studies. *BMJ (Clinical Research Ed.)*, 339(nov12 1), b4254. DOI: 10.1136/bmj.b4254 PMID: 19910400

Harpending, H. (1992). Age differences between mates in Southern African pastoralists. *Behavioral and Brain Sciences*, 15(1), 102–103. DOI: 10.1017/S0140525X00067716

Hartarto, R. B., & Wibowo, W. T. (2023). Conditional cash transfer and early marriage: A case study of Mataram City, West Nusa Tenggara. *International Journal of Development Issues*, 22(1), 57–71. DOI: 10.1108/IJDI-08-2022-0171

Hashemi, K. (2017). Religious legal traditions, Muslim states and the convention on the rights of the child: An essay on the relevant UN documentation. *International Law and Islamic Law*, 535–568. https://doi.org/DOI: 10.4324/9781315092515-24/RELIGIOUS-LEGAL-TRADITIONS-MUSLIM-STATES-CONVENTION-RIGHTS-CHILD-ESSAY-RELEVANT-UN-DOCUMENTATION-KAMRAN-HASHEMI

Hassan, S., & Nader, R. (2021). Socio-economic implications of early marriage in low-income countries. *Journal of Global Health*, 11(2), 345–359. DOI: 10.7189/jogh.11.02001

Hayes, B., & Protas, M. (2021). Child Marriage and Intimate Partner Violence: An Examination of Individual, Community, and National Factors. *Journal of Interpersonal Violence*, 37(21-22), NP19664–NP19687. DOI: 10.1177/08862605211042602 PMID: 34476987

Heaton, T. B. (1996). Socio-economic and familial status of women associated with age at first marriage in three Islamic societies. *Journal of Comparative Family Studies*, 27(1).

Hegazy, M., & Elsadek, A. (2019). Early marriage and associated health consequences among female children in giza governorate. *Egyptian Journal of Health Care*, 10(1), 420–435. DOI: 10.21608/ejhc.2019.213861

Henrion, R. (2003). Mutilations génitales féminines, mariages forcés et grossesses précoces. *Bulletin de l'Académie Nationale de Médecine*, 187(6), 1051–1066. DOI: 10.1016/S0001-4079(19)33937-8 PMID: 14978867

Hertler, S. C., Figueredo, A. J., Peñaherrera-Aguirre, M., Fernandes, H. B., Woodley of Menie, M. A., Hertler, S. C., ... & Woodley of Menie, M. A. (2018). Urie Bronfenbrenner: Toward an evolutionary ecological systems theory. *Life history evolution: A biological Meta-theory for the social sciences*, 323-339.

Hertrich, V. (2002). Nuptiality and gender relationships in Africa: an overview of first marriage trends over the past 50 years, session on family change in Africa and Latin America. Population Association of America Annual Meeting, Atlanta, 9-11 May.

Hirschman, C., & Rindfuss, R. (1982). The sequence and timing of family formation events in Asia. *American Sociological Review*, 47(5), 660–680. DOI: 10.2307/2095165

Hofferth, S. L., & Moore, K. A. (1979). Early childbearing and later economic well-being. *American Sociological Review*, 44(5), 784–815. DOI: 10.2307/2094528 PMID: 533035

Hoffman, S. D. (2006). *By the numbers: The public costs of adolescent childbearing*. National Campaign to Reduce Teen Pregnancy.

Hoffman, S. D., & Maynard, R. A. (2008). *Kids Having Kids: Economic Costs and Social Consequences of Teen Pregnancy*. Urban Institute Press.

Hofmann, V., & Müller, C. M. (2018). Avoiding antisocial behavior among adolescents: The positive influence of classmates' prosocial behavior. *Journal of Adolescence*, 68(1), 136–145. https://doi.org/https://doi.org/10.1016/j.adolescence.2018.07.013. DOI: 10.1016/j.adolescence.2018.07.013 PMID: 30077085

Holcamp, G. (2009). Researching the girls' dropout rate in Malawi. Why girls dropout of primary schools and in what way this rate can be reduced. Master Thesis Special Education.

Home, A. M. (1998). Predicting role conflict, overload and contagion in adult women university students with family and jobs. *Adult Education Quarterly*, 48(2), 85–97. DOI: 10.1177/074171369804800204

Hossain, A., & Uddin, E. M. (2023). Physical school environment and infectious diseases: A case of primary school context in Bangladesh. In Azeez, P. A., Nikhil Raj, P. P., & Mohanraj, R. (Eds.), *Ecological and evolutionary perspectives on infections and morbidity* (pp. 126–151). IGI Global. DOI: 10.4018/978-1-7998-9414-8.ch006

Hossain, M. G., Mahumud, R. A., & Saw, A. (2016). Prevalence of child marriage among Bangladeshi women and trend of change over time. *Journal of Biosocial Science*, 48(4), 530–538. Advance online publication. DOI: 10.1017/S0021932015000279 PMID: 26286142

Human Rights Watch. (2013). Child marriage: Legal reform needed to protect rights. https://www.hrw.org/news/2013/06/14/child-marriage-legal-reform-needed-protect-rights

Human Rights Watch. (2014). When I grow up, I'll be forced to marry: Child and forced marriage in South Sudan. https://www.hrw.org/report/2014/02/20/when-i-grow-ill-be-forced-marry/child-and-forced-marriage-south-sudan

Human Rights Watch. (2015). Bangladesh: End child marriage. https://www.hrw.org/news/2015/06/08/bangladesh-end-child-marriage

Hynek, K., Abebe, D., Liefbroer, A., Hauge, L., & Straiton, M. (2022). The association between early marriage and mental disorder among young migrant and non-migrant women: A norwegian register-based study. *BMC Women's Health*, 22(1), 258. Advance online publication. DOI: 10.1186/s12905-022-01836-5 PMID: 35761261

ICDDRB. (2007). *Health and demographic surveillance system- Matlab* (Vol. 39). International Centre for Diarrheal Disease Research, Bangladesh.

ICDDRB. (2007a). *Health and Demographic Surveillance System- Matlab* (Vol. 39). International Centre for Diarrhoeal Disease Research, Bangladesh.

ICDDRB. (2007b). Consequences of early marriage on female schooling in rural Bangladesh. *Health Science Bulletin*, 5(4), 13–18.

ICRW (International Center for Research on Women). (2019). *Accelerating action to end child marriage: Insights from the Frontline*. ICRW.

IIPS and ICF. (2022). *India National Family Health Survey NFHS-5 (2019-21)*. Mumbai, India: IIPS and ICF. Retrieved from https://www.dhsprogram.com/pubs/pdf/FR375/FR375.pdf

International Center for Research on Women. (2005). *Too Young To Wed: Education & Action Toward Ending Child Marriage*. The International Center for Research on Women.

International Center for Research on Women. (2014). Too young to wed: The lives, rights, and health of young married girls. https://www.icrw.org/wp-content/uploads/2016/10/Too-Young-to-Wed-Full-Report.pdf

International Labour Organization. (1999). Worst forms of child labour convention, 1999 (No. 182). https://www.ilo.org/dyn/normlex/en/f?p=NORMLEXPUB:12100:0:NO:P12100_ILO_CODE:C182

International Women's Rights Action Watch Asia Pacific. (2013). Child marriage and the law: Legislative reform initiative paper. https://www.iwraw-ap.org/wp-content/uploads/2013/10/IWRAWAP-MY-CM-Legislative-Reform-Initiative-Book.pdf

Irani, M., & Roudsari, R. (2019). Reproductive and Sexual Health Consequences of Child Marriage: A Review of literature. *Journal of Midwifery & Reproductive Health*, 7, 1584–1590. DOI: 10.22038/JMRH.2018.31627.1342

Irani, M., & Roudsari, R. L. (2019). Reproductive and sexual health consequences of child marriage: A review of literature. *Journal of Midwifery & Reproductive Health*, 7(1), 1584–1590. DOI: 10.22038/jmrh.2018.31627.1342

Islam, A. (2016). Prevalence and Determinants of Contraceptive use among Employed and Unemployed Women in Bangladesh. [IJMA]. *International Journal of MCH and AIDS*, 5(2). Advance online publication. DOI: 10.21106/ijma.83 PMID: 28058196

Islam, M. N., & Ahmed, A. U. (1998). Age at first marriage and its determinants in Bangladesh. *Asia-Pacific Population Journal*, 13(2), 73–92. DOI: 10.18356/f31b417e-en PMID: 12321742

Itebiye, B. (2016). Forced and early marriages: Moral failures vs religious nuances. *European Scientific Journal*, 12(17), 305. DOI: 10.19044/esj.2016.v12n17p305

Iustitiani, N., & Ajisuksmo, C. (2018). Supporting factors and consequences of child marriage. *Anima Indonesian Psychological Journal*, 33(2), 100–111. DOI: 10.24123/aipj.v33i2.1581

Jain, S., Gupta, P., & Bhatt, S. (2017). Early marriage and HIV/AIDS: Risk factors among young women aged 15–24 years in India. *Journal of Family Medicine and Primary Care*, 6(4), 703–709. DOI: 10.4103/jfmpc.jfmpc_121_16

Java, W., Yayan, I., Univeristas, S., Negeri, I., Hidayatullah, S., Zezen, J., & Muttaqin, Z. (2023). Child exploitation by parents in early marriage: Case study in Cianjur West Java, Indonesia. *Samarah: Jurnal Hukum Keluarga Dan Hukum Islam*, 7(3), 1921–1942. DOI: 10.22373/sjhk.v7i3.14804

Jensen, R., & Thornton, R. (2003). Early female marriage in the developing world. In Oxfam, G. B. (Ed.), *In gender, development and Marriage, Caroline Sweetman*. DOI: 10.1080/741954311

Jin, X., Li, S., & Feldman, M. W. (2005). Marriage form and age at first marriage: A comparative study in three counties in contemporary rural China. *Social Biology*, 52(1-2), 18–46.

John, N. A., Kapungu, C., Sebany, M., & Tadesse, S. (2023). Do gender-based pathways influence mental health? Examining the linkages between early child marriage, intimate partner violence, and psychological well-being among young Ethiopian women (18–24 years Old). *Youth & Society*, 55(6), 1155–1172. DOI: 10.1177/0044118X221079375

John, N., Edmeades, J., & Murithi, L. (2019). Child marriage and psychological well-being in Niger and Ethiopia. *BMC Public Health*, 19(1), 1029. Advance online publication. DOI: 10.1186/s12889-019-7314-z PMID: 31370825

Johnson, M. P. (1995). Patriarchal terrorism and common couple violence: Two forms of violence against women. *Journal of Marriage and Family*, 57(2), 283–294. DOI: 10.2307/353683

Johnson, M. P. (2008). *A typology of domestic violence: Intimate terrorism, violent resistance, and situational couple violence*. Northeastern University Press.

Jumarim, J. (2024). The practice of adoption in the Sasak community and Its implications for marriage law in Indonesia. *Samarah: Jurnal Hukum Keluarga Dan Hukum Islam*, 8(1), 445–467. DOI: 10.22373/sjhk.v8i1.18581

Kabeer, N. (2020). Empowering women or pleasing parents? The tension between women's rights and cultural values in the transition to adulthood in Pakistan. *Gender & Society*, 34(1), 74–98. DOI: 10.1177/0891243219899717

Kahraman, A. B., & Şenateş, T. (2020). Çocuk gelinler (Siverek örneği). *Journal of Social Sciences*, 29(29), 380–392.

Kakar, S. (2020). Child/forced/servile marriages ⇄ Human trafficking. *The Palgrave international handbook of human trafficking*, 503–519.

Kalamar, A. M., Lee-Rife, S., & Hindin, M. J. (2016). Interventions to prevent child marriage among people in low- and middle-income countries: A systematic review of the published and gray literature. *The Journal of Adolescent Health*, 59(3), 16–21. DOI: 10.1016/j.jadohealth.2016.06.015 PMID: 27562449

Kalmuss, D., & Namerow, P. (1994). Subsequent childbearing among teenage mothers: The determinants of a closely spaced second birth. *Family Planning Perspectives*, 26(4), 149–153. DOI: 10.2307/2136238 PMID: 7957815

Kamal, S. M. M., Hassan, C. H., Alam, G. M., Ying, Y., Sakib, N., & Bhuiya, A. (2015). Child marriage in Bangladesh: Trends and determinants. *Journal of Biosocial Science*, 47(1), 120–139. DOI: 10.1017/S0021932013000746 PMID: 24480489

Kanji, S., Carmichael, F., Darco, C., Egyei, R., & Vasilakos, N. (2024). The impact of early marriage on the life satisfaction, education and subjective health of young women in India: A longitudinal analysis. *The Journal of Development Studies*, 60(5), 705–723. DOI: 10.1080/00220388.2023.2284678

Kaplan, V. (2023). Mental health states of housewives: An evaluation in terms of self-perception and codependency. *International Journal of Mental Health and Addiction*, 21(1), 666–683. DOI: 10.1007/s11469-022-00910-1 PMID: 36091486

Kapur, R. (2019). Understanding the societal problem of child marriage. Downloaded from https://researchgate.net.≥civil law < marriage

Kara, B. (2015). Değişen Aile Dinamikleri Açisindan Erken Yaşta Evlilikler Sorunu ve Toplumsal Önemi. *Süleyman Demirel Üniversitesi İktisadi ve İdari Bilimler Fakültesi Dergisi*, 20(2), 59–72.

Kartika, N. Y., Efendi, M., Normelani, E., Heru, H., & Sopyan, S. (2021). The influence of education, welfare and residential area on adolescent marriages. *Journal of Anthropologic: Isu-Isu Sosial Budaya*, 23(1), 18. DOI: 10.25077/jantro.v23.n1.p18-26.2021

Kasturirangan, A., Krishnan, S., & Riger, S. (2004). The impact of culture and minority status on women's experience of domestic violence. *Trauma, Violence & Abuse*, 5(4), 318–332. DOI: 10.1177/1524838004269487 PMID: 15361586

Kayes, S. (1995). Cultural change of Santal community of Rajshahi district: An anthropological study. M. Phil Dissertation, The Institute of Bangladesh Studies, Rajshahi: University of Rajshahi, Unpublished.

Kelly, C. A., Chalasani, S., Mensch, B. S., & Soler-Hampejsek, E. (2014). Adolescent pregnancy and education trajectories in Malawi. Paper presented at 2013 27th IUSSP International Population Conference. Busan, Republic of Korea, 28 August.

Kelly, L. (1988). *Surviving sexual violence*. Polity Press.

Kemkes-Grottenthaler, A. (2004). For better or worse, till death do us part: Spousal age gap and differential longevity- evidence from historical demography. *Collegium Antropologicum*, 28, 203–219. PMID: 15571094

Kiernan, K. (1986). Teenage marriage and marital breakdown: A longitudinal study. *Population Studies*, 40(1), 35–54. DOI: 10.1080/0032472031000141826

Kıran, E. (2017). Toplumsal cinsiyet rolleri bağlamında türkiye'de çocuk gelinler. Balkan Sosyal Bilimler Dergisi, (ICOMEP 2017 Özel Sayısı), 1-8.

Kishore, P. (2023). Child marriages: A curse for humanity. Downloaded from http://www.brighterkashmir.com › child-marriages-a-cur... Kumar, S. (2023). Exploring the socioeconomic factors behind girl-child marriage in India. *Indian Journal of Health, Sexuality, and Culture*, 9(1), 142-151.

Klepinger, D., Lundberg, S., & Plotnick, R. (1999). How does adolescent fertility affect the human capital and wages of young women. *The Journal of Human Resources*, 34(3), 421–448. DOI: 10.2307/146375

Klinger-Vartabedian, L., & Wispe, L. (1989). Age differences in marriage and female longevity. *Journal of Marriage and Family*, 51(1), 195–202. DOI: 10.2307/352380

Klugman, J., Hanmer, L., Twigg, S., Hasan, T., McCleary-Sills, J., & Santamaria, J. (2014). Voice and Agency: Empowering Women and Girls for Shared Prosperity. In *Voice and Agency: Empowering Women and Girls for Shared Prosperity*. DOI: 10.1596/978-1-4648-0359-8

Ko, C. F., Heer, D. M., & Wu, H. Y. (1985). Social and biological determinants of age at first marriage in Taiwan, 1970. *Social Biology*, 32(1-2), 115–128. PMID: 4081802

Koenig, M. A., Lutalo, T., Zhao, F., Nalugoda, F., Wabwire-Mangen, F., Kiwanuka, N., & Gray, R. (2003). Coercive sex in rural Uganda: Prevalence and associated risk factors. *Social Science & Medicine*, 57(4), 783–797. PMID: 14672593

Kok, M. (2021). Adolescent pregnancy and health outcomes: A global perspective. *International Journal of Women's Health*, 13, 111–124. DOI: 10.2147/IJWH.S296773

Kok, M. C., Kakal, T., Kassegne, A. B., Hidayana, I. M., Munthali, A., Menon, J. A., Pires, P., Gitau, T., & van der Kwaak, A. (2023). Drivers of child marriage in specific settings of Ethiopia, Indonesia, Kenya, Malawi, Mozambique and Zambia – findings from the Yes I Do! baseline study. *BMC Public Health*, 23(1), 1–16. DOI: 10.1186/s12889-023-15697-6 PMID: 36624437

Komter, A. (1989). Hidden power in marriage. *Gender & Society*, 3(2), 187–216. DOI: 10.1177/089124389003002003

Köseli, A., & Çelik, K. (2020). *Çocuk Yaşta, Erken ve Zorla Evliliklerin Sağlık Riskleri ve Sonuçlarına Çok Sektörlü Yaklaşım*. UNFPA, Birleşmiş Milletler Nüfus Fonu.

Kruger, D. I., Berthelon, M., & Navia, R. (2009). Adolescent motherhood and secondary schooling in Chile. Institute for the Study of Labor (IZA) Discussion Paper No. 4552. Bonn, Germany: November.

Kuhn, A., & Wolter, S. C. (2023). The strength of gender norms and gender-stereotypical occupational aspirations among adolescents. *Kyklos*, 76(1), 101–124. DOI: 10.1111/kykl.12320

Kumar, A. (2011). Mental health services in rural India: Challenges and prospects. *Health (Irvine, Calif.)*, 3(12), 757–761. https://papers.ssrn.com/sol3/papers.cfm?abstract_id=1978314. DOI: 10.4236/health.2011.312126

Kumari, N., & Shekhar, C. (2023). Trend and determinants of early marriage in Rajasthan: Evidence from the national family health survey. *Children and Youth Services Review*, 145, 106746. DOI: 10.1016/j.childyouth.2022.106746

Kumar, V. (2022). The socio-cultural changes in Indian society: A sociological perspective. In Thanavathi, C., & Ramya, S. (Eds.), *Women education in India* (pp. 18–26). Island Publishers.

Kusumadewi, H., & Wiswayana, W. M. (2024). Enforcing preventions of child marriage cases in ASEAN member states Within the framework of Sustainable Development Goals. *PROIROFONIC, 1*(1), 407–419. https://proirofonic.upnjatim.ac.id/index.php/proirofonic/article/view/46

Kusumayati, A. (2018). Child marriage in Indonesia: Analysis of data from Indonesia Demographic and Health Surveys 2002, 2007 and 2012. *Jurnal Studi Pemuda, 7*(2), 171–185.

Kuswanto, H., Oktaviana, P. P., Efendi, F., Nelwati, N., & Malini, H. (2024). Prevalence of and factors associated with female child marriage in Indonesia. *PLoS One, 19*(7), e0305821. DOI: 10.1371/journal.pone.0305821 PMID: 38968277

Lal, B. S. (2015). Child marriage in India: Factors and problems. [IJSR]. *International Journal of Scientific Research, 4*(4), 2993–2998.

Lamb, S., Markussen, E., Teese, R., Sandberg, N., & Polesel, J. (Eds.). (2011). *School dropout and completion: International comparative studies in theory and practice.* Springer Publishing Company. DOI: 10.1007/978-90-481-9763-7

Lapa, T. Y., Kozhukhar, N. G., & Kozhukhar, T. V. (2019). Gender-based violence in the family: Theoretical and practical aspects. *Pravo.Zhurnal Vysshei Shkoly Ekonomiki, 2*, 114–135.

Law on Child Protection. (No. 5395). (2005). https://www.mevzuat.gov.tr/MevzuatMetin/1.5.5395.pdf (24.03.2024)

Law on Foreigners and International Protection-LFIP. (No. 6458) (2013). resmigazete.gov.tr/eskiler/2013/04/20130411-2.htm (20.03.2024).

Law on Protection of the Family and the Prevention of Violence against Women (No. 6284) (2012). https://www.mevzuat.gov.tr/File/GeneratePdf?mevzuatNo=17030&mevzuatTur=KurumVeKurulusYonetmeligi&mevzuatTertip=5 (24.03.2024)

Lazarus, R. S., & Folkman, S. (1984). *Stress, appraisal, and coping.* Springer Publishing company.

Lebni, J. Y., Solhi, M., Azar, F. E. F., Farahani, F. K., & Irandoost, S. F. (2023). Exploring the consequences of early marriage: A conventional content analysis. *Inquiry: The Journal of Health Care Organization, Provision, and Financing, 60*, 1–14.

Lee, D. (2010). The early socioeconomic effects of teenage childbearing: A propensity score matching approach. *Demographic Research, 23*, 697–736. DOI: 10.4054/DemRes.2010.23.25

Lee, H. Y. (1971). A study of changing family values in a Korean middle-town. *International Population Conference*, London, 1969, vol.1, pp. 467-468.

Lee, H. Y. (1982). Age at first marriage in Peninsular Malaysia. *Journal of Marriage and Family*, 44(3), 785–798. DOI: 10.2307/351600

Lee-Rife, S. M. (2010). Women's empowerment and reproductive experiences over the lifecourse. *Social Science & Medicine*, 71(3), 634–642. DOI: 10.1016/j.socscimed.2010.04.019 PMID: 20621752

Lee-Rife, S., Malhotra, A., Warner, A., & Glinski, A. M. (2012). What works to prevent child marriage: A review of the evidence. *Studies in Family Planning*, 43(4), 287–303. DOI: 10.1111/j.1728-4465.2012.00327.x PMID: 23239248

Lekanova, E. E. (2020). Legal Regulation of the Minimum Marriage Age: The Past and the Present. *Actual Problems of Russian Law*, 15(8), 84–95. Advance online publication. DOI: 10.17803/1994-1471.2020.117.8.084-095

Levine, D. L., & Painter, G. (2003). The schooling costs of teenage out-of-wedlock childbearing: Analysis with a within-school propensity score-matching estimator. *The Review of Economics and Statistics*, 85(4), 884–900. DOI: 10.1162/003465303772815790

Lewis, J. (Ed.). (1996). Social age for marriage, context: Southeast Asians and other newcomers in California's classrooms, 16(122), 12-23.

Liang, W., & Chikritzhs, T. (2011). Brief report: Marital status and alcohol consumption behaviours. *Journal of Substance Use*, 17(1), 84–90. DOI: 10.3109/14659891.2010.538463

Lim, S., & Raymo, J. M. (2016). Marriage and women's health in Japan. *Journal of Marriage and Family*, 78(3), 780–796. DOI: 10.1111/jomf.12298 PMID: 30774150

LIoyd. C. (2005). Growing up global: The changing traditions to adulthood in developing countries. Panel on transitions to adulthood in developing countries. Committee on Population, National Research Council and Institute of Medicine. Washington, D. C.: The National Academic Press.

Lioyd, C. B., & Mensch, B. S. (2008). Marriage and childbirth as factors in dropping out from school: An analysis of DHS data from sub-Saharan Africa. *Population Studies*, 62(1), 1–13. DOI: 10.1080/00324720701810840 PMID: 18278669

Livesey, L. (2017). *A literature review on early marriage*. University of Gloucestershire. Downloaded from https://eprints.glos.ac.uk › Research › Research Repository

Lloyd, C. B., & Mensch, B. S. (2006). *Marriage and childbirth as factors in school exit: An analysis of DHS data from sub-Saharan Africa* (Population council Working Paper No.219). New York: Population Council.

Lloyd, K. M. (2006). Latinas' transition to first marriage: An examination of four theoretical perspectives. *Journal of Marriage and Family*, 68(4), 993–1014. DOI: 10.1111/j.1741-3737.2006.00309.x

Loaiza, E., & Wong, S. (2012). Marrying too young: End child marriage. *UNFPA Journal*, 3(5), 1–55.

Lobenstine, D. (Ed.). (2015). *Early and Child Marriage in India: A Landscape Analysis*. Nirantar Trust.

Lofstedt, P., Ghilagaber, G., Shusheng, L., & Johansson, A. (2005). Changes in marriage age and first birth interval in Huaning County, Yunnan Province, PR China. *The Southeast Asian Journal of Tropical Medicine and Public Health*, 36(5), 1329–1338. PMID: 16438167

Loomis, C. P. (1936). The study of the life cycle of families. *Rural Sociology*, 1, 180–199.

Lowe, G., Hughes, D., & Witt, D. (1989). Changes in the influence of early marriage on the educational attainment of men and women. *Sociological Spectrum*, 9(2), 163–173. DOI: 10.1080/02732173.1989.9981881

Luke, N. (2005). Confronting the 'Sugar Daddy' stereotype: Age and economic asymmetries and risky sexual behavior in urban Kenya. *International Family Planning Perspectives, 31* (1), 6–14. doi:. JSTOR 3649496. PMID 15888404.DOI: 10.1363/3100605

Lundgren, R., & Amin, A. (2015). Addressing intimate partner violence and sexual violence among adolescents: emerging evidence of effectiveness.. *The Journal of adolescent health: official publication of the Society for Adolescent Medicine*, 56 1 Suppl, S42-50 . https://doi.org/.DOI: 10.1016/j.jadohealth.2014.08.012

Lutz, C., Berges, M., Hafemann, J., & Sticha, C. (2018). In Pozdniakov, S. N., & Dagienė, V. (Eds.), *Piaget's cognitive development in bebras tasks - A descriptive analysis by age groups BT - Informatics in schools. Fundamentals of Computer Science and Software Engineering* (pp. 259–270). Springer International Publishing.

Mady, C. (2023). Women's rights campaigns in Lebanon: A Bakhtinian-Foucauldian approach to voice and visibility. *Feminist Media Studies*, 23(7), 3324–3336. DOI: 10.1080/14680777.2022.2108877

Mahato, S. K. (2016). Causes and consequences of child marriage: A perspective. *International Journal of Scientific and Engineering Research*, 7(7), 697–702. DOI: 10.14299/ijser.2016.07.002

Mahmuddin, M., Mansari, M., & Melayu, H. A. (2023). Community's role in preventing child marriage: An analysis of models and community compliance with village policies. *Gender Equality: International Journal of Child and Gender Studies*, 9(2), 235–244. DOI: 10.22373/equality.v9i2.19673

Maitra, P. (2004). Effects of socioeconomic characteristics on age at marriage and total fertility in Nepal. *Journal of Health, Population and Nutrition*, 22(1), 84–96. PMID: 15190816

Major, B., Appelbaum, M., Beckman, L., Dutton, M. A., Russo, N. F., & West, C. (2009). Abortion and mental health: Evaluating the evidence. *The American Psychologist*, 64(9), 863–890. DOI: 10.1037/a0017497 PMID: 19968372

Males, M. A. (2010). *Teenage sex and pregnancy: Modern myths, unsexy realities.* Bloomsbury Publishing USA. DOI: 10.5040/9798216023890

Malhotra, A., & Elnakib, S. (2021). 20 Years of the Evidence Base on What Works to Prevent Child Marriage: A Systematic Review.. *The Journal of adolescent health: official publication of the Society for Adolescent Medicine.* https://doi.org/.DOI: 10.1016/j.jadohealth.2020.11.017

Malhotra, A. (1997). Gender and the timing of marriage: Rural-urban differences in Java. *Journal of Marriage and Family*, 59(2), 434–450. DOI: 10.2307/353481

Malhotra, A., & Tsui, A. O. (1996). Marriage timing in Sri Lanka: The role of modern norms and ideas. *Journal of Marriage and Family*, 58(2), 476–490. DOI: 10.2307/353511

Malhotra, A., Warner, A., McGonagle, A., & Lee-Rife, S. (2011). *Solutions to end child marriage: What the evidence shows.* International Center for Research on Women.

Malhotra, A., Warner, A., Mcgonagle, A., & Lee-Rife, S. (2011). *WHAT THE EVIDENCE SHOWS Solutions to End Child Marriage Solutions to End Child Marriage.* International Center for Research on Women.

Malmberg, L.-E., & Sumra, S. (2001). Socio-cultural factors and Tanzanian primary school students' achievements and school experience. [New Series]. *Utafiti*, 4(Special Issue), 207–219.

Maloney, C. T., Aziz, K. M. A., & Sarker, P. C. (1981). *Beliefs and fertility in Bangladesh*. International Centre for Diarrhoeal Disease Research, Bangladesh.

Manandhar, N., & Joshi, S. (2020). Health co-morbidities and early marriage in women of a rural area of nepal: A descriptive cross-sectional study. *JNMA; Journal of the Nepal Medical Association*, 58(230). Advance online publication. DOI: 10.31729/jnma.5205 PMID: 34504369

Mandal, M., & Hindin, M. J. (2013). From child marriage to marital rape: The Indian context. *Violence Against Women*, 19(9), 1315–1328.

Manlove, J. (1998). The influence of high school dropout and school disengagement on the risk of school-age pregnancy. *Journal of Research on Adolescence*, 8(2), 187–220. DOI: 10.1207/s15327795jra0802_2 PMID: 12294323

Manlove, J., Terry-Humen, E., Ikramullah, E., & Moore, K. A. (2006). The role of parent religiosity in teens' transitions to sex and contraception. *The Journal of Adolescent Health*, 39(4), 578–587. DOI: 10.1016/j.jadohealth.2006.03.008 PMID: 16982394

Mansory, A. (2007). *Dropout study in basic education level of schools in Afghanistan*. Swedish Committee for Afghanistan.

Maree, J. G. (2021). The psychosocial development theory of Erik Erikson: Critical overview. *Early Child Development and Care*, 191(7–8), 1107–1121. DOI: 10.1080/03004430.2020.1845163

Marini, M. M. (1984). Age and sequencing norms in the transition to adulthood. *Social Forces*, 63(1), 229–244. DOI: 10.2307/2578867

Marphatia, A. A., Ambale, G. S., & Reid, A. M. (2017). Women's marriage age matters for public health: A review of the broader health and social implications in South Asia. *frontiers in Public Health, 5*:269. DOI: 10.3389/fpubh.2017.00269

Marphatia, A. A., Ambale, G. S., & Reid, A. M. (2016). Women's marriage age matters for public health: A review of the broader health and social implications in South Asia. *Frontiers in Public Health*, 4, 1–10. DOI: 10.3389/fpubh.2016.00070 PMID: 29094035

Mas'udah, S. (2021). Power relations of husbands and wives experiencing domestic violence in dual-career families in Indonesia. *Milennial Asia*, 14(1), 5–27. DOI: 10.1177/09763996211039730

Mashreque, M. S. (1984). The traditional village family in Bangladesh: An anthropological survey. *The Journal of BARD. Comilla*, 13(1/2), 44–72.

Matras, J. (1965). The social strategy of family formation: Some variations in time and space. *Demography*, 2(1), 349–362. DOI: 10.2307/2060123

Maynard, E. M., & Pearsall, S. J. (1994). What about male mature students? A comparison of the experiences of men and women students. *Journal of Access Studies*, 9, 229–240.

Maynard, R. A. (1996). *Kids having kids: Economic costs and social consequences on teen pregnancy*. National Campaign to Reduce Teen Pregnancy.

Mayor, S. (2004). Pregnancy and childbirth are leading causes of death in teenage girls in developing countries. *BMJ (Clinical Research Ed.)*, 328(7449), 328. DOI: 10.1136/bmj.328.7449.1152-a PMID: 15142897

Mazurana, D., & Marshak, A. (2019). Addressing data gaps on child, early, and forced marriage in humanitarian settings. *Save the Children, White Paper and Discussion Draft December*.

Mbamba, C. R., Yeboaa, P. A., Gyimah, C., & Mccarthy, M. (2023). When child marriage and child welfare intersect: Understanding the barriers to education. *Children & Society*, 37(3), 966–978. DOI: 10.1111/chso.12640

McAlpine, A., Hossain, M., & Zimmerman, C. (2016). Sex trafficking and sexual exploitation in settings affected by armed conflicts in africa, asia and the middle east: Systematic review. *BMC International Health and Human Rights*, 16(1), 34. Advance online publication. DOI: 10.1186/s12914-016-0107-x PMID: 28031024

McDougall, J., Toliver, S., & Najmabadi, A. (2016). *Ending child marriage in the Americas: A review of legislative initiatives*. UNICEF.

McKenzie, L. (2021). Age-dissimilar couple relationships: 25 years in review. *Journal of Family Theory & Review*, 13(4), 496–514. DOI: 10.1111/jftr.12427

McLeod, S. (2011). *Albert Bandura's social learning theory*. Simply Psychology.

McNiss, C., Kalarchian, M., & Laurent, J. (2021). Factors associated with childhood sexual abuse and adolescent pregnancy. *Child Abuse & Neglect*, 120, 105183. Advance online publication. DOI: 10.1016/j.chiabu.2021.105183 PMID: 34245975

Melhado, L. (2008). Teenage parents' educational attainment is affected more by available resources than by parenthood. *Perspectives on Sexual and Reproductive Health*, 39, 184–185.

Mensah, E. O. (2023). Husband is a priority: Gender roles, patriarchy and the naming of female children in Nigeria. *Gender Issues*, 40(1), 44–64. DOI: 10.1007/s12147-022-09303-z

Mensch, B. (1986). Age differences between spouses in first marriage. *Social Biology*, 33, 229–240. PMID: 3563546

Meyer, S. (2016). *Domestic violence and vulnerabilities: Intersecting inequalities*. Routledge.

Michael, R. T., & Tuma, N. B. (1985). Entry into marriage and parenthood by young men and women: The influence of family background. *Demography*, 22(4), 515–544. DOI: 10.2307/2061586 PMID: 4076482

Michel, M., & Tener, D. (2023). "The problem is that a kibbutz is standing in front of you and you have no name or face for it": Child sexual abuse risk factors and disclosure in the collective kibbutz community. *Children and Youth Services Review*, 148, 106918. DOI: 10.1016/j.childyouth.2023.106918

Miller, E., & Roca, M. (2022). The intersection of early marriage and health: A review of current research. *Health Policy and Planning*, 37(4), 529–540. DOI: 10.1093/heapol/czac021

Mitra, S. N., Ali, M. N., Islam, S., Cross, A. R., & Saha, T. (1994). *Bangladesh demographic and health survey 1993–1994*. Mitra and Associates.

Mohney, C., & Anderson, W. (1988). The effect of life events and relationships on adult women's decisions to enroll in college. *Journal of Counseling and Development*, 66(6), 271–274. DOI: 10.1002/j.1556-6676.1988.tb00866.x

Molla, R. R., Rahman, M. S., Khan, M. M. R., Islam, M. M., Rahman, M. A., Billah, S. M., & Alam, M. M. (2018). Trends, prevalence and determinants of early marriage in Bangladesh: An overview. *Sexual & Reproductive Healthcare: Official Journal of the Swedish Association of Midwives*, 16, 91–99. DOI: 10.1016/j.srhc.2018.02.006

Mondain, N., Legrand, T., & Sabourin, P. (2007). Changing patterns in men's first marriage among Sereer in rural Senegal. [September.]. *Journal of Comparative Family Studies*, 38(2), 22. DOI: 10.3138/jcfs.38.4.627

Moore, K. A., & Waite, L. J. (1977). Early childbearing and educational attainment. *Family Planning Perspectives*, 9(5), 220–225. DOI: 10.2307/2134432 PMID: 902716

Morgan, S. P., & Rindfuss, R. R. (1982). Household structure and tempo of family formation in comparative perspective. Paper presented at the Annual Meetings of the Population Association of America, San diego.

Morgan, S. P., & Teachman, J. D. (1988). Logistic regression: Description, examples, and comparison. *Journal of Marriage and Family*, 50(4), 929–936. DOI: 10.2307/352104

Morrels, S., Matthijs, K., & Leuven, K. U. (2008). The age at first marriage in three Belgian cities: Antwerp, Aalst and Ghent, 1800-1906. Paper presented in the 9th International Conference on Urban history "Comparative History of Urban Cities" Loyn, 27th-30th August 2008.

Morrow, G., Yount, K. M., Bergenfeld, I., Laterra, A., Kalra, S., Khan, Z., & Clark, C. J. (2023). Adolescent boys' and girls' perspectives on social norms surrounding child marriage in Nepal. *Culture, Health & Sexuality*, 25(10), 1277–1294. DOI: 10.1080/13691058.2022.2155705 PMID: 36573269

Mott, F. L., & Marsiglio, W. (1976). Early childbearing and completion of high school. *Family Planning Perspectives*, 17(5), 234–237. DOI: 10.2307/2135098 PMID: 3842664

Mourtada, R., Schlecht, J., & DeJong, J. (2017). A qualitative study exploring child marriage practices among Syrian conflict-affected populations in Lebanon. *Conflict and Health*, 11(S1, Suppl 1), 27. DOI: 10.1186/s13031-017-0131-z PMID: 29167699

Mpilambo, J. E., Appunni, S. S., Kanayo, O., & Stiegler, N. (2017). Determinants of early marriage among young women in Democratic Republic of Congo. *Journal of Social Sciences*, 52(1-3), 82–91. DOI: 10.1080/09718923.2017.1322393

Muharry, A., Hakimi, M., & Wahyuni, B. (2018). Family structure and early marriage on women in indramayu regency. *Journal of Kesehatan Masyarakat*, 13(3), 314–322. DOI: 10.15294/kemas.v13i3.8946

Muhith, A., Fardiansyah, A., Saputra, M. H., & Nurmiyati, . (2018). Analysis of causes and impacts of early marriage on madurese sumenep East Java Indonesia. *Indian Journal of Public Health Research & Development*, 9(8), 1495–1499. DOI: 10.5958/0976-5506.2018.00944.0

Mukharrom, T., & Abdi, S. (2023). Harmonizing Islam and human rights through the reconstruction of classical Islamic tradition. *Samarah: Jurnal Hukum Keluarga Dan Hukum Islam*, 7(1), 40–57. DOI: 10.22373/sjhk.v7i1.16436

Mukherjee, P. and Agarwal, M. (2023). Factors influencing female workforce participation in urban India: A case study. *International Journal of Indian Economic Light*, 1-7. https://doi.org/DOI: 10.36713/epra12849

Munley, P. H. (1975). Erik Erikson's theory of psychosocial development and vocational behavior. *Journal of Counseling Psychology*, 22(4), 314–319. DOI: 10.1037/h0076749

Murdock, G. P. (1960). *Social structure*. Macmillan Publishing Company.

Murphy-Graham, E., & Lloyd, C. (2015). Empowering adolescent girls in developing countries: The potential role of education. *Policy Futures in Education*, 14(5), 556–577. DOI: 10.1177/1478210315610257

Murphy, M., Pande, R., & Malhotra, A. (2018). *International Child Marriage Laws: Policy and Practice*. Springer.

Muthengi, E., & Erulkar, A. S. (2016). Violence against adolescent girls in lower-income countries: An overview of findings from the violence against children and youth surveys. *The Journal of Adolescent Health*, 59(3), 318–322. PMID: 27320034

Nabila, R., Roswiyani, R., & Satyadi, H. (2022). A literature review of factors influencing early marriage decisions in Indonesia. *Advances in Social Science, Education and Humanities Research*, 655, 1392–1402. DOI: 10.2991/assehr.k.220404.223

Naghizadeh, S., Mirghafourvand, M., Mohammadi, A., Azizi, M., Taghizadeh-Milani, S., & Ganbari, H. (2021). Knowledge and viewpoint of adolescent girls regarding child marriage, its causes and consequences. *BMC Women's Health*, 21(1), 351. Advance online publication. DOI: 10.1186/s12905-021-01497-w PMID: 34615510

Naher, M. S. (1985). Marriage pattern: Customs and changes in rural Bangladesh. *The Journal of Social Studies*, 20(30), 121–132.

Nam, C. E., & Terrie, E. W. (1981). *Measurement of socioeconomic status: Current issues*. Westview Press.

Naruka, R., Kumar, V., Singh, H., & Kaushik, T. K. (2023). Domestic child adoption in India: The problem and prospectives. *Tuijin Jishu Journal of Propulsion Technology*, 44(6), 1162–1174.

Natanael, M. J., & Fajar, M. R., and M. R. (2013). Prevalence of Child Marriage and Its Determinants among Young Women in Indonesia. *Child Poverty and Social Protection Conference*.

Neath, J., & Schriner, K. (1998). Power to people with disabilities: Empowerment issues in employment programming. *Disability & Society*, 13(2), 217–228. DOI: 10.1080/09687599826795

Nevangga, R. P., Ardlianawati, N., Wicaksono, D., Arisyna, A., & Sasmita, N. S. (2023, November). Situational analysis of the mental health of referral COVID-19 hospital staff. In *AIP Conference Proceedings* (Vol. 2739, No. 1). AIP Publishing. DOI: 10.1063/5.0126737

Nguyen, M. C., & Wodon, Q. (2014). Impact of child marriage on literacy and education attainment in Africa. Available from http://allinschool.org/wp-content/uploads/2015/02/OOSC-2014-QW-Child-Marriage-final.pdf

Nguyen, M. C., & Wodon, Q. (2014). Impact of child marriage on literacy and education attainment in Africa. *Global Partnership for Education, September.*

Nirantar Trust. (2015). *Early and child marriages in India: A landscape analysis.* Drishti Printers.

Nishat, J., Shovo, T., Ahammed, B., Islam, M., Rahman, M., & Hossain, M. (2023). Mental health status of early married girls during the covid-19 pandemic: A study in the southwestern region of bangladesh. *Frontiers in Psychiatry*, 13, 1074208. Advance online publication. DOI: 10.3389/fpsyt.2022.1074208 PMID: 36683997

Noor, M., Fatimah, H., Rahman, F., Laily, N., & Yulidasari, F. (2021). The impact of physical and psychological health of early married behaviors in adolescents. *Journal Berkala Kesehatan*, 7(1), 16. DOI: 10.20527/jbk.v7i1.9618

Norton, A. J. (1980). Family life cycle: 1980. *Journal of Marriage and Family*, 45(2), 267–275. DOI: 10.2307/351506

Nour, N. M. (2006). Health consequences of child marriage in Africa. *Emerging Infectious Diseases*, 12(11), 1644–1649. DOI: 10.3201/eid1211.060510 PMID: 17283612

Nour, N. M. (2009). Child marriage: A silent health and human rights issue. *Reviews in Obstetrics & Gynecology*, 2(1), 51. PMID: 19399295

Novianti, D., Fatonah, S., Abadi, M. T. D., Haq, M. F., & Sagita, V. A. (2023). Social Media and Early Marriage During the Covid-19 Pandemic in Indonesia. *Journal of Social and Political Sciences*, 6(4), 35–46. DOI: 10.31014/aior.1991.06.04.443

Nurfieni, A. (2023). The impact of law number 16 of 2019 marriage dispensation and child marriage gap. *Indonesian Journal of Law and Islamic Law (Ijlil)*, 5(2), 50–61. DOI: 10.35719/ijlil.v5i2.330

Nurmila, N., & Windiana, W. (2023). Understanding the Complexities of Child Marriage and Promoting Education to Prevent Child Marriage in Indramayu, West Java. *Ulumuna*, 27(2), 823–853. DOI: 10.20414/ujis.v27i2.680

Nyamongo, I. (2000). Factors influencing education and age at first marriage in an arid region: The case of the Borana of Marsabit district, Kenya. *African Study Monographs*, 21(2), 55–65.

O'Donnell, A., & Elliott, K. (2021). *Children, human rights and the law: An introduction*. Routledge.

Obeisat, S. (2021). The lived experience of early marriage in jordan: The perspective of adolescent girls and young women. *SAGE Open*, 11(3), 215824402110488. DOI: 10.1177/21582440211048895

Omoeva, C., & Hatch, R. (2014). *Teenage, married, and out of school: Effects of early marriage and childbirth on school dropout*. Education Policy and Data Center Working Paper.

Opesemowo, O. A., & Odumosu, E. T. (2023). The sway of early marriage on the girl child education among some ethnic groups in Lagos state, Nigeria. *Journal of Culture and Values in Education*, 6(3), 26–41. DOI: 10.46303/jcve.2023.18

Oppenheimer, V. K. (1970). *The female labor force in the United States: Demographic and economic factors determining its growth and changing composition*. Population Monograph Series, N. 5, Institute of International Studies. Berkeley: University of California.

Oppenheimer, V. K. (1988). A theory of marriage timing. *American Journal of Sociology*, 94(3), 563–591. DOI: 10.1086/229030

Oppenheimer, V. K. (1997). Women's employment and the gain to marriage. The specialization and trading model. *Annual Review of Sociology*, 23(1), 431–453. DOI: 10.1146/annurev.soc.23.1.431 PMID: 12348280

Osakinle, E., & Tayo-Olajubutu, O. (2017). Child marriage and health consequences in Nigeria. *American Scientific Research Journal for Engineering, Technology, and Sciences (ASRJETS), 30*(1), 351-356. https://core.ac.uk/download/pdf/235050181.pdf

Osofsky, J. D., & Osofsky, H. J. (2001). The psychological effects of war and violence on children. *Paediatrics*, 108(2), 301–309.

Otto, L. B. (1979). Antecedents and consequences to marital timing. In Burr, W. R. (Eds.), *contemporary theories about family: research based theories* (Vol. 1, pp. 101–126). Free Press.

Öztürk, A. B., Albayrak, H., Karataş, K., & Aslan, H. (2021). Dynamics of Child Marriages among Syrian and Afghan Refugees in Turkey. *Atatürk Üniversitesi Sosyal Bilimler Enstitüsü Dergisi*, 25(1), 251–269.

Padalıhasanoğlu, E. Ç., & Yaman, Ö. M. (2022). Gayriresmî Erken Evlilikler: 18 Yaş Altı Evlilik Yapan Kadınların Evlilik Öncesi Aile Yaşantılarının İncelenmesi. Turkish Studies-Social Sciences, 17(5).

Pallitto, C. C., & Murillo, V. (2008). Childhood Abuse as a Risk Factor for Adolescent Pregnancy in El Salvador. *The Journal of Adolescent Health*, 42(6), 580–586. Advance online publication. DOI: 10.1016/j.jadohealth.2007.11.148 PMID: 18486867

Pampapathi, N. L. (2018). Child marriages in India: Causes and consequences. *IJCRT*, 6(1), 1436–1439.

Parpart, J. L., Connelly, P., & Barriteau, E. (Eds.). (2000). *Theoretical perspectives on gender and development*. IDRC.

Parrado, E. A., & Zenteno, R. M. (2002). Gender differences in union formation in Mexico: Evidence from marital search model. *Journal of Marriage and Family*, 64(3), 756–773. DOI: 10.1111/j.1741-3737.2002.00756.x

Parsons, J., Edmeades, J. D., Kes, A., Petroni, S., Sexton, M. W., & Wodon, Q. (2015). Economic Impacts of Child Marriage: A Review of the Literature. *The Review of Faith & International Affairs*, 13(3), 12–22. DOI: 10.1080/15570274.2015.1075757

Parsons, J., & McCleary-Sills, J. (2014). *Preventing Child Marriage*. EnGender Impact.

Parsons, T. (1954). *Essays in sociological theory*. Free Press.

Parvez, N., & Gauhar, F. R. (2024). Child in conflict with law in India: Changing concerns and constraints. *Sprin Journal of Arts, Humanities, and Social Sciences*, 3(7), 1–6. DOI: 10.55559/sjahss.v3i7.367

Pascall, G., & Cox, R. (1993). Education and domesticity. *Gender and Education*, 5(1), 17–35. DOI: 10.1080/0954025930050102

Patankar, S. (2021). Fighting social acceptance of child marriage in India. Downloaded from https://borgenproject.org › The Blog

Patowari, P., Huirem, R., & Loganathan, K. (2019). The Paradoxical Problem of Child Marriage in India. *Department of Social Work*, 10(1), 117. http://www.aus.ac.in/social-work-department/wp-content/uploads/sites/15/2021/02/Vol-10_No-1_Social-Work-Journal.pdf#page=118

Paul, P. (2019). Child marriage and its association with morbidity and mortality of children under 5 years old: Evidence from India. *Journal of Public Health (Berlin)*, 28(3), 331–338. DOI: 10.1007/s10389-019-01038-8

Paul, P. (2020). Child Marriage Among Girls in India: Prevalence, Trends and Socio-Economic Correlates. *Indian Journal of Human Development*, 14(2), 304–319. DOI: 10.1177/0973703020950263

Paul, P., & Mondal, D. (2020). Child marriage in India: A human rights violation during the COVID-19 pandemic. *Asia-Pacific Journal of Public Health*, 33(1), 162–163. DOI: 10.1177/1010539520975292 PMID: 33233942

Pearse, R., & Connell, R. (2016). Gender Norms and the Economy: Insights from Social Research. *Feminist Economics*, 22(1), 30–53. DOI: 10.1080/13545701.2015.1078485

Phiri, M., Namayawa, S., Sianyeuka, B., Sikanyiti, P., & Lemba, M. (2023). Determinants of spousal physical violence against women in Zambia: A multilevel analysis. *BMC Public Health*, 23(1), 934. DOI: 10.1186/s12889-023-15927-x PMID: 37221522

Pillai, V. K. (1985). Predicting age at first marriage: A review of recent models. *The Journal of Family Welfare*, 32(1), 41–49.

Pocuca, M. B., Krstinic, D. M., & Šarkić, N. (2023). Prohibition of Minor Marriages. *Kultura Polisa*, 20(2), 101–129. DOI: 10.51738/Kpolisa2023.20.2r.101pks

Pope, D. H., McMullen, H., Baschieri, A., Philipose, A., Udeh, C., Diallo, J., & McCoy, D. (2023). What is the current evidence for the relationship between the climate and environmental crises and child marriage? A scoping review. *Global Public Health: An International Journal for Research, Policy and Practice*, 18(1), 2095655. Advance online publication. DOI: 10.1080/17441692.2022.2095655 PMID: 36403290

Porter, S. A. (2016). Girls' education, development and social change. *Policy Futures in Education*, 14(5), 517–538. DOI: 10.1177/1478210315625904

Pourtaheri, A., Mahdizadeh, M., Tehrani, H., Jamali, J., & Peyman, N. (2024). Socio-ecological factors of girl child marriage: A meta-synthesis of qualitative research. *BMC Public Health*, 24(428), 1–23. DOI: 10.1186/s12889-023-17626-z PMID: 38341573

Pourtaheri, A., Sany, S. B. T., Aghaee, M. A., Ahangari, H., & Peyman, N. (2023). Prevalence and factors associated with child marriage, a systematic review. *BMC Women's Health*, 23(1), 1–15. DOI: 10.1186/s12905-023-02634-3 PMID: 37817117

Presser, H. (1975). Age differences between spouses: Trends, patterns, and social implications. *The American Behavioral Scientist*, 19(2), 190–205. DOI: 10.1177/000276427501900205

Prisco, G. (2023). "Girls giving birth to babies". A pedagogical perspective for the self-determination and existential planning of young mothers. *Women &Education*, (2), 088-093.

Putri, U. F. W., Prasetyo, B., & Salim, L. A. (2022). Causes of Early Marriage on Socio-Ecological Levels. *Budapest International Research and Critics Institute-Journal*, 5(3), 18869–18876. DOI: 10.33258/birci.v5i3.5884

Pyke, K., & Adams, M. (2010). What's age got to do with it? A case study analysis of power and gender in husband-older marriages. *Journal of Family Issues*, 31(6), 748–777. DOI: 10.1177/0192513X09357897

Quentin, W., Montenegro, C., Nguyen, H., & Onagoruwa, A. (2018). Missed opportunities: the high cost of not educating girls. In *World Bank*. Issue July.

Quisumbing, A. R., & Hallman, K. (2003). Marriage in transition: Evidence on age, education, and assets from six developing countries. Policy Research Division Working Papers, Population Council, 2003, Retrieved from www.popcouncil.org/publications/wp/prd/rdwplist.html

Raffe, D. (2010). Scotland: System of education. In Baker, E., Peterson, P., & McGaw, B. (Eds.), *The international encyclopedia of education* (3rd ed., Vol. 5, pp. 770–775). Elsevier. DOI: 10.1016/B978-0-08-044894-7.01429-9

Rahaman, S. M. Z. (1995). Muslim marriage practices in a village of Bangladesh. *Rajshahi University Studies*, 3, (Part-C), 131-149.

Rahaman, S. M. Z. (1995). *Muslim marriage practices in a village of Bangladesh. Rajshahi University Studies* (Vol. 3). Part-C.

Rahayu, W., & Wahyuni, H. (2020). The influence of early marriage on monetary poverty in Indonesia. *Journal of Indonesian Economy and Business*, 35(1). Advance online publication. DOI: 10.22146/jieb.42405

Rahman, M. A., Tohan, M. M., Zaman, S., Islam, M. A., Rahman, M. S., Howlader, M. H., & Kundu, S. (2024). A structural equation modelling to explore the determinants of mental health disorders among reproductive-aged women in Nepal: A nation-wide cross-sectional survey.

Raj, A. (2010). When the mother is a child: The impact of child marriage on the health and human rights of girls. *Archives of Disease in Childhood*, 95(11), 931–935. DOI: 10.1136/adc.2009.178707 PMID: 20930011

Raj, A., & McDougal, L. (2017). Sexual violence and girls' vulnerability to child marriage in humanitarian settings. *Reproductive Health Matters*, 25(51), 49–54.

Raley, R. K., Durden, T. E., & Wildsmith, E. (2004). Understanding Mexican American marriage patterns using a life course approach. *Social Science Quarterly*, 85(4), 872–890. DOI: 10.1111/j.0038-4941.2004.00249.x

Rashid, T., & Karim, M. (2022). Empowering girls through education and economic opportunities: Strategies to delay early marriage. *Development Studies Research*, 9(3), 234–249. DOI: 10.1080/21665095.2022.2117739

Rasmussen, B., Maharaj, N., Kumnick, M., & Sheehan, P. (2021). Evaluating interventions to reduce child marriage in India. *Journal of Global Health Reports*, 5, e2021044. DOI: 10.29392/001c.23619

Raval, D., & Bharad, B. (2021). EARLY MARRIAGE: NEGLECTED FORM OF CHILD ABUSE. *GAP GYAN -. Global Journal of Social Sciences*, 4(4), 58–62. Advance online publication. DOI: 10.47968/gapgyan.440011

Raymo, J., & Iwasawa, M. (2005). Marriage market mismatches in japan: An alternative view of the relationship between women's education and marriage. *American Sociological Review*, 70(5), 801–822. DOI: 10.1177/000312240507000504

Reley, R. K., & Sweeney, M. M. (2009). Explaining race and ethnic variation in marriage: Directions for future research. *Race and Social Problems*, 3(3), 132–142. DOI: 10.1007/s12552-009-9013-3

Reupert, A. (2017). A socio-ecological framework for mental health and well-being. *Advances in Mental Health Promotion. Advances in Mental Health*, 15(2), 105–107. DOI: 10.1080/18387357.2017.1342902

Revillard, A. (2006). Work/family policy in France. *International Journal of Law, Policy and the Family*, 20(2), 133–150. DOI: 10.1093/lawfam/ebl009

Ribar, D. (1994). Teen fertility and high school completion. *The Review of Economics and Statistics*, 76(3), 413–424. DOI: 10.2307/2109967

Richman, J. (1977). Bargaining for sex and status: the dating service and sex role change. In Stein, P., Richman, J., & Hannon, N. (Eds.), *the family: functions, conflicts, and symbols* (pp. 158–165). Addison Wesley.

Roberts, T. A., Auinger, P., & Klein, J. D. (2005). Emotional problems among adolescents and young adults and their association with sexual behavior. *Paediatrics*, 115(6), 1727–1734.

Rodgers, R. H. (1964). Toward a theory of family development. *Journal of Marriage and Family*, 26(3), 262–270. DOI: 10.2307/349456

Roest, J. (2016). Child Marriage and Early Childbearing in India: Risk Factors and Policy Implications. The final version is available online from Young Lives at: https://www.younglives.org.uk/content/child-marriage-and-early-child-bearing-india-risk-factors-and-policy-implications

Roest, J. (2016). Child marriage and early child-bearing in India: Risk factors and policy implications. *Young Lives Policy Paper, 10*, 12-34. https://www.younglives-india.org/sites/default/files/syndicated/YL-PolicyPaper-10-Sep16_0.pdf

Roy, K. T. (2008). Determinants of early marriage in Rajshahi, Bangladesh. *Pakistan Journal of Social Sciences*, 5(6), 606–611.

Rozelle, S., Guo, L., Shen, M., Hughart, A., & Giles, J. (1999). Leaving China's farms: Survey results of new paths and remaining hurdles to rural migration. *The China Quarterly*, 158, 367–393. DOI: 10.1017/S0305741000005816

Rumberger, R. W. (2011). High school dropout in the United States. Lamb, S., Markussen, E., Teese, R., Sandberg, N., & Polesel, J. Editors, *School dropout and completion: International comparative studies in theory and practice* (pp. 275-294). London: Springer Publishing Company. DOI: 10.1007/978-90-481-9763-7_16

Rumble, L., Peterman, A., Irdiana, N., Triyana, M., & Minnick, E. (2018). An empirical exploration of female child marriage determinants in Indonesia. *BMC Public Health*, 18(1), 407. Advance online publication. DOI: 10.1186/s12889-018-5313-0 PMID: 29587705

Sagade, J. (2005). *Child marriage in India: Socio-legal and human rights dimensions*. OUP India Publishers.

Sagalova, V., Nanama, S., Zagré, N., & Vollmer, S. (2021). Long-term consequences of early marriage and maternity in West and Central Africa: Wealth, education, and fertility. *Journal of Global Health*, 11, 13004. Advance online publication. DOI: 10.7189/jogh.11.13004 PMID: 34484711

Salam, A. (2023). *Analysis of The Impact of Early Marriage On Children's Parenting Patterns*. Journal Transnational Universal Studies., DOI: 10.58631/jtus.v1i1.1

Saleh, A., Othman, S., Ismail, K., & Shabila, N. (2022). Exploring Iraqi people's perception about early marriage: A qualitative study. *BMC Women's Health*, 22(1), 393. Advance online publication. DOI: 10.1186/s12905-022-01980-y PMID: 36175884

Saleheen, A., Afrin, S., Kabir, S., Habib, M., Zinnia, M., Hossain, M., Haq, I., & Talukder, A. (2021). Sociodemographic factors and early marriage among women in Bangladesh, ghana and iraq: An illustration from multiple indicator cluster survey. *Heliyon*, 7(5), e07111. DOI: 10.1016/j.heliyon.2021.e07111 PMID: 34095593

Sampedro, R. (2021). The Sustainable Development Goals (SDG). *Carreteras*, 4(232), 253–257. Advance online publication. DOI: 10.4324/9780429282348-52

Samsuddin, S. N. A., Masroom, M. N., & Wan Mohd Yunus, W. M. A. (2019). Mental Health of Muslim Unwed Pregnant Teenagers. *Malaysian Journal of Medicine & Health Sciences, 15*.

Santhya, K. G., & Jejeebhoy, S. J. (2007). Early marriage and HIV/AIDS risk factors among young women in India. *Economic and Political Weekly*, 42(14), 1229–1297.

Santhya, K. G., Ram, U., Acharya, R., Jejeebhoy, S. J., Ram, F., & Singh, A. (2010). Associations between early marriage and young women's marital and reproductive health outcomes: Evidence from India. *International Perspectives on Sexual and Reproductive Health*, 36(3), 132–139. DOI: 10.1363/3613210 PMID: 20880798

Santrock, J. W. (2010a). *Child Development* (13th ed.). McGraw-Hill.

Sarah, D., Media, G., & Hough-Stewart, L. (2019). *The State of Girls' rights in the UK 2019-2020*. Lecturer in Social Anthropology.

Sarkar, S. (2021). Local crime and early marriage: evidence from India. WIDER Working Paper. https://doi.org/DOI: 10.35188/UNU-WIDER/2021/975-4

Sarker, P. C. (1997). *Social structure & fertility behavior: a cross-cultural study*. Dhaka, Bangladesh: Center for development Services.

Sattar, M. A. (1984). A comparison of age and sex patterns of participation in economic activities in Tribal and Non-Tribal communities in Bangladesh. In Qureshi, M. S. (Ed.), *Tribal cultures in Bangladesh*. Institute of Bangladesh Studies.

Sattar, T., Yasin, G., & Afzal, S. (2012). Socio-cultural and economic impediments of inequality in provision of educational rights to female: A case of Southern Punjab (Pakistan). *International Journal of Human Resource Studies*, 2(1), 122–138. DOI: 10.5296/ijhrs.v2i1.1210

Save the Children. (2012). Ending child marriage: How elevating the status of girls advances U.S. foreign policy objectives. https://www.savethechildren.org/content/dam/usa/reports/advocacy/ending-child-marriage-report-2012.pdf

Sawhill, I. V. (2006). *Teenage Pregnancy Prevention: Welfare Reform's Missing Component*. Brookings Institution.

Say, L., Chou, D., Gemmill, A., Tunçalp, Ö., Moller, A. B., Daniels, J., Gülmezoglu, A. M., Temmerman, M., & Alkema, L. (2014). Global causes of maternal death: A WHO systematic analysis. *The Lancet. Global Health*, 2(6), e323–e333. Advance online publication. DOI: 10.1016/S2214-109X(14)70227-X PMID: 25103301

Scala, M. A. (1996). Going back to school: Participation motives and experiences of older adults in an undergraduate classroom. *Educational Gerontology*, 22(8), 747–773. DOI: 10.1080/0360127960220804

Schoen, R., Wooldredge, J., & Thomas, B. (1989). Ethnic and educational effects on marriage choice. *Social Science Quarterly*, 70, 617–630.

Schreck, L. (1998). Expectation about marriage and childbearing vary by race and ethnicity among girls in grades 6-8. *Family Planning Perspectives*, 30(5), 252–253. DOI: 10.2307/2991619

Schwartz, C. R. (2013). Trends and variation in assortative mating: Causes and consequences. *Annual Review of Sociology*, 39(1), 451–470. DOI: 10.1146/annurev-soc-071312-145544

Scott, S., Nguyen, P. H., Neupane, S., Pramanik, P., Nanda, P., Bhutta, Z. A., Afsana, K., & Mcnon, P. (2021). Early marriage and early childbearing in South Asia: Trends, inequalities, and drivers from 2005 to 2018. *Annals of the New York Academy of Sciences*, 1491(1), 60–73. DOI: 10.1111/nyas.14531 PMID: 33258141

Sekine, K., & Hodgkin, M. E. (2017). Effect of child marriage on girls' school dropout in Nepal: Analysis of data from the multiple indicator cluster survey 2014. *PLoS One*, 20(7), 1–13. DOI: 10.1371/journal.pone.0180176 PMID: 28727793

Semaan, S., Haddad, C., Awad, E., Sacre, H., Hallit, R., Akel, M., Salameh, P., Obeid, S., & Hallit, S. (2023). Caring for a mentally ill patient at home, mental health, religiosity, and spirituality and their association with family caregivers' quality of life in Lebanon. *The Primary Care Companion for CNS Disorders*, 25(4), 47977. DOI: 10.4088/PCC.22m03333 PMID: 37471477

Sen, S., & Ghosh, A. (Eds.). (2021). *Love, labour, and law: Early and child marriage in India*. SAGE Publications Pvt. Ltd.

Şen, S., & Kavlak, O. (2011). Çocuk Gelinler: Erken Yaş Evlilikleri ve Adölesan Gebeliklere Yaklaşım. *Journal of Social Policy Studies*, 7(25).

Seta, R. (2023). Child marriage and its impact on health: A study of perceptions and attitudes in Nepal. *Journal of Global Health Reports*, 7, e2023073. DOI: 10.29392/001c.88951

Seth, R., Bose, V., Qaiyum, Y., Chandrashekhar, R., Kansal, S., Taneja, I., & Seth, T. (2018). Social determinants of child marriage in rural India. *the Ochsner Journal*, 18(4), 390–394. DOI: 10.31486/toj.18.0104

Setiawan, H. H., Wardianti, A., Yusuf, I., & Asikin, A. (2020). ANAK SEBAGAI PELAKU TERORISME DALAM PERSPEKTIF EKOLOGI SOSIAL. *Sosio Informa : Kajian Permasalahan Sosial Dan Usaha Kesejahteraan Sosial*, 6(3), 252–263. DOI: 10.33007/inf.v6i3.2400

Setyanto, A., Kewuel, H. K., & Zurinani, S. (2024). The phenomenon and impact of early marriage- A case study of Islamic communities in East Java, Indonesia-. *Kurdish Studies*, 12(1), 2297–2307. DOI: 10.58262/ks.v12i1.160

Sezgin, A., & Punamäki, R. (2019). Impacts of early marriage and adolescent pregnancy on mental and somatic health: The role of partner violence. *Archives of Women's Mental Health*, 23(2), 155–166. DOI: 10.1007/s00737-019-00960-w PMID: 30955087

Shafer, K., & James, S. L. (2013). Gender and socioeconomic status differences in first and scond marriage formation. *Journal of Marriage and Family*, 75(3), 544–564. DOI: 10.1111/jomf.12024

Shahidul, S. M. (2012). Marriage market and an effect on girls' school dropout in Bangladesh. *Journal of Alternative Perspectives in the Social Sciences*, 4(2), 552–564.

Shahidul, S. M. (2014). Parents' class background and hypergamy in the marriage market of Bangladesh: Does the dowry affect school dropout among girls? *The Asia-Pacific Education Researcher*, 23(3), 709–715. DOI: 10.1007/s40299-013-0142-5

Sheela, M. S. J., & Audinarayana, N. (2000). Determinants of female age at first marriage in Tamil Nadu: An analysis of NFHS data. *The Journal of Family Welfare*, 46(2), 25–32.

Shehan, C. L., Berardo, F. M., Vera, H., & Carley, S. M. (1991). Women in age-discrepant marriages. *Journal of Family Issues*, 12(3), 291–305. DOI: 10.1177/019251391012003003

Sheth, C. (2021). A community-based approach to preventing child marriage. *India Development Review*. https://idronline.org › a-community-based-approach-to-...
Shrestha. I. K., & Khanal S. P. (2024). Factors associated with time to first birth after marriage: A systematic review. *BIBECHANA 21*(2), 180-194.

Shukla, S., Ezebuihe, J. A., & Steinert, J. I. (2023). Association between public health emergencies and sexual and reproductive health, gender-based violence, and early marriage among adolescent girls: A rapid review. *BMC Public Health*, 23(1), 1–14. DOI: 10.1186/s12889-023-15054-7 PMID: 36650493

Siddiquee, M. A. R. (1997). The nature of participation of marginal community in politics: An analysis of Santal Tribe, Unpublished Ph. D. Dissertation, Rajshahi, Bangladesh: University of Rajshahi.

Silva, T., & Percheski, C. (2024). Age-heterogamous partnerships: Prevalence and partner differences by marital status and gender composition. *Demographic Research*, 50, 625–642. DOI: 10.4054/DemRes.2024.50.23

Singh, R., & Vennam, U. (2016). Factors shaping trajectories to child and early marriage: Evidence from Young Lives in India. https://ora.ox.ac.uk/objects/uuid: 14005c76-8e23-4817-b74f-64578861af18/download_file?safe_filename=YL -WP149-Trajectories%2Bto%2Bearly%2BMarriage.pdf&file_format=application %2Fpdf&type_of_work=General+item

Singh, A. (2020). Psychological impacts of early marriage on adolescent girls: A literature review. *The Journal of Adolescent Health*, 67(5), 654–661. DOI: 10.1016/j.jadohealth.2020.06.025

Singh, P., Pattanaik, F., & Singh, A. (2023). Beyond the Clock: Exploring the Complexities of Women's Domestic Roles in India Through the Lenses of Daughters and Daughters-in-Law. *The Indian Journal of Labour Economics : the Quarterly Journal of the Indian Society of Labour Economics*, 66(2), 535–559. DOI: 10.1007/s41027-023-00441-w

Singh, S., & Kaur, M. (2024). Child marriage in India: The chains of tradition. *Educational Administration: Theory and Practice*, 30(1), 1425–1434.

Singh, S., & Samara, R. (1998). Early marriage among women in developing countries. *International Family Planning Perspectives*, 22(4), 148–157. DOI: 10.2307/2950812

Skinner, G. W. (1997). Family systems and demographic processes. In Kertzer, D. I., & Fricke, T. (Eds.), *anthropological demography: toward a new synthesis* (pp. 53–95). University of Chicago Press.

SmithBattle, L.SmithBattle. (2007). Legacies of advantage and disadvantage: The case of teen mothers. *Public Health Nursing (Boston, Mass.)*, 24(5), 409–420. DOI: 10.1111/j.1525-1446.2007.00651.x PMID: 17714225

Smith, P. C. (1980). Asian marriage patterns in transition. *Journal of Family History*, 5(1), 58–96. DOI: 10.1177/036319908000500104

Snyder, A. R., Brown, S. L., & Condo, E. P. (2004). Residential differences in family formation: The significance of cohabitation. *Rural Sociology*, 69(2), 255–260. DOI: 10.1526/003601104323087598

Snyder, T. (1994). [IES: The National Center for Education Statistics.]. *Digest of Educational Statistics*, •••, 1994.

Solhi, M., Azar, F., Farahani, F., & Lebni, J. (2021). Exploring the consequences of early marriage among Kurdish women: a qualitative study in western Iran. https://doi.org/DOI: 10.21203/rs.3.rs-55314/v2

Solomon, B. B. (1987). Empowerment: Social work in oppressed communities. *Journal of Social Work Practice*, 2(4), 79–91. DOI: 10.1080/02650538708414984

South, S. (2001). The variable effects of family background on the timing of first marriage: United States 1969-1993. *Social Science Research*, 30(4), 606–626. DOI: 10.1006/ssre.2001.0714

South, S. J. (1991). Sociodemographic differentials in mate selection preferences. *Journal of Marriage and Family*, 53(4), 928–940. DOI: 10.2307/352998

South, S. J., & Croder, K. D. (2000). The declining significance of neighborhoods? Marital transitions in community context. *Social Forces*, 78(3), 1067–1099. DOI: 10.2307/3005942

Souza, M. T. D., Silva, M. D. D., & Carvalho, R. D. (2010). Integrative review: What is it? How to do it? *Einstein (Sao Paulo, Brazil)*, 8(1), 102–106. DOI: 10.1590/s1679-45082010rw1134 PMID: 26761761

Spanier, G., & Glick, P. (1980). Mate selection differentials between whites and blacks in the United States. *Social Forces*, 58(3), 707–735. DOI: 10.2307/2577180

Speizer, I. S., & Pearson, E. (2011). Association between early marriage and intimate partner violence in India: A focus on youth from Bihar and Rajasthan. *Journal of Interpersonal Violence*, 26(10), 1963–1981. DOI: 10.1177/0886260510372947 PMID: 20587462

Stanko, E. A. (1985). *Intimate intrusions: Women's experience of male violence*. Routledge & Kegan Paul.

Stark, E. (2007). *Coercive control: How men entrap women in personal life*. Oxford University Press. DOI: 10.1093/oso/9780195154276.001.0001

Stark, L. (2018). Early marriage and cultural constructions of adulthood in two slums in Dar es Salaam. *Culture, Health & Sexuality*, 20(8), 888–901. Advance online publication. DOI: 10.1080/13691058.2017.1390162 PMID: 29111880

St-Germain, A., Kirby, R., & Urquia, M. (2022). Reproductive health among married and unmarried mothers aged less than 18, 18–19, and 20–24 years in the United States, 2014–2019: A population-based cross-sectional study. *PLoS Medicine*, 19(3), e1003929. Advance online publication. DOI: 10.1371/journal.pmed.1003929 PMID: 35271581

Stone, L. (1994). *Family values in a historical perspective*. University of Utah Press.

Stoyanova, V. (2016). United Nations against slavery: Unravelling concepts, institutions, and obligations. *Mich. J. Int'l L.*, 38, 359.

Strat, Y., Dubertret, C., & Foll, B. (2011). Child marriage in the united states and its association with mental health in women. *Pediatrics*, 128(3), 524–530. DOI: 10.1542/peds.2011-0961 PMID: 21873691

Strungaru, S. (2024). Understanding Child Marriage: Law and Practice. In *The Hidden Child Brides of the Syrian Civil War: Vulnerable and Voiceless in Human Rights Law and Practice* (pp. 13–33). Springer Nature Singapore. DOI: 10.1007/978-981-97-2159-7_2

Subramanee, S. D., Agho, K., Lakshmi, J., Huda, M. N., Joshi, R., & Akombi-Inyang, B. (2022). Child Marriage in South Asia: A Systematic review. *International Journal of Environmental Research and Public Health*, 19(22), 15138. DOI: 10.3390/ijerph192215138 PMID: 36429857

Sulistiawati, I., & Pratiwi, C. S. (2021). Psychological disorders found on the early-age married teenagers who are under 18. *International Journal of Health Science and Technology*, 2(3), 177–189. DOI: 10.31101/ijhst.v2i3.1969

Sütlü, S. (2022). Policies On Gender Equality. In Sütlü, S., & Say Şahin, D. (Eds.), *Disadvantaged Groups: A Social Policy Perspective* (pp. 17–28). Nobel Publishing.

Suveren, Y., & Turan, Z. (2022). Erken Evlilik Sorunu ve Kadın Sağlığı: Güncel Bir Değerlendirme. *Universal Journal of History and Culture*, 4(1), 78–99. DOI: 10.52613/ujhc.1010759

Sweet, S., & Moen, P. (2006). Advancing a career focus on work and family: Insights from the life course perspective. In Pitt-Catsouphes, M., Kossek, E. E., & Sweet, S. (Eds.), *The work and family handbook: Multidisciplinary perspectives, methods, and approaches* (pp. 189–208). Erlbaum.

Syria - United States Department of State. (2023, December 7). United States Department of State. https://www.state.gov/reports/2023-trafficking-in-persons-report/syria/

Taber, K. S. (2020). In Akpan, B., & Kennedy, T. J. (Eds.), *Mediated learning leading development—The social development theory of Lev Vygotsky BT - Science education in theory and practice: An introductory gGuide to learning theory* (pp. 277–291). Springer International Publishing., DOI: 10.1007/978-3-030-43620-9_19

Taplak, A., & Yılmaz, F. (2022). Adolescent marriage and motherhood in turkey: A qualitative study exploring determinants, impacts and opinions about preventive strategies. *Journal of Advanced Nursing*, 78(8), 2537–2547. DOI: 10.1111/jan.15211 PMID: 35285542

Teachman, J. D., Tedrow, L. M., & Crowder, K. D. (2000). The changing demography of America's families. *Journal of Marriage and Family*, 62(4), 1234–1246. DOI: 10.1111/j.1741-3737.2000.01234.x

Tembo, G. (2021). *Causes and effects of early marriages in Zambia*: A case study of the University of Zambia.

Thi, H. D., Huong, T. B. T., Tuyet, M. N. T., & Van, H. M. (2023). Socio-cultural norms and gender equality of ethnic minorities in Vietnam. *Journal of Racial and Ethnic Health Disparities*, 10(5), 2136–2144. DOI: 10.1007/s40615-022-01393-5 PMID: 36006587

Thompson, N. (2006). *Power and Empowerment*. Russell House Publishing Ltd.

Tinago, C. B., Frongillo, E. A., Warren, A. M., Chitiyo, V., Jackson, T. N., Cifarelli, A. K., Fyalkowski, S., & Pauline, V. (2024). Testing the effectiveness of a community-based peer support intervention to mitigate social isolation and stigma of adolescent motherhood in Zimbabwe. *Maternal and Child Health Journal*, 28(4), 657–666. DOI: 10.1007/s10995-023-03821-2 PMID: 37957412

Tong, R. (2012). Gender Roles. In *Encyclopedia of Applied Ethics* (pp. 399–406). Elsevier., DOI: 10.1016/B978-0-12-373932-2.00307-0

Toso, K., Cock, P., & Leavey, G. (2020). Maternal exposure to violence and offspring neurodevelopment: A systematic review. *Paediatric and Perinatal Epidemiology*, 34(2), 190–203. Advance online publication. DOI: 10.1111/ppe.12651 PMID: 32026500

Trickett, P., Noll, J., & Putnam, F. (2011). The impact of sexual abuse on female development: Lessons from a multigenerational, longitudinal research study. *Development and Psychopathology*, 23(2), 453–476. DOI: 10.1017/S0954579411000174 PMID: 23786689

Tripathi, N., & Sekher, T. V. (2013). Youth in India ready for sex education? Emerging evidence from national surveys. *PLoS One*, 8(8), e71584. DOI: 10.1371/journal.pone.0071584 PMID: 23951197

Turkish Penal Code. (2004). https://www.mevzuat.gov.tr/mevzuat?MevzuatNo=5237&MevzuatTur=1&MevzuatTertip=5 (23.03.2024)

Uddin, M. E. (2008). Cross-cultural comparison of family size and composition between Muslim and Santal communities in rural Bangladesh. *World Cultures eJournal, 16*(1), 1-18.

Uddin, M. E. (2008). Cross-cultural comparison of family size and composition between Muslim and Santal communities in rural Bangladesh. *World Cultures eJournal, 16*(1), 1-20.

Uddin, M. E. (2009b). Cross-cultural comparison of marriage relationship between Muslim and Santal communities in a village of Bangladesh. *World Cultures eJournal, 17*(1), 1-17.

Uddin, M. E. (2010). *Family structure: A cross-cultural comparison between Muslim and Santal communities in rural Bangladesh*. Saarbruchen: Lambert Academic Publishing.

Uddin, J., Pulok, M. H., Johnson, R. B., Rana, J., & Baker, E. (2019). Association between child marriage and institutional delivery care services use in Bangladesh: Intersections between education and place of residence. *Public Health*, 171, 6–14. DOI: 10.1016/j.puhe.2019.03.014 PMID: 31071578

Uddin, M. E. (2007). Marital duration and sexual frequency among the Muslim and Santal couples in rural Bangladesh: A cross-cultural Perspective. *International Journal of Humanities and Social Science*, 2(8), 444–453.

Uddin, M. E. (2009a). Age at first marriage for husband and wife between Muslim and Santal communities in rural Bangladesh. *International Journal of Humanities and Social Science*, 3(4), 318–326.

Uddin, M. E. (2009c). Correlates of family cultural background and family status and role between Muslim and Santal communities in rural Bangladesh. *Antrocom: Online Journal of Anthropology*, 5(1), 15–27.

Uddin, M. E. (2009c). Cross-cultural value orientations among the Muslim, Hindu, Santal and Oraon communities in rural Bangladesh. *International Journal of Humanities and Social Science*, 4(10), 754–765.

Uddin, M. E. (2009d). Family structure between Muslim and Santal communities in rural Bangladesh. *International Journal of Humanities and Social Science*, 5(6), 438–447. DOI: 10.5281/zenodo.1058249

Uddin, M. E. (2009e). Cross-cultural socio-economic status attainment between Muslim and Santal couple in rural Bangladesh. *International Journal of Humanities and Social Science*, 4(11), 779–786. DOI: 10.5281/zenodo.1075058

Uddin, M. E. (2010). *Family structure: A cross-cultural comparison between Muslim and Santal communities in rural Bangladesh. Saarbruchen*. Lambert Academic Publishing.

Uddin, M. E. (2011). Cross-cultural social stress among Muslim, Hindu, Santal and Oraon communities in Rasulpur of Bangladesh. *The International Journal of Sociology and Social Policy*, 31(5/6), 361–388. DOI: 10.1108/01443331111141318

Uddin, M. E. (2012). Cross-cultural family structure among Muslim, Hindu, Santal and Oraon communities in Bangladesh. *Journal of GLBT Family Studies*, 8(4), 334–360. DOI: 10.1080/1550428X.2012.705620

Uddin, M. E. (2012). Socio-cultural factors affecting family size between Muslim and Santal communities in rural Bangladesh. *Antrocom: On-Line Journal of Anthropology*, 8(2), 395–410.

Uddin, M. E. (2015). Family socio-cultural values affecting early marriage between Muslim and Santal communities in rural Bangladesh. *The International Journal of Sociology and Social Policy*, 35(3/4), 141–164. DOI: 10.1108/IJSSP-06-2014-0046

Uddin, M. E. (2015a). Exploration and implication of value orientation patterns in social policy-practice with ethnic communities in Bangladesh. *Global Social Welfare : Research, Policy & Practice*, 2(3), 129–138. DOI: 10.1007/s40609-014-0018-5

Uddin, M. E. (2015c). Ethnic disparity in family socio-economic status in Bangladesh: Implication for family welfare policy-practice. *Global Social Welfare : Research, Policy & Practice*, 2(2), 29–38. DOI: 10.1007/s40609-014-0021-x

Uddin, M. E. (2017). Disparity in family status attainment between majority and minority ethnic groups in Bangladesh. *International Journal of Social Economics*, 44(4), 530–546. DOI: 10.1108/IJSE-07-2015-0187

Uddin, M. E. (2017). Family demographic mechanisms linking of socioeconomic status to subjective physical health in rural Bangladesh. *Social Indicators Research*, 130(3), 1263–1279. DOI: 10.1007/s11205-015-1209-x

Uddin, M. E. (2017a). Ecological framework for primary school attainment in the tri-ethnic communities in rural Bangladesh. *Child Indicators Research*, 10(3), 693–713. DOI: 10.1007/s12187-016-9401-3

Uddin, M. E. (2021). Teenage marriage and high school dropout among poor girls: A narrative review for family pathways in Bangladesh. *Journal of Research in Social Sciences and Language*, 1(1), 55–76. https://www.jssal.com/index.php/jssal/article/view/15

Uddin, M. E. (2023). Understanding ethnic disparities in family status attainment: Implications for family welfare policy-practice in Bangladesh. In Chandan, H. (Ed.), *Implications of marginalization and critical race theory on social justice* (pp. 197–219). IGI Global. DOI: 10.4018/978-1-6684-3615-8.ch010

Uddin, M. E. (2024). Family socioeconomic inequalities between majorities and minorities across the globe: Implication for policy practice. In Baikady, R. (Eds.), *The Palgrave handbook of Global social problems*. Springer. DOI: 10.1007/978-3-030-68127-2_441-1

Uddin, M. E., & Arefin, M. S. (2007). Family authority pattern and gender dimension of birth control methods adoption in the Santal and Oraon ethnic communities in rural Bangladesh. *International Journal of Humanities and Social Science*, 2(8), 430–437.

Udgiri, R. (2017). Socio-demographic factors for early marriage and early pregnancy - A community based study. *Journal of Comprehensive Health*, 5(2), 59–66. DOI: 10.53553/JCH.v05i02.009

Udry, J. R., & Cliquet, R. L. (1982). A cross-cultural examination of the relationship between ages at menarche, marriage, and first birth. *Demography*, 19(1), 53–64. DOI: 10.2307/2061128 PMID: 7067870

Uecker, J. (2012). Marriage and mental health among young adults. *Journal of Health and Social Behavior*, 53(1), 67–83. DOI: 10.1177/0022146511419206 PMID: 22328171

Uecker, J. E., & Stokes, C. E. (2008). Early marriage in the United States. *Journal of Marriage and Family*, 70(4), 835–846. DOI: 10.1111/j.1741-3737.2008.00530.x PMID: 20305796

UNESCO. (b). (2014). UNESCO Priority Gender Equality Action Plan for 2014-2021. *United Nations Educational, Scientific and Cultural Organization*.

UNFPA (2012). *Marrying too young: Ending child marriage*. New York: United Nations Population fund.

UNFPA. (2013). *Adolescent pregnancy*. United Nations Population Fund.

UNFPA. (2018). Empowering young people to end child marriage and address gender-based violence through the provision of comprehensive sexuality education. https://asiapacific.unfpa.org/en/publications/empowering-young-people-end-child-marriage-and-address-gender-based-violence-through

UNFPA. (2019). *Çocuk Yaşta, Erken ve Zorla Evliliklerin Önlenmesine Yönelik Birleşmiş Milletler Ortak Programı*. https://www.cocukyastaevliligeson.org/#/?id=ba%c5%9flarken

UNFPA. (2020). *Türkiye'de Çocuk Yaşta Erken ve Zorla Evlilikler: 1993-2018 Türkiye Nüfus ve Sağlık Araştırmaları Veri Analizi*. https://turkiye.unfpa.org/sites/default/files/pub-pdf/turkce_web_son_pdf.pdf

UNFPA. (2022). *Taking the Field Forward: Investing in Knowledge to End Child Marriage*. UNFPA-UNICEF. Retrieved May 7, 2024 from https://www.unicef.org/documents/child-marriage-publication-catalogue-2020-2021

UNFPA-UNICEF. (2023). UNFPA-UNICEF Global Programme to Accelerate Action to End Child Marriage. *Unfpa, January*.

UNHCR. (2021). Yüksek Yarar Prosedürü Kılavuz İlkeleri: Çocuğun Yüksek Yararının Değerlendirilmesi ve Belirlenmesi. Birleşmiş Milletler Mülteciler Yüksek Komiserliği (BMMYK). https://www.unhcr.org/sites/default/files/2024-04/guidelines-on-supervised-independent-living-for-unaccompanied-children-turkish.pdf (22.03.2024)

UNICEF, & UNFPA. (2010). Marrying Too Young. In *United Nations Population Fund UNFPA* (Vol. 11, Issue 1).

UNICEF. (2005). Early marriage: A harmful traditional practice. https://www.unicef.org/publications/index_26902.html

UNICEF. (2012). *Latest trends and future prospects Child Marriage*. UNICEF.

UNICEF. (2015). Ending child marriage: Progress and prospects. https://data.unicef.org/resources/ending-child-marriage-progress-and-prospects/

UNICEF. (2017). *Çocuk Yaşta Evliliklerin Önlenmesi Hizmet Sağlayıcılar için Uygulama Rehberi*. UNICEF.

UNICEF. (2017). Gender and Equality: Glossary Of Terms And Concepts. In *The Qur an, Morality and Critical Reason* (Issue November).

UNICEF. (2018). A Profile of Child Marriage in the Middle East and North Africa, UNICEF, New York. https://www.unicef.org/mena/media/2641/file/MENA-ChildMarriageReport.pdf.pdf (21.03.2024)

UNICEF. (2018). Progress for every child in the SDG era. https://data.unicef.org/resources/progress-child-sdg-era-2018/

UNICEF. (2019). Child Marriage IN South Asia: An Evidence Review. New York: UNICEF. Downloaded from http://digitalrepository.fccollege.edu.pk/bitstream/123456789/949/1/Child%20marriage%20in%20south%20asia%20An%20Evidence%20Review.pdf

UNICEF. (2020). Child Marriage. New York: UNICEF. Downloaded from https://www.unicef.org/protection/child-marriage

UNICEF. (2021). *Evolution in the evidence base on child marriage (2000-2019)*. https://www.unicef.org/media/91991/filc/Child-marriage-evidence-report-2021.pdf

UNICEF. (2023). Child marriage data and statistics. Retrieved from https://www.unicef.org/reports/child-marriage-data-and-statistics

UNICEF. (2023). *Child-marriage global Database*. https://data.unicef.org/topic/child-protection/child-marriage/

UNICEF. (2024). Child marriage, https://www.unicef.org/protection/child-marriage (20.03.2024)

United Nations (2015). The world's women 2015: Trends and statistics.

United Nations Children's Fund (UNICEF). (2001). *Early marriage: child spouses*. UNICEF.

United Nations Children's Fund. (2014). Ending child marriage: Progress and prospects. https://www.unicef.org/media/files/Child_Marriage_Report_7_17_LR.pdf

United Nations Development Programme. (2016). Ending child marriage: Progress and prospects. https://www.undp.org/content/dam/undp/library/Democratic%20Governance/Women%27s%20Empowerment/Ending-Child-Marriage-Global-Initiative-Progress-and-Prospects-2016.pdf

United Nations Economic and Social Council. (2006). General Comment No. 18: The Right to Non-Discrimination in Economic, Social and Cultural Rights. https://www.refworld.org/docid/4538838d0.html

United Nations Fund for Population Activities. (2012). Marrying too young: end child marriage. UNFPA. Retrieved on May 6, 2024, from https://www.unfpa.org/publications/marrying-too-young

United Nations General Assembly. (1966). International Covenant on Civil and Political Rights. https://www.ohchr.org/en/professionalinterest/pages/ccpr.aspx

United Nations Human Rights Office of the High Commissioner. (2001). Child marriage. https://www.ohchr.org/Documents/Publications/Factsheet23en.pdf

United Nations Population Fund (UNFPA) (2012). "Marrying Too Young: End Child Marriage."

United Nations Population Fund. (2001). *Socio-cultural aspects of reproductive health*. UNFPA.

United Nations Population Fund. (2012). Marrying too young: End child marriage. https://www.unfpa.org/sites/default/files/pub-pdf/MarryingTooYoung.pdf

United Nations Population Fund. (2020). Ending child marriage in Africa: A briefing for journalists. https://www.unfpa.org/sites/default/files/resource-pdf/Ending_child_marriage_in_Africa%2C_a_briefing_for_journalists_EN_LR.pdf

United Nations. (1966). International Covenant on Economic, Social and Cultural Rights. https://www.ohchr.org/en/professionalinterest/pages/cescr.aspx

United Nations. (1979). Convention on the Elimination of All Forms of Discrimination against Women. https://www.un.org/womenwatch/daw/cedaw/

United Nations. (1988). *First marriage: Patterns and determinants*. Population Division.

United Nations. (1989). Convention on the Rights of the Child. https://www.ohchr.org/en/professionalinterest/pages/crc.aspx

United Nations. (1990). *Patterns of first marriage: Timing and prevalence*. Population Division.

United Nations. (2000). Optional Protocol to the Convention on the Rights of the Child on the Sale of Children, Child Prostitution and Child Pornography. https://www.ohchr.org/en/professionalinterest/pages/OPSCCRC.aspx

United Nations. (2000). *World marriage patterns*. Population Division.

United Nations. (2017). Child marriage laws around the world. https://www.unwomen.org/en/what-we-do/ending-violence-against-women/facts-and-figures/child-marriage

Upchurch, D. M., & McCarthy, J. (1990). The timing of a first birth and high school completion. *American Sociological Review*, 55(2), 224–234. DOI: 10.2307/2095628

Utomo, A. J. (2014). Marrying up? Trends in age and education gaps among married couples in Indonesia. *Journal of Family Issues*, 35(12), 1683–1706. DOI: 10.1177/0192513X14538023

Vera, H., Berardo, D., & Berardo, F. M. (1985). Age heterogamy in marriage. *Journal of Marriage and Family*, 47(3), 553–566. DOI: 10.2307/352258

Veronese, G., Mahmid, F. A., & Bdier, D. (2023). Gender-based violence, subjective quality of life, and mental health outcomes among Palestinian women: The mediating role of social support and agency. *Violence Against Women*, 29(5), 925–948. DOI: 10.1177/10778012221099988 PMID: 36042012

Vettriselvan, R., Rengamani, J., James, F. A., Srinivasan, R., & Poongavanam, S. (2019). Issues and challenges of women employees in Indian technical industries. *International Journal of Engineering and Advanced Technology, 8*(2S2), 2019.

Vettriselvan, R., Rengamani, J., James, F. A., Srinivasan, R., & Poongavanam, S. (2019b). Issues and Challenges of Women Employees in Indian Technical Industries. *International Journal of Engineering and Advanced Technology, 8*(2S2), 404-409.

Vettriselvan, R., Anto, R., & Rajan, F. S. A. (2018b). Pathetic Health Status and Working Condition of Zambian Women. *Indian Journal of Public Health Research & Development*, 9(9), 259–264. DOI: 10.5958/0976-5506.2018.01006.9

Vettriselvan, R., & Arunkumar, N. (2018a). Child labour in unorganized mechanical engineering industries of Tamil Nadu: A situation analysis. *International Journal of Mechanical Engineering and Technology*, 9(10), 809–819.

Vettriselvan, R., Rajan, F. S. A., & Arunkumar, N. (2019a). Occupational Health Issues Faced by Women in Spinners. *Indian Journal of Public Health Research & Development*, 10(1), 500–512. DOI: 10.5958/0976-5506.2019.00098.6

Vikram, K. (2023). Modern marriage in a traditional society: The influence of college education on marriage in India. *Journal of Family Issues*, 45(5), 1116–1141. DOI: 10.1177/0192513X231155591

Vikram, K., Visaria, A., & Ganguly, D. (2023). Child marriage as a risk factor for non-communicable diseases among women in India. *International Journal of Epidemiology*, 52(5), 1303–1315. DOI: 10.1093/ije/dyad051 PMID: 37159526

Vilán, A. (2023). The evolution of the global movement to end child marriage. *Human Rights on the Edge*, 110–127. DOI: 10.4324/9781003394464-8

Vogler, C., & Pahl, I. (1994). Money, power and inequality in marriage. *The Sociological Review*, 42(2), 263–288. DOI: 10.1111/j.1467-954X.1994.tb00090.x

Vygotsky, L. S. (1986). *Thought and language*. The MIT Press.

Wahyudi, T., Hasanbasri, M., Kusnanto, H., & Hakimi, M. (2019). Social determinants of health of child marriage (analysis of ifls 2000, 2007, 2014). *Journal of Kesehatan Masyarakat*, 15(1), 62–68. DOI: 10.15294/kemas.v15i1.16514

Walker, L. E. A. (1979). *The battered woman*. Harper & Row Publishers.

Wallerstein, J. (1991). The long-term effects of divorce on children: A review. *Journal of the American Academy of Child and Adolescent Psychiatry*, 30(3), 349–360. DOI: 10.1097/00004583-199105000-00001 PMID: 1810276

Ward, A. C. (2009). The role of causal criteria in causal inferences: Bradford Hill's aspects of association. *Epidemiologic Perspectives & Innovations*, 6(1), 2. DOI: 10.1186/1742-5573-6-2 PMID: 19534788

Wardani, I. H. (2022, December). Legal Protection of Underage Women in Early Marriage. In *Proceeding International Seminar and Conference on Islamic Studies (ISCIS)* (Vol. 1, No. 1).

Wardlaw, T., You, D., Hug, L., Amouzou, A., & Newby, H. (2014). UNICEF Report: Enormous progress in child survival, but more significant focus on newborns urgently needed. *Reproductive Health*, 11(1), 1–4. DOI: 10.1186/1742-4755-11-82

Ward, T., & Birgden, A. (2007). Human rights and correctional cinical prctice. *Aggression and Violent Behavior*, 12(6), 628–643. DOI: 10.1016/j.avb.2007.05.001

Warner, E. (2011). Behind the Wedding Veil: Child Marriage as a Form of Trafficking in Girls. *The American University Journal of Gender, Social Policy & the Law*, 12, 1.

Warria, A. (2017). Forced child marriages as a form of child trafficking. *Children and Youth Services Review*, 79, 274–279. DOI: 10.1016/j.childyouth.2017.06.024

Watts, C., & Zimmerman, C. (2002). Violence against women: Global scope and magnitude. *Lancet*, 359(9313), 1232–1237. DOI: 10.1016/S0140-6736(02)08221-1 PMID: 11955557

West, C. M. (Ed.). (2002). *Violence in the lives of Black women: Battered, black, and blue*. Haworth Press.

Westoff, C. F. (1992). Age at marriage, age at first birth and fertility in Africa. World Bank Technical Paper # 169. Washington D. C., US: the World Bank.

Whitley, R., & Whitley, R. (2021). Family ties: marriage, divorce, and the mental health of men and boys. *Men's Issues and Mental Health: An Introductory Primer*, 207-234.

WHO. (2004). *Adolescent pregnancy*. Retrieved from: (https://apps.who.int/iris/bitstream/handle/10665/42903/9241591455_eng.pdf;jsessionid=4EE656F1D73E523CA32062208E4D280C? Sequence WHO. (2011). *Preventing Early Pregnancy and Poor Reproductive Outcomes Among Adolescents in Developing Countries*. Retrieved from https://iris.who.int/bitstream/handle/10665/44691/9789241502214_eng.pdf

WHO. (2011). Global strategy to stop health-care providers from performing female genital mutilation. https://www.who.int/reproductivehealth/publications/fgm/rhr_11_18/en/

WHO. (2017). *Mental health of adolescents*. Geneva: World Health Organization. Retrieved from https://www.who.int/

WHO. (2020). Child marriage. https://www.who.int/news-room/q-a-detail/child-marriage

WHO. (2022). *Adolescent pregnancy: Overview*. Geneva: World Health Organization. Retrieved from https://www.who.int/news-room/fact-sheets/detail/adolescent-pregnancy

WHO. (2024). *Gender and health*. https://www.who.int/health-topics/gender#tab=tab_1

Wijayati, N. A., & Soemanto, R. B. (2017). Socioeconomic and cultural determinants of early marriage in Ngawi, East Java: Application of the PRECEDE-PROCEED Model. *Journal of Health Promotion and Behavior*, 2(4), 302–312. DOI: 10.26911/thejhpb.2016.02.04.02

Williams, K. (2003). Has the future of marriage arrived? a contemporary examination of gender, marriage, and psychological well-being. *Journal of Health and Social Behavior*, 44(4), 470. DOI: 10.2307/1519794 PMID: 15038144

Wilson, B. (1982). Age differences between spouses and marital instability. Paper presented at the meeting of Population Association of America, San Diego.

Wodon, Q., Male, C., Nayihouba, A., Onagoruwa, A., Savadogo, A., Yedan, A., ... & Petroni, S. (2017). Economic impacts of child marriage: global synthesis report.

Wodon, Q., Malé, C., Nayihouba, K. A., Onagoruwa, A. O., Savadogo, A., Yedan, A., Edmeades, J., Kes, A., John, N., Murithi, L., Steinhaus, M., & Petroni, S. (2017). Economic impacts of child marriage: global synthesis report. *MINISTERIO DE EDUCACIÓN*, 1–99.

Wodon, Q. (2016). Early Childhood Development in the Context of the Family: The Case of Child Marriage. *Journal of Human Development and Capabilities*, 17(4), 590–598. Advance online publication. DOI: 10.1080/19452829.2016.1245277

Wolfe, D. M. (1959). Power and authority in the family. In D. Cartwright (Ed.): *Studies in social power*. The University of Michigan and an Arbor.

World Bank. (2015). Child marriage: A silent health and human rights issue. https://openknowledge.worldbank.org/bitstream/handle/10986/22788/9781464805007.pdf

World Bank. (2017). *Economic impacts of child marriage: Global synthesis report*. World Bank.

World Health Organization (WHO). (2013). *Global and regional estimates of violence against women: Prevalence and health effects of intimate partner violence and non-partner sexual violence*. World Health Organization.

World Health Organization. (2011). Global strategy to stop health-care providers from performing female genital mutilation. https://www.who.int/reproductivehealth/publications/fgm/rhr_11_18/en/

World Health Organization. (2020). Child marriage. https://www.who.int/news-room/q-a-detail/child-marriage

World Health Organization. (2022). Adolescent pregnancy: Overview. Retrieved from https://www.who.int/news-room/fact-sheets/detail/adolescent-pregnancy

Xing, C., Betancor, V., Chas, A., & Rodríguez-Pérez, A. (2022). Gender inequality in incivility: Everyone should be polite, but it is fine for some of us to be impolite. *Frontiers in Psychology*, 13, 966045. Advance online publication. DOI: 10.3389/fpsyg.2022.966045 PMID: 36225692

Yadav, K. P. (2006). *Child marriage in India*. Adhyayan Publishers.

Yağmur, S. K. (2023). Early and forced marriages, child brides. *International Journal of Arts, Humanities, and Social Sciences*, 4(7), 26–30. DOI: 10.56734/ijahss.v4n7a4

Yakoob, T. (2012). Socio-cultural constraints faced by girls regarding access to their secondary education in Mardan, Khyber Pakhtunkhuwa. *International Journal of Management Sciences and Business Research*, 1(12), 11–19.

Yoosefi Lebni, J., Solhi, M., Ebadi Fard Azar, F., Khalajabadi Farahani, F., & Irandoost, S. F. (2023). Exploring the consequences of early marriage: A conventional content analysis. *Inquiry*, 60, 00469580231159963. Advance online publication. DOI: 10.1177/00469580231159963 PMID: 37073489

Yount, K. M., Krause, K. H., & Miedema, S. S. (2017). Preventing gender-based violence victimization in adolescent girls in lower-income countries: Systematic review of reviews. *Social science & medicine (1982), 192*, 1–13. DOI: 10.1016/j.socscimed.2017.08.038

Yount, K. M., Crandall, A., Cheong, Y. F., Osypuk, T. L., Bates, L. M., Naved, R. T., & Schuler, S. R. (2016). Child marriage and intimate partner violence in rural Bangladesh: A longitudinal multilevel analysis. *Demography*, 53(6), 1821–1852. DOI: 10.1007/s13524-016-0520-8 PMID: 27812927

Youvan, D. C. (2024). Child marriage and legal paradoxes: India's battle with tradition and child protection laws. DOI:DOI: 10.13140/RG.2.2.10715.17446

Yüksel, F., & Koçtürk, N. (2021). Investigation of Factors Associated with the Child Marriage in Turkey. *Journal of Child Sexual Abuse*, 30(6), 653–666. DOI: 10.1080/10538712.2021.1956664 PMID: 34323160

Yuliastuti, A., Mubin, M. F., Ernawati, E., & Pranata, S. (2024). Bibliometric Analysis of the Impact of Early Marriage on Adolescents. *Indonesian Journal of Global Health Research*, 6(2), 759–770.

Zastrow, C. (2010). *Introduction to social work and social welfare: Empowering people* (10th ed.). Brooks/Cole Cengage Learning.

Zeejin, V. M., & Kumar, G. S. (2020). A study on child marriage in a multilateral approach with special reference to Gudiyatham, Vellore district, Tamil Nadu. *Mukt Shabd Journal*, 9(4), 2557–2578.

Zegeye, B., Keetile, M., Ahinkorah, B. O., Ameyaw, E. K., Seidu, A., & Yaya, S. (2021). Utilization of deworming medication and its associated factors among pregnant married women in 26 sub-Saharan African countries: A multi-country analysis. *Tropical Medicine and Health*, 49(1), 53. Advance online publication. DOI: 10.1186/s41182-021-00343-x PMID: 34193313

About the Contributors

Emaj Uddin is a Professor at the Department of Social Work, Rajshahi University, Bangladesh. He graduated in Social Work and earned his Doctoral degree from the Institute of Bangladesh Studies (IBS), Rajshahi University. His research interest includes family studies, health, and child development. He writes several articles on child development and education in international abstracted and indexed Journals. He is an editorial board member in some international journals.

***

A. Balakrishnan, Professor & Head, Department of Applied Research, Gandhigram Rural Institute specialized in Rural Development, Labour Studies, Interdisplinary Research, Human Resource Management having 28 years of teaching and research experience

Deepan A. is an Assistant Professor at Sambhram University in Uzbekistan, with over 7 years of marketing experience in multinational corporations and 8 years of teaching across Central Africa, India, and Uzbekistan. His professional background includes expertise in strategic marketing, brand management, and market analysis, complemented by a strong academic career involving curriculum development and student mentoring. Deepan's research interests focus on contemporary challenges in marketing and business education, reflecting his commitment to bridging industry knowledge with academic inquiry, making him a valuable asset in both corporate and educational environments.

Sema Beserek is a social worker. She has been working with migrants, asylum seekers and refugees in various NGOs for many years.

Bilal Ahmad Bhat is presently working as Professor (Statistics) and Head, Division of social Sciences, Faculty of Fisheries, Ganderbal, SKUAT. Dr. Bilal has published more than 400 research papers in reputed journals and has organised a number of national/ international conferences, Dr. Bilal has received many awards and is a member of advisory board in well known journals of repute

Tripti Bhushan is currently working as Assistant Professor at O. P Jindal Global Law School and as Fellow at Centre for Law and Humanities at JGU. Earlier she was working as Teaching and Research for Intellectual Pursuit (TRIPS) Fellow and Academic Tutor at Jindal Global Law School. She has also worked as an Assistant Professor at Kalinga University, Raipur. She has completed her undergraduate program (B.A, LL. B)(Hons) from Amity Law School, Lucknow. She further pursued her Post Graduate Program (LL.M) in Intellectual Property Rights from Hidayatullah National Law University, Raipur. She has also obtained distinction with Grade 'A' in her Dissertation during her LL.M. She has also taught various courses as Visiting Faculty at Indore Law Institute, ARKA Jain University, Maharashtra National Law University Aurangabad. She has been invited as a Resource Person for delivering lectures/Sessions at various International/National Organizations such as " Asiatic International Business Academy', Peruvian Bar Association, International Congress, Legal Desire Summit, Path Lexis, NMIMS Mumbai, MNLU, Amity Universities, MSME Gangtok, MSME New Delhi, Department of Forensic Science & Criminology, Madurai, Parul University, JECRC University Jaipur. Aligarh Muslim University, Aligarh. She has various Publication in journals like Indonesian Journal of International Law Economic and Political Weekly (EPW), NTUT Journal of Intellectual Property and Management, Oxford University Hub, Law School Policy Review NLSIU Bangalore, International Journal of Public Law and Policy, UNHRC, Journal of Intellectual Property Rights. She has edited Book on "Handbook on Legal Contemporary Issues in India" ISBN-978-93-5668-453-9 published by Blue Rose Publishers which is forwarded by Hon'ble Justice Vineet Kothari (Former Chief Justice Gujarat High Court) and Authored Book on Facets of Media Law and Intellectual Property Rights.She has also completed various National & International Courses from W.I.P.O, CISCO Networking Academy, United States Institute of Peace, Dr. Ram Manohar Lahiya National Law University, Lucknow, The Law Learners, ADBI Institute, University of De Geneva, Amity University, Alison. She has also completed Professional Development Program from University of Buraimi. She has also completed IP Awareness / Training Program under National Intellectual Property Awareness Mission #NIPAM organized by Intellectual Property Office. She is also the Advisory Board Member of International Centre for Intellectual Property Laws (IC-IPL) & Young Member at Young ICCA(International Council for Commercial Arbitration). She has been Invited to judge the Preliminary Rounds of Third GDGU International Virtual Law and Technology Moot Court Competition,2022 in association with Cyber Law

University Goenka University She has also been Invited as a Jury member to judge the First National Justice Dipak Misra Moot Court Competition & also to judge the First I-Win-IP National I.P.R Moot Court in collaboration with Centre of IPR & Patent Facilitation & University of Osmania. Earlier she has also worked with The National T.V as Content Writer & Nexus Legal Associates. She has attended various International/National Conferences at NALSAR University of Law, Hyderabad, International Conference on Environmental Law at Gujarat National Law University, Gandhinagar, International Trade & I.P.R Conference by Intellectual Society of Entrepreneurship & Research Development (ISERD India). Cambridge University, Staffordshire University,UK,Kent Law School, U.K. She has Interned at various organizations/ Law Firms during her law school including Bharucha & Partners, Chiramrit Legal, The Law Desk, Neeraj Associates, Indian Oil Corporation, N.T.P.C(National Thermal Power Corporation), Judicial Training & Research Institute (J.T.R.I), U.P Human Rights Commission. Awards and Recognitions 'Award for Research Excellence:' Jindal Global University (2021-2022). 'Award for Best External Paper:' in Annual conference organized by Kent Law School, U.K (2021). 'Recipient of 'Emerging Scientist Award in the field of Law In year (2020).

Ajay Chandel is working as an Associate Professor at Mittal School of Business, Lovely Professional University, Punjab. He has 14 years of teaching and research experience. He has published papers in SCOPUS, WOS, and UGC listed Journals in areas like Social Media Marketing, E-Commerce, and Consumer Behaviour. He has published cases on SMEs and Social Entrepreneurship in The Case Centre, UK. He also reviews The Case Journal, Emerald Group Publishing, and International Journal of Business and Globalisation, Inderscience. He has authored and developed MOOCs on Tourism and Hospitality Marketing under Epg-Pathshala- A gateway to all postgraduate courses (a UGC-MHRD project under its National Mission on Education Through ICT (NME-ICT).

Ramy El-Kady is a Full Professor of Criminal Law at the Police Academy and holds the position of Head of the Criminal Law Department. He was rewarded with the State Encouragement Award in Legal and Economic Sciences, Citizenship and Human Rights Branch, on the topic of "the right of persons cooperating with justice for protection in international conventions and national legislation. He graduated from the Police College in 1999. He obtained a postgraduate diploma in criminal sciences and public law, which is equivalent to a master's degree in criminal law, in 2003. He obtained a PhD in criminal law from the Faculty of Law, Cairo University, on the topic of (Mediation as an Alternative to a Criminal Case: A Comparative Study. He currently teaches criminal law subjects to college students. He supervised numerous studies submitted for doctoral degrees and higher diplomas and authored a host of research in the criminal law field. He has previously judged numerous research papers in a number of refereed regional scientific journals. He published a host of research in refereed and indexed periodicals and took part in a number of international and local conferences and symposia.

Lalhriatpuii Fanai is working in the field of addiction among emerging adults. She has completed her Masters in clinical psychology and is currently pursuing a doctoral degree in Psychology. Her research interests lie in developing culturally appropriate interventions; ethnocultural moderators of treatment outcomes; assessing and enhancing motivation to change; and improving interventions for individuals with alcohol and other substance use disorders (SUDs).

Ritu Gautam, Sr. Assistant Professor, Academic Coordinator, Sharda School of Law, Sharda University, is having more than 11 yr. of diverse experience in the field of Law. Dr. Ritu has earned her Ph.D. in Cyber laws along with LL.M, MBA, B.Com, LLB, and PGCCL. Dr. Ritu is an expert in family mediation and heading a very successful Family Dispute Resolution, in Greater Noida, U.P. Dr. Ritu is having experience in dealing with more than 600 family dispute cases. She has published 6 books on different social issues, 30 Research papers in UGC care and SCOPUS journals, and 50 book chapters on different issues. She has been awarded by National Commission for Women (NCW) and Uttar Pradesh Police (Women and Safety Wing) for her excellent work. Her previous books have received many accolades in the academic circle.

Bekir Güzel is an associate professor in the Department of Social Work at Recep Tayyip Erdoğan University, Türkiye. His main areas of research are social work, refugees, asylum seekers, immigrants, migration policies, international migration movements, labor migration and child labor.

Nyi. R. Irmayani Intermediate expert researcher at the Research Center for Social Welfare, Villages and Connectivity; National Research and Innovation Agency (BRIN). Born in Jakarta on February 20, 1968. Graduated from the Faculty of Law, Trisakti University, Jakarta 1992 and the Department of Social Psychology at the Faculty of Psychology, Gadjah Mada University, Yogyakarta, in 2002. Research focus for the last 5 years has been on Social Resilience in Rural Communities, Children in Conflict with the Law, Family Development Session (FDS) Family Hope Program (PKH), Mapping of Social Companions and Volunteers, Digital Social Innovation in Rural Areas.

Geetanjali Jaiswani, MBBS, MS ENT Dr. Geetanjali Jaiswani is a distinguished medical professional specializing in Ear, Nose, and Throat (ENT) medicine. An alumnus of Banaras Hindu University (BHU), she earned her MBBS degree followed by a Master of Surgery (MS) in ENT, where she honed her skills and deepened her knowledge in the field. With a passion for teaching, Dr. Jaiswani has dedicated herself to educating future healthcare professionals. Her commitment to academia is reflected in her involvement in various educational initiatives, mentoring students, and contributing to curriculum development. In addition to her teaching endeavors, Dr. Jaiswani is actively engaged in research aimed at advancing ENT practices. Her work focuses on innovative treatment methodologies and improving patient outcomes, which has led to several publications in reputable medical journals. Dr. Jaiswani's contributions to the field of ENT, combined with her dedication to education and research, make her a respected figure in the medical community. She continues to inspire her students and peers alike through her expertise and unwavering commitment to advancing medical knowledge.

Vaishnavi Jeyachandran is a PhD Scholar at Christ University. She is also a practicing counsellor and a researcher. Her research interests include coping strategies, cultures' influence on mental health, and enhancing the well-being of children, young adults, educators, and mental health professionals.

Christian Kaunert is Professor of International Security at Dublin City University, Ireland. He is also Professor of Policing and Security, as well as Director of the International Centre for Policing and Security at the University of South Wales. In addition, he is Jean Monnet Chair, Director of the Jean Monnet Centre of Excellence and Director of the Jean Monnet Network on EU Counter-Terrorism.

Deepthi Jose Maliakkal is a doctoral research scholar from the Department of Psychology at CHRIST University, India. Her research interests include emotional abuse, domestic and interpersonal violence, counseling, and mental health.

R. Sakthivel, Professor & Deputy Vice Chancellor (Research & Innovation) at DMI – St. Eugene University, Zambia holds Ph.D. in Plant Biology and Plant Biotechnology from Madras University, M.Phil. & M.Sc. Degree from Madras University, B.Sc. Degree from Bharathidasan University, Master in Education from Tamil Nadu Teacher Education University and Bachelor in Education from Bharathiyar University. He has served in various capacities from Assistant Lecturer, Lecturer, Senior Lecturer, Assistant Professor, Professor, Head of the Department, Vice Principal, Principal – Academic, Registrar and Deputy Vice Chancellor (Research & Innovation) in Colleges such as DMI – St. Eugene University, Zambia - Central Africa, St. Joseph University College of Agricultural Sciences and Technology, Songea, Tanzania, East Africa and St. Joseph University in Tanzania, Arusha Campus, Arusha, Tanzania, East Africa. Presently he is working as Deputy

Vice Chancellor (Research & Innovation) for DMI – St. Eugene University, Zambia, Central Africa. His outstanding work has been widely recognized as he has won the Best Researcher Award, Top 50 International Distinguished Academic Leaders 2020, Academic Excellence Awards - 2019 for Distinguished Principal, Outstanding Contribution in Leadership - 2019, Young Scientist Award - 2018, the Bharat Ratna Dr. A. P. J. Abdul Kalam award - 2011 and he was awarded Senior Research Fellow by the Defence Research and Development Organization (DRDO). As a researcher, he has published 45 research articles in both International and National peer reviewed journals with Impact factor, NCBI – Genbank publications 30, Blog Publications 1, Patent 1 and he has published 6 books.

R. Vettriselvan, an Associate Professor, AMET University, specialised in HRM and Marketing. He is acting as Mentor, Saraswathi Institute of Medical Sciences, Hapur. He served as Review Board member, National Council for Higher Education, Malawi, Head of the Department, School of Commerce and Management Studies, St. Eugene University, Zambia, and Director, Research and Publication, St. John the Baptist University, Malawi. He has published 28 books and 80 articles in peer reviewed journals and edited book chapters. Under his guidance two have completed and five are pursuing their PhD.

Iranna Ronad, MSW, KSET: Iranna Ronad, MSW, KSET: Iranna Ronad, Head of the Department of Social Work at Shree Sangameshwara Arts and Commerce College in Chadchan, Karnataka, India, makes significant contributions to the field of social work education. He is an academic with over a decade of experience in teaching and research. Ronad gained invaluable insights and practical experience working as a social worker and counselor in the development sector before entering academia, which he now shares with his students. Additionally, he is a dedicated academic writer with 30 publications to his credit. Ronad's passion lies in counseling, professional social work, and social development. He makes a substantial contribution to the theoretical and practical facets of social work education by actively mentoring students at the graduate and postgraduate levels, creating a dynamic learning environment.

Hari Harjanto Setiawan, Born in Klaten, on November 2, 1973. He completed his Bachelor's degree in 1998 at the College of Social Welfare (STKS) Bandung. In 2001, he graduated from the University of Indonesia in the Sociology Study Program with a specialization in Social Welfare. In 2014 he completed his Doctoral education at the University of Indonesia, Social Welfare Study Program. Since 2007 until 2021 Social Affairs as a functional staff of Associate Expert Research at the Center for Research and Development of Social Welfare, Ministry of the

Republic of Indonesia. Starting January 1, 2022, he will change his office to the National Research and Innovation Agency, Republic of Indonesia. The studies of interest are studies on Social Welfare, children's social problems and Social Entrepreneurship. Various studies have been conducted and published in the form of books and scientific journals. Another experience, as the editorial board of the Journal of "Sosio Konsepsia".

Bhupinder Singh working as Professor at Sharda University, India. Also, Honorary Professor in University of South Wales UK and Santo Tomas University Tunja, Colombia. His areas of publications as Smart Healthcare, Medicines, fuzzy logics, artificial intelligence, robotics, machine learning, deep learning, federated learning, IoT, PV Glasses, metaverse and many more. He has 3 books, 139 paper publications, 163 paper presentations in international/national conferences and seminars, participated in more than 40 workshops/FDP's/QIP's, 25 courses from international universities of repute, organized more than 59 events with international and national academicians and industry people's, editor-in-chief and co-editor in journals, developed new courses. He has given talks at international universities, resource person in international conferences such as in Nanyang Technological University Singapore, Tashkent State University of Law Uzbekistan; KIMEP University Kazakhstan, All'ah meh Tabatabi University Iran, the Iranian Association of International Criminal law, Iran and Hague Center for International Law and Investment, The Netherlands, Northumbria University Newcastle UK,

Sevinc Sutlu She graduated from Ankara University Faculty of Medicine. She completed her master's degree in Isparta Süleyman Demirel Faculty of Medicine, Department of Public Health, and her doctorate in Ege University Faculty of Medicine, Department of Geriatrics. She works as an associate professor of public health at Burdur Mehmet Akif Ersoy University, Faculty of Health Sciences.

Huy Hung Ta lecture in Economics and Management, International School, Vietnam National University Hanoi, former of Vice Director International Program cooperate between Toulon University and Academy of Finance

Adhani Wardianti Born in Mataram on December 9 1975. Completed his Bachelor's Degree in 1997 at the Social Welfare Polytechnic (POLTEKKESOS) Bandung, in 2010 he completed his Master's Degree at the Social Welfare Polytechnic (POLTEKKESOS) Bandung. Currently serving as a Functional Community Advisor at the Class I Bandung Correctional Center (BAPAS) under the Ministry of Law and Human Rights, West Java Regional Office. Active as a member of the Indonesian Community Guidance Association and part of the assessment team for the functional position of community counselor. The study of interest is the study of social problems, especially the study of social problems of children in conflict with the law (ABH).

Yanuar Wismayanti In 2020, she received a Doctoral degree from Griffith University, Australia, from the School of Human Services and Social Work with the research project Understanding Child Sexual Abuse in Indonesia: A Critical Analysis. After completing her Doctoral education at Griffith University, Wismayanti returned to serve as a researcher at the Ministry of Social Affairs. Then, in 2021, he joined the National Research and Innovation Agency (BRIN). As a researcher, some of his research focuses include social science topics, especially issues of child protection, women, gender, poverty, and social protection, and focus on social policy topics. Several studies have been carried out through collaboration with research institute partners, including universities both at home and abroad, as well as ministries/institutions and local government partners.

Dr. Mohit Yadav is an Associate Professor in the area of Human Resource Management at Jindal Global Business School (JGBS). He has a rich blend of work experience from both Academics as well as Industry. Prof. Mohit holds a Ph.D. from Department of Management Studies, Indian Institute of Technology Roorkee (IIT Roorkee) and has completed Master of Human Resource and Organizational Development (MHROD) from prestigious Delhi School of Economics, University of Delhi. He also holds a B.Com (Hons.) degree from University of Delhi and UGC-JRF scholarship. He has published various research papers and book chapters with reputed publishers like Springer, Sage, Emerald, Elsevier, Inderscience etc. and presented research papers in national and International conferences both in India and abroad. He has many best paper awards on his credit too. He is reviewer of various international journals like Computers in Human Behavior, Policing etc. His areas of interest are Organizational Behavior, HRM, Recruitment and Selection, Organizational Citizenship Behavior, Quality of work life and role.

Index

A

Age-heterogamy 1, 3, 4, 5, 6, 7, 8, 10, 11, 13, 14, 15, 16, 17, 18, 21
Age-Homogamy 1, 4, 5, 6, 7, 8, 10, 11, 13, 14, 15, 16, 19
Anxiety 67, 68, 142, 145, 163, 164, 165, 169, 170, 171, 172, 173, 174, 175, 178, 180, 191, 193, 194, 197, 207, 238, 239, 248, 255, 270, 275, 299, 301, 302, 329, 332, 333, 334, 335
Arab Laws 293
Asylum Seekers 369, 373, 374, 375, 376, 377, 378, 384

B

Bangladesh 1, 2, 3, 4, 5, 6, 7, 8, 9, 10, 11, 16, 19, 20, 21, 22, 23, 24, 25, 27, 28, 29, 30, 31, 32, 34, 35, 36, 37, 38, 39, 40, 42, 43, 44, 45, 46, 47, 48, 49, 50, 51, 52, 54, 55, 56, 57, 58, 85, 86, 87, 88, 89, 91, 94, 110, 113, 114, 115, 116, 118, 119, 120, 130, 131, 138, 139, 150, 162, 179, 182, 183, 185, 186, 192, 200, 211, 224, 229, 232, 242, 243, 244, 259, 287, 288, 298, 316, 321, 338, 339, 364, 366, 367, 387, 388

C

Child marriage 22, 29, 53, 63, 64, 70, 72, 75, 76, 77, 78, 81, 82, 84, 85, 86, 87, 88, 89, 90, 91, 93, 94, 95, 96, 97, 98, 100, 101, 102, 103, 104, 105, 107, 108, 109, 110, 111, 112, 113, 114, 133, 137, 138, 139, 141, 142, 143, 150, 151, 152, 153, 154, 155, 156, 157, 158, 159, 160, 161, 162, 164, 172, 177, 178, 179, 180, 182, 183, 184, 185, 186, 187, 188, 192, 194, 200, 206, 210, 211, 212, 219, 220, 221, 231, 232, 233, 234, 236, 237, 240, 245, 246, 247, 248, 249, 250, 251, 253, 254, 256, 257, 258, 259, 260, 273, 274, 276, 282, 283, 285, 287, 288, 292, 294, 295, 302, 303, 304, 305, 307, 309, 316, 317, 318, 322, 323, 324, 325, 326, 339, 342, 343, 344, 346, 347, 348, 349, 350, 351, 352, 353, 354, 355, 356, 357, 358, 359, 360, 361, 362, 363, 364, 365, 366, 367, 370, 387, 388, 389, 391
Children's Rights 77, 78, 94, 97, 99, 102, 104, 251, 267, 293, 298, 357, 359, 361, 372, 377, 378, 383
child trafficking 291, 292, 293, 294, 295, 309, 316, 319, 326
communities 4, 8, 24, 25, 32, 34, 35, 36, 37, 38, 39, 40, 42, 44, 45, 47, 49, 50, 56, 57, 58, 63, 64, 65, 67, 68, 70, 71, 72, 79, 80, 81, 82, 83, 89, 113, 118, 138, 139, 142, 147, 150, 152, 155, 157, 162, 163, 172, 173, 175, 176, 177, 181, 186, 194, 207, 209, 211, 220, 251, 259, 265, 266, 268, 269, 270, 271, 273, 274, 277, 278, 279, 280, 281, 284, 288, 296, 303, 307, 318, 333, 338, 339, 341, 343, 344, 346, 347, 353, 356, 357, 359, 360, 361, 362, 366, 370, 373, 374, 377, 388
Contraception 243, 248, 328, 329, 330, 336, 338
Cross-Cultural Comparison 24, 25, 57, 58, 138, 139, 186, 338
Cultural Norms 34, 61, 65, 66, 69, 78, 80, 113, 142, 167, 171, 172, 173, 177, 180, 192, 193, 194, 195, 224, 263, 271, 284, 328, 346, 370

D

Depression 67, 68, 142, 145, 152, 155, 163, 164, 165, 169, 171, 172, 174, 175, 178, 180, 191, 193, 194, 197, 207, 238, 239, 270, 275, 294, 299, 300, 301, 302, 329, 332, 333, 334, 350, 351, 361

463

E

Early Marriage 9, 23, 25, 27, 28, 29, 30, 31, 32, 33, 34, 35, 37, 38, 39, 40, 44, 45, 47, 49, 50, 51, 54, 56, 57, 58, 59, 61, 62, 63, 64, 65, 66, 68, 69, 70, 71, 72, 73, 74, 75, 76, 77, 78, 79, 80, 81, 82, 83, 84, 85, 87, 88, 89, 94, 95, 96, 98, 102, 105, 106, 107, 110, 113, 114, 115, 116, 117, 118, 119, 120, 122, 123, 124, 126, 130, 131, 133, 137, 138, 141, 142, 143, 144, 145, 146, 150, 151, 152, 154, 155, 156, 160, 161, 162, 163, 164, 165, 166, 167, 168, 169, 170, 171, 172, 173, 174, 175, 176, 177, 178, 179, 180, 181, 182, 183, 184, 185, 186, 189, 190, 191, 192, 193, 194, 195, 196, 197, 198, 199, 200, 201, 202, 203, 204, 205, 206, 207, 208, 209, 210, 211, 213, 214, 216, 219, 220, 222, 223, 224, 228, 229, 234, 235, 236, 238, 239, 240, 241, 242, 243, 244, 246, 248, 249, 251, 252, 253, 254, 255, 256, 257, 258, 259, 260, 261, 262, 263, 264, 265, 266, 267, 268, 269, 270, 271, 272, 273, 274, 275, 276, 277, 278, 279, 280, 281, 282, 283, 284, 286, 287, 288, 291, 292, 293, 294, 295, 296, 298, 299, 300, 301, 302, 303, 304, 307, 309, 310, 316, 319, 320, 321, 322, 324, 325, 339, 341, 342, 344, 345, 346, 347, 348, 349, 351, 352, 356, 357, 360, 364, 365, 366, 367, 369, 370, 371, 372, 373, 374, 376, 377, 379, 380, 382, 383, 384, 385, 386, 387, 388, 389, 390
Economic Consequences 85, 193, 261, 270, 272
Egyptian Law 310, 312, 313, 314, 315
Empowerment 61, 62, 65, 69, 71, 73, 74, 75, 79, 80, 82, 83, 84, 86, 88, 107, 119, 123, 150, 163, 176, 177, 194, 201, 203, 204, 206, 207, 208, 209, 271, 274, 280, 281, 316, 317, 336, 357, 360, 369, 373, 374, 376, 377, 378, 381, 384, 385, 386, 387, 388

Empowerment-Based Practice 369, 378
Ethnic Groups 5, 6, 27, 28, 29, 30, 49, 51, 52, 58, 168, 242, 287

F

Family Life Course Pathways 116, 122, 123, 130
Family Life Course Perspective 115, 122
Family Socio-Cultural Value 45, 47
Family structure 1, 11, 13, 14, 15, 16, 18, 24, 25, 58, 128, 139, 194, 223, 229, 276, 287, 383
forced marriage 68, 85, 86, 110, 153, 171, 177, 182, 219, 220, 221, 231, 282, 292, 293, 295, 307, 321, 322, 324, 370

G

Gender 1, 2, 3, 4, 9, 16, 17, 20, 21, 22, 23, 24, 25, 28, 29, 31, 35, 36, 39, 49, 52, 54, 62, 63, 64, 65, 66, 67, 69, 70, 71, 72, 75, 76, 78, 79, 80, 81, 82, 83, 84, 85, 86, 87, 88, 89, 93, 94, 95, 96, 97, 101, 103, 104, 105, 107, 111, 112, 113, 114, 116, 119, 120, 123, 124, 125, 129, 132, 133, 137, 142, 151, 152, 155, 158, 162, 163, 164, 166, 168, 170, 171, 172, 173, 175, 177, 180, 184, 186, 187, 190, 192, 193, 194, 217, 218, 219, 220, 221, 222, 223, 224, 229, 230, 231, 234, 235, 236, 237, 238, 241, 243, 245, 246, 249, 251, 252, 255, 260, 261, 262, 264, 268, 269, 270, 271, 274, 275, 276, 278, 279, 281, 282, 284, 287, 295, 298, 307, 309, 317, 325, 326, 328, 344, 346, 347, 348, 357, 360, 362, 365, 370, 372, 383, 386, 391, 392
Gender-based violence 62, 63, 65, 70, 72, 76, 78, 82, 84, 88, 89, 113, 162, 172, 186, 218, 221, 224, 231, 245, 246, 260, 326, 347, 372, 391
Gender equality 62, 63, 65, 66, 67, 69, 70, 71, 75, 76, 78, 80, 83, 84, 86, 94, 95, 96, 104, 107, 112, 113, 142, 175, 177, 218, 219, 220, 235, 262, 271,

274, 278, 279, 281, 282, 307, 309, 357, 360, 365, 370, 372, 386
Gender Inequality 62, 64, 65, 70, 72, 79, 82, 84, 93, 95, 104, 105, 114, 124, 133, 163, 166, 172, 173, 190, 192, 193, 222, 229, 230, 236, 237, 252, 261, 262, 264, 268, 269, 271, 276, 284, 346, 362, 391, 392
Girls' rights 65, 70, 74, 75, 78, 79, 80, 83, 219, 223, 234, 241, 268, 309, 320, 359
Global Context 237, 241

H

Health 22, 23, 29, 50, 54, 55, 59, 62, 63, 64, 65, 67, 68, 71, 72, 73, 74, 75, 79, 80, 83, 84, 85, 86, 87, 88, 89, 91, 93, 94, 95, 101, 102, 103, 104, 108, 109, 111, 112, 113, 114, 116, 119, 123, 124, 125, 132, 136, 139, 141, 142, 143, 144, 146, 147, 149, 151, 152, 153, 155, 156, 157, 158, 159, 160, 161, 162, 163, 164, 165, 167, 168, 169, 170, 171, 172, 173, 174, 175, 176, 178, 179, 180, 182, 183, 184, 185, 186, 187, 188, 189, 190, 191, 192, 193, 194, 195, 196, 197, 198, 199, 200, 201, 202, 203, 204, 205, 206, 207, 208, 209, 210, 211, 212, 213, 214, 216, 218, 219, 220, 221, 222, 223, 228, 229, 230, 231, 232, 233, 234, 235, 236, 237, 238, 239, 240, 241, 243, 245, 246, 247, 248, 249, 250, 251, 253, 254, 255, 256, 257, 258, 259, 260, 262, 271, 273, 274, 275, 276, 277, 280, 281, 282, 283, 284, 286, 287, 288, 289, 291, 292, 293, 299, 300, 302, 307, 308, 311, 312, 315, 316, 319, 321, 322, 323, 324, 325, 326, 327, 328, 330, 331, 332, 333, 334, 335, 336, 337, 338, 339, 342, 344, 350, 351, 352, 356, 358, 360, 361, 362, 363, 364, 365, 366, 367, 370, 371, 374, 377, 378, 379, 380, 382, 383, 387, 388, 390, 391, 392
High School Dropout 89, 114, 115, 116, 117, 118, 119, 120, 122, 125, 126, 128, 130, 131, 136, 137, 139, 162, 186, 211, 259, 288, 339, 367, 388
Human Capital Theory 261, 263
Human rights 51, 62, 63, 65, 66, 72, 75, 76, 79, 82, 86, 89, 90, 91, 94, 95, 99, 100, 112, 114, 158, 160, 167, 168, 188, 192, 194, 213, 214, 215, 218, 220, 221, 234, 245, 253, 259, 264, 265, 267, 278, 279, 292, 295, 309, 324, 342, 343, 351, 360, 362, 366, 372, 373, 387
human trafficking 229, 292, 293, 295, 310, 311, 312, 313, 314, 319, 321, 322, 323, 378

I

India 28, 52, 53, 61, 85, 87, 94, 118, 141, 142, 143, 144, 148, 150, 151, 152, 153, 154, 155, 156, 158, 159, 160, 161, 162, 163, 169, 182, 189, 192, 200, 201, 204, 211, 212, 219, 229, 231, 237, 238, 239, 242, 244, 245, 246, 249, 256, 257, 258, 259, 260, 261, 282, 286, 287, 288, 304, 327, 341, 343, 344, 345, 346, 347, 349, 351, 352, 356, 357, 363, 364, 365, 366, 367
Intergenerational Impact 163, 165, 174, 270
International Mechanisms 369, 370, 372, 376, 383, 384, 385
Intersectionality 168, 183, 255, 261, 264, 286, 370, 373
Interventions 62, 63, 69, 74, 77, 78, 81, 82, 83, 84, 85, 108, 156, 163, 164, 165, 167, 168, 171, 173, 176, 177, 179, 180, 191, 193, 197, 200, 201, 203, 204, 206, 207, 208, 209, 210, 233, 241, 247, 257, 262, 264, 271, 274, 279, 280, 281, 282, 283, 284, 316, 317, 323, 328, 336, 337, 343, 356, 357, 359, 360, 362, 366, 369, 380

L

Long-Term Wellbeing 189, 193

M

Marriage pattern 3, 5, 8, 9, 11, 12, 14, 16, 20, 28, 31, 33, 51, 55, 242

Mental Health 68, 85, 86, 109, 111, 141, 142, 143, 144, 146, 152, 155, 156, 158, 159, 161, 163, 164, 165, 168, 169, 170, 171, 172, 173, 174, 175, 176, 178, 180, 182, 183, 184, 185, 186, 187, 189, 191, 193, 194, 197, 198, 207, 208, 235, 237, 239, 240, 241, 248, 249, 254, 255, 257, 258, 260, 275, 282, 302, 321, 325, 326, 332, 333, 336, 338, 339, 344, 352, 358, 362, 388, 390

Mental Well-being 315

Morbidity 62, 110, 183, 189, 193, 200, 207, 222, 245, 287, 344

P

policies 65, 72, 73, 77, 78, 79, 82, 84, 94, 95, 98, 100, 102, 105, 107, 112, 116, 153, 156, 157, 179, 193, 203, 205, 206, 207, 208, 209, 213, 214, 240, 247, 264, 274, 280, 284, 316, 321, 336, 360, 365, 377

Poverty 5, 29, 33, 36, 51, 61, 62, 63, 64, 65, 69, 72, 80, 83, 95, 96, 102, 103, 104, 105, 106, 107, 110, 114, 116, 119, 123, 126, 128, 133, 143, 147, 152, 154, 156, 173, 174, 175, 190, 191, 192, 193, 194, 196, 198, 199, 200, 220, 223, 224, 228, 229, 230, 233, 238, 241, 243, 244, 250, 252, 254, 261, 262, 268, 269, 270, 271, 273, 274, 276, 277, 280, 284, 286, 288, 291, 296, 300, 301, 304, 307, 316, 327, 330, 331, 333, 344, 346, 348, 349, 354, 356, 357, 362, 383

Prevention strategies 107

PTSD 68, 145, 163, 164, 165, 169, 170, 171, 172, 178, 180, 238, 302

Puberty 30, 36, 105, 106, 118, 154, 248, 266, 296, 298, 299, 304, 329, 346

Public Health Interventions 193, 247

R

Religion 28, 35, 39, 100, 102, 103, 105, 106, 120, 121, 122, 224, 242, 264, 265, 266, 267, 309, 375

Reproductive Health 59, 67, 68, 71, 72, 74, 80, 84, 89, 93, 94, 95, 101, 102, 113, 136, 139, 149, 156, 161, 183, 193, 194, 201, 202, 204, 205, 206, 208, 210, 211, 218, 220, 221, 229, 232, 235, 238, 245, 246, 247, 254, 256, 258, 260, 280, 282, 307, 323, 325, 328, 330, 336, 364, 374, 380, 382

Right To Health 311

S

Social and Legal Interventions 63

Social Implications 23, 88, 193, 211, 233, 257, 262, 275, 277, 387

Social Norms Theory 218, 265

Social Reproduction Theory 261, 263

society 1, 3, 4, 7, 22, 28, 30, 35, 52, 71, 81, 83, 84, 87, 96, 100, 101, 102, 104, 105, 106, 107, 111, 112, 114, 118, 124, 142, 144, 145, 147, 148, 151, 153, 156, 161, 166, 172, 175, 177, 184, 217, 218, 232, 239, 240, 242, 247, 263, 264, 267, 270, 271, 273, 282, 286, 291, 292, 294, 296, 300, 309, 311, 312, 319, 320, 322, 323, 324, 334, 341, 343, 344, 346, 347, 349, 350, 352, 354, 356, 361, 364, 365, 367, 371, 374, 376, 377, 383, 387

socioeconomic status 1, 2, 5, 9, 11, 23, 24, 65, 67, 89, 114, 119, 162, 186, 191, 197, 211, 259, 288, 295, 339, 366, 388

Socio-Legal Implications 237, 241

T

Teenage 89, 103, 114, 115, 116, 118, 119, 120, 124, 125, 126, 127, 128, 129, 130, 131, 132, 133, 134, 135, 136, 137, 139, 145, 149, 162, 186, 211, 238, 240, 245, 247, 248, 259, 265, 288, 299, 305, 307, 317, 322, 324, 327,

328, 329, 330, 331, 332, 333, 334, 335, 336, 337, 338, 339, 342, 367, 388

Türkiye 228, 231, 233, 235, 369, 373, 374, 375, 376, 377, 378, 380, 381, 383, 384, 385, 386, 390, 392

W

well-being 2, 61, 63, 64, 68, 69, 74, 75, 77, 79, 80, 83, 99, 111, 134, 143, 145, 146, 147, 156, 157, 159, 161, 164, 166, 168, 170, 174, 175, 176, 179, 183, 184, 187, 193, 194, 202, 204, 209, 238, 239, 241, 248, 265, 271, 272, 273, 277, 278, 296, 300, 301, 302, 315, 316, 323, 336, 342, 351, 352, 362, 371, 377, 382, 383

Women's Education 222, 261, 264, 284, 288

Workforce Participation 261, 263, 287